UNDERSTANDING FEDERAL INCOME TAXATION

UNDERSTANDING FEDERAL INCOME TAXATION

Fourth Edition

J. Martin Burke
Regents Professor of Law
University of Montana School of Law

Michael K. Friel
Professor of Law and Director, Graduate Tax Program
University of Florida Levin College of Law

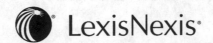

ISBN: 978-0-7698-5282-9 (print)
ISBN: 978-0-3271-8305-1 (eBook)

Library of Congress Cataloging-in-Publication Data
Burke, J. Martin.
  Understanding federal income taxation / J. Martin Burke, Regents Professor of Law, University of
Montana School of Law, Michael K. Friel, professor of law and director, Graduate Tax Program, University
of Florida College of Law. -- Fourth edition.
     pages cm
  Includes index.
  ISBN 978-0-7698-5282-9
  1. Income tax--Law and legislation--United States. I. Friel, Michael K. II. Title.
  KF6369.85.B87 2013
  343.7305'2--dc23
                                                                                              2012037649

NOTE TO USERS

To ensure that you are using the latest materials available in this area, please be sure to periodically check the LexisNexis Law School web site for downloadable updates and supplements at www.lexisnexis.com/lawschool.

Editorial Offices
121 Chanlon Rd., New Providence, NJ 07974 (908) 464-6800
201 Mission St., San Francisco, CA 94105-1831 (415) 908-3200
www.lexisnexis.com

MATTHEW◆BENDER

DEDICATION

To Jackie and Jonathan
and My Mother and Father
— MKF

To My Mother and Father
and My Eleven Brothers and Sisters
— JMB

PREFACE

As experienced tax professors, we know that students encountering the complexities of the tax code for the first time are often frustrated by its difficulties and look to their casebooks or to supplemental material for an adequate overview of the principles and policies underlying federal income tax law and for a detailed explanation of the interpretation and application of pertinent provisions of the Internal Revenue Code. Thus, such overviews and explanations have been principal features of the authors' casebook, *Taxation of Individual Income*. This book in turn adapts material from *Taxation of Individual Income* for those students using other casebooks who seek such supplemental material to assist them in their study. We have specifically designed this book to supplement other casebooks used in traditional courses in federal individual income taxation.

This book consists of forty-four chapters with each chapter addressing a basic topic in individual income taxation, e.g., the taxation of personal injury awards, the interest deduction, installment sales. Because the provisions of the Internal Revenue Code are necessarily at the heart of tax study, we have included in each chapter a part or all of the Code section(s) pertinent to the specific topic. Likewise, the chapters contain summaries of leading cases and relevant administrative rulings as well as numerous examples explaining the application of the law

For students in law schools or business programs, we suggest that, before turning to this book, students first read the cases and other materials assigned by their professors. With that reading as background, students should then read the corresponding materials in this book to acquire a broader overview of the area including the development of the law related to a specific topic.

While this book is designed primarily for students, we recognize that it may also prove valuable to the general practitioner. Before representing a client in a divorce or some property transaction, the attorney may be well advised to read the chapter(s) relevant to the representation. Not only will this book provide the attorney with helpful overviews of the tax law related to a client matter, it will also serve as a tool for locating cases and other relevant authority.

In sum, we have written this book as a basic guide for students studying the tax law for the first time and for general practitioners handling transactions with an individual income tax dimension. A word of caution: neither this guide nor any casebook or supplemental material should be viewed as a substitute for careful reading of the Internal Revenue Code. Lawyers and accountants must ultimately base their decisions on the Code and the judicial and administrative interpretations of the Code. Our hope is that this book will aid in the study of the Code and the application of its provisions.

ACKNOWLEDGMENTS

We are indebted to a number of people for their assistance in the development of this book. We have benefitted greatly from the comments and suggestions by our colleagues and our students at the University of Montana School of Law and the University of Florida College of Law, and we wish to acknowledge their help and that of our tax colleagues at other schools. We are also indebted to Linda Kirby of the University of Florida College of Law. Her assistance and support in the preparation of this manuscript were indispensable, and for that we are most grateful and appreciative.

TABLE OF CONTENTS

TABLE OF CONTENTS

TABLE OF CONTENTS

TABLE OF CONTENTS

TABLE OF CONTENTS

TABLE OF CONTENTS

TABLE OF CONTENTS

TABLE OF CONTENTS

TABLE OF CONTENTS

TABLE OF CONTENTS

TABLE OF CONTENTS

TABLE OF CONTENTS

TABLE OF CONTENTS

TABLE OF CONTENTS

TABLE OF CONTENTS

TABLE OF CONTENTS

Chapter 1

INTRODUCTION TO FEDERAL INCOME TAX

§ 1.01 A BRIEF HISTORY OF FEDERAL INCOME TAX

The federal income tax as we know it today had its beginning with the ratification of the 16th Amendment to the U.S. Constitution in 1913. The amendment provides:

> The Congress shall have the power to lay and collect taxes on incomes, from whatever source derived, without apportionment among the several states and without regard to any census or enumeration.

This amendment set the stage for the 1913 Income Tax Act, an act imposing a very low rate of taxes. Given the high exemption levels established in that act, only a small portion of the American public paid income taxes. In 1920, for example, there were only about five and one-half million taxable individual income tax returns filed, although 62,667,000 Americans were 20 years of age or older. In 1920, a family earning $10,000 a year (quite a sum for that time) would have paid only $558 in income tax. Because of World War I, tax rates were considered high at that time. By 1928, the family earning $10,000 would pay only $40 in federal income tax.

While initially only the well-to-do were subject to income taxes, the pool of taxpayers radically increased in the 1940s primarily as a result of the government's need for additional revenues to fund the American war effort in World War II. Thus, while only 14.7 million individual income tax returns were filed in 1940, 49.8 million individual income tax returns were filed in 1945. The adage "two things in life are inevitable: taxes and death" took on new meaning in the World War II era. Today, the great majority of adult Americans are required to file individual income tax returns, with approximately 140 million individual income tax returns being filed each year.

Needless to say, the almost overnight movement from a system which taxed relatively few people to a mass tax system created serious administrative problems. To alleviate some of the collection difficulties and to assure taxpayer compliance, the modern tax withholding system was created. Under the system, employers are required to withhold from their employees' compensation a sum determined by reference to a specially formulated schedule and approximating the federal income taxes an employee will owe. Amounts withheld by employers are periodically remitted to the Treasury. The success of our federal income tax system is largely attributable to this withholding system.

Our federal income tax system serves a number of functions, the most obvious being raising revenues to operate the government. The tax system also serves to allocate the cost of public goods and services among Americans on an ability-to-pay basis. This is accomplished through a progressive rate structure whereby high income taxpayers pay a larger fraction of their income in taxes than low income taxpayers. Exactly how progressive our system is and ought to be are topics of ongoing debate. Changes in deductions, exclusions and credits, as well as changes in tax rates and tax brackets, all affect the progressivity of the system.

The federal income tax is also used as a tool of social policy. Various Internal Revenue Code provisions reflect social concerns of the Congress. For example, Section 163 allows taxpayers to deduct home mortgage interest. Congress' stated purpose in allowing the deduction of such a personal expense is to encourage home ownership. Likewise, Section 121, providing a substantial exclusion for gain on the sale of a principal residence, not only encourages home ownership, but minimizes tax as a factor in deciding whether to sell one's home. Another familiar example of the use of tax as a tool of social policy is Section 170, the charitable deduction provision. Providing a deduction for charitable contributions indirectly subsidizes various social programs benefitting large segments of our population.

Finally, the federal income tax often is used to implement economic policy. For example, the accelerated cost recovery system of Section 168 stimulates the economy by allowing businesses to depreciate certain tangible property rapidly, thereby encouraging businesses to invest in new equipment.

The propriety of using the tax system to influence an individual's economic or personal decisions may be questioned. To take advantage of tax breaks, taxpayers often significantly alter their economic behavior. For example, historically many of the tax shelters in which taxpayers invested represented activities almost certain to generate economic losses but which were nevertheless attractive because of the tax benefits they produced. In response, Congress enacted legislation substantially limiting tax shelter activity and forcing taxpayers to focus on the economic viability of an undertaking, rather than merely on the potential tax benefits.

This shifting interplay of revenue-raising, social and economic considerations is an ever-present feature of our tax system.

§ 1.02   RESOLUTION OF TAX ISSUES THROUGH THE JUDICIAL PROCESS

[A]   Trial Courts

If the Commissioner of the Internal Revenue Service asserts a deficiency in income tax, *i.e.*, claims that the taxpayer has failed to pay all that is owed, the taxpayer may:

(1)   refuse to pay the tax and petition the Tax Court for a redetermination of the deficiency; or

(2)   pay the deficiency, file an administrative claim for refund, and upon denial of the claim, sue for refund in federal district court or the United States Court of Federal Claims.

There are thus three courts which have original jurisdiction in federal tax cases: the Tax Court, the United States District Courts and the United States Court of Federal Claims.

[1] The Tax Court

Of the three courts having original jurisdiction in tax cases, the Tax Court is undoubtedly the most important. The Tax Court has often been referred to as the "poor man's court" because the taxpayer commences an action in that court for redetermination of a deficiency *without first paying the asserted deficiency.* In contrast, actions for refund in the federal district courts and the Court of Federal Claims are, as the nature of the action indicates, commenced only after an asserted deficiency has been paid.

Because the Tax Court hears only tax cases, it is the most sophisticated trial court from the standpoint of tax expertise. The Tax Court has 19 members. The Tax Court, known as the Board of Tax Appeals until 1943, was established in 1924. Prior to the Tax Reform Act of 1969, the Tax Court was technically an independent agency of the executive branch of the federal government. The 1969 Act renamed the court the "United States Tax Court" and gave it "constitutional status" under Article 1, Section 8, Clause 9 of the Constitution, so that it is now part of the judicial branch. The change to constitutional status gives the Tax Court the power to punish for contempt and to issue writs to enforce its decisions.

The Tax Court has its headquarters in Washington, D.C., but the court holds hearings in principal cities throughout the United States on a fairly regular schedule. Cases are tried without a jury by one judge, who submits an opinion to the chief judge for consideration. The chief judge will either allow the decision to stand or refer it to the full court for review. Reviewed opinions of the Tax Court are likely to be accorded greater weight. Published opinions of the Tax Court always indicate if the opinion has been reviewed. Dissenting opinions are published.

[2] Federal District Courts

The United States District Courts have jurisdiction in any tax case against the United States seeking a refund of tax, regardless of the amount involved. Unlike actions before the Tax Court, suits in the federal district courts may be tried before juries. The taxpayer must bring tax actions against the United States in the district in which the taxpayer resides, or, in the case of a corporation, in the district in which it has its principal place of business. A taxpayer, as indicated above, cannot litigate a tax action in the federal district courts without first paying the amount in dispute and then commencing a refund action.

[3] The United States Court of Federal Claims

The United States Court of Federal Claims was created by the Federal Courts Improvement Act of 1982. It inherited substantially all of the jurisdiction formerly exercised by the United States Court of Claims. The Court of Federal Claims has jurisdiction over all tax suits against the United States regardless of amount. Jury trial is not available in the Court of Federal Claims. The jurisdiction of the Court of Federal Claims extends throughout the United States; where a taxpayer resides makes no difference. The principal office of the Court of Federal Claims is in the District of Columbia, but it may hold court at such times and in such places as it may fix by rule of the court. Like the federal district courts, the Court of Federal Claims has no jurisdiction to hear deficiency cases. The taxpayer must pay the deficiency, thus converting the suit into a refund suit, before bringing an action before the court.

[B] Appellate Courts

Appeals from the Tax Court are heard as a matter of right by the Federal Courts of Appeals of the United States. Jurisdiction is in the court for the circuit in which the taxpayer resides. Prior to its 1970 decision in *Golsen v. Commissioner,*[1] the Tax Court did not regard itself as bound by the decisions of any particular federal court of appeals, even the court which would hear the case in question on appeal. In *Golsen,* the Tax Court reversed itself and announced that it would follow a decision of the federal court to which an appeal from a Tax Court decision would be made, if the federal appeals court decision were squarely on point.

Prior to 1982, decisions of the Court of Claims were reviewed by the Supreme Court under the certiorari procedure. The 1982 Court Improvement Act created the United States Court of Appeals for the Federal Circuit, which has exclusive jurisdiction of an appeal from a final decision of the United States Court of Federal Claims. Decisions of the Court of Appeals for the Federal Circuit are reviewable by the Supreme Court.

Decisions of the federal district courts may, as a matter of right, be appealed to the appropriate federal court of appeals.

[C] Selection of Forum

As the above brief description of the various trial courts indicates, the taxpayer aggrieved by a decision of the Internal Revenue Service has a choice regarding the forum in which resolution of the tax issue may be sought. As a practical matter, a taxpayer's finances may prove controlling in choosing a court. Thus, because a taxpayer is not entitled to sue in federal district court or the United States Court of Federal Claims unless a deficiency is paid and a refund claim pursued, the Tax Court will often be the favored forum because one may commence an action there without having paid the asserted deficiency. Other factors likely to influence taxpayers and their advisors in choosing a forum will be the desire for a jury trial, the expertise of the Tax Court judges, and the past record of the particular court on a given issue. For example, if a taxpayer's claim for refund raises an issue on which the Court of Federal Claims has ruled favorably for other taxpayers, a taxpayer could be expected to bring a refund action in the Claims Court.

---

[1] 54 T.C. 742 (1970).

§ 1.03   COMPUTATION OF TAX LIABILITY

[A]   Basic Questions Addressed by an Income Tax System

Our income tax law addresses a number of fundamental questions:

(1)   *What* items of economic income or gain will be includable in gross income?

(2)   *What* items of expense will be allowable as deductions?

(3)   *When* is an amount included in income? *When* is the taxpayer entitled to claim a deduction for an amount that is clearly deductible?

(4)   *Who* is the taxpayer — *who* is going to be taxed on items of income?

(5)   What is the *character* of the items of income or the deductions?

[B]   Evaluating Tax Liability

To determine the income tax liability of an individual, it is necessary to answer two questions:

(1)   What is the applicable tax rate?

(2)   What is the tax rate applied to — that is, what is the tax base?

The answer to the first of these two questions is relatively simple. Internal Revenue Code Section 1 sets forth the rates for various taxpayers. Section 1(a), for example, applies to married individuals filing joint returns; section 1(b) applies to heads of households; section 1(c) applies to unmarried individuals; section 1(d) applies to married individuals filing separate returns. Tax rates have varied considerably over the years. For example, a major change in the rates occurred as part of the Tax Reform Act of 1986, when tax rates were significantly reduced — immediately prior to 1986 the maximum individual income tax rate was 50%; and five years prior to that, the top rate was as high as 70%. Under current law, the maximum rate for individuals is 39.6%, although there is a 28% maximum rate on "net capital gain" income and a 20% cap on "adjusted net capital gain."[2] The income levels at which the higher rates apply vary according to the taxpayer's filing status.

The appropriate tax rate is applied to the "taxable income" of the taxpayer. In calculating the taxpayer's taxable income, the five questions discussed above become important. Section 63 defines "taxable income." Section 63(b) provides that, for individuals who do not itemize their deductions, the term "taxable income" means "adjusted gross income minus (1) the standard deduction, and (2) the deduction for personal exemptions provided in section 151." For all other taxpayers, "taxable income" means "gross income minus the deductions allowed by this chapter [Chapter 1 of Subtitle A of the Internal Revenue Code] (other than standard deduction)."[3]

---

[2] I.R.C. § 1(a), (h), (i). Capital gains from the most common transactions, *e.g.*, the sale of stock, are taxed at a maximum of 15% for most taxpayers, but at a rate of 20% for those in the 39.6% bracket.

[3] I.R.C. § 63(a).

[1] Gross Income

The first order of business then is to determine gross income.

§ 61. Gross income defined.

(a) **General definition. Except as otherwise provided in this subtitle, gross income means all income from whatever source derived, including (but not limited to) the following items:**

(1) Compensation for services, including fees, commissions, fringe benefits, and similar items;

(2) **Gross income derived from business;**

(3) **Gains derived from dealings in property;**

(4) **Interest;**

(5) **Rents;**

(6) **Royalties;**

(7) **Dividends;**

(8) **Alimony and separate maintenance payments;**

(9) **Annuities;**

(10) **Income from life insurance and endowment contracts;**

(11) **Pensions;**

(12) **Income from discharge of indebtedness;**

(13) **Distributive share of partnership gross income;**

(14) **Income in respect of a decedent; and**

(15) **Income from an interest in an estate or trust.**

[Note: The reference in Section 61 to "this subtitle" is to subtitle A of Title 26 of the United States Code. Subtitle A includes all income tax provisions beginning with Section 1 and ending with Section 1563.] Since "gross income" is defined as "all income," the definition is not particularly helpful. Although the courts have struggled with the precise meaning of the term "gross income," they have generally been expansive in their definition of income.

Example: Caroline Taxpayer is a self-employed consultant whose business is unincorporated.

(1) She receives $130,000 in checks and $15,000 in cash this year as consulting fees;

(2) She is owed $15,000 from clients for consulting work they have done this year; and

(3) She receives $5,000 in interest on corporate bonds and bank deposits.

Question: What is Caroline Taxpayer's gross income?

Answer: The various items are dealt with as follows:

(1) The $145,000 in cash and checks represents gross receipts from the consulting business and is includable in gross income under Section 61. The costs incurred by Caroline to produce these receipts cannot be deducted from the $145,000 in arriving at the gross income figure; Section 61 says nothing about net income. The Code, however, specifically authorizes deductions for expenses incurred in one's trade or business.[4]

(2) Whether the $15,000 Caroline is owed from clients for work performed during the current year is includable in her gross income for the year depends on her method of accounting. If she is a "cash method" taxpayer, she is not required to include the $15,000 in gross income.[5] If she is an "accrual method" taxpayer, the $15,000 is included in gross income currently because she earned it this year.[6] For purposes of this example, assume Caroline, like most individuals, uses the cash method and thus does not include the $15,000 in gross income.

(3) The $5,000 interest clearly constitutes gross income, as reflected in Section 61(a)(4).

Caroline's gross income is thus, $145,000 + $5,000 = $150,000.

[2] The Concept of Adjusted Gross Income

Assuming the taxpayer in the above example had no other income in the current year, her gross income is $150,000. The next step is to determine her adjusted gross income. Section 62 defines adjusted gross income as gross income less certain deductions. Note that Section 62 simply defines adjusted gross income; *it is not a deduction granting provision.* In general, only those deductions listed in Section 62 are taken into account in computing adjusted gross income. Thus, there are two categories of deductions. The first category is comprised of deductions, enumerated in Section 62, which a taxpayer may consider in determining his or her adjusted gross income; these are referred to as *"above the line"* deductions. The second category of deductions consists of those deductions a taxpayer may take into account only after the adjusted gross income has been determined; these are referred to as *"below the line"* deductions.[7]

Adjusted gross income may be viewed as an interim measure of taxable income. Prior to 1944, taxpayers simply itemized all of their deductions. All of their allowable business deductions and personal deductions had to be listed separately

---

[4] *See* Chapter 12, *infra.*

[5] *See* I.R.C. § 451(a); Treas. Reg. § 1.446-1(c)(1)(i). A cash method taxpayer includes income only when it is actually or constructively received. *See* Chapter 28, *infra.*

[6] *See* I.R.C. § 461(a); Treas. Reg. § 1. 451-1(a). An accrual method taxpayer includes income when all events have occurred which fix his right to the income and the amount can be determined with reasonable accuracy. *See* Chapter 29, *infra.*

[7] A taxpayer may deduct either the below the line deductions or the standard deduction (discussed below), not both. Below the line deductions are thus effectively deductible only if in the aggregate they exceed the standard deduction. If the standard deduction exceeds the below the line deductions, then the below the line deductions provide no tax benefit and are in effect wasted.

on the return. In the early years of modern American tax history, this required itemization was manageable from an administrative standpoint because relatively few people were required to file returns. In the early 1940s, however, when the United States adopted a mass system of taxation, the required itemization of all deductions came to be viewed as extremely burdensome not only for the taxpayer attempting to complete a tax return, but also for the Internal Revenue Service in reviewing the tax returns filed.

In 1944, as part of a tax simplification act, Congress decided that, in lieu of itemizing their *personal deductions,* taxpayers should be given a "standard deduction." In effect, Congress would simply assume that all taxpayers had incurred a certain amount of deductible *personal* expenses. If the taxpayer chose to use the standard deduction, the taxpayer would be entitled to deduct the amount specified by Congress regardless of what deductible personal expenses the taxpayer had actually incurred. All taxpayers, however, would be allowed to deduct their *trade or business* expenses and many investment expenses regardless of whether they elected the standard deduction. The standard deduction was thus largely intended to eliminate the itemizing of deductible personal expenses.

Congress initially provided that the standard deduction would be a percentage of the income determined after taking into account trade or business expenses but before taking into account deductible personal expenses. There was not in existence, however, any interim measure of gross income less business expenses to which the standard deduction percentage could be applied. Congress therefore created an interim measure known as "adjusted gross income." Beginning with the 1944 Act, a taxpayer would compute taxable income by deducting business expenses from gross income. This figure was the taxpayer's adjusted gross income. The taxpayer would then elect either to itemize other deductions or to take the standard deduction. Disregarding the personal exemptions available, the taxpayer's taxable income then equaled the difference between the adjusted gross income and either the taxpayer's itemized deductions or the standard deduction.

Note that the standard deduction under current law is a set dollar amount that is adjusted annually for inflation, rather than a percentage of adjusted gross income.[8]

Adjusted gross income (AGI) continues to serve as a dividing line between those deductions allowed to all taxpayers regardless of whether they itemize (the "above the line" deductions) and those deductions which may be taken only if the taxpayer itemizes (the "below the line" deductions).[9] AGI is also important because it is used to limit the deduction for certain personal expenses (*e.g.,* the charitable deduction is limited to a percentage of AGI) and is used as a basis in calculating various other "tax-related" amounts.

---

[8] For example, the "basic standard deduction" of $5,000 on a joint return has risen to $12,200 for calendar year 2013 on account of inflation adjustments. *See* I.R.C. § 63(c)(2)(A), (4); Rev. Proc. 2013-15, I.R.B. 2013–5.

[9] *See* I.R.C. § 63(e).

[3] Deductions

The deduction provisions of the Code begin with Section 161. Most deductions reflect the notion that our tax system ought to permit a deduction for the costs incurred in producing income. As discussed previously, however, the Code allows a number of deductions, *e.g.*, the deduction for home mortgage interest, which are not integral to our tax system. These deductions exist only because of certain economic and social policies Congress seeks to implement. While defining gross income expansively, the courts view deductions as a matter of "legislative grace" and therefore narrowly construe them.

Deductions are expenditures; not all expenditures, however, are deductible. Rather, every deduction must be authorized by a specific Code section. Some expenditures, *e.g.*, wages paid to an employee,[10] are generally currently deductible — that is, they may be deducted in their entirety on the current year's tax return. Other expenditures are never deductible. Personal expenses, for example, are generally not deductible.[11] Some expenditures which are deductible, but not all at once; rather, they are accounted for over a period of time. For example, the cost of a building purchased for use in one's business will not be deductible in the year of purchase but rather will be deductible during the life of the building.[12]

Example: Caroline Taxpayer pays the following expenses this year:

(1) $10,000 home mortgage loan ($7,000 interest + $3,000 principal);

(2) $30,000 for office rent and supplies and employee wages for her consulting business;

(3) $1,000 investment newsletter;

(4) $6,000 charitable contribution.

Question: Which of these expenditures are deductible? Are they deductible above the line or below the line?

Answer: (1) The $3,000 portion of the mortgage loan representing payment of principal is not deductible. Mortgage payments on one's personal residence represent a personal expenditure, and personal expenditures are generally not deductible.[13]

The $7,000 interest portion of the mortgage payment is a personal expense just as the principal payment is a personal expense. Section 163(a), however, specifically allows a deduction for "all interest paid or accrued within the taxable year on indebtedness." Section 163(h) qualifies this general rule by providing that personal interest is generally not deductible. Personal interest, however, does not include so-called "qualified residence interest." The home mortgage interest paid by Caroline may be "qualified residence interest" and thus may be deductible. For purposes of this

---

[10] I.R.C. § 162.

[11] I.R.C. § 262.

[12] I.R.C. §§ 167(a), 168.

[13] I.R.C. § 262.

example, assume the interest is deductible under Section 163. To the extent Section 163(a) permits Caroline to deduct interest on personal debt such as a home mortgage, it represents an exception to the general rule that personal expenditures are not deductible. Indeed, this section provides one of the significant tax breaks enjoyed by homeowners. Certainly, this deduction is not one which is mandated by a system which seeks to tax only net income.

Having determined that the $7,000 interest payment is deductible, the next question is whether the deduction is above or below the line. Section 62 lists above-the-line deductions. While interest expense may be an above-the-line deduction if it is incurred in a trade or business (Section 62(a)(1)), interest expense incurred with respect to a personal debt is not listed as an above-the-line deduction. Thus, the $7,000 interest deduction may not be used in computing adjusted gross income. Instead, it will be taken into account in computing Caroline's below-the-line deductions.

(2) The rent Caroline paid for her business office is deductible as a trade or business expense pursuant to Section 162(a)(3). As such, it is an above the line deduction according to Section 62(a)(1). Similarly, the amounts paid in employee wages and for office supplies in connection with the business likewise constitute deductible business expenses under Section 162(a), and are also above the line deductions under Section 62(a)(1).

(3) The $1,000 Caroline paid for the investment newsletter is a deductible business expense under Section 162 if she uses the newsletter for business purposes. However, if she subscribes to the newsletter only for the information it provides about investments she has made, the expense is not a deductible trade or business expense.

Carrying on one's own investment activities has been held not to constitute a trade or business within the meaning of Section 162.[14] Section 212, however, specifically provides a deduction for expenses paid or incurred during the taxable year "for the production or collection of income." Thus, depending on the facts, the newsletter may be deductible either as a business expense under Section 162 or as an investment activity expense under Section 212.

For purposes of our example, assume the cost of the newsletter is deductible under Section 212. As such, it is deductible below the line. Under Section 62, only limited types of Section 212 expenses are deductible above the line and the newsletter expense is not one of them. This is a curious result because it seems that taxpayers should always be allowed to deduct expenses incurred in the production of taxable income. There is no good policy reason to deny above the line treatment to this expense, and yet Congress has done so. Thus, the expense will serve to reduce the taxpayer's taxable income, and hence the taxpayer's tax liability, only if the taxpayer has aggregate below the line expenses greater than the standard deduction. By contrast, were the newsletter cost to be considered a business expense,

---

[14] Higgins v. Commissioner, 312 U.S. 212 (1941).

it would be deductible above the line and would not be subject to the potential disallowance that below the line deductions face.[15]

(4) Finally, Caroline made a charitable contribution of $6,000. Although contributions to charities are classic examples of personal expenditures, Section 170, as noted earlier, provides a deduction for charitable contributions. There are limits, however, on charitable deductions. In this case, Section 170(b)(1)(A) limits Caroline's deduction to 50% of her "contribution base." Section 170(b)(1)(F) provides that "contribution base" means "adjusted gross income." Thus, as long as Caroline has an adjusted gross income of at least $12,000, she will be entitled to a full $6,000 deduction for the charitable contribution. The charitable contribution deduction, as you might expect, is not among those listed in Section 62, and is instead a below the line deduction.

[4]　Calculating Adjusted Gross Income

Based on the foregoing, Caroline is thus "allowed" the following deductions:

above the line deductions:

office rent, supplies & employee wages	$30,000
TOTAL	$30,000

below the line deductions:

interest	$7,000
newsletter	1,000
charitable contributions	6,000
TOTAL	$14,000

Returning to the definition of adjusted gross income in Section 62(a):

AGI = Gross income, less the above the line deductions

Thus, AGI = $150,000 − $30,000 = $120,000

[5]　Taxable Income

[a]　Itemize or Elect Standard Deduction

Next, Caroline must determine her taxable income. As noted earlier, the formula for computing taxable income depends on whether the taxpayer itemizes deductions, i.e., elects to claim below the line deductions rather than taking the standard deduction. If the taxpayer does not itemize deductions, the taxpayer is entitled only to the standard deduction in lieu of any below the line deductions (other than the personal exemption, discussed *infra*).[16] Clearly, if a taxpayer's below the line deductions exceed the standard deduction, as will be the case with Caroline, the taxpayer should be advised to itemize.

---

[15] *See* I.R.C. § 62(a)(1).

[16] Note the definition of "itemized deductions" in Section 63(d).

If she elects to itemize, Caroline will determine her taxable income by subtracting from her gross income of $150,000 all of her allowable deductions.[17] For taxpayers itemizing deductions, the computation of adjusted gross income is not specifically required by Section 63(b); however, for taxpayers who have made charitable contributions or have other expenses, the deductibility of which depend on the amount of the adjusted gross income, their adjusted gross income must be determined. Having already computed Caroline's adjusted gross income, the only deductions which remain to be taken in computing her taxable income are the below the line deductions (or standard deduction) and the personal exemption.

[b] Section 67: The 2% Floor on Miscellaneous Itemized Deductions

Section 67 provides that certain itemized deductions, called "miscellaneous itemized deductions," may not be deducted except to the extent that in the aggregate such deductions exceed 2% of the taxpayer's adjusted gross income. For example, if one has adjusted gross income of $100,000 and aggregate miscellaneous itemized deductions of $2,000 or less, none of the miscellaneous itemized deductions may be deducted. If the miscellaneous itemized deductions total $2,500, they may be deducted to the extent of $500.

This 2% floor on miscellaneous itemized deductions not only reduces the tax benefits of certain deductions, but also the number of taxpayers claiming the deductions. The floor relieves taxpayers of the burden of recordkeeping with respect to certain expenditures unless they expect that in the aggregate the expenditures will exceed the floor. In turn, the Internal Revenue Service's work in auditing returns is reduced. With respect to each below the line deduction, it is necessary to determine whether it is a miscellaneous itemized deduction and thus subject to this 2% floor. Under Section 67(b), Caroline's deductions for home mortgage interest ($7,000) and charitable contributions ($6,000) are not miscellaneous itemized deductions and are not subject to the 2% rule of Section 67(a). The newsletter expense ($1,000), however, has been assumed to be a section 212 expense; as such it is subject to the rule. The aggregate miscellaneous itemized deduction thus total $1,000. It is clear that $1,000 does not exceed 2% of the adjusted gross income of $120,000; therefore the $1,000 expense will not be deductible. Thus, Caroline's below the line deductions are disallowed by section 67 to the extent of $1,000; her itemized deductions are cut back from $14,000 to $13,000 by Section 67.

[c] The Section 68 Overall Limitation on Itemized Deductions

There is, moreover, yet another hurdle that taxpayers seeking to itemize deductions must surmount. Section 68 provides that otherwise allowable itemized deductions are reduced by the lesser of: (1) 3% of the amount by which the taxpayer's adjusted gross income exceeds an inflation-adjusted "applicable

---

[17] I.R.C. § 63(a).

amount" or (2) 80% of otherwise allowable itemized deductions.[18] As a result, a taxpayer will not be subject to the Section 68 cutback unless the taxpayer's adjusted gross income exceeds the applicable amount. The applicable amount for 2013 is $300,000 on a joint return and $250,000 for an unmarried individual (not a surviving spouse or head of household).[19] Because Caroline's adjusted gross income of $120,000 does not exceed the applicable amount, her allowable itemized deductions will not be reduced by Section 68.

However, in order to illustrate the operation of Section 68, assume an applicable amount of $250,000 and a single taxpayer with adjusted gross income of $400,000 and otherwise allowable itemized deductions of $30,000.[20] Because the taxpayer's adjusted gross income exceeds the applicable amount by $150,000, the taxpayer would be subject to the Section 68 limitations. Under the "lesser of" rule of Section 68, the cutback is determined as follows: (1) 3% of $150,000 is $4,500; (2) 80% of the otherwise allowable itemized deductions ($30,000) is $24,000. The lesser amount is $4,500, so the taxpayer's allowable itemized deductions would be reduced to $25,500 from the $30,00 otherwise allowed.

To return to Caroline: After applying Section 67 (disallowed itemized deductions: $1,000) and Section 68 (disallowed itemized deductions: $0), Caroline's remaining itemized deductions are $13,000.

If the standard deduction for Caroline is less $13,000, she will itemize her deductions. Otherwise, she will the standard deduction in lieu of itemizing. In point of fact, the standard deduction, which is adjusted annually for inflation, is currently less than $13,000.[21] Caroline will therefore itemize her deductions.

[d]   Personal Exemptions

Next, it is necessary to determine the deduction for the personal exemption. Section 151(a) provides a deduction for personal exemptions. Section 151(d)(1) sets the exemption amount, in general, at $2,000, adjusted for inflation after 1989 as set forth in Section 151(d)(4).[22] In addition, Congress has added a provision under which the exemption amount may be reduced, and potentially eliminated, for high-income taxpayers. Under Section 151(d)(3), the exemption amount is reduced by two percentage points for each $2,500 (or fraction thereof) by which the taxpayer's adjusted gross income exceeds the inflation-adjusted "applicable amount" in effect under Section 68(b). Because Caroline's adjusted gross income of $120,000 does not

---

[18] I.R.C. § 68(a).

[19] See I.R.C. § 68(b)(1) for the apoplicable amounts for 2013 for various categories of taxpayers, inflation-adjusted after 2013 under I.R.C. §68(b)(2).

[20] The reference to "otherwise allowable itemized deductions" requires that the Section 67 2% floor be applied first; then Section 68 is applied to the remaining allowable itemized deductions. See I.R.C. §68(d).

[21] The "basic standard deduction" on a joint return is $5,000 adjusted for inflation after 1988. I.R.C. § 63(c)(2), (5). For 2013, the inflation-adjusted basic standard deduction on a joint return is $12,200 and $6,100 on the return of an unmarried individual, such as Caroline, who is not a surviving spouse or head of household. Rev. Proc. 2013-15, *supra*.

[22] For 2013, the inflation-adjusted personal exemption is $3,900. Rev. Proc. 2013-15, *supra*.

exceed the applicable amount,[23] any personal exemptions to which she is entitled will not be subject to reduction under Section 151(d)(3).

Caroline may claim one personal exemption. In the case of married taxpayers filing a joint return, there are two taxpayers, and therefore there will be two personal exemptions.[24] In addition to the exemptions provided for each taxpayer, there are additional exemptions for each dependent who meets the requirements set out in Section 152. Here, we assume Caroline has no dependents. Taxpayers who have minor children will typically be able to claim an exemption for each child under Section 152 and the "qualifying child" provisions of Section 152(c). Assume the current inflation-adjusted exemption amount is $3,900. With one exemption, Caroline will claim a total deduction of $3,900. Even if Caroline did not elect to itemize, Section 63(b) makes it clear that she is entitled to claim personal exemptions in addition to the standard deduction.

The personal exemption and the standard deduction provide a floor assuring that taxpayers will not be taxed unless they have income greater than the combined amount of the personal exemptions allowed and the standard deduction. As noted in the legislative history of the 1986 Tax Reform Act, "[a]n overriding goal of the Committee is to relieve families with the lowest incomes from Federal income tax liability. Consequently, the Bill increases the amounts of both the personal exemption and the standard deduction . . . so that the income level at which individuals begin to have tax liability (the tax threshold) will be raised sufficiently to free millions of poverty-level individuals from Federal income tax liability."[25]

[e]   Calculating Taxable Income

Caroline Taxpayer's taxable income therefore is:

Adjusted Gross Income	$120,000
less: itemized deductions	13,000
personal exemptions	3,900
	16,900
Taxable Income	$103,100

[6]   Tax Rates

Next, Caroline must apply the appropriate tax rate under Section 1. Section 1(a) and (i) together provide six different rates, or brackets: 10%, 15%, 25%, 28%, 33%, 35%, and 39.6%. The income level at which the higher rates begin to apply depends on a taxpayer's filing status. In addition, the dollar ranges to which the different

---

[23] For 2013, the applicable amount for an unmarried individual who is not a surviving spouse or head of household is $250,000. I.R.C. § 68(b)(1).

[24] Treas. Reg. § 1.151-1(b).

[25] H.R. 99-426 p.82 (1985); Senate Rep. 99-313 p.31, 32 (1986). *See also* General Explanation of the Tax Reform Act of 1986 prepared by the Staff of the Joint Committee on Taxation, p.15.

brackets apply themselves are to be adjusted for inflation.[26] For example, for 2013, under the tax rate tables of Section 1(c) and (i), as adjusted for inflation,[27] the tax on the return of an unmarried individual (not a surviving spouse or head of household) with taxable income of $103,100 is 10% on the first $8,925 of taxable income (or $892.50); 15% on the next $27,325 (or $4,098.75); 25% on the next $51,600 (or $12,900); and 28% on the remaining $15,250 (or $4,270). Caroline's tax liability would thus be $22,161.25.[28]

[7] Credits

One final computation must be made. Caroline must determine whether there are any credits which may be taken against the tax. The Code sections providing credits are generally Sections 21-53.[29] The most common credit is found in Section 31 — the credit for withholding taxes paid through the year by employers on behalf of the employees. Allowance of this credit makes sense since, in effect, employees are prepaying their income taxes via the payment of the withholding tax.

On the facts of the problem, Caroline is not subject to withholding tax because she is self-employed. She would, however, be required to make advance payments on the tax. This type of advance payment is referred to as an estimated tax payment. Assuming Caroline paid estimated tax as required, the tax paid would be deducted from the $22,161.25 tax liability figure.[30]

§ 1.04 CONCLUSION

This chapter has provided an overview of the federal income tax system. The chapters that follow will provide the details of the individual income tax system.

---

[26] I.R.C. § 1(f).

[27] The tax rate tables for 2013 are in Rev. Proc. 2013-15, *supra*.

[28] This liability is preliminary because it can be affected by the maximum capital gains rate provision of Section 1(h). Section 1(h) will apply when the taxpayer has a net capital gain, including qualified dividend income. The taxpayer here does not. The purpose of Section 1(h) is to provide preferential tax rates for qualified dividend income or other net capital gain. The preferential rates may vary based on the taxpayer's bracket and on the components of the net capital gain. Section 1(h) is remarkably complex and will be studied in detail in Chapter 31, *infra*.

[29] A credit reduces one's tax on a dollar for dollar basis, whereas a deduction reduces taxable income, thus providing a reduction in tax that is dependent on the tax bracket of the individual. For example, a $1,000 deduction results in a $396 tax savings for a person in a 39.6% tax bracket, but only a $150 tax savings for a person in a 15% tax bracket. On the other hand, a $1,000 tax credit saves a person $1,000 in taxes regardless of tax bracket.

[30] In addition, because Caroline is self-employed, she must pay a self-employment tax.

Chapter 2

GROSS INCOME CONCEPTS AND LIMITATIONS

§ 2.01 THE SEARCH FOR A DEFINITION OF INCOME

The most basic question confronted in the federal income tax system is "What is income?" The answer to that question is not simple. One cannot merely rely on common usage, nor will one find much solace in the definitions of economists. Rather, the answer is found in an examination of the interplay of congressional purpose, administrative goals, accounting concepts and public policy as defined by the Congress, the courts and the Treasury.

§ 61. Gross income defined.

(a) General definition.

Except as otherwise provided in this subtitle, gross income means all income from whatever source derived, including (but not limited to) the following items:

(1) **Compensation for services, including fees, commissions, fringe benefits, and similar items;**

(2) **Gross income derived from business;**

(3) **Gains derived from dealings in property;**

(4) **Interest;**

(5) **Rents;**

(6) **Royalties;**

(7) **Dividends;**

(8) **Alimony and separate maintenance payments;**

(9) **Annuities;**

(10) **Income from life insurance and endowment contracts;**

(11) **Pensions;**

(12) **Income from discharge of indebtedness;**

(13) **Distributive share of partnership gross income;**

(14) **Income in respect of a decedent; and**

(15) **Income from an interest in an estate or trust.**

Modern federal income tax originated with the Sixteenth Amendment, adopted in 1913, which provides:

> The Congress shall have the power to lay and collect taxes on incomes, *from whatever source derived*, without apportionment among the several states and without regard to any census or enumeration. (Emphasis added).

This amendment set the stage for the 1913 Tax Act which included the following definition of net income:

> The net income of a taxable person shall include *gains, profits, and income* derived from salaries, wages, or compensation for personal services of whatever kind and in whatever form paid, or from professions, vocations, businesses, trade, commerce, or sales, or dealings in property, whether real or personal, growing out of the ownership or use of or interest in real or personal property; and also from interest, rent, dividends, securities, or the transaction of any lawful business carried on for gain or profit, or *gains or profits and income* derived from any source whatever.[1]

Both this provision and the current definition of "gross income" in Section 61(a) of the Internal Revenue Code of 1986, *supra*, are very broad. The 1913 Act provided that income includes "gains or profits and income derived from any source," whereas the Section 61(a) definition is simpler — gross income is "all income from whatever source derived." Both definitions enumerate items constituting gross income. Both, for example, list such common forms of income as wages and salaries, rents, dividends and interest. The list provided in current Section 61(a), however, is much broader and includes items one might not otherwise consider income, *e.g.*, fringe benefits, cancellation of indebtedness, and alimony and separate maintenance payments.

Neither the 1913 definition nor the current definition of income provides any concise, all-encompassing standard for determining income. As the history of judicial and administrative rulings suggests, however, Congress cannot be faulted for failing to provide such a standard. Arguably, both Section 61(a) and its 1913 predecessor were never intended to be the exclusive definition of income, but rather were little more than descriptions of a necessary step in a mathematical formula for computing "taxable income." Thus, in defining "gross income" in Section 61, Congress was merely describing the first step in the calculation of "adjusted gross income" and "taxable income."

More importantly, as the Supreme Court noted in *Commissioner v. Glenshaw Glass*,[2] Congress, in defining "gross income," intended to exert "the full measure of its taxing power." As soon became apparent, the early judicial efforts to express the concept of income in some simply stated standard were unsatisfactory. In *Eisner v. Macomber*,[3] the Court defined "income" as: "[T]he gain derived from capital, from labor, or from both combined, provided it be understood to include profit gained through a sale or conversion of capital assets. . . ."

---

[1] Tax Law of October 3, 1913. H.R. 3321, II, sub. B. (emphasis added).

[2] 348 U.S. 426 (1955).

[3] 252 U.S. 189, 206–207 (1920).

The *Eisner v. Macomber* standard embodied many of the notions contained in the 1913 Act. Nonetheless, the definition was incomplete. The Board of Tax Appeals so indicated in *Hawkins v. Commissioner,*[4] when it noted:

> . . . it is conceivable that since the income tax is primarily an application of the idea of measuring taxes by financial ability to pay, as indicated by the accretion to one's economic wealth during the year, there may be cases in which taxable income will be judicially found although outside the precise scope of the description already given.[5]

The words of the Board of Tax Appeals were prophetic. Eleven years after its decision in *Eisner v. Macomber,* the Supreme Court, in *U.S. v. Kirby Lumber Co.,*[6] considered whether the discharge of a corporate debt for an amount less than the face of the debt resulted in income to the debtor. The Court ruled it did. Obviously, the *Eisner v. Macomber* definition of income would not have readily accommodated discharge of debt, and yet the taxpayer had clearly benefitted economically from the discharge. Although not citing the *Macomber* definition, the Court, in an apparent reference to it, commented that it saw "nothing to be gained by the discussion of judicial definitions."

The Supreme Court, in *Commissioner v. Glenshaw Glass,*[7] laid to rest any lingering question regarding the continued viability of the *Eisner v. Macomber* definition of income. Glenshaw Glass had received, in settlement of litigation, payment of punitive damages for fraud and antitrust violations. The question for the Court was whether the punitive damages constituted gross income under the Code, or, as the taxpayer argued, a windfall beyond the scope of the statutory definition of gross income. The Court, after noting that Congress intended by its definition of gross income to tax all gains except those specifically exempted, rejected the taxpayer's reliance on *Eisner v. Macomber*. The Court noted that the *Macomber* definition "was not meant to provide a touchstone to all future gross income questions." According to the Court, the punitive damages received by Glenshaw Glass were "instances of undeniable accessions to wealth, clearly realized, and over which the taxpayers have complete dominion." Absent congressional intent to exempt such payments from taxation, the Court concluded they constitute gross income.

While the many court decisions addressing the question of "What is gross income?" may not have resulted in a simple definition, the decisions are nonetheless instructive. Decisions like *Glenshaw Glass* emphasize that the concept of "income" as developed by the Congress, the courts and the Treasury is both widely inclusive and elastic. The decisions reflect that, except for items which congressional drafters did not or could not foresee, such as cancellation of indebtedness income or income of a finder, the statutory definition of income has been adequate and has not created any significant uncertainty in our tax law.

---

[4] 6 B.T.A. 1023 (1927).

[5] *Id.* at 1024.

[6] 284 U.S. 1 (1931).

[7] 348 U.S. 426 (1955).

Congress over the years has done much to resolve any questions which might exist regarding whether an item is income. Not only has Congress expanded the Section 61(a) list of items specifically included in "gross income," it has also added a number of sections expressly characterizing certain receipts as income. In almost every case, in expanding the scope of gross income, Congress has been motivated by a desire to clarify the law, to make the tax laws more equitable, or to expand the tax base. For example, Section 86 provides that taxpayers with income over a certain level must report part of their Social Security or Railroad Retirement payments as gross income. This extension of the income concept reflects primarily a concern for equity, since such payments can appropriately be viewed as merely deferred compensation. Section 61(a)(1), amended to add the words "fringe benefits," clarifies that those fringe benefits not specifically excluded are includable in gross income since they, in effect, represent additional compensation for services. Section 85 requires the inclusion of unemployment benefits in gross income regardless of a recipient's income level, reflecting the view that unemployment compensation constitutes wage replacement payments and should not receive more favorable tax treatment than wages.

For a variety of policy reasons, Congress has specifically excluded certain items from gross income. Section 102, for example, excludes gifts and bequests. Several subsequent chapters address the more important statutory exclusions.

In sum, Section 61 and its enumeration of specific items of gross income, together with the other statutory provisions characterizing certain items as gross income, describe most of the items constituting income. Items not specifically addressed by the statute should be evaluated by reference to those which are. It will be seen that income generally includes items that increase the taxpayer's net worth. Statutory exclusions as well as certain limited judicial and administrative exclusions discussed in later chapters limit the scope of gross income and must always be considered when one attempts to determine whether an item is includable in gross income.

§ 2.02 INCOME REALIZED IN ANY FORM

The regulations tell us explicitly that gross income may be realized in any form, whether money, property or services.[8] Neither the Code nor the regulations provide a definition of "realization," although the term is nonetheless a common and important one in the tax lexicon. It may be useful to think of income as being realized when some event occurs that, by explicit rule or common practice, causes the tax system to take account of income that previously existed in a form too inchoate to tax, i.e., "potential income" rather than "realized income." Thus, the system does not seek to tax the taxpayer's ideas or talents, or the income-producing potential of the taxpayer's assets; it seeks to tax the realization — the "making real" — of the income therein. In the examples in the coming pages, the concept of realization will be further fleshed out.

If services are paid for in property, the fair market value of the property is the measure of compensation; if paid for in the form of services, the value of the services

---

[8] Treas. Reg. § 1.61-1(a).

received is the amount of compensation.[9] Fair market value is generally defined as the price a willing buyer would pay a willing seller, with neither under a compulsion to buy or sell, and both having reasonable knowledge of relevant facts.[10] It seems obvious that a tax system cannot depend on the taxpayer's receipt of cash as the *sine qua non* of income. Although most taxpayers presumably cannot dictate the form of their payments and would have to accept cash, some taxpayers could occasionally or routinely receive payment in services or property, and to that extent receive an unwarranted tax advantage. For example, if Lawyer prepares a will for Plumber, it would be anomalous to charge Lawyer with $500 of income when Lawyer receives $500 cash from Plumber and then hires Plumber to do $500 worth of plumbing work, but to charge Lawyer with no income when the cash is dispensed with and Plumber does the plumbing in exchange for the will. Similarly, if Lawyer owes Accountant $500, Lawyer cannot avoid income on the will preparation by directing Plumber to pay $500 to Accountant, or by directing Plumber to provide $500 in plumbing services to Accountant.

Cash payment, of course, serves as a very convenient measure of the amount of Lawyer's income; measurement may be much less certain when valuation of goods or services is necessary, but the difficulty of measurement should not obscure the fact of payment. Nonetheless, one might begin to consider how far to take the principle that the form of income is irrelevant. Should non-cash receipts of minor value be disregarded due to problems in administration and enforcement by the Internal Revenue Service, and record-keeping or valuation problems for taxpayers? How minor is minor? If hard-to-value property is received, should taxation await its disposition by the taxpayer when valuation will presumably be ascertainable? What if its value increases or decreases in the meantime? Should enforcement be particularly vigorous — or relatively relaxed — if taxpayers believe no one really reports all non-cash income? While no definitive answers exist to these questions, the questions are nonetheless worthy of discussion and debate. As a specific example of the administrative, valuation, and timing problems associated with the taxing of noncash receipts, consider the frequent flyer miles accumulated by a taxpayer as a result of business travel paid for by the taxpayer's employer. Conceptually, one might argue that the miles constitute additional compensation to the taxpayer. For reasons of administrative convenience, however, the Service has announced that it will "not assert that any taxpayer has understated his federal income tax liability by reason of the receipt or personal use of frequent flyer miles . . . attributable to the taxpayer's business or offical travel."[11]

§ 2.03   REALIZATION, IMPUTED INCOME AND BARGAIN PURCHASES

Gross income nevertheless does not encompass *all* "accessions to wealth." This section considers some very real limits on the meaning of gross income, limits no less real for the fact that they are not explicitly expressed in any provision of the

---

[9] Treas. Reg. § 1.61-2(d)(1).

[10] *See* Estate Tax Treas. Reg. § 20.2031-1(b).

[11] Announcement 2002-18, 2002-1 C.B. 621.

Internal Revenue Code.

[A] The Realization Requirement

Example 1: George buys $100 worth of XYZ stock at the beginning of the year. At the end of the year the stock is worth $150.

Analysis: Given low or moderate rates of inflation, it seems clear that by any common understanding of the term — and by economic definitions as well — George is wealthier now than he was when he bought the stock. Is he therefore taxed on this increased wealth, *i.e.*, on the $50 of "income" reflected in the increased value of the stock? The instinctive answer one gives is that mere appreciation in value of property is not taxable. That is the correct answer under our income tax system, as well. The technical reason for this non-taxation is that the appreciation has not been "realized"; George will not be charged with income until such realization occurs.

Example 2: Assume the facts of Example 1 and that George sells the XYZ stock for $150.

Analysis: George will now be taxed on $50 of income because that amount of income has been "realized." Indeed, the sale of property for cash is the most obvious of the "realization events."

As was emphasized earlier, income is not found in cash alone. Similarly, realization events are not limited to cash sales. For example, Treasury regulations speak of gain or loss as being realized on the conversion of property into cash or the exchange of property for other property differing materially either in kind or in extent.[12] The Code itself refers to an amount "realized" on the "sale or other disposition" of property.[13] In any case, although the mere appreciation in value of George's stock is not realization of income, it should be equally clear that George is wealthier, and a system that taxes *all* accessions to wealth could and should tax that increase.

One of the early tax cases, *Eisner v. Macomber*,[14] discussed above in connection with the definition of income, also addressed the realization requirement. Mrs. Macomber owned stock in Standard Oil of California. She and the other shareholders received a 50% stock dividend — that is, a dividend in the form of additional corporate stock rather than a cash dividend. Under the Revenue Act of 1916, the stock dividend was taxable, but the Supreme Court held (5-4) that no gain and no income had been realized by reason of the stock dividend and that Congress had no power to tax it under the Constitution.

The majority opinion suggested that realization is a constitutional requirement, *i.e.*, Congress could not constitutionally tax unrealized gain. In that sense, *Macomber* was the high-water mark of the realization requirement. By 1940,

---

[12] Treas. Reg. § 1.1001-1(a).

[13] I.R.C. § 1001(b).

[14] 252 U.S. 189, 206–207 (1920).

however, in *Helvering v. Horst*,[15] the Supreme Court was suggesting in dicta the realization requirement was merely a rule of "administrative convenience." Today, there appears to be a broad consensus that realization is not a constitutionally-required prerequisite to taxation. In the Supreme Court's 1991 decision in *Cottage Savings Association v. Commissioner*,[16] the issue presented was whether a savings and loan association "realized" losses on the exchange of its interests in one group of home mortgage loans for interests in a different group of home mortgage loans. The Court began by affirming "the concept of realization is 'founded on adminis-trative convenience.' "[17] The Court concluded the losses had in fact been realized because, based on the regulations under Section 1001, an exchange of property gives rise to a realization event as long as the exchanged properties are "materially different — that is, as long as they embody legally distinct entitlements. Cottage Savings' transactions at issue here easily satisfy this test. Because the participation interests exchanged . . . derived from loans that were made to different obligors and secured by different homes, the exchanged interests did embody legally distinct entitlements. Consequently, we conclude that Cottage Savings realized its losses at the point of the exchange."[18]

To suggest Congress could tax unrealized gain is not to suggest that Congress intends to do so. The realization requirement is a pervasive, popularly-supported aspect of our tax system, and there is no indication Congress is about to reverse course in this regard. Assuming Congress could tax "mere appreciation," there are policy reasons for and against doing so. On the one hand, taxing each year's appreciation would more nearly match tax income and economic income; it would thus tend to place on the same tax footing persons who are economically similarly situated. One might also argue the tax laws should not discourage the sale of property, and the realization requirement does so by permitting each year's unrealized appreciation to go untaxed, thus levying the entire tax in the year of disposition.

On the other hand, and without attempting a complete cataloging, two major reasons are typically offered in support of the present system. First, measuring the appreciation (and, presumably, depreciation) in all of the property of every taxpayer every year would present enormous administrative problems for taxpayers and the Internal Revenue Service. Accurate, easy valuation may not be possible with assets having no established market. As a practical (and political) matter, there are obviously very real limits on how much time, cost, and complexity can reasonably be imposed on the average taxpayer. Furthermore, the Service itself cannot be expected to scrutinize every valuation. It might be suggested, however, that such administrative problems would be adequately resolved by a more limited change in the rule. Perhaps the realization requirement would be discarded only with respect to particularly liquid assets, such as publicly traded stock, or with respect to investments of a type or magnitude — real estate investments of a certain size, for example — that one presumes the taxpayer has ready access to reliable valuation

---

[15]   311 U.S. 112 (1940).

[16]   499 U.S. 554 (1991).

[17]   *Id.* at 559.

[18]   *Id.* at 566.

assistance. Perhaps, however, the line would simply be too difficult to draw, or too arbitrary to accept.

Second, some argue it is fundamentally unfair to treat unrealized gains as income because taxpayers might lack the cash to pay resulting taxes and might thus be forced to sell assets — perhaps at artificially low prices, given the need for cash — to pay the tax. This problem might be sufficiently ameliorated by limiting the scope of any rule dispensing with the realization requirement.

In the end, whatever the merits of the realization requirement, consider what is at stake. To return to the example at the outset of this section, George does not go forever untaxed on the economic gain associated with the appreciation of his XYZ stock. When George "realizes" the gain, it will be taxed. Realization is thus fundamentally a matter of timing. The unrealized total gain, of course, may fluctuate from time to time as the property's value changes, but that total will be treated as income only on realization. To describe realization as a matter of timing should, nonetheless, not be seen as a dismissive comment. In taxes, timing can be everything — a proposition explored in some detail in chapters to come.

[B] Imputed Income

The concept of imputed income is often difficult to grasp initially. One technically has "income" from self-help activities, such as mowing the lawn, shaving, or repairing a leaky pipe, and from the use of one's own property, such as the homeowner's occupancy of a home. Imputed income is not taxed, even though the Internal Revenue Code contains no specific exclusion to that effect. The exclusion is rather a matter of administrative practice, but no less firmly established for that reason. It may be helpful to divide imputed income into two categories, imputed income from services and imputed income from property, and, in order to appreciate the economic benefit involved, to approach the topic by way of example.

Imputed income from owning and using one's own property is typically illustrated by a homeowner-versus-renter example.

> **Example 1:** John and Mary each have $250,000 to invest. John uses his $250,000 to buy a house, which he lives in, and which has a rental value of $25,000 per year. Mary invests her $250,000 in an investment paying 10% per year ($25,000). Mary then rents a house identical to John's for $25,000 per year.

> **Analysis:** Ignoring homeowner's or renter's costs, consider John's and Mary's situations: each has a $250,000 asset, each derives a $25,000 per year benefit from that asset — John in the form of the $25,000 rental value of his home, Mary in the form of $25,000 cash — but Mary's return on her investment is taxed, while John's equivalent return is nontaxable. Their economic positions and income are identical, but their tax positions are not.

Similar, though less significant or dramatic, examples could be developed with respect to ownership and use of other property, from automobiles, boats and washing machines, to pencil sharpeners, bottle cap openers and steak knives, and everything in between. Should such economic benefits be taxed? How would the value of the benefit be determined? In general, the administrative nightmare summoned forth is so powerful that even theorists limit their tax proposals to such big-ticket items as houses. The problem of determining rental value, it is suggested, may be overcome by applying a uniform percentage to the house's value as determined for local property tax purposes. The resulting amount would then be the rental value for federal income tax purposes. Arguably, if rental value were taxed, a deduction for "rental expenses" would be appropriate. Consider some of the implications of the existing system, which neither taxes the rental value of a home one owns and uses nor allows a deduction for rent paid on a home for personal use. Tax commentators frequently note that the existing system, even disregarding such matters as the tax deduction for mortgage interest (Section 163) and real property taxes (Section 164) favors home ownership over renting. Perhaps the tax benefits derived by homeowners are justified on the ground they promote societal goals such as maintaining stability of families and communities.

Imputed income is also present — but again, not treated as income and not taxed — in the economic benefit arising from self-help, *i.e.*, from performing services for oneself, one's family or others.

Example 1: The going rate for mowing lawns is $50. John mows his own lawn.

Analysis: Despite the clear value of the services he has performed for himself, John has no taxable income — only economic imputed income.

Example 2: John and his neighbor mow each other's identical lawns.

Analysis: Assume John and his neighbor are not making gifts to each other. Since income can be realized in any form, John and his neighbor presumably each have $50 of income as a result of the benefit received (the mowing of one's own lawn) from the labor performed (the mowing of the other's lawn). But if each mows his own lawn, there is, as noted earlier, a different tax result: no income. Nonetheless, it seems clear that our tax system cannot function satisfactorily if it ignores barter arrangements.

Finally, consider a somewhat different example.

Example 3: Doctor A and Doctor B have each been earning $200,000 a year from practicing medicine. Doctor A decides to spend most of her time treating the poor for free and reduces her paid practice to $100,000 per year. Doctor B, by contrast, continues to earn $200,000 annually, but gives away $100,000 of it to various poor people so that they can pay for needed medical services.

Analysis: Doctor A will not be taxed on the value of the free services she renders; a taxpayer may simply waive payment without being charged with income. This happens, in a sense, whenever we assist others without expecting or seeking compensation. Doctor B, on the other hand, has $200,000 in income. Unless he receives a deduction for his gifts to poor people (which he does not, as discussed in Chapter 26 dealing with charitable deductions) his income greatly exceeds Doctor A's, although their economic situations are identical.

The list of self-help activities that produce some economic benefit is endless, from relatively marketable activities such as lawyers drafting their own wills and doctors diagnosing their own ailments, to the most trivial, mundane and nonmarketable of activities. It has not been seriously proposed that self-help activities be taxed.

One special type of service, however, raises very serious tax policy questions. The value of full-time household services performed by homemakers — taking care of the house, taking care of children and family — is obviously quite substantial. Assume, for purposes of illustration, a value of $40,000 per year on these services and a 20% tax rate; contrast the family with a full-time homemaker spouse with the family where the parents work outside the home and hire homemaker services. The former receives, in effect, $40,000 of economic benefits tax-free; the latter obtains the benefits only after earning $50,000 and paying $10,000 in taxes. To put it another way, if the employer pays the housekeeper $40,000 per year, the housekeeper pays $8,000 to the government, and the employer-housekeeper unit thus has $8,000 less than it had at the outset. But if employer and housekeeper marry, with the housekeeping services performed as before, that same $8,000 stays within the two-person unit. The difference in the two situations reflects one of the tax benefits the Code accords married couples. Various tax provisions (see, for example, the child-care credit in Section 21 and the exclusion rule of Section 129) ameliorate the situation of the individual who hires services.

The most common tax questions related to imputed income are those associated with self-employment or employment activities. In *Morris v. Commissioner*,[19] the Board of Tax Appeals held the value of farm products consumed by the owner was not income. "If products of a farm consumed thereon are income to the producer, it would seem to follow that the rental value of the farmer's home, the gratuitous services of his wife and children, and the value of the power derived from draft animals owned by the farmer and used without cost should also be so considered. It is obvious that such items are comparable to the rental value of a private residence, which has never been regarded as income or as a factor in the determination of tax liability." A number of cases involve commissions paid to salespersons purchasing for their own account. The taxpayers claim the transaction should be viewed as a reduction in purchase price, a bargain purchase, in effect. (Bargain purchases are discussed below.) In *Commissioner v. Daehler*,[20] the taxpayer, a real estate salesman, purchased property listed with a broker who was not his employer. The broker divided the commission with the taxpayer's employer-broker, who in turn paid a commission to taxpayer. The Fifth Circuit, reversing the Tax Court, held the taxpayer's commission was income to him, not a reduction in purchase price. Earlier, in *Commissioner v. Minzner*,[21] also reversing the Tax Court, the Fifth Circuit held that an insurance agent was taxable on the commissions he received on life insurance he purchased on his own life. Thus, in these and other commission

---

[19] 9 B.T.A. 1273, 1278 (1928) (acq.).

[20] 281 F.2d 823 (5th Cir. 1960).

[21] 279 F.2d 338 (5th Cir. 1960).

cases, the taxpayers have been viewed as receiving taxable income, not non-taxable imputed income. Perhaps the difference lies in the presence of another party — the employer or an independent contractor — who is viewed as making payment to the taxpayer through reduction of the purchase price or application of the commission in accordance with the taxpayer's wishes.

[C]   Bargain Purchases

This chapter concludes with some brief comments on bargain purchases, but the brevity should not be considered a measure of the topic's significance. Assume a taxpayer purchases an asset for less than its fair market value. While it may be fair and accurate to surmise the taxpayer's wealth has increased and the taxpayer thus has taxable income, the common law of taxation concludes otherwise.

> **Example 1:** Mary buys a house for $275,000 in an arm's length transaction. The house, however, is worth $300,000, as any competent appraisal would confirm — but the seller needed money quickly and was willing to sell the house for less than its market value.

> **Analysis:** Mary has made a bargain purchase. In the absence of any indication that the sale/purchase was not an arm's length transaction, she has no income. See, for example, *Pellar v. Commissioner*.[22]

The reasons for the bargain purchase rule are not hard to discern. It would be administratively unworkable to require taxpayers and the Service to look behind every acquisition to determine whether one of the participants received a taxable bargain, and if so, in what amount. It makes obvious good sense to assume no bargain element is present in the vast bulk of arm's length transactions, and if one is, it is too speculative to measure, or is minimal enough to ignore. The occasional, obvious and measurable bargain purchase can thus perhaps be tolerated for the sake of the basic rule.

The same rule should not and does not apply where the transaction is not at arm's length. Recall the most common type of gross income — compensation for services.

> **Example 2:** As in the prior example, Mary buys a house for $275,000. The house is worth $300,000, but the seller owes Mary, who is a lawyer, $25,000 for legal services, so he satisfies his obligation by selling her the house for only $275,000.

> **Analysis:** Mary has $25,000 of income. The bargain element cannot be ignored where it represents compensation for services and Mary will be taxed accordingly.

The regulations are quite explicit on this point. If property is transferred as compensation for services in an amount less than its fair market value, the difference between the fair market value and the amount paid is gross income.[23] The rule is easy to state; determining whether a bargain element is present or

---

[22] 25 T.C. 299 (1955) (acq.).

[23] Treas. Reg. § 1.61-2(d)(2)(i).

whether it represents compensation for services is, on occasion, somewhat more difficult. (Even when there is no doubt about the presence of a bargain and its relationship to the provision of services, one might, as a matter of policy, choose to exclude the bargain element, within limits, from income. Section 132, for example, deliberately excludes certain fringe benefits from income. See the later discussion of Section 132 in Chapter 11.)

It is important not to misapply the realization requirement in connection with a compensatory bargain purchase triggering gross income. Assume, for example, an employer transfers to an employee, as compensation, stock worth $500 in return for payment of $100. Under Regulation Section 1.61-2(d)(2)(i), the employee has gross income of $400. It would be incorrect to state that the employee had no income because the $400 gain had not been realized and would not be realized until the employee disposed of the stock. The $400 difference simply does not constitute appreciation in the stock's value while in the hands of the employee. The property was given to the employee as compensation and the fair market value of that property must be used to measure the compensatory element in the transaction.

Chapter 3

THE EFFECT OF AN OBLIGATION TO REPAY

§ 3.01 LOANS

Loans are not gross income. No code provision or regulation announces this rule, but the rule is absolutely clear and fixed, and the rationale for it is straightforward. A loan does not represent an "accession to wealth" or increase the taxpayer's net worth because the loan proceeds are accompanied by an equal and offsetting liability: the borrower has an obligation to repay the loan; this repayment obligation negates treatment of a loan as income.

As a corollary to this rule, it logically follows that repayment of a loan does not reduce gross income, *i.e.*, repayment does not result in a deductible expense. A lender has no income when a loan is repaid. The lender has no deduction when the loan is made; the repayment is merely a recovery of capital for him.[1] In a federal tax system based on one's income instead of one's consumption, loans and repayments do not enter or reduce the income tax base.

It is, of course, true that not every loan is fully repaid by its borrower. Since the rationale for not treating the loan as income was the taxpayer's offsetting obligation to repay the loan, a failure to repay may generate tax consequences. Suppose, for example, a third party repays the loan on behalf of the borrower. In *Old Colony Trust Company v. Commissioner*,[2] the Court held the compensatory payment of the employee's tax liability by his employer gave rise to gross income. It was as though the employer paid the employee additional compensation and the employee then paid his own taxes. Obviously, under those circumstances, the employee has additional income in the form of salary or wages. That the process is short-circuited by the employer paying the employee's taxes directly does not change the tax results. Generalizing upon *Old Colony*, it is appropriate to conclude that the payment of one's liabilities by another may give rise to gross income.[3]

---

[1] An internally consistent tax system that reversed these rules could exist. For example, the borrower's loan proceeds could be subject to tax and loan repayments could then be deductible. Proposals for a so-called consumption tax incorporate such provisions. Loan proceeds available for consumption purposes would be subject to the consumption tax. Loan repayments, which effectively reduce the amount available for consumption, would reduce the consumption tax base and hence the consumption tax.

[2] 279 U.S. 716 (1929).

[3] However, not every payment of another's liability is compensatory in nature. For example, the payment could in some circumstances represent a gift to the borrower and therefore be excludable from income under Section 102. *See* Chapter 5, *infra*.

If, however, all or part of one's debt is forgiven by the lender, this is functionally equivalent to the lender's making payment (to itself) on behalf of the borrower to the extent of the amount forgiven. If the lender is also the employer, applying the principles of *Old Colony Trust* will result in discharge-of-indebtedness income to the employee.[4] Our tax system does not take advantage of hindsight, return to the original loan transaction and recast it as income. The loan remains a loan; it is the forgiveness that constitutes income.

While loan proceeds do not constitute income, a taxpayer may not avoid taxation by disguising compensation as a loan.

> **Example:** Andrew agrees to perform services for Patrick in Year 2. Patrick agrees to pay Andrew $10,000 in Year 2 for the services. Andrew arranges for Patrick to give Andrew a loan for $10,000 in Year 1 repayable in Year 2. In Year 2, Andrew writes a check to Patrick for $10,000 in full payment of the Year 1 loan; at the same time, Patrick writes a check to Andrew for $10,000 as compensation for the services provided by Andrew.

> **Analysis:** The Year 1 loan appears under these facts to represent a prepayment of the compensation owing to Andrew and not a true loan. In effect, Andrew received the $10,000 bargained for compensation in Year 1 and must report $10,000 of gross income in Year 1. The "loan" arrangement and the exchange of checks in Year 2 will be viewed as meaningless.

It may not always be obvious whether a transfer is a loan or a taxable payment. For example, suppose a corporation makes substantial cash disbursements to a shareholder, permits the shareholder to use the corporation's credit card for personal purposes, and pays tax liabilities owed by the shareholder. In *Morrison v. Commissioner*,[5] the Tax Court looked to the totality of the circumstances and concluded that, despite the absence of a note or other written instrument, the payments were loans, not constructive dividends; the court found that the corporation had enough funds to make the loans, that the shareholder had enough income to repay them, and that there was in fact evidence of repayment, including interest.

§ 3.02 CLAIM OF RIGHT

The proceeds of a loan are not income because the borrower is subject to an unconditional obligation to make repayment. However, money or other property received subject to a *contingent* repayment obligation is income; the contingency of the repayment obligation does not transform the receipt of income into a loan. The leading case regarding this issue is *North American Oil Consolidated v. Burnet*,[6] in which the United States Supreme Court announced a standard known as the "claim of right" doctrine:

> If a taxpayer receives earnings under a claim of right and without restriction as to its disposition, he has received income which he is required

---

[4] See the discussion of this topic in Chapter 9, *infra.*

[5] T.C. Memo. 2005–53.

[6] 286 U.S. 417 (1932).

to return [that is, to report on his tax return], even though it may still be claimed that he is not entitled to retain the money, and even though he may still be adjudged liable to restore its equivalent.[7]

North American Oil involved a dispute between the government and North American Oil Company regarding the beneficial ownership of certain oil properties. As a result of a suit instituted by the government, the net profits from the oil lands in 1916 were held in receivership. In 1917, however, a federal district court concluded that North American Oil Company was the rightful owner of the profits and the receiver paid the profits to the company. The government appealed the district court decision but the decision was affirmed. A further appeal by the government to the U.S. Supreme Court was dismissed in 1922.

The issue raised by these facts was the proper year for the inclusion of the profits in income by North American Oil Company, *i.e.*, should the profits be included in 1916, the year earned, or 1917, the year received, or 1922, the year the government's suit was ultimately dismissed? The resolution of this issue apparently made a difference to the taxpayer because of the different tax rates applicable to these different years.

Applying the claim of right doctrine noted above, the Supreme Court concluded that North American Oil Company had to include the net profits in its income for 1917. The Court noted the company actually received the profits in 1917 and did so acknowledging no obligation to repay them. The Court stated that, if the government had ultimately prevailed and the company were required to return the profits, the company would be entitled to a deduction in the amount which it had been required to include.

Thus, a taxpayer who properly reports income under the claim of right doctrine is entitled to a deduction[8] if subsequently required to return the money. But the taxpayer may never be required to return the money, and, under the claim of right doctrine, one does not await the resolution of a contingency to decide whether the receipt of the money is income. Money received under a claim of right, without restriction as to disposition, is income; the contingent repayment obligation does not allow the receipt to be treated as a loan.

Example: Publisher miscalculates the royalty owed to Author on a recently published novel and pays Author $10,000 more than Author is entitled to receive. Author receives the royalty check in Year 1 and reports it as income on her income tax return for Year 1. In Year 2, Publisher discovers its error, notifies Author, and Author returns the $10,000. May Author properly file an amended tax return for Year 1 reporting $10,000 less income?

Analysis: Under the claim of right doctrine, Author appropriately included the entire royalty payment received in Year 1. As a result of returning $10,000 of the royalty, Author will be entitled to claim a deduction or a special reduction of her Year 2 taxes. Author, however, may not recalculate

---

[7] *Id.* at 424.

[8] Or possibly a reduction in taxes under Section 1341, discussed in Chapter 30, *infra*.

her Year 1 income; she may not file an amended return as a means of correcting the problem resulting from Publisher's mistake.

The boundaries of the claim of right doctrine are less easy to state than the rule itself. What degree of restriction, for example, negates its application? Suppose the taxpayer sets aside the amounts received, retains control over them, and elects not to use them pending resolution of the dispute. The Court in *Commissioner v. Alamitos Land Co.*,[9] applied the claim of right doctrine in a case of such self-imposed voluntary restraint in which a utility company placed disputed revenues in a bank account (jointly controlled by the utility and its bonding company) to be available for repayment if required on ultimate settlement of the dispute.[10] By contrast, where the taxpayer, under court order, was required to deposit with the clerk of the court possible excess commissions collected, the amounts so deposited were not income.[11]

It has also been held that funds over which the taxpayer acts only as a conduit are not received under a claim of right. Thus, in a case where a city employee received what the government characterized as bribes, but promptly passed all the funds on to another official, the employee was held to be merely a conduit for the flow of funds, and was not taxed on them.[12] In *Ford Dealers Advertising Fund v. Commissioner,*[13] a nonprofit corporation received funds that were to be utilized solely for its nonprofit purposes. The court held the funds were received "in trust," destined for a specific use, with no gain accruing to the taxpayer, and thus were not includable in gross income.

§ 3.03 ILLEGAL INCOME

The tax treatment of illegal payments has been marked by uncertainty and course reversal. It has long been clear that gains from an illegal business may be taxed.[14] But should an embezzler's gain be taxable? Such illegally seized money can be analogized to a loan in the sense that the embezzler's receipts are subject to an offsetting absolute, unconditional obligation to make repayment. There is not even a semblance of a claim of right to the funds, and hence the application of claim of right notions seems inappropriate. By contrast, it may seem troubling or intolerable to some for an embezzler to be legally entitled to tax-free treatment on his illegally acquired funds, precisely because of their illegal provenance. To make crime a tax shelter and vice its own reward may not be a completely satisfactory tax policy.

The Supreme Court's 1961 decision in *James v. United States,*[15] holds embezzled funds includable in gross income, and is the rule today. Earlier, in *Commissioner v.*

---

[9] 112 F.2d 648 (9th Cir. 1940).

[10] *See also* Rev. Rul. 55-137, 1955-1 C.B. 215.

[11] Rev. Rul. 69-242, 1969-2 C.B. 9.

[12] Pierson v. Commissioner, T.C. Memo. 1976-281.

[13] 55 T.C. 761 (1971), *aff'd,* 456 F.2d 255 (5th Cir. 1972).

[14] *See* U.S. v. Sullivan, 274 U.S. 259 (1927).

[15] 366 U.S. 213 (1961).

Wilcox,[16] the Court had held embezzled funds not includable in income, because of the obligation to repay. Subsequently, in *Rutkin v. United States,*[17] the Court distinguished between embezzlement and extortion, and held that extorted funds constituted income, reasoning that the extortioner's victim is considerably less likely than the embezzler's victim to demand repayment. Several years later, *James* eliminated this nice distinction and overruled *Wilcox.* The Court in *James* noted the broad principle articulated by the Court in *Glenshaw Glass*[18] that the Section 61 language "all income from whatever source derived" encompassed all "accessions to wealth, clearly realized, and over which the taxpayer has complete dominion." In view of this broad principle, the Court rejected the taxpayer's argument that unlawful gains resulting from embezzlement are not subject to tax:

> When a taxpayer acquires earnings, lawfully or unlawfully, without the consensual recognition, express or implied, of an obligation to repay and without restriction as to their disposition, he has received income which he is required to return, even though he may still be adjudged liable to restore its equivalent.[19]

Although *James* appears to stand for the proposition that all illegal receipts are within gross income, questions may arise on the margins. In *Gilbert v. Commissioner,*[20] the taxpayer made unauthorized withdrawals of corporate funds and subsequently pleaded guilty to state and federal charges of having unlawfully withdrawn the funds. However, he had promptly informed several of the corporate officers and directors of the withdrawals, and apparently believed he was acting in the best interests of the corporation as well as his own in withdrawing the funds to meet a "margin call" on stock he had purchased. Finding for the taxpayer, the Second Circuit concluded the taxpayer did not realize income under the *James* test because the taxpayer fully intended to repay the withdrawn funds, expected with a reasonable certainty to be able to repay them, believed that the withdrawals would be approved by the corporation, and made a prompt assignment of assets sufficient to secure the amount owed. The corporation was not able to recover fully the amounts withdrawn, but in these circumstances both the taxpayer and the Second Circuit regarded the transaction as being in the nature of a loan.

The *James* case suggests, and the Service concedes, that repayment of illegal income entitles the taxpayer to a deduction.[21] Suppose in the same year the embezzlement occurs, the embezzler is caught, promises to make repayment, and executes a confession of judgment in favor of the victim. Does the embezzlement still constitute gross income? The Second Circuit said "yes" in *Buff v. Commissioner,*[22] reversing the Tax Court, and rejecting the argument that the "consensual recognition" of indebtedness within the same tax year transformed the transaction

---

[16]   327 U.S. 404 (1946).

[17]   343 U.S. 130 (1952).

[18]   Comm'r v. Glenshaw Glass, 348 U.S. 426 (1955). *See* Chapter 2, *supra.*

[19]   366 U.S. at 219.

[20]   552 F.2d 478 (2d Cir. 1971).

[21]   Rev. Rul. 65-254, 1965-2 C.B. 50.

[22]   496 F.2d 847 (1974).

into a loan; it also noted that no payment had actually been made on the judgment.

In any event, it may not always be easy to distinguish loans from illegal income, to differentiate the swindler from the failed, but legitimate promoter who has lost the funds loaned to or invested in his enterprise. The taxpayers in *Kreimer v. Commissioner*,[23] had been convicted of obtaining loans under false pretenses amounting to fraud, and the Commissioner sought to tax the funds as income. The Tax Court held that, although the taxpayers had misrepresented the transactions, nonetheless the proceeds they obtained were loans, not gross income, since the taxpayers had always regarded and treated the obligations as bona fide debt they intended to repay. By contrast, where there is a consistent pattern of fraudulent dealing demonstrating an absence of an intent to repay, merely labeling the funds obtained as "loans" will not avoid gross income.[24]

The receipt of illegal income may raise significant Fifth Amendment questions. May a taxpayer successfully assert his constitutional rights against compulsory self-incrimination, and decline on that basis to report his illegal income? The boundaries of the Fifth Amendment protections are not completely clear in regard to tax returns and proceedings. The Supreme Court in *United States v. Sullivan*,[25] stated that:

> If the form of return provided called for answers that the defendant was privileged from making, he could have raised the objection on the return, but could not on that account refuse to make any return at all. . . . It would be an extreme if not an extravagant application of the Fifth Amendment to say that it authorized a man to refuse to state the amount of his income because it had been made in crime. But if the defendant desired to test that or any other point, he should have tested it in the return so that it would be passed upon. He could not draw a conjurer's circle around the whole matter by his own deduction that to write any word upon the government blank would bring him into danger of the law.[26]

§ 3.04 DEPOSITS

An advance payment of income is still income. The regulations explicitly provide that rent paid in advance generally constitutes gross income in the year it is received regardless of the period covered or the taxpayer's method of accounting.[27] By contrast, a loan is not income because there is an offsetting obligation of repayment. The question then arises regarding how "deposits" should be treated. They could be treated as analogous to loans under the duty-to-repay rationale, and thus nontaxable, or they could be treated like advance payments of income and taxable on receipt. The question arises most frequently with respect to "security deposits" in connection with landlord-tenant leases, although utility company

---

[23] T.C. Memo 1983-672.

[24] U.S. v. Rochelle, 384 F.2d 748 (5th Cir. 1967); U.S. v. Rosenthal, 470 F.2d 837 (2d Cir. 1972).

[25] 274 U.S. 259 (1927).

[26] *Id.* at 263–64.

[27] Treas. Reg. § 1.61-8(b).

deposit cases have presented the issue as well. The result often turns on a "facts and circumstances" analysis.

In a 1990 case, the Supreme Court considered whether certain utility deposits were advance payments and therefore includable in income, or more like loans and thus not includable in income because of the offsetting obligation to repay. In *Commissioner v. Indianapolis Power & Light Company,*[28] most customers of the taxpayer were not required to make deposits. The customers making deposits had the right to control the ultimate disposition of the deposit. They could require a refund from the company if they met creditworthiness standards. Only customers who did not pay their bills could not get a refund. Thirty-one to forty percent of the deposits were refunded by check, indicating that customers were aware of their right to demand a refund. Most of the customers, of course, simply directed that their refund be applied to what they owed. The utility company had only minimal rights vis-a-vis the deposits; among other things, unclaimed deposits had to be turned over to the state and the utility company could exercise control over the deposit only when the customer failed to pay his utility bills. The utility always treated the deposits as belonging to the customer; it paid interest on many of the deposits and gave the customers a receipt indicating their cash was on deposit.

In determining whether the customer deposits were advance payments, the Court examined the "nature of the rights and obligations" the utility had on receiving the deposits. Focusing on whether the utility enjoyed "complete dominion" over the deposits, the Court concluded it did not, since the deposits were subject to an "express obligation to repay." "The key [in determining complete dominion] is whether the taxpayer has some guarantee that he will be allowed to keep the money." That the deposits were commingled with other funds was not dispositive, given the obligation to repay. Similarly, while Indianapolis Power and Light did pay interest on "deposits," the Supreme Court eschewed the opportunity to rely on this to any degree.

The Supreme Court rejected the Commissioner's advance payment argument because by its nature an advance payment "protects against the risk that the purchaser will back out of the deal before the seller performs," whereas the deposits the utility received provided no such protection. The fact that deposits were frequently applied to utility bills was a matter of customer choice, not proof of advance payment. On this point, as the Court noted, utility deposits are "less plausibly regarded as income than lease deposits would be," since the lease deposit reflects a contractual obligation to pay rent for a specified period, and the utility deposit reflects no analogous contractual obligation. Nonetheless, the Court pointed out that its decision was consistent with the Tax Court's treatment of lease deposits, a treatment that stresses, as part of a facts and circumstances analysis, the question of control: does the landlord or the tenant control the ultimate disposition of the funds? The Tax Court subsequently applied *Indianapolis Power and Light* in the rental context, holding that refundable amounts received from tenants were not income to the taxpayer, in light of the tenants' control over the refunds and the

---

[28] 493 U.S. 203 (1990).

taxpayer's lack of "unfettered dominion" over the funds.[29]

Similarly, in *Perry Funeral Home, Inc. v. Commissioner*,[30] the Tax Court, relying on the "complete dominion" or "control" rationale of *Indianapolis Power & Light*, concluded that amounts received by the taxpayer funeral home pursuant to so-called "preneed funeral contracts" constituted nontaxable deposits and would therefore be includable in the taxpayer's income only upon the taxpayer's actual provision of goods and services pursuant to the contract. Under the preneed funeral contract, a buyer prepaid the taxpayer for certain goods and services to be provided by the taxpayer upon the buyer's death. State regulations, however, specifically provided that preneed funeral contracts could be cancelled by the buyer or the buyer's legal representative at any time prior to the actual provision of the goods and services by the taxpayer. The taxpayer's records indicated that, during a six-year period through the time of the trial in the case, only six preneed contracts were cancelled.

The Tax Court rejected the Service's argument that prepayments under the preneed contracts were not the equivalent of a refundable security deposit or loan and, hence, were not controlled by the standards set forth in *Indianapolis Power & Light*. Just as in *Indianapolis Power & Light*, the buyer or the buyer's legal representative controlled the conditions under which money paid to the taxpayer would be refunded; and the taxpayer had no guaranty it could keep the money received and thus no "unfettered dominion" over it. The taxpayer's unrestricted use of the money in the interim, the nonpayment of interest, and the later application of the money to goods and services were not dispositive in determining whether the taxpayer had the necessary level of dominion to treat the prepayments as gross income. The low level of cancellations did not warrant disregarding the buyer's cancellation right because, according to the Tax Court, "it is the bona fide existence of such a right, not the exercise or frequency of exercise, which controls." To the extent an advance payment serves to protect a taxpayer against the risk a buyer will back out before the taxpayer has a chance to perform, the taxpayer in *Perry Funeral Home* had no such protection — the taxpayer's opportunity to provide the goods and services that would eliminate the cancellation right was contingent upon the later choice of the buyer's legal representative to call upon the taxpayer to act under the contract.

---

[29] Highland Farms, Inc. v. Comm'r, 106 T.C. 237 (1996).

[30] T.C. Memo. 2003-340.

Chapter 4

GAINS DERIVED FROM DEALINGS IN PROPERTY

§ 4.01 COMPUTING GAIN DERIVED FROM DEALINGS IN PROPERTY

Section 61(a)(3) specifies that gross income includes "gains derived from dealings in property." Determining such gain involves several important concepts, including "recovery of capital," "basis," "adjusted basis," and "amount realized." These concepts must be examined in order to understand the tax treatment of even the most common property transactions.

Consider the following example which demonstrates the gain-as-income notion:

> **Example:** Melissa purchased stock in XYZ Corporation for $800 last year. During the next 12 months, the stock increased at the rate of $10 per month. Melissa sold the stock this year for $2,000. How much income must Melissa report?

As discussed in Chapter 2, appreciation on property is not reportable as income until it is realized. Realization occurs when there is a sale, exchange or other disposition of property. Thus, although her stock may be publicly traded and its increasing value documented daily in the reports of the New York Stock Exchange, Melissa "realizes" no income as long as she owns the stock. Her sale of the stock is a realization event. Section 61(a)(3), however, taxes "*gain* derived from dealings in property." Melissa will be taxed only on the *gain* from the sale of the stock.

§ 1001. Determination of Amount of and Recognition of Gain or Loss.

(a) Computation of Gain or Loss. The gain from the sale or other disposition of property shall be the excess of the amount realized therefrom over the adjusted basis provided in section 1011 for determining gain, and the loss shall be the excess of the adjusted basis provided in such section for determining loss over the amount realized.

(b) Amount Realized. The amount realized from the sale or other disposition of property shall be the sum of any money received plus the fair market value of the property (other than money) received . . .

(c) Recognition of Gain or Loss. Except as otherwise provided in this subtitle, the entire amount of the gain or loss, determined under this section, on the sale or exchange of property shall be recognized.

[G]ain is the excess of the amount realized over the unrecovered cost or other basis for the property sold or exchanged. The specific rules for computing the amount of gain or loss are contained in Section 1001 and the regulations thereun der."[1] Section 1001 contains a comparable definition of gain with one exception — instead of "unrecovered cost," Section 1001(a) speaks of "adjusted basis." "Unrecovered cost" is the same as adjusted basis.

The "amount realized" on the sale or disposition of property equals the money received plus the fair market value of any other property received.[2] Melissa's amount realized is thus $2,000. Her adjusted basis in the stock is her "unrecovered cost," in this case, $800, the amount Melissa paid for the stock. Statutorily, Section 1001(a) directs the taxpayer to Section 1011 for a definition of adjusted basis. Section 1011(a) provides that adjusted basis is equal to the basis as determined under Section 1012 (or other appropriate section) adjusted as provided in Section 1016.

While numerous provisions in the Code address basis, the most significant is Section 1012. It prescribes that basis equals cost "except as otherwise provided . . . ." Subsequent chapters will address other basis provisions which give meaning to the "except-as-otherwise-provided" language in Section 1012. In Melissa's case, her basis is her "cost." Most commonly, cost is the amount paid for an item. Thus, Melissa's basis in the stock is $800.

Determination of adjusted basis requires a consideration of Section 1016, which requires a taxpayer to adjust her basis to reflect recovery of investment or any additional investment. In other words, adjusted basis reflects the impact events occurring subsequent to one's acquisition of property may have on the amount of one's investment in the property. Two brief examples will demonstrate the necessity of adjustments to basis:

> **Example 1:** Jackie purchased a home for $350,000 and subsequently added a room to the home at a cost of $75,000. Although Jackie's original basis in the home was $350,000, *i.e.*, the amount she paid for the home, she must adjust the basis in her home to reflect the additional investment which the new room represents. Therefore, Jackie's adjusted basis (or unrecovered cost) is $425,000.

> **Example 2:** Assume the same facts as Example 1 but also that a small greenhouse attached to Jackie's home was completely destroyed in a hail storm and Jackie recovered $10,000 from her insurance company for the destruction of the greenhouse. Instead of investing the $10,000 in replacing the greenhouse, she used the $10,000 to take a cruise. Because the insurance proceeds represent a partial recovery of the cost of the home, Jackie must adjust her basis to reflect that recovery. Her adjusted basis (or unrecovered cost) in the home would therefore be $415,000, *i.e.*, $425,000 less the $10,000 recovery.

Unlike the taxpayer in either of the above examples, Melissa has neither invested more in the XYZ company nor recovered any of her cost. Therefore, no adjustments may be made to Melissa's basis. Her adjusted basis is the same as her original basis — $800.

---

[1] Treas. Reg. § 1.61-6(a).

[2] I.R.C. § 1001(b).

Once the amount realized and adjusted basis are known, the amount of Melissa's gain, and therefore her income from the sale of the stock is readily computed. The amount realized of $2,000 less the adjusted basis of $800 equals $1,200 of gain which, according to Section 61(a)(3), constitutes gross income.[3]

This example demonstrates a fundamental principle in our income tax system — the taxpayer may recover tax-free her investment (capital) in property before being charged with income from a disposition of the property. Melissa, having paid $800 for the stock, was entitled to recover $800 from the sale of the stock tax-free. Had Melissa sold the stock for only $800, she would have had no gain and thus no income. Had she sold the stock for less than $800, she would have had a loss. Only the excess of the amount realized over her investment of $800 constituted income. This principle is often referred to as the "recovery of capital" or "return of capital" concept. As the example demonstrates, "basis" and "adjusted basis" implement the recovery of capital concept by providing a measure of the capital (or investment) the taxpayer is entitled to recover tax-free. Briefly stated, basis prevents previously taxed dollars from being taxed a second time.

That the recovery of capital concept is implicit in the notion of "income" was recognized by the Supreme Court in *Doyle v. Mitchell Bros. Co.*,[4] a case interpreting the Corporation Excise Tax Act of 1909. The issue in *Mitchell Bros.* was whether gross receipts from the conversion of assets constituted gross income. Concluding that a business computing its gross income may deduct its cost in the assets sold from its gross receipts, the Court noted:

> [W]e think, that by the true intent and meaning of the act the entire proceeds of a mere conversion of capital assets were not to be treated as income. Whatever difficulty there may be about a precise and scientific definition of "income," it imports . . . something entirely distinct from principal or capital either as a subject of taxation or as a measure of the tax; conveying rather the idea of gain or increase . . . . Understanding the term in this natural and obvious sense, it cannot be said that a conversion of capital assets invariably produces income. If sold at less than cost, it produces rather loss or outgo. Nevertheless, in many if not in most cases there results a gain that properly may be accounted as a part of the "gross income" received "from all sources"; and by applying to this the authorized deductions we arrive at "net income." In order to determine whether there has been gain or loss, and the amount of the gain if any, we must withdraw from the gross proceeds an amount sufficient to restore the capital value that existed at the commencement of the period under consideration.[5]

As demonstrated above, Sections 61(a)(3) and 1001 reflect the very standard discussed by the Court in *Mitchell Bros.*

---

[3] Melissa's XYZ stock would be classified as a "capital asset" under Section 1221, and the gain on its sale would be characterized as long term capital gain if she had held the stock for more than one year. In turn, this gain would be subject to preferential tax rates under Section 1(h). Characterization and the preferential treatment accorded to long term capital gains will be discussed in detail in Chapter 31, *infra*.

[4] 247 U.S. 179 (1918).

[5] *Id.* at 184, 185.

If, prior to selling her stock, Melissa had received a $10 dividend from XYZ Company, that dividend, unlike the insurance proceeds in the greenhouse example above, would not constitute a tax-free return of capital. Nor would it be reflected by a downward adjustment of Melissa's basis in the stock, thus increasing her gain when she sold the stock. Rather, the dividend would constitute profit from Melissa's investment in XYZ and would be treated as gross income.[6] Congress could have provided that dividends paid by corporations to their shareholders are tax free until the shareholder has recovered her basis (investment) in the stock, but it chose not to do so. Instead, a dividend is viewed as earnings on or profit from one's investment much the way rent represents earnings on one's property or interest represents earnings on one's money. Just as rents[7] and interest[8] are gross income, so too are dividends. Thus, because Melissa must report the $10 dividend as gross income, she is not treated as having recovered any of her investment in the stock, and her basis in the stock is not adjusted to reflect the receipt of the dividend.

The recovery of capital concept is applicable in contexts other than that involving the disposition of property. A common example of its application is found in the borrowing context. As noted in Chapter 3, loans are not gross income to the borrower. Conversely, when a loan is repaid, the lender has no income and has merely recovered the amount he had loaned. For the borrower, the repayment of the loan principal represents a recovery of capital. Other examples of the application of the concept will be considered in later Chapters in this text.

§ 4.02   TAX COST BASIS

If a taxpayer receives property in lieu of cash compensation for services rendered, the fair market value of that property is taxable to him as income (*see* Chapter 2). The taxpayer is then treated as having a basis in the property equal to the fair market value upon which he was taxed. This basis is commonly referred to as a "tax cost basis."

Assume, for example, a taxpayer received from his employer a car in lieu of cash compensation. The car had a fair market value of $25,000 — exactly equal to the compensation owing to the taxpayer. The taxpayer upon receiving the car had $25,000 of compensation income. If the taxpayer subsequently sells the car for $25,500, he has only $500 of gain — the excess of the amount received over his basis. The $25,000 upon which he was already taxed is his "tax cost basis." The total income from the receipt and sale of the car is thus $25,500, just as though the taxpayer first received $25,000 in cash from his employer, purchased the car from the employer for that amount, and then sold the car for $25,500.

A further issued raised by the above example is the tax impact on the employer who transfers the car in lieu of cash to satisfy an obligation owed to the employee. If the employer's adjusted basis in the car were $20,000, the employer would "realize" gain in the amount of $5,000, *i.e.*, the difference between the employer's

---

[6] I.R.C. § 61(a)(7).

[7] I.R.C. § 61(a)(5).

[8] I.R.C. § 61(a)(4).

amount realized ($25,000 obligation satisfied) and the employer's adjusted basis in the car ($20,000).[9]

Assume in the above example the car was worth $35,000 and the taxpayer paid the employer $10,000 for the car. One might be tempted to conclude that the taxpayer has simply made a bargain purchase and therefore need not report any income. As a result, the taxpayer's basis in the car would be $10,000. Given, however, the relationship of the parties and the circumstances of the transfer (*i.e.*, the intention of the employer to compensate the taxpayer for services rendered), the $25,000 "bargain element" must be characterized as compensation and the taxpayer must report $25,000 of income. The taxpayer's basis will therefore be $35,000, *i.e.*, the $10,000 cash paid plus the $25,000 of compensation of income reported.[10] If taxpayer were subsequently to sell the car for $36,000, the taxpayer would recognize gain of $1,000.

§ 4.03 IMPACT OF LIABILITIES

[A] Impact on Basis

The amount of a taxpayer's investment in property, and therefore the taxpayer's initial basis in property, is clear when there are no liabilities encumbering the property and the taxpayer pays cash for the property. However, computation of the taxpayer's basis is complicated if property is not paid for in full at the time of purchase, *e.g.*, if the purchaser remains obligated to the seller for part of the purchase price, assumes a liability of the seller, takes the property subject to the liability, or borrows money from a third party to pay the purchase price. Consider the following examples:

> **Example 1:** Julie purchases a tract of unimproved land from Paul for $100,000 and borrows the full $100,000 from the Last National Bank. Assume Julie gives the bank a promissory note for $100,000 secured by a mortgage on the land. The note is a recourse note, *i.e.*, if Julie should fail to make loan payments as required, the Bank could look not only to the land for purposes of repayment but also to Julie's other assets. What basis does Julie have in the land?

> **Analysis:** It is clear that, in borrowing the funds to purchase the land, Julie has incurred an obligation to repay the Last National Bank. Presumably, she will repay the loan and thus actually make a $100,000 investment in the land. Her cost is really $100,000. As noted by the Supreme Court in *Commissioner v. Tufts*,[11] "[b]ecause of the obligation to repay, the taxpayer

---

[9] Assuming the car were one which the employer held for personal purposes, the gain on the transfer of the car would be characterized as a capital gain. See Chapter 31, *infra*, for a discussion of capital gains and losses. By contrast, if one assumes the employer used the car for business purposes and claimed depreciation deductions with respect to the car, the character of the gain would be ordinary to the extent the gain is attributable to depreciation deductions allowed to the employer. See Chapter 33, *infra*, for a detailed discussion of depreciation recapture.

[10] Treas. Reg. § 1.61–2(d)(2)(i).

[11] 461 U.S. 300, 307 (1983).

is entitled to include the amount of the loan in computing his basis in the property; the loan under Section 1012, is part of the taxpayer's cost of the property." Thus, whether the funds Julie uses to purchase the land are borrowed or were from her savings, her basis in the land is the same — $100,000.

Example 2: Assume the same facts as in Example 1 except Julie borrows the $100,000 from Paul instead of the Last National Bank, *i.e.*, Paul will sell the land to Julie under a contract requiring Julie to pay Paul the purchase price over a period of time. What basis does Julie have in the property?

Analysis: It makes no difference that the "lender" is also the seller. Julie's basis in the property is $100,000, the same basis as in Example 1.

Example 3: Assume the same facts as in Example 2 except Julie is not personally liable for repayment of the borrowed funds. Thus, if she should default on the contract, her property, other than the land, would not be subject to Paul's claims. (Where there is no personal liability associated with borrowing, the borrowing is considered "nonrecourse.") What basis does Julie have in the property?

Analysis: The nonrecourse nature of the loan does not change the taxpayer's basis. The Commissioner in *Crane v. Commissioner*,[12] argued that nonrecourse and recourse debt should be accorded the same treatment and the Supreme Court agreed.[13] Julie will therefore have a $100,000 basis in the property just as before.

As the above rules indicate, by reflecting in the basis of property the debt incurred by a taxpayer in acquiring the property, the tax system gives credit to a taxpayer for an investment the taxpayer has yet to make. Because depreciation deductions are computed with reference to one's basis in property,[14] this treatment of debt can be beneficial to a taxpayer acquiring depreciable assets. Having received advance credit for making the investment, however, the taxpayer is not permitted to increase her basis when the debt is paid. Thus, as Julie makes payments on the $100,000 borrowed to purchase the property, there will be no change (adjustment) in her basis.

[B]   Impact on Amount Realized

Determination of the amount realized by a seller is likewise not straightforward when the property sold is encumbered by liabilities for which the purchaser directly or indirectly becomes responsible. Consider the following example:

Example: Assume Daniel purchased a home for $400,000. Daniel borrowed $300,000 of the purchase price and gave the lender a recourse note secured

---

[12] 331 U.S. 1 (1947).

[13] The *Crane* rationale and the special problems associated with nonrecourse liabilities are discussed in Chapter 37, *infra*. This chapter focuses exclusively on the impact of recourse liabilities on basis and amount realized.

[14] See Chapter 14, *infra*, for a thorough discussion of depreciation.

by a mortgage on the property. The other $100,000 of the purchase price was paid from Daniel's savings. Three years later, when Daniel still owed $275,000 to the lender, Daniel sold the home to Michael for $500,000. Michael paid Daniel $225,000 cash (Daniel's equity in the home) and assumed the $275,000 liability encumbering the home. What is Daniel's amount realized? $225,000 or $500,000?

Analysis: In defining amount realized, Section 1001(b) does not mention liabilities but only cash or other property. If one considered only the $225,000 of cash actually received by Daniel, an anomalous result would follow. Daniel's basis (adjusted basis) in the home is $400,000. (See the previous discussion of the impact of liabilities on basis. Note that, in paying $25,000 on his mortgage, Daniel did not increase his basis in the home. As explained previously, he had already received advance credit for making that payment.) If Daniel's amount realized is only $225,000, then Daniel has sustained a $175,000 loss. That, of course, is absurd; the home appreciated $100,000 in value from the time Daniel purchased it. Therefore, rather than a loss, Daniel should have a gain of $100,000. If the liability assumed by Michael is included in Daniel's amount realized, the correct result is reached: Daniel will realize $100,000 of gain, *i.e.*, the difference between his amount realized of $500,000 ($225,000 cash plus $275,000 liability assumed) and the adjusted basis of the home ($400,000).

Thus, a necessary corollary to the inclusion of liabilities in basis is the inclusion in amount realized of liabilities of the taxpayer assumed by the purchaser.[15] This conclusion is supported by the principle announced in *Old Colony Trust Company v. Commissioner*,[16] discussed in Chapter 2, *i.e.*, the payment of one's obligation by another may constitute income. Where, as part of the purchase price, a buyer agrees to assume the seller's liability, it is just as though the buyer paid the amount of the liability directly to the seller and the seller used the amount received to pay the liability. Given those circumstances, the payment by the buyer of the liability amount to the seller would be included in the seller's amount realized. No different result occurs when the buyer pays the seller's creditor directly.

At this juncture, two general rules are apparent: (1) recourse liabilities assumed by a taxpayer in the acquisition of property are included in the taxpayer's basis in that property; and (2) a seller must include in her amount realized on a sale of encumbered property the recourse liabilities assumed by the purchaser.[17]

---

[15] Treas. Reg. § 1.1001-2(a)(1) and (4)(i), (ii). See *Commissioner v. Tufts*, 461 U.S. 300, 309–310 (1983), which is discussed in Chapter 37, *infra*.

[16] 279 U.S. 716 (1929).

[17] As will be discussed in Chapter 38, *infra*, comparable rules are applicable to nonrecourse indebtedness.

§ 4.04   BASIS OF PROPERTY ACQUIRED IN TAXABLE EXCHANGES

Section 1012 states that the basis of property is generally its cost. If an individual, in a taxable exchange, "pays" for newly acquired property with other property, the cost, and thus the basis, of that newly acquired property is not always, as one might expect, the value of the property given in exchange. Rather, as discussed below, the rule is that the basis of property acquired in a taxable exchange is the fair market value of the property acquired.

Assume, for example, Joe exchanges his 100 shares of stock in XYZ Co. for George's 100 shares of stock in ABC Co. Joe's basis in his XYZ stock is $5,000 and the stock is worth $10,000. George's ABC stock is worth $10,000. Joe's gain is clearly $5,000: his amount realized is $10,000, the value of the ABC stock he receives; and his basis in the XYZ stock he gives up is $5,000. But what basis does Joe take in the ABC stock? On the facts of this example, where the property received and the property given up have the same value, the answer is easy — Joe's basis in the ABC stock is $10,000 regardless of whether we look to the value of the property received or the value of the property given up.

A different example, however, will demonstrate why, in point of fact, the basis of the acquired property should be based on the value of that property. Assume Joe and George agreed to the exchange when their properties had the same value, $10,000. But some time later, when Joe and George actually exchanged stock certificates, the value of George's stock had fallen to $9,000 while Joe's stock retained its $10,000 value. Joe's amount realized on the exchange of his XYZ stock is $9,000, the value of the ABC stock received. Joe's adjusted basis in the XYZ stock was $5,000. Therefore, Joe's gain under Section 1001(a) is $4,000. If Joe's basis in the $9,000 of ABC stock he received in the exchange were $10,000, i.e., the value of his XYZ stock he gave up, there would be a $1,000 loss inherent in the ABC stock. Were Joe to sell that stock for its fair market value of $9,000 the day after the exchange, Joe would recognize the $1,000 loss, i.e., the amount realized ($9,000) less the adjusted basis ($10,000) equals a loss of $1,000. Combining the $4,000 gain on the exchange with the $1,000 loss on the hypothetical sale, Joe would have realized a net gain of $3,000. If, instead of exchanging the XYZ stock for ABC stock and then immediately converting the ABC stock into $9,000 of cash, Joe had merely sold the XYZ stock for $9,000, Joe would have recognized $4,000 of gain. Clearly, the result should be no different where there is first an exchange for other stock worth $9,000 followed by a conversion of the stock into $9,000 of cash. And yet, if Joe's basis in the ABC stock is $10,000, there will be a difference, i.e., Joe's net gain will be $3,000 instead of $4,000 — an obvious understatement of the gain inherent in the overall transaction.

Consider George's situation. His amount realized on the exchange with Joe is $10,000, the value of the XYZ stock George receives. Assume George's adjusted basis in the ABC stock was $12,500. Therefore, his Section 1001(a) loss on the exchange is $2,500. If his basis in the $10,000 of newly acquired XYZ stock were only $9,000, the value of the ABC stock he gave up at the time of the exchange, he would have a potential gain of $1,000 in the XYZ stock received from Joe. Were he to sell the XYZ stock the next day for $10,000, he would recognize this $1,000 gain.

Combining the loss of $2,500 on the exchange and the gain of $1,000 on the sale, George's net loss would only be $1,500. Again, if one were to eliminate the exchange and assume that George merely sold his ABC stock for $10,000 cash, George's loss would be $2,500. Thus, to treat George's basis in the property received in the exchange as equaling the value of the ABC stock he gave up at the time of the exchange is to understate George's loss, *i.e.*, George would have only $1,500 of loss instead of the $2,500 of loss he has actually sustained.

The issue raised by the above example was considered by the Court of Claims (now known as the United States Court of Federal Claims) in *Philadelphia Park Amusement Co. v. U.S.*[18] The taxpayer in that case operated an amusement park in Philadelphia. Under the circumstances presented, the Court of Federal Claims rejected the view that the cost basis of property received in a taxable exchange is the fair market value of the property *given* in the exchange. Rather, the court held that "the cost basis of the property received in a taxable exchange is the fair market value of the property *received* in the exchange" (emphasis added). The court reasoned as follows:

> When property is exchanged for property in a taxable exchange, the taxpayer is taxed on the difference between the adjusted basis of the property given in exchange and the fair market value of the property received in exchange. For purposes of determining gain or loss, the fair market value of the property received is treated as cash and taxed accordingly. To maintain harmony with the fundamental purpose of these sections, it is necessary to consider the fair market value of the property received as the cost basis to the taxpayer. The failure to do so would result in allowing the taxpayer a stepped-up basis, without paying a tax therefor, if the fair market value of the property received is less than the fair market value of the property given, and the taxpayer would be subjected to a double tax if the fair market value of the property received is more than the fair market value of the property given.[19]

Applying this reasoning to the example of the stock exchange between Joe and George above, gain and loss are distorted if the cost basis of property received in a taxable exchange is considered to be equal to the fair market value of property given in the exchange. In effect, when that incorrect standard was applied to Joe, he took a stepped-up basis in the ABC stock, *i.e.*, he received a basis of $10,000 instead of the $9,000 basis which *Philadelphia Park* required and, in turn, Joe's net gain was ultimately reduced. By contrast, George was incorrectly subject to a double tax in that the amount of loss he actually sustained on the transaction was understated. Applying the standard established by *Philadelphia Park*, these distortions are eliminated, *i.e.*, Joe's basis in the ABC stock will be $9,000 rather than $10,000; George's basis in the XYZ stock will be $10,000 rather than $9,000. The standard enunciated in *Philadelphia Park* has specific application to those exchanges where the properties exchanged differ in value as in the above example. If the properties exchanged do not differ in value, one can confidently determine the

---

[18] 126 F. Supp. 184 (Ct. Cl. 1954).

[19] *Id.* at 188.

basis in the property received by reference to the value of the property relinquished.

The foregoing example did not involve liabilities associated with either the property exchanged or the property received. The following example addresses a taxable exchange involving a liability which is assumed and demonstrates the complex analysis which can be entailed in dealing with liabilities and basis.

Example: Dory exchanged a truck for a vacant lot owned by Kevin. Dory's adjusted basis in the truck was $25,000 and the truck had a fair market value of $30,000. Kevin's land was worth $40,000 but was encumbered by a liability in the amount of $10,000 which Dory assumed. What are the tax consequences to Dory?

Analysis: Dory's amount realized is $40,000, the fair market value of the land received from Kevin. Dory's adjusted basis for purposes of the Section 1001 gain calculation is not only the adjusted basis she had in her truck ($25,000) but also the $10,000 she has agreed to pay as a result of her assumption of Kevin's liability. In other words, Dory is giving up both a truck and ultimately $10,000 in cash when she pays the liability she assumed. As discussed previously, Dory will be given advance credit in basis for paying the $10,000 liabilities, *i.e.*, she will be viewed as investing currently another $10,000 in the deal. Thus, Dory's gain is $5,000, *i.e.*, amount realized ($40,000) less adjusted basis ($25,000 plus $10,000) equals $5,000. According to *Philadelphia Park*, her basis in Kevin's lot will equal the fair market value of the lot — her amount realized, *i.e.*, $40,000. If, subsequent to the exchange, Dory were to make a payment on the mortgage principal, her basis would not be affected because she has already been credited in basis with paying the full $10,000 mortgage balance.

Chapter 5

GIFTS, BEQUESTS AND INHERITANCE

§ 5.01 EXCLUSION OF GIFTS FROM INCOME

Gifts are given and received on a variety of occasions. Despite the holding of *Glenshaw Glass*[1] that accessions to wealth generally constitute income, and a gift is clearly an accession to wealth, Congress has specifically excluded gifts from income in each income tax act since 1913.[2]

§ 102. Gifts and Inheritances.

(a) General rule

Gross income does not include the value of property acquired by gift, bequest, devise, or inheritance.

The continued exclusion of gifts can be justified for both public policy and administrative reasons. Most gifts occur within the family unit. Indeed, the sharing of goods and services is common in any household. Sometimes that sharing manifests itself in a formal way through a gift from one family member to another on a special occasion, such as a birthday or Christmas; at other times the sharing is informal, such as daily meals shared by members of the same household, cars and other equipment used in common by family members, etc. Such formal and informal sharing arrangements are natural and important aspects of family life and should not be burdened with tax considerations. Furthermore, administratively it would be impossible to enforce a rule that such sharing arrangements give rise to income.

The exclusion for gifts, however, is not limited to intrafamily wealth transfers. Friends exchange gifts and gifts even occur in the employment setting between employers and employees. Certainly, the further a transfer is removed from the family context, the more strained becomes the justification for a gift exclusion and the more likely the Service and the courts are to question whether the transfer really rises to the level of a gift.

[A] The Nature of a Gift

Section 102 excludes gifts as well as property acquired from a decedent through bequest, devise or inheritance. Thus, property which we receive as a result of the generosity of a person either during his lifetime or at his death is excluded from income.

---

[1] *Comm'r v. Glenshaw Glass*, 348 U.S. 426 (1955), is discussed in Chapter 1, *supra*.

[2] The donor may be required to pay a gift tax on some transfers. Discussion of gift tax issues are beyond the scope of this book.

A threshold question under Section 102 is whether that which is received can be characterized as a gift, bequest, devise or inheritance. If it cannot be so characterized, then the Section 102 exclusion obviously is inapplicable. Identifying excludable gifts is generally no problem when transfers are between family members or close friends. By contrast, gifts made in a commercial or business setting raise troubling characterization questions. Taxpayers receiving "gifts" in those settings have, as a matter of course, claimed the shelter of Section 102, thus placing considerable strain on that section and forcing the courts to attempt to define its scope.

The motive of the donor is critical in characterizing receipts as gifts under Section 102. The leading case in this area is the Supreme Court decision in *Commissioner v. Duberstein.*[3]

Duberstein and Berman were presidents of companies that did business with one another. On a number of occasions, Duberstein provided the names of potential customers to Berman. Berman subsequently told Duberstein this information proved so helpful that he wanted to give Duberstein a Cadillac as a gift. After some initial protest to the effect that he had not intended to be compensated, Duberstein accepted the car. Berman's company apparently deducted the value of the car as a business expense. Duberstein claimed the car was a gift and not reportable as gross income. The Tax Court held for the Commissioner, concluding the car was intended as compensation for services. The Seventh Circuit reversed. The Supreme Court, on review, declined to promulgate a "test for determining whether a transfer constituted a gift," but noted that its prior cases had established that, "[a] gift in the statutory sense . . . proceeds from a 'detached and disinterested generosity . . . out of affection, respect, admiration, charity or like impulses.' . . . And in this regard, the most critical consideration . . . is the transferor's 'intention.' "[4]

This language has been repeatedly cited by the courts as establishing the criteria for evaluating whether the receipt of property constitutes a gift. However, the Court specifically states in *Duberstein*: "Decision of the issue presented in these cases must be based ultimately on the application of the fact-finding tribunal's experience with the mainsprings of human conduct to the totality of the facts of each case."[5] In commercial and business settings, this application has proven a challenge and, not surprisingly, has produced very inconsistent results. In *Duberstein* itself, the Court, relying on the Tax Court's conclusions as the trier of facts, reinstated the Tax Court's decision in favor of the government.

---

[3] 363 U.S. 278 (1960).

[4] *Id.* at 285–86.

[5] *Id.* at 289.

[1]   Employer-Employee "Gifts"

§ 102.   Gifts and inheritances.

(c)   Employee Gifts.

(1)   In General.

Subsection (a) shall not exclude from gross income any amount transferred by or for an employer to, or for the benefit of, an employee.

(2)   Cross references.

For provisions excluding employee achievement awards from gross income, see section 74(c). For provisions excluding certain de minimis fringes from gross income, see section 132(e).

Recognizing the difficulties associated with distinguishing gifts from compensation, Congress has enacted specific Code provisions which eliminate or reduce many of the characterization problems. Perhaps the most significant limitation denies a Section 102(a) exclusion for amounts transferred by an employer to, or for the benefit of, an employee. See Section 102(c)(1), enacted in 1986.[6]

Note that, if Section 102(c)(1) had existed at the time, it would not have been applicable in *Duberstein* because Berman was not Duberstein's employer.

> **Example 1:** Martha gives John a new car as a gift. Martha is John's employer.
>
> **Analysis:** The Section 102(a) gift exclusion is inapplicable, and John has gross income. (Section 102(c)(2) suggests that employee achievement awards [*see* Chapter 7] and *de minimis* fringe benefits [*see* Chapter 11] remain excludable, but these provisions are clearly not applicable here.)
>
> **Example 2:** Same facts as prior example, except that John is also Martha's son.
>
> **Analysis:** Proposed regulations except "extraordinary transfers to the natural objects of an employer's bounty" from the rule of Section 102(c); thus, Section 102(c) does not apply to transfers to related parties, where the transfer "can be substantially attributed to the familial relationship", not to the employment.[7]

---

[6] As will be discussed in Chapter 11, *infra*, Section 132 provides an exclusion for certain fringe benefits including so-called "de minimis" fringe benefits. The legislative history to Section 102 (c)(1) specifically notes that "the rule under present law whereby de minimis fringe benefits may be deductible by the employer but are not taxable to the employee can apply to employee awards of low value, including traditional awards (such as gold watch) upon retirement after lengthy service for an employer." H.R. Rep. 99-426, 99th Cong. 1st Sess., p. 105.

[7] Prop. Treas. Reg. § 1.102-1(f)(2).

[2]   Business Gifts

In 1962, long prior to the enactment of Section 102(c) but after the *Duberstein* decision, Congress added a provision that has limited significantly the number of gifts made by businesses. Section 274(b) disallows a deduction under Section 162 or Section 212 for gifts to individuals in excess of $25. Thus, a business making "gifts" is faced with a choice: on the one hand, it can transfer property to an individual and characterize the transfer as compensation and presumably entitle itself to a business deduction. Considering the emphasis placed by *Duberstein* on the "donor's" motive, the effect of such characterization by the business is almost assuredly a denial of a Section 102 exclusion to the recipient. On the other hand, the business can support the recipient's characterization of the transfer as an excludable gift, thereby losing the right to claim a deduction. In any event, one must keep in mind that Section 102(c)(1) negates gift status for transfers from employers to employees. Such transfers, as a result, do not implicate Section 274(b), which applies only to items excludable as gifts under Section 102.

[B]   The Nature of a Bequest or Inheritance

With respect to cash or other property received as the result of another's death, *i.e*, bequests, devises, and inheritance, a threshold question similar to that in the gift context is raised: is the cash or property received a bequest, devise or inheritance, or is it compensation or some other form of taxable item? For example, heirs of a decedent sometimes challenge the validity of the decedent's will. The Supreme Court, in *Lyeth v. Hoey*,[8] considered "[w]hether property received by an heir from the estate of his ancestor is acquired by inheritance, when it is distributed under an agreement settling a contest by the heir of the validity of the decedent's will. . . ." While acknowledging that state law is determinative on matters such as the validity of the will or the identification of the heirs of a decedent, the Court emphasized that characterization of a distribution from the estate for federal tax purposes is a federal question. Finding that Congress, in enacting Section 102, intended a uniform rule, and that through the use of the language "bequest, devise, or inheritance" in Section 102, "Congress used comprehensive terms embracing all acquisitions in the devolution of a decedent's estate,"[9] the Court concluded that the amounts received through the settlement agreement were excludable.

Wolder v. Commissioner,[10] presents another characterization question similar to that in *Duberstein*. Wolder and his client agreed that Wolder would render legal services to the client at her request and not bill her for the services; the client, in turn, agreed to leave certain property to Wolder by her will. Wolder rendered the requested legal services (apparently largely revisions to the client's will) and the client bequeathed the promised property. The tax question was whether the amounts received by an attorney under the terms of a client's will were compensation for services or an excludable bequest. The same analysis used in

---

[8]   305 U.S. 188, 191 (1938).

[9]   *Id.* at 194.

[10]   493 F.2d 608 (2d Cir. 1974).

Duberstein is applicable. The bequest was simply the form chosen to provide compensation for services; the property's status as a "bequest" for state law purposes was irrelevant to its characterization for federal tax purposes, and the amounts received were held to be income.

Although the language of Section 102(a) is deceptively simple, a case-by-case approach to characterization is necessary, applying one's "experience with the mainsprings of human conduct" to the facts presented, and recognizing that the Supreme Court's definition of excludable gift does not "satisfy an academic desire for tidiness, symmetry and precision."[11]

[C]   Statutory Limitations on the Exclusion — Section 102(b)

§ 102.   Gifts and inheritances.

(b)   Income. Subsection (a) shall not exclude from gross income —

(1) the income from any property referred to in subsection (a), or

(2) where the gift, bequest, devise, or inheritance is of income from property, the amount of such income.

Where, under the terms of the gift, bequest, devise, or inheritance, the payment, crediting, or distribution thereof is to be made at intervals, then, to the extent that it is paid or credited or to be distributed out of income from property, it shall be treated for purposes of paragraph (2) as a gift, bequest, devise, or inheritance of income from property. Any amount included in the gross income of a beneficiary under subchapter J shall be treated for purposes of paragraph (2) as a gift, bequest, devise, or inheritance of income from property.

As is so often the case in the tax law, Congress gives and Congress takes away; an exclusion is provided and then the exclusion is limited. Section 102 reflects such a give-and-take arrangement. Specifically, Section 102(b) provides two limitations on the exclusion. First, the income from property excluded as gift, bequest, devise, and inheritance is not excluded.[12]

> **Example:** Martha gives Peter a share of IBM stock which pays a dividend every three months.
>
> **Analysis:** The value of the stock is excluded from Peter's income under Section 102(a), but, under Section 102(b)(1), the dividends which IBM distributes to Peter are not excluded. They will constitute income under Section 61(a)(7).

A second limitation is provided by Section 102(b)(2), which denies an exclusion to gifts, whether made during life or at death, of income from property. Consider the following common example:

---

[11] Comm'r v. Duberstein, 363 U.S. 278, 289 (1960).

[12] I.R.C. § 102(b)(1).

Example: Mother dies leaving a portfolio of stocks and bonds in trust for the benefit of her son and her grandchildren. The trust provides that Trust Company will manage the portfolio and will distribute all income from the stocks and bonds annually to the son. When the son dies, the trust will terminate and all of the trust property will be distributed in equal shares to the grandchildren who are then alive. The son thus has an equitable life estate while the grandchildren have a contingent remainder interest. The son and the grandchildren have both received as "gifts" an interest in the same property. Will these "gifts" be excluded from income?

Analysis: The "gift" to the son will be taxable pursuant to Section 102(b)(2). From Section 102(b)(1), we know that, if Mother had merely given the stocks and bonds outright to her son, the son could have excluded the value of the stocks and bonds but not the income from them. Section 102(b)(2) prevents Mother from avoiding Section 102(b)(1) by merely dividing the ownership in the stocks and bonds between an income beneficiary, the son, and remainderpersons, the grandchildren.

Section 102(b)(2) codifies the holding of *Irwin v. Gavit*,[13] which presented a fact pattern similar to that in the example. Examining the applicable provisions of the Code, the Court noted:

> The statute . . . provides that there shall be levied a tax "upon the entire net income arising or accruing from all sources. . . ." If these payments properly may be called income by the common understanding of that word and the statute has failed to hit them it has missed so much of the general purpose that it expresses at the start. . . . [T]he net income is to include "gains or profits and income derived from any source whatever, including the income from but not the value of property acquired by gift, bequest, devise or descent." . . . [T]he trustees are to make "return of the net income of the person for whom they act, subject to this tax," and . . . trustees and others having the control or payment of fixed or determinable gains of another person who are required to render a return on behalf of another are "authorized to withhold enough to pay the normal tax." The language quoted leaves no doubt in our minds that if a fund were given to trustees for A for life with remainder over, the income received by the trustees and paid over to A would be income of A under the statute. It seems to us hardly less clear that even if there were a specific provision that A should have no interest in the corpus, the payments would be income none the less. . . . In the first case, it is true that the bequest might be said to be of the corpus for life, in the second it might be said to be of the income. But we think that the provision of the act that exempts bequests assumes the gift of a corpus and contrasts it with income arising from it, but was not intended to exempt income properly so-called simply because of a severance between it and the principal fund.[14]

---

[13] 268 U.S. 161 (1925).

[14] *Id.* at 166–67.

Notice in the preceding example that the grandchildren get the benefit of the Section 102(a) exclusion, not the son. Although it would be possible to divide the exclusion between the son and the grandchildren in proportion to the value of the property interest each received, and to exclude a proportionate share of income from each, this is not the law — the entire exclusion flows to the grandchildren.

§ 5.02 BASIS OF PROPERTY RECEIVED BY GIFT, BEQUEST OR INHERITANCE

§ 1015. Basis of property acquired by gifts and transfers in trust.

(a) Gifts after December 31, 1920.

If the property was acquired by gift after December 31, 1920, the basis shall be the same as it would be in the hands of the donor or the last preceding owner by whom it was not acquired by gift, except that, if such basis (adjusted for the period before the date of the gift as provided in section 1016) is greater than the fair market value of the property at the time of the gift, then for the purpose of determining loss the basis shall be such fair market value. If the facts necessary to determine the basis in the hands of the donor or the last preceding owner are unknown to the donee, the Secretary shall, if possible, obtain such facts from such donor or last preceding owner, or any other person cognizant thereof. . . .

[A] Gifts of Appreciated Property

As should be clear from Chapter 4, the taxpayer's basis in property is critical in determining the gain or loss realized by the taxpayer upon disposition of the property. One therefore needs to be concerned about basis when gifts of property excludable under Section 102(a) are made. Consider the following example involving a gift of appreciated property.

> **Example:** Claude purchases a share of XYZ stock for $200 and gives the stock to Mary when the stock is worth $400 per share. Has Claude realized $200 of gain? What basis does Mary have in the stock?

> **Analysis:** Claude does not realize gain. Mary's basis in the stock will be $200.

The donor's gain and the donee's basis are necessarily related. There is untaxed, unrealized gain of $200 in Claude's stock prior to the gift. The gain should not disappear merely because Claude gives the stock to Mary. One possible approach would treat Claude as having realized the gain inherent in the stock at the time of the gift. Were that case, the basis Mary takes in the stock should be the fair market value of the stock *i.e.*, her basis should reflect that there is no further gain inherent in the stock at that time. In other words, if Claude realizes $200 gain, then Mary's basis should be $400. Thus, if she were to sell the stock for $400, no gain would be realized.

But the disposition of property by gift is not treated as a realization event, and Claude realizes no taxable gain on the gift. Such an approach would presumably discourage gifts as well as create valuation problems. However, the gain does not simply disappear untaxed. The $200 gain potential is preserved by requiring Mary to retain the same basis in the stock that Claude had.[15] Thus, if Mary were to sell the stock for its fair market value of $400, she would realize $200 of taxable gain.

Recall from Chapter 4 the cost basis rule of Section 1012. Section 1015 provides a different basis rule in the case of gifts.[16] Mary's basis is referred to as a "substituted basis" or a "transferred basis."

The transferred basis rule assures that the $200 of gain inherent in the stock when the gift was made remains subject to taxation. The effect of the transferred basis rule is to shift the tax burden associated with the appreciated value of the stock from Claude to Mary. In *Taft v. Bowers*,[17] the Supreme Court rejected a donee's challenge to the constitutionality of such a shift. In that case, a father gave his daughter shares of stock that had increased in value during the time the father owned them. After a further increase in value, the daughter sold the stock. She conceded she was taxable on any appreciation in the stock occurring while she owned the stock, but argued she was not taxable on appreciation that occurred during the period her father owned the stock. The Supreme Court disagreed:

> If, instead of giving the stock to petitioner, the donor had sold it at market value, the excess over the capital he invested (cost) would have been income therefrom and subject to taxation under the Sixteenth Amendment. He would have been obliged to share the realized gain with the United States. He held the stock — the investment — subject to the right of the sovereign to take part of any increase in its value when separated through sale or conversion and reduced to his possession. Could he, contrary to the express will of Congress, by mere gift enable another to hold this stock free from such right, deprive the sovereign of the possibility of taxing the appreciation when actually severed, and convert the entire property into a capital asset of the donee, who invested nothing, as though the latter had purchased at the market price? And after a still further enhancement of the property, could the donee make a second gift with like effect, etc.? We think not.

> In truth the stock represented only a single investment of capital — that made by the donor. And when through sale or conversion the increase was separated therefrom, it became income from that investment in the hands of the recipient subject to taxation according to the very words of the Sixteenth Amendment. By requiring the recipient of the entire increase to pay a part into the public treasury, Congress deprived her of no right and subjected her to no hardship. She accepted the gift with knowledge of the statute and, as to the property received, voluntarily assumed the position of her donor. When she sold the stock she actually got the original sum invested, plus the entire appreciation; and out of the latter only was she called on to pay the tax demanded. . . .

---

[15] I.R.C. § 1015(a).

[16] To the extent that Claude paid any gift tax attributable to the appreciation in the stock, Section 1015(d)(1) and (d)(6) would increase Mary's basis by that amount.

[17] 278 U.S. 470 (1929).

There is nothing in the Constitution which lends support to the theory that gain actually resulting from the increased value of capital can be treated as taxable income in the hands of the recipient only so far as the increase occurred while he owned the property. . . .[18]

In effect, *Taft v. Bowers* confirms that another limitation exists with respect to the general exclusion rule for gifts, *i.e.*, the appreciation inherent in gifts may ultimately be taxed to the donee.

[B]   Gifts of Property — Basis in Excess of Fair Market Value

Our tax law generally prohibits the shifting of income from one taxpayer to another. Nevertheless, as demonstrated above, the transferred basis rule of Section 1015(a) and the rule of *Taft v. Bowers* together enable a donor to shift potential gain (income) to a donee. Considering that ours is a progressive tax system, a taxpayer in a high bracket may therefore be encouraged to make gifts of appreciated property to a related taxpayer in a lower tax bracket so as to assure that gain will be taxed at the lowest possible rates.

Suppose, however, the property in question is not appreciated but has declined in value, and has a fair market value less than the donor's basis. Although a donor may shift potential gain, Section 1015 prevents the shifting of loss to the donee.

Example 1: Claude is in a 10% tax bracket while Mary is in a 30% bracket. Assume Claude purchased stock for $200 and when it was only worth $100 gave it to Mary. A $100 loss deduction on the sale of the stock would be worth only $10 to Claude in his tax bracket (*i.e.*, 10% x $100 = $10) whereas the loss deduction would be worth $30 to Mary (*i.e.*, 30% x $100 = $30).

Analysis: Section 1015 provides that, where the fair market value of property is less than the donor's adjusted basis in the property, the donee *for loss purposes only* will take a basis equal to the fair market value of the property.[19] In these circumstances, where Claude's basis exceeds the value of the property, Mary's basis will be only $100, the value of the property. Thus, if Mary were to sell the stock for $100, no loss would be realized and the $100 loss which was inherent in the stock while Claude held it would simply disappear. Under these circumstances, Claude should sell the stock for its $100 value, thereby enabling him both to make a $100 gift to Mary and at the same time assure that the $100 loss would be realized and not simply disappear. (As will be discussed in Chapter 15, Claude will be entitled to deduct the loss when he sells the stock.)

Example 2: Claude buys XYZ stock for $200. When its value is $100, he gives it to Mary. The value further declines to $75 and Mary then sells it for that amount.

---

[18] *Id.* at 482–84.

[19] I.R.C. § 1015(a).

Analysis: For loss purposes, Mary's basis under Section 1015(a) is $100. Her realized loss is thus $25. The unrealized loss of $100 at the time of the gift from Claude simply disappears.

Example 3: Same facts as the prior example, except that the stock's value increases to $300, and Mary thereupon sells it for that amount.

Analysis: Mary's gain is $100. Note that the special loss rule of Section 1015(a) is inapplicable. Mary does not have a loss here; she has a gain. Mary is therefore entitled to use the general rule of Section 1015(a), which means her basis is $200, the same as Claude's basis, and her gain on a sale of the stock for $300 is $100.

Thus, when property is given away with inherent unrealized loss, Section 1015(a) really provides a donee with two possible basis calculations — one basis to use when determining gain, and another basis to use when determining loss. Consider the possibility that the stock in our example increases somewhat in value following the gift to Mary, but not so dramatically as in the last example.

Example 4: Same facts as before — Claude buys stock for $200 and gives it to Mary when it is worth $100 — but the stock subsequently increases in value to $125, whereupon Mary sells it for that amount.

Analysis: Mary has no gain and no loss. Because the value of the stock was less than Claude's basis, Mary's basis *for determining loss* is only $100. Thus, on a sale for $125, she has no loss. For purposes of determining gain, she is entitled to use the general rule of Section 1015(a) and to use a transferred basis of $200. Using this basis, she has no gain.

Note that, for any sale between $100 and $200, Mary will have neither gain nor loss. Her "loss basis" of $100 will prevent a loss. Her "gain basis" of $200 will prevent a gain.[20]

[C]   Basis of Property Received by Bequest or Inheritance

§ 1014.   Basis of property acquired from a decedent.

(a)   In general — Except as otherwise provided in this section, the basis of property in the hands of a person acquiring the property from a decedent or to whom the property passed from a decedent shall, if not sold, exchanged, or otherwise disposed of before the decedent's death by such person, be —

(1) the fair market value of the property at the date of the decedent's death. . . .

To an expanding list, another basis provision must be added — Section 1014(a)(1). In effect, this provision "steps-up" (or "steps-down") the basis of property acquired from a decedent to the fair market value of the property at the time of the decedent's death.[21] Thus, in the case of appreciated property, Section

---

[20] *See* Treas. Reg. § 1.1015-1(a)(1), (2).

[21] Section 1014(a)(2), (3) and (4) provides different basis rules in the cases of alternative valuation under Section 2032, special valuation under Section 2032A, or exclusion under Section 2031(c). These estate and gift tax provisions are beyond the scope of this book.

1014 provides tax amnesty for the gain inherent in the property at the time of a person's death. The devisee or heir receiving the "stepped-up basis" can sell the property for its value as of the decedent's death and not realize any gain. Only that appreciation occurring after the decedent's death will be subject to tax. By contrast, if property decreased in value during the lifetime of the decedent so that the decedent's basis exceeded the value of the property, Section 1014(a) will negate the loss inherent in the property.[22]

> **Example 1:** Claude buys XYZ stock for $200. At his death the stock, now worth $400, is bequeathed to Mary.
>
> **Analysis:** Neither Claude nor his estate is taxed on the built-in gain. Mary takes a $400 basis under Section 1014(a). The built-in gain simply disappears, untaxed.
>
> **Example 2:** Claude buys XYZ stock for $200. At his death the stock is worth $100 and is bequeathed to Mary.
>
> **Analysis:** The loss disappears because Mary will take a $100 basis in the stock under Section 1014(a). In the circumstances, Claude would be advised to sell the stock prior to death so as to realize and recognize the loss and prevent a later step-down in basis.

Section 1014(a) applies not only to property owned by the decedent at the time of his death which is transferred by the decedent's will or pursuant to the intestate succession laws of a jurisdiction, but also to property acquired from a decedent through other means, e.g., joint tenancy or community property.[23]

§ 1014. Basis of property acquired from a decedent —

(b) Property acquired from the decedent — For purposes of subsection (a), the following property shall be considered to have been acquired from or to have passed from the decedent:

(1) Property acquired by bequest, devise, or inheritance, or by the decedent's estate from the decedent;

. . .

(6) In the case of decedents dying after December 31, 1947, property which represents the surviving spouse's one-half share of community property held by the decedent and the surviving spouse under the community property laws of any State, or possession of the United States or any foreign country, if at least one-half of the whole of the community interest in such property was includible in determining the value of the decedent's gross estate under

---

[22] The basis rules of Section 1014 were briefly replaced during 2010 by Section 1022, which provided that property acquired from a decedent would generally take a basis equal to the lower of decedent's basis or the value of the property at decedent's death, although basis increases in limited amounts, beyond this general rule, were available. Section 1022 was enacted as a trade-off for the 2010 repeal of the federal estate tax. When estate tax repeal was not extended beyond 2010, Section 1022 was allowed to sunset as well, and Section 1014 resumed its historic role as the governing basis provision for property acquired from a decedent.

[23] *See* I.R.C. § 1014(b).

chapter 11 of subtitle B (section 2001 and following, relating to estate tax)....

. . .

(9) **In the case of decedents dying after December 31, 1953, property acquired from the decedent by reason of death, form of ownership, or other conditions (including property acquired through the exercise or non-exercise of a power of appointment) if by reason thereof the property is required to be included in determining the value of the decedent's gross estate under chapter 11 of subtitle B or under the Internal Revenue Code of 1939.**

Particular attention should be paid to Section 1014(b)(6) which makes Section 1014 applicable to a surviving spouse's one-half share of community property "if at least one-half of the whole of the community interest in such property was includable in determining the value of the decedent's gross estate" for federal estate tax purposes.

> **Example 1:** Tom and Sue, a married couple, own ABC stock in joint tenancy. Assume they each contributed $50 to purchase the stock, so the stock's basis is $100. They do not reside in a community property state. Tom dies when the stock in worth $200.

> **Analysis:** Tom's half interest is includable in his estate under Section 2040. Under Section 1014(b)(9), Sue will hold the stock with a basis of $150: Tom's half interest was worth $100 at his death and will get a basis step-up to $100. Sue acquires that interest by reason of "form of ownership," the joint tenancy. Sue's half interest will continue to have a basis of $50, her half of the original basis of $100.

> **Example 2:** Same facts as in previous example, except that Tom and Sue live in a community property state.

> **Analysis:** Under Section 1014(b)(6), Sue will hold the ABC stock with a basis of $200. Tom's half interest will be included in his estate, and will get a basis step-up to $100 as one would expect. But Section 1014(b)(6) gives Sue's half interest a basis step-up to $100 as well, for an aggregate stock basis of $200.

Considering the potentially significant tax breaks associated with Section 1014(a), a taxpayer may attempt to give highly appreciated properties to a terminally ill relative knowing the taxpayer will soon receive the properties back by way of devise or inheritance. If the relative's taxable estate were small enough (as a general rule, less than the applicable exclusion amount for federal estate tax purposes, i.e., $5,250,000 in 2013), there would probably be no federal estate tax generated by the inclusion of the property in the relative's estate and the taxpayer would thus receive the benefits of a stepped-up basis tax-free. The following provision addresses this issue:

§ 1014.   **Basis of property acquired from a decedent** —

(e) **Appreciated property acquired by decedent by gift within 1 year of death** —

(1)   **In general — In the case of a decedent dying after December 31, 1981, if —**

(A)   **Appreciated property — The term "appreciated property" means any property if the fair market value of such property on the day it was transferred to the decedent by gift exceeds its adjusted basis.**

(B)   **Treatment of certain property sold by estate — In the case of any appreciated property described in subparagraph (A) of paragraph (1) sold by the estate of the decedent or by a trust of which the decedent was the grantor, rules similar to the rules of paragraph (1) shall apply to the extent the donor of such property (or the spouse of such donor) is entitled to the proceeds from such sale.**

> **Example:** Mary owns stock worth $100,000, which she purchased several years ago for $25,000. Mary gives the stock to her father, who dies six months later when the stock's value is $100,000. Father bequeaths the stock to Mary.

> **Analysis:** Father's basis in the stock is $25,000 under Section 1015. But for Section 1014(e), Mary would take a $100,000 basis in the stock under Section 1014(a)(1). Under Section 1014(e), however, Mary will take Father's basis instead, *i.e.*, $25,000. But note that Section 1014(e) is avoided if Father lives more than one year after the gift, or if Father bequeaths the property to anyone other than Mary or her spouse.

§ 5.03   PART-GIFT, PART-SALE

Some transfers are in part a gift and in part a sale. The sale of property for less than fair market value is common between family members and even close friends. Substantively, the transaction involves a sale in part and a gift in part. Recognizing the potential for confusion in such a mixed transaction, the Treasury has promulgated regulations which resolve the questions that may arise. Under Regulation Section 1.1001-1(e) the seller-donor has gain to the extent that the amount realized exceeds her adjusted basis in the property. The same regulation also appropriately provides that no loss is recognized on such a transaction. The examples provided by this regulation are helpful and should be carefully read.[24]

Regulation Section 1.1015-4 also addresses this issue. The regulation favors the taxpayer by providing that the donee's basis will be the greater of the amount the donee paid for the property or the adjusted basis of the donor (plus any gift tax paid). Consistent with Section 1015(a), a special rule limits the donee's basis, for purposes of computing loss, to the fair market value of the property at the time of the transfer to the donee.

> **Example 1:** Sally sells a lake-front lot to her favorite grandchild, Erin, for $10,000. Sally had paid $20,000 for the lot 5 years before and the lot had a value of $50,000 at the time of the sale to Erin. What are the tax consequences?

---

[24]   Different rules exist in the case of a part-gift, part-sale to charity. *See* I.R.C. § 1011(b); Chapter 26, *infra*.

Analysis: This is a part-gift, part-sale. Sally has no gain or loss. Regulation Section 1.1001-1(e). Erin's basis in the lot is $20,000, under the "greater of" rule (greater of donor's basis or amount paid) of Regulation Section 1.1015-4.

Example 2: Same facts as in previous example, except Sally sells the lot for $30,000.

Analysis: Sally has a realized gain of $10,000. Erin's basis, under the "greater of" rule of Regulation Section 1.1015-4, is $30,000.

Example 3: Same facts as in Example 1, except the lot is worth only $15,000 when Sally sells it for $10,000.

Analysis: Sally has no gain or loss under Regulation Section 1.1001-1(e). Erin's basis *for determining loss* under the "greater of" rule is $15,000 (not $20,000) because basis for loss purposes cannot exceed the value at transfer.[25] For gain purposes, Erin's basis would be $20,000 under the "greater of" rule.

Example 4: Suppose that the lot in Example 1 were subject to a liability of $10,000, and that Erin, in lieu of paying Sally $10,000 in cash, assumes the $10,000 liability when receiving the property.

Analysis: The same result obtains as in Example 1: the transaction is still in part a gift, and in part a sale; the amount realized by Sally, on account of the assumption of the liability, is still $10,000, pursuant to Regulation Section 1.1001-2(a)(1), (4)(ii),(iii), and neither gain nor loss is recognized on the transaction. Erin is treated as having paid $10,000 by reason of the liability assumption. Erin's basis under the "greater of" rule is $20,000.

Note that gain can be recognized on a part-gift, part-sale if the liability assumed exceeds the seller-donor's basis in the property. Thus, in Example 4, if the liability Erin assumed were $25,000 (and Sally's basis remained $20,000), Sally's amount realized would be $25,000, and she would recognize gain of $5,000 on the part-gift, part-sale.[26] Because Erin's assumption of the liability would be treated as an amount paid, her basis under the "greater of" rule would be $25,000, the amount paid.

---

[25] Treas. Reg. § 1.1015-4.

[26] *See also* Diedrich v. Commissioner, 457 U.S. 191 (1982).

Chapter 6

SALE OF A PRINCIPAL RESIDENCE

The Internal Revenue Code encourages home ownership. Chapter 22 considers the popular deduction for home mortgage interest; Chapter 23 addresses the deduction for property taxes. This chapter focuses on perhaps the most significant tax benefit enjoyed by homeowners — the exclusion available under Section 121 for gains realized on the sale or exchange of one's principal residence. In 1997 Congress dramatically changed the treatment of gain from the sale of one's principal residence. To appreciate the nature of these changes, a brief review of Section 121 as it existed prior to the 1997 Act and of Section 1034, which was repealed in 1997, is necessary.

§ 6.01 SECTIONS 1034 AND 121 BEFORE THE TAXPAYER RELIEF ACT OF 1997

Whether necessitated by a change in employment, a growing family or a desire to live in a different neighborhood, most individuals will likely occupy a number of residences during their lifetimes. That pattern in American life began to emerge as Americans became more mobile after World War II. Because of rising prices, the great majority of homeowners selling their homes in those post-war years realized gain equal to the difference between the sale price and the adjusted basis of their home. In many instances, that gain was merely a reflection of post-war inflation in the housing market. Furthermore, those selling their homes were likely, either immediately prior or subsequent to the sale, to purchase another home, using as a down payment all or most of the proceeds from the sale of the former home. Congress recognized in 1951 that to tax the gain from the sale of one's home would only reduce the money available to the homeowner for reinvestment in a new home and, in turn, could discourage homeowners from making any but the most necessary of moves.

To eliminate tax considerations from the decision of whether to move from one home to another, Congress in 1951 enacted a provision (Section 1034 — repealed by the 1997 Taxpayers Relief Act) enabling taxpayers to avoid recognition of gain on the sale of their home as long as they "bought up," *i.e.*, purchased (within a given period of time) a new home costing at least as much as the sale price of the old home. Any gain realized but not recognized on the sale of the old residence was preserved in the basis of the new residence.

Under Section 1034, if a taxpayer failed to purchase a new residence costing at least as much as the selling price of the old residence, the taxpayer had to recognize gain in an amount equal to the difference between the selling price of the old residence and the cost of the new residence (but not in excess of gain realized on the sale of the old residence). Any unrecognized gain would, of course, be preserved in the basis of the new residence.

While Section 1034 did much to negate tax considerations associated with the move from one principal residence to another, the relief provided by Section 1034 was not always adequate. For example, older individuals who no longer needed a family home or could no longer maintain a home might choose to sell their home and purchase a smaller, less expensive one or might opt to move instead into a rented apartment. In these circumstances, Section 1034 was either inapplicable or did not completely defer the gain. Considering that many older people selling their homes viewed the proceeds of the sale as a form of retirement savings, the inadequacy of Section 1034 to defer tax on their realized gain was a serious problem.

To respond to the needs of these taxpayers, Congress enacted a provision enabling older taxpayers to exclude a portion of the gain they realized on the sale of their home. Unlike Section 1034, Section 121 (prior to its amendment in 1997 — hereinafter referred to as "old Section 121") provided a permanent exclusion of gain. Taxpayers electing to take advantage of old Section 121 did not have to purchase a new principal residence and, if they did, the gain excluded by that provision did not serve to reduce the basis of their new principal residence.

Old Section 121 permitted qualifying taxpayers to exclude from income $125,000 of the gain realized from the sale or exchange of property owned and used as the taxpayer's principal residence. Unlike Section 1034, however, old Section 121 provided only a once-in-a-lifetime benefit: once a taxpayer or taxpayer's spouse had taken advantage of the exclusion, it was never again available. Old Section 121 imposed (1) age requirements generally limiting the exclusion to those individuals 55 years of age or older; and (2) ownership and use requirements on the residence covered by its provisions (a taxpayer had to own and use the property as her principal residence for periods aggregating three years or more during the five year period ending on the date of the sale or exchange).

While affording significant tax relief to homeowners, both sections 1034 and 121 had inherent problems. Aside from interpretational difficulties, Section 1034, by requiring taxpayers to "buy-up," often resulted in taxpayers investing in housing far greater than their needs. For example, to avoid capital gains tax on the sale of her home, a taxpayer, whose company transferred her from a high cost city to a town where housing costs were considerably lower, might purchase a home in the new location that was larger and more substantial than she needed or wanted.[1] In addition, because Section 1034 merely deferred gain, a taxpayer would be required to maintain records regarding improvements to the home in order to be able to establish the home's adjusted basis. The exclusion provided by old Section 121 alleviated some of these problems for eligible taxpayers but the excludable amount was considered by many to be too modest given rapidly appreciating real estate markets.

---

[1] Capital gains and the preferential tax rates applicable to long term capital gains are discussed in Chapter 31, *infra.* I.R.C. § 121(a).

§ 6.02   SECTION 121 AFTER THE TAXPAYER RELIEF ACT OF 1997

The 1997 Taxpayer Relief Act repealed Section 1034 and repealed the language of old Section 121, replacing it with the provisions discussed herein. Current Section 121 provides a very substantial exclusion for gains from the sale of a residence taxpayer has owned and used as her principal residence for periods aggregating two years or more during the five year period ending on the date of the sale or exchange.

[A]   Ownership and Use Requirements

§ 121.   Exclusion of Gains from Sale of Principal Residence.

(a)   Exclusion. Gross income shall not include gain from the sale or exchange of property, if during the 5-year period ending on the date of the sale or exchange, such property has been owned and used by the taxpayer as the taxpayer's principal residence for periods aggregating 2 years or more.

Under current Section 121, taxpayers may exclude up to $250,000 ($500,000 with respect to certain joint returns) of the gain on the sale or exchange of a qualifying principal residence. To qualify for the exclusion, the statute requires that the taxpayer have owned and used the property as a principal residence "for periods aggregating 2 years or more" during the preceding five year period.[2] Consider the following examples:

> **Example 1:** Erik and Liz purchased a home in Seattle in January 2005 and made that home their principal residence until March 1, 2010 when Liz was transferred to Portland. Although the condominium they rented in Portland became their principal residence and they intended to live in Portland permanently, they kept the Seattle home so that their daughter, Emily, a second year law student, would have a place to live until she graduated. Erik and Liz sold their Seattle home on December 1, 2012 and realized a very substantial gain on the sale. Will Erik and Liz be entitled to claim the benefit of Section 121?

> **Analysis:** Although Erik and Liz were not using the Seattle home as their principal residence at the time of the sale, they had owned and used the home as their principal residence during more than two of the five years before the sale. Assuming all other requirements of Section 121 are satisfied, Erik and Liz would be entitled to exclude their gain up to the statutory limits discussed below.

> **Example 2:** Assume the same facts as in Example 1 except that Erik and Liz did not sell their Seattle home in December 2012 but instead moved back to Seattle on January 1, 2013 after being in Portland more than two years. They took up residence again in their Seattle home where their daughter had continued to live since she completed law school. They made the Seattle home their principal residence until January 1, 2014 when they

---

[2] I.R.C § 121(a).

sold the home at a substantial gain. Is Section 121 available to them under these circumstances?

Analysis: Again, they would be eligible for the Section 121 exclusion because the home was their principal residence for periods aggregating two years or more during the five year period before the sale. [January 1, 2009 — March 1, 2010 and January 1, 2013 — January 1, 2014.] Note that the statute does not require two years of continuous occupancy of a home as one's principal residence but only periods of such occupancy totaling two years during the five year period.

The ownership and use requirements may be satisfied during nonconcurrent periods as long as the taxpayer satisfies each of them within the five year period ending on the date of the sale or exchange.[3]

Example 3: Assume the facts of Example 1 except that Erik and Liz rented the Seattle home in 2005 instead of purchasing it. Assume also that in March 2010 they purchased the home. Their daughter Emily lived in the home while she attended law school. As in Example 1, Erik and Liz moved to Portland in March 2010 and sold the Seattle home on December 1, 2012.

Analysis: The Section 121 exclusion will apply to the sale of the Seattle home because Erik and Liz owned the home for at least two years out of the five years preceding the sale (March 2010 until December 1, 2012) and they used the Seattle home as their principal residence for at least two years during the five year period preceding the sale (from December 1, 2007 until March 1, 2010).[4]

Regulation § 1.121–1(c)(2) defines "use" as requiring occupancy. Short temporary absences, such as absences because of vacations or seasonal absence (even if accompanied by rental of the residence) will be counted as periods of use.

Example 4: Pat, a college professor, purchased a home on February 2, 2010 for use as his principal residence. During 2010 and 2011, Pat traveled to Italy each summer for two months to teach in a summer program. Pat sold the home on March 2, 2012.

Analysis: Although, in the five year period preceding the date of the sale, Pat used the residence for a total of less than two years (21 months), the Section 121 exclusion will apply to the gain from the sale of the residence because the two month periods during which Pat was in Italy each summer are short temporary absences and are counted as periods of use in determining whether Pat used the residence for the requisite period.[5] By contrast, if, instead of spending two months each summer in Italy, Pat had spent his sabbatical lasting from September 1, 2010 until August 30, 2011 in Italy, Pat's absence would not be considered a short temporary absence

---

[3] Treas. Reg. § 1.121-1(c)(1).

[4] Treas. Reg. § 1.121-1(c)(4) Ex. 3.

[5] Treas. Reg. § 1.121-1(c)(4) Ex. 5.

and could not be counted towards Pat's use of the property. As a result, Pat would not be eligible for the Section 121 exclusion.[6]

Section 121 contains a number of special rules related to the ownership and use requirements of Section 121(a). If an unmarried individual sells or exchanges property subsequent to the death of his or her spouse, the individual's use and ownership periods for purposes of Section 121(a) will include the period the deceased spouse owned and used the property.[7]

Example 5: Martha has owned and used a house as her principal residence since July 1, 1997. Martha and Bill marry on July 1, 2011 and from that date they use Martha's house as their principal residence. Martha dies on August 15, 2012 and Bill inherits the property and continues to use the property as his principal residence. Bill sells the property on May 1, 2013, at which time he has not remarried.

Analysis: Although Bill has owned and used the house for less than two years, Bill will be considered to have satisfied the ownership and use requirements of Section 121 because Bill's period of ownership and use includes the period that Martha owned and used the property before her death.[8]

If an individual receives property in a transaction described in Section 1041 (*i.e.*, a transfer of property between spouses or former spouses), that individual's ownership period for purposes of Section 121(a) will include the ownership period of the transferor.[9]

Example 6: Anna and Bob divorce. Under the terms of a property settlement, Anna transfers title to a home she owned to Bob. Although Bob never had any previous ownership interest in the home, for purposes of Section 121(a), Bob will be considered to have owned the home for the period that Anna owned the home.

Likewise, if an individual continues to have an ownership interest in a residence but is not living in the residence because the individual's spouse or former spouse is granted use of the residence under a divorce or separation instrument, the individual will nonetheless be deemed to use the property during the period her spouse or former spouse is granted the use of the property.[10]

Example 7: Mary and Pat divorce. Under the divorce decree, Mary is required to move out of the family home but will continue to have an ownership interest in it. The divorce decree provides that Pat may continue to live in the home until the couple's child (who will be living with Pat) attains the age of 18. The home is then to be sold and the proceeds are to be divided equally between Mary and Pat. Assume that the couple's child

---

[6] Treas. Reg. § 1.121-1(c)(4) Ex. 4.

[7] I.R.C. § 121(d)(2).

[8] This example is based on the one provided in Treas. Reg. § 1.121-4(a)(2).

[9] I.R.C. § 121(d)(3)(A); Treas. Reg. § 1.121-4(b)(1).

[10] I.R.C. § 121(d)(3)(B); Treas. Reg. § 1.121-4(b)(2).

attains the age of 18 five years later and the home is then sold at a significant gain. Although Mary has not used the home as her principal residence during the five year period before the sale, she will be deemed to have so used it during that period as a result of the application of Section 121(d)(3)(B).

If an individual becomes physically or mentally incapable of self-care, the use rules are modified. If the individual owns and uses the residence for one year in the five year period prior to the sale, the individual will be treated as using the residence as his principal residence for any period during the five year period in which the individual, while owning the property, resides in a facility satisfying certain requirements.[11]

[B] Amount Excludable

§ 121(b). Limitations.

(1) In General. The amount of gain excluded from gross income under subsection (a) with respect to any sale or exchange shall not exceed $250,000.

(2) Special Rules for Joint Returns. In the case of a husband and wife who make a joint return for the taxable year of the sale or exchange of the property —

(A) $500,000 limitation for certain joint returns. Paragraph (1) shall be applied by substituting "$500,000" for "$250,000" if

(i) either spouse meets the ownership requirements of subsection (a) with respect to such property; and

(ii) both spouses meet the use requirements of subsection (a) with respect to such property;

(iii) neither spouse is ineligible for the benefits of subsection (a) with respect to such property reason of paragraph (3).

(B) Other joint returns.

If such spouses do not meet the requirements of subparagraph (A), the limitation under paragraph (1) shall be the sum of the limitations under paragraph (1) to which each spouse would be entitled if such spouses had not been married. For purposes of the preceding sentence, each spouse shall be treated as owning the property during the period that either spouse owned the property.

(3) Application to Only 1 Sale or Exchange Every 2 Years.

(A) In general. Subsection (a) shall not apply to any sale or exchange by the taxpayer if, during the 2-year period ending on the date of such sale or exchange, there was any other sale or exchange by the taxpayer to which subsection (a) applied.

(4) Special Rule for Certain Sales by Surviving Spouses. In the case of a sale or exchange of property by an unmarried individual whose spouse is

---

[11] I.R.C. § 121(d)(7).

deceased on the date of such sale, paragraph (1) shall be applied by substituting "$500,000" for "$250,000" if such sale occurs not later than 2 years after the date of death of such spouse and the requirements of paragraph (2)(A) were met immediately before such date of death.

As a general rule, Section 121 allows a taxpayer to exclude up to $250,000 of gain. The exclusion applies to only one sale or exchange every two years.[12] Note the special exception to this rule under Section 121(c), discussed *infra*. If taxpayers file a joint return, the taxpayers may exclude up to $500,000 of the gain if certain requirements are met. Those requirements are: (1) one of the spouses must satisfy the ownership requirements; (2) both spouses must satisfy the use requirement; and (3) neither spouse has used the exclusion within the past two years. Consider the following examples:

> **Example 1:** Joe and Pam have been married for many years and have resided in the same home throughout their marriage. Title to the home is in Joe's name alone. Joe and Pam sell the home this year at a gain of $300,000 and move into an apartment. They file a joint return. What tax benefits are available to them under Section 121?

> **Analysis:** They will be entitled to exclude all $300,000 of the gain on the home as a result of the application of Section 121(b)(2) which eliminates the need for Pam to meet the ownership requirement. This special rule can be viewed as a recognition by Congress that it is not uncommon for title to property to be in the name of just one spouse. For example, title may be in the name of only one spouse because that spouse owned the home prior to the marriage and title was never changed into both spouses' names.

Other circumstances also enable a married couple to claim exclusions totaling up to $500,000 on the sale of homes without satisfying the specific requirements of Section 121(b)(2). For example, assume a husband and wife each owned their own home before they married and the couple sold both of the homes shortly after they married. If all of the other general requirements of Section 121 were satisfied, the husband and the wife would each be entitled to exclude up to $250,000 of gain from his or her sale. (Note, if one spouse had used the exclusion within the past two years, the other spouse may nonetheless claim an exclusion of up to $250,000 on the sale of her principal residence.) Similarly, a husband and wife who work in different parts of the country and have separate principal residences are entitled to exclude up to $250,000 of the gain on the sale of each of the residences. If, however, the gain on the husband's residence were $200,000 and the gain on the wife's residence were $300,000, the couple could only exclude a total of $450,000 of gain, *i.e.*, the husband could exclude $200,000 and the wife could exclude only $250,000 — she may not use her husband's unused exclusion of $50,000 to exclude gain in excess of her $250,000 exclusion limit. The couple would therefore have to report $50,000 of the $500,000 of gain.[13]

In December 2007, Congress amended Section 121(b) by adding (b)(4) addressing a situation of considerable concern to some individuals selling a home not long

---

[12]　I.R.C. § 121(b)(3).

[13]　Treas. Reg. § 1.121-2(a)(4) Ex. 3.

after the death of a spouse. Consider the following example:

> **Example 2:** Bill's wife, Martha, died September 1, 2006. On December 31, 2006, Bill sold the home he and Martha had jointly owned and lived in for almost fifty years. Bill realized $450,000 of gain on the sale of the home. [Note: Bill would have been entitled to a stepped-up basis for Martha's one-half of the home under Section 1014(a)(9).] Pursuant to Section 6013, Bill was allowed to file a joint return for Martha and himself for 2006, the year of Martha's death. He, however, could not file a joint return thereafter unless he remarried. Because Bill was entitled to file a joint return for 2006, all $450,000 of the gain from the sale of the home may be excluded under Section 121(b)(2). In the alternative, assume Bill sold the home two days later — on January 2, 2007. Bill obviously may not file a joint return with Martha for 2007. As a result, Bill could only exclude $250,000 of the gain on the sale of the home.

As the above example illustrates, where a taxpayer decided to sell the family home after the death of his spouse, the timing of the sale could make a huge difference in terms of the amount of the exclusion available. To prevent a widowed spouse from having to rush to complete a sale within the same year as the death of the spouse, Congress enacted Section 121(b)(4) effective for sales or exchanges after December 31, 2007. This provision allows a widowed taxpayer who has not remarried to sell or exchange his principal residence and claim an exclusion of up to $500,000 if the sale or exchange occurs *not later than 2 years after the date of death of the taxpayer's spouse and the requirements of Section 121(a)(2)(A) were met immediately before the date the spouse's death.* Thus, in the above example, if Bill's sale of the home occurred January 2, 2008 (or for that matter, any time before September 1, 2008), Bill would have the benefit of an exclusion of up to $500,000.

Under Section 121, two people who are not married but who jointly owned and used the same home as their principal residence would each be eligible to exclude up to $250,000 of their respective gain, assuming all other requirements of Section 121 were satisfied.

> **Example 3:** Scott and Russell purchased a home as tenants-in-common with each owning one half of the value of the home. They used the home as their principal residence for five years and then sold it at a significant gain. The gain would be split evenly between Scott and Russell and each of them could exclude up to $250,000 of the gain.

In 2008, Congress added Section 121(b)(5), which provides that the Section 121 exclusion shall not apply to the gain allocated to periods of "nonqualified use." The gain allocation is based on the ratio that nonqualified use periods bear to the period the taxpayer has owned the property. Generally speaking, a period of nonqualified use is a period (after 2008) during which the property was not used as the taxpayer's principal residence (or the principal residence of the taxpayer's spouse or former spouse). § 121(b)(5)(C)(i). There are, however, exceptions, including an exception for any portion of the five-year period in § 121(a) that is after the last date the property was used as a principal residence by the taxpayer or the taxpayer's spouse.

§ 121(b)(5).   Exclusion of Gain Allocated to Nonqualified Use.

(A) In general - Subsection (a) shall not apply to so much of the gain from the sale or exchange of property as is allocated to periods of nonqualified use.

(B) Gain allocated to periods of nonqualified use. For purposes of subparagraph (A), gain shall be allocated to periods of nonqualified use based on the ratio which -

(i) the aggregate periods of nonqualified use during the period such property was owned by the taxpayer, bears to

(ii) the period such property was owned by the taxpayer.

(C) Period of nonqualified use. For purposes of this paragraph -

(i) In general. The term "period of nonqualified use" means any period (other than the portion of any period preceding January 1, 2009) during which the property is not used as the principal residence of the taxpayer of the taxpayer's spouse or former spouse.

(ii) Exceptions. The term "period of nonqualified use" does not include -

(I) any portion of the 5-year period described in subsection (a) which is after the last date that such property is used as the principal residence of the taxpayer or the taxpayer's spouse

. . . .

Example 4: Mary, a single woman, owned her home from January 1, 2009 to December 31, 2014, when she sold it at a gain of $150,000. Mary occupied her home as her principal residence only for the period from January 1, 2009 to December 31, 2012. She rented out the home from January 1, 2013 to December 31, 2014, the date of the sale.

Analysis: At first glance, it appears that during the 6-year period of Mary's ownership (January 2009 - December 2014) there were two years of nonqualified use (January 2013 - December 2014). If so, this would mean that 33% of the gain (2 years out of 6 years), or $50,000, was allocated to a period of nonqualified use and was not excludable under § 121. However, under the exception noted above, a period of nonqualified use does not include any portion of the § 121(a) 5-year period which is after the last date the property was used as the taxpayer's principal residence. As a result, there is no period of nonqualified use in this example, and the entire $150,000 gain is excludable.[14]

Example 5: Given the strong rental market, Alexis (a single person) purchased a residence on January 1, 2009 with the intent of holding the residence as a rental property. Alexis paid $200,000 for the residence. Alexis

---

[14] Note, however, that if the taxpayer was allowed depreciation deductions during the rental period, the gain allocable to the depreciation is not excluded. Section 121(d)(6). Section 121(b)(5)(D) provides that the nonqualified use rule is to be applied after Section 121(d)(6), and that the allocation of gain to a period of nonqualified use is made without regard to Section 121(d)(6). Depreciation is discussed in detail in Chapter 14.

rented the residence to university students for the first two years she owned it, i.e., from January 1, 2009 through December 31, 2010. On January 1, 2011 Alexis moved into the residence and made it her principal residence until January 1, 2013 when she moved out of the residence and put it up for sale. She sold the residence on January 1, 2014 for $500,000. Assume that Alexis' adjusted basis in the residence was still $200,000. (For purposes of this example, ignore the depreciation deductions Alexis would be allowed with respect to the residence during the period she rented the residence.) Assume the only reason Alexis sold the home was that she wanted a larger home and that Alexis has never taken advantage of Section 121.

Analysis: Under these circumstances, Alexis has two years of nonqualified use during the five years she owned the property. As a result, 2/5 or $120,000 of her $300,000 of realized gain on the sale of the home is not eligible for exclusion under Section 121. The remaining 3/5 of the gain or $180,000 of gain will be eligible for exclusion under Section 121.

[C]　Exclusion for Taxpayers Failing to Meet Certain Requirements

§ 121(c)(1).　In General.

In the case of a sale or exchange to which this subsection applies, the ownership and use requirements of subsection (a) and subsection (b)(3) shall not apply; but the dollar limitation under paragraph (1) or (2) of subsection (b) whichever is applicable, shall be equal to

(A) the amount which bears the same ratio to such limitation (determined without regard to this paragraph) as

(B) the shorter of

(i) the aggregate periods, during the 5 year period ending on the date of such sale or exchange, such property has been owned and used by the taxpayer as the taxpayer's principal residence; or

(ii) the period after the date of the most recent sale or exchange by the taxpayer to which subsection (a) applied and before the date of such sale or exchange, bears to 2 years.

If a sale or exchange occurs because of "a change in place of employment, health, or . . . [certain] unforseen circumstances," and a taxpayer consequently fails to meet the ownership and use requirements of Section 121(a) or the once-every-two-year rule of Section 121(b)(3), Section 121(c) provides that some or all of the gain may still be excluded. The maximum excludable amount of gain will be a fraction of the $250,000 ($500,000 in the case of a joint return where the requirements of Section 121(b)(2) are met) limit. The following examples demonstrate common application of Section 121(c).

Example 1: Sean purchases a home and lives in it for a year and then is transferred by his employer to a different city. Sean sells the home and realizes a gain of $600,000. May Sean claim the benefit of Section 121? Assume Sean has never previously taken advantage of Section 121.

Analysis: Because of the circumstances, Sean's failure to satisfy the two year ownership and use requirement will not negate the availability of an exclusion. Under the formula in Section 121(c)(1), the exclusion will be limited to a fraction of the $250,000 exclusion otherwise available. That fraction will have as its numerator the length of time Sean owned and used the home as his principal residence (here one year) and the denominator will be two years. Thus, the fraction is 1/2. Sean will therefore be entitled to exclude up to $125,000 of gain. Since the gain realized on the sale was $600,000 Sean will be required to recognize $475,000 of gain.

Example 2: Sean owned a home he had used as his principal residence since 2000. On July 1, 2012, Sean married Trish and the couple made Sean's home their principal residence. On July 1, 2013, Sean and Trish sell their home (which had remained titled in Sean's name) because of a change in the location of both of their jobs from the East coast to the West coast. Neither Sean nor Trish had used the Section 121 exclusion previously. The gain on the sale of the home was $400,000. Sean and Trish file a joint return.

Analysis: Because Sean and Trish have not both used the home as their principal residence for at least two years during the five year period preceding the sale of the home, the maximum dollar limitation amount that may be claimed by Sean and Trish will not be $500,000, but rather will be the sum of each spouse's limitation amount determined as if they had not been married although Trish will be treated as owning the home for the period Sean owned it. (Section 121(b)(2)(B).) Sean is eligible to exclude up to $250,000 of gain because he meets the requirements of Section 121. Trish is not eligible to exclude the maximum dollar limitation amount. Instead, she is eligible to claim a reduced exclusion. Because the sale of the home is due to a change in place of employment, Trish is eligible to exclude up to $125,000 of the gain (12 months/24 months or 1/2 of $250,000). Therefore, Sean and Trish are eligible to exclude up to $375,000 of the $400,000 gain on the sale of the home.

Example 3: Ron owned a home he had used as his principal residence since 1997. On July 1, 2012, Ron's longtime companion Sally moved into Ron's home and, on the same day, Ron transferred a one-half interest in the home to Sally as a tenant-in-common. On December 1, 2012, Sally gave birth to Mark, Ron and Sally's first child. Sally resigned from her position as comptroller of a company so that she could be at home to take care of Mark. On July 1, 2013, Ron and Sally sold their home because Ron's employer transferred him to the employer's main office located hundreds of miles away in another state. The gain on the sale of their home was $500,000. Ron and Sally purchase a new home near the place of Ron's new employment. Sally did not seek employment in the new location. Neither Ron nor Sally had previously taken advantage of Section 121. Ron and Sally are not married and are therefore not eligible to file a joint return. What are the tax consequences of the sale to Ron and Sally?

Analysis: Ron's share of the gain on the sale of the home is $250,000. Because he owned and used the home as his principal residence for at least two years prior to the sale, Ron is entitled to exclude the entire $250,000 of gain allocable to him. Sally, by contrast, is not eligible to exclude all $250,000 of her gain since she had owned and used the home for only one year. Instead, she is eligible to claim a reduced exclusion because the sale of the home was due to a change in her co-owner's place of employment. Regulation § 1.121-3(c) provides that a sale will be treated as a sale by reason of a change in place of employment if the primary reason for the sale is a change in the location of a "qualified individual's" employment. A "qualified individual" is defined in Regulation § 1.121-3(f)(3) to include the co-owner of the taxpayer's residence. Sally will be entitled to an exclusion equal to a fraction of the maximum exclusion ($250,000) which would otherwise be available to her. As in Example 2, that fraction will have as its numerator the length of time Sally owned and used the home as her principal residence (here, one year) and the denominator will be two years. The fraction is 1/2, thus allowing Sally to exclude up to $125,000 of gain.

Note that, under Regulation § 1.121-3(f), "qualified individuals," for purposes of the reduced maximum exclusion, include not only the co-owner of the taxpayer's residence, as in the above example, but also the taxpayer, the taxpayer's spouse, and persons who have the same principal place of abode as the taxpayer. (The list of "qualified individuals" is further expanded where the change of residence is by reason of health.)

Regulation § 1.121-3, addressing the reduced maximum exclusion under Section 121(c), provides so-called "safe harbors" relating to sales or exchanges by reason of change in employment, health, or other unforseen circumstances. Regulation § 1.121-3(e)(1) provides that "a sale or exchange is by reason of unforeseen circumstances if the primary reason for the sale or exchange is the occurrence of an event that the taxpayer could not reasonably have anticipated before purchasing and occupying the residence." Regulation § 1.121-3(e)(2) provides a safe harbor by identifying specific events that will be deemed unforseen circumstances, including (1) the involuntary conversion of the residence; (2) natural or man-made disasters or acts of war or terrorism resulting in a casualty to the residence (without regard to deductibility under Section 165(h); (3) death; (4) divorce or legal separation under decree of divorce or separate maintenance; or (5) multiple births resulting from the same pregnancy. This same regulation clarifies that a sale or exchange (not within the unforeseen circumstances safe harbor) will not qualify for the reduced maximum exclusion if the primary reason for the sale or exchange is a preference for a different residence or an improvement in financial circumstances.

[D] Limitation on Exclusion for Depreciation Claimed

Although it is premature to discuss depreciation (which will be discussed in detail in Chapter 14), Section 121(d)(6) provides that the exclusion shall not apply to the gain realized on a sale of one's principal residence to the extent that the taxpayer claimed depreciation deductions with respect to that residence at any time after May 6, 1997. This provision is commonly applicable when a taxpayer has used part of her home as a home office and has claimed depreciation deductions with respect to that part of the home. For example, if after May 6, 1997, the taxpayer had properly claimed a total of $15,000 in depreciation deductions with respect to her home office, and the taxpayer sold the home and realized $75,000 in gain, under Section 121(d)(6) only $60,000 of that gain would be subject to exclusion under Section 121(a). The $15,000 balance would be subject to capital gains tax, discussed in Chapter 31. Thus, to the extent a taxpayer has claimed depreciation deductions with respect to property, the Section 121 exclusion will be reduced.

[E]   Principal Residence

Section 121 requires that a residence be "used by the taxpayer as a principal residence for periods aggregating two years." There are two prongs to this requirement. First, the residence must be the taxpayer's principal residence. Second, once the principal residence is determined, one must determine whether the property was used (occupied) as the taxpayer's principal residence for the requisite period. PLR 200645001. *See* Section IV.A., *supra*, for discussion of "use" of a residence as a principal residence.

With regard to whether a property constitutes one's principal residence, the Tax Court in *Gates v. Commissioner*, 135 T.C. 1 (2010) emphasized that "Congress intended Section 121 to mean the primary dwelling or house that a taxpayer occupied as his principal residence. Nothing in the legislative history indicates that Congress intended Section 121 to exclude gain on the sale of property that does not include a house or other structure used by the taxpayer as his principal place of abode. Although a principal residence may include land surrounding the dwelling, the legislative history supports a conclusion that Congress intended the Section 121 exclusion to apply only if the dwelling the taxpayer sells was actually used as his principal residence for the period required by Section 121(a)." In *Gates*, the taxpayers demolished an old residence in which they had lived and, in its stead, built on the same property a new residence in which they intended to live. The taxpayers, however, never lived in the new residence. As a result, the court denied any exclusion under Section 121 on the sale of the new residence even though the taxpayers could establish they had met the Section 121 requirements with regard to the old residence they had demolished.

Under the regulations interpreting Section 121, if a taxpayer alternates between two residences, the residence the taxpayer uses a majority of the time during the year will ordinarily be considered the taxpayer's principal residence.[15]

> **Example:** During a five-year period, Taxpayer spends five months per year at a home she owns on the coast and seven months each year at her home in the city. Taxpayer sells the home on the coast. Although Taxpayer has owned and used the home on the coast as her residence for a period aggregating more than two years during the five year period prior to the sale, the home on the coast will ordinarily not be considered her principal residence.

This majority-of-time test, however, is not dispositive. The regulations also include a nonexclusive list of other factors relevant in identifying a property as a

---

[15] Treas. Reg. § 1.121-1(b)(2).

taxpayer's principal residence: (1) the taxpayer's place of employment; (2) the principal place of abode of family members; (3) the address listed on the taxpayer's federal and state tax returns, driver's license, automobile registration, and voter registration card; (4) the taxpayer's mailing address for bills and correspondence; (5) the location of taxpayer's banks; and (6) the location of religious organizations and recreational clubs with which the taxpayer is affiliated.[16]

An important issue related to the determination of "principal residence" is the extent to which the property owned in conjunction with the dwelling place may be considered to be part of the principal residence. In *Bogley v. Commissioner*,[17] the taxpayer's home was on a 13-acre tract of land. The taxpayer unsuccessfully sought to sell as a unit his home and the thirteen acres on which it was situated. He finally subdivided the property and sold the house together with three acres of land. Thereafter, within the year, the taxpayer sold the remaining land as two five-acre tracts. The purchaser of the taxpayer's house bought one of the five-acre tracts. The taxpayer, claiming the house and all thirteen acres constituted his principal residence, argued the gain from the sale of each part of the property should be treated as gain from the sale of a principal residence. The Fourth Circuit concluded that the two five-acre tracts had been used as part of the principal residence of the taxpayer and had never been converted to any other use. Therefore, these tracts retained their character as part of the principal residence even after the house and the three acres were sold. Regulation § 1.121-1(b)(3)(i) follows *Bogley* and provides specific requirements for the exclusion of gain from the sale of vacant land used as part of the taxpayer's principal residence. How much land surrounding a home can be considered part of the principal residence? That determination will obviously depend on all of the facts and circumstances.

Vacation homes are typically located in recreational areas where property values often increase rapidly. The ability to exclude large amounts of gain associated with the sale of such homes will tempt taxpayers to convert their vacation homes into principal residences for the requisite two year period prior to selling the vacation home.

Example 2: Assume Maurice owns a highly appreciated summer home located on a lake 60 miles from the city in which Maurice lives and works. If Maurice moves to the lake home and lives there for two years, commuting each day to work, will Maurice be entitled to claim the benefit of Section 121 when he sells the lake home? In other words, will the lake home have been converted to Maurice's principal residence for a two year period?

Analysis: Because of the weight accorded the amount of time spent using a property as one's residence, Maurice appears to have a strong argument that the lake home qualifies as Maurice's principal residence. It is not uncommon for individuals to commute significant distances to work each day. Thus, for example, an individual may live on Long Island and spend

---

[16] Treas. Reg. § 1.121-1(b)(2). See *Guinan v. U.S.*, 2003 U.S. Dist. LEXIS 11923 (D. Ariz. April 9, 2003), for a case applying the various factors for determining a taxpayer's principal residence.

[17] 263 F.2d 746 (4th Cir. 1959).

hours commuting by train to New York City to work each day. The individual's Long Island home will be considered to be that individual's principal residence. Maurice should be treated no differently. See, however, Regulation § 1.121-1(b)(2) for a list of other factors relevant to the determination of Maurice's principal residence.

Example 3: Assume the facts of Example 2, except Maurice lives at the lake for five months each year during the five years before he sells the lake home and commutes to work during those five months. During seven months of each year, Maurice lives in a home he owns in the same city in which he is employed. Will Maurice be eligible for Section 121 on the basis that he has used the lake home as his principal residence for periods aggregating two years or more during the five year period before the sale?

Analysis: "If a taxpayer alternates between two properties, using each as a residence for successive periods of time, the property that the taxpayer uses a majority of time during the year will ordinarily be considered the taxpayer's principal residence."[18] Based upon the language of the regulation, it would appear Maurice's lake home will not be considered Maurice's principal residence in any of the five years. Thus, Maurice may not be eligible for the exclusion under Section 121. This result, however, is not entirely free from doubt considering that the regulation does not make the majority-of-the-time-during-the-year test dispositive. One suspects that the Service and the courts will find themselves in coming years spending considerable time evaluating whether a residence is the taxpayer's principal residence.

[F] Conclusion

The 1997 changes in Section 121 provide an enormous benefit to homeowners. Although some taxpayers will realize gain on the sale of their homes in excess of the excludable limits of Section 121, Section 121 will exclude the gain from most home sales in this country.

---

[18] Treas. Reg. §§ 1.121-1(b)(2), 1.121-1(b)(4) Ex. 1.

Chapter 7

SCHOLARSHIPS AND PRIZES

Prior to 1954, no statute explicitly addressed the taxability of prizes and awards and scholarships, and as a result, they were excluded from income only if they qualified as "gifts" under the forerunner of present Section 102. Section 74, enacted in 1954, generally included prizes and awards in gross income, but made a major exception for awards based on "religious, charitable, scientific, educational, artistic, literary, or civic achievement," provided the recipient was selected without action on his part to enter the contest, and also was not required to render substantial future services.[1] Section 117, also first enacted in 1954, excluded "scholarships and fellowships" from gross income for both degree candidates and non-degree candidates. The exclusionary provisions of both statutes, however, were significantly narrowed in 1986.

§ 7.01 PRIZES AND AWARDS

§ 74. Prizes and awards.

(a) **General rule. Except as otherwise provided in this section or in section 117 (relating to qualified scholarships), gross income includes amounts received as prizes and awards.**

(b) **Exception for certain prizes and awards transferred to charities. Gross income does not include amounts received as prizes and awards made primarily in recognition of religious, charitable, scientific, educational, artistic, literary, or civic achievement, but only if —**

(1) **the recipient was selected without any action on his part to enter the contest or proceeding;**

(2) **the recipient is not required to render substantial future services as a condition to receiving the prize or award; and**

(3) **the prize or award is transferred by the payor to a governmental unit or organization described in paragraph (1) or (2) of section 170(c) pursuant to a designation made by the recipient.**

[A] Prizes and Awards Generally Taxable

Prizes and awards are now generally taxable. The pre-1986 exception applicable to recipients of "meritorious achievement" awards had often been criticized on policy grounds. Prizes and awards represent a clear accession to wealth, it was argued, and ought to be taxed, particularly since the value of the exclusion

---

[1] I.R.C. § 74(b)(1), (2).

increases with the tax bracket of the recipient, and since the presence of the exclusion may provide a temptation to disguise taxable compensation as a tax-exempt prize. This argument prevailed, Section 74(b)(3) was added to the Code, and the meritorious achievement exception now applies only if the recipient gives up the prize. Specifically, in addition to meeting the pre-1986 requirements (religious, charitable, etc., achievement, no action to enter, no substantial future services) in order to qualify for the exclusion, the recipient must also designate a governmental unit or qualifying charity to which the payor transfers the prize.[2] A timely designation must be made and carried out before the award is used.[3] Since the recipient of such a prize or award could presumably avoid gross income by simply rejecting the award (*see, e.g.,* Rev. Rul. 57-374),[4] the statutory scheme, in a sense, broadens the right to reject: in addition to outright rejection, a qualifying designation and transfer also avoids gross income. Note that since no gross income is generated, no charitable deduction is allowed either.[5] The tax consequences are not necessarily the same as if the recipient accepted the prize (receiving gross income) and then transferred it to a qualifying charity (receiving a charitable deduction). If, for example, the taxpayer's itemized deductions were less than the standard deduction or if the taxpayer's charitable contributions for the year exceeded the Section 170(b) limitations,[6] the transfer-to-charity rule would be useful.

[B]   Employee Achievement Awards Exempt

§ 74(c).   Exception for certain employee achievement awards.

(1)   In general.

Gross income shall not include the value of an employee achievement award (as defined in section 274(j)) received by the taxpayer if the cost to the employer of the employee achievement award does not exceed the amount allowable as a deduction to the employer for the cost of the employee achievement award.

(2)   Excess deduction award.

If the cost to the employer of the employee achievement award received by the taxpayer exceeds the amount allowable as a deduction to the employer, then gross income includes the greater of —

(A) an amount equal to the portion of the cost to the employer of the award that is not allowable as a deduction to the employer (but not in excess of the value of the award), or

(B) the amount by which the value of the award exceeds the amount allowable as a deduction to the employer.

The remaining portion of the value of such award shall not be included in the gross income of the recipient.

---

[2] I.R.C. § 74(b)(3).

[3] Prop. Treas. Reg. § 1.74-1(c)(1), (d), (e)(2).

[4] 1957-2 C.B. 69.

[5] Prop. Treas. Reg. § 1.74-1(f).

[6] *See* Chapter 26, *infra.*

§ 274(j)(3).   Definitions.

For purposes of this subsection —

(A)   Employee achievement award.

The term "employee achievement award" means an item of tangible personal property which is

(i) transferred by an employer to an employee for length of service achievement of safety achievement,

(ii) awarded as part of a meaningful presentation, and

(iii) awarded under conditions and circumstances that do not create a significant likelihood of the payment of disguised compensation.

(B)   Qualified plan award.

(i)   In general. — The term "qualified plan award" means an employee achievement award awarded as part of an established written plan or program of the taxpayer which does not discriminate in favor of highly compensated employees (within the meaning of section 414(q)) as to eligibility of benefits.

(ii)   Limitation.

An employee achievement award shall not be treated as a qualified plan award for any taxable year if the average cost of all employee achievement awards which are provided by the employer during the year, and which would be qualified plan awards but for the subparagraph, exceeds $400. For purposes of the preceding sentence, average cost shall be determined by including the entire cost of qualified plan awards, without taking into account employee achievement awards of nominal value.

The principal exclusion now in Section 74 is for "employee achievement awards."[7] The exclusion for employee achievement awards constitutes congressional approval and encouragement of "double" tax benefits — that is, a deduction for the employer and an exclusion for the employee — in certain restricted circumstances. The statutory scheme requires, in part, that the award consist of tangible personal property, given in recognition of a qualifying length of service or safety achievement. A "qualified plan award" is an employee achievement award under a written plan that does not discriminate in favor of highly compensated employees, provided the average annual cost for all employee achievement awards does not exceed $400.[8] The employer's deduction for the cost of employee achievement awards is limited to $400 per year for each employee, except that the limit may increase to a maximum of $1600 with respect to qualified plan awards. If the cost of the award is fully deductible to the employer, the employee may exclude the award from income. If the cost is not fully deductible, the award constitutes gross income to the extent its value or cost (whichever is greater) exceeds the deduction limit. (The "excess cost" amount, however, cannot be greater than the value of the award itself.)

Example 1: Employer provides to Employee an employee achievement award of tangible personal property. This is the only such award provided

---

[7] I.R.C. §§ 74(c), 274(j).

[8] I.R.C. § 274(j)(3)(B).

to Employee this year. The employee achievement award, which does not qualify as a "qualified plan award," has a value of $300 and cost Employer $300.

Analysis: The award is fully deductible to Employer, and Employee has no gross income, because the value of the award does not exceed $400.

Example 2: Same facts as above, however, the award has a value of $600 and cost Employer $500.

Analysis: Employee has gross income of $200. Since Employer's deduction for employee achievement awards (not qualified plan awards) is limited to $400 per year for each employee, Employee has gross income to the extent value or cost, whichever is greater, exceeds $400. Since the value, $600, is greater than the cost, $500, Employee has income of $200 ($600 minus $400).

Comment:

Note that Employer can deduct up to $1,600 per year with respect to "qualified plan awards"— *i.e.*, employee achievement awards under a written plan, nondiscriminatory in favor of highly compensated employees, where the average cost of such awards does not exceed $400. If this were a qualified plan award, it would be fully deductible to Employer, and as a result, Employee would have no income.

This statutory exclusion of Section 74(c) is complemented by the congressional determination that employee awards should generally not be classified as gifts, and that Section 102 should not apply to transfers from employer to employee.[9] In addition to the provisions of Section 74(c), an independent basis for excluding certain employee awards may be found in the *de minimis* fringe benefit provisions.[10] The fringe benefit rules are studied in detail in Chapter 11.

The fact that prizes and awards are generally taxable means that difficult valuation issues may be presented when an award is not in cash. The regulations state that the measure of income is fair market value.[11]

§ 7.02 QUALIFIED SCHOLARSHIPS

§ 117. Qualified scholarships.

(a) In general.

Gross income does not include any amount received as a qualified scholarship by an individual who is a candidate for a degree at an educational organization described in § 170(b)(1)(A)(ii).

(b) Qualified scholarship.

For purposes of this section —

---

[9] I.R.C. §§ 102(c)(1), 274(b).

[10] *See* I.R.C. § 132(e)(1); Prop. Treas. Reg. § 1.74-2(e).

[11] Treas. Reg. § 1.74-1(a)(2).

(1)   In general —

The term "qualified scholarship" means any amount received by an individual as a scholarship or fellowship grant to the extent the individual establishes that, in accordance with the conditions of the grant, such amount was used for qualified tuition and related expenses.

(2)   Qualified tuition and related expenses.

For purposes of paragraph (1), the term "qualified tuition and related expenses" means

(A) tuition and fees required for the enrollment or attendance of a student at an educational organization described in section 170(b)(1)(A)(ii), and

(B) fees, books, supplies, and equipment required for courses of instruction at such an educational organization.

[A]   Limitation of Exclusion

The exclusion for scholarships and fellowships is now limited to "qualified scholarships" received by degree-seeking students at qualifying educational institutions. There is no exclusion for scholarships or fellowships received by those who are not candidates for degrees.[12] The term "candidate for a degree" includes students attending a primary or secondary school, and undergraduate or graduate students pursuing an academic or professional degree at a college or university; it also includes students pursuing, at educational institutions, certain qualifying employment-training programs or programs acceptable for full credit towards a bachelor or higher degree.[13]

Prior to 1986, there was no limit on the statutory exclusion for amounts received by degree candidates as scholarships, and the exclusion thus extended to amounts used to cover ordinary living expenses, including meals and lodging. A "qualified scholarship," in contrast, is limited to that portion of a scholarship or fellowship used for tuition and certain related expenses. The change thus eliminates the perceived inequity of allowing a tax benefit for personal living expenses to scholarship recipients, while denying it to non-scholarship students and to non-students generally. The exclusion, of course, still provides a tax benefit to scholarship students with respect to tuition and fees.

Although the statute requires that the scholarship be used for "qualified tuition and related expenses" (a term that encompasses required tuition, required fees, and required books, supplies, and equipment) in accordance with the conditions of the grant, actual "tracing" of funds is not required.[14] The student is entitled to exclude an otherwise qualifying scholarship up to the aggregate amount incurred

---

[12] However, educational costs that qualify as trade or business expenses are deductible. *See* Treas. Reg. § 1.162-5. In addition, certain postsecondary educational expenses may qualify for a tax credit under Section 25A. The deductibility of educational expenses generally and the availability of various education tax incentives are examined in Chapter 18, *infra*.

[13] Prop. Treas. Reg. § 1.117-6(c)(4).

[14] I.R.C. § 117(b)(2); Prop. Treas. Reg. § 1.117-6(e).

for qualified tuition and related expenses; no exclusion is allowed for scholarship amounts earmarked for nonqualifying purposes, such as room and board.[15]

> **Example 1:** Mary receives a $10,000 scholarship to attend State University, where she is a candidate for a bachelor's degree. Qualified tuition and related expenses for the year total $8,500.

> **Analysis:** Mary has income of $1,500. The scholarship is a qualified scholarship to the extent of $8,500, the amount of the year's qualified tuition and related expenses.

> **Example 2:** Assume the same facts as Example 1, except that Mary was required by the terms of the scholarship to apply $4,000 of the scholarship to room and board at State University.

> **Analysis:** Qualified tuition and related expenses do not include room and board. Since $4,000 of the scholarship must be applied to room and board, that $4,000 will constitute gross income. Mary's qualified tuition and related expenses are $8,500 (*see* Example 1). The remaining $6,000 of the scholarship will not constitute gross income, since it does not exceed $8,500.

[B]   Scholarships as Compensation

§ 117(c).   Limitation.

(1) . . . [S]ubsections (a) and (d) shall not apply to that portion of any amount received which represents payment for teaching, research, or other services by the student required as a condition for receiving the qualified scholarship or qualified tuition reduction.

No exclusion is allowed for scholarship amounts that represent payment for services.[16]

> **Example:** Mary receives a $10,000 scholarship, but is required to work in the library for 10 hours a week as a condition of the scholarship.

> **Analysis:** Some portion of Mary's scholarship apparently constitutes payment for services. That portion of the "scholarship" will constitute gross income under Section 117(c).

Indeed, there has been considerable litigation as to whether payments made in an educational setting constituted an excluded scholarship or fellowship, or compensation for services.[17] In *Bingler v. Johnson*,[18] taxpayers were employees of Westinghouse Electric Corporation. Taxpayers received payments from their employer under a Fellowship Program while they were on "educational leave" from their job, pursuing postgraduate study in engineering. During a preliminary work-study phase of the program, the taxpayers were required to hold their

---

[15] Prop. Treas. Reg. § 1.117-6(c)(1).

[16] I.R.C. § 117(c)(1). There is a limited exception for National Health Service Corps and Armed Forces Health Professions scholarships. I.R.C. §117(c)(2).

[17] *See* Prop. Treas. Reg. § 1.117-6(d).

[18] 394 U.S. 741 (1969).

positions with Westinghouse; following their educational leave they were required to return to work for Westinghouse for at least two years. The stipends they received while on leave were clearly related to their salaries, and their fringe benefits were maintained. The Supreme Court held that the payments received were in the nature of a *quid pro quo* for services rendered (whether in the past, present, or future) and were not excludable as scholarships, but were taxable as compensation under applicable regulations.

Particularly litigious, and particularly likely to lose, have been medical interns and residents trying to cast their remuneration as a fellowship grant.[19] Graduate teaching and research assistants have also litigated frequently, losing where it was found they were primarily being paid to teach rather than paid to study.[20] In the case of employer-employee scholarships generally, it is difficult, as one might expect, to avoid application of the *quid pro quo* reasoning of *Bingler v. Johnson* that holds the "scholarship" to be taxable compensation.

[C] Tuition Reduction

§ 117(c). Qualified tuition reduction.

(1) In general.

Gross income shall not include any qualified tuition reduction.

(2) Qualified tuition reduction.

For purposes of this subsection, the term "qualified tuition reduction' means the amount of any reduction in tuition provided to an employee of an organization described in section 170(b)(1)(A)(ii) for the education (below the graduate level) at such organization (or another organization described in section 170(b)(1)(A)(ii)) of —

(A) such employee, or

(B) any person treated as an employee (or whose use is treated as an employee use) under the rules of section 132(h).

Although employer-employee scholarships may be unlikely to qualify under Section 117(a), some employer-provided educational benefits are nonetheless tax-free. "Qualified tuition reduction" programs, essentially a special fringe benefit for employees of educational organizations and their family members, are nontaxable, provided they do not discriminate in favor of highly compensated employees, even though the programs are clearly compensatory in nature, of potentially great value, and limited to one category of employees.[21]

---

[19] *See, e.g.*, Burstein v. U.S., 622 F.2d 529 (Ct. Cl. 1980).

[20] *See, e.g.*, Ellenwood v. Comm'r, T.C. Memo 1982-137; Sebberson v. Comm'r, T.C. Memo 1984-605.

[21] *See* I.R.C. § 117(d) (note the limitation in subsection (c)).

[D]   Educational Assistance Programs

§ 127.   Educational assistance programs.

(a) Exclusion from gross income.

(1) In general.

Gross income of an employee does not include amounts paid or expenses incurred by the employer for educational assistance to the employee if the assistance is furnished pursuant to a program which is described in subsection (b).

(2) $5,250 maximum exclusion.

If, but for this paragraph, this section would exclude from gross income more than $5,250 of educational assistance furnished to an individual during a calendar year, this section shall apply only to the first $5,250 of such assistance so furnished.

(b) Educational assistance program.

(1) In general.

For purposes of this section, an educational assistance program is a separate written plan of an employer for the exclusive benefit of his employees to provide such employees with educational assistance. The program must meet the requirements of paragraphs (2) through (6) of this subsection.

Education-related fringe benefits of more general applicability are the educational assistance programs described in Section 127. Employer payments for educational assistance to the employee are excluded from gross income, up to a maximum of $5,250 per year. The program cannot discriminate in favor of highly compensated employees and is subject to various other requirements. Educational assistance includes tuition and course-related expenses, but payments for meals, lodging, transportation and certain other expenditures do not qualify.[22] There is no requirement that the education be job-related or part of a degree program, and purely personal educational benefits may thus be obtained on a tax-free basis.[23]

Scholarship treatment may apply as well to grants from a private foundation established by a corporation to provide scholarships to children of employees, or to employees themselves. The Service has announced that scholarship treatment obtains if the grants are controlled and limited by substantial non-employment-related factors so that the employment relationship is no more than an initial qualifying condition.[24]

---

[22] I.R.C. § 127(c)(1).

[23] Treas. Reg. § 1.127-2(a)(4).

[24] Rev. Proc. 76-46, 1976-2 C.B. 670.

[E] Gifts

Finally, the relationship between Section 117 and the provisions dealing with prizes and awards and with gifts must be considered. Non-qualifying scholarships and fellowships are generally includable in income, by virtue of Section 74(a); the Section 102 gift exclusion is inapplicable.[25]

---

[25] *See* Prop. Treas. Reg. § 1.117-6(b)(1). See also Treas. Reg. § 1.102-1(a), stating that Section 102 does not apply to prizes and awards or to scholarships and fellowships.

Chapter 8

LIFE INSURANCE, ANNUITIES, AND INDIVIDUAL RETIREMENT ACCOUNTS

A full account of the tax treatment of life insurance is extremely complex and technical, and beyond the scope of this book. This overview will concentrate only on some fundamental rules, with a brief discussion of the tax advantages current law provides.

§ 8.01 LIFE INSURANCE

§ 101. **Certain death benefits —**

(a) **Proceeds of life insurance contracts payable by reason of death —**

(1) **General rule — Except as otherwise provided in paragraph (2), subsection (d), and subsection (f), gross income does not include amounts received (whether in a single sum or otherwise) under a life insurance contract, if such amounts are paid by reason of the death of the insured.**

[A] Exclusion of Mortality Gains

With respect to life insurance, the basic rule is clear: life insurance proceeds paid "by reason of the death of the insured" are excluded from gross income.[1] To grasp the full significance of this exclusion, it is helpful to distinguish between the "risk element" and the "savings element" in life insurance. The portion of an insurance premium that purchases insurance against the risk of dying at a given time represents the risk element; the portion, if any, that exceeds the actuarial cost of pure risk insurance represents the savings element.[2]

The simplest form of life insurance, "term insurance," is pure risk insurance and contains no savings element. Assume, for example, Taxpayer pays a $100 premium for a $50,000 one-year term life insurance policy on his life. If Taxpayer dies during the one-year period, the insurance company pays $50,000 to Taxpayer's beneficiary. If Taxpayer does not die during the one-year period, Taxpayer receives nothing when the year is up, and has no coverage unless the insurance is renewed.[3] The tax consequences of Taxpayer's dying, or not dying, during the one-year period are

---

[1] I.R.C. § 101(a)(1).

[2] An insurance premium also contains a "loading component" that reflects the insurance company's expenses and profit margin. For ease of illustration, we will regard the loading component as simply absorbed within the risk and savings elements of a premium.

[3] In a real sense, of course, it is incorrect to say Taxpayer receives nothing for his $100 premium, since Taxpayer has in fact received the insurance coverage, and the security and peace-of-mind that come with it.

straightforward. If Taxpayer dies, his beneficiary receives $50,000 on Taxpayer's $100 "investment," but this $49,900 "mortality gain" is tax-free under Section 101(a)(1). Conversely, if Taxpayer survives the period, he has "lost" his $100 bet with the insurance company; and has a "mortality loss." Taxpayer is ordinarily not entitled to any tax deduction for the premium; it is a nondeductible personal expense.[4] The insurance company, of course, is insuring many other individuals, and has set its premium on an actuarially sound basis, so that in the aggregate the premiums collected, and any earnings on them, will not only cover the payments that must be made for insured individuals who die and "win" their gambles, but pay the company's expenses and provide a profit as well.

A number of reasons for the tax-free treatment of mortality gains could be advanced. Life insurance proceeds may be viewed as somewhat equivalent to gifts and bequests, excludable from gross income under Section 102. The exclusion of the increase in the "value" of the policy (in our example, from $100 at the time of purchase to $50,000 at death) is similar to the exclusion provided by the basis step-up rules of Section 1014 for property passing at death.[5] In addition, by providing tax-free treatment to life insurance proceeds under Section 101, and nondeductibility of their premiums under Section 262, the whole matter can be seen, in the aggregate at least, as roughly a wash from the standpoint of the government. Assuming taxation of the proceeds would entail allowing a deduction for premiums, or for recovery of basis in some fashion, the present system may be viewed as the simplest and most efficient way of addressing the issue. Moreover, the government may simply want to use the tax system to encourage people to provide some protection against sudden loss of family earnings. Finally, of course, the circumstance in which life insurance proceeds are received — upon the death of the insured, who may perhaps be the family breadwinner — may obviously be regarded as a particularly inappropriate time to tax the beneficiary.

The preceding discussion has concerned term insurance with a one-year term. Assume Taxpayer, having survived Year 1, wants to take out a $50,000 policy for another year. In that event, all else being equal, Taxpayer's Year 2 premium will be greater than $100 for the simple reason that, being one year older, Taxpayer has, statistically speaking, an increased risk of dying. As each year passes, the premium for a one-year term policy will increase. Suppose Taxpayer wishes to buy term insurance for a five-year period, but pay the same premium each year. Since Taxpayer's risk factor increases each year, a level premium means the first year premium must be set at a level greater than the actuarial cost of pure risk insurance for that year; the excess portion of the premium, and earnings on it, in effect supplement the later years' premiums which, in themselves, do not cover the actuarial costs for those years.

---

[4] I.R.C. § 262. In some instances, payment of a premium on life insurance may constitute a deductible expense, as when an employer pays the premium on an employee's life insurance as a form of compensation to the employee. It is assumed in the discussion, however, that the life insurance is purchased for personal purposes, and the premiums are nondeductible under Section 262. (Even where Section 262 is not applicable, deduction of premiums may be disallowed by other provisions. *See, e.g.,* I.R.C. §§ 263(a), 264, 265(a)(1).)

[5] *See* Chapter 5, *supra.*

The savings element of life insurance is certainly present in this type of multi-year, level-premium term insurance. But term insurance builds up no cash value. Other types of life insurance, such as "ordinary life insurance," "whole life insurance," "variable life insurance," "universal life insurance," and numerous variations, are designed to do more than provide risk insurance over a period of time; they also act as investment vehicles. With ordinary life insurance, a constant level premium is paid to provide a given amount of insurance over the life of the insured. The premium paid is necessarily greater than it would be for the same amount of term insurance. Only part of the premium insures the taxpayer against the risk of dying; the remainder is, in effect, invested by the insurance company on behalf of the insured, and over the years a "cash value" builds up, reflecting not only the excess portions of the premiums, but the earnings on them. The later the insured's death occurs, the greater the amount of cash value build-up inherent in the insurance proceeds. The owner of the policy may typically borrow against the cash value, or obtain it outright by termination of the policy by surrendering it. Under current law, however, neither the insured nor the insurance company is taxed on this "inside build-up" while it accumulates. This tax deferral is a central advantage of life insurance as an investment vehicle.

Suppose, for example, Taxpayer purchases term insurance. The annual premium for the same amount of ordinary life insurance will, of course, cost him more than the annual premium for the term insurance. Assume Taxpayer places the difference between the cost of the term insurance and the cost of ordinary life insurance in the bank to draw interest. The interest on bank savings is taxable, so the bank savings would grow more slowly than the untaxed "savings" that accrue on the amount invested in ordinary life insurance.

The following example illustrates the interaction of the risk element and savings element and the Section 101(a)(1) exclusion.

Example: Assume Taxpayer has owned for 15 years an ordinary life policy with a face value of $50,000, and has paid $1,200 per year, or a total of $18,000, in premiums. Also assume that pure risk (term) insurance would have cost only $10,000 over the same period, and that the insurance company has earned $4,000 for Taxpayer on the "excess" $8,000 in premiums; the cash value of the policy is thus $12,000 ($8,000 plus $4,000). Taxpayer dies, and his beneficiary receives the $50,000.

Analysis: The tax consequences are clear: the entire $50,000 is tax-free under Section 101(a)(1). That $50,000 actually consists of:

(1) $8,000:   return of the "excess" portion of the premium;
(2) $4,000:   interest earned by the "excess" amount;
(3) $10,000:   return of the risk portion of premium;
(4) $28,000:   the net mortality gain. (Recall that the policy had a cash value of $12,000. Thus, $38,000 of the proceeds are properly allocable to term insurance. Since the actuarial cost of that insurance would be $10,000, the net mortality gain was $28,000.)

Mortality gains on life insurance are untaxed. The return of the savings element, the "excess" portion of the premium, is also properly tax-free under normal return-of-capital principles. However, the *interest* earned on the savings element is not merely tax-deferred, but ultimately tax-exempt as well. Tax reform proposals have often attacked this element of life insurance taxation, arguing that no policy justification exists for affording such favored treatment to savings in the form of life insurance. It is thus often proposed that this "inside build-up" in life insurance be currently taxed.

The exclusion applies to the proceeds of "life insurance contracts," a term defined in Section 7702. The essential elements of insurance generally are the shifting of risk from policyholder to insurer and the distribution of risk among the policyholders. The purpose of the statutory definition is to permit the full tax advantages associated with life insurance to be available only to those contracts where the risk element is real and substantial, and not to permit what are basically investment programs with a minor life insurance element to qualify as life insurance for tax purposes. Thus, if the contract in question is a life insurance contract under local law, but does not meet the requirements of Section 7702, mortality gains are excluded from income, but the interest earnings on the investment portion of the contract are taxed currently to the policyholder; tax-free inside build-up is lost. For purposes of this chapter, an assumption is made that what is labeled a life insurance contract satisfies Section 7702.

[B] Death of the Insured

Even though the contract in question is a life insurance contract, the proceeds received under the contract must be payable "by reason of the death of the insured" to qualify for the Section 101 exclusion. This requirement typically poses no problem. Suppose, however, a seller of property on the installment basis takes out insurance on the life of the purchaser in an amount equal to the unpaid balance of the purchase price. The Service has ruled that the insurance proceeds do not qualify under Section 101(a) since they are paid not "by reason of the death of the insured," but rather, in effect, by reason of the unpaid debt; they are instead collections of the unpaid purchase price.[6]

[C] Accelerated Death Benefit

In addition to death benefits, insurance companies now offer insurance contracts designed to provide so-called "living benefits" as well. One type of living benefit is an "accelerated death benefit," pursuant to which payment on a policy insuring a terminally ill individual may be "accelerated" — that is, paid prior to death, in recognition of the substantial medical and other expenses not infrequently encountered in protracted terminal illnesses. Similar benefits may also be provided to severely disabled chronically ill individuals who may, for example, require long term nursing care or hospitalization. Furthermore, even if such benefits are not available under the terms of the life insurance contract, it may be possible to sell or assign the death benefit under the contract to a third party. Such pre-death

---

[6] Rev. Rul. 70-254, 1970-1 C.B. 31.

payments or proceeds are excludable under Section 101(a) pursuant to Section 101(g). Under the detailed special rules of this section, enacted in 1996, qualifying amounts under a life insurance contract on the life of an insured who is a terminally or chronically ill individual will be excluded from income as an amount paid by reason of the death of the insured.[7]

[D] Surrender for Value

If an insured individual, who is neither terminally nor chronically ill, surrenders an ordinary life insurance policy for its cash value, the proceeds are not payable by reason of death, and Section 101 does not apply. What applies instead are the rules of Section 72(e), and those rules extend an additional tax advantage to life insurance because they provide that the proceeds are taxable only to the extent they exceed the total consideration paid for the policy (*i.e.*, the insured's basis in the policy).[8] In effect, the taxpayer is permitted to deduct otherwise nondeductible premiums.

> **Example:** Taxpayer received $10,000 on the surrender of her ordinary life policy after having paid total premiums over the years equal to $9,000. Assume only $4,000 of the premiums represented the actuarial cost of term insurance.

> **Analysis:** Taxpayer's income is only $1,000. Conceptually, of the $9,000 in premiums paid, $4,000 was the cost of the insurance coverage Taxpayer actually received and the other $5,000 was the savings element discussed above. This $5,000 in "savings" produced the $10,000 return and thus the return-of-capital amount should only be $5,000 and the income reported $5,000. Section 72(e) permits not only the $5,000 savings element to offset the $10,000 in proceeds but also the $4,000 actual risk portion of the premiums paid. Thus, Taxpayer's income is only $1,000. The normally nondeductible "mortality loss" of $4,000 is thus made deductible. By way of contrast, had Taxpayer paid $4,000 for term insurance (and survived) and also paid $5,000 for an investment that grew to $10,000 over the years — and this is the functional equivalent of the example — Taxpayer would ultimately be required to report as income the $5,000 of appreciation on the investment and the cost of term insurance would be nondeductible under Section 262.

[E] Interest Income

§ 101. Certain death benefits —

(c) **Interest — If any amount excluded from gross income by subsection (a) is held under an agreement to pay interest thereon, the interest payments shall be included in gross income.**

(d) **Payment of life insurance proceeds at a date later than death —**

---

[7] *See* I.R.C. §§ 101(g), 7702B.

[8] I.R.C. § 72(e)(6).

(1)   General rule — The amounts held by an insurer with respect to any beneficiary shall be prorated (in accordance with such regulations as may be prescribed by the Secretary) over the period or periods with respect to which such payments are to be made. There shall be excluded from the gross income of such beneficiary in the taxable year received any amount determined by such proration. Gross income includes, to the extent not excluded by the preceding sentence, amounts received under agreements to which this subsection applies.

(2)   Amount held by an insurer — An amount held by an insurer with respect to any beneficiary shall mean an amount to which subsection (a) applies which is —

(A) held by any insurer under an agreement provided for in the life insurance contract, whether as an option or otherwise, to pay such amount on a date or dates later than the death of the insured, and

(B) equal to the value of such agreement to such beneficiary

(i) as of the date of death of the insured (as if any option exercised under the life insurance contract were exercised at such time), and

(ii) as discounted on the basis of the interest rate used by the insurer in calculating payments under the agreement and mortality tables prescribed by the Secretary.

(3)   Application of subsection — This subsection shall not apply to any amount to which subsection (c) is applicable.

Life insurance proceeds on account of the insured's death may be paid either in a lump-sum or in installments. Section 101(a)(1) applies to both cases. The exclusion, however, is not intended to cover post-death earnings on the proceeds. Thus, interest payments on amounts withheld by the insurer under an agreement to pay interest are taxable.[9]

> **Example 1:** Assume life insurance proceeds are $100,000, to be paid to Beneficiary two years after Taxpayer's death. In the interim, Beneficiary receives $6,000 per year interest from the insurance company on the insurance proceeds.
>
> **Analysis:** The interest payments are taxable; the $100,000 paid two years hence is not.
>
> **Example 2:** Alternatively, assume life insurance proceeds of $100,000 are to be paid in five annual installments of $25,000 each.
>
> **Analysis:** $20,000 of each annual payment is excluded. $5,000 is taxable. ($100,000 divided by 5 years of equal payments equals an exclusion of $20,000 per year.) In this case there is plainly an interest component built into the installments to compensate for the delayed payment of the death benefits. In effect, Section 101(d) provides that the principal portion of each installment shall be tax-free, and the interest portion taxable. The excluded amount, the "amount held by the insurer" in the statutory phrase, is to be prorated equally over the installments if the installments are for a fixed

---

[9] I.R.C. § 101(c).

number of years; the proration will be over the beneficiary's life expectancy (in accordance with the insurer's mortality table) if the installments are to be paid for the life of the beneficiary. Payments in excess of the prorated portions are taxable.[10] This mechanism for distinguishing the taxable portion of a payment from the nontaxable portion is similar to that used with regard to annuities under Section 72, and is discussed at greater length below.

[F]   Transfer for Value

§ 101.   Certain death benefits —

(a)   Proceeds of life insurance contracts payable by reason of death —

. . .

(2)   Transfer for valuable consideration —

In the case of a transfer for a valuable consideration, by assignment or otherwise, of a life insurance contract or any interest therein, the amount excluded from gross income by paragraph (1) shall not exceed an amount equal to the sum of the actual value of such consideration and the premiums and other amounts subsequently paid by the transferee. The preceding sentence shall not apply in the case of such a transfer

(A) if such contract or interest therein has a basis for determining gain or loss in the hands of a transferee determined in whole or in part by reference to such basis of such contract or interest therein in the hands of the transferor, or

(B) if such transfer is to insured, to a partner of the insured, to a partnership in which the insured is a partner, or to a corporation in which the insured is a shareholder or officer.

The term "other amounts" in the first sentence of this paragraph includes interest paid or accrued by the transferee on indebtedness with respect to such contract or any interest therein if such interest paid or accrued is not allowable as a deduction by reason of section 264(a)(4).

To this point, the assumption has been that Taxpayer was the insured and the owner of the insurance policy. Section 101(a)(1), however, does not require the insured to be the owner of the policy, nor does it prohibit the owner of a policy from also being the beneficiary of insurance on the life of another. Thus, if A has an insurable interest in the life of B, A may take out a policy in which B is the insured and A is the beneficiary; the proceeds A receives by reason of B's death will be within the Section 101(a)(1) exclusion. [Note, however, section 101(j) (added in 2006), which generally provides, in the case of employer-owned life insurance contracts, the amount excluded as a death benefit by the applicable policyholder (as defined in section 101(j)(3)(B)) cannot exceed the sum of the premiums and other amounts paid by the policyholder for the contract.]

---

[10] Treas. Reg. § 1.101-4(a)–(c).

Suppose, however, that A purchased the policy from B. The transfer for value rules of Section 101(a)(2) now apply. Unless one of the exceptions apply, the exclusion will be limited to the consideration A paid B plus any premiums or other amounts subsequently paid by A. Insurance proceeds in excess of these payments will be taxable.

> **Example:** B sells the policy described above to A for $5,000. The policy has a face amount of $25,000, and on B's death A receives the $25,000. A may exclude from income only $5,000 plus any additional premiums or other amounts paid by A.

The reasons for the transfer-for-value provisions are not completely clear. Legislative history suggests that Congress found the prospect of speculating in life insurance sufficiently distasteful to warrant denial of tax free treatment in profitable transactions. Note, however, that Section 101(a)(2) applies not just to arm's length commercial transactions, but to intra-family purchases as well. Also note that A could avoid the unfavorable tax results by simply purchasing a new policy on B's life directly from the insurer.

[G] Group-term Life Insurance

Congress has encouraged employers to provide group-term life insurance for their employees by treating the employer-paid cost of providing up to $50,000 of such insurance as a tax-free fringe benefit. The employer's cost for insurance in excess of the $50,000 level is taxable compensation. Special rules apply to employee benefit plans that discriminate in favor of so-called "key employees."[11]

§ 8.02 ANNUITIES

§ 72. Annuities; certain proceeds of endowment and life insurance contracts —

(a) **General rule for annuities —**

Except as otherwise provided in this chapter, gross income includes any amount received as an annuity (whether for a period certain or during one or more lives) under an annuity, endowment, or life insurance contract.

(b) **Exclusion ratio —**

(1) **In general — Gross income does not include that part of any amount received as an annuity under an annuity, endowment, or life insurance contract which bears the same ratio to such amount as the investment in the contract (as of the annuity starting date) bears to the expected return under the contract (as of such date).**

(2) **Exclusion limited to investment — The portion of any amount received as an annuity which is excluded from gross income under paragraph (1) shall not exceed the unrecovered investment in the contract immediately before the receipt of such amount.**

---

[11] I.R.C. § 79(d).

(3) Deduction where annuity payments cease before entire investment recovered —

(A) In general — if —

(i) after the annuity starting date, payments as an annuity under the contract cease by reason of the death of an annuitant, and

(ii) as of the date of such cessation, there is unrecovered investment in the contract, the amount of such unrecovered investment (in excess of any amount specified in subsection (e)(5) which was not included in gross income) shall be allowed as a deduction to the annuitant for his last taxable year.

An annuity may be defined as a series of payments over a period of time. For tax purposes, the regulations under Section 72 describe "amounts received as an annuity" as amounts payable at regular intervals over more than a year, provided the time period or the total amount payable is determinable on the date payments are deemed to begin.[12] For example, an annuity might consist of monthly payments for ten years, or for the life of the annuitant.

Suppose Taxpayer purchases an annuity for $10,000 from an insurance company. In return, the company agrees to pay Taxpayer $1,000 a year for the next 25 years. Taxpayer will thus receive a total of $25,000 which, in substance, consists of: (1) a $10,000 tax-free return of her investment; and (2) a $15,000 profit on her investment, which is the functional equivalent of interest on the $10,000 and properly taxable.

The statute provides a method for determining how much of each $1,000 payment is taxable, and how much is excluable as a return of basis. The statutory language provides an "exclusion ratio,"[13] in which the numerator is the "investment in the contract" and the denominator is the "expected return" under the contract. These terms, defined in Section 72(c)(1) and (c)(3), are $10,000 and $25,000, respectively, in this example. The fraction or exclusion ratio is $10,000/$25,000, or 40%. Section 72(b)(1) provides "that part" (*i.e.,* 40%) of the "amount received as an annuity" (*i.e.,* each $1,000 payment) is not gross income. The non-excluded portion is included in gross income pursuant to Section 72(a). Thus, with a $10,000 investment and $25,000 in total payments, 10/25 (40%) of each payment is nontaxable return of basis. The $15,000 of income is 60% (15/25) of the $25,000 total, so 60% of each payment is income. As a result, $600 of each $1,000 payment is gross income and $400 is nontaxable. At the end of 25 years, Taxpayer will have received $10,000 tax-free ($400 × 25) and been taxed on $15,000 ($600 × 25).

To summarize, the excluded portion is:

$$\text{Amount received as an annuity} \quad \times \quad \frac{\text{Investment in the Contract}}{\text{Expected Return}}$$

or

$$\$1,000 \quad \times \quad \frac{\$10,000}{\$25,000} = \$400$$

---

[12] Treas. Reg. § 1.72-1(b).

[13] I.R.C. § 72(b)(1).

Although this method of spreading income over the term of the payments is simple, it does not really make economic sense. Rather than spreading the $15,000 "interest" element evenly over the payments, it would be more realistic economically to allocate more interest in the first year (when the principal sum held by the insurer is greatest) and to allocate less interest thereafter as the remaining principal balance also decreases by reason of the $1,000 payments.

The example previously given involved payments over a stated number of years. Suppose, as is commonly the case, that the annuity was to be paid for as long as Taxpayer lived. Although it cannot be known in advance how many years Taxpayer will live, by consulting mortality tables, it can be determined how many years Taxpayer is actuarially "expected" to live, and in that way an "expected return" under the annuity contract can be constructed.[14] For example, if Taxpayer is 59 years old on the annuity starting date[15] she can be actuarially expected to receive 25 payments of $1,000, or $25,000.[16] The exclusion ratio under Section 72(b)(1) would thus, as before, be 40%, and $400 of each $1,000 payment she received would be excluded from income.

Suppose, however, that Taxpayer lives for something more or less than 25 years. Living more than 25 years will result in a "mortality gain" for Taxpayer, i.e., Taxpayer will receive more than the expected 25 payments; living less than 25 years will cause a "mortality loss" to Taxpayer. (Thus, whereas with life insurance Taxpayer bets on an early death, with a lifetime annuity Taxpayer gambles on a long life.)

Prior to 1986, mortality gains and losses under annuity contracts were effectively ignored — that is, a taxpayer who died before fully recovering her investment in the contract received no deduction for the unrecovered basis; conversely, a taxpayer who lived out her life expectancy, and thus had fully recovered her investment, was nonetheless permitted to continue to apply the exclusion ratio to subsequent payments — in other words, to recover more than her investment tax-free. Much criticized, these rules on mortality gains and losses were changed in 1986 so that once the investment in the annuity contract is fully recovered, further payments are fully taxable.[17] If a taxpayer dies before fully recovering her investment, the unrecovered investment is deductible for her last tax year.[18] In the above example, if Taxpayer survives 25 years, the full $1,000 will be taxable starting with the 26th payment. By contrast, if Taxpayer dies after receiving 20 payments, she will only have recovered $8,000 ($400 × 20) of her investment; the unrecovered investment of $2,000 will be deductible for her last taxable year.

---

[14] I.R.C. § 72(c)(3)(A).

[15] See I.R.C. § 72(c)(4).

[16] Treas. Reg. § 1.72-9, Table V. Many annuities are two-life joint and survivor annuities, i.e., payable for the life of the survivor of two persons; Table VI in the regulations provides actuarial calculations for such cases. For example, if an annuity is payable for the life of the survivor of Taxpayer and Spouse, and if on the annuity starting date, Taxpayer is 59 years old and Spouse is 58, the multiple is 31.1, or, in the $1,000 annual payment example, the expected return is $31,100.

[17] I.R.C. § 72(b)(2).

[18] I.R.C. § 72(b)(3).

The discussion to this point assumed that lifetime annuities have no "refund feature." For example, if Taxpayer pays $10,000 for a lifetime annuity of $1,000 per year, but dies after receiving only one payment, it has been assumed that Taxpayer in effect "loses" $9,000. It is far more likely that the annuity contract contains a refund feature of some sort. For example, the insurer may guarantee payments for a certain number of years, or guarantee that, if the consideration paid exceeds the amounts paid out up to death, the excess will be paid to the annuitant's estate or beneficiary. The presence of a refund feature requires that the "investment in the contract" (used in computing the exclusion ratio) be decreased.[19] Decreasing the investment in the contract reduces the exclusion ratio fraction, thus reducing the amount of each annuity payment excluded from income.

Annuities provide excellent tax advantages. Annuities are typically deferred payment annuities; premiums are paid in for a number of years before payment commences. During those "pay in" years the premiums are earning investment income free of tax, and the earnings are not taxed until the annuity starting date. At one time, funds withdrawn before the annuity starting date were simply treated as tax-free returns-of-capital up to the amount of the taxpayer's investment. This was perceived as an abuse of the annuity rules, and now such withdrawals (including loans) are taxable to the extent of earnings on the investment.[20] Moreover, premature distributions from an annuity contract may also be subject to a 10% penalty tax on that portion of the distribution that constitutes income.[21] Nonetheless, the tax-deferral on annuity earnings prior to payment makes annuities an attractive long-term investment. Employer pension plans, for example, are often funded by means of annuity contracts. So-called "qualified" pension plans enjoy favored tax treatment, but they must comply with a great number of special requirements.[22] To make it less attractive to employers to use deferred annuity contracts as a way to fund nonqualified pensions for the benefit of highly compensated employees — and thus avoid the requirements and limitations of qualified pension plans, while still obtaining the tax deferral benefits of such annuities — Congress enacted Section 72(u). Under that provision, subject to some exceptions, investment earnings are subject to tax on a current basis if the annuity contract is not held by a natural person — if, for example, it is held by a corporation.

Annuities are ordinarily issued by commercial insurers, but Section 72 and its fundamental tax rules apply to so-called private annuities as well. Private annuities, however, may raise some additional tax issues. For example, when one person transfers money or property to another in return for an annuity, the parties may not be dealing at arm's length, and the money or property transferred may be worth more or less than the annuity received. A question arises as to how the differential is characterized for tax purposes. Is it a gift, dividend, compensation, etc.? The answer to the question will depend on the facts and circumstances of each case.

---

[19] I.R.C. § 72(c)(2)(A).

[20] I.R.C. § 72(e)(2), (3), (4).

[21] I.R.C. § 72(q).

[22] *See* I.R.C. § 401.

§ 8.03   INDIVIDUAL RETIREMENT ACCOUNTS

As an encouragement to savings and investment, principally for retirement purposes, Congress has authorized tax-favored devices commonly known as "IRAs" (individual retirement accounts or annuities) to which taxpayers may make annual contributions. (Section 7701(a)(37) defines the term "individual retirement plan" to include individual retirement accounts, described in Section 408(a), and individual retirement annuities, described in Section 408(b). For convenience, this chapter will simply refer to them as IRAs.) There are various types of IRAs, with differing tax attributes. All IRAs, however, share with annuities the tax advantage that funds invested in an IRA grow on a tax-free basis until distributed. This discussion considers the deductible IRA, the nondeductible IRA and the Roth IRA.[23]

[A]   Deductible IRAs

Section 219 authorizes an annual deduction of up to $5,000 (adjusted for inflation) for qualifying cash contributions to an IRA.[24] Under Section 219(b)(5)(B), the maximum deduction amount is increased by $1,000 for taxpayers 50 or older. Thus, the $5,000 limit becomes $6,000 for an individual 50 or older. The deduction, however, is phased out where the taxpayer, or the taxpayer's spouse, is an active participant in certain pension plans and has an adjusted gross income in excess of a specified dollar amount (the "applicable dollar amount").[25] For example, for 2007 and thereafter, the applicable dollar amount for a taxpayer who is an active participant filing a joint return is $80,000 (adjusted for inflation). At that level, the deduction limit starts to phase out, and is reduced to zero when adjusted gross income reaches $100,000 (adjusted for inflation). (Under Section 219(g)(7), a separate, much higher applicable amount of $150,000 [adjusted for inflation] applies to a taxpayer who is not an active participant and is filing a joint return.) No deduction is allowed for contributions once the taxpayer reaches age 70½. The maximum allowed as a deduction cannot exceed the amount of the taxpayer's compensation income. For married persons filing a joint return, however, the compensation of the taxpayer's spouse is taken into account in determining compensation. In effect, a homemaker spouse with no employment income is thus allowed to contribute each year to an IRA an amount equal to the inflation-adjusted deduction limit.

The individual retirement accounts themselves are subject to the rules of Section 408. Under Section 408(e)(1), the accounts are exempt from taxation. The accrued income in an IRA is not taxed until distributed. Distributions from IRAs are includable in gross income under the annuity rules of Section 72.[26] Thus, where the contributions to an IRA are deductible, and the income accrued by the IRA has

---

[23] So-called Coverdell Education Savings Accounts, authorized by Section 530, will be summarized in Chapter 18, *infra*, which deals with education expenses. These accounts are not retirement accounts, but are tax-favored vehicles to pay for higher education expenses. Their provisions are not coordinated with those of the IRAs discussed in this chapter.

[24] I.R.C. § 219(a), (b)(1), (5), (e).

[25] I.R.C. § 219(g).

[26] I.R.C. § 408(d)(1).

not been taxed, all distributions from the IRA will be fully taxable. The investment-for-retirement purpose of the IRA is effectuated in two ways. Distributions from an IRA must commence by April 1 of the year following the year the taxpayer reaches age 70½.[27] There is, conversely, a 10% penalty tax on "early distributions" from an IRA.[28] The penalty, which applies only to the income portion of the distribution, does not apply to distributions after age 59½, or on retirement after reaching age 55, or in certain other enumerated circumstances. A similar penalty tax applies to early distributions from an annuity that is not an IRA.[29]

[B] Nondeductible IRAs

Active participants in certain pension plans, with adjusted gross incomes greater than the phase-out limits, cannot make deductible contributions to IRAs. Such taxpayers are, however, permitted to make nondeductible contributions to an IRA.[30] Total annual contributions, deductible and nondeductible, which any taxpayer makes to one or more IRAs cannot exceed the deduction limit dollar amount — $5,000 in 2008 and thereafter (adjusted for inflation). Excess contributions can result in the imposition of an excise tax. The increased limit for those 50 or older, noted above, applies here as well. As is the case with deductible contributions, nondeductible contributions cannot be made once the taxpayer reaches age 70½. Similarly, although the contributions may be nondeductible, they at least enjoy the advantage of tax-deferral: the income earned by the IRA is not currently taxed and thus grows tax-free until distribution. Under the annuity rules of Section 72, pursuant to Section 408(d)(1), distributions attributable to nondeductible contributions are prorated between the contributions and the income earned on them, and such distributions are thus taxable only to the extent of the income portion.

> **Example:** Don contributed $10,000 in nondeductible contributions to his IRA over a multi-year period. When the IRA balance is $15,000, Don receives a $3,000 distribution. Since two-thirds of the balance represented nondeductible contributions and one-third represented income earned on the contributions, two-thirds, or $2,000 of the distribution is nontaxable; $1,000 of the distribution will be includable in income.

"Early distributions" are subject to the 10% penalty tax noted above with respect to the income portion of a distribution, and mandatory distributions must commence by April 1 of the year following the year the taxpayer reaches age 70½.

---

[27] I.R.C. §§ 401(a)(9)(C), 408(a)(6), (b)(3); Treas. Reg. § 1.408–8 Q & A 3.

[28] I.R.C. §§ 72(t), 4974(c).

[29] *See* I.R.C. § 72(q).

[30] *See* I.R.C. § 408(o).

[C]   Roth IRAs

In 1997, Congress created a new type of IRA, formally named after a former chair of the Senate Finance Committee and thus known as a "Roth IRA." A Roth IRA must be so designated when it is established.[31] Contributions to Roth IRAs are nondeductible.[32] However, the distinguishing feature of a Roth IRA is that qualifying distributions from a Roth IRA are completely tax-free.

Contributions to all of one's IRAs — deductible, nondeductible, Roth — cannot exceed the annual deduction limit of Section 219.[33] Contributions to a Roth IRA are further limited based on the taxpayer's modified adjusted gross income. In the case of a joint return, for example, the maximum contribution is phased out to zero for a modified adjusted gross income between $150,000 and $160,000 (adjusted for inflation).[34] ("Rollovers" to a Roth IRA from another IRA are not subject to the contribution limitations based on modified gross income.)

"Qualified distributions" from a Roth IRA are excluded from income.[35] In general, qualified distributions are those that meet two conditions: (1) They satisfy a five-year holding period, *i.e.*, they do not take place within the five-tax-year period that begins with the first tax year for which a contribution is made to a Roth IRA; and (2) they are made after the taxpayer attains age 59½, dies, or is disabled.[36] (Under an additional exception, distributions to pay for "qualified first-time homebuyer expenses," as defined in Section 72(t)(2)(F), may also constitute qualified distributions.) Furthermore, unlike the deductible and nondeductible IRAs, contributions may be made to a Roth IRA after age 70½, and there is no requirement that distributions from a Roth IRA commence once the taxpayer reaches 70½.[37] These features somewhat undercut the retirement-income purpose of an IRA. There are also special rules relating to the "rollover" of amounts from other IRAs to a Roth IRA.[38]

Because of the rules relating to income limits and to active-participant status in a given year, some taxpayers will not be able to make a contribution either to a deductible IRA or to a Roth IRA. For those taxpayers, only the nondeductible IRA will be available that year. Other taxpayers may be eligible to make a contribution to a Roth IRA, but not to a deductible IRA; given the potential tax-exempt treatment of the earnings, such taxpayers will presumably choose to make a contribution to a Roth IRA rather than to a traditional nondeductible IRA. Similarly, those taxpayers eligible for a deductible IRA because they are not active participants, but ineligible for a Roth IRA because of their income levels, would presumably choose the deductible rather than the nondeductible IRA. Finally,

---

[31] I.R.C. § 408A(b).

[32] I.R.C. § 408A(c)(1).

[33] *See* I.R.C. § 408A(c)(2).

[34] I.R.C. § 408A(c)(3).

[35] I.R.C. § 408A(d)(1)(A).

[36] I.R.C. § 408A(d)(2).

[37] I.R.C. § 408A(c)(4), (5).

[38] I.R.C. § 408A(c)–(e).

some taxpayers may have the choice between contribution to a deductible IRA or to a Roth IRA. Assuming full funding of the IRA, identical investment results and unchanging tax rates, a present value analysis indicates that a Roth IRA provides the better economic return over the same time span. However, given such factors as the unpredictability of future tax rates and each individual taxpayer's interest or lack of interest in an immediate deduction, one can anticipate that different taxpayers will make different choices.

Chapter 9

DISCHARGE OF INDEBTEDNESS

§ 61.   Gross Income Defined.

(a)   General Definition. Except as otherwise provided in this subtitle, gross income means all income from whatever source derived, including (but not limited to) the following items:

. . .

(12) Income from discharge of indebtedness;

Because there is an obligation to repay them, loan proceeds do not represent an accession to wealth and are thus not gross income.[1] As a corollary to this principle, no deduction is allowed when loans are repaid. A related question is whether forgiveness of all or part of the loan generates income. It would seem that a person who borrows more than she is required to pay back has obviously been enriched and to that extent has an item of gross income. Although that supposition seems reasonable, it is not completely accurate.

§ 9.01   HISTORICAL BACKGROUND

The history of the legislative, judicial and administrative treatment of the forgiveness of debt is rife with confusion and inconsistency. The ambivalence of the courts regarding the proper treatment of debt forgiveness is disturbing. A brief review of the pertinent case law is revealing.

In its 1926 decision in *Bowers v. Kerbaugh-Empire Co.*,[2] the Supreme Court considered whether a taxpayer who had borrowed money repayable in German marks had realized income when the taxpayer repaid the loan with greatly devalued marks. Stated another way, did the taxpayer have income because it required far fewer dollars to repay the loan than the dollar equivalent of the original loan proceeds? The Court ruled for the taxpayer. It reasoned that, because the borrowed money was entirely lost in a business venture, repayment of the loan with devalued marks only reduced the taxpayer's loss. The Court concluded that "the mere diminution of loss is not gain, profit or income."

On the bare facts of *Kerbaugh-Empire*, one may have concluded that if the taxpayer borrowed German marks and repaid German marks no income would be realized. Note, however, that, in finding for the taxpayer, the Court did not adopt that simple rationale. Our tax system computes gain, loss, and income in terms of dollars — not foreign currency. Thus, in *Kerbaugh-Empire*, the taxpayer was

---

[1] *See* Chapter 3, *supra*.

[2] 271 U.S. 170 (1926).

deemed to have borrowed X dollars but to have repaid only Y dollars. It is the excess of the X dollars deemed borrowed over the Y dollars deemed repaid that concerned the Commissioner and was addressed by the Court. While inflation is addressed in certain Code provisions, *e.g.*, tax rates are indexed for inflation, the Code does not pervasively address distortions created by inflation. Thus, a taxpayer does not have income merely because the taxpayer repays a loan with dollars which, because of inflation, have a purchasing power equal to less than the purchasing power of the dollars borrowed.

The Court in *Kerbaugh-Empire* emphasized that the borrowed funds were lost in an unsuccessful enterprise. Theoretically, the success of a venture to which borrowed funds are applied should not be relevant to a determination of whether income is triggered when one repays less than the amount borrowed. The exclusion of loan proceeds from income is based on the existence of an offsetting obligation to repay the loan. If the loan is not repaid in full, the taxpayer-debtor should be required to report the excess of the loan proceeds over the amount repaid as income.

In *U.S. v. Kirby Lumber Co.*,[3] the Supreme Court had an opportunity to reconsider the *Kerbaugh-Empire* treatment of debt repayment. In *Kirby Lumber*, the taxpayer corporation had issued bonds for which it had received the par value of the bonds. Later, in the same year, the corporation repurchased some of the bonds on the open market for almost $140,000 less than par. (While the Court does not explain the reason for this lower price, fluctuation in interest rates might account for the difference.) The issue before the Court was whether that difference constituted gross income. In cursory fashion, the Court concluded the corporation should recognize gross income in the amount of the difference between the amount it received for the bonds when issued and the amount it paid for the bonds upon repurchase. Instead of rejecting the analysis of *Kerbaugh-Empire*, however, the Court distinguished the case noting that in *Kerbaugh-Empire* the "transaction as a whole was a loss." By contrast, as a result of its repurchase of some of the bonds, the taxpayer in *Kirby Lumber* had freed or made available approximately $140,000 in assets previously offset by the obligation of those bonds. The Court's analysis thus ensured the continuing viability of *Kerbaugh-Empire*.

While the Court's reasoning in *Kirby Lumber* is not entirely clear, the Court's holding emphasizes that (a) the taxpayer was solvent at all relevant times and (b) the balance sheet of the taxpayer reflected an increased net worth (or a "clear gain" in the Court's words) as a result of the reduction of liabilities without a dollar-for-dollar reduction of assets. As in *Kerbaugh-Empire*, one may ask why such facts should be significant in determining whether income is realized when one repays less than one has borrowed. Conceptually, those facts should not make a difference. But *Kirby Lumber* teaches they do and its teaching has proven a lasting and, arguably, an unfortunate legacy.

In adding Section 61(a)(12) in 1954 providing that "income from discharge of indebtedness" constitutes income, Congress did not alter the effect of either *Kirby Lumber* or *Kerbaugh-Empire*. Rather, Congress merely codified the understanding

---

[3] 248 U.S. 1 (1931).

that under some circumstances the discharge of indebtedness constitutes income. Congress made no effort to identify those circumstances, apparently assuming the courts and the Treasury would hammer out that detail. They have, and *Kirby Lumber* and *Kerbaugh-Empire* are part of the detail. Congress, however, re-entered the picture with Section 108 in 1980 providing an exclusion from gross income in instances where discharge of indebtedness occurs in certain listed circumstances, including a bankruptcy case or when the taxpayer is insolvent.

§ 9.02   SPECIFIC RULES GOVERNING EXCLUSION

[A]   Discharge of Indebtedness When Taxpayer Is Insolvent

[1]   Case Law Pre-1980 Bankruptcy Tax Act

Assume A, who leases a commercial building from B, has fallen substantially behind in his lease payments. Assume also that, at the beginning of this year, A is insolvent and A and B negotiate a settlement whereby A agrees to pay B 25% of the lease payments in arrears and B, hoping to keep A occupying the building, agrees to cancel the balance of the delinquent payments and to reduce A's rent in the future. Even after the cancellation, however, A remains insolvent. Does A have income as a result of this cancellation of debt? Is this a *Kirby Lumber* case or is it closer to *Kerbaugh-Empire*?

In the example, A has had the beneficial use of B's property, but, considering the cancellation, is not returning to B equal value. On similar facts, the Commissioner in *Dallas Transfer and Terminal Warehouse v. Commissioner*,[4] argued that a lessee-taxpayer had income. Rejecting the Commissioner's argument, the Fifth Circuit compared the situation to a bankruptcy proceeding where a debtor surrenders property to pay part of his debts and the remainder of the debts are discharged. The court reasoned the discharge of debt "did not result in the debtor acquiring something of exchangeable value in addition to what he had before. There is a reduction or extinguishment of liabilities without any increase of assets. There is an absence of such gain or profit as is required to come within the accepted definition of income." The Fifth Circuit, distinguishing *Kirby Lumber*, noted that Kirby Lumber's "assets having been increased by the cash received for the bonds, by the repurchase of some of those bonds at less than par, the taxpayer, to the extent of the difference between what it received for those bonds and what it paid in repurchasing them, had an asset which had ceased to be offset by any liability, with a result that after that transaction *the taxpayer had greater assets than it had before.*" (Emphasis added).[5]

Cases like *Dallas Transfer & Terminal Warehouse Co.* established that, if a taxpayer were insolvent before and after the discharge or cancellation of a debt, no income resulted. While it might be viewed as mean-spirited for the courts to find income when debt is discharged because of a debtor's insolvency, in such insolvency

---

[4] 70 F.2d 95 (5th Cir. 1934).

[5] *Id.* at 96.

circumstances such a finding is nonetheless theoretically correct.

In the above example, assume instead that, as a result of the discharge, A were again solvent. Now is there income and, if so, how much? In *Lakeland Grocery Co. v. Commissioner*,[6] the Board of Tax Appeals held that a debtor realized income to the extent a discharge of indebtedness made the debtor solvent. In *Lakeland Grocery*, the creditors seeking to permit the taxpayer to remain in business agreed to a plan resulting in the forgiveness of approximately $90,000 of debt. As a result, the taxpayer-debtor became solvent to the extent of almost $40,000. Relying on *Kirby Lumber Co.*, the Board concluded that the taxpayer had realized approximately $40,000 of gain when "it obtained assets clear of liabilities."

[2] The Insolvency Exclusion Under Section 108

§ 108(a). **Exclusion from Gross Income.**

(1) **Gross income does not include any amount which (but for this subsection) would be includible in gross income by reason of the discharge (in whole or in part) of indebtedness of the taxpayer if —**

. . .

(B) **the discharge occurs when the taxpayer is insolvent,**

. . .

(3) **Insolvency exclusion limited to amount of insolvency. — In the case of a discharge to which paragraph 1(B) applies, the amount excluded under paragraph 1(B) shall not exceed the amount by which the taxpayer is insolvent.**

. . .

———————

§ 108(d). **Meaning of terms; special rules relating to certain provisions —**

. . .

(3) **Insolvent. —**

For purposes of this section, the term "insolvent" means the excess of liabilities over the fair market value of assets. With respect to any discharge, whether or not the taxpayer is insolvent and the amount the taxpayer is insolvent, shall be determined on the basis of the taxpayer's assets and liabilities immediately before the discharge.

In 1980, Congress specifically addressed the discharge of indebtedness of bankrupt or insolvent taxpayers by enacting Section 108. That section not only codifies the judicial and administrative exclusions discussed previously, but literally replaces them. Thus, except as provided in Section 108, there is "no insolvency exception from the general rule that gross income includes income from the discharge of indebtedness."[7]

———————

[6] 36 B.T.A. 289 (1937).

[7] I.R.C. § 108(e)(1).

Example 1: Bill borrowed $50,000 from Kevin. Later, when Bill was insolvent, Kevin accepted $25,000 from Bill in satisfaction of the debt. Immediately prior to Bill's payment to Kevin, Bill's only asset was cash in the amount of $60,000. In addition to the $50,000 he owed Kevin, Bill also owed Judy $40,000. Thus, Bill was insolvent to the extent of $30,000. What tax results to Bill as a result of Kevin's forgiveness of $25,000 of the debt?

Analysis: After paying Kevin $25,000 in satisfaction of the $50,000 debt, Bill is still insolvent to the extent of $5,000, *i.e.*, Bill has $35,000 of cash but his debt to Judy is $40,000. Thus, under Section 108(a)(1)(B), Bill has no income as a result of the forgiveness of the debt by Kevin.

Example 2: Assume the same facts as Example 1 except that Bill owes Judy only $30,000.

Analysis: Prior to the arrangement with Kevin, Bill was insolvent to the extent of $20,000, *i.e.*, his debts to Judy and Kevin totaled $80,000 and Bill had only $60,000 in assets. Section 108(a)(3) therefore limits Bill's insolvency exclusion to $20,000. As a result, Bill must report $5,000 of income when Kevin forgives $25,000 of Bill's debt.

Section 108 specifically provides a discharge of indebtedness will not generate gross income if "the discharge occurs in a title 11 [bankruptcy] case" or if "the discharge occurs when the taxpayer is insolvent." Note that Section 108(a)(3), like *Lakeland Grocery*, limits the insolvency exclusion to "the amount by which the taxpayer is insolvent."

Merkel v. Commissioner addressed the issue of whether contingent liabilities — for example, the potential liability a taxpayer may have as a result of personally guaranteeing another person's loan — should be treated as "liabilities" for purposes of applying the insolvency exception under Section 108(a)(1)(B). The Ninth Circuit affirmed the Tax Court's determination that, to claim the benefit of the insolvency exception, the taxpayer must prove, with respect to any obligation, that it is more likely than not that the taxpayer will be called upon to pay it. The Ninth Circuit noted:

> The origins of § 108(a)(1)(B) demonstrate that Congress intended for only those liabilities in the amount that actually offset assets to be considered in calculating insolvency for purposes of the income tax exclusion. We agree with the Tax Court's conclusion that "an indiscriminate inclusion of obligations to pay . . . in the statutory insolvency calculation . . . without any consideration of how speculative those obligations may be, would render meaningless any inquiry into whether assets are freed upon the discharge of indebtedness." We also agree, based upon Congress' purpose of not burdening an insolvent debtor with an immediate tax liability, that Congress considered a debtor's ability to pay an immediate tax on discharge of indebtedness income the "controlling factor" in determining whether the § 108(a)(1)(B) exception applies. Accordingly, a taxpayer claiming to be insolvent for purposes of § 108(a)(1)(B) and challenging the Commissioner's determination of deficiency must prove by a preponderance of the evidence that he or she will be called upon to pay

an obligation claimed to be a liability and that the total amount of liabilities so proved exceed the fair market value of his or her assets.[8]

The relief afforded debtors by Section 108(a), however, is not without its costs. Specifically, Section 108(b) requires certain tax attributes of the taxpayer-debtor be reduced. While the reduction rules are complex and their detail is beyond the scope of this book, it should be noted that among the tax attributes subject to reduction is the taxpayer's basis in property.[9]

Note the special limitation on basis reduction provided by Section 1017(b)(2) in case of discharge of indebtedness as a result of insolvency or bankruptcy.[10] The effect of lowering a taxpayer's basis in property is, of course, either to increase the gain realized or decrease the loss realized when taxpayer sells, exchanges or otherwise disposes of the property. In addition, if the property is depreciable property, reduction in basis will decrease the total amount of depreciation deductions allowable.[11] Thus, Section 108, rather than always providing a permanent exclusion for income, may often merely defer reporting of income and may reduce other tax benefits such as depreciation deductions.

Example 3: Kevin borrowed $150,000 from Bill. Later, when Kevin was insolvent, Bill accepted $75,000 from Kevin in satisfaction of the debt. Immediately prior to Kevin's payment to Bill, Kevin's assets were $100,000 cash and business equipment worth $40,000 with an adjusted basis of $60,000. Thus, Kevin's assets totaled $140,000 and his liability to Bill was $150,000, leaving Kevin insolvent to the extent of $10,000. As a result of Bill's forgiveness of $75,000 of the debt, Kevin is solvent to the extent of $65,000, *i.e.*, Kevin has $25,000 of cash and business equipment worth $40,000. What tax results to Kevin?

Analysis: Section 108(a)(3) will exclude only $10,000 of the $75,000 of canceled debt. Kevin will thus have $65,000 of cancellation of indebtedness income. As a result of the operation of Sections 108(b)(2)(E) and 1017(b)(2), Kevin's adjusted basis in the equipment will be reduced to $50,000. Thus, although Section 108(a)(1)(B) allowed Kevin to exclude $10,000 in income, there is a price to be paid, *i.e.*, the reduction in the basis of the equipment. That reduced basis means that Kevin will ultimately lose $10,000 in depreciation deductions, *i.e.*, he will only be allowed $50,000 in depreciation deductions instead of $60,000 with respect to the property. Alternatively, if Kevin were to sell the equipment the following year for its fair market value of $40,000, he would report a $10,000 loss (amount realized $40,000 less

---

[8] 192 F.3d 844, 850 (9th Cir. 1999), *aff'g* 109 T.C. 463 (1997).

[9] I.R.C. § 108(b)(2)(E). For provisions governing the reduction of basis, see Section 1017.

[10] The special limitation generally limits the required basis reduction to the excess of the taxpayer's aggregate property bases over the taxpayer's aggregate liabilities. In effect, to the extent this special limit is applicable, the taxpayer is able to exclude debt discharge from income without making a corresponding basis reduction.

[11] Depreciation is examined in detail in Chapter 14, *infra*.

adjusted basis $50,000) rather than a $20,000 loss (amount realized $40,000 less adjusted basis $60,000).[12]

[B] Discharge of Qualified Real Property Business Indebtedness

Section 108(a)(1)(D) provides an exclusion for income from the discharge of "qualified real property business indebtedness," as defined in Section 108(c)(3). Under Section 108(c)(3)(C) a taxpayer must make an election for real property business indebtedness to qualify for the exclusion.

The amount excluded may not exceed the outstanding principal amount of the debt (immediately before the discharge) less the value (immediately before the discharge) of the business real property securing the debt. (This value is reduced by any *other* qualified real property business indebtedness secured by the property immediately before the discharge. Section 108(c)(2)(A).) In no event shall the amount excluded under Section 108(a)(1)(D) exceed the aggregate adjusted bases of taxpayer's depreciable real property held immediately before the discharge. Section 108(c)(2)(B).

As in the case of the insolvency exclusion discussed above, a taxpayer pays a price for taking advantage of the qualified real property business indebtedness exclusion of Section 108(a)(1)(D). Specifically, Section 108(c)(1)(A) provides that the amount excluded shall be applied to reduce the basis of the depreciable real property owned by the taxpayer.

Example: In expanding her automobile sales business, Cathy purchased a large, unimproved tract of land adjacent to her business. The cost of the lot was $350,000 and Cathy borrowed $300,000 from a local lending institution to finance the purchase, giving the lender a mortgage on the land purchased. A few years later when the outstanding balance on the loan was $275,000, Cathy encountered problems making the payments on the loan because of a downturn in the local economy. Under the circumstances, the lender agreed to forgive $25,000 of the loan balance. Cathy was solvent at the time of the loan forgiveness. Assume the adjusted basis in the land was $350,000. The land had a fair market value of $250,000. Assume also that Cathy, in conjunction with her business, owned depreciable real property with a fair market value of $500,000 and an adjusted basis of $140,000. Cathy owned no other depreciable real property.

Analysis: Assuming that Cathy makes the appropriate election, the debt on the land appears to constitute "qualified real property business indebted- ness" as defined in Section 108(c)(3) and (c)(4). The limitations of Section 108(c)(2)(A) and (B) discussed above should pose no problem; all $25,000 of the forgiveness will qualify. Section 108(c)(1)(A) provides that the basis of Cathy's depreciable real property (here $140,000) must be reduced by the amount excluded from gross income (here $25,000). The cost to Cathy

---

[12] See Section 108(d)(9) for rules regarding the time for making an election.

therefore of excluding from income the $25,000 in debt forgiveness is the reduction in her adjusted basis in the depreciable real property from $140,000 to $115,000.[13]

[C]   Discharge of Indebtedness on Principal Residence Before January 2014

As a result of the subprirne mortgage crisis, home foreclosure sales have become common. In many cases, because of a slump in housing prices, the proceeds of a foreclosure sale were inadequate to cover the balance of the outstanding mortgage on the foreclosed home. Given the financial condition of the borrower, lenders often simply forgave the remaining indebtedness. For the unfortunate borrower/taxpayer who had lost her home another problem loomed: the amount of forgiven indebtedness would normally constitute discharge of indebtedness income under Section 61(a)(12). Congress enacted the Mortgage Forgiveness Debt Relief Act of 2007 to provide relief to these taxpayers. Specifically, Congress added new subsection (a)(1)(E) to Section 108 providing an exclusion for indebtedness discharged *on or after January 1, 2007 and before January 1, 2014* that is "qualified principal residence indebtedness." (Congress has previously extended the expiration date of the provision and may do so again.) [Note that the provision is not limited to foreclosure sales but rather is applicable to the discharge of any qualified principal residence indebtedness so long as the discharge is directly related to a decline in the value of the residence or to the financial condition of the taxpayer. Section 108(a)(1)(E), (h)(3). "Qualified principal residence indebtedness" is defined as up to $2 million of indebtedness secured by the taxpayer's principal residence so long as the indebtedness is acquisition indebtedness, *i.e.*, indebtedness incurred in constructing, acquiring or substantially improving the residence. Section 108(h)(2), (3). Section l08(h)(5) provides that the term "principal residence" shall have the same meaning as it does for purposes of the Section 121 exclusion. (*See* Chapter 6.) The new exclusion provision takes precedence over the insolvency exclusion unless the taxpayer otherwise elects. Section 108(a)(2)(C).

A taxpayer taking advantage of the exclusion under subsection 108(a)(1)(E) must reduce (but not below zero) her basis in her principal residence by the amount excluded. In this regard, consider two situations. First, assume a situation where the lender does not foreclose but the lender and borrower renegotiate the loan terms including monthly payments and the amount of the loan. Although excluded by Section 108(a)(1)(E), the amount of indebtedness discharged as a result of the renegotiation will reduce the borrower's/taxpayer's basis in his principal residence. Second, assume a foreclosure sale. For purposes of computing gain on that sale, the borrower's/taxpayer's basis will be reduced by the amount of the Section 108(a)(1)(E) exclusion. Of course, in the case of a foreclosure sale, the Section 121 exclusion is available to the taxpayer so long as he satisfies the ownership, use and other requirements of that provision.

---

[13] See Section 1017 for the specific provisions regarding the reduction in adjusted basis required by Section 108(c)(1)(A).

[D]   Purchase-Money Debt Reduction for Solvent Debtors

§ 108(e)(5).   Purchase-money debt reduction for solvent debtor treated as price reduction.

If —

(A) the debt of a purchaser of property to the seller of such property which arose out of the purchase of such property is reduced,

(B) such reduction does not occur in

(i) a title 11 case or

(ii) when the purchaser is insolvent, and

(C) but for this paragraph,

such reduction would be treated as income to the purchaser from the discharge of indebtedness, then such reduction shall be treated as a purchase price adjustment.

Section 108(e)(5) codifies another judicial exclusion related to the discharge of debt. Assume a taxpayer purchases property agreeing to pay the purchase price to the seller over a period of time. Subsequent to the purchase, the taxpayer refuses to pay the entire balance of the purchase price because of irregularities associated with the sale or because of defects in the property. The parties resolve their dispute by agreeing to a reduction in the balance of the purchase price. While it is true that the debt of the taxpayer has been canceled in part, the courts considering such circumstances held that no income resulted but rather merely a retroactive reduction in the purchase price.[14] As a result, the basis of the taxpayer in the property was correspondingly reduced.[15] The codification of this exception in Section 108(e)(5) extends the exception beyond the dispute settlement area. In the 1980 Bankruptcy Tax Act, the Senate Finance Committee indicated the purpose of the provision was to "eliminate disagreements between the Internal Revenue Service and the debtor as to whether, in a particular case to which the provision applies, the debt reduction should be treated as a discharge of income or a true price adjustment."

> **Example:** Martin agreed to purchase a mountain cabin from Mike for $200,000. Martin, who planned to use the cabin for personal purposes, agreed to pay Mike the $200,000 under a contract extending over a 20 year period. Five years after the purchase, mining activity in the area caused the value of the cabin to decline to $125,000. Martin still owed $175,000 on the cabin at the time. Fearing Martin would default on the cabin payments, Mike agreed to reduce the balance owing under the contract to $100,000. Assume Martin was solvent at all times.
>
> **Analysis:** This appears to be a classic purchase price adjustment covered by Section 108(e)(5). As such, the $75,000 reduction in price does not trigger discharge of indebtedness income to Martin. Rather, under Section

---

[14] Hirsch v. Comm'r, 115 F.2d 656 (1940); Helvering v. A.L. Killian Co., 128 F.2d 433 (1948).

[15] Comm'r v. Sherman, 135 F.2d 68 (6th Cir. 1943).

108(e)(5), it is just as though the purchase price for the cabin had been $125,000 instead of $200,000. Martin's basis in the cabin will be $125,000.

Contrast the situation presented in the above example to one where the taxpayer has borrowed money from a third party lender in order to purchase property from another.

Example: Martin used a credit card issued by a bank to purchase a variety of merchandise and services. When Martin owed $20,000 on the credit card, he experienced financial difficulties and could not make the minimum monthly payments required by the credit card company. Martin, who is solvent, entered into an agreement whereby the credit card company agreed to accept $5,000 (payable over a six month period) in full satisfaction of the $20,000 credit card balance. Does Section 108(e)(5) apply?

Analysis: Section 108(e)(5) requires more than a mere creditor/debtor relationship.[16] Instead, Section 108(e)(5)(A) specifically focuses on the reduction of a debt of *the purchaser of the property to the seller arising out of the purchase*; it thus requires a purchaser/seller relationship. A generic credit card transaction does not constitute the sale of property under Section 108(e)(5). In this case, the company issuing the credit card sold nothing to Martin, rather it acted solely as a third party lender. In Rev. Rul. 92-92,[17] the Service addressed a situation in which A borrowed money from C to purchase property from B. When, because of an economic downturn, C modified the terms of the loan by reducing the loan's principal amount, the Service concluded that Section 108(e)(5) was inapplicable and found that A had discharge of indebtedness income. As emphasized by the Service, the debt in this case was reduced by an agreement between C (the third-party lender) and A (the purchaser) of the property. Even though the debt arose in connection with the purchase of the property by A from B, it was not a debt of the purchaser (A) "to the seller" (B), as required by Section 108 (e)(5)(A) of the Code. Thus, the debt reduction by C does not qualify as a purchase price adjustment under Section 108(e)(5) of the Code. As noted in the Revenue Ruling, even under common law: "An agreement to reduce a debt between a purchaser and a third-party lender is not a true adjustment of the purchase price paid for the property because the seller has received the entire purchase price from the purchaser and is not a party to the debt reduction agreement. The debt reduction relates solely to the debt and results in discharge of indebtedness income to the debtor."

[E]   Acquisition of Indebtedness by Person Related to Debtor

§ 108(e)(4).   Acquisition of Indebtedness by Person Related to Debtor. —

(A)   Treated as acquisition by debtor. — **For purposes of determining income of the debtor from discharge of indebtedness, to the extent provided in regulations prescribed by the Secretary, the acquisition of outstanding indebtedness by a person bearing a relationship to the debtor specified in section**

---

[16] *See* Payne v. Commissioner, T.C. Memo 2008-66.

[17] 1992-2 C.B. 35.

267(b) or 707(b)(1) from a person who does not bear such a relationship to the debtor shall be treated as the acquisition of such indebtedness by the debtor . . . .

For purposes of determining how much income a taxpayer has from the discharge of indebtedness, Section 108(e)(4) specifically provides that, if a person related to a debtor acquires the indebtedness, the acquisition shall be treated as an acquisition by the debtor. Among the relationships addressed in Section 267(b) and Section 707(b)(1) are an individual and that individual's family members, a shareholder and a corporation in which the shareholder owns more than 50% of the outstanding stock, and a partnership and a person owning more than 50% of the capital or profits interest in the partnership.

> **Example:** Assume Jackie owns more than 50% of the stock in XYZ Corporation and is therefore "related" to XYZ within the meaning of Section 108(e)(4). XYZ issues its own bonds for which it receives par value. Subsequently, Jackie repurchases the bonds on the open market for an amount considerably less than par. Under the rationale of *Kirby Lumber*, does XYZ have discharge of indebtedness income?

> **Analysis:** Considering that Jackie, and not XYZ, repurchased the bonds, one might conclude XYZ has no discharge of indebtedness income. Section 108(e)(4), however, attributes Jackie's acquisition of the bonds to XYZ and thus prevents XYZ from avoiding discharge of indebtedness income.

In Revenue Ruling 91-47,[18] taxpayer sought to avoid discharge of indebtedness income and Section 108(e)(4) by arranging for an unrelated person to form a corporation for the purpose of acquiring the taxpayer's indebtedness. Shortly after the corporation was formed and the indebtedness acquired, the taxpayer purchased all of the stock in the corporation. According to the Service, to permit the taxpayer to avoid discharge of indebtedness under these circumstances would elevate form over substance and frustrate the policy underlying Section 108(e)(4).

[F]   Discharge of Deductible Debt

§ 108(e)(2).   Income not realized to extent of lost deductions. —

No income shall be realized from the discharge of indebtedness to the extent that payment of the liability would have given rise to a deduction.

Recall the earlier example involving the landlord who canceled rent payments owed by an insolvent commercial tenant. The example illustrated the judicial development of the insolvency exception to cancellation of indebtedness income. Suppose, however, the commercial tenant was not insolvent when the past due rent was forgiven. Section 108(e)(2) provides that forgiveness of a debt does not generate income if the payment of the debt would have been deductible. The rationale is that, if discharge of indebtedness income were to be imputed to the tenant, the tenant would be entitled to an above the line deduction for the past due rent which would completely offset the discharge of indebtedness income.

---

[18] 1991-2 C.B. 16.

Example: Finn's small technology firm suffered a significant decline in business. Finn owes Jessica $20,000 for services she has provided the firm. Finn pays Jessica $15,000 and Jessica forgives Finn the other $5,000 of the debt. Assuming the cost of Jessica's services would be deductible by Finn as business expenses when paid, what are the tax consequences of the debt forgiveness to Finn?

Analysis: Because the cost of Jessica's services are deductible, Finn will have no income when Jessica forgives $5,000 of the debt.

[G]   Discharge of Certain Student Loans

To encourage students to engage in public service in occupations or areas with unmet needs, such as doctors or teachers working in low-income or rural areas, Congress enacted Section 108(f)(1), excluding from gross income amounts otherwise includable in gross income by reason of the discharge of indebtedness in whole or in part of any student loan. The discharge must be pursuant to a provision of such loan under which all or part of the indebtedness of the individual would be discharged "if the individual worked for a certain period of time in certain professions for any of a broad class of employers." Unlike the other provisions of section 108, Section 108(f) excludes discharge of debt from gross income without requiring any reduction in the taxpayer's other tax attributes.

For purposes of Section 108(f), a "student loan" includes any loan made by qualified lenders (which include the United States, states and their political subdivisions, certain tax-exempt public benefit corporations, and educational institutions themselves under certain conditions) to assist an individual in attending educational institutions with a regular faculty, curriculum and enrolled student body. Qualifying student loans may also include refinancing by educational institutions of student loans that assisted individuals in attending the educational institution, where the refinancing is pursuant to a program designed to encourage students to engage in public service.[19]

§ 9.03   DISPUTED OR CONTESTED DEBTS

If the amount of a debt is disputed, settlement of the amount does not constitute a discharge of indebtedness. As noted in *Preslar v. Commissioner*,[20]

> The "contested liability" or, as it is occasionally known, "disputed debt" doctrine rests on the premise that if a taxpayer disputes the original amount of a debt in good faith, a subsequent settlement of that dispute is "treated as the amount of debt cognizable for tax purposes." . . . In other words, the "excess of the original debt over the amount determined to have been due" may be disregarded in calculating gross income.

---

[19] *See* Revenue Ruling 2008-34, 2008-2 C.B. 76, where the Service concluded that the Section 108(f) exclusion applied to the discharge of loans made under a law school's Loan Repayment Assistance Program, which was applicable to employment of the law school's graduates in law-related public service positions with tax-exempt charitable organizations or governmental units.

[20] 167 F.3d 1323, 1327–28 (10th Cir. 1999).

The origins of the contested liability doctrine can be traced to *N. Sobel, Inc. v. Commissioner*, 40 B.T.A. 1263 (1939), a case arising during the Great Depression. In that case, a New York corporation purchased 100 shares of a bank's stock and signed a $21,700 note as payment. When the note matured, the stock was worthless. The corporation sued the bank for rescission, insisting the loan contravened state law and the bank had failed to fulfill its promise to guarantee the corporation against loss. Shortly thereafter, the state superintendent of banks closed the bank because of insolvency and initiated a countersuit against the corporation for the amount of the note. The parties ultimately settled the consolidated proceedings with the corporation paying the superintendent $10,850 in return for discharge of the debt. The corporation then took a $10,850 deduction in the year of settlement. The Commissioner disallowed the deduction and assessed a $10,850 deficiency, representing the amount of the original loan over the settlement figure. The Board of Tax Appeals reversed the ruling and upheld the deduction, concluding the corporation's ownership of the shares and the degree of liability on the note were highly unclear. ("There is question whether the taxpayer bought property in 1929 and question as to its liability and the amount thereof."). The Board found the corporation's financial obligations could not be assessed definitively prior to resolution of its dispute with the superintendent and, since settlement compromised the parties' claims and precluded recognition of their legal rights, the existence and amount of the corporation liability were not fixed until the date of settlement. Thus, release of the note did not amount to a gain for the corporation.

According to the Tenth Circuit in *Preslar*, "to implicate the contested liability doctrine, the original amount of the debt must be unliquidated," that is, the amount of the debt must be disputed.[21]

The Tenth Circuit was critical of the Third Circuit's 1990 decision in *Zarin v. Commissioner* which concluded that a liquidated debt, if unenforceable, would implicate the contested liability doctrine.[22] In *Zarin*, the taxpayer incurred a $3,435,000 gambling debt he disputed on the basis that the debt was unenforceable under state law. Ultimately, the taxpayer and the casino settled the dispute for $500,000. The Third Circuit, relying on the contested liability doctrine rejected the Commissioner's argument that the taxpayer had discharge of indebtedness income equal to the difference between the gambling debt and the $500,000. The Commissioner argued the contested liability doctrine was inapplicable because the debt was liquidated, *i.e.*, Zarin did not contest the amount of the debt but rather based his contest on the unenforcability of the debt. According to the Commissioner, the contested liability doctrine is only applicable when there is an unliquidated debt. The Third Circuit rejected this rationale emphasizing that, when a debt is unenforceable, the amount of the debt is in dispute. According to the court, the settlement of the debt at $500,000 fixed the amount of the debt that is cognizable for

---

[21] *Id.* at 1328.

[22] 916 F.2d 110 (3d Cir. 1990).

tax purposes. Because Zarin paid the $500,000, there can be no discharge of indebtedness income.

In criticizing *Zarin*, the Tenth Circuit in *Preslar* noted:

> The whole theory behind requiring that the amount of a debt be disputed before the contested liability exception can be triggered is that only in the context of disputed debts is the IRS unaware of the exact consideration initially exchanged in a transaction. The mere fact that a taxpayer challenges the enforceability of a debt in good faith does not necessarily mean he or she is shielded from discharge-of-indebtedness income upon resolution of the dispute . . . . A total denial of liability is not a dispute touching upon the amount of the underlying debt . . . . "If the parties initially treated the transaction as a loan when the loan proceeds were received, thereby not declaring the receipt as income, then the transaction should be treated consistently when the loan is discharged and income should be declared in the amount of the discharge." . . . A holding to the contrary would strain IRS treatment of unenforceable debts and, in large part, disavow the Supreme Court's mandate that the phrase "gross income" be interpreted as broadly as the Constitution permits.[23]

The Tax Court subsequently followed *Preslar* in concluding that a taxpayer who settled a credit card dispute with the issuing bank had discharge of indebtedness income. The court emphasized that a significant part of the debt owed by the taxpayer was uncontested and liquidated. Discharge of liability for any of such debt therefore constituted discharge of indebtedness income.[24]

§ 9.04 DISCHARGE OF INDEBTEDNESS AS GIFT, COMPENSATION, ETC.

Kirby Lumber did not mark the end of the Supreme Court's consideration of debt repayment issues. In *Commissioner v. Jacobson*,[25] the Court considered whether a discharge of indebtedness could be considered an excludable gift under Section 102(a) and its predecessors. The Court faced with a fact pattern similar to *Kirby Lumber* concluded the gift exclusion was not applicable where a debtor purchased his own obligations at a discount. The Court noted the sellers in *Jacobson* sought to minimize their loss by getting as high a price as possible for the bonds; the taxpayer (maker of the bonds), by contrast, sought to reduce his obligation by purchasing the bonds as cheaply as possible. According to the Court, there was no evidence of any intent on the part of the bondholders to make a gift to the taxpayer, an intent that would be extraordinary in a commercial context. In light of *Jacobson*, it is doubtful any taxpayer will be successful in arguing the discharge of indebtedness in a commercial context constitutes an excludable gift.[26]

---

[23] 167 F.3d at 1328.

[24] Earnshaw v. Commissioner, T.C. Memo. 2002-191.

[25] 336 U.S. 28 (1949).

[26] In this regard, consider the Court's later landmark decision in *Comm'r v. Duberstein*, 363 U.S. 278 (1960), discussed in Chapter 5, *supra*.

Notwithstanding *Jacobson*, however, in certain contexts the cancellation of indebtedness can be an excludable gift. For example, if a parent lends money to a child and subsequently forgives the debt, the forgiveness of the debt would likely be considered a gift excludable under Section 102(a).

Likewise, the cancellation of indebtedness under some circumstances may represent a form of compensation or some other form of payment which should not be considered "income from the discharge of indebtedness" within the meaning of Section 61(a)(12).

> **Example:** Smith enters into a contract to purchase certain goods from Brown to be held for sale in Smith's business. Brown ships some of the goods and then refuses to ship others. Smith refuses to pay Brown the $10,000 owed for the goods Brown shipped. Brown sues to recover the $10,000. Smith counterclaims for breach of contract, claiming damages for lost profit. Smith and Brown settle the suit with Smith agreeing to pay Brown $7,500 for the goods Brown shipped and Brown forgiving the remaining $2,500 in return for the execution of a release of the breach of contract counterclaim.

> **Analysis:** Had Smith actually received the $2,500 from Brown and then paid Brown $10,000, Smith and Brown would have been in the same financial situation. From a tax standpoint, it would be clear, however, that Smith had received $2,500 in damages for lost profits. The result should be the same under the circumstances presented in the example. Smith should be treated as receiving damages for lost profits in the amount of $2,500 and should not be deemed to have any discharge of indebtedness income. As a result of this analysis, Section 108 is inapplicable.[27]

§ 9.05 INAPPLICABILITY OF SECTION 108 TO GAIN REALIZED ON TRANSACTIONS INVOLVING DISCHARGE OF INDEBTEDNESS

Section 61 identifies a broad range of income items as gross income, including "income from the discharge of indebtedness." Section 108 provides an exclusion for income from the discharge of indebtedness under specified circumstances. An issue arises as to whether Section 108 excludes income other than that described in Section 61(a)(12), most particularly whether Section 108 excludes gain (Section 61(a)(3) income) when gain is realized on a transfer of appreciated property by an insolvent debtor to a creditor in partial satisfaction of a debt. The Eighth Circuit in *Gehl v. Commissioner*,[28] held that Section 108 "grants an exclusion to insolvent taxpayers only as to income from the discharge of indebtedness. It does not preclude the realization [and recognition] of income from other activities and sources."

---

[27] *See* Rev. Rul. 84-176, 1984-2 C.B. 34.

[28] 50 F.3d 12 (8th Cir. 1995).

Example: Aaron owes Barney $50,000. In view of Aaron's financial difficulties, Barney agrees to accept a tract of land owned by Aaron in full satisfaction of the $50,000 debt. Aaron's land has a fair market value of $30,000 and an adjusted basis of $20,000. Assume Aaron was insolvent both before and after the transfer of the land to Barney in satisfaction of the debt.

Analysis: Aaron will have $20,000 of discharge of indebtedness income which is clearly excludable under Section 108. At the same time, Aaron will also have $10,000 of gain as a result of using an appreciated asset to satisfy part of the debt. It is just as though Aaron had sold the land for $30,000 and then paid the $30,000 to Barney in full satisfaction of the $50,000 debt. Under those circumstances, Aaron would have recognized $10,000 of gain on the sale of the land and would have had $20,000 of discharge of indebtedness as a result of Barney's acceptance of the $30,000 in full satisfaction of the $50,000 debt. According to *Gehl*, while the $20,000 of discharge of indebtedness income is excludable under Section 108, the $10,000 of gain is not. In other words, *Gehl* requires a bifurcated analysis, *i.e.*, the transfer of the land in satisfaction of $30,000 of the debt is treated outside of Section 108 while the forgiveness of the remaining $20,000 of the debt falls within Section 108.

Chapter 10

COMPENSATION FOR PERSONAL INJURY AND SICKNESS

§ 10.01 INTRODUCTION

A taxpayer can recover damages for many reasons, including breach of contract, property damage, personal injuries, or injuries resulting from another's violation of any number of laws (civil rights law, consumer fraud laws, securities laws, etc.). The general rule regarding the taxation of such damages is to ask "in lieu of what were the damages awarded?" However, a set of important special rules applies to damages on account of personal physical injury or physical sickness, and the bulk of this chapter will be concerned with these special rules.

Sections 104 and 105 exclude from gross income certain amounts received on account of personal physical injury or sickness. These provisions are now commonly regarded as an expression of congressional compassion for those who suffer personal physical injury or illness; such payments are exempt from taxation. The predecessor of the current provisions dates back to the Revenue Act of 1918, at which time considerable doubt existed as to whether personal injury payments or accident insurance proceeds constituted income in a constitutional sense, or rather represented a type of nontaxable conversion of capital lost through the injury or illness. While Congress did not expressly address this constitutional question, its enactment in 1918 of the predecessor to sections 104 and 105 made clear that, even if amounts received on account of personal injury or sickness are within Congress' power to tax, they should nonetheless be excluded in calculating gross income. Although courts and tax counsel have generally assumed such payments are within the reach of the congressional taxing power, the exclusion enacted in 1918 has persisted, albeit with a number of alterations enacted over the intervening years.[1]

---

[1] The U.S. Court of Appeals for the D.C. Circuit rejected a taxpayer's argument that compensatory damages for personal injuries are not within Congress' power to tax. *Murphy v. U.S.*, 493 F.3d 170 (D.C. Cir. 2007), *cert. denied*, 2008 U.S. Lexis 3544 (Apr. 21, 2008). The *Murphy* court concluded that a compensatory award for a nonphysical personal injury was gross income under Section 61 and that the tax upon the award was in the nature of an excise tax and was thus within Congress' taxing power.

§ 10.02 DAMAGES

[A] Business or Property Damages

Damage awards (other than those covered by the exclusion rules noted above) are taxed as the underlying item they are replacing would have been taxed. The general rule is exemplified, with respect to business or property damages, in the leading case of *Raytheon Products Corp. v. Commissioner*,[2] which instructs that the question be asked "in lieu of what were the damages awarded?" For example, unless there is a specific rule to the contrary, damages awarded on account of lost profits would be taxable; a recovery for property damage would be measured against the basis for the property to determine the taxpayer's realized gain or loss.

In *Raytheon Products Corp.*, the corporate taxpayer settled its suit for damages under the antitrust laws and claimed it was entitled to exclude from income as a nontaxable return of capital most of the proceeds it received. The First Circuit disagreed:

> Damages recovered in an antitrust action are not necessarily nontaxable as a return of capital. As in other types of tort damage suits, recoveries which represent a reimbursement for lost profits are income . . . . The reasoning is that since the profits would be taxable income, the proceeds of litigation which are their substitute are taxable in like manner.

> Damages for violation of antitrust acts are treated as ordinary income where they represent compensation for loss of profits . . . .

> The test is not whether the action was one in tort or contract but rather the question to be asked is, "In lieu of what were the damages awarded?" . . . Where the suit is not to recover lost profits but is for injury to goodwill, the recovery represents a return of capital and, with certain limitations to be set forth below, is not taxable.

> . . .

> But, to say that the recovery represents a return of capital in that it takes the place of the business goodwill is not to conclude that it may not contain a taxable benefit. Although the injured party may not be deriving a profit as a result of the damage suit itself, the conversion thereby of his property into cash is a realization of any gain made over the cost or other basis of the goodwill prior to the legal interference. A buys Blackacre for $5,000. It appreciates in value to $50,000. B tortiously destroys it by fire. A sues and recovers $50,000 tort damages from B. Although no gain was derived by A from the suit, his prior gain due to the appreciation in value of Blackacre is realized when it is turned into cash by the money damages.

> Compensation for the loss of Raytheon's goodwill in excess of its cost is gross income.[3] . . .

---

[2] 144 F.2d 110, 113 (1st Cir. 1944).

[3] *Id.* at 113, 114.

The "in lieu of" test is regularly applied in business litigation to determine the character of judgments and settlements.

Example: Assume Maria, a sole proprietor, ordered $10,000 in Christmas merchandise from Distributor and prepaid Distributor the full $10,000. Distributor failed to deliver the merchandise until after Christmas. Maria returned the merchandise and demanded repayment of the $10,000 prepayment. When Distributor refused to repay the $10,000, Maria filed suit seeking recovery of the $10,000 as well as $20,000 in lost profits. Distributor settled the matter by paying Maria $15,000.

Analysis: Under the "in lieu of" test, $10,000 of the $15,000 recovery should be treated as a return of the prepayment and thus will not constitute income to Maria. The other $5,000, however, represents lost profits, *i.e.*, a substitute for the profits Maria would have realized had Distributor not been negligent in delivering the merchandise ordered. Maria therefore has $5,000 of ordinary income.

[B] Damages Received on Account of Personal Physical Injuries or Physical Sickness

§ 104. Compensation for injuries or sickness —

(a) In general — Except in the case of amounts attributable to (and not in excess of) deductions allowed under section 213 (relating to medical, etc., expenses) for any prior taxable year, gross income does not include —

. . .

(2) the amount of any damages (other than punitive damages) received (whether by suit or agreement and whether as lump sums or as periodic payments) on account of personal physical injuries or physical sickness . . . .

For purposes of paragraph (2), emotional distress shall not be treated as a physical injury or physical sickness. The preceding sentence shall not apply to an amount of damages not in excess of the amount paid for medical care (described in subparagraph (A) or (B) of section 213(d)(1)) attributable to emotional distress.

Section 104(a)(2) excludes from income any damages received, whether by suit or agreement, as a lump-sum or periodic payment, on account of personal physical injuries or physical sickness. Section 104(a)(2) thus distinguishes between (a) personal physical injuries and physical sickness and (b) nonphysical personal injuries and injuries to one's business or property. The damages excluded under Section 104(a)(2) are those received through prosecution or settlement of "tort or tort type rights."[4]

The policy justification for the Section 104(a)(2) exclusion has never been articulated by Congress. The exclusion is often presumed to rest on compassion, but it has also been suggested that damages for personal injury do not constitute

---

[4] Treas. Reg. § 1.104-1(c).

income because they do not add to wealth but merely restore a loss of capital.[5] This exclusion might be justified in part because of the involuntary nature of the "conversion of capital" that occurred. Indeed, the historic definition of "damages" as "tort or tort type" recoveries has been relied on to deny exclusions to amounts received pursuant to contracts permitting others to take actions which, but for the contract, would have been tortious. For example, in *United States v. Garber*,[6] the court denied the benefit of a Section 104(a)(2) exclusion to a taxpayer who periodically sold her blood plasma, and contended the payments she received constituted damages for the personal injury she sustained each time she gave blood. According to the Fifth Circuit, the statutory exclusion as interpreted by former Regulation § 1.104–1(c) necessitated some sort of tort claim against the payor, and merely because the taxpayer experienced pain and discomfort in giving blood did not make the purchaser's actions tortious.

Early judicial and administrative decisions excluding personal injury recoveries from income did not rely on the statutory predecessor to Section 104(a)(2), but instead found — wholly apart from the statutory exclusion — that such recoveries simply did not constitute gross income within the meaning of the forerunner of present Section 61. A 1922 administrative ruling held there was "no gain, and therefore no income" derived from damages received for alienation of affection or for defamation of personal character.[7] An early Tax Court decision similarly held that payment received for injury to personal reputation was nontaxable because it "in no event involves income . . . . [The] compensation . . . adds nothing to the individual . . . . It is an attempt to make the plaintiff whole as before the injury."[8]

In *Eisner v. Macomber*,[9] the Court defined "income" as "the gain derived from capital, from labor, or from both combined, provided it be understood to include profit gained through a sale or conversion of capital assets . . . ." Even after this characterization of income had been firmly supplanted by the broader definition of income articulated by the U.S. Supreme Court in *Glenshaw Glass*, the practice of excluding damages from income on nonstatutory grounds persisted. Revenue Ruling 56-518,[10] for example, held that certain damages received on account of wartime persecution were "in the nature of reimbursement for the deprivation of civil and personal rights and [did] not constitute taxable income." Indeed, as late as 1974, the Service, without mentioning Section 104(a)(2), held that amounts received on account of alienation of affection or in consideration of surrendering custody of a minor child were not income; the ruling held that Solicitor's Opinion 132 was superseded since its position — that the damages were excluded because they did not constitute income, not because they came within the terms of the statutory exclusion — was also set forth under the current statute and regulations.[11] Since the early 1970s, however, the cases and rulings consistently look to Section 104(a)(2)

---

[5] *See* Starrels v. Comm'r, 35 T.C. 646 (1961), *aff'd*, 304 F.2d 574 (9th Cir. 1962).

[6] 589 F.2d 843 (5th Cir. 1979).

[7] Solicitor's Opinion 132, I-1 C.B. 92 (1922).

[8] Hawkins v. Comm'r, 6 B.T.A. 1023, 1025 (1927).

[9] 252 U.S. 189, 206–207 (1920).

[10] 1956-2 C.B. 25.

[11] Rev. Rul. 74-77, 1974-1 C.B. 33.

as the basis for holding damages received on account of personal injury (or today, "personal physical injury or physical sickness") nontaxable. In effect, modern cases and rulings assume that, except to the extent excluded by section 104(a)(2), damages on account of personal injury are gross income under section 61.[12]

In enacting the predecessor to Section 104(a)(2), Congress likely intended to exclude only those damages received on account of physical injuries. Nonetheless, the courts and even the Service did not distinguish between physical and non-physical injuries prior to a legislative amendment in 1996. For example, the Tax Court held that damages for defamation of personal reputation were excludable under Section 104(a)(2).[13] Historically, the dividing line between excludable and nonexcludable damages under Section 104(a)(2) was not between physical and non-physical injuries, but rather between personal and non-personal injuries. Because neither the Code nor the regulations defined "personal injury," it fell to the courts to determine what injuries would be considered "personal." In an important decision excluding damages received on account of injuries to a taxpayer's professional reputation, the Tax Court in *Threlkeld v. Commissioner*,[14] held that "personal injury" for purposes of Section 104(a)(2) referred to "any invasion of the rights that an individual is granted by virtue of being a person in the sight of the law." This definition easily encompassed not only traditional non-physical injuries such as defamation but a broad array of newly-minted, and generally employment-related, actions for non-physical injuries. For example, damages awarded under 42 U.S.C. 1983 for violation of free speech rights were held nontaxable,[15] as were damages on account of discrimination on the basis of sex and national origin.[16]

In addition to providing an expansive definition to the term "personal injury" as used in Section 104(a)(2), *Threlkeld* also emphasized that the exclusion could not properly be limited only to those components of an award that compensate for non-economic losses; economic losses were also excludable:

> [W]hether the damages received are paid on account of "personal injuries" should be the beginning and the end of the inquiry. To determine whether the injury complained of is personal, we must look to the origin and character of the claim . . . and not to the consequences that result form the injury.[17]

As a result, prior to the 1996 amendments restricting the exclusion to "physical" injury or "physical" sickness awards or settlements, employees recovering awards for wrongful discharge, sex discrimination or any other employment-related claim constituting a "personal injury" within the *Threlkeld* definition could exclude not only the damages received on account of emotional distress or other psychological injuries suffered, but also lost wages.

---

[12] See, however, footnote 1, *supra*.

[13] Seay v. Comm'r, 58 T.C. 32 (1972) (acq.).

[14] 87 T.C. 1294 (1986), *aff'd*, 848 F.2d 81 (6th Cir. 1988).

[15] Bent v. Comm'r, 87 T.C. 236, *aff'd*, 835 F.2d 67 (3d Cir. 1987).

[16] Metzger v. Comm'r, 88 T.C. 834, *aff'd*, 845 F.2d 1013 (3d Cir. 1988).

[17] 87 T.C. at 1299.

[C]   Supreme Court Limitations on the Pre-1996 Version of Section 104(a)(2)

The first significant limitations on the increasingly broad scope of Section 104(a)(2) are to be found in two important U.S. Supreme Court decisions, *Burke v. United States*,[18] and *Commissioner v. Schleier*.[19]

[1]   What is a "Personal Injury"?

Burke was the first Supreme Court decision to interpret Section 104(a)(2). In *Burke*, employees of the Tennessee Valley Authority (TVA) brought, and ultimately settled, an action against TVA under Title VII of the Civil Rights Act of 1964, alleging that the TVA had engaged in illegal sex discrimination. In reversing the lower court's decision holding the settlement amount excludable, the Supreme Court emphasized that the regulation interpreting Section 104(a)(2) links "personal injury" as used in section 104(a)(2) to tort principles by defining damages received as an amount received through prosecution or settlement of a claim "based on tort or tort-type rights."[20] Therefore, according to the Court, the question to be asked in Section 104(a)(2) cases was whether the injury complained of is a tort type personal injury.

While acknowledging that discrimination is "an invidious practice that causes grave harm to its victims," the Court noted such harm "does not automatically imply, however, that there exists a tort-like 'personal injury' for purposes of the federal income tax law." The Court stressed that "remedial principles . . . figure prominently in the definition and conceptualization of torts. One of the hallmarks of traditional tort liability is the availability of a broad range of damages to compensate the plaintiff." The Court noted the limited nature of the remedies afforded by Title VII, *i.e.*, backpay and injunctive relief. Because of the circumscribed remedies available, the Court concluded that the amounts received by the taxpayers in settlement of their claims were not "damages received on account of personal injuries" within the meaning of Section 104(a)(2). Although *Burke* thus limited the Section 104(a)(2) exclusion to some extent, it did so by focusing on the remedial scheme of the underlying statutory cause of action, not on the scope of the Section 104(a)(2) exclusion itself. [The tort-type requirement of the regulations was eliminated in 2012 by amendments to Regulation § 1.104–1(c), which specifically provide that an injury "need not be defined as a tort under state common law."]

---

[18]   504 U.S. 229 (1992).

[19]   515 U.S. 323 (1995).

[20]   Treas. Reg. § 1.104-1(c). (This regulation was substantially amended in 2012 to eliminate the requirement that the claim be based on tort or tort-type rights.)

[2] When are Damages Received "On Account Of" a Personal Injury?

Commissioner v. Schleier[21] addressed the excludability of awards for backpay and liquidated damages under the Age Discrimination in Employment Act (ADEA). Accourding to the Court, the key question to be asked in applying Section 104(a)(2) is whether the damages received were "on account of," *i.e.*, actually compensated for, personal injury. Prior to *Schleier*, considerable confusion existed in the lower courts as to the excludibility of ADEA awards. The confusion centered on the interpretation of *Burke, i.e.*, on whether the remedies available under the ADEA rendered an ADEA action a tort or tort-type action, rather than on the question of whether the damages received in an ADEA action were "on account of," *i.e.*, compensated for, personal injuries.[22]

The standard articulated by the Court in *Schleier* appears to be that the only damages which are "on account of" personal injuries for Section 104(a)(2) purposes are those that bear a close nexus to the personal injury, *i.e.*, "the injury justifies [the] damages" or the damages are intended to compensate the taxpayer for the personal injury and the consequences causally linked to the injury. The *Schleier* Court used the following example to demonstrate the required nexus between the injury and the excludable damages under Section 104(a)(2):

> Assume that a taxpayer is in an automobile accident, is injured, and as a result of that injury suffers (a) medical expenses, (b) lost wages, and (c) pain, suffering, and emotional distress that cannot be measured with precision. If the taxpayer settles a resulting lawsuit for $30,000 (and if the taxpayer has not previously deducted her medical expenses, see Section 104(a)), the entire $30,000 would be excludable under Section 104(a)(2). The medical expenses for injuries arising out of the accident clearly constitute damages received "on account of personal injuries." Similarly, the portion of the settlement intended to compensate for pain and suffering constitutes damages "on account of personal injury." Finally, the recovery for lost wages is also excludable as being "on account of personal injuries," as long as the lost wages resulted from time in which the taxpayer was out of work as a result of her injuries.[23]

If the appropriate nexus between the damages and personal injuries does not exist, no exclusion is available. For example, in *Schleier*, because the Court concluded the liquidated damages available under the ADEA were not intended to compensate the taxpayer for any personal injuries, *e.g.*, psychological harm, but rather were intended to punish the wrongdoer, no exclusion for the liquidated damages was appropriate. Similarly, the backpay recovered by the taxpayer was not excludable because the necessary nexus between the backpay and a personal injury did not exist, *i.e.*, regardless of whether the taxpayer suffered any personal injury as a result of his discharge from employment at age 60, he was still entitled to the backpay under the ADEA. In other words, the backpay was not intended to

---

[21] 515 U.S. 323.

[22] *See, e.g.*, Downey v. Comm'r, 100 T.C. 634 (1993), *rev'd*, 33 F.3d 836 (7th Cir. 1994).

[23] 515 U.S. at 329.

compensate the taxpayer for a personal injury or its consequences but rather to ensure that the taxpayer received those wages he would have earned had he not been illegally discharged.

In some respects, the standard adopted by the *Schleier* Court is identical to the historic "in lieu of what" test of *Raytheon Products Corp. v. Commissioner* discussed previously. That test arguably provides the narrowest interpretation of the "on account of" language, ensuring that only damages for personal injury are excludable. Strictly applied, however, the "in lieu of what" test would result in backpay, lost wages and other damages for nonpersonal harms never being excluded unless it could be established they were intended as a measure of the personal injury. *Schleier*, at least in its car accident hypothetical, suggests a more generous test regarding economic losses. The Service apparently agrees that economic losses are excludable under Section 104(a)(2) provided the requirements of that provision are satisfied.[24]

[D] Exclusion for Personal Physical Injury or Physical Sickness: The 1996 Amendments to Section 104

[1] Distinction Between Physical and Non-Physical Injuries

Despite the *Schleier/Burke* limitations on the scope of Section 104(a)(2), Congress nonetheless viewed Section 104(a)(2) as too broad in scope, allowing taxpayers, particularly those who were victims of employment discrimination, to exclude awards primarily intended to compensate them for lost wages or lost profits. Congress therefore chose to limit the exclusion by restricting it to those damages received on account of "physical" injuries or "physical" sickness. In addition, Congress specifically provided that "emotional distress" is not to be treated — save only for related medical care expenses — as a physical injury or physical sickness. Thus, as a result of the 1996 amendments limiting § 104(a)(2) to physical injuries or physical sickness, damages that had historically been excludable, e.g., damages received on account of libel, slander, wrongful discharge, and employment discrimination, became taxable.

For purposes of determining excludability under § 104(a)(2), the legislative history of the 1996 act amending that provision relies on an "origin-of-the-claim" standard. Thus, the House Committee Report states: "if an action has its origin in a physical injury or physical sickness, then all damages (other than punitive damages) that flow therefrom are treated as payments received on account of physical injury or physical sickness . . ." The legislative history thus suggests congressional adoption of the *Schleier* standard, i.e., that § 104(a)(2) excludes all damages intended to compensate a taxpayer for a physical injury or physical sickness and the consequences, including economic consequences, e.g., lost wages or income, resulting from that injury or sickness. Consider the following examples in assessing whether, as a matter of policy, it is appropriate to exclude economic

---

[24] *See* P.L.R. 200041022 (citing favorably the *Schleier* hypothetical); Rev. Rul. 85-97, 1985-2 C.B. 50 (providing that lost income is excludable in an action for damages stemming from a physical injury).

damages such as lost wages even if a causal connection exists between those damages and a physical injury or physical sickness.

Example 1: Doctor, a surgeon in a solo-practice, is seriously injured in a ski accident and brings a negligence action against the owner of the ski resort. Doctor seeks damages for all past and future medical expenses associated with the accident, damages for pain and suffering, and damages for lost income as a result of being unable to perform surgery for more than a year following the accident. Doctor and ski resort owner settle the matter out of court for $1,500,000.

Analysis: The personal physical injury requirement of Section 104(a)(2) is clearly satisfied in this case. In addition, under the *Schleier* standard, the award is recovered "on account of" the personal physical injury. The requisite linkage exists between the damage award and a personal physical injury, i.e., the ski resort owner intended to compensate Doctor for the personal injury and the consequences stemming therefrom. As a result, all damages flowing from the personal injury, including the lost income, will be excludable.

Example 2: A newspaper printed a story falsely accusing Doctor (the same individual in the prior example) of committing a serious felony. As a result, Doctor was suspended from practicing surgery, was required to defend herself in a grueling license revocation proceeding before the state medical board, and ultimately lost a significant number of her patients. Doctor suffered severe emotional distress and, at one point was hospitalized for depression. The pressures experienced by Doctor's family as a result of the problems associated with the libelous statements in the press and the license revocation procedures and Doctor's resulting psychological problems had a deleterious impact on Doctor's marriage and ultimately resulted in divorce. In settlement of the libel action brought by Doctor, the newspaper paid Doctor $1,500,000 in compensation for her loss of personal and business reputation, the emotional distress that she suffered and is suffering, her medical costs, and her lost income.

Analysis: Under the law as it existed before the 1996 amendments to Section 104(a)(2), Doctor would presumably have been entitled to exclude the entire amount of the award. All of the requirements of the old Section 104(a)(2) as interpreted by *Schleier* are satisfied. However, post 1996, as a result of the amendments to Section 104(a)(2), the award (except for amounts paid for medical costs) will be taxable. Because Doctor's libel action did not have its origin in a personal physical injury, she is not entitled to exclude any part of the award other than the amount allocable to her medical costs. As in the prior example, it is likely that a significant portion of the award is allocable to lost income. Here, no exclusion exists for this economic award whereas in the prior example the amount received for lost income is excludable.

One might question whether the dichotomy between physical and non-physical injuries is justifiable as a matter of policy. In *Young v. United States*,[25] the Sixth Circuit rejected a Fifth Amendment Equal Protection challenge to amended Section 104(a)(2), finding the distinction between physical and non-physical injury to be rationally related to articulated government purposes, i.e., the establishment of a uniform policy regarding taxation of damage awards and the reduction of litigation.[26] The Sixth Circuit suggests that the amendments were intended to reduce litigation. A review of the post-1996 Act case law suggests that Congress may have failed in that regard.

[2] Personal Physical Injury or Physical Sickness

Section 104(a)(2) does not define "physical injury" or "physical sickness." Likewise, there is no regulation defining these terms. The Service issued a private letter ruling (PLR 200041022) in 2000 that provides some limited guidance. PLR 200041022 states "direct unwanted or uninvited physical contacts resulting in *observable bodily harms* such as bruises, cuts, swelling, and bleeding are personal physical injuries under § 104(a)(2)." (emphasis added) In this ruling, the Service refused to issue a ruling regarding the application of the Section 104(a)(2) exclusion to damages on account of a "pain incident" where the physical contact did not manifest itself in the form of a cut, bruise or other similar bodily harm. The Service, noting general rules regarding issuance of letter rulings, stated "a letter ruling will not ordinarily be issued because of the factual nature of the problem. Because the perception of pain is essentially subjective, it is a factual matter."

Since the issuance of the private letter ruling, there has been some additional guidance provided by the Service and courts regarding the interpretation to be given "personal physical injury and physical sickness." Thus, in PLR 200121031, the Service recognized that a sheetrocker who had contracted and suffered asbestos-related lung cancer and other asbestos related diseases as a result of his long-term exposure to asbestos in his work had suffered a "physical injury" within the meaning of that term in § 104(a)(2). In *Domeny v. Commissioner*,[27] the flare-up of the taxpayer's multiple sclerosis condition caused by a hostile workplace was held to constitute a physical injury or physical sickness. Likewise, in *Parkinson v. Commissioner*,[28] the court held that a heart attack and its physical aftereffects suffered by a taxpayer as a result of emotional distress inflicted upon the taxpayer in his workplace constituted a "physical injury or physical sickness" for Section 104(a)(2) purposes.

---

[25] 332 F.3d 893 (6th Cir. 2003).

[26] Taxation of damages awarded on account of non-physical injuries has been held to be both constitutional and within the scope of § 61. *See* Murphy v. IRS, 493 F.3d 170 (D.C. Cir. 2007), *cert. denied*, 553 U.S. 1004 (2008); Stadnyk v. Commissioner, T.C. Memo 2008-289, *aff'd* in unpublished opinion, 2010 U.S. App. Lexis 4209 (6th Cir. 2010).

[27] T.C. Memo 2010-9. See, however, *Blackwood v. Commissioner*, T.C. Memo 2012–190, distinguishing *Domeny*. In *Blackwood*, the taxpayer, who suffered from depression, was fired by her employer. As a result, she suffered symptoms such as insomnia, migraines, nausea, vomiting and back pain. The court concluded these were merely symptoms of emotional distress and did not constitute physical injury or physical sickness under § 104(a)(2).

[28] T.C. Memo 2010-142.

While the Service in PLR 200041022 indicated its refusal to issue a ruling regarding whether pain unaccompanied by a cut or bruise constituted a "physical injury, the Tax Court in *Amos v. Commissioner*,[29] concluded that some of the damages awarded a taxpayer were excludable under Section 104(a)(2) apparently without a showing of bruises, cuts or other observable bodily harms. *Amos v. Commissioner* involved former professional basketball player Dennis Rodman. In a 1997 game pitting Rodman's Chicago Bulls against the Minnesota Timberwolves, Rodman twisted his ankle when he fell into a group of photographers, including the taxpayer Amos. Rodman kicked Amos in the groin. Amos was taken by ambulance to a hospital where he complained he had experienced considerable pain. Hospital personnel observed that Amos was able to walk, but that he was limping and complained of pain. There apparently was no observable swelling or bruising in the groin area. Amos immediately retained a lawyer and shortly afterward the matter was settled by Rodman's payment of $200,000 to Amos. The settlement agreement provided, without allocation, that the settlement covered not only any physical injuries Amos suffered but also Amos' agreement not to defame Rodman, disclose the existence or terms of the agreement, or assist in any criminal prosecution against Rodman with respect to the matter. The court concluded that a significant part of the settlement was intended to compensate Rodman for a personal physical injury within the meaning of § 104(a)(2) and held that $120,000 of the settlement was excludable under that provision. *Amos* appears to indicate that some physical contacts, e.g., a kick in the groin, constitute a personal physical injury even though there is no cut, bruise or other *observable* bodily harm.

Does false imprisonment constitute a personal physical injury? In view of the fact that states and the federal government often provide compensation to individuals who have been wrongly incarcerated, the question is anything but academic. Authority on the issue, however, is limited. In *Stadnyk v. Commissioner*,[30] the court rejected taxpayer's argument that "physical restraint and detention and the resulting deprivation of personal liberty is [itself] a physical injury." In that case, the taxpayer was wrongfully detained for only about eight hours. In a deposition, the taxpayer had indicated she had not suffered any physical injury as a result of her arrest and detention, i.e., in arresting and detaining her, no one had "put their hands on her, grabbed her, jerked her around, bruised her or hurt her." Nonetheless, the taxpayer argued the physical loss of her freedom constituted a "personal physical injury" within the meaning of Section 104(a)(2). The Sixth Circuit, affirming the Tax Court, stated that taxpayer sought "to create a *per se* rule that every false imprisonment claim necessarily involves a physical injury, even though physical injury is not a required element of false imprisonment under [applicable state law]. The court conceded that false imprisonment might result in a physical injury, such as an injured wrist as a result of being handcuffed. "But the mere fact that false imprisonment involves a physical act — restraining the victim's freedom — does not mean that the victim is *necessarily* physically injured *as a result* of that physical act." What difference, if any, would or should it make if, instead of being

---

[29] T.C. Memo 2003-329.

[30] T. C. Memo 2008-289, *aff'd* in an unpublished opinion, 2010 U.S. App. Lexis 4209 (6th Cir. 2010).

wrongly detained for a matter of hours, a taxpayer were wrongly imprisoned for years?

[3] Emotional Distress

As noted, Section 104(a)(2) specifically provides that "emotional distress shall not be treated as a physical injury or physical sickness." Just as the statute and regulations do not define "personal physical injury or physical sickness" for purposes of § 104(a)(2), they do not define "emotional distress." The House Committee report for the 1996 Act, however, does note "the term emotional distress includes physical *symptoms* (e.g., insomnia, headaches, and stomach disorders) which may result from such emotional distress.[31] The Report notes that, since emotional distress is not a physical injury or physical sickness, "[t]he exclusion from gross income does not apply to any damages received (other than for medical expenses . . .) based on a claim of employment discrimination or injury to reputation accompanied by a claim for emotional distress."[32] If, however, the claim had its origin in a personal physical injury, a recovery for emotional distress may be excludable. In this regard, the Report states: [T]he exclusion . . . applies to any damages received based on a claim of emotional distress that is attributable to a physical injury or physical sickness." Regulation § 1.104-1(c)(1) specifically provides for the exclusion of damages for emotional distress attributable to a physical injury or physical sickness.

What constitutes a "symptom" of emotional distress? As noted above, the legislative history provides three examples, insomnia, headaches, and stomach disorders. Since the 1996 amendments to § 104(a)(2), courts have identified other symptoms of emotional distress including loss of appetite, emotional instability, anxiety and depression. In *Parkinson v. Commissioner*,[33] the Tax Court concluded that a taxpayer who suffered a heart attack as a result of the emotional distress he experienced in the workplace had suffered a physical injury within the meaning of § 104(a)(2). In rejecting the Commissioner's argument that the settlement in that case was entirely for emotional distress, the Court noted:

> In a medical context, a "symptom" is "subjective evidence of disease or of a patient's condition, i.e., such evidence as perceived by the patient." *The Sloane-Dorland Annotated Medical-Legal Dictionary*, 496 (Supp. 1992). A "symptom" is distinguished from a "sign", defined as "any objective evidence of a disease, i.e., such evidence as is perceptible to the examining physician, as opposed to the subjective sensations (symptoms) of the patient . . .

> It would seem self-evident that a heart attack and its physical aftereffects constitute physical injury or sickness rather than mere subjective sensations or symptoms of emotional distress . . .

---

[31] House Committee Report on Small Business Job Protection Act of 1996 (H.R. 3448) at 142-43, n. 24.

[32] *Id.* At 143.

[33] T.C. Memo 2010-142.

Insofar as respondent means to suggest that claims of physical injury or sickness are not compensable in a cause of action for intentional infliction of emotional distress, respondent is mistaken. When it first recognized the tort of intentional infliction of emotional distress, the Court of Appeals of Maryland in *Harris v. Jones*, 281 Md. 560, 380 A.2d 611, 613 (1977), looked to the Restatement, Torts 2d, Sec. 46(1) (1965), which states:

> One, who by extreme and outrageous conduct intentionally or reck-lessly causes severe emotional distress to another, is subject to liability for such emotional distress, and *if bodily harm to the other results from it, for such bodily harm.* [Emphasis added.]

The provision in the 1996 Act negating emotional distress as a physical injury or physical sickness has generated considerable controversy. In her 2009 report to Congress, the National Taxpayer Advocate noted:

> Although the medical community increasingly believes that mental illness is caused by physical/chemical abnormalities or changes in the body and may produce physical symptoms as well — effectively blurring the line between physical suffering and mental suffering — the tax code continues to treat taxpayers differently according to their illnesses. Under current law, if a taxpayer is awarded compensation for depression or anxiety resulting from sexual harassment in the workplace, for example, the award would be includible in gross income because current law provides an exclusion only for awards received on account of physical injury or sickness. The National Taxpayer Advocate recommends that Congress amend IRC Section 104(a)(2) to exclude from gross income any payments received as a settlement or judgment for mental anguish, emotional distress and pain and suffering.[34]

Do you agree?

[4] Recoveries by Individuals Other than Individuals Suffering Physical Injury or Sickness

The legislative history of the 1996 Act is clear that, if a claim has its origin in a physical injury or physical sickness, it is not necessary that the recipient of damages be the individual who suffered the physical injury or sickness. The House Report states: "if an action has its origin in a physical injury or physical sickness, then all damages (other than punitive damages) that flow therefrom are treated as payments received on account of physical injury or physical sickness *whether or not the recipient of the damages is the injured party.*" (Emphasis added) The Report provides the following example: "damages (other than punitive damages) received by an individual on account of a claim for loss of consortium due to the physical injury or physical sickness of such individual's spouse are excludable from gross income."[35] Thus, in PLR 200121031 addressing damages received by a taxpayer for

---

[34] National Taxpayer Advocate's 2009 Annual Report to Congress (December 31, 2009), IRS Publication 2104C (Rev. 12-2009) p. 31.

[35] House Report on Small Business Job Protection Act of 1996 (H.R. 3448) at 143.

the asbestos-related lung cancer and other asbestos related diseases that killed her husband, a sheetrocker, the Service noted:

> Husband contracted physical diseases from exposure to asbestos. These diseases were the proximate cause of the circumstances giving rise to Taxpayer's loss of consortium claim, survival action and wrongful death action. Because there exists a direct link between the physical injury suffered and the damages recovered, Taxpayer may exclude from gross income any economic damages compensating for such injury. These would include damages received for the survival action, loss of consortium and wrongful death of Taxpayer's spouse.

[E] Punitive Damages

The excludability of punitive damages under Section 104(a)(2) has been the subject of numerous conflicting court decisions and administrative rulings. In 1989, Congress, in an effort to clarify the law in this regard, amended Section 104(a)(2) to provide that the statutory exclusion did not apply "to any punitive damages in connection with a case not involving physical injury or sickness." This amendment addressed only punitive damages arising out of non-physical personal injuries. The statute failed to address the tax status of punitive damages arising out of physical personal injuries or physical sickness. The Supreme Court in *O'Gilvie v. United States*,[36] held that Section 104(a)(2) (prior to the 1996 amendments) did not exclude punitive damages. Relying specifically on the interpretation it had given in *Schleier* to the "on account of" language of Section 104(a)(2), the Supreme Court reasoned that "punitive damages are not covered [by Section 104(a)(2)] because they are an element of damages not designed to compensate victims, rather they are punitive in nature." The 1996 amendments to Section 104(a)(2) make clear that the Section 104(a)(2) exclusion does not apply to punitive damages.[37]

> **Example:** Assume the facts of the earlier example regarding Doctor, who was injured in a ski accident. Assume Doctor seeks punitive damages in addition to the damages for past and future medical expenses, pain and suffering, and lost income. When the matter is settled for $1,500,000, $500,000 of the settlement is allocated to punitive damages.

> **Analysis:** As noted in the prior example, the settlement, except for the $500,000 allocated to punitive damages, is within the Section 104(a)(2) exclusion and will not be taxed. The $500,000 amount allocated to punitive damages will be includible in gross income.

---

[36] 519 U.S. 79 (1996).

[37] However, Section 104(c) provides that prior law continues to apply to a limited category of punitive damages, namely to punitive damages received in a wrongful death action if the "applicable State law (as in effect on September 13, 1995 and without regard to any modification after such date) provides . . . that only punitive damages may be awarded in such an action." Apparently, Congress believed it would be unfair to deny an exclusion for damages recovered on account of wrongful death in states which characterized wrongful death recoveries as "punitive damages" and yet allow an exclusion for such recoveries in states which did not characterize them as "punitive damages."

[F]   Allocation of Awards

Because punitive damages are not excludable, a taxpayer negotiating the settlement of a case involving a physical personal injury may seek to allocate the entire settlement amount to the physical injury even though the taxpayer's pleadings requested both compensatory and punitive damages.[38] The tortfeasor/payor may be indifferent to the characterization of the settlement and agree to the proposed allocation. It is uncertain whether the Service will respect the settlement agreement's characterization of the entire award as compensation for the physical injuries. The Service, however, is likely to scrutinize settlements carefully and to dispute allocations resulting from settlement negotiations it does not consider to be arms-length. For example, in *Robinson v. Commissioner*,[39] the Tax Court held it was not bound by a state court judgment allocating 95% of certain settlement proceeds to tort-like personal injuries. In that case, following a jury verdict which awarded the taxpayers amounts for lost business profits and personal injuries as well as $50 million in punitive damages, the taxpayer entered into an agreement with the defendant settling their lawsuit for a specific sum considerably less than the verdict amount. The taxpayers unilaterally prepared a final judgment making the allocation in question. The defendant bank, apparently anxious to settle the suit and recognizing the taxpayers' desire to avoid tax, acquiesced in the allocation. The presiding judge, without reviewing the allocation, signed the judgment. The Tax Court, emphasizing that it could make its own determination of the proper allocation of the settlement proceeds, ultimately held that the taxpayers could exclude 37.3% of the settlement under Section 104(a)(2) with the balance being includable in gross income.

Similarly, in *Bagley v. Commissioner*,[40] the Tax Court agreed the Service should not be bound by a settlement agreement allocating all of the $1.5 million settlement to personal injuries. A jury had previously awarded the taxpayer $1,000,000 for personal injuries and $5,000,000 in punitive damages. According to the court, the critical question in determining the tax status of settlement amounts was "in lieu of what" was the settlement amount paid. Based on the facts presented, the court concluded the taxpayer could not have expected to recover more than $1,000,000 for the personal injuries; the balance of the settlement proceeds therefore represented a payment in lieu of punitive damages.

By contrast, in *McKay v. Commissioner*,[41] the court respected an allocation in a settlement agreement of approximately three-fourths of the settlement award to personal injury claims and one-fourth to taxpayer's contract claims. In *McKay*, a jury had awarded taxpayer over $1.6 million for lost compensation and over $12.8

---

[38] A related issue can arise with respect to the allocation of expenses incurred in pursuing personal injury claims. In general, expenses otherwise deductible will not be allowed if they are allocated to tax-exempt income. *See* I.R.C. § 265. Consider, therefore, the taxpayer who pays attorney's fees to obtain a personal injury award, where some portion of the award is excludable under Section 104(a)(2), but the remainder is taxable. To the extent the attorney's fees are properly allocable to the tax-exempt income, they will be nondeductible. *See* Chapters 12, 27, *infra*.

[39] 102 T.C. 116 (1994), *aff'd in part*, 70 F.3d 34 (5th Cir. 1995), *cert. denied*, 519 U.S. (1996).

[40] 105 T.C. 396 (1995).

[41] 102 T.C. 465 (1994).

million for "future damages" as a result of taxpayer's wrongful discharge. These damages were then trebled to over $43 million for the employer's violation of Racketeer Influenced and Corrupt Organizations Act (RICO). Following the jury verdict, the parties engaged in negotiations resulting in a $16 million settlement, three-fourths of which was allocated to the taxpayer's wrongful discharge tort claim. In upholding the allocation, the Tax Court emphasized the adversarial nature of the negotiations that led to the allocation of the award. Specifically, the court stressed that the tortfeasor in *McKay* had insisted none of the settlement be allocated to the RICO violations or punitive damages.

> **Example:** Assume the facts of the prior example except that Doctor settles her case, as before, for $1,500,000. Although Doctor had sought punitive damages as well as damages for medical expenses, pain and suffering and lost income, the settlement agreement, alternatively (1) allocates the entire award solely to medical expenses, pain and suffering and lost income or (2) makes no allocation at all.

> **Analysis:** No bright-line rules exist to answer allocation questions. Ultimately, one must determine whether, on the basis of all the facts and circumstances, some portion of the award must be allocated to punitive damages and thus be included in gross income. Doctor should be prepared to document, to the extent possible, the arm's length nature of the settlement and the reasons for the allocations that were made. Doctor is perhaps more susceptible to a claim that some portion of the award must be allocated to punitive damages, since Doctor sought such damages, and there is no indication that Doctor abandoned her punitive damage claim. In these circumstances, if Doctor quantified her demands — for example, in her pleadings — the Commissioner may assert that whatever percentage of the total demand represented punitive damages, that same percentage of the unallocated settlement award should be deemed the amount of punitive damages received.[42]

[G] Periodic Payments

Section 104(a)(2) explicitly provides that periodic payments qualify for the exclusion. A simple example illustrates the significance of this provision.

> **Example 1:** Victor sues George in a personal physical injury action. Pursuant to a settlement agreement, George agrees to pay Victor $3,000 per month for the next ten years.

> **Analysis:** This is a periodic payment and, under the statute, Victor will be entitled to exclude the entire amount he receives over the next ten years even though a significant portion of the payments in effect constitutes interest income.

Consider a simple contrasting example:

---

[42] *See* Rev. Rul. 58-418, 1958-2 C.B. 18 (in such circumstances the complaint provided the best evidence as the proper allocation).

Example 2: Victor receives a lump sum payment, and invests it in an annuity paying exactly $3,000 per month for the next ten years.

Analysis: Victor would be entitled to exclude the lump sum received, but would have to report a portion of each month's annuity payments as income pursuant to Section 72.[43] This income portion is the economically identical interest income or investment income that was untaxed in the prior example. Section 104(a)(2) thus encourages injured taxpayers to structure their settlement awards so as to exclude the interest component of periodic payments.

§ 10.03 PAYMENT UNDER ACCIDENT AND HEALTH INSURANCE POLICIES

§ 104. Compensation for injuries or sickness —

(a) **In general — Except in the case of amounts attributable to (and not in excess of) deductions allowed under section 213 (relating to medical, etc., expenses) for any prior taxable year, gross income does not include —**

. . .

(3) **amounts received through accident or health insurance (or through an arrangement having the effect of accident or health insurance) for personal injuries or sickness (other than amounts received by an employee, to the extent such amounts (A) are attributable to contributions by the employer which were not includible in the gross income of the employee, or (B) are paid by the employer); . . .**

---

§ 105. Section 105. Amounts received under accident and health plans —

(a) **Amounts attributable to employer contributions — Except as otherwise provided in this section, amounts received by an employee through accident or health insurance for personal injuries or sickness shall be included in gross income to the extent such amounts (1) are attributable to contributions by the employer which were not includible in the gross income of the employee, or (2) are paid by the employer.**

(b) **Amounts expended for medical care — Except in the case of amounts attributable to (and not in excess of) deductions allowed under section 213 (relating to medical, etc., expenses) for any prior taxable year, gross income does not include amounts referred to in subsection (a) if such amounts are paid, directly or indirectly, to the taxpayer to reimburse the taxpayer for expenses incurred by him for the medical care (as defined in section 213(d)) of the taxpayer, his spouse, and his dependents (as defined in section 152). Any child to whom section 152(e) applies shall be treated as a dependent of both parents for purposes of this subsection.**

(c) **Payments related to absence from work — Gross income does not include amounts referred to in subsection (a) to the extent such amounts —**

---

[43] *See* Chapter 8, *supra.*

(1) constitute payment for the permanent loss or loss of use of a member or function of the body, or the permanent disfigurement, of the taxpayer, his spouse, or a dependent (as defined in section 152), and

(2) are computed with reference to the nature of the injury without regard to the period the employee is absent from work.

---

§ 106.   Contributions by employer to accident and health plans —

(a)   General Rule. Except as otherwise provided in this section, gross income of an employee does not include employer-provided coverage under an accident or health plan.

It is appropriate to consider Sections 104(a)(3), 105, and 106(a) together. Under Section 104(a)(3), payments received through accident or health insurance policies are excluded from gross income, provided the policy was not financed by the taxpayer's employer or by employer contributions not includible in the taxpayer's income. In effect, if the taxpayer is willing to finance his own accident and health insurance with after-tax dollars, payments thereunder will be tax-free.

Such is not the case with employer-financed plans. Payments made by employer-financed accident and health plans are not exempt under Section 104(a)(3), but instead are governed by Section 105. Section 105(a) generally includes such payments in the employee's gross income but provides exceptions for medical expense reimbursements and certain payments for permanent bodily injury or disfigurement.[44]

> **Example:** Tom receives $10,000 in "sick pay" or wage continuation payments for the time he is off work due to illness.
>
> **Analysis:** If the sick pay or wage continuation payments are made under an employer financed insurance policy, they are taxable. If they are made under a policy Tom purchased with his own (after tax) dollars, they are not.

Similarly, contrast the tax treatment of medical expense payments under self-financed and employer-financed insurance plans. The Section 105(b) exclusion for medical care for the taxpayer, spouse and dependents is limited to the actual medical expenses incurred; under Section 104(a)(3), however, payments that exceed medical expenses incurred remain tax-free. Revenue Ruling 69-154,[45] illustrates the difference:

> **Example 1:** The taxpayer has two self-financed health insurance policies that in combination make medical payments totaling $1,200 when actual medical expenses are only $900.
>
> **Analysis:** All of the payments (including the excess $300) are nontaxable.
>
> **Example 2:** Both policies in the prior example are employer-financed.

---

[44] I.R.C § 105(b), (c).
[45] 1969-1 C.B. 46.

Analysis: Reimbursement of $900 for actual medical expenses is not taxed, but the $300 excess reimbursement would be includible in gross income.

If one policy is employer-financed and the other is self-financed, the excess reimbursement is allocated in proportion to the relative payments made by each policy.

Example 3: As before, actual medical expenses were $900, but total payments of $1,200 were made by the two policies — 70%, or $840, by the employer-financed policy and 30%, or $360, by the self-financed policy.

Analysis: Since 70% of the total payments were made by the employer-financed policy, 70%, or $210, of the excess reimbursement of $300 would be attributed to that policy and included in income. The remaining 30% ($90) of the excess reimbursement would be allocated to the self-financed policy and excluded from income under Section 104(a)(3).

Suppose, however, a single policy is in part self-financed and in part financed by the employer. Payment under such a policy is treated as self-financed in proportion to that part of the total premiums paid by the taxpayer.

Example 4: Assume the employer policy in Example 3 was financed half by employer contributions and half by after-tax employee contributions.

Analysis: Again, since that policy made 70% of the total payments made by both policies, 70%, or $210, of the excess reimbursement is attributable to it. However, since the employer made only half of the contributions to the total premium, only half of the excess reimbursement ($105) is attributable to the employer's contribution, and thus only $105 is includible in gross income.

Note at this point the Section 106(a) exclusion for employer-provided coverage under accident and health plans. Section 106(a) permits employer contributions to accident and health plans to be made on a tax-free basis to the employee, but Section 105(a) makes payments under such employer-financed plans taxable, except to the extent Sections 105(b) or (c) applies.

As noted previously, payments under employer-financed plans are excluded to the extent they compensate for permanent bodily injury or disfigurement of the taxpayer, spouse, or dependents, provided the payments are computed with reference to the nature of the injury and not the period of absence from work.[46] If such amounts are paid under a workers' compensation act, they are excluded by Section 104(a)(1).[47] Section 105(c), however, could apply to, and exclude, any amounts paid in excess of the applicable workers' compensation act, since such excess amounts would not be excludable under Section 104(a)(1).

---

[46] I.R.C. § 105(c).

[47] Treas. Reg. § 1.105-3. *See* § 10.05, *infra.*

§ 10.04 PREVIOUSLY DEDUCTED MEDICAL EXPENSES

Section 213 allows a deduction for unreimbursed medical expenses in excess of a floor based on the taxpayer's adjusted gross income. Medical expenses incurred on account of a personal physical injury or physical sickness, unreimbursed and thus deducted in the year paid, may be reimbursed in a later year as part of a claim for damages on account of personal physical injury or physical sickness.

Amounts attributable to previously deducted medical expenses are not excluded from income under either Section 104 or Section 105.[48] The reason is an obvious one: to allow an expenditure to be deducted from income, and then to allow the reimbursement of the expense to be excluded from income would constitute a double tax benefit for the same amount, and the Code properly prohibits that. Reimbursements for nondeductible medical expenses, however, are excluded from income under Sections 104 and 105.[49]

In some instances, a payment for personal injury or sickness, based in part on the taxpayer's medical expenses, may be made in the form of an undifferentiated lump sum. In Revenue Ruling 75-230,[50] the Service required that a lump sum award in a personal injury suit settled out of court be allocated between medical expenses and other components of the award. The ruling stated that the Service would respect an allocation made by the parties unless the allocation were unreasonable; where no allocation was made, the settlement would be presumed to be attributable first to medical expenses previously deducted, and thus includible in income to the extent of the prior medical expense deduction allowed. Awards for future medical expenses were addressed by Revenue Ruling 75-232.[51] Such awards may be excluded from income, but to the extent of the allocations to future medical expenses, the taxpayer may not deduct those future medical expenses under Section 213[52] when they are incurred.

§ 10.05 WORKERS' COMPENSATION

§ 104. Compensation for injuries or sickness —

(a) **In general — Except in the case of amounts attributable to (and not in excess of) deductions allowed under section 213 (relating to medical, etc., expenses) for any prior taxable year, gross income does not include —**

(1) **amounts received under workmen's compensation acts as compensation for personal injuries or sickness;**

Section 104(a)(1) excludes from income amounts received under workers' compensation acts as compensation for personal injuries or sickness. The regulations provide that the exclusion also extends to payments under a statute "in the nature of a workmen's compensation act," but not to retirement payments to the extent

---

[48] I.R.C. §§ 104(a), 105(b).

[49] *See* Treas. Reg. § 1.213–1(g).

[50] 1975-1 C.B. 93.

[51] 1975-1 C.B. 94.

[52] *See* Chapter 25, *infra*.

based on age, length of service, or employee contributions, even where retirement is caused by occupational injury or illness.[53] Conversely, compensation for nonoccupational injury or illness is not within Section 104(a)(1), even if the label of workers' compensation is placed upon the payment.

§ 10.06 CERTAIN DISABILITY PENSIONS

Military disability pensions and certain other government disability pensions are excluded from income under Section 104(a)(4). However, except for certain grandfathered pensions, this exclusion is now sharply limited by Section 104(b) to persons receiving compensation for combat-related injuries and to those who would on application receive disability compensation from the Veterans' Administration. A special provision also provides an exclusion for disability income attributable to injuries suffered in a terrorist attack upon an employee of the United States engaged in performance of official duties outside the United States.[54]

---

[53] Treas. Reg. § 1.104-1(b).

[54] I.R.C. § 104(a)(5).

Chapter 11

FRINGE BENEFITS

Although it might seem that any benefit accorded an employee in connection with his employment constitutes compensation, the Service, the courts and the Congress have applied disparate treatment to fringe benefits during the last 80 years. As a result of such treatment, the law regarding the tax treatment of fringe benefits is to be found in a patchwork of legislative, judicial and administrative rules.

§ 11.01 MEALS AND LODGING

[A] The Treatment of Meals and Lodging Prior to 1954

The uncertain and piecemeal tax treatment of fringe benefits is perhaps best exemplified in the historic treatment of meals and lodging provided by an employer to an employee. The earliest rulings of the Service established the excludability of meals and lodging provided to employees. For example, the Service, in a 1919 ruling, excluded the room and board furnished seamen aboard a ship.[1] A 1920 ruling exempted "'supper money' paid by an employer to an employee, who voluntarily performs extra labor for his employer after regular business hours."[2] These and similar meals and lodging exclusions were premised on the notion that the benefits given employees were for the convenience of the employer. This so-called "convenience of employer doctrine" soon was adopted by the Treasury and the courts as the standard for determining whether employer-provided meals and lodging were excludable. The convenience of employer doctrine required taxpayers to establish that benefits accorded them as employees were grounded in business necessity. For example, the Service held:

> [W]here the employees of a hospital are subject to immediate service on demand at any time during the twenty-four hours of the day and on that account are required to accept quarters and meals at the hospital, the value of such quarters and meals may be considered as being furnished for the convenience of the hospital and does not represent additional compensation to the employees. On the other hand, where the employees . . . could, if they so desired, obtain meals and lodging elsewhere than in the hospital and yet perform the duties required of them by such hospital, the ratable value of the board and lodging furnished is considered additional compensation.[3]

---

[1] O.D. 265, 1 C.B. 71 (1919).

[2] O.D. 514, 2 C.B. 90 (1920).

[3] O.D. 915, 4 C.B. 85–86 (1921).

Similarly, in *Benaglia v. Commissioner,*[4] the court held that the value of a suite of rooms provided free of charge to the manager of a resort hotel was excludable from his income. The manager's employer expected him to live at the hotel because his managerial duties were continuous and required him to be available at a moment's call.

The convenience of employer doctrine was not a tidy one. The Service and the courts were inconsistent in their treatment of employer-provided meals and lodging. In 1950, the Service took the position that, if the employer characterized a benefit as compensation, the benefit would be treated as income regardless of whether the employee could establish that the benefit was provided for the convenience of the employer. Some courts rejected this position while others embraced it. As a result, similarly situated taxpayers were treated differently depending on which standard was used.

[B] Section 119 — Meals or Lodging Furnished for the Convenience of the Employer

§ 119. Meals or lodging furnished for the convenience of the employer.

(a) Meals and lodging furnished to employee, his spouse, and his dependents, pursuant to employment. — There shall be excluded from gross income of an employee the value of any meals or lodging furnished to him, his spouse, or any of his dependents by or on behalf of his employer for the convenience of the employer, but only if —

(1) in the case of meals, the meals are furnished on the business premises of the employer, or

(2) in the case of lodging, the employee is required to accept such lodging on the business premises of his employer as a condition of his employment.

To resolve the confusion regarding the proper treatment of employer provided meals and lodging, Congress added Section 119 in 1954. Section 119(b)(1) retains the convenience of employer doctrine. The regulations provide:

> . . . condition of employment means that [the employee] be required to accept the lodging in order to enable him properly to perform the duties of his employment. Lodging will be regarded as furnished to enable the employee properly to perform the duties of his employment when, for example, the lodging is furnished because the employee is required to be available for duty at all times or because the employee could not perform the services required of him unless he is furnished such lodging.[5]

This regulation appears to be merely an application of the convenience of the employer standard as developed in the early rulings.

Although the provision of meals or lodging may be for the convenience of the employer, the fact remains that personal needs of the employee are satisfied. As suggested by a dissenting opinion in *Benaglia*, perhaps the value of the benefit to

---

[4] 36 B.T.A. 838 (1937).

[5] Treas. Reg. § 1.119-1(b)(3).

the employee should be treated as income. In that case, there was evidence that, given the taxpayer's income and family responsibilities, the taxpayer would have incurred expenses of $3,600 per year if he lived elsewhere. One might well concede that the greater value of the accommodations provided the manager at the resort hotel should not be taxed to him since he apparently would never have rented such luxurious accommodations if he had been required to pay for them himself. Nonetheless, it can be argued that Benaglia should have been required to report as income at least the $3,600 per year that he saved by not having to rent housing at all. However, in justifying the exclusion of benefits provided for the convenience of the employer, the Tax Court, in *Van Rosen v. Commissioner*[6] reasoned:

> . . . [T]hough there was an element of gain to the employee, in that he received subsistence and quarters which otherwise he would have had to supply for himself, he had nothing he could take, appropriate, use and expend according to his own dictates, but rather, the ends of the employer's business dominated and controlled, just as in the furnishing of a place to work and in the supplying of the tools and machinery with which to work. The fact that certain personal wants and needs of the employee were satisfied was plainly secondary and incidental to the employment.[7]

In addition to providing meals and lodging to employees, employers, as in *Benaglia*, often provide meals and lodging to the employee's family. Section 119 initially did not address this matter. In 1959, the Service issued Revenue Ruling 59-409,[8] which would have triggered additional income to an employee for the value of benefits provided to members of his family, but this ruling was withdrawn without comment the following year. In 1978, Congress amended Section 119 to exclude meals and lodging provided to an employee's spouse and dependents. One might argue that conceptually at least the Service's position anticipated in the withdrawn revenue ruling was correct. By contrast, however, one might also argue that the position ultimately taken by Congress has merit in that it avoids the administrative problems that might be involved in valuing benefits passing to an employee's family.

Not surprisingly, the enactment of Section 119 did not end disputes between taxpayers and the Service regarding the exclusion of meals and lodging. Rather, it focused attention on the "business premises," "condition of employment" and "convenience of employer" requirements. For example, in *Caratan v. Commissioner*[9] the Service contended that owner-employees of a farming corporation could not exclude the value of the living accommodations provided them because they had failed to establish that they were required to accept the lodging as a condition of their employment. The Tax Court agreed, noting that, since there was available housing in a residential area ten minutes from the farm, it was not necessary to the performance of their duties that the taxpayers live in the housing provided by their corporation. The Ninth Circuit, in reversing, relied on the regulations, which provide in relevant part:

---

[6] 17 T.C. 834 (1951).

[7] *Id.* at 838.

[8] 1959-2 C.B. 48.

[9] 442 F.2d 606 (9th Cir. 1971).

. . . [L]odging will be regarded as furnished to enable the employee properly to perform the duties of his employment when, for example, the *lodging is furnished because the employee is required to be available for duty at all times* or because the employee could not perform the services required of him unless he is furnished such lodging.[10]

The court stressed that pursuant to the regulation, it was enough for the taxpayer to establish that he was required to be available for duty at all times. "It is not necessary to show that the duties would be impossible to perform without such lodging being available." The availability of nearby housing was therefore irrelevant.

In *Commissioner v. Kowalski*,[11] the Supreme Court considered whether cash payments made to state police troopers as meal allowances were excludable under Section 119. The Court concluded that cash payments were not excludable under that section which, according to the Court, excluded only meals in kind. The taxpayer's reliance on the general convenience of employer doctrine developed in the case law was misplaced, according to the Court, because Section 119 places specific limitations on the exclusion for meals and lodging. As will be discussed below, occasional supper money is excludable as a *de minimis* fringe benefit.[12] That provision, however, and the regulations interpreting it would not be applicable to the meal allowance provided to the state troopers in *Kowalski* since it was regularly paid and thus could not be considered "occasional."

In sum, the convenience of employer doctrine, utilized first by the Service to exclude meals and lodging, has been codified in Section 119. The convenience of employer doctrine, however, has an existence beyond Section 119 as is demonstrated by the 1968 decision in *U.S. v. Gotcher*.[13] In that case, the court excluded the value to the taxpayer of a twelve-day, all-expenses-paid trip to Germany to tour the Volkswagen facilities there. Volkswagen, as part of a campaign to attract dealers for its cars, developed a program whereby prospective dealers were brought to Germany to inspect its manufacturing plants and to experience first hand the stability of post-war Germany. Although some of the time spent by the taxpayer on the trip was not business related, the dominant purpose of the trip was clearly business and not pleasure. The court viewed Volkswagen as the primary beneficiary of the program since the trip was designed to induce Gotcher to invest in a Volkswagen dealership. The benefits to the Gotchers were subordinate to the benefits to Volkswagen. Therefore, Gotcher had no income. The court, however, did find that the cost of the trip attributable to Mrs. Gotcher, who accompanied her husband, was income to him since the court considered her trip to be primarily a vacation.

---

[10] Treas. Reg. § 1.119-1(b) (emphasis added).

[11] 434 U.S. 77 (1977).

[12] I.R.C. § 132(a)(4).

[13] 401 F.2d 118 (5th Cir. 1968).

§ 11.02　FRINGE BENEFITS AND SECTION 132

The piecemeal approach Congress originally took with respect to fringe benefits is reflected in a number of other exclusion provisions. A non-exhaustive list of so-called "statutory fringe benefits" would include employee group term life insurance under $50,000 (Section 79); employer-provided accident and health benefits (Sections 105, 106(a)); group legal services (Section 120); and dependent care assistance programs (Section 129). Qualified retirement plans (Section 401 *et seq.*) constitute a particularly significant fringe benefit for many employees.

In addition to statutory fringe benefits, a host of non-statutory employer-provided fringe benefits existed, but generally were ignored by the Service or treated as nontaxable. For example, in 1921, the Service ruled that "personal transportation passes issued by a railroad company to its employees and their families . . . are considered gifts and the value does not constitute taxable income to the employees."[14]

The Service's hands-off approach to non-statutory fringe benefits invited employers and employees to negotiate compensation packages laden with "nontaxable" fringe benefits. Both the employer and the employee benefitted from such arrangements — on the one hand, it was typically cheaper for the employer to provide fringe benefits than to increase employee's salaries; on the other hand, the employee receiving fringe benefits was able to satisfy certain personal needs or desires without any tax cost. The only loser was the federal fisc. Yet, it was not until the early 1970s that Treasury finally moved to address the tax status of fringe benefits. By that time, the notion that most nonstatutory fringe benefits were nontaxable was firmly entrenched. The Treasury's regulatory efforts were sufficiently controversial that they were blocked by a congressional moratorium on fringe benefit regulations. It was not until 1984 that Congress enacted the first comprehensive treatment of fringe benefits.

The centerpiece of the fringe benefit legislation of 1984 is Section 132. Initially recognizing four categories of excludable fringe benefits, Section 132 today lists eight categories of excludable benefits: (1) no-additional-cost service; (2) qualified employee discount; (3) working condition fringe; (4) *de minimis* fringe; (5) qualified transportation fringe; (6) qualified moving expense reimbursement; (7) qualified retirement planning services; and (8) qualified military base realignment and closure fringe.[15]

[A]　No-Additional-Cost Service

§ 132.　Certain fringe benefits.

(b)　No-additional-cost service defined. — For purposes of this section, the term "no-additional-cost service" means any service provided by an employer to an employee for use by such employee if —

---

[14]　O.D. 946, 4 C.B. 110 (1920).

[15]　Qualified moving expense reimbursement is discussed in detail in Chapter 19, *infra*, and will not be discussed here. Qualified retirement planning services and qualified military base realignment and closure will not be discussed in this text.

(1) such service is offered for sale to customers in the ordinary course of the line of business of the employer in which the employee is performing services and

(2) the employer incurs no substantial additional cost (including forgone revenue) in providing such service to the employee (determined without regard to any amount paid by the employee for such service).

Congress recognized that companies engaged in the airline, railroad, or hotel businesses often have excess capacity (*e.g.*, extra seats on a scheduled airline flight) which will remain unused for lack of paying customers. As a result, such businesses commonly make their excess capacity available free of charge to employees and their families. Because there is essentially no cost incurred by the employer in allowing an employee to occupy an otherwise empty seat on a company aircraft or an empty room in a hotel, Congress opted to exclude from income the entire value of such services, subject to a number of restrictions.

First, the service must be one offered for sale to customers in the ordinary course of business. For example, if an employee of a corporation has personal business in Emerald City and the company allows the employee to occupy an otherwise empty seat on the corporate jet which is being flown to Emerald City for business reasons, the benefit enjoyed by the employee fails the "for sale to customers" standard.

A second requirement contained in Section 132(b)(1) is the line of business requirement. This requirement is best explained by the following excerpt from the legislative history:

> Under this limitation, for example, an employer which provides airline services and hotel services to the general public is considered to consist of two separate lines of business. As a consequence, the employees of the airline business of the employer may not exclude the value of free hotel rooms provided by the hotel business of the employer and vice versa. The purpose of the line of business limitation is to avoid, to the extent possible, the competitive imbalances and inequities which would result from giving the employees of a conglomerate or other large employer with several lines of business a greater variety of tax free benefits than could be given to the employees of a small employer with only one line of business. Thus, small businesses will not be disadvantaged in their ability to compete with large businesses providing the same goods or services. . . .[16]

While this requirement is easily applied to the employees of the airline business in the legislative history example, a problem may arise if an employee does work for more than one line of the business. The regulations provide that the performance of substantial services directly benefitting more than one line of business is treated as the performance of substantial services in all such lines of business.[17] Thus, an accountant who does all of the accounting work for both the airline and the hotel divisions of a company will be deemed employed in each line of the airline's business,

---

[16] H.R. Rep. 98–432, 98th Cong., 2d Sess., p. 1594–95 (1984).

[17] Treas. Reg. § 1.132-4(a)(1)(iv).

thereby qualifying the free travel and hotel accommodations provided the accountant for exclusion under the no-additional-cost standard.

Section 132(b)(2) provides a third requirement, *i.e.*, that the employer incur no substantial additional cost (including forgone revenue). "[F]or purposes of determining whether any revenue is forgone, it is assumed that the employee would not have purchased the service unless it were available to the employee at the actual price charged to the employee."[18] Permitting airline employees to take personal flights at no charge and to receive reserved seats results in forgone revenue (from the reserved seats which are no longer available for sale to the public); therefore employees receiving the free flights are not eligible for the no-additional-cost exclusion.[19] Section 132(b)(2) also provides that whether an employer incurs any substantial additional cost be determined without regard to any amount which an employee might be required to pay. Thus, employee payment does not serve to transform an employer-provided service into a "no-additional-cost" service, although such payment may obviously be quite relevant in measuring the income, if any, the employee receives from the employer's provision of the service. Finally, note that the statute refers to "substantial" additional costs. The cost of services "merely incidental" to the primary service, such as the housekeeping costs associated with maintenance of hotel rooms or the cost of an additional airline meal, are generally not "substantial."[20]

It is also worth noting that the regulations, after listing several "excess capacity services" that qualify as no-additional-cost services, specifically state that non-excess capacity services, which do not so qualify, may nonetheless be fully or partially excluded from income under the "qualified employee discount" rules discussed below.[21]

A fourth requirement is contained in Section 132(j)(1) which prohibits discrimination in favor of highly compensated employees, a term which, as defined in Section 414(q), can include officers and owners.[22] If the nondiscrimination rule is violated, only the members of the highly compensated group, rather than all employees receiving benefits, will be subject to tax.[23]

Section 132(i) provides a special rule authorizing reciprocal agreements between employers in the same line of business, thus enabling the employers to provide tax-free benefits to one another's employees. Such reciprocal agreements must be in writing and the employers may not incur any substantial additional costs (including forgone revenues) in providing such services. This rule resulted in part from the lobbying efforts of airline flight attendants who had come to depend on interline passes which enable many attendants to "commute" by air to their jobs.

---

[18] Treas. Reg. § 1.132-2(a)(5).

[19] Treas. Reg. § 1.132-2(c).

[20] Treas. Reg. § 1.132-2(a)(5)(ii).

[21] Treas. Reg. § 1.132-2(a)(2).

[22] *See* Treas. Reg. § 1.132-8(a)(1).

[23] Treas. Reg. § 1.132-8(a)(2).

The exclusion of no-additional-cost services is limited to services provided "employees." Section 132(f) defines employee to include one's spouse and dependent children as well as certain retired and disabled employees and the surviving spouse of a deceased employee. Section 132(h)(3) provides a special rule treating the use of air transportation by the parent of an employee as use by the employee. Section 132(j)(5) also provides favorable treatment for affiliates of airlines.

> **Example:** Fred is a flight attendant for Blue Sky Airline. The airline provides free travel on a standby basis to Fred and Fred's parents. The value of the free trips taken by Fred's parents are excludable from Fred's income.

In *Charley v. Commissioner*,[24] the taxpayer argued that Section 132(a)(1) excluded from income amounts he received for frequent flyer miles he converted to cash. Taxpayer was president of a company engaged in a business which investigated the causes of industrial accidents. The taxpayer and his wife owned a majority of the shares in the company. In his capacity as an employee of the company, the taxpayer traveled to various accident sites. The company had an "unwritten policy" that frequent flyer miles earned by an employee as a result of travel for the company became the sole property of the employee.

When a client's work required the taxpayer to travel by air, the company charged the client for a round-trip, first class ticket. The taxpayer would instruct the company's travel agent to arrange round-trip coach service to the destination but to charge the company for first class travel. The taxpayer would then use his frequent flyer miles, most of which were earned on company travel, to upgrade the coach ticket to first class. The taxpayer would instruct the travel agent to transfer funds to his personal travel account in an amount equal to the difference between the coach ticket and the amount which the company was charged for the round-trip first class ticket. The Service argued that the funds credited to the taxpayer's personal travel account constituted taxable income.

Rejecting the taxpayer's novel argument that the amounts credited represented a "no-additional-cost service," excludable under Section 132(a)(1), the court noted that the taxpayer's company did not offer frequent flyer miles for sale to customers in the ordinary course of its business. (The court specifically refused to reach the issue of whether the frequent flyer miles which the company allowed the taxpayer to keep in and of themselves constituted gross income.) Instead, the court concluded that either the travel credit arrangement represented additional compensation to the taxpayer from his company or the taxpayer had simply sold his frequent flyer miles in which he had a zero basis. Under either analysis, the amount credited to his personal travel fund constituted gross income.

In what may reflect administrative realities, however, the Service has announced it will not seek to tax the receipt or personal use of frequent flyer miles or other in-kind promotion benefits attributable to business travel, and any future guidance it may provide will be applied prospectively.[25]

---

[24] 91 F.3d 72 (9th Cir. 1996).

[25] Announcement 2002-18, 2002-1 C.B. 621.

[B]   Qualified Employee Discount

§ 132.   Certain fringe benefits.

(c)   Qualified employee discount defined. — For purposes of this section —

(1)   Qualified employee discount. —   The term "qualified employee discount" means any employee discount with respect to qualified property or services to the extent such discount does not exceed —

(A) in the case of property, the gross profit percentage of the price at which the property is being offered by the employer to customers, or

(B) in the case of services, 20 percent of the price at which the services are being offered by the employer to customers.. . .

(3)   Employee discount defined. The term "employee discount" means the amount by which —

(A) the price at which the property or services are provided by the employer to an employee for use by such employee, is less than

(B) the price at which such property or services are being offered by the employer to customers.

(4)   Qualified property or services. — The term "qualified property or services" means any property (other than real property and other than personal property of a kind held for investment) or services which are offered for sale to customers in the ordinary course of the line of business of the employer in which the employee is performing services.

The exclusion for qualified employee discounts reflects congressional recognition of the long-standing practice of businesses to provide discounts to their employees on the same goods and services they sell to the general public. Retailers appeared before the congressional subcommittee considering the fringe benefit legislation and argued for continuation of the exclusion of discounts on goods and services which employees enjoyed. The following excerpt suggests the kind of concerns which Congress addressed in enacting the legislation:

> Providing discounts stimulates a company's sales to a natural group of customers who might not otherwise buy as much of the company's merchandise. Since the discounted price generally is higher than the employer's cost, by offering employees a discount, a company can increase overall sales as well as profits. . . .

> Providing discounts to employees serves another important interest of the employer — namely the stimulation of sales to the general public. By encouraging employees to purchase the employer's merchandise, employee discounts help the employer to educate his employees about the merchandise he sells. Employees who have had personal experience with the store's merchandise make more effective sales persons; their morale is higher, and they are often more loyal advocates of their employer and his goods. . . . In addition, providing employee discounts is an effective means to advertise a store's merchandise. Seeing a salesperson wearing apparel and accessories sold at the store may encourage customers to try on and purchase similar goods. Finally, providing employee discounts causes an effective

stimulus to sales by a "multiplier effect." This effect results from employees being accompanied on shopping trips by others who become customers as a result of the trip.

Employee discounts have not been taxed since the income tax was enacted in 1913. Unlike wages which compensate employees for services rendered, employee discounts bear no relationship to job performance. The value of the discount to any individual employee depends not on the quality of his or her job performance but on the quantity of his or her purchase. Accordingly, employee discounts do not constitute compensation and should not be treated as such for tax purposes.

. . . Moreover, a change in policy to impose a tax on employee discounts would also raise a difficult question of valuation. . . . [F]air market value is fraught with numerous deficiencies. It is not always readily or clearly determinable. The objective dollar value of a discount simply does not accurately measure its real value. For example, comparable merchandise may be available at a promotional sale or at a nearby store at the same or even a lower net price than the employee pays with the discount. If store X's $100 item is regularly available in store Y for $75, why should an employee recognize income if X permits him or her to buy the item for $75 (a 25% discount). It is difficult in a case such as this to identify the value that is being taxed.[26]

Section 132(c) limits the amount of discount which will be excludable and provides separate limitations for property and for services. The exclusion for employee discounts on services is limited to 20% of the price at which the services are being offered by the employer to customers. By contrast, the exclusion for employee discounts on property is limited to the gross profit percentage which is the excess of the aggregate sales price for the property sold by the employer over the aggregate cost of such property to the employer, divided by the aggregate sales price. Consider the following example provided by the legislative history:

. . . [I]f total sales of . . . merchandise during a year were $1,000,000 and the employer's cost for the merchandise was $600,000, then the gross profit percentage for the year is 40% [$1,000,000 minus $600,000 equals $400,000 which is 40% of $1,000,000]. Thus, an employee discount with respect to such merchandise is excluded from income to the extent it does not exceed 40% of the selling price of the merchandise to nonemployee customers. If in this case the discount allowed to the employee exceeds 40% (for example 50%), the excess discount on a purchase (10% in the example) is included in the employee's gross income.[27]

Section 132(c)(4) defines "qualified property or services." Note that the definition contains the same "for sale to customers" and "line of business" requirements of

---

[26] Testimony of Mr. Dexter Tight, Senior Vice President and General Counsel of the GAP Stories, Inc. on Behalf of the national Retail Merchants Association on H.R. 3525, "Permanent Tax Treatment of Fringe Benefits Act," Before the Ways and Means Subcommittee on Select Revenue Measures (August 1, 1983).

[27] H.R. 98–432, 98th Cong., 2d Sess., p.1599.

Section 132(b). In addition, note that real property and personal property held for investment do not qualify for the Section 132(c) exclusion. For example, the exclusion would not apply to employee purchases of stocks or bonds, gold coins or residential and commercial real estate. In imposing this limitation, Congress explained that it was concerned that such property could typically be sold by employees "at close to the same price at which the employer sells the property to its nonemployee customers."[28]

The scope of the term "employee" as used in Section 132(c) is the same as that in Section 132(b), and the anti-discrimination rules applicable to the no-additional-cost service exclusion are also applicable to the qualified employee discount exclusion.[29] Note, however, that the reciprocal agreement rules of Section 132(i) are not applicable to qualified employee discounts.

> **Example:** Fred, a Blue Sky flight attendant and his parents, spouse and children are entitled to a 50% discount on any reserved seat purchased by them on a regularly scheduled Blue Sky flight. Fred's child flies to New York on Blue Sky and saves 50% on his ticket which would normally have cost $500. Thus, the child saved $250.

> **Analysis:** The child is treated as an employee for purposes of both the no-additional cost and qualified employee discount rules.[30] The no-additional-cost rule, however, is inapplicable because the seat is reserved. Regulation Section 1.132-2(c) provides that the airline forgoes potential revenue under these circumstances and therefore the benefit doesn't fall within the no-additional-cost rule. However, Regulation Section 1.132-2(a)(2) provides that the employee may be eligible to claim a qualified employee discount of up to 20% of the value provided. Regulation Section 1.132-3(e) provides a specific example confirming that Fred may exclude 20% of the value of his child's ticket or $100. The other $150 of the discount provided will be income to Fred.[31]

[C]　Working Condition Fringe

§ 132.　Certain fringe benefits.

(d)　Working condition fringe defined. — For purpose of this section, the term "working condition fringe" means any property or services provided to any employee of the employer to the extent that, if the employee paid for such property or services, such payment would be allowable as a deduction under section 162 or 167.

---

[28] *Id.* at 1597.

[29] *See* I.R.C. § 132(j)(1). A special rule treats the leased section of a department store as part of the line of business of the person operating the department store treats employees in the leased section as employees of that person. I.R.C. § 132(j)(2).

[30] I.R.C. § 132(h)(2).

[31] Treas. Reg. § 1.61-21(a)(4). The fact that the income will be taxed to Fred should be emphasized. The benefit provided is in the nature of compensation to the employee, Fred. Although the benefit may be enjoyed or consumed by a family member or other third party, the benefit arises out of the employment relationship, and is taxable to the employee.

Employers typically provide their employees with all the tools, office space, and supplies they need. In addition, the employer may provide necessary transportation, subscriptions to current literature in the employee's particular field, and other property or services to facilitate the employee's work. Such property and services are so closely connected to job performance that were the employee, rather than the employer, to pay for them, the employee would be entitled to deduct their cost as a business expense. Thus, when they are provided by the employer, they should not be considered compensation to the employee. Indeed, Congress in Section 132(a)(3) has excluded these so-called "working condition fringe benefits." The anti-discrimination rules do not apply to working condition fringe benefits since, for example, it may be appropriate to provide a well appointed office for the president of a business but not provide such an office for other employees.

The regulations provide that cash payments to the employee do not qualify as working condition fringe benefits unless the employee is required to use the payments for expenses incurred in a specific or pre-arranged qualifying activity, verify such use, and return any excess to the employer.[32] Rules are also provided for determining the working condition fringe benefit portion of vehicle usage, where an employee uses an employer-provided vehicle for both business and personal purposes.[33] Consumer product testing, *i.e.,* the use by employees of employer-manufactured consumer goods, such as automobiles, for testing and evaluation outside the employer's office, was an area of some particular concern to Congress, and the regulations, drawing on legislative history to Section 132, delineate the requirements for such employee use to qualify as a working condition fringe.[34]

In Revenue Ruling 92-69[35] the Service concluded that employer-provided outplacement services were excludable by employees as working condition fringe benefits. According to the ruling, "if [an] employer . . . derives a substantial business benefit from the provision of such outplacement services that is distinct from the benefit it would derive from the mere payment of additional compensation, such as promoting a positive corporate image, maintaining employee morale, and avoiding wrongful termination suits, the service may generally be treated as a working condition fringe."[36]

In one case, the Eighth Circuit held that the annual fishing trip provided by the taxpayer to its employees constituted a working condition fringe benefit, excludable from employee income and deductible to the employer as a business expense. Following its annual two-day meeting, the taxpayer sponsored a four-day, expense-paid fishing trip to a resort in Canada. The testimony indicated that, although the trips were voluntary, nearly all employees felt an obligation to attend. There was also considerable testimony regarding the business discussions that took place among those attending. The court concluded that the taxpayer "had a realistic expectation to gain concrete benefits from the trip based on its knowledge of its own

---

[32] Treas. Reg. § 1.132-5(a)(1)(v).

[33] Treas. Reg. § 1.132-5(b).

[34] Treas. Reg. § 1.132-5(n).

[35] 1992-2 C.B. 51.

[36] *Id.* at 53.

small company, its knowledge of the utility of interpersonal interactions that probably would not occur but for the trip, and its knowledge of its own past experience."[37]

[D]   De Minimis Fringe Benefits

§ 132.   Certain fringe benefits.

(e)   De minimis fringe defined. — For purposes of this section —

(1)   In general. — The term "de minimis fringe" means any property or service the value of which is (after taking into account the frequency with which similar fringes are provided by the employer to the employer's employees) so small as to make accounting for it unreasonable or administratively impracticable.

Reflecting a congressional desire for administrative convenience, Section 132(a)(4) excludes "*de minimis* fringe benefits," which are defined in Section 132(e). Note the emphasis placed on "frequency" as a factor for determining whether a benefit is *de minimis*. Note also that unlike no-additional-cost service, qualified employee discount, and working condition fringe, the *de minimis* exception does not necessitate an employer-employee relationship between the provider and recipient. Thus, for example, benefits received by a director of a corporation may constitute excludable *de minimis* fringe benefits.

The regulations provide special rules for excluding as *de minimis* fringe benefits meals and occasional meal money.[38] The regulations also list a variety of common benefits that do or do not qualify as *de minimis*.[39] For example, occasional cocktail parties, picnics for employees and their guests, flowers provided to employees at time of sickness or family crisis — all are excludable as *de minimis* fringe benefits. By contrast, season tickets to theater or sporting events or the use of an employer-owned facility such as a hunting lodge for a weekend are not excluable as *de minimis* fringe benefits. *De minimis* fringe status is explicitly denied to any cash or cash equivalent benefits, other than those allowed by the special rules.[40] The anti-discrimination rules do not apply to *de minimis* fringe benefits.

[E]   Qualified Transportation Fringe

§ 132.   Certain fringe benefits.

(f)   Qualified transportation fringe —

(1)   In general. For purposes of this section, the term "qualified transportation fringe" means any of the following provided by an employer to an employee:

(A) Transportation in a commuter highway vehicle if such transportation is in connection with travel between the employee's residence and place of

---

[37] Townsend Industries v. United States, 342 F.3d 890 (8th Cir. 2003).

[38] Treas. Reg. § 1.132-6(d)(2).

[39] Treas. Reg. § 1.132-6(e).

[40] Treas. Reg. § 1.132-6(c).

employment.

      (B) Any transit pass.

      (C) Qualified parking.

      (D) Any qualified bicycle commuting reimbursement...

    (5) Definitions. For purposes of this subsection —

      (C) Qualified parking. — The term "qualified parking" means parking provided to an employee on or near the business premises of the employer or on or near a location from which the employee commutes to work by transportation described in subparagraph (A) [mass transit facilities], in a commuter highway vehicle, or by carpool. Such term shall not include any parking on or near property used by the employee for residential purposes.

Section 132(a)(5) excludes from income "qualified transportation fringe" benefits. A qualified transportation fringe is (1) transportation in a commuter highway vehicle in connection with travel between the employee's residence and place of employment; (2) a transit pass; (3) qualified parking; or (4) qualified bicycle commuting reimbursement.[41] The Code defines each of these terms.[42] Cash reimbursements for these items are also excludable.[43] The exclusion, however, is subject to specified dollar limitations. Thus, the Code limits the aggregate excludable benefits in the nature of transit passes or transportation in a commuter highway vehicle in connection with travel between taxpayer's residence and place of employment to $100 per month. Qualified parking is limited to $175 per month. These figures are adjusted annually for inflation.[44] Bicycle commuting reimbursement is $20 per month.[45]

Qualified parking includes parking on or near the employee's business premises but specifically does not include parking on or near property used by the employee for residential purposes.[46]

> **Example:** Cathy lives in a plush apartment on Park Avenue in New York City and works in an investment banking business located ten blocks away. The business pays the $400 per month parking rental for Cathy's vehicle in the garage located across the street from Cathy's apartment. Cathy either walks to work or takes a taxi.

> **Analysis:** Cathy's parking is not "qualified parking" within the meaning of Section 132(f)(5)(C) and therefore no part of the amount paid by Cathy's employer for Cathy's parking rental is excludable as a qualified transportation fringe.

---

[41] I.R.C. § 132(f)(1).

[42] I.R.C. § 132(f)(5)(A)–(C), (F).

[43] I.R.C. § 132(f)(3).

[44] I.R.C. § 132(f)(2), (6). But note that on a temporary basis, currently through the year 2013 unless retroactively extended, the exclusion limit for transit passes and commuter highway vehicles is increased to be the same as the qualified parking limit, an inflation-adjusted $245 for 2013. I.R.C. § 132(j)(2) (flush language).

[45] I.R.C. § 132(f)(5)(F).

[46] I.R.C. § 132(f)(5)(C).

[F] On-Premises Gyms and Other Athletic Facilities

Congressional concern for employee health is reflected in the special exclusion provided in Section 132(j)(4) for on-premises athletic facilities provided by the employer. The exclusion is applicable, however, only if the use of such facilities is limited to employees, their spouses and their dependent children.[47]

§ 11.03 VALUATION

Fringe benefits that are not excluded from income under Section 132 or another section of the Code are, of course, subject to tax pursuant to Section 61(a)(1). The regulations make clear that the measure of income is the fair market value of the fringe benefit, less any excludable portion of the fringe benefit and any amount paid by the recipient.[48] Special, and extensive, valuation rules are provided, however, with respect to employer-provided vehicles, chauffeur services, commercial and non-commercial air travel, and eating facilities. As noted previously, the regulations explicitly tax the value of the fringe benefit to the employee, even though the benefit may actually be received by someone else.[49]

---

[47] I.R.C. § 132(j)(4)(B)(iii).

[48] Treas. Reg. § 1.61-21(b)(1).

[49] Treas. Reg. § 1.61-21(a)(4).

Chapter 12

BUSINESS AND PROFIT SEEKING EXPENSES

The business deduction of Section 162 and the "profit-seeking" deduction of Section 212 reflect the principles that (1) "net income," rather than gross income, should be subject to tax; and (2) expenses necessary to the earning of items of gross income generally ought to be allowed as deductions. There are two notable exceptions. First, "personal" expenses — those expenses not within the business or profit-seeking classification — generally will not be deductible in determining the net income subject to tax.[1] Second, some expenditures are regarded as "capital expenditures" because they were made to obtain an asset or benefit that lasts for some substantial or indefinite period of time. For that reason, capital expenditures of the business or profit-seeking type generally may not be deducted in full at the time of the expenditure. Rather, they must be deducted in increments over some period, or perhaps deducted, in effect, only on disposition of the asset when the asset's adjusted basis is subtracted from the amount realized to determine gain or loss.[2] This chapter focuses on the line between business or profit-seeking expenses on the one hand, and personal expenses on the other.

§ 12.01 BUSINESS DEDUCTIONS — SECTION 162

§ 162. Trade or business expenses —

(a) In general — There shall be allowed as a deduction all the ordinary and necessary expenses paid or incurred during the taxable year in carrying on any trade or business . . . .

While courts have historically viewed deductions as a matter of legislative grace,[3] the fact is that Congress has authorized deductions for most expenses incurred in producing income. The Internal Revenue Code taxes gain, profit or net income — not gross receipts. The Section 61(a)(2) language "gross income derived from business" has been interpreted to mean "the total sales, less the cost of goods sold."[4] For example, if a retailer pays $10,000 for the inventory she sells to the public for $20,000, her gross income is not $20,000, but $10,000. Similarly, if a house painter is paid $25,000 for his services but pays $5,000 for the paint he uses, he will be taxed on $20,000 and not $25,000, i.e., his gross income will be $25,000, but he will be entitled to deduct the $5,000 paint cost. Section 162 supports the painter's deduction for the paint costs.

---

[1] I.R.C. § 262(a).

[2] See Chapter 13, *infra*, for a complete discussion of capital expenditures.

[3] *See, e.g.*, Interstate Transit Lines v. Comm'r, 319 U.S. 590 (1943).

[4] Treas. Reg. § 1.61-3(a).

Section 162 is the business deduction workhorse of the Code; more dollars are deducted on the authority of this provision than any other in the Internal Revenue Code. Most Section 162 deductions may be taken "above the line" (that is, they are deducted in computing adjusted gross income, and may therefore be taken regardless of whether the taxpayer itemizes or claims the standard deduction). As a result, they are generally not subject to the Section 67 limitation on certain itemized deductions.[5]

The first 27 words of Section 162(a) establish a number of significant requirements for the deduction of costs associated with a business: (1) the cost must be an "expense"; (2) the expense must be "ordinary"; (3) it must be "necessary"; (4) it must be "paid or incurred during the taxable year"; and (5) it must be paid or incurred in "carrying on" a "trade or business." Whether a cost constitutes an "expense" (as opposed to a capital expenditure) will be considered in the next chapter. Requirement (4) relates to timing and will be discussed in Chapters 28 and 29. The "ordinary and necessary" and "carrying on a trade or business" requirements will be considered in detail in this chapter.

[A] The Expense Must be "Ordinary and Necessary"

[1] Is the Expense "Ordinary"?

The Supreme Court considered the meaning of the term "ordinary" in *Welch v. Helvering*.[6] The taxpayer in that case had been employed by a company that became bankrupt and was discharged from its debts. The taxpayer established his own business, providing the same services as his former employer. To "strengthen his own standing and credit" in reestablishing relations with customers of his former employer, the taxpayer began to pay the former employer's discharged debts. The tax question was whether such payments were deductible business expenses under the predecessor of Section 162. According to the Court, the term "ordinary" requires that a cost be customary or expected in the life of a business. As to what is customary or expected in a business, the Court stated that, "Life in all its fullness must supply the answer . . . ." The Court in *Welch v. Helvering* found that the "fullness of life" indicated business people did not "ordinarily" make payments such as those in question, but the Court's decision raised more questions than it answered. The case may be viewed merely as a failure of proof case — that is, the taxpayer simply failed to provide evidence that business people in his situation would act as he did — or it may suggest that taxpayers may not deduct payments they are not legally obligated to pay.

In *Jenkins v. Commissioner*,[7] however, the Tax Court allowed country songwriter and singer, Harold L. Jenkins, whose stage name was Conway Twitty, to deduct as a business expense amounts he repaid to investors in his defunct fast food venture, Twitty Burgers, Inc. Jenkins argued that he repaid investors to protect his

---

[5] Above- and below-the-line deductions, as well as the Section 67 limitation, are discussed in Chapter 1, *infra*.

[6] 290 U.S. 111 (1933).

[7] T.C. Memo 1983-667.

business as a country singer and performer. Testifying regarding his motivation for repaying the Twitty Burger investors, Jenkins stated:

> I'm 99 percent entertainer. That's just about all I know. The name Conway Twitty, and the image that I worked so hard for since 1955 and 1956 is the foundation that I, my family and the 30 some odd people that work for me stand on. They depend on it and they can depend on it.
>
> . . . I handled it that way . . . because of the image. And second . . . I handled it that way because I think it is morally right, and if you owe a man something, you pay him.
>
> . . . When we got the letter from Walter Beach and from [Merle] Haggard's lawyer . . . my people said, hey, you know, we've got some letters from people saying they are going to sue you, and that you might have done something wrong as far as securities and all that stuff goes. It just scares you to death.
>
> . . . A lawsuit like that with — say Merle Haggard sued Conway Twitty . . . and you're in court and they are saying it's fraud and something to do with the securities thing, and, you know, all the years I've worked for are gone. If my fans didn't give up on me, it would warp me psychologically. I couldn't function any more because I'm the type of person I am.

Expert testimony on Jenkins' behalf was presented by the Director of the Country Music Foundation in Nashville. He testified that:

> Had . . . Conway Twitty allowed investors to be left dangling with heavy losses following the collapse of the Twitty Burgers chain, the multiple lawsuits, unfavorable news stories and disgruntled investors would have all damaged the very reputation which was a key element in Conway's image as an artist. Though he would have continued to perform . . . there exists serious doubt that he would have achieved the unparalleled success he enjoyed during the 1970's had his reputation been so injured.[8]

---

[8] Judge Irwin closed his opinion in *Jenkins* with the following "Ode to Conway Twitty":

Twitty Burgers went belly up
But Conway remained true
He repaid his investors, one and all
It was the moral thing to do.
His fans would not have liked it
It could have hurt his fame
Had any investors sued him
Like Merle Haggard and Sonny James.
When it was time to file taxes
Conway thought what he would do
Was deduct those payments as a business expense
Under section one-sixty-two.
In order to allow these deductions
Goes the argument of the Commissioner
The payments must be ordinary and necessary
To a business of the petitioner.
Had Conway not repaid the investors
His career would have been under cloud,
Under the unique facts of this case
Held: The deductions are allowed.

Apparently, the Tax Court viewed *Welch v. Helvering* as a failure-of-proof case. By contrast to the taxpayer in *Welch*, Conway Twitty provided enough evidence to justify a business deduction for amounts he repaid those who invested in Twitty Burgers.

In *Welch v. Helvering*, the Supreme Court also appeared to give a second meaning to the Section 162 term "ordinary." "Ordinary" expenses are apparently to be distinguished from capital expenditures such as reputation (goodwill) or learning. *Welch* could also have been decided on the basis that the costs in question were capital expenditures in the nature of goodwill.[9]

In *Deputy v. Dupont*,[10] decided subsequent to *Welch*, the Supreme Court's discussion of "ordinary" was somewhat more illuminating:

> Ordinary has the connotation of normal, usual or customary. To be sure, an expense may be ordinary though it happens but once in the taxpayer's lifetime . . . . Yet the transaction which gives rise to it must be of common or frequent occurrence in the type of business involved . . . . Hence, the fact that a particular expense would be an ordinary or common one in the course of one business and so deductible . . . does not necessarily make it such in connection with another business . . . . As stated in *Welch v. Helvering*, ". . . [w]hat is ordinary, though there must always be a strain of constancy within it, is nonetheless a variable affected by time and place and circumstance." One of the extremely relevant circumstances is the nature and scope of the particular business out of which the expense in question accrued. The fact that an obligation to pay has arisen is not sufficient. It is the kind of transaction out of which the obligation arose and its normalcy

---

In a poetic riposte, the Service responded to the opinion as follows:

> Our reaction to the Court's opinion is reflected in the following "Ode to Conway Twitty: A Reprise":

Harold Jenkins and Conway Twitty
They are both the same
But one was born
The other achieved fame.
The man is talented
And has many a friend
They opened a restaurant
His name he did lend.
They are two different things
Making burgers and song
The business went sour
It didn't take long.
He repaid his friends
Why did he act
Was it business or friendship
Which is fact?
Business the court held
It's deductible they feel
We disagree with the answer
But let's not appeal.
Recommendation: Nonacquiescence.

AOD 1984-022.

[9] See Chapter 13, *infra*, for a discussion of capital expenditures.

[10] 308 U.S. 488, 495–496 (1940).

in the particular business which are crucial and controlling.[11]

A quarter of a century later, in *Commissioner v. Tellier*, 383 U.S. 687 (1966), in allowing a deduction for legal expenses incurred by a taxpayer in defending himself in a criminal action, the Court noted: "[t]he principal function of the term 'ordinary' in § 162(a) is to clarify the distinction, often difficult, between those expenses that are currently deductible and those that are in the nature of capital expenditures, which, if deductible at all, must be amortized over the useful life of the asset . . . The legal expenses deducted by the respondent were not capital expenditures. They were incurred in his defense against charges of past criminal conduct, not in the acquisition of a capital asset. Our decisions establish that counsel fees comparable to those here involved are ordinary business expenses, even though a 'lawsuit affecting the safety of a business may happen once in a lifetime.' "

While determining whether costs incurred in day-to-day conduct of a business are "ordinary" is generally easy, the courts and the Service nonetheless regularly encounter cases demanding careful consideration.

For example, in *Goedel v. Commissioner*,[12] a New York securities firm purchased a term insurance policy on the life of President Franklin Roosevelt, seeking to secure its large inventory of stock from loss should the death of the President occasion a fall in stock prices. The firm deducted the insurance premiums as a business expense. The Service challenged the deduction. The Board of Tax Appeals concluded the premiums paid by a securities firm on a life insurance policy covering President Roosevelt were not deductible. The court doubted other businesses "accustomed to buying insurance in connection with their business" would use funds to purchase an insurance policy of the nature acquired by the firm. If a securities firm presented the same case today, would *Goedel* mean the firm could never deduct the premium? Would an insurance company even issue to kind of policy issued in *Goedel*? If it did, the taxpayer seeking to deduct the premiums could make a forceful argument that merely because an expenditure is unprecedented in a business is not reason enough to find that it is not "ordinary" and therefore not deductible under Section 162.

In *Gilliam v. Commissioner*,[13] the taxpayer, an artist with a history of mental and emotional problems, created a major disturbance on an airline while flying to Memphis to lecture and teach. The taxpayer, who was indicted for violating certain federal criminal statutes and sued by a passenger whom he injured, sought to deduct as business expenses (1) the legal fees incurred in defending the criminal action and (2) the settlement paid to the injured passenger. Disallowing the claimed deductions, the Tax Court reasoned that artists and teachers while traveling on business do not generally engage in conduct like the taxpayer's; the costs incurred were not part of the taxpayer's transportation costs and the actions of the taxpayer aboard the aircraft did not further the taxpayer's trade or business. In short, the taxpayer's costs were not "ordinary" within the meaning of Section 162.

---

[11] *Id.* at 495–6.

[12] 29 B.T.A. 1 (1939).

[13] T.C. Memo 1986-81.

The Tax Court in *Gilliam* distinguished its decision in *Dancer v. Commissioner*[14] allowing a deduction for the costs incurred by a taxpayer in settling a negligence action arising from an automobile accident that occurred while he was traveling on business. The *Dancer* court noted:

> It is true that the expenditure in the instant case did not further petitioner's business in any economic sense; nor is it, we hope, the type of expenditure that many businesses are called upon to pay. Nevertheless, neither factor lessens the direct relationship between the expenditure and the business. Automobile travel by petitioner was an integral part of this business. As rising insurance rates suggest, the cost of fuel and routine servicing are not the only costs one can expect in operating a car. As unfortunate as it may be, lapses by drivers seem to be an inseparable incident of driving a car . . . . Costs incurred as a result of such an incident are just as much a part of overall business expenses as the cost of fuel.[15]

By contrast, Gilliam, while a passenger on a plane, committed acts that, but for his successful temporary insanity defense, would have been criminal. Such acts cannot be said to be "inseparable incidents" of traveling on an airplane. The Tax Court in *Gilliam* emphasized that the taxpayer's "activities were not directly in the conduct of his trades or businesses" but "merely occurred in the course of transportation connected with Gilliam's trades or businesses." Quoting from *Dancer*, the Tax Court noted "in cases like this where the cost is an adjunct of and not a direct cost of transporting an individual, we have not felt obliged to routinely allow the expenditure as a transportation costs deduction."[16]

[2] Is the Expense "Necessary"?

In *Welch v. Helvering*, the Court interpreted the term "necessary" to mean "appropriate and helpful" and indicated it would be slow to "override" the judgment of a business person regarding the necessity of any costs incurred. Given the *Welch* interpretation of the "necessary" standard, it is not surprising that few cases have focused on the determination of whether a cost was "necessary." In *Palo Alto Town & Country Village, Inc. v. Commissioner*,[17] the Ninth Circuit reversed a Tax Court decision holding the cost incurred in having an airplane on a standby basis was not an ordinary and necessary expense. The Tax Court found the taxpayers' evidence regarding the necessity of having a plane available was inconsistent with the business taxpayers actually conducted. The court concluded the taxpayers "did not use the airplane with sufficient frequency to justify the expense of maintaining it on a permanent standby basis as ordinary and necessary for the conduct of [their] business."[18] The Ninth Circuit, however, noted ". . . the Tax Court didn't deny that on one occasion the immediate availability of the plane, arising from its standby status, led to a saving of almost $1,000,000 in interest on a

---

[14] 73 T.C. 1103 (1980).

[15] *Id.* at 1108–09.

[16] T.C. Memo 1986-81.

[17] 565 F.2d 1388 (9th Cir. 1977).

[18] T.C. Memo 1973-223.

loan, or that not having the plane on standby would result in delays in getting Palo Alto personnel back home from their business trips, or that chartering a plane and keeping it on standby would be much more expensive than taxpayers' standby arrangement."[19] According to the Ninth Circuit, the facts indicated that the cost incurred in having a plane "on a standby basis was certainly appropriate and helpful to the business, and it was a response one would normally expect a business in taxpayers' circumstances to make."[20] The expense was thus both ordinary and necessary.

Contrast *Palo Alto* with *Henry v. Commissioner*,[21] where the Tax Court denied deductions to a taxpayer for depreciation and maintenance costs associated with his yacht. The taxpayer, an accountant, argued that his yacht, which flew a flag bearing the number "1040" (a reference to the individual income tax form) was used to advertise his business. The court rejected the taxpayer's argument, noting the taxpayer did not use the yacht to entertain or meet clients. The court noted "in determining that which is 'necessary' to a taxpayer's trade or business, the taxpayer is ordinarily the best judge on the matter and we would hesitate to substitute our own discretion for his with regard to whether an expenditure is 'appropriate and helpful' in the purposes of his business. But where, as in this case, the expenditures may well have been made to further ends which are primarily personal, this ordinary constraint does not prevail; petitioner must show affirmatively that his expenses were 'necessary' to the conduct of his professions."[22] The court examined the facts and concluded the taxpayer had not established he had taken up boating "solely or even primarily to serve the needs of his practice or that he would not have operated [the yacht] regardless of whatever business advantages he hoped to derive from this sport . . . . [T]he claimed expenses, when considered in relation to the fees which petitioner attributes to yachting, are inordinate and do not indicate the requisite proximate relationship between his sporting activities and his business . . . . The pennant may have some relationship to the conduct of taxpayer's business. But the evidence does not show how any specific fee resulted from his operating a yacht."[23] As *Palo Alto* and *Henry* suggest, the determination of whether an expense is "necessary" is a factual determination.

---

[19]   565 F.2d at 1390.

[20]   *Id.* at 1391.

[21]   36 T.C. 879 (1961). See also *Dobbe v. Commissioner*, T.C. Memo. 2000–330, *aff'd*, 2003-1 U.S.T.C. ¶ 50,377 (9th Cir. 2003), rejecting a corporation's attempt to deduct landscaping around the personal residence of the corporation's sole shareholders. Although the corporation was engaged in the business of importing and growing flower bulbs, it offered little evidence that the landscaping was appropriate or necessary to the maintenance of its business.

[22]   36 T.C. at 884.

[23]   *Id.* at 885.

[3]   "Reasonable" Salaries

§ 162.   Trade or business expenses —

(a) In general —

There shall be allowed as a deduction all the ordinary and necessary expenses paid or incurred during the taxable year in carrying on any trade or business including —

(1) a reasonable allowance for salaries or other compensation for personal services actually rendered.

Salaries and other compensation represent one of the most common types of expenses incurred by any business. Section 162(a)(1) specifically addresses salaries and provides that only reasonable salaries may be deducted. This "reasonableness" requirement does not add anything to the "ordinary and necessary" standard; the element of reasonableness is inherent in the phrase "ordinary and necessary." An unreasonably large salary is not an ordinary and necessary expense of a business. However, if there is some tax advantage to shifting income from one party to another related party, a business may choose to pay an unreasonably large salary to a related person.

The best example of this is found in the context of closely held corporations where the owners of the corporation are also likely to be corporate employees. Although the corporation may be owned by one or two people, the corporation is nevertheless a separate taxable entity, thus affording both the possibility and the desirability of income shifting. Profits generated by the corporation are taxed to it and profits distributed as dividends by the corporation are taxed to the shareholders.[24] This double tax can be eliminated if the corporation can successfully characterize its distributions to shareholders as deductible salaries or compensation; hence, the temptation to disguise dividends as deductible wages. Through the use of large salaries, a successful corporation can reduce its own tax and at the same time distribute profits to its owners. If the owners of the business have determined they want the corporation to distribute rather than accumulate profits, the corporation might just as well save taxes by characterizing the distributions as salaries. The reasonableness standard is the primary obstacle to this strategy.

While the reasonableness standard is easy to understand, its application is at best difficult. According to the Ninth Circuit in *Elliots, Inc. v. Commissioner*,[25] the reasonableness of compensation paid to a shareholder-employee, particularly a sole shareholder, should be evaluated from the perspective of a hypothetical independent investor:

> A relevant inquiry is whether an inactive, independent investor would be willing to compensate the employee as he was compensated. The nature and quality of the services should be considered, as well as the effect of those services on the return the investor is seeking on his investment. The corporation's rate of return on equity would be relevant to the independent

---

[24] These comments are applicable to so-called C corporations — that is, corporations taxed under Subchapter C of Chapter 1 of Subtitle A of the Internal Revenue Code.

[25] 716 F.2d 1241 (9th Cir. 1983).

investor in assessing the reasonableness of compensation in a small corporation where excessive compensation would noticeably decrease the rate of return.[26]

As noted by the Ninth Circuit, courts have historically used some combination of the following factors in determining the reasonableness of compensation: (1) the position held by the employee; (2) hours worked and duties performed; (3) the general importance of the employee to the success of the company; (4) a comparison of past duties and salary with current responsibilities and compensation; (5) a comparison of the employee's salary with those paid by similar companies for similar services; (6) the size of the company, the complexities of the company's business and the general economic conditions; (7) the existence of a potentially exploitable relationship between the taxpaying company and its employees; and (8) the existence of a bonus system that distributes all or nearly all of the pre-tax earnings of the company.[27] The court emphasized that no single factor is determinative but, rather, the employment situation must be viewed as a whole. The court repeatedly invoked as a touchstone whether the compensation formula would allow a reasonable return on equity to an independent investor.

The independent investor test suggested by the Ninth Circuit has been adopted by some courts, including the Seventh Circuit in *Exacto Spring Corporation v. Commissioner.*[28] According to the Seventh Circuit, the multi-factor test, "invites the Tax Court to set itself up as a superpersonnel department for closely held corporations, a role unsuitable for courts . . . . The judges of the Tax Court are not equipped by training or experience to determine the salaries of corporate officers. No judges are."[29] With respect to the independent investor test, the Seventh Circuit added:

> There is, fortunately, an indirect market test, as recognized by the Internal Revenue Service's expert witness. A corporation can be conceptualized as a contract in which the owner of assets hires a person to manage them. The owner pays the manager a salary and in exchange the manager works to increase the value of the assets that have been entrusted to his management; that increase can be expressed as a rate of return to the owner's investment. The higher the rate of return (adjusted for risk) that a manager can generate, the greater the salary he can command. If the rate of return is extremely high, it will be difficult to prove that the manager is being overpaid, for it will be implausible that if he quit if his salary was cut, and he was replaced by a lower-paid manager, the owner would be better off; it would be killing the goose that lays the golden egg. The Service's expert believed that investors in a firm like Exacto would expect a 13 percent return on their investment. Presumably they would be delighted with more. They would be overjoyed to receive a return more than 50

---

[26] *Id.* at 1245.

[27] *Id.* at 1245–48. *See, e.g.,* Charles McCandless Tile Service v. U.S., 422 F.2d 1336 (Ct. Cl. 1970); Wechsler & Co., Inc. v. Commissioner, T.C. Memo. 2006–173 (listing another factor, *i.e.,* internal consistency in compensation).

[28] 196 F.3d 833 (7th Cir. 1999).

[29] *Id.* at 835.

percent greater than they expected — and 20 percent, the return that the Tax Court found that investors in Exacto had obtained, is more than 50 percent greater than the benchmark return of 13 percent.[30]

In *Menards Inc. v. Commissioner*,[31] the Service argued that the $20.6 million compensation paid by the taxpayer to its CEO was not reasonable and therefore disallowed part of the deduction claimed by the company under Section 162. The taxpayer, one of the nation's top retail home improvement chains, is engaged in the retail sale of hardware, building supplies, paint, garden equipment and similar items. The Tax Court concluded that, under the independent investor test articulated in *Exacto Spring*, the compensation paid the CEO would be presumed to be reasonable in view of the rate of return on investment generated by the taxpayer. According to the court, however, this presumption of reasonableness was rebutted when one considered the amount paid to CEOs by other comparable publicly traded companies such as Home Depot, Lowes, Target, and Staples. In that regard, the Tax Court relied on Treas. Reg. § 1.162-7(b)(3) providing that reasonable compensation "is only such amount as would ordinarily be paid for like services by like enterprises under like circumstances." The court concluded that the compensation paid to taxpayer's CEO was reasonable only to the extent of approximately $7 million with the balance paid the CEO constituting a nondeductible constructive dividend.

The Tax Court decision in *Menards* was reversed by the Seventh Circuit.[32] The appellate court, in an opinion written by Judge Posner, concluded that the Tax Court erred in disallowing a deduction for the compensation in excess of $7 million, reasoning that:[33]

> All businesses are different, all CEOs are different, and all compensation packages for CEOs are different. . . . The main focus of the Tax Court's decision . . . was on whether Menard's compensation exceeded that of comparable CEOs in 1998 — that is, whether it was objectively excessive . . .
>
> The CEO of Home Depot was paid that year only $2.8 million, though it is a much larger company than Menards; and the CEO of Lowe's, also a larger company, was paid $6.1 million. But salary is just the beginning of a meaningful comparison, because it is only one element of a compensation package. Of particular importance to this case is the amount of risk in the compensation structure. . . . A risky compensation structure implies that the executive's salary is likely to vary substantially from year to year — high when the company has a good year, low when it has a bad one. Mr. Menard's average annual income may thus have been considerably less than $20 million — a possibility the Tax Court ignored. Had the corporation lost money in 1998, Menard's total compensation would have been only $157,500 — less than the salary of a federal judge — even if the loss had not been his fault . . .

---

[30] *Id.* at 838–39.

[31] T.C. Memo. 2004-207.

[32] Menards, Inc. v. Commissioner, 560 F.3d 620 (7th Cir. 2009).

[33] Id. at 623, 626–28.

Nor did the Tax Court consider the severance packages, retirement plans, or perks of the CEOs with whom it compared Menard (though it did take account of their stock options), even though such differences can make an enormous difference to an executive's compensation. . . . [The adjustment the Tax Court made to arrive at its conclusion that the compensation in excess of $7.1 million was nondeductible] disregarded differences in the full compensation packages of the three executives being compared, differences in whatever challengers faced the companies in 1998, and differences in the responsibilities and performance of the three CEOs.

We have discussed risk; with regard to responsibilities there is incomplete information about the compensation paid other senior management besides Mr. Menard himself, and no information about the compensation paid the senior management of Home Depot and Lowe's other than those companies CEOs. The relevance of such information is that it might show that Menard was doing work that in other companies is delegated to staff, or conversely that staff was doing all the work and Menard was, in substance though not if form, clipping coupons. The former inference is far more likely, given the undisputed evidence of Menard's workaholic, micromanaging ways and the fact the Menard's board of directors is a tiny dependency of Mr. Menard. He does the work that in publicly held companies like Home Depot or Lowe's is done by boards that have more than two directors besides the CEO. Of course they are larger companies — Home Depot's revenues were seven times as great as Menard's in 1998 — so we would expect them to have more staff. But we are given no information on how much more staff they had.

We know that besides Menard himself, Menards — already a $3.4 billion company in 1998 — had only three corporate officers. The Tax Court thought it suspicious that they were modestly compensated. . . . The Tax Court did not consider the possibility, which the evidence supports, that Menard really does do it all himself . . .

We conclude that in ruling that Menard's compensation was excessive in 1998, the Tax Court committed clear error, and its decision is therefore reversed.

[4]   Clothing Expenses

As noted in *Bernardo v. Commissioner*,[34] "[g]enerally, the cost of a business wardrobe required as a condition of employment is considered a nondeductible personal expense within the meaning of section 262 if the purchased clothing is suitable for general or personal wear." In this regard, the Tax Court has required that a taxpayer, seeking to deduct clothing costs, satisfy a three-part standard. Specifically, under the Tax Court standard, the taxpayer must establish that (1) the clothing is not suitable for general or personal wear by the taxpayer (a subjective test); (2) the clothing is required or essential in the taxpayer's employment; and (3) the clothing is not, in fact, used for taxpayer's general or personal wear. By

---

[34] T.C. Memo 2004-199.

contrast, the IRS disavows the use of the subjective test and utilizes as its standard an objective test, i.e., the clothing is not adaptable to general usage as ordinary clothing. The Service's position was endorsed by the Fifth Circuit in *Pevsner v. Commissioner* in disallowing a deduction for the expensive designer clothing purchased and used as business attire by a manager of a designer boutique.

In some cases, because of the taxpayer's inability to satisfy the burden of the Tax Court's subjective test, the Tax Court test and the objective test of *Pevsner* may actually produce the same results. In this regard, consider the facts of *Bernardo v. Commissioner*. There, the taxpayer, in her position as district manager for Mervyn's, was required by her employer to wear black or white dresses or suits while on the job. To acquire the clothing necessary for her position, the taxpayer had no need to go to "specialized" stores. Furthermore, there was no company logo required to be on taxpayer's clothing. Taxpayer contended that she owned no black or white dresses or suits and thus was required to purchase a new wardrobe, the cost of which she sought to deduct. Rejecting the taxpayer's position, the Tax Court noted that she did not satisfy two of its three tests: she failed the Tax Court's subjective test as she provided no evidence that the clothing was unsuitable, in terms of price, quality, or style for her personal wear; and she also failed to provide evidence that she never wore the clothing away from work. Thus, the Tax Court reached the same result, i.e., denial of deduction, that would have been reached by a court employing the *Pevsner* objective test.

In Revenue Ruling 70-474,[35] the Service ruled deductible the uniform acquisition and maintenance costs for police officers, firemen, letter carriers, nurses, bus drives and railway men "required to wear distinctive types of uniforms while at work . . . Which are not suitable for ordinary wear.[36] In Revenue Ruling 67-115,[37] the cost of required military fatigue uniforms, the off-duty wearing of which was prohibited, was held deductible. When work clothing may be worn off-duty, however, who decides upon its "suitability" for such wear?

[5] Public Policy Considerations

Historically, courts sometimes denied a business deduction solely on the grounds that its allowance would frustrate public policy. For example, the Supreme Court, in *Tank Truck Rentals v. Commissioner*,[38] disallowed a truck company's deduction of fines paid for violation of state maximum weight laws, concluding such costs could not be considered necessary "if allowance of the deduction would frustrate sharply defined national or state policies proscribing particular types of conduct, evidenced by some governmental declaration thereof." According to the Court, "the test of nondeductibility always is the severity and immediacy of the frustration resulting from the allowance of the deduction. The flexibility of such a standard is necessary if we are to accommodate both the congressional intent to

---

[35] 1970-2 C.B. 34, 35.

[36] *See also* Treas. Reg. § 1.262-1(b)(8) relating to "equipment" of members of the armed services and the uniforms of reservists.

[37] 1967-1 C.B. 30.

[38] 356 U.S. 30 (1958).

tax only net income, and the presumption against congressional intent to encourage violation of declared public policy."[39] The Court concluded that to permit deduction of the fines imposed by the state would only encourage noncompliance by taking the "sting" out of the penalty.

By contrast, the same day it decided *Tank Trunk Rentals*, the Court concluded in *Commissioner v. Sullivan*,[40] that rent and wage expenses incurred in operating an illegal bookmaking establishment were deductible. The Court reasoned that, if it denied the deduction, it "would come close to making [such a gambling enterprise] taxable on the basis of its gross receipts, while all other business would be taxable on the basis of net income. If that choice is to be made, Congress should do it."[41] *Tank Trunk Rentals* was distinguished on the basis that allowance of a deduction for the fines would have been a device for avoiding the consequences of violating the state maximum weight limits.

Recognizing the difficulty in determining what constituted "sharply defined national or state policies" and in applying the "severity and immediacy" test of *Tank Trunk Rentals*, Congress in 1969 and 1971 amended Section 162 by adding provisions disallowing deductions for certain fines, penalties, bribes and antitrust payments.[42] The Senate Finance Committee report for the 1969 legislation states: "The provision for the denial of deductions for payments in [the situations covered by the 1969 legislation] is intended to be all inclusive. Public policy, in other circumstances, generally is not sufficiently clearly defined to justify the disallowance of deductions."[43] Explaining the 1971 legislation, the Senate report noted: "The Committee continues to believe that the determination of when a deduction should be denied should remain under the control of Congress."[44]

[6]   Lobbying Expenses

In 1993, Congress reversed 30-year old legislation allowing the deduction of lobbying expenses. As amended, Section 162(e) disallows any deduction for amounts paid or incurred in connection with (1) influencing legislation or (2) any direct communication with a covered executive branch official in an attempt to influence official actions or positions of the official.[45] "Influencing legislation" is

---

[39] *Id.* at 33–35.

[40] 356 U.S. 27 (1958).

[41] *Id.* at 29.

[42] *See* I.R.C. § 162(c), (f), (g). Note that Section 280E disallows a deduction or credit for costs incurred in a trade or business which consists of "trafficking in controlled substances . . . which is prohibited by Federal law or the law of any State in which such trade or business is conducted."

[43] S. Rep. No. 91–552, 91st Cong., 1st Sess. (1969), 1969-3 C.B. 597.

[44] S. Rep. No. 92–437, 92d Cong., 1st Sess. (1971), 1972-1 C.B. 559. While Congress may have preempted the courts from using public policy as a basis for denying deductions for trade or business expenses otherwise deductible under Section 162, the courts and the Service continue to use the public policy rationale as a basis for denying deductions under Section 165. Thus, in Revenue Ruling 81-24, 1981-1 C.B. 79, the Service, relying on public policy grounds, denied a loss deduction to a taxpayer for the destruction of a building as a result of arson committed by him. *See also* Holt v. Comm'r, 69 T.C. 75 (1977).

[45] I.R.C. § 162(e)(1)(A), (D).

broadly defined to mean "any attempt to influence any legislation through communication with any member or employee of a legislative body, or with any government official or employee who may participate in the formulation of legislation."[46] The disallowance rule for influencing legislation does not apply to "legislation of any local council or similar governing body."[47] For example, boards of county commissioners, city councils and tribal councils come within this exception.

[B] "Carrying On a Trade or Business"

[1] What Constitutes a "Trade or Business"?

The existence of a trade or business is key to deductions under Section 162. And yet, neither the Code nor the regulations contain a definition of "trade or business." Nevertheless, only on rare occasions since 1913 have the courts considered the meaning of "trade or business." Both *Higgins v. Commissioner*[48] and *Commissioner v. Groetzinger*[49] represent such occasions.

The taxpayer in *Higgins* sought to deduct as ordinary and necessary business expenses substantial salary, rental and other costs he incurred in managing his extensive investments.[50] The taxpayer "merely kept records and collected interest and dividends from his securities, through managerial attention for his investments." The Court held for the Commissioner, on the grounds that "no matter how large the estate or how continuous or extended the work [of managing his investments] may be," the Commissioner's determination that Higgins was not engaged in a trade or business would not be overturned.

As in its 1941 decision in *Higgins*, the Court in *Groetzinger* some 45 years later concluded that the status of an enterprise as a trade or business will depend on the facts. The taxpayer in *Groetzinger* devoted himself full-time to gambling on dog races; he had no other employment and hoped to earn a living from the gambling. In the year at issue, however, he had a small net loss. The tax question was whether the gambling losses were business losses. If they were not business losses, the taxpayer would be subject to the alternative minimum tax, with a resulting greater tax liability for the year in question. Thus, the taxpayer argued that his gambling constituted a trade or business. In affirming a judgment for the taxpayer, the Supreme Court provided some guidance regarding the meaning of "trade or business." Specifically, the Court rejected, as the test for the existence of a "trade or business," the formulation of Justice Frankfurter in a concurring opinion in *Deputy v. Dupont*[51] that ". . . carrying on any trade or business involves holding one's self out to others as engaged in the selling of goods or services." In a more

---

[46] I.R.C. § 162(e)(4)(A).

[47] I.R.C. § 162(e)(2).

[48] 312 U.S. 212 (1941).

[49] 480 U.S. 23 (1987).

[50] At the time of *Higgins*, the Code contained no provision comparable to current Section 212 allowing a deduction for expenses for the production of income. Section 212 is discussed in § 12.02, *infra*.

[51] 308 U.S. 488 (1940).

positive vein, the Court in *Groetzinger* stated "We accept the fact that to be engaged in a trade or business, the taxpayer must be involved in the activity with continuity and regularity and the taxpayer's primary purpose for engaging in the activity must be for income or profit. A sporadic activity, a hobby, or an amusement diversion does not qualify." On this basis, the Court held for the taxpayer, and reaffirmed the "general position" of *Higgins* that resolution of the trade or business issue depends on the facts of the case.

Whether the taxpayer has a bona fide objective of making a profit must be determined each year by considering all the facts and circumstances related to the activity during the year. Regulation § 1.183-2(a) lists the following factors for determining whether an activity is engaged in for profit: (1) the manner in which the taxpayer carries on the trade or business; (2) the expertise of the taxpayer or his or her advisers; (3) the time and effort expended by the taxpayer in carrying on the activity; (4) the expectation that assets used in the activity may appreciate in value; (5) the success of the taxpayer in carrying on other similar or dissimilar activities; (6) the taxpayer's history of income or losses with respect to the activity; (7) the amount of occasional profits, if any, which are earned; (8) the financial status of the taxpayer; and (9) elements of personal pleasure or recreation. Although this regulation interprets Section 183 addressing so-called "hobby losses," the factors listed in the regulation are equally applicable to the trade or business determination that is made for Section 162 purposes.[52] As noted in Regulation § 1.183-2(b), no one factor listed in the regulation is determinative, and whether the taxpayer is engaged in the activity does not depend upon merely counting those factors suggesting the presence of a profit motive and comparing the number to those factors indicating the opposite.

While the Court in *Higgins* determined that the management of one's own investments is not a trade or business, other courts have nevertheless distinguished so-called "traders" from "investors." A "trader" is considered to be engaged in a trade or business; and an "investor," like Mr. Higgins, is not. A "trader's" activities are directed toward short-term trading with income being derived principally from the sale of securities rather than from the dividends and interest "investors" typically seek. Thus, a taxpayer's investment intent, the nature of the income to be derived from the activity, and the extent and regularity of the taxpayer's securities transactions will be relevant in determining whether the taxpayer is a "trader" engaged in a trade or business, or an "investor" who is not.[53]

[2] The "Carrying On" Requirement

The development of a new business typically involves two stages before the trade or business becomes operational. First, there is the investigatory stage where a person may review various kinds of businesses before deciding to acquire or to enter into a specific business. The leading case involving investigatory expenses, *Frank v. Commissioner*,[54] involved a taxpayer who sought to purchase and operate a

---

[52] *See, e.g.*, Keanini v. Commissioner, 94 T.C. 41 (1990).

[53] Moller v. U.S., 721 F.2d 810 (Fed. Cir. 1983); Purvis v. Comm'r, 530 F.2d 1332 (9th Cir. 1976).

[54] 20 T.C. 511 (1953).

newspaper or radio station. The taxpayer, who ultimately purchased a newspaper, made trips to numerous cities to investigate possible purchases, incurring various travel expenses and legal fees in connection with the investigations. The Tax Court denied a deduction:

> The travel expenses and legal fees spent in searching for a newspaper business with a view to purchasing the same cannot be deducted under the provisions of section [162], Internal Revenue Code. The petitioners were not engaged in any trade or business at the time the expenses were incurred. The trips made by the taxpayers were not related to the conduct of the business that they were then engaged in but were preparatory to locating a business venture of their own. The expense of investigating and looking for a new business and trips preparatory to entering a business are not deductible as an ordinary and necessary business expense incurred in carrying on a trade or business . . . . The word "pursuit" in the statutory phrase "in pursuit of a trade or business" is not used in the sense of "searching for" or "following after," but in the sense of "in connection with" or "in the course of" a trade or business. It presupposes an existing business with which petitioner is connected.[55]

The legislative history to Section 195, addressing so-called "start-up" expenses, reinforces the point:

> Business investigatory expenses generally are nondeductible regardless of whether they are incurred by an existing business in relation to another business or by a taxpayer who is not in any business. However, taxpayers may be able to deduct a loss for business investigatory expenses incurred in an unsuccessful attempt to acquire a specific business. Nevertheless, business investigatory expenses of a general nature normally are viewed as being either nondeductible personal expenses or as not being ordinary and necessary trade or business expenses, *viz.*, because no business exists, within the meaning of section 162 of the Code.[56]

The second stage in developing a new business occurs after the taxpayer has decided to acquire or establish a specific business and commences preparations for its operation. In *Richmond Television Corporation v. U.S.*,[57] the taxpayer sought to deduct certain personnel training expenses incurred prior to receiving the Federal Communications Commission [FCC] license necessary to operate. The Fourth Circuit, considering the deductibility of these expenses, held "[e]ven though a taxpayer has made a firm decision to enter into business and over a considerable period of time spent money in preparation for entering that business, he still has not engaged in carrying on any trade or business within the intendment of Section 162(a) until such time as the business has begun to function as a going concern and performed those activities for which it was organized."[58] The taxpayer was required to treat these pre-operating expenses as capital expenditures.

---

[55] *Id.* at 513, 14.

[56] H. Rpt. No. 96–1278, 96th Cong., 2d Sess., p. 9.

[57] 345 F.2d 901 (4th Cir.), *rev'd and remanded on another issue*, 382 U.S. 68 (1965).

[58] *Id.* at 907.

The "carrying on" requirement, which, as in *Richmond Television*, results in a distinction between pre-opening or start-up costs and operating costs of a business, can be justified on the ground that costs incurred in investigating a business, training personnel, lining-up distributors, suppliers, or potential customers, setting up books and records, and otherwise placing a new business in an operational posture provide benefits long beyond the current tax year and therefore should not be currently deductible. Such expenses are viewed as being no different than the costs incurred in acquiring an existing business, or buildings and equipment for an existing business. As discussed in the next chapter, those acquisition costs generally cannot be currently deducted but must be capitalized.

The "carrying on" requirement also assists in preventing taxpayers from deducting personal expenses. The excerpt from the legislative history to Section 195 suggests the concern that investigation expenses may actually be personal expenses that should not be deductible. As later chapters indicate, drawing the line between nondeductible personal expenses and deductible business expenses has been an enormously difficult job for Congress, the Service and the courts. The "carrying on" requirement forces the taxpayer to establish that expenses are actually associated with the *operation* of a trade or business, making it more likely that the expenses are genuinely business-related, as opposed to being merely personal expenses.

[3] Section 195 and the Amortization of Certain Pre-Operational or Start-Up Costs

§ 195. Start-up expenditures —

(a) Capitalization of expenditures —

Except as otherwise provided in this section, no deduction shall be allowed for start-up expenditures.

(b) Election to deduct —

(1) Allowance of deduction — If a taxpayer elects the application of this subsection with respect to any start-up expenditures —

(A) the taxpayer shall be allowed a deduction for the taxable year in which the active trade or business begins in an amount equal to the lesser of —

(i) the amount of start-up expenditures with respect to the active trade or business, or

(ii) $5,000, reduced (but not below zero) by the amount by which such start-up expenditures exceed $50,000, and

(B) the remainder of such start-up expenditures shall be allowed as a deduction ratably over the 180-month period beginning with the month in which the active trade or business begins.

(2) Dispositions before close of amortization period — In any case in which a trade or business is completely disposed of by the taxpayer before the end of the period to which paragraph (1) applies, any deferred expenses attributable to such trade or business which were not allowed as a deduction

by reason of this section may be deducted to the extent allowable under section 165.

(c)   Definitions — For purposes of this section —

(1)   Start-up expenditures — The term "start-up expenditure" means any amount —

(A) paid or incurred in connection with —

(i) investigating the creation or acquisition of an active trade or business, or

(ii) creating an active trade or business, or

(iii) any activity engaged in for profit and for the production of income before the day on which the active trade or business begins, in anticipation of such activity becoming an active trade or business, and

(B) which, if paid or incurred in connection with the operation of an existing active trade or business (in the same field as the trade or business referred to in subparagraph (A)), would be allowable as a deduction for the taxable year in which paid or incurred.

The term "start-up expenditure" does not include any amount with respect to which a deduction is allowable under section 163(a), 164, or 174.

(2)   Beginning of trade or business —

(A)   In general — Except as provided in subparagraph (B), the determination of when an active trade or business begins shall be made in accordance with such regulations as the Secretary may prescribe.

(B)   Acquired trade or business — An acquired active trade or business shall be treated as beginning when the taxpayer acquires it.

In many cases, drawing the line between pre-operating and operating expenses is not as easy as in *Richmond Television*, where the date of the issuance of the FCC license provided a bright dividing line. Considerable controversy developed in the courts regarding the characterization of expenses as either start-up or operating expenses. To reduce the controversy and litigation in this area and to encourage the formation of new businesses, Congress in 1979 added Section 195 to the Code. As originally enacted, Section 195 permitted the taxpayer to elect to amortize (*i.e.*, to pro-rate at an even level) business start-up expenditures over a period of not less than 60 months.

Congress amended Section 195 in 2004 to allow a taxpayer to deduct up to $5,000 of start-up expenditures in the taxable year in which the active trade or business begins. However, the $5,000 amount is reduced (but not below zero) by the amount the start-up expenditures exceed $50,000. The remainder of the start-up expenditures are amortized over a 180-month period (or the same 15-year amortization period used for Section 197 intangibles as discussed in Chapter 41) beginning with the month in which the active trade or business begins. Note that to claim a current deduction for or to amortize start-up expenditures under Section 195, one must actually engage in the trade or business.

As the House Report accompanying the 1979 Act explained:

. . . expenditures eligible for amortization must satisfy two requirements. First, the expenditure must be paid or incurred in connection with creating, or investigating the creation or acquisition of, a trade or business *entered into by the taxpayer*. Second, the expenditure involved must be one which would be allowable as a deduction for the taxable year in which it is paid or incurred if it were paid or incurred in connection with the expansion of an existing trade or business in the same field as that entered into by the taxpayer. Under the provision, eligible expenses consist of *investigatory costs* incurred in reviewing a prospective business prior to reaching a final decision to acquire or to enter that business. These costs include expenses incurred for the analysis or survey of potential markets, products, labor supply, transportation facilities, etc. Eligible expenses also include *startup costs* which are incurred subsequent to a decision to establish a particular business and prior to the time when the business begins.[59]

Consider the following example:

Example: Linda decides to open an art gallery to buy and sell fine works of art. Prior to opening the art gallery, Linda spends $10,000 in rental costs for the building in which the gallery is located, $15,000 in pre-opening wages to employees of the gallery, and $6,000 in advertising. Are these costs deductible?

Analysis: The listed expenses are start-up expenditures. Because the expenditures do not exceed $50,000, Linda may elect to deduct $5,000 of the $31,000 in costs. She must amortize the remaining $26,000 over a 180-month period.

[4] Application of the "Carrying On" Requirement to Employees

The pre-operating/operating distinction reflected in *Frank* and *Richmond Television* has carried over into the employment-seeking context. The courts and the Service agree that a taxpayer may be in the trade or business of being an employee.[60] Furthermore, an employee can have more than one trade or business. For example, a person who works full time as a tax specialist with an accounting firm and at the same time regularly teaches tax as an adjunct professor at a local college will be deemed engaged in two businesses: tax accounting and teaching. If an employee incurs costs in seeking a job with a new employer, whether the employee may deduct those costs as trade or business expenses under Section 162 turns on whether the employee can establish that the costs were incurred in "carrying on" a trade or business. If the expenses were incurred in an effort to commence a new trade or business, they will not satisfy the "carrying on" requirement and, like the pre-operating expenses in *Richmond Television*, will be treated as capital expenditures. By contrast, if the expenses were incurred by an employee seeking work in the same trade or business, the "carrying on" requirement would be satisfied and the costs (*e.g.*, resume costs, postage, etc.) would be

---

[59] H.R. Rep. No. 96–1278, 96th Cong., 2d Sess., p. 10 (emphasis added).

[60] *See* Primuth v. Comm'r, 54 T.C. 374 (1970).

deductible. Note that deductible employee business expenses are generally below-the-line expenses and are subject to the 2% floor imposed by Section 67.

The scope of an employee's current trade or business is obviously critical in evaluating the deductibility of costs incurred in seeking new employment. Determining that scope, however, has proven difficult. In *Primuth v. Commissioner*,[61] the taxpayer was the secretary-treasurer for a small corporation. He paid a fee to an employment agency to assist him in securing new employment, and through its services he obtained a new job with increased responsibilities as secretary-controller with a larger corporation. The Tax Court found that the taxpayer was carrying on the trade or business of being a "corporate executive" and held the employment agency expense was deductible since it was incurred "to permit [the taxpayer] to continue to carry on that very trade or business — albe it with a different corporate employer."[62] A concurring opinion in *Primuth* suggested that, whether the employment-seeking expenses were incurred in the employee's current trade or business or a new trade or business, could be determined by "comparing the position which the taxpayer occupied before and after the change [of employment]. Perhaps the categorization of corporate executive will not always be applicable, but, in this case, petitioner was at all times a financial corporate executive."[63]

The courts subsequently extended the *Primuth* principle to other contexts involving payment of employment counseling fees. In *Cremona v. Commissioner*,[64] for example, the taxpayer-employee was held to be in the trade or business of being an "administrator," and the job counseling fees he incurred to improve his job opportunities in that business were held to be deductible even though the taxpayer did not succeed in obtaining new employment. The Tax Court in *Cremona* rejected the Commissioner's argument that employment-seeking costs were only deductible if new employment were actually secured. The Service advocated this seeking/securing standard presumably to assure that the expenses were business related. But following its loss in *Cremona*, the Service accepted the proposition that the expenses of seeking employment, even if not successful, could be deducted. Revenue Ruling 75-120[65] carefully preserves the rule of nondeductibility for pre-operating expenses while at the same time eliminating the distinction between seeking and securing employment as a test for deductibility.[66] Specifically, the Service stated:

> In view of [*Primuth* and *Cremona*], it is now the position of the Service that expenses incurred in seeking new employment in the same trade or business are deductible under section 162 of the Code if directly connected with such trade or business as determined by all the objectives facts and circumstances. However, such expenses are not deductible if an individual

---

[61] 54 T.C. 374 (1970).

[62] *Id.* at 379.

[63] *Id.* at 382.

[64] 58 T.C. 219 (1972).

[65] 1975-1 C.B. 55.

[66] Nothing in the legislative history of Section 195 indicates that Congress intended employment seeking expenses to be amortizable investigation costs under Section 195.

is seeking employment in a new trade or business even if employment is secured.[67]

A final issue in the employment setting is how long a taxpayer may be unemployed and still be considered to be in the trade or business of his former employment. In *Furner v. Commissioner*,[68] a teacher who took a leave from teaching for a year to obtain a master's degree in her field was held to be "carrying on" her trade or business for the year, thus allowing her educational expenses to be deducted. The "obvious principle," according to *Primuth*, "is that it is possible for an employee to retain, at least temporarily, his status of carrying on his own trade or business independent of receiving any compensation from a particular employer."[69] Equally obvious, however, is the fact that a prolonged period of unemployment will terminate one's status as being engaged in a trade or business. The Service addressed this issue in Revenue Ruling 75-120, noting:

> If the individual is presently unemployed, his trade or business would consist of the services previously performed for his past employer if no substantial lack of continuity occurred between the time of the past employment and the seeking of the new employment. Such expenses are not deductible by an individual where there is a substantial lack of continuity between the time of his past employment and the seeking of the new employment, or by an individual seeking employment for the first time.[70]

What remains uncertain is how long a person can be unemployed without losing her trade or business status. The Service appears to have embraced a one-year period as a guideline.[71]

§ 12.02 SECTION 212 DEDUCTIONS

§ 212. **Expenses for production of income —**

In the case of an individual, there shall be allowed as a deduction all the ordinary and necessary expenses paid or incurred during the taxable year —

(1) for the production or collection of income;

(2) for the management, conservation, or maintenance of property held for the production of income; or

(3) in connection with the determination, collection, or refund of any tax.

---

[67] Rev. Rul. 75-120, 1975-1 C.B. 55, 56.

[68] 393 F.2d 292 (7th Cir. 1968), reversing 47 T.C. 165 (1966).

[69] 54 T.C. 374, 378 (1970).

[70] 1975-1 C.B. 55, 56. The ruling goes on to add that, in addition, "[s]uch expenses are not deductible under section 212(1) of the Code which applies only to expenses incurred with respect to an existing profit-seeking endeavor not qualifying as a trade or business."

[71] *See* Rev. Rul. 68-591, 1968-2 C.B. 73.

Congress enacted the forerunner of Section 212 in 1942 in response to the Supreme Court's decision in *Higgins v. Commissioner*[72] that one could not be in the trade or business of investing. Section 212, sometimes referred to as the non-trade-or-business analog to Section 162, allows a deduction for the "ordinary and necessary" expenses of producing or collecting income, maintaining property held for the production of income, or determining, collecting or refunding any tax. The regulations provide some delineation and elaboration and a variety of examples of expenditures falling within or without the statutory provisions.[73] For example, ordinary and necessary investment fees, custodial fees, office rent and clerical help are all deductible in connection with Section 212 activities, as are rental property expenses and administration expenses of a trust or estate, except to the extent allocable to tax-exempt income.[74] By contrast, commuting expenses, rental costs for a safe deposit box for jewelry and other personal items, home residence expenses, and the expense of defending or perfecting title to property are not deductible under Section 212.[75] Most Section 212 deductions are below-the-line deductions (available only if the taxpayer itemizes). Moreover, most Section 212 deductions are treated as miscellaneous itemized deductions under Section 67, which limits their deductibility. (See, however, Section 62(a)(4) allowing an above-the-line deduction for expenses attributable to property held for the production of rents or royalties.) Also, no deduction is allowable for expenditures allocable to tax-exempt income.[76]

> **Example 1:** Sam incurs $500 investment fees attributable to $10,000 in tax-exempt bond interest. The investment fees are non-deductible because they are allocable to the tax-exempt income.

> **Example 2:** The taxpayer pays attorney's fees to collect tax-exempt damages for a personal physical injury. The fees are nondeductible.

The taxpayers in *Frank v. Commissioner*,[77] discussed earlier in this chapter, who sought to enter the newspaper business, were unsuccessful in their efforts to deduct as a Section 162 business expense the costs of investigating the purchase of a newspaper. They also were unsuccessful in their attempt to deduct the costs under Section 212:

> Neither are the travel and legal expenses incurred by the petitioners in their attempt to find and purchase a business deductible under section [212], Internal Revenue Code, which allows the deduction of expenses incurred in the production or collection of income or in the management, conservation, or maintenance of property held for the production of income. There is a basic distinction between allowing deductions for the expense of producing or collecting income, in which one has an existent interest or right, and expenses incurred in an attempt to obtain income by the creation of some new interest . . . . The expenses here involved are of the latter

---

[72] 312 U.S. 212 (1941).

[73] Treas. Reg. § 1.212-1.

[74] Treas. Reg. § 1.212-1(g)-(i).

[75] Treas. Reg. § 1.212-(f), (h), (k).

[76] Treas. Reg. § 1.212-1(e).

[77] 20 T.C. 511 (1953).

classification. The traveling costs were incurred in an endeavor to acquire a business which might, in the future, prove productive of income. It might reasonably be said that petitioners were engaged in the active search of employment as newspaper owners, but that cannot be regarded as a business. It is much like the situation . . . found in *McDonald v. Commissioner*, 323 U.S. 57, where it was held that a Pennsylvania court of common pleas judge seeking reelection could not deduct under section [212] expenses of such campaign. The Supreme Court said ". . . his campaign contributions were not expenses incurred in being a judge but in trying to be a judge for the next ten years."[78]

---

[78] *Id.* at 514. See Rev. Rul. 75-120, 1975-1 C.B. 55, to the same effect on this point.

Chapter 13

CAPITAL EXPENDITURES

§ 13.01 DEDUCTIBLE EXPENSE OR CAPITAL EXPENDITURE?

§ 263. Capital Expenditures.

(a) **General Rule. No deduction shall be allowed for**

(1) **Any amount paid out for new buildings or for permanent improvements or betterments made to increase the value of any property or estate** . . . .

(2) **Any amount expended in restoring property or in making good the exhaustion thereof for which an allowance is or has been made.**

Our tax system taxes net income and therefore Section 162 generally permits business expenses to be deducted from gross income. But as Section 161 cautions, Section 162 deductions are subject to exceptions. Perhaps the most important is found in Section 263, denying deductions for capital expenditures. Specifically, Section 263 denies a deduction for the cost of new buildings or for permanent improvements or betterments increasing the value of the property, and for restoration costs for which an allowance is made.

The regulations list examples of capital expenditures, including the cost of acquisition or production or improvement of real or personal tangible property and the cost of acquisition or creation of intangible property.[1]

The rationale for the prohibition on deduction of capital expenditures is that a capital expenditure provides a benefit that persists, that contributes to income over a period of years; its value is not consumed or dissipated within the current year. Since a capital expenditure contributes to income over a period of years, to allow its cost to be deducted currently would result in mismatching income and the expenses related to the production of that income. Indeed, it is the matching of current expenditures with future income that is at the heart of the capitalization requirement.

This is not to say that the cost of a capital expenditure can never be recovered; indeed, the regulations, while denying a deduction, also alert us to the prospect of such recovery with the phrase "except as otherwise provided in Chapter 1 of the Internal Revenue Code.[2] Chapter 14 will address the recovery of capital expenditures by way of depreciation deductions and Chapter 15 will consider loss

---

[1] Treas. Reg. § 1.263(a)-IT(c).

[2] Treas. Reg. § 1.263(a)-IT(a).

deductions as another means of cost recovery. This chapter will focus on identifying capital expenditures.

What is typically at stake in distinguishing capital expenditures from current deductions is timing. Is the expense fully recoverable — *i.e.*, deductible — now? Is it instead recoverable bit by bit over a number of years? Or, worse yet for the taxpayer, is it recoverable only at the end of the line, when the property in question is disposed of? If substantial time and money are involved, the answer to the timing question can be expensive. By contrast, where the amounts and time periods involved are minimal, it may make good administrative sense to permit current deductions even for expenses that arguably produce some hard-to-measure benefit in future years. For example, a current deduction for "incidental" materials and supplies is allowed where no records of consumption or inventories are kept and where taxable income is clearly reflected.[3]

> **Example:** Assume that during a year a taxpayer purchases incidental cleaning materials for her business but fails to use all of the cleaning materials during the year. Assume no records of consumption or inventory are kept.

> **Analysis:** The regulation permits the taxpayer to deduct the entire cost of the cleaning materials "provided [her] taxable income is clearly reflected by this method." The taxpayer will be allowed a current deduction for the entire cost of the materials rather than only a deduction for the cost of the materials actually used during the year.

§ 13.02   DEFINING CAPITAL EXPENDITURES — *INDOPCO*

Distinguishing capital expenditures from currently deductible expenses is sometimes difficult. As the Supreme Court reiterated in *INDOPCO, Inc. v. Commissioner*,[4] "the 'decisive distinctions' between current expenses and capital expenditures 'are those of degree and not of kind.' " Commenting on the relationship between deductions and capital expenditures, the Court added:

> The notion that deductions are exceptions to the norm of capitalization finds support in various aspects of the Code. Deductions are specifically enumerated and thus are subject to disallowance in favor of capitalization. See §§ 161 and 261. Nondeductible capital expenditures, by contrast, are not exhaustively enumerated in the Code; rather than providing a "complete list of nondeductible expenditures" . . . § 263 serves as a general means of distinguishing capital expenditures from current expenses . . . . For these reasons, deductions are strictly construed and allowed only "as there is a clear provision therefor."[5]

---

[3] Treas. Reg. § 1.162–3T(a)(2). See also Treas. Reg. § 1.162–12, allowing farmers to deduct the cost of "ordinary tools of short life or small cost, such as hand tools, including shovels, rakes, etc. . . ."

[4] 503 U.S. 79, 86 (1992).

[5] *Id.* at 84.

In *INDOPCO*, the Court affirmed the Third Circuit's decision in *National Starch and Chemical Corporation v. Commissioner*,[6] holding that consulting and legal fees incurred by a company in deciding whether to accept another company's friendly takeover bid provided a long term benefit and therefore had to be capitalized. On appeal, the taxpayer argued that, contrary to the Third Circuit's decision, the longevity of the benefits derived from an expenditure was irrelevant in determining current deductibility. According to the taxpayer, the Supreme Court's decision in *Lincoln Savings & Loan Association*,[7] had established a new test — the "separate and distinct asset" test — for determining whether expenditures had to be capitalized. In *Lincoln Savings & Loan Association*, the Court required the taxpayer to capitalize the "additional premium," which it and other state savings and loan associations were required to pay to the Federal Savings and Loan Insurance Corporation for the purpose of insuring their deposits, because the "additional premium" created a "separate and distinct asset." Rejecting the taxpayer's argument in *INDOPCO*, the Supreme Court noted:

> *Lincoln Savings* stands for the simple proposition that a taxpayer's expenditure that "serves to create or enhance . . . a separate and distinct" asset should be capitalized under Section 263. It by no means follows, however, that *only* expenditures that create or enhance separate and distinct assets are to be capitalized under Section 263 . . . . In short, *Lincoln Savings* holds that the creation of a separate and distinct asset well may be a sufficient but not a necessary condition to classification as a capital expenditure . . . .

> Nor does our statement in *Lincoln Savings* . . . that "the presence of an ensuing benefit that may have some future aspect is not controlling" prohibit reliance on future benefit as a means of distinguishing an ordinary business expense from a capital expenditure. Although the mere presence of an incidental future benefit . . . may not warrant capitalization, a taxpayer's realization of benefits beyond the year in which the expenditure is incurred is undeniably important in determining whether the appropriate tax treatment is immediate deduction or capitalization . . . . Indeed, the text of the Code's capitalization provision, § 263(a)(1), which refers to "permanent improvements or betterments," itself envisions an inquiry into the duration and extent of the benefits realized by the taxpayer.[8]

Focusing on the facts of the case, the Supreme Court concluded that the taxpayer had failed to carry its burden of establishing that the expenses were "ordinary and necessary" within the meaning of Section 162(a). Rather, the facts indicated "the transaction produced significant benefits to National Starch that extended beyond the tax year in question."[9] Among other benefits, the Court noted that, as a result of the takeover, the taxpayer would benefit from the enormous resources, especially basic technology, of the acquiring company. National Starch

---

[6] 918 F.2d 426 (3d Cir. 1990).

[7] 403 U.S. 345 (1971).

[8] 503 U.S. at 86, 87 (quoting from *Welch v. Helvering*, 290 U.S. 111, 114 (1933)).

[9] *Id.* at 88.

also "obtained benefits through its transformation from a publicly held, freestanding corporation into a wholly owned subsidiary of Unilever."[10] The Court emphasized its decision was consistent with other decisions holding that expenses "incurred for the purpose of changing the corporate structure for the benefit of future operations are not ordinary and necessary business expenses."[11] The *INDOPCO* decision thus appeared to focus, in deciding capitalization questions, on whether the expenditure at issue generated future benefits and whether those benefits were significant.

The guidance *INDOPCO* provides leaves room for ambiguity and disagreement. In that regard, it may be useful to bear in mind it is the concern with matching income and related expenses that underlies the capitalization requirement, and that such matching ought therefore ordinarily be carried out, and capitalization imposed, at least in the absence of administrative or compliance burdens significant enough to make matching impractical or unwarrranted. Consider in this regard the following excerpt from the decision by the Seventh Circuit Court of Appeals in *US Freightways Corp. v. Commissioner*:

> Freightways is a long-haul freight trucking company that operates throughout the continental United States . . . . Every year it is required to purchase a large number of permits and licenses and to pay significant fees and insurance premiums in order legally to operate its fleet of vehicles . . . . None of the licenses and permits at issue was valid for more than twelve months, nor did the benefits of any of the fees and insurance premiums paid extend beyond a year from the time the expense was incurred . . . . After auditing Freightways' tax return, the Commissioner concluded that Freightways should have capitalized its 1993 . . . expenses and deducted them ratably over the 1993 and 1994 tax years . . . .

> We turn . . . to the central reason the Commissioner, as affirmed by the Tax Court, gave: that no matter what other characteristics an expenditure has, if it is made in one tax year and its useful life extends "substantially" (an undefined term) beyond the close of that year, then it must be capitalized. Perhaps this rule works in some simple cases. It relies on an implicit spectrum between things that are consumed immediately and those that last well beyond a year . . . . The problem is that many things fall somewhere in the middle of this hypothetical spectrum . . . .

> Even the Commissioner concedes the ordinariness of Freightways' . . . expenses for companies in the trucking business. Not only are they ordinary, but as Freightways points out, they recur, with clockwork regularity, every year. Both this court and the IRS have recognized this type of regularity as something that tends to support a finding of deductibility . . . .

> The Commissioner responds that some distortion remains as long as the expenses are not capitalized . . . . In his appellate brief, the Commissioner

---

[10] *Id.* at 88–89.

[11] *Id.* at 89.

asserts that expensing was allowing Freightways in a sense to borrow deductions from later years and thus to lower its tax burdens year after year . . . . We agree with him that the mere fact that certain expenditures recur does not negate the distorting effect of expensing that predictably occurred here — the interest-free government loan that comes from the deduction remains the same regardless of whether the . . . expenses are unchanged throughout the corporate life of Freightways.

But perfection is a lot to ask for, even in the administration of the tax laws . . . .

Freightways final point is that perfection in temporal matching comes at too high a price for these kinds of expenses. At some point the "administrative costs and conceptual rigor" of achieving a more perfect match become too great . . . . Here, there is a considerable administrative burden that Freightways and any similarly situated taxpayer will bear if it must always allocate one-year expenses to two tax years, year in and year out. It argues that the gain in precision for the taxing authorities is far outweighed by the administrative burden it will bear in performing this task . . . .

We conclude that, for the particular kind of expenses at issue in this case, fixed one-year items where the benefit will never extend beyond that term, that are ordinary, necessary, and recurring expenses for the business in question, the balance of factors under the statute and regulations cuts in favor of treating them as deductible expenses under I.R.C. § 162(a). We therefore reverse the Tax Court's ruling to the contrary.[12]

See the discussion below regarding the "12-month rule" that is now part of the regulations governing the capitalization of intangibles.

§ 13.03   SELECTED CATEGORIES OF CAPITAL EXPENDITURES

As emphasized by the Supreme Court in *INDOPCO* and as demonstrated by the facts of that case, the capitalization concept is fundamental and pervasive in the tax law and manifests itself in many guises. This section considers several common classes of capital expenditures.

[A]   Cost of Acquisition and Costs Incurred in Perfecting and Defending Title

As the regulations explicitly state, acquisition costs constitute capital expenditures. The application of this rule is straightforward enough when the taxpayer incurs costs in purchasing such tangible property as a building, machine or vehicle, or such intangible property as a copyright, a patent, or an interest in a corporation or a partnership. The asset produces a continuing, long term benefit, and its cost must be capitalized, which means the taxpayer will take a basis in the

---

[12]   270 F.3d 1137, 1139, 1143, 1145–47 (7th Cir. 2001).

asset equal to the cost. For example, if a taxpayer pays $500,000 for a building to be used in the taxpayer's business, the building cost must be capitalized and becomes the taxpayer's initial basis in the building.

In this example, costs other than the $500,000 purchase price incurred in purchasing the building, such as brokerage fees, would also be capitalized as part of the cost of the building.[13] Such costs will, like the actual purchase price, become part of the building's basis. If, two years later, the taxpayer were to spend $300,000 to expand the building, that expansion cost would likewise be capitalized and would result in an upward adjustment of the taxpayer's basis in the building under Section 1016(a)(1).

Temporary regulations issued in 2011 with respect to tangible property expand significantly on the prior regulations as they relate to acquisition costs. The temporary regulations require capitalization of amounts paid to acquire or produce a unit of real or personal property, including the purchase or invoice price, transaction costs, and costs for work performed prior to the date the unit of property is placed in service by the taxpayer.[14] Under the temporary regulations, transaction costs are costs paid to facilitate acquisition of real or personal property and include, among other items, amounts paid for: (1) negotiating the terms or structure of the acquisition and obtaining tax advice on the acquisition; (2) preparing and reviewing the documents that effectuate the acquisition, such as preparing the bid, offer, sales contract, or purchase agreement; (3) conveying property between the parties, including sale and transfer taxes and title registration costs; and (4) broker's commissions.[15]

Determining whether a particular expense is properly classifiable as an acquisition cost has sometimes been controversial. For example, in *Woodward v. Commissioner*,[16] and its companion case, *United States v. Hilton Hotels Corp.*,[17] the issue was the deductibility of appraisal and litigation costs the taxpayers incurred in determining the price of stock they were required to purchase from dissenting shareholders under applicable state law. The taxpayers argued that under a "primary purpose" standard, the costs were not acquisition costs, since title to the stock was not at issue. The Supreme Court, however, held that the "origin of the claim" was in the acquisition of the stock, that this was the proper standard to apply, and the costs were thus capital expenditures.

Costs incurred in defending or perfecting title are also capital expenditures and cannot be deducted currently.[18] Such costs are generally functionally equivalent to typical acquisition costs. Thus, for example, in *Georator Corp. v. United States*,[19] legal fees incurred in resisting efforts to cancel the registration of taxpayer's trademark were held to be capital expenditures, as were the legal fees incurred in

---

[13] Treas. Reg. § 1.263(a)-2T(a), (f).

[14] Treas. Reg. § 1.263(a)-2T(d)(1).

[15] Treas. Reg. § 1.263(a)-2T(f)(1)(i), (ii).

[16] 397 U.S. 580 (1970).

[17] 397 U.S. 572 (1970).

[18] Treas. Reg. §§ 1.263(a)-2T(e).

[19] 485 F.2d 283 (4th Cir. 1973).

a trademark infringement action brought by the taxpayer in *Medco Products Co. v. Commissioner.*[20] Note that under the regulations it is not merely the costs incurred in perfecting a recently-acquired title, but those incurred in the defense of a pre-existing one that must be capitalized. However, where the dispute does not relate to the title to property but to the income from it, the expense has been held deductible.[21]

In a sense, the cost of disposing of an asset may also be regarded as part of the cost of its acquisition. The *Woodward* opinion, for example, explicitly states that disposition costs are to be treated as capital expenditures.[22] The practical consequence is that on disposition of the asset, the gain is reduced or the loss is increased by treating the disposition costs as a reduction in the amount realized.

Another aspect of the acquisition-cost rule is presented in *Commissioner v. Idaho Power.*[23] *Idaho Power* addressed the question of how a taxpayer, a utility company, should treat the depreciation on equipment used in the construction of its own facilities. The taxpayer argued that the depreciation deductions should be allowable for the current year while the Service argued that the depreciation on the equipment should be capitalized as part of the cost of the facilities under construction. The Court found for the Commissioner on a number of grounds. First, the Court noted that construction related expenses are part of the acquisition cost of the property being constructed. Thus, just as wages paid to employees constructing the facility must be capitalized as part of the facilities cost, construction-related depreciation should be capitalized. Second, "capitalization of construction-related depreciation by the taxpayer who does its own construction work maintains tax parity with the taxpayer who has its construction work done by an independent contractor." The depreciation on the contractor's equipment during the performance of the job will be an element of the cost charged by the contractor for his construction services, and the taxpayer, of course, would have to capitalize the entire cost of the contractor's services. Finally, the Court noted the priority ordering directive of Section 161 which requires that the capitalization provision — Section 263 — take precedence over deduction provisions, including Section 167 depreciation. Thus, costs that may ordinarily be regarded as currently deductible, such as wages or rent, take on a different status when they are part of the "acquisition cost" of constructed property.

Idaho Power principles were applied by the Seventh Circuit in *Encyclopedia Britannica v. United States.*[24] In that case, Encyclopedia Britannica sought to deduct currently the amounts which they had agreed to pay another publishing company for researching, preparing, editing, and arranging the manuscript for a book. The Seventh Circuit disagreed with Encyclopedia Britannica's

---

[20] 523 F.2d 137 (10th Cir. 1975).

[21] See, for example, *Southland Royalty Co. v. United States*, 582 F.2d 604 (Ct. Cl. 1978), allowing a deduction for expenses incurred in an action to recover additional royalty payments but disallowing a current deduction for expenses incurred in a suit to determine the longevity of an intervening leasehold interest.

[22] 397 U.S. at 575. *See also* Treas. Reg. § 1.263(a)-1T(d).

[23] 418 U.S. 1 (1974).

[24] 685 F.2d 212 (7th Cir. 1982).

characterization of the payments as payments for services. The Seventh Circuit concluded that the payments were for the acquisition of an asset, a book which would yield income to Encyclopedia Britannica over a period of years. As the court noted: "From the publisher's standpoint a book is just another rental property; and just as the expenditures in putting a building into shape to be rented must be capitalized, so, logically at least, must the expenditures used to create a book . . . . If you hire a carpenter to build a tree house that you plan to rent out, his wage is a capital expenditure to you. *See Commissioner of Internal Revenue v. Idaho Power Co. . . .*"[25]

Congress, in 1986, enacted Section 263A, which incorporates the principles of *Idaho Power* and requires capitalization of direct and indirect costs — including certain interest costs — incurred by taxpayers who manufacture, construct, or produce real or tangible personal property, or who acquire or hold inventory property for resale.[26] Voluminous regulations have been issued to implement the statutory directive.

[B] Retirement and Removal

It is clear that acquisition-related costs constitute capital expenditures. However, the costs incurred in retiring and removing an asset are generally currently deductible. In Revenue Ruling 2000-7,[27] the taxpayer removed and discarded telephone poles and installed new ones. The ruling notes that the "costs of removing an asset have been historically allocable to the removed asset and, thus, generally deductible when the asset is retired and the costs are incurred." The removal costs in question were properly allocable to the retired poles and were not required to be capitalized. The fact that their retirement might be part of a project that replaced them with new poles did not change the result, since the removal costs were held to be related to the retired poles, not to assets with a useful life substantially beyond the current year (the new poles). The ruling cautions that its analysis would not apply to the removal of a "component of a depreciable asset," the costs of which would be deductible or not depending on whether the removal and replacement of the component constituted a repair or an improvement.

Another "retirement" issue arose in the case of *Steger v. Commissioner*.[28] Upon retirement from law practice, the taxpayer purchased a malpractice insurance policy, the purpose of which was to provide insurance coverage for an indefinite period of time for any malpractice that the taxpayer may have committed prior to the retirement (but for which no claim had arisen as of retirement). The cost of the policy was held deductible. The court noted that "it is a longstanding rule of law that if a taxpayer incurs a business expense [that is nondeductible] either as a current expense or through yearly depreciation deductions, the taxpayer is allowed to deduct the expense for the year in which the business ceases to operate." Thus,

---

[25] *Id.* at 214.

[26] *See* § 263A(a), (b), (f), (g).

[27] 2000-7 I.R.B. 712.

[28] 113 T.C. 227 (1999).

the Tax Court held that even if the insurance policy constituted a capital asset, its cost was nonetheless deductible because the taxpayer purchased it in the year the taxpayer's business ceased.

[C] Repair or Improvement

[1] Historic Rules

It has long been axiomatic that expenditures for repairs or maintenance, which do not materially add to value or appreciably prolong useful life, are deductible; replacements or improvements, on the contrary, are not. The Tax Court decisions in *Midland Empire Packing Co. v. Commissioner*[29] and *Mt. Morris Drive-In Theatre v. Commissioner*,[30] exemplify the struggle courts have had with the distinction. In *Midland Empire Packing Co.*, the taxpayer was forced to install a concrete liner in the basement of its packing plant to oil-proof it against the oil nuisance created by a neighboring refinery which was constructed long subsequent to the time the taxpayer had started to operate its packing plant. Quoting *Illinois Merchants Trust Co., Executor*,[31] the court defined "repair" as follows:

> To repair is to restore to a sound state or to mend, while a replacement connotes a substitution. A repair is an expenditure for the purpose of keeping the property in an ordinarily efficient operating condition. It does not add to the value of the property, nor does it appreciably prolong its life. It merely keeps the property in an operating condition over its probable useful life for the uses for which it was acquired. Expenditures for that purpose are distinguishable from those for replacements, alterations, improvements, or additions which prolong the life of the property, increase its value, or make it adaptable to a different use. The one is a maintenance charge, while the others are additions to capital investment which should not be applied against current earnings.[32]

Applying this standard, the court concluded the concrete liner constituted a repair since it merely permitted the plant to continue its normal operations and did not expand the plant or change the scale of its operation.

Mt. Morris Drive-In Theatre Co. addressed the question of whether the costs of a drainage system added to a newly developed drive-in theater had to be capitalized. There, an landowner whose property was adjacent to that of the taxpayer complained that the taxpayer's construction of a drive-in theater resulted in an acceleration and concentration of rain run-off onto his land. The landowner sued to restrain the taxpayer from permitting the run-off. The parties settled the dispute with the taxpayer agreeing to construct a drainage system. The court concluded the cost of the drainage system represented a capital expenditure. It distinguished *Midland Empire Packing* on the ground that the need for the drainage system was

---

[29] 14 T.C. 635 (1950).

[30] 25 T.C. 272 (1955).

[31] 4 B.T.A. 103, 106 (1926).

[32] 14 T.C. at 640.

foreseeable whereas the need for a concrete liner in *Midland Empire Packing* was not. In a concurring opinion, Judge Raum noted that the drainage system was "plainly capital in nature." He emphasized it was "wholly irrelevant whether the necessity for the drainage system could have been foreseen." Applying Judge Raum's analysis, one might as readily conclude the concrete liner in *Midland Empire Packing* was "plainly capital in nature." Dissenting, Judge Rice urged that the drainage system, like the concrete liner, "did not improve, better, extend, increase or prolong the useful life of [the drive-in theater]." As these various opinions suggest, reconciling the two cases may be difficult.

Even in light of *INDOPCO*, not all repairs need be capitalized on the theory their benefits extend beyond the current year. Despite the fact amounts paid or incurred for incidental repairs may have some future benefit, *INDOPCO* "does not affect the treatment of [those costs] as business expenses which are generally deductible under Section 162 of the Code."[33]

Conversely, a series of repairs may in the aggregate bring about an "improvement" to the property in question. For example, in *United States v. Wehrli*,[34] the taxpayer, the owner of an office building, sought to deduct as repairs the costs involved in preparing the building for a new tenant. The court discussed the boundary line between repairs and capital expenses:

> In our search for a more definite formula for the resolution of the line-drawing process, we evolved what may be called the "one-year" rule of thumb, under which an expenditure should be capitalized "if it brings about the acquisition of an asset having a period of useful life in excess of one year or if it secures a like advantage to the taxpayer which has a life of more than one year . . . ." We think, however, that it was intended to serve as a mere guidepost for the resolution of the ultimate issue, not as an absolute rule requiring the automatic capitalization of every expenditure providing the taxpayer with a benefit enduring for a period in excess of one year. Certainly the expense incurred in the replacement of a broken window-pane, a damaged lock, or a door, or even a periodic repainting of the entire structure, may well be treated as a deductible repair expenditure even though the benefits endure quite beyond the current year.

> In the continuing quest for formularization, the courts have superimposed upon the criteria in the repair regulation an overriding precept that an expenditure made for an item which is part of a "general plan" of rehabilitation, modernization, and improvement of the property, must be capitalized, even though, standing alone, the item may appropriately be classified as one of repair. Whether the plan exists, and whether a particular item is part of it, are usually questions of fact to be determined by the fact finder based upon a realistic appraisal of all the surrounding facts and circumstances, including, but not limited to, the purpose, nature, extent, and value of the work done, *e.g.*, whether the work was done to suit the needs of an incoming tenant, or to adapt the property to a different use,

---

[33] Rev. Rul. 94-12, 1994-1 C.B. 36.

[34] 400 F.2d 686 (10th Cir. 1968).

or, in any event, whether what was done resulted in an appreciable enhancement of the property's value.[35]

The repair or improvement question may simply be one more aspect of the acquisition issue discussed previously. The principles applicable to the repair or improvement question were summarized by the Service in Revenue Ruling 2001-4, discussed below.

[2] Temporary Regulations — Improvements and Repairs

For several years, the Service has recognized the need to provide further clarification with regard to the deduction-versus-capitalization rules relating to repair or improvement of tangible property. In 2004, the Service announced its intent to propose regulations that "provide clear, consistent and administrable rules that will reduce the uncertainty and controversy in this area, while also preventing the distortion of income."[36]

Proposed regulations under Section 263(a) were issued originally in 2006 and then withdrawn and reproposed in 2008. Finally, at the end of 2011, temporary regulations were issued, the text of which also serves as yet a third set of proposed regulations. The issuance of the temporary regulations, which generally took effect in 2012, suggests that the issuance of final regulations is closer than ever before. The temporary regulations provide considerable guidance in this area. Unlike the prior regulations which, among other matters, focused on whether expenditures materially increase the value of property, the temporary regulations steer clear of focusing on value in addressing amounts paid to improve tangible property. The temporary regulations provide general rules for determining the appropriate unit of property to which the improvement regulations apply, and require capitalization of amounts paid to bring about a betterment to a unit of property, to restore a unit of property, or to adapt a unit of property to a new or different use.[37]

Determination of the appropriate unit of property is critical in the application of the temporary regulations. For example, to decide whether a cost associated with property is to be treated as a deductible repair cost or a capitalization improvement cost, one must first identify the unit of property that will be the focus of the repair/improvement analysis. Although the prior regulations did not provide rules for identifying a unit of property, courts prior to the temporary regulations nonetheless had to determine the unit of property to be considered in applying the repair/improvement analysis. For example, in *FedEx Corporation v. United States*,[38] the court, in determining whether a taxpayer could deduct currently the costs associated with maintenance of its jet aircraft engines and auxiliary power units, noted that, in applying the repair regulations, it first had to decide whether the aircraft themselves, rather than the engines or power units, were the appropriate unit of property to which to apply the regulations. Applying factors similar to the factors discussed below and included in the temporary regulations, the court

---

[35] *Id.* at 689, 690.

[36] 2004-3 I.R.B. 308, Notice 2004-6.

[37] Treas. Reg. § 1.263(a)-3T(d).

[38] 291 F. Supp. 2d 699 (W.D. Tenn. 2003), *aff'd*, 412 F.3d 617 (6th Cir. 2005).

concluded the aircraft themselves were the appropriate units of property for purposes of applying the repair regulations. Having made that determination, the court concluded the maintenance performed on the engines and power units preserved, but did not prolong, the life of the aircraft. Obviously, had the engines themselves been the unit of property to be analyzed, the court would likely have reached a different conclusion.

The temporary regulations provide, in general, that the unit-of-property determination will be made using a functional interdependence standard. For property other than buildings, "all components that are functionally interdependent comprise a single unit of property. Components of property are functionally interdependent if the placing in service of one component by the taxpayer is dependent on the placing in service of the other component by the taxpayer."[39] In one example, the temporary regulations conclude that a laptop computer and a printer used in providing legal services constitute separate units of property because they are not components that are functionally interdependent, that is, the placing in service of the computer is not dependent on the placing in service of the printer.[40] The temporary regulations contain a special rule for buildings whereby a building and its structural components are generally (but not always) treated as a single unit of property for purposes of these temporary regulations.[41]

Under the temporary regulations, an amount paid results in the betterment of property only if it "(i) ameliorates a material condition or defect that . . . existed prior to the taxpayer's acquisition of the unit of property . . . (ii) results in a material addition . . . to the unit of property; or (iii) results in a material increase in capacity . . . productivity, efficiency, strength, or quality of the unit of property . . ."[42] The regulations provide examples of amounts that must be capitalized because they constitute a "betterment" since they ameliorate a pre-existing material condition, e.g., to prevent further leakage of gasoline and resultant soil contamination, a purchaser of land removes the underground gasoline storage tanks left by the prior occupant.[43] By contrast, under a fact pattern identical to that of *Midland Empire Packing Co.*, the regulations find no betterment as a result of the addition of the concrete liner to the walls of the packing plant.[44]

The regulations identify a range of situations in which an amount will be treated as being paid to restore a unit of property, including: (1) if it returns the unit of property to its ordinarily efficient operating condition after the property has deteriorated to a state of disrepair and is no longer functional for its intended use; (2) if it results in the rebuilding of the unit of property to a like-new condition after the end of the economic useful life of the property; and (3) if it is for the replacement of a major component or a substantial structural part of the unit of property.[45]

---

[39] Treas. Reg. § 1.263(a)-3T(e)(3)(i).

[40] Treas. Reg. § 1.263(a)-3T(e)(6) Ex. 9.

[41] Treas. Reg. § 1.263(a)-3T(e)(2)(i).

[42] Treas. Reg. § 1.263(a)-3T(h)(1).

[43] Treas. Reg. § 1.263(a)-3T(h)(4) Ex. 1.

[44] Treas. Reg. § 1.263(a)-3T(h)(4) Ex. 12.

[45] Treas. Reg. § 1.263(a)-3T(i)(1).

Significantly, these regulations provide that the replacement of a major component or a substantial structural part requires consideration of "all the facts and circumstances [including] the quantitative or qualitative significance of the part or combination of parts in relation to the unit of property. A major component or substantial structural part includes a part or combination of parts that comprise a large portion of the physical structure of the unit of property or that perform a discrete and critical function in the operation of the unit of property."[46] In this regard, the regulations provide an example whereby an entirely new roof of a business building is treated as a major component or substantial part of the building.[47]

The temporary regulations indicate that an amount will be treated as paid to adapt a unit of property to a new or different use "if the adaptation is not consistent with the taxpayer's intended ordinary use of the unit of property at the time originally placed in service by the taxpayer."[48] As an example of such an adaptation, the regulations identify a situation in which a manufacturing facility is converted to a showroom.[49]

The temporary regulations also contain a safe harbor rule for routine maintenance on property other than buildings whereby an amount will not be deemed to improve the unit of property.[50] Routine maintenance includes recurring activities a taxpayer performs to keep the unit of property in its ordinarily efficient operating condition, e.g., the inspection, cleaning and testing of the unit of property, and the replacement of parts of the unit of property with comparable and commercially available and reasonable replacement parts. Factors such as industry practice and manufacturers' recommendations are considered in determining whether the maintenance is routine.

Compare in this regard Revenue Ruling 2001-4,[51] issued prior to the regulations and generally favorable to the airline industry, in which the Service addressed the deductibility of the costs of "heavy maintenance visits" on commercial aircraft, visits which must be performed every eight years of aircraft operation. The purpose of a heavy maintenance visit, according to the aircraft maintenance manual, is "to prevent deterioration of the inherent safety and reliability levels of the aircraft equipment and, if such deterioration occurs, to restore the equipment to their inherent levels."[52] A heavy maintenance visit involves primarily the inspection, testing, servicing, repairing, reconditioning, cleaning, stripping, and repainting of numerous airframe parts and components. It does not involve replacements, alterations, improvements or additions to the airframe that appreciably prolong its useful life or materially increase its value. According to the ruling, "the heavy maintenance visit merely [keeps] the airframe in an ordinarily efficient operating

---

[46] Treas. Reg. § 1.263(a)-3T(i)(4).

[47] Treas. Reg. § 1.263(a)-3T(i)(5) Ex. 12.

[48] Treas. Reg. § 1.263(a)-3T(j)(1).

[49] Treas. Reg. § 1.263(a)-3T(j)(3) Ex. 1.

[50] Treas. Reg. § 1.263(a)-3T(g)(1).

[51] 2001-1 C.B. 295.

[52] Rev. Rul. 2001-4, 2001-1 C.B. 295.

condition over its anticipated useful life for the uses for which the property was acquired."[53] The Service emphasized that "although the high cost of the work performed may be considered in determining whether an expenditure is capital in nature, cost alone is not dispositive."

The Service considered three situations involving heavy maintenance visits. In the first situation, the only work done was that normally associated with a heavy maintenance visit. Given the nature of the heavy maintenance visits as described above, the Service held the cost of the heavy maintenance visit was deductible.

The second situation considered by the ruling involved a heavy maintenance visit at which time certain other work was done, *i.e.*, the replacement of all of the skin panels on the belly of the aircraft fuselage, the installation of a cabin smoke and fire detection and suppression system, a ground proximity warning system and an airphone system. The Service concluded the cost of these additional improvements had to be capitalized although it permitted the deduction of the costs of the balance of the work associated with a standard heavy maintenance visit. According to the ruling, the fact that these capital improvements were done at the same time as the heavy maintenance visit did not render the costs of the heavy maintenance visit a capital expenditure under the general rehabilitation doctrine discussed above in *Wehrli*. Whether a general plan of rehabilitation exists is a question of fact. According to the ruling, the airline under the circumstances of this second situation did not plan to rehabilitate the aircraft but "merely to perform discrete capital improvements to the airframe."

The third situation involved not only a heavy maintenance visit but also the replacement of major components and significant portions of substantial structural parts that materially increased the value and substantially prolonged the useful life of the airframe. As a result of the work, the aircraft's value was materially increased. The Service concluded all of the work, including the heavy maintenance work, was incurred pursuant to a general plan of rehabilitation. Therefore, consistent with the *Werhli* analysis, all of the costs had to be capitalized.

Expenditures for employee training also raise capitalization issues. The question arises whether the costs of maintaining the quality of a business' workforce are to be viewed as comparable to incidental repairs and therefore currently deductible, or whether those costs provide long-term benefits and thus constitute capital expenditures. Historically, training costs, including the costs of trainers and expenses incurred in updating training manuals, have been deemed currently deductible expenses. *INDOPCO* does not change that result. Revenue Ruling 96-62[54] acknowledges there may be some future benefits to be derived from employee training, but nonetheless states that training costs will generally be deductible business expenses. The ruling cites examples of costs associated with training employees to operate new equipment, and training new employees of an ongoing business. According to the ruling, training costs must be capitalized only in unusual circumstances where the training provides benefits significantly beyond those traditionally associated with training in the ordinary course of business. For

---

[53] *Id.* at 298.

[54] 1996-2 C.B. 9.

example, the training costs incurred by an electric utility company in preparing employees to operate a nuclear power plant must be capitalized. The ruling addresses only those employee training costs incurred while a taxpayer is actually carrying on a trade or business. The ruling does not apply to start-up costs.

[D] Intangible Assets

Sustained uncertainties and disagreements as to the application of *INDOPCO* led the Service in 2002 to issue proposed regulations relating to the capitalization of intangibles. The preamble to the proposed regulations described the approach the Service was taking with respect to *INDOPCO*:

> A fundamental purpose of section 263(a) is to prevent the distortion of taxable income through current deduction of expenditures relating to the production of income in future years. Thus, in determining whether an expenditure should be capitalized, the Supreme Court has considered whether the expenditure produces a significant future benefit. *INDOPCO v. Commissioner*, 503 U.S. 79 (1992). A "significant future benefit" standard, however, does not provide the certainty and clarity necessary for compliance with, and sound administration of, the law. Consequently, the IRS and Treasury Department believe that simply restating the significant future benefit test, without more, would lead to continued uncertainty on the part of taxpayers and continued controversy between taxpayers and the IRS. Accordingly, the IRS and Treasury Department have initially defined the exclusive scope of the significant future benefit test through the specific categories of intangible assets for which capitalization is required in the proposed regulations. The future benefit standard underlies many of those categories. . . . [However, if] an expenditure is not described in one of the categories in the proposed regulations or in subsequent future guidance, taxpayers and IRS field personnel need not determine whether that expenditure produces a significant future benefit.

In 2004, the Service issued final regulations adopting the same approach:

> As in the proposed regulations, the final regulations provide that an amount paid to acquire or create an intangible not otherwise required to be capitalized by the regulations is not required to be capitalized on the ground that it produces significant future benefits for the taxpayer, unless the IRS publishes guidance requiring capitalization of the expenditure.

The general rule of the final regulations requires the capitalization of amounts paid to acquire or create an intangible, to "facilitate" the acquisition or creation of an intangible, or to create or enhance a separate and distinct asset.[55]

Among the examples given of "acquired intangibles" are ownership interests in corporations, partnerships or other entities; debt instruments; options to provide or acquire property; leases; patents or copyrights; and franchises or trademarks.[56] The cost of acquiring such intangibles must be capitalized.

---

[55] Treas. Reg. § 1.263(a)-4(b)(1).

[56] Treas. Reg. § 1.263(a)-4(c)(1).

"Created intangibles" include financial interests (which in turn include ownership interests in corporations, partnerships and other entities; debt instruments; and options to provide or acquire property); prepaid expenses; certain membership fees; amounts paid to create (or terminate) certain contracts for property or services; and amounts paid to defend title to intangible property.[57] Again, the costs of creating the intangibles must be capitalized.[58]

It is hardly surprising that capitalization is required for such intangibles. The Service has, for example, taken the position for many years that prepaid expenses must generally be capitalized, pointing to the First Circuit opinion in *Commissioner v. Boylston Market Association*, which, in requiring the capitalization of the purchase of three years' fire insurance, stated:

> Advance rentals, payments of bonuses for acquisition and cancellation of leases, and commissions for negotiating leases are all matters which the taxpayer amortizes over the life of the lease . . . . [T]he payments are prorated primarily because the life of the asset extends beyond the taxable year. To permit the taxpayer to take a full deduction in the year of payment would distort his income. Prepaid insurance presents the same problem and should be solved in the same way.[59]

The regulations also provide for capitalizing amounts paid to "facilitate" the acquisition or creation of an intangible — or in the language of the regulations, to facilitate a "transaction." The rule of the regulations is that an amount facilitates a transaction, and thus must be capitalized, if the amount is "paid in the process of investigating or otherwise pursuing the transaction."[60] There are, however, significant simplifying conventions under which (1) employee compensation and overhead, and (2) de minimis costs (amounts not in excess of $5,000) are treated as amounts that do not facilitate the acquisition or creation of intangibles, an thus need not be capitalized.[61] In effect, the regulations opt for ease of administration and record-keeping over the more accurate measurement of income that would in theory emerge from precise allocations of employee time, overhead and minor costs to each of the taxpayer's transactions.

Another significant simplification provision is a "12-month rule," under which capitalization is not required for amounts paid for a right or benefit that does not extend beyond either (1) 12 months from first realizing the right or benefit, or (2) the end of the tax year following the year of payment.[62]

Example: Mia purchases a 12-month license for her business on June 15, Year 1, where the license period runs from July 1, Year 1, to June 30, Year 2.

---

[57] Treas. Reg. § 1.263(a)-4(d)(2)-(9).

[58] Treas. Reg. § 1.263(a)-(4)(d)(1).

[59] Commissioner v. Boylston Market Association, 131 F.2d 966, 968 (1st Cir. 1942).

[60] Treas. Reg. § 1.263(a)-4(e)(1)(i).

[61] Treas. Reg. § 1.263(a)-4(e)(4).

[62] Treas. Reg. § 1.263(a)-4(f)(1).

Analysis: Because the right or benefit does not extend more than 12 months beyond July 1, the date it is first realized, and because the right or benefit does not extend beyond Year 2 (the end of the year following the year of payment), the payment need not be capitalized.

Suppose, however, the license period runs from June 15, Year 1 to July 1, Year 2; or alternatively, suppose Mia pays for a 12-month license on December 30, Year 0 with the license period extending from February 1, Year 1 to January 31, Year 2. In either case, the regulations would require capitalization of the payment: in the first case, because the right or benefit extends more than 12 months beyond the date it is first realized; in the alternative case, because the right or benefit extends beyond Year 1, the year following the year of payment.

Is there an echo of the *US Freightways* reasoning in the 12-month rule? Note that renewal rights may need to be taken into account in determining compliance with the rule.[63]

Amounts paid to facilitate the acquisition of a trade or business or to change the business' capital structure must also be capitalized. The simplifying conventions relating to employee compensation and overhead and to de minimis costs also apply here.[64] The regulations also identify, with respect to certain common types of business acquisitions, "inherently facilitative" amounts that must always be capitalized (such as the cost of appraisals, of preparation and review of purchase agreements, and of property transfers between parties to the transaction); otherwise, amounts paid to investigate and pursue the transaction, but which are not inherently facilitative, are deemed to facilitate the transaction (and thus require capitalization) only with respect to activities performed after a letter of intent has been executed or the material terms of the transaction have been approved by the governing authority of the taxpayer.[65] Costs incurred prior to these trigger events to investigate and otherwise pursue an acquisition are not subject to this capitalization requirement.

[E]   Expansion Costs

A related topic is how expenditures incurred to expand an existing business should be treated. As noted in Chapter 12, expenses incurred prior to "carrying on a trade or business" are not currently deductible. The question raised is whether a taxpayer engaged in expansion activities incurs currently deductible expenses, analogous to "maintenance" of property.

In *Briarcliff Candy Corp. v. Commissioner*,[66] a pre-*INDOPCO* case, the taxpayer's costs in establishing a "franchise" division to promote sales in new retail outlets were held to be deductible. The *Briarcliff* court found the facts there brought the case "squarely within the long recognized principle that expenditures

---

[63]   Treas. Reg. § 1.263(a)-4(f)(5). For additional applications of the 12-month rule to prepaid expenses, see Treas. Reg. § 1.263(a)-4(f)(8), Examples (1) and (2).

[64]   Treas. Reg. § 1.263(a)-5(a), (d).

[65]   Treas. Reg. § 1.263(a)-5(e).

[66]   475 F.2d 775 (2d Cir. 1973).

for the protection of an existing investment or the continuation of an existing business or the preservation of existing income from loss or diminution" are currently deductible and not capital in nature. The *Briarcliff* court noted the organizational changes the taxpayer had made in that case in order to spread its sales into a new territory "were not comparable to the acquisition of a new additional branch or division to make and sell a new and different product."[67]

In *Colorado Springs National Bank v. U.S.*,[68] the issue was whether costs incurred by a bank in creating credit card services for customers were currently deductible or had to be capitalized. The Tenth Circuit found that credit cards represented merely a new method for banks to provide letters of credit to their customers. Relying on *Briarcliff*, the court held the bank had no property interest in the credit card procedures. Under these circumstances, the costs it incurred in establishing the credit card operation were currently deductible.

Clearly the costs of entering a new line of business ought not to be currently deductible, but in light of *INDOPCO*, the question arises as to whether even the expansion costs of an existing business must be capitalized on the grounds they are necessarily productive of significant future benefits. The Service appears not to take this position. In Revenue Ruling 2000-4,[69] the Service seemingly re-affirmed the *Briarcliff* holding of deductibility. The issue in that ruling was whether the taxpayer could deduct the costs incurred in obtaining, maintaining and renewing certifications of compliance with certain international quality standards, known as "ISO 9000," intended to ensure the provision of quality services or products. In the course of holding the ISO 9000 certification costs to be deductible because, under *INDOPCO*, they did not result in future benefits that were more than incidental, the Service specifically cited *Briarcliff* in support of the statement that "even if ISO 9000 certification facilitates the expansion of the taxpayer's existing business, the mere ability to sell in new markets and to new customers, without more, does not result in significant future benefits."

Costs associated with business "down-sizing" can also raise capitalization questions. In Revenue Ruling 94-77,[70] the Service considered whether severance payments made by a taxpayer to its employees were deductible as business expenses or, in view of *INDOPCO*, had to be capitalized. Concluding the severance payments did not have to be capitalized but could be deducted currently, the Service stated: ". . . although severance payments made by a taxpayer to its employees in connection with a business down-sizing may produce some future benefits, such as reducing operating costs and increasing operating efficiencies, these payments principally relate to previously rendered services of those employees. Therefore, such severance payments are generally deductible as business expenses."

---

[67] *Id.* at 787.

[68] 505 F.2d 1185 (10th Cir. 1974).

[69] 2000-1 C.B. 331.

[70] 1994-2 C.B. 19.

[F]   Advertising Expenses

Advertising expenses may often provide benefits that continue well beyond the current taxable year. A case could presumably be made for capitalizing all advertising costs except to the extent the taxpayer can demonstrate their benefits are sufficiently short-lived. Nonetheless, the long-standing administrative practice is generally to treat advertising expenses as currently deductible. In the aftermath of the Supreme Court's decision in *INDOPCO*, discussed *supra*, the Service reaffirmed the deductibility of advertising expenses.

> The *Indopco* decision does not affect the treatment of advertising costs under section 162(a) of the Code. These costs are generally deductible under that section even though advertising may have some future effect on business activities, as in the case of institutional or goodwill advertising. *See* section 1.162-1(a) and section 1.162-20(a)(2) of the regulations. Only in the unusual circumstance where advertising is directed towards obtaining future benefits significantly beyond those traditionally associated with ordinary product advertising or with institutional or goodwill advertising, must the costs of that advertising be capitalized.[71]

In *RJR Nabisco Inc. v. Commissioner*,[72] the Commissioner sought to distinguish between the costs of developing advertising campaigns and the costs of executing or carrying out those campaigns. The Commissioner argued that advertising execution expenditures generate principally short-term benefits and are thus currently deductible, whereas advertising campaign expenditures provide only long-term benefits and ought to be capitalized. The Tax Court rejected the distinction:

> Although the case law admits the possibility of allocation between the short- and long-term benefits of advertising expenditures and, thus, would provide a basis for the Commissioner to insist that a taxpayer prove the portion of his advertising expenditures allocable to current benefits, the authorities previously cited, section 1.162-20(a)(2), Income Tax Regs., and Rev. Rul. 92-80, establish that the Secretary and the Commissioner, respectively, have eschewed that approach with respect to ordinary business advertising, even if long-term benefits (*e.g.*, goodwill) are the taxpayer's primary objective . . . . The result, as a practical matter, is that, notwithstanding certain long-term benefits, expenditures for ordinary business advertising are ordinary business expenses if the taxpayer can show a sufficient connection between the expenditure and the taxpayer's business.[73]

The intangibles regulations appear to follow this approach. See, for example, Treas. Reg. § 1.263(a)-4(l) Ex. 7, which concludes that capitalization is not required for "product launch costs" that include payments "to develop and implement a marketing strategy and an advertising campaign to raise consumer awareness" for a new pharmaceutical product. (The example notes the payments are not amounts

---

[71]   Rev. Rul. 92-80, 1992-2 C.B. 57.

[72]   T.C. Memo 1998-252.

[73]   *Id.* at *45–47.

paid (1) to acquire or create, or facilitate the acquisition or creation of, one of the specified self-created intangibles subject to capitalization; or (2) to create a separate and distinct intangible asset.)

§ 13.04   PURCHASE OR LEASE

Section 162(a)(3) specifically authorizes the deduction of rental payments with respect to property used in a trade or business but only if the taxpayer does not take title and has no equity in the property. The line between a lease and a purchase agreement may in some cases be unclear, causing the Service to question the deductibility of "rent" the taxpayer is paying. Are the rental payments being made by the taxpayer really disguised acquisition costs, routinely capital in nature, or are they what they purport to be, rental payments applicable to the current year and routinely deductible?

> **Example:** Taxpayer "leased" a fire sprinkler system from Sprinkler, Inc. Sprinklers, Inc. custom designed the fire sprinkler system for Taxpayer's business. The four year lease required Taxpayer to make "lease payments" of $4,000 annually. At the end of the four year lease term, Taxpayer had the option of purchasing the system for $100. Had Taxpayer purchased the system outright instead of "leasing" it, the cost would have been $14,500.

> **Analysis:** The Ninth Circuit considered comparable facts in *Estate of Starr v. Commissioner*.[74] The Ninth Circuit concluded that the taxpayer was actually purchasing the sprinkler system rather than leasing it. If the taxpayer had been successful in characterizing the transaction as a lease, the taxpayer could deduct the lease payments currently. By contrast, given the court's characterization, the taxpayer would be required to capitalize the cost of the system and could only recover the cost over time through depreciation deductions. In effect, the taxpayer's characterization would have accelerated deductions while the court's characterization lengthened the period over which the taxpayer would recover the cost of the system. The court noted that the difference between the purchase price of the sprinkler system and the aggregate amount of lease payments represented interest.

> This same analysis would presumably be applied to the facts presented in this example. Thus, assuming the sprinkler system were classified as five year property for depreciation purposes, the taxpayer would be required to depreciate the cost of the system ($14,500) over a five year period. Amounts paid by Taxpayer in excess of $14,500 would presumably be deductible as interest.

---

[74] 274 F.2d 294 (1959).

Chapter 14

DEPRECIATION

§ 14.01   DEPRECIATION

Clear reflection of income is a general goal of the Internal Revenue Code. Because our tax system taxes only net income, those costs incurred in producing income are generally deductible. To provide a mechanism whereby taxpayers could deduct the costs associated with the use of business or investment property, Congress developed a cost recovery system allowing taxpayers to claim depreciation deductions with respect to properties used in their trade or business or for investment. The Code's depreciation rules allow taxpayers to write-off or deduct their capital investment (or cost) over a specified period of time — the recovery period. The Supreme Court in *Commissioner v. Idaho Power* (discussed in Chapter 13) explained depreciation as follows:

> Depreciation is an accounting device which recognizes that the physical consumption of a capital asset is a true cost, since the asset is being depleted. As the process of consumption continues, and depreciation is claimed and allowed, the asset's adjusted income tax basis is reduced to reflect the distribution of its cost over the accounting periods affected . . . . "The purpose of depreciation accounting is to allocate the expense of using an asset to the various periods which are benefitted by that asset . . . ." When the asset is used to further the taxpayer's day-to-day business operations, the periods of benefit usually correlate with the production of income.[1]

Certain fundamental questions must be addressed by any depreciation system: What property is subject to depreciation? Over what period may one's costs be recovered through depreciation deductions? What method will be used for computing the amount of the depreciation deductions?

[A]   Depreciable Property

Section 167, the principal depreciation provision, defines "depreciation deduction" as "a reasonable allowance for the exhaustion, wear and tear (including a reasonable allowance for obsolescence) — (1) of property used in the trade or business, or (2) of property held for the production of income." The trade, business, or investment limitation is applicable because our tax system does not generally allow deductions for personal expenses. As a result, one may not claim depreciation deductions with respect to property held for personal use, *e.g.*, one's personal

---

[1] 418 U.S. 1, 10–11 (1974).

residence. (See, however, Chapter 21 addressing home office deductions.) Although one's home has a limited useful life, the wear and tear on it is a nondeductible personal expense.

Not only must the trade, business, or investment use standard be satisfied, the property must also be ". . . subject to wear and tear, decay or decline from natural causes, exhaustion, or obsolescence. Land, . . . stock, and other assets that . . . do not decline in value predictably [are] not depreciable."[2] Likewise, a taxpayer may not depreciate property held as inventory or held primarily for sale to customers.[3]

In the past, some taxpayers sought to render land depreciable by carving out term interests in land with the remainder interest being held by a related person. Section 167(e), however, prevents such arrangements.[4]

> **Example:** Dan is interested in purchasing a tract of farmland. Rather than purchasing a fee simple interest in the land, Dan makes the following arrangement with the seller: Dan will purchase a 25-year term interest in the land and Dan's daughter, Cathy (a related person under the terms of the statute), will purchase the remainder interest in the land. Because a term interest by its very nature has a limited life, Dan expects to be able to write-off the cost of the term interest by means of depreciation-type deductions.

> **Analysis:** Since the remainder interest is held by a related person, Section 167(e) disallows any depreciation deduction with respect to the term interest.

If an asset is not depreciable because it is not subject to wear, tear or exhaustion or because it is not used in the taxpayer's trade or business or for the production of income, the taxpayer may recover the cost of the asset upon disposing of it. As discussed in detail in Chapter 4, gain realized in a transaction equals the excess of the amount realized over the taxpayer's adjusted basis; loss realized equals the excess of the taxpayer's adjusted basis over the amount realized on the transaction[5] Basis represents one's cost; and "adjusted basis," as the term suggests, merely refers to the basis adjusted to reflect certain tax significant items, *e.g.*, depreciation deductions, which affect basis. In accord with Section 1001(c), a taxpayer must generally recognize (i.e., include in income) the realized gain. By contrast, realized loss will only be deductible if the taxpayer meets the requirements of Section 165.

> **Example 1:** Taxpayer purchases a summer home for $300,000, uses it exclusively for personal purposes for ten years and then sells it for

---

[2] *General Explanation of the Economic Recovery Tax Act of 1981*, Staff of the Joint Committee on Taxation, H. Rep. 4242, 97th Cong., p. 67.

[3] *See* Treas. Reg. § 1.167(a)-2; Rev. Rul. 89-25, 1989-1 C.B. 79 (holding that houses used temporarily by a homebuilder as models and/or sales offices are not depreciable).

[4] Section 167(e)(1) provides: "No depreciation deduction shall be allowed under this section . . . to the taxpayer for any term interest in property for any period during which the remainder interest in such property is held (directly or indirectly) by a related person."

[5] I.R.C. § 1001(a).

$750,000. What are the tax consequences to Taxpayer assuming that taxpayer is not eligible for the Section 121 exclusion discussed in Chapter 6?

Analysis: Because Taxpayer uses the summer home for personal purposes and not for business or for the production of income, the home is not depreciable. Taxpayer's basis in the house is $300,000, *i.e.*, the cost of the home. As a result of the sale, Taxpayer will realize and recognize $450,000 of gain, *i.e.*, Section 1001(a) defines gain as the difference between the amount realized on the sale ($750,000) and Taxpayer's adjusted basis ($300,000). [Note that the example assumes Taxpayer did not invest additional amounts in the home and that nothing else occurred that would require an adjustment to the home's basis. Thus, the adjusted basis is the same as Taxpayer's original basis.] Under this Section 1001(a) formula, Taxpayer is allowed to recover her cost tax-free; only amounts received in excess of her cost will constitute gain.

Example 2: Taxpayer purchases for $100,000 a tract of land for use in her business. Four years later, Taxpayer sells the land for $90,000. What are the tax consequences to Taxpayer?

Analysis: Because land is not subject to wear, tear or exhaustion, it is not depreciable. Taxpayer's adjusted basis in the land at the time of the sale is thus the same as the purchase price, *i.e.*, $100,000. Taxpayer realizes a $10,000 loss on the sale — the adjusted basis of the land ($100,000) exceeds the amount realized ($90,000) by $10,000. As will be discussed in detail in Chapter 15, Taxpayer will be entitled to deduct the $10,000 loss.[6] Taxpayer in effect has been permitted to recover in full her $100,000 investment in the land, *i.e.*, she received $90,000 from the purchaser and was allowed a $10,000 loss deduction.

[B] Recovery Period — The Useful Life Concept

[1] Historical Development

If the most accurate measurement of the cost of producing income is sought, depreciation deductions should be taken throughout the period an asset is used in the production of income. Of course, one doesn't know at the time an asset is acquired exactly how many years the taxpayer will use the asset in a trade or business or for investment. One can, however, estimate how long a particular asset is expected to be useful in an income-producing activity. An asset's useful life is not necessarily coextensive with its actual physical life. For example, a car may be in running condition for twenty or thirty years; its usefulness in a particular business, however, may be limited to only a few years. The determination of useful life thus requires an asset by asset determination.

A direct correlation exists between the useful life of an asset and the size of the depreciation deduction allowable in a given year. The longer the useful life, the

---

[6] I.R.C. § 165.

smaller the annual deduction. Early in our tax history, the taxpayer had the burden of establishing the useful life of an asset. Considering the speculative nature of this determination, it is not surprising that considerable controversy ensued between the Service and taxpayers regarding useful lives. To alleviate some of the problems, the Treasury in 1942 issued so-called "Bulletin F," which provided average useful lives for a multitude of assets. While taxpayers were not required to adopt the useful life indicated in Bulletin F for a given asset, the use of a shorter life was risky. In 1962, the Treasury issued guidelines prescribing useful lives for classes of assets, rather than on an asset-by-asset basis as in Bulletin F. These guidelines, by comparison to Bulletin F, authorized far shorter useful lives.

Congress in 1971 enacted Section 167(m), authorizing the Treasury to create an Asset Depreciation Range (ADR) providing an industry-wide set of useful lives for classes of assets. With respect to a given asset, a taxpayer could select a useful life 20% longer or shorter than the so-called midpoint life of the class of assets to which a taxpayer's asset belonged. Not only did ADR reduce disputes regarding the useful lives of assets, it also permitted taxpayers to write off the cost of acquiring assets over a much shorter period. With certain exceptions, however, the ADR system did not prescribe useful lives for real property. The 1962 Guidelines, therefore, continued to be used with respect to real property, providing useful lives ranging from 40 years for apartment buildings to 60 years for warehouses.

Notwithstanding the shorter useful lives authorized by the 1962 guidelines and the 1971 ADR system, one could argue that some correlation existed between the useful lives provided in these safe harbor standards and the actual economic lives of assets. Any such correlation which might have existed, however, was negated in 1981 when Congress, both as a simplification measure and as a stimulant to the economy, provided a new system for depreciating tangible property. The Accelerated Cost Recovery System, known as ACRS, significantly de-emphasized the useful life concept by assigning all tangible property to one of five recovery periods based on the asset's "class life" which is defined in Section 168(i)(1) as the class life (if any) applicable to the property under Section 167(m) (the ADR System).

Under the ACRS as originally enacted in 1981 and applicable to tangible depreciable property placed in service after December 31, 1981, most real property was classified as 15-year property, meaning that the cost of buildings such as an office complex could be written off over a 15-year period. In addition, most tangible personal property was classified as 3-year property or 5-year property and could be written off over three or five years. Property with no assigned class life under ACRS was treated as 5-year property. These shortened useful lives, combined with accelerated methods of computing depreciation, enabled taxpayers to write-off the cost of newly acquired property far more rapidly than before.

[2] Current Recovery Periods — Modified Accelerated Cost Recovery System (MACRS)

§ 168. Accelerated Cost Recovery System.

(c) **Applicable recovery period. — For purposes of this section, the applicable recovery period shall be determined in accordance with the following table:**

In the case of:	The applicable recovery period is:
3-year property	3 years
5-year property	5 years
7-year property	7 years
10-year property	10 years
15-year property	15 years
20-year property	20 years
Residential Rental Property	27.5 years
Nonresidential real property	39 years

Congress in 1986 amended ACRS, creating the current depreciation system, the so-called Modified Accelerated Cost Recovery System (MACRS) which is applicable to tangible depreciable property placed in service after December 31, 1986. This modified system, by comparison to ACRS, expands the number of recovery periods and lengthens the recovery period of real property and, to some extent, certain tangible personal property. Thus, under current law "nonresidential real property" is depreciated over 39 years and "residential rental property" is depreciated o ver 27.5 years. Property other than "nonresidential real property" and "residential rental property" must generally be classified within one of six recovery periods — three, five, seven, ten, fifteen, and twenty years. The most important of these categories are the 3-year, 5-year and 7-year classes.

Each of these classes is defined by reference to the "class life" of assets.[7] The "class life" of an asset is its midpoint life in the Asset Depreciation Range (ADR) discussed previously.[8] Congress specifically provided, however, that 5-year property would include, among other items, automobiles or light general purpose trucks despite the fact that these assets technically have the same class life as 3-year property and thus might otherwise be considered 3-year property. In addition, 5-year property includes computers, copying equipment, and heavy general purpose trucks.[9] The 7-year property class is now the catchall class and includes all personal property with no assigned class life under ADR, such as office furniture, fixtures and equipment.

As noted, Congress, in enacting ACRS and the current MACRS, significantly de-emphasized the useful life concept. Historically, only assets with a determinable useful life were depreciable. Thus, a valuable art piece was not considered depreciable property because it did not have a determinable useful life.[10] A question which has sparked considerable disagreement between the courts and the Service is whether, in view of the changes wrought by ACRS and MACRS, a taxpayer must still establish that an asset has a determinable useful life for the asset to be depreciable. With respect to this issue, the courts ruled in favor of the taxpayers in

---

[7] I.R.C. § 168(e)(1).

[8] See the excerpt from Rev. Proc. 87-56, reprinted at the end of this chapter.

[9] I.R.C. § 168(e)(3)(B)(i).

[10] Rev. Rul. 68-232, 1968-1 C.B. 79.

Simon v. Commissioner,[11] (allowing professional violinists to depreciate their nineteenth-century violin bows) and *Liddle v. Commissioner*,[12] (allowing a professional musician to depreciate a seventeenth-century bass viol). In finding these antique instruments to be depreciable, the courts emphasized that Congress sought to simplify depreciation by eliminating disputes regarding the useful life of assets. To accomplish its goal, Congress defined broad classes, *e.g.*, 3-year, 5-year and 7-year property, to which assets were assigned and over which periods the assets were depreciable. According to the *Simon* and *Liddle* courts, therefore, the key requirement was no longer the determination of useful life but rather a determination that the asset was subject to wear and tear or exhaustion. Because of the use of the instruments by the taxpayers, the courts concluded the instruments were subject to wear and tear.

In *Selig v. Commissioner*,[13] *Simon* and *Liddle* were followed and the taxpayer was allowed to take depreciation deductions on "exotic automobiles" he owned and exhibited for a fee at car shows. The question, according to the Tax Court, was whether a depreciation deduction was allowable for automobiles held in a "pristine condition" and exhibited for a fee in the taxpayer's trade or business:

> The long and the short of it is yes, provided the automobiles are subject to obsolescence. We have found that the exotic automobiles were state-of-the-art, high technology vehicles with unique design features or equipment. We have no doubt that, over time, the exotic automobiles would, because of just those factors, become obsolete in petitioner's business. *The fact that petitioners have failed to show the useful lives of the exotic automobiles is irrelevant.*[14]

Although there was no evidence that the automobiles were subject to wear and tear, the court was nevertheless convinced that by their very nature they "had a useful life as show cars shorter than their ordinary useful life and, thus, suffered obsolescence" and also that they "were not museum pieces of indeterminable useful life."

[C]   Depreciation Methods

§ 168.   **Accelerated Cost Recovery System.**

(b)   **Applicable depreciation methods. — For purposes of this section —**

(1)   **In general. — Except as provided in paragraphs (2) and (3), the applicable depreciation method is —**

(A) **the 200 percent declining balance method,**

(B) **switching to the straight line method for the 1st taxable year for which using the straight line method with respect to the adjusted basis as of the beginning of such year will yield a larger allowance.**

---

[11]   103 T.C. 247, *aff'd*, 68 F.3d 41 (2d Cir. 1995).

[12]   103 T.C. 285, *aff'd*, 65 F.3d 329 (3d Cir. 1995).

[13]   T.C. Memo. 1995-519.

[14]   *Id.* (emphasis added).

· · ·

(3)   **Property to which straight line method applies. — The applicable depreciation method shall be the straight line method in the case of the following property:**

(A) **Nonresidential real property.**

(B) **Residential rental property.**

Just as Congress has manipulated the useful life concept to increase or decrease depreciation rates, it has also varied the methods used to compute depreciation. Depreciation methods may be separated into two categories: straight line depreciation and accelerated depreciation. Currently, the Code utilizes both depreciation methods. The straight line method is the simplest. "Under the straight line method the cost or other basis of the property less its estimated salvage value is deductible in equal annual amounts over the period of the estimated useful life of the property."[15] In general, under the straight line method, one merely divides the cost of the asset by the number of years in the recovery period to determine the depreciation allowance for the given year.

> **Example:** Assume Taxpayer builds an apartment building costing $1,000,000 and qualifying as residential rental property with a useful life of 27.5 years. Assume also that the salvage value at the end of the 27.5 year period is $0. In theory, the taxpayer should be entitled to deduct 3.6% (*i.e.*, 100%/27.5) of the $1,000,000 cost or $36,000 per year so that after 27.5 years Taxpayer would have deducted the full $1,000,000 cost of the building. The 3.6% is the straight line rate of depreciation. If there were a salvage value to the property at the end of the 27.5 years, the annual depreciation deductions would be computed by subtracting the salvage value from the $1,000,000 cost and dividing the balance by 27.5. Section 168(b)(4), however, provides that salvage value under MACRS is treated as zero, thereby allowing a taxpayer to recover the entire cost of property during the recovery period.

Acknowledging that property does not wear out at an even rate and desiring to stimulate the economy by authorizing more rapid depreciation, Congress has authorized accelerated methods of recovery. The effect of these methods is to permit larger depreciation deductions in the early years of the recovery period than in the later years, *i.e.*, the depreciation deductions are "front-loaded." One such accelerated method is known as the declining balance method. It differs from the straight line method in that a greater fixed rate is used and is applied, not to the total cost of property each year as in the straight line example above, but to the cost less the depreciation deductions claimed for prior years (*i.e.*, the adjusted basis).[16] The most common declining balance methods are the so-called 200% or double declining balance method and the 150% declining balance method.

Consider the following example which demonstrates the 200% or double declining balance method:

---

[15]   Treas. Reg. § 1.167(b)-1.

[16]   See the definition of declining balance method in Treas. Reg. § 1.167(b)-2(a).

Example: Taxpayer purchases a used truck for business use for $10,000. The truck has a useful life of five years. How will Taxpayer's depreciation deductions be computed using the double declining balance method?

Analysis: The straight line rate of depreciation would be 20%, *i.e.*, 100% divided by 5. As its name suggests, the 200% or double declining balance method authorizes Taxpayer to use a depreciation rate double that of straight line, or, in this example, 40%. That depreciation rate is then applied, year by year, to a declining balance — the unrecovered cost of the asset. Note the difference between the depreciation which the taxpayer may claim under the straight line and double declining balance methods:

	straight line	double declining balance
Year 1	$2,000	$4,000 (40% × $10,000)
Year 2	$2,000	$2,400 (40% × $6,000)
Year 3	$2,000	$1,440 (40% × $3,600)
Year 4	$2,000	$864 (40% × $2,160)
Year 5	$2,000	$518 (40% × $1,296)[17]

The front-loading effect of the double-declining balance is obvious from this example.

Section 168(b)(1) provides that, with respect to 3-year, 5-year and 7-year property, the 200% or double declining balance method shall be used, but the taxpayer shall shift to the straight line method in the year that method, if applied to the adjusted basis at the beginning of such year, would produce the larger deduction.[18] The taxpayer, however, may elect an alternative depreciation system, allowing the taxpayer to depreciate property over a longer time period using the straight line method. Presumably, taxpayers would seldom elect to use this system.

Section 168(b)(3) requires taxpayers to use the straight line method to depreciate residential rental property and nonresidential real property, as well as a range of other specialized properties including qualified leasehold improvement property described in Section 168(e)(6) and qualified restaurant property described in Section 168(e)(7). (An alternative depreciation method[19] may be elected by a taxpayer with respect to real property and will have the effect of lengthening the period over which depreciation deductions are claimed. For example, a taxpayer may elect to depreciate residential rental property over a 40-year period rather than a 27.5-year period.)

---

[17] The 200% or double declining balance method always leave a balance at the end of the asset's useful life (*i.e.*, $778 in the example) because by definition it authorizes a deduction of only a portion — here, 40% — of the remaining balance. Under the declining balance method, any unrecovered balance may be deducted upon retirement of the asset.

[18] I.R.C. §§ 168(9)(2), 168(g)(7). See § 14.02, *infra*, for the application of this method to the facts of the example above.

[19] I.R.C. § 168(g)(2).

[D]　Conventions

§ 168.　Accelerated Cost Recovery System.

(d)　Applicable convention. — For purposes of this section —

(1)　In general. — Except as otherwise provided in this subsection, the applicable convention is the half-year convention.

(2)　Real property. — In the case of

(A) nonresidential real property,

(B) residential rental property . . . .

the applicable convention is the mid-month convention.

. . .

(4)　Definitions. —

(A)　Half-year convention. — The half-year convention is a convention which treats all property placed in service during any taxable year (or disposed of during any taxable year) as placed in service (or disposed of) on the mid-point of such taxable year.

(B)　Mid-month convention. — The mid-month convention is a convention which treats all property placed in service during any month or disposed of during any month) as placed in service (or disposed of) on the mid-point of such month.

(C)　Mid-quarter convention. — The mid-quarter convention is a convention which treats all property placed in service during any quarter of a taxable year (or disposed of during any quarter of a taxable year) as placed in service (or disposed of) on the mid-point of such quarter.

The applicable recovery period during which depreciation may be claimed begins when the property is placed in service. "Placed in service" means "placed in a condition or state of readiness and availability for the specifically assigned function."[20] To avoid difficulties associated with computing depreciation for fractions of a year, Congress adopted a number of conventions. Residential rental property and nonresidential real property placed in service during any month are deemed placed in service on the mid-point of such month.[21] The depreciation amount for the full year is then prorated according to the number of months during which the property was in service for the particular year. For example, if a calendar year taxpayer places residential rental property in service on the last day of January, the property will be deemed to have been placed in service at the middle of the month. The depreciation amount for the first year will equal 11.5/12 or 23/24 of the annual depreciation amount. In the year of disposition, the taxpayer will likewise prorate the annual depreciation deduction over the number of months that the property was in service during that year and will take the mid-month convention into account. For example, if a taxpayer sells residential rental property on June 2, the taxpayer will be deemed to have sold the property at the midpoint of the month

---

[20]　Treas. Reg. § 1.46-3(d)(1)(ii).

[21]　I.R.C. § 168(d)(2), (4)(B).

and will be entitled to claim 5½ months of depreciation in the year of sale. No depreciation deduction is allowed for property placed in service and disposed of during the same taxable year.[22]

All the other classes of property are generally subject to a half-year convention, *i.e.*, any property placed in service during the tax year (or disposed of during any taxable year) is deemed placed in service (or disposed of) on the mid-point of the tax year.[23] For example, a calendar year taxpayer who purchases a truck for business use on December 1 will ordinarily be deemed to have placed the truck in service on July 1, and will therefore be entitled to one-half year's depreciation on the truck instead of only one month's. Similarly, placing the truck in service on February 1 would give rise to one-half year's depreciation, not eleven months. In the year in which the truck is disposed of, the taxpayer will generally compute the depreciation deduction, if any, for the year on the assumption that the truck was sold on July 1 of that year. In other words, the taxpayer will only be entitled to one-half year's depreciation in the year of sale.

To prevent taxpayers from taking undue advantage of the half-year convention, Congress has provided that if the properties placed in service (other than nonresidential real and residential rental property) during the last three months of the year have aggregate bases greater than 40% of the aggregate bases of *all* properties placed in service that year, a mid-quarter convention will apply instead of the half-year convention.[24] (Nonresidential real property and residential rental property are not subject to the mid-quarter convention and are therefore not taken into account in the "greater-than-40%" calculation.) For example, if a business truck placed in service on December 1 is the only depreciable property placed in service that year, the greater-than-40% test is necessarily met, and the mid-quarter convention will apply. The truck will be deemed placed in service midway through the fourth quarter, so one-eighth of a year's depreciation will be allowed. The Treasury has published Revenue Procedure 87-57, included in part at the end of this chapter, providing tables incorporating the various conventions, enabling depreciation deductions to be computed quickly. In the year of disposition, the taxpayer is entitled to claim depreciation subject to the above conventions. If another truck of equal cost had been placed in service in January of the same year, the greater-than-40% test would still be met (because 50% of the aggregate bases would have been placed in service in the last 3 months of the year). The January truck would be deemed placed in service midway through the first quarter, so 7/8 of the year's depreciation would be allowed. The December truck, as noted, would be entitled to 1/8 of a year's depreciation.

As previously noted, Section 168 is generally applicable to tangible, depreciable property placed in service after 1986. Intangible property like patents and

---

[22] Treas. Reg. § 1.168(d)-1(b)(3)(ii).

[23] I.R.C. § 168(d)(1), (4)(A).

[24] I.R.C. § 168(d)(3). Under the mid-quarter convention, property placed in service during any calendar quarter of a taxable year (or disposed of during any quarter of a taxable year) is treated as placed in service (or disposed of) on the mid-point of such calendar quarter. Section 168(d)(3)(B) also provides that any property placed in service and disposed of during the same taxable year will likewise not be considered in determining whether the mid-quarter convention is applicable.

copyrights continues to be subject to the depreciation rules of Section 167, unless otherwise treated under Section 197 (discussed below.)[25]

§ 14.02　COMPUTING THE DEPRECIATION DEDUCTION

§ 168.　Accelerated Cost Recovery System.

(a)　**General rule. — Except as otherwise provided in this section, the depreciation deduction provided by section 167(a) for any tangible property shall be determined by using —**

(1) the applicable depreciation method,

(2) the applicable recovery period, and

(3) the applicable convention.

There are four steps to computing the depreciation deductions authorized by the Code:

(1)　Determine the adjusted basis of the property.

(2)　Determine the applicable recovery period.

(3)　Determine the applicable depreciation method.

(4)　Determine the applicable convention.

Example: Assume a taxpayer purchases for $10,000 on March 1 a used light general purpose truck to be used in the taxpayer's business and acquires no other depreciable property this year. How will the taxpayer compute her depreciation deductions?

Analysis: First, consider the four steps outlined above.

(1) In the case of purchased property, the adjusted basis will generally be its cost. Therefore, the adjusted basis is $10,000, and depreciation for the first year will be computed with reference to that amount.

(2) Section 168(e)(3) classifies automobiles and light general purpose trucks as 5-year property; Section 168(c)(1) provides that the applicable recovery period for 5-year property is five years.

(3) Section 168(b)(1) provides that the 200% declining balance method (switching to straight line) is the appropriate method for 5-year property.

(4) Generally, according to Section 168(d)(1), the applicable convention for 5-year property is the half-year convention, and that convention applies here.[26]

---

[25] See Section 167(f)(1), providing that computer software shall be depreciated over a 36-month period using the straight line method.

[26] Since the truck was the only depreciable property placed in service this year and since this did not occur in the last three months of the year, the mid-quarter convention will not apply.

Second, the rates in the tables in Revenue Procedure 87-57 (included at the end of the Chapter) will be applied. The appropriate table in this case is Table 1 because it is the table which incorporates 5-year property, double-declining balance switching to straight line, and the half-year convention. According to that table, the depreciation rate for the first year will be 20%. (The reason the first year rate is 20% is that only half a year's depreciation is allowed; hence, half of 40% is the appropriate rate for the first year.) Applying that rate to the "unadjusted basis"[27] of the truck, the taxpayer will be entitled to claim a depreciation deduction of $2,000 in Year 1 (*i.e.*, $10,000 X .20 = $2,000). In Year 2, the depreciation rate will be 32%, yielding a depreciation deduction of $3,200 (*i.e.*, $10,000 X .32 = $3,200). Using this same method of computation, the depreciation in Years 3 through 6 will be $1,920, $1,152, $1,152, and $576. Note that, because of the half-year convention, the recovery period for 5-year property will actually extend over six calendar years.

In sum, using Table 1 of Revenue Procedure 87-57, the depreciation schedule for the truck is as follows:

Recovery Year	"Unadjusted Basis"	Depreciation Rate	Depreciation
1	$10,000	20%	$2,000
2	$10,000	32%	$3,200
3	$10,000	19.20%	$1,920
4	$10,000	11.52%	$1,152
5	$10,000	11.52%	$1,152
6	$10,000	5.76%	$ 576
TOTAL		100%	$10,000

Note that the taxpayer will claim depreciation deductions totaling $10,000 (the full cost of the truck) over six calendar years.

The depreciation tables provided in the Revenue Procedure are fully consistent with the language of Section 168(b)(1), which provides for a 200% declining balance method switching to straight line when the straight line method produces a greater deduction. For example, the Year 2 rate in the table, 32% of $10,000, is the same as the double declining rate of 40% applied against an adjusted basis of $8,000 (*i.e.*, $10,000 less first year depreciation of $2,000). Table 1 merely applies the congressional directive of Section 168(b)(1) in a fashion that makes computation of depreciation a simpler process for taxpayers.

Similarly, the tables incorporate the switch to straight line depreciation in the appropriate year. In the above example, at the beginning of Year 5 there are one and one-half years left in the recovery period. Year 5 itself represents two-thirds of

---

[27] The tables set forth in this Revenue Procedure provide the appropriate depreciation rate to be applied to the "unadjusted basis" of the property in each year of the recovery period. Simply stated, the term "unadjusted basis" means the adjusted basis of the property, disregarding any depreciation deductions claimed by the taxpayer. Thus, the unadjusted basis of the automobile is $10,000 in each of the six years of the recovery period.

the remaining recovery period, so a switch to straight line depreciation will allow a deduction in Year 5 of two-thirds of the unrecovered cost. The double declining balance method would result in deducting only forty percent of the unrecovered cost so the switch will be made to straight line depreciation in Year 5.[28]

The same approach used above to compute depreciation deductions for tangible personal property should be used for computing depreciation deductions for nonresidential real property or residential rental property. In the case of such real property, however, the straight line method will be used together with the mid-month convention.

§ 14.03 ADDITIONAL FIRST YEAR DEPRECIATION

Congress has amended Section 168 to provide "bonus depreciation" for certain property *acquired after December 31, 2007 and placed in service before January 1, 2014*. The following quote from the legislative history describes the operation of Section 168(k) providing for bonus (or "additional first year") depreciation:

> The provision [Section 168(k)] allows an additional first-year depreciation deduction equal to 50 percent of the adjusted basis of qualified property. . . . The basis of the property and the depreciation allowances in the year the property is placed in service and later years are appropriately adjusted to reflect the additional first year-year depreciation deduction. . . . The taxpayer may elect out of additional first-year depreciation for any class of property for any taxable year.

> The interaction of the additional first-year depreciation allowance with the otherwise applicable depreciation allowance [under the rules of Section 168 discussed above] may be illustrated as follows. Assume that in 2009, a taxpayer purchases new depreciable property and places it in service. The property's cost is $1,000, and it is five-year property subject to the half-year convention. The amount of the additional first-year depreciation allowed under the provision is $500. The remaining $500 of the cost of the property is deductible under the rules applicable to five-year property. Thus, 20 percent [of $500], or $100, is also allowed as a depreciation deduction in 2009. The total depreciation deduction with respect to the property for 2009 is $600. The remaining $400 cost of the property is recovered under otherwise applicable rules for computing depreciation. [In other words, assuming she does not sell the property, the taxpayer would be allowed to claim the following deductions with respect to the property in subsequent years: 32% of $500 in 2010; 19.2% of $500 in 2011; 11.52% of $500 in both 2012 and 2013; and 5.76% of $500 in 2014.]

---

[28] Technically, the switch does not occur in Year 4 because straight line depreciation would result in a deduction equal to, but not greater than, the double declining balance method. At the outset of Year 4, there are two and one-half years left in the recovery period. Year 4 itself is two-fifths, or forty percent, of that two and one-half year period. So, straight line depreciation would allow a deduction in Year 4 of forty percent of the unrecovered cost, exactly equal to the forty percent allowed under the double declining balance method.

Property qualifying for the additional first-year depreciation deduction must meet all of the following requirements. First, the property must be property to which the Modified Accelerated Cost Recovery System (MACRS) applies with an applicable recovery period of 20 years or less. . . . Second, the original use [the first use to which the property is put] of the property must commence with the taxpayer after December 31, 2007. Third, the taxpayer must purchase the property within the applicable time period. Finally, the property must be placed in service after December 31, 2007 and before January 1, [2014]. . . .

§ 14.04   AMORTIZATION OF INTANGIBLES — SECTION 197

In 1993, Congress added Section 197, allowing taxpayers to amortize certain intangibles ratably over a 15-year period. Section 197 should, in large part, negate disputes between the Service and taxpayers regarding whether an intangible has a limited useful life. Most notably, Section 197 allows for the first time the amortization of goodwill and going concern value. Because of its importance in the sale and purchase of a business, detailed examination of Section 197 is deferred until Chapter 41.

§ 14.05   RELATIONSHIP BETWEEN BASIS AND DEPRECIATION

As previously stated, depreciation is the means whereby a taxpayer recovers the cost of property used in a trade or business or investment activity. Since adjusted basis reflects the unrecovered cost of property, it is appropriate to adjust the basis of property for depreciation deductions allowable. Section 1016(a)(2) provides that basis must be reduced by the depreciation claimed "but not less than the amount allowable." A taxpayer failing to claim an allowable depreciation deduction with respect to an asset must still adjust the basis of the asset to reflect the allowable depreciation amount. This latter requirement prevents a taxpayer from choosing when depreciation will be deducted.

Example: Marcella purchases a building for $1,000,000, uses it in her business during a 10-year period, and then sells it for $900,000. Assuming the depreciation allowable during the years Marcella owned the building equaled $375,000, how much gain must Marcella report on the sale?

Analysis: Marcella's gain on the sale of the building would be computed using the Section 1001 formula: amount realized less adjusted basis equals gain realized. Since Marcella's adjusted basis would be $625,000, on account of the allowable depreciation of $375,000, her gain on the sale would be $275,000. Even though Marcella sold the property for less than she paid for it, she still recognizes gain because the depreciation deductions she was allowed exceeded the actual decline in the value of the building. In effect, the gain is attributable to the excess of the depreciation deductions allowed over the actual economic depreciation of the property. Section 1016(a)(2) requires Marcella to adjust the basis of the building to reflect the allowable depreciation amounts even if she never actually claimed them.

§ 14.06   SECTION 179 — EXPENSING TANGIBLE PERSONAL PROPERTY

§ 179.   Election to expense certain depreciable business assets.

(a)   Treatment as expenses. — A taxpayer may elect to treat the cost of any section 179 property as an expense which is not chargeable to capital account. Any cost so treated shall be allowed as a deduction for the taxable year in which the section 179 property is placed in service.

. . .

(b)   Limitations. —

(1) Dollar limitation. The aggregate cost which may be taken into account under subsection (a) for the taxable year shall not exceed —

(A) $250,000 in the case of taxable years beginning after 2007 and before 2010,

(B) $500,000 in the case of taxable years beginning in 2010, 2011, 2012 or 2013 and

(C) $25,000 in the case of taxable years beginning after 2013.

(2) Reduction in limitation. The limitation under paragraph (1) for any taxable year shall be reduced (but not below zero) by the amount by which the cost of section 179 property placed in service during such taxable year exceeds —

(A) $800,000 in the case of taxable years beginning after 2007 and before 2010,

(B) $2,000,0000 in the case of taxable years beginning in 2010, 2011, 2012 or 2013, and

(C) $200,000 in the case of taxable years beginning after 2013.

(3)   Limitation based on income from trade or business. —

(A)   In general. — The amount allowed as a deduction under subsection (a) for any taxable year (determined after the application of paragraphs (1) and (2)) shall not exceed the aggregate amount of taxable income of the taxpayer for such taxable year which is derived from the active conduct by the taxpayer of any trade or business during such taxable year.

. . .

(c)   Election. —

(1)   In general. — An election under this section for any taxable year shall —

(A) specify the items of section 179 property to which the election applies and the portion of the cost of each of such items which is to be taken into account under subsection (a)

. . .

(d)   Definitions and special rules —

(1) **Section 179 property. — For purposes of this section, the term "section 179 property" means any tangible property (to which section 168 applies) . . . (B) which is section 1245 property (as defined in section 1245(a)(3))[29] and (C) which is acquired by purchase for use in the active conduct of a trade or business . . . .**

Despite the general rule that no current deduction is allowable for costs incurred in acquiring an asset with a useful life extending substantially beyond the tax year, Congress in enacting Section 179 has authorized taxpayers to expense (*i.e.*, to deduct currently) the cost of acquisition of certain depreciable business assets. This provision is applicable only to "Section 179 property," which generally is tangible personal property acquired by purchase for use in the active conduct of a trade or business. Section 179 is elective.

Section 179(b)(1) limits the amount that can be expensed under Section 179 with respect to qualifying property placed in service during a year. As the Code provision set out above indicates, Congress has changed the Section 179 limits a number of times during recent years. While for 2014, Section 179 provides that the cost of Section 179 property can be expensed only up to $25,000, one suspects that Congress, in its continuing efforts to stimulate the economy, is likely to increase that limit once again.

Section 179(b)(2) provides a reduction in the limitation specified in Section 179(b)(1) for the amount by which the cost of Section 179 property placed in service by a taxpayer during the taxable year exceeds a specified dollar amount. The limitations under Section 179(b)(1) and (2) suggest that Congress intends Section 179 as a break for small businesses. Section 179(b)(3) further limits the Section 179 deduction to the amount of income from the taxpayer's trade or business during the year allowing, however, a carryover of any amount of the deduction which would otherwise be allowable.[30]

> **Example:** In 2013, Judy purchased and placed in service a $400,000 piece of equipment for use in her business. Judy could expense, *i.e.*, deduct currently, up to a maximum of $500,000 of the purchase price of Section 179 property under Section 179(b)(1). Furthermore, the amount eligible to be expensed by Judy would be reduced by $1 for every dollar by which the aggregate cost of qualifying property placed in service during the year by Judy exceeded $2,000,000.[31] A third limitation would prevent Judy from expensing an amount greater than the taxable income she derived from her business during the year. Assuming Judy is allowed to expense all $400,000 of the cost of the equipment, her adjusted basis in the equipment will be zero as explained *infra*.

Congress has limited the amount of the cost of "sports utility vehicles" that can be taken into account by taxpayers under Section 179. Specifically, Congress added Section 179(b)(5)(A) limiting the amount of a sports utility vehicle's cost that can be deducted under Section 179 to $25,000. The term "sports utility vehicles" is specially

---

[29] Section 1245 property is primarily tangible personal property.

[30] I.R.C. § 179(b)(3)(A) & (B).

[31] I.R.C. § 179(b)(2).

defined in Section 179(b)(5)(B) and includes vehicles that are not subject to the luxury automobile limitations under Section 280F (*see* Chapter 21) and for which the specific features of such vehicles are not necessary for purposes of conducting the taxpayer's business.

The legislative history[32] for the Jobs and Growth Tax Relief Reconciliation Act of 2003 makes the following instructive comments about the congressional policy underlying Section 179:

> The [House Ways and Means] Committee believes that section 179 expensing provides two important benefits for small businesses. First, it lowers the cost of capital for tangible property used in a trade or business. With a lower cost of capital, the Committee believes small business will invest in more equipment and employ more workers. Second, it eliminates depreciation record keeping requirements with respect to expensed property.

Section 179 is merely a means of recovering one's cost in property. Therefore, an adjustment must be made to the basis of Section 179 property placed in service during the year to the extent a Section 179 deduction with respect to that property was claimed.[33] The remaining basis is still eligible for depreciation deductions.

Example 1: Assume that in 2013 a taxpayer purchases a $400,000 piece of equipment (classified as 5-year property) for business use. The taxpayer elects to expense only $100,000 of the equipment's cost under Section 179. How much depreciation may the taxpayer claim under Section 168 in 2013?

Analysis: Even though the taxpayer has elected the benefit of Section 179, the taxpayer is still allowed to claim a depreciation deduction under Section 168 for the year that the equipment is placed in service; however, the basis in the equipment must first be adjusted to reflect the Section 179 deduction claimed.[34] Thus, the adjusted basis to which the depreciation percentage will be applied for the first year will be $300,000 rather than $400,000. Because the equipment is 5-year property, depreciation deductions will be computed using the rates set out in Table 1 of Revenue Procedure 87-57. Thus, in 2013 the taxpayer may claim a Section 168 depreciation deduction of $60,000 ($300,000 x 0.20) in addition to the Section 179 deduction of $100,000. The rates set out in that table will be applied in each subsequent year to the $300,000 figure. If no adjustment were made to the basis for the Section 179 deduction, the taxpayer, through the combination of the Section 179 deduction plus the deductions under Section 168, would ultimately deduct more than 100% of the cost of the equipment — clearly an improper result.

Example 2: Assume the facts of Example 1 except that the taxpayer is allowed a 50% additional first-year deduction under Section 168.

---

[32] H.R. Rep. No. 108-94 (2003).

[33] Treas. Reg. § 1.179-1(f).

[34] It is here that the historic characterization of Section 179 as providing "*additional* first year depreciation" is helpful.

Analysis: First, one must reduce the taxpayer's basis by the $100,000 the taxpayer expensed under § 179. The taxpayer's adjusted basis for purposes of § 168(k) is thus $300,000 as in Example 1. Under § 168(k), the taxpayer will be allowed additional first-year depreciation equal to 50% of the $300,000 adjusted basis or a $150,000 deduction. The taxpayer's unadjusted basis for purposes of the general rules of § 168 will be $150,000 and taxpayer will be entitled to a depreciation deduction equal to 20% of the $150,000 or $30,000. The taxpayer will deduct a total of $280,000 of the $400,000 cost of the equipment this year, leaving taxpayer with a $120,000 adjusted basis.

§ 14.07   THE RELATIONSHIP OF DEBT TO DEPRECIATION

As discussed in Chapter 4, a taxpayer who borrows money to purchase property is considered to have a basis in the property equal to the cost of the property, even though that cost has been financed initially by another. That basis is used for purposes of computing the depreciation deduction. For example, if a taxpayer borrows $50,000 to purchase a $50,000 piece of heavy equipment for use in a business, the taxpayer will be entitled to depreciate the equipment using $50,000 as the basis for depreciation. It makes no difference whether the taxpayer borrowed the money from a third person or borrowed the money from the party selling the equipment. The possible advantages to the taxpayer under these circumstances should be obvious — the taxpayer has not yet incurred any out-of-pocket expense but nonetheless is permitted to claim depreciation deductions. As will be discussed in Chapter 43, taxpayers have availed themselves of the tax breaks associated with this relationship between debt and depreciation. Congress, however, has enacted legislation significantly reducing the tax shelter opportunities previously available.

Excerpt From REVENUE PROCEDURE 87–56
1987-2 C.B. 674

SEC. 5. TABLE OF CLASS LIVES AND RECOVERY PERIODS

.01   Except for property described in section 5.02, below, the class lives (if any) and recovery periods for property subject to depreciation under section 168 of the Code appear in the tables below. These tables are based on the definition of class life in section 2.02 of this revenue procedure and the assigned items described in section 3 of this revenue procedure.

.02   For purposes of depreciation under the general depreciation system, residential rental property has a recovery period of 27.5 years and nonresidential real property has a recovery period of 31.5 years. For purposes of the alternative depreciation system, residential rental and non-residential real property each has a recovery period of 40 years . . . .

Asset class	Description of assets included	Class Life (in years)	Recovery Periods (in years) General Depreciation System	Recovery Periods (in years) Alternative Depreciation System
00.11	**Office Furniture, Fixtures, and Equipment:** Includes Furniture and fixtures that are not a structural component of a building. Includes such assets as desks, files, safes, and communications equipment. Does not include communications equipment that is included in other classes.	10	7	10
00.12	**Information Systems:** Includes computers and their peripheral equipment used in administering normal business transactions and the maintenance of business records, their retrieval and analysis . . . . Also, does not include equipment of a kind used primarily for amusement or entertainment of the user	6	5	5
00.13	**Data Handling Equipment, except Computers:** Includes only typewriters, calculators, adding and accounting machines, copiers, and duplicating equipment	6	5	6
00.21	**Airplanes (airframes and engines), except those used in commercial or contract carrying of passengers or freight, and all helicopters (airframes and engines)**	6	5	6
00.22	**Automobiles, Taxis**	3	5	5
00.23	**Buses**	9	5	9
00.241	**Light General Purpose Trucks:** Includes trucks for use over the road (actual unloaded weight less than 13,000 pounds)	4	5	5
00.242	**Heavy General Purpose Trucks:** Includes heavy general purpose trucks, concrete ready mix-truckers, and ore trucks, for use over the road (actual unloaded weight 13,000 pounds or more)	6	5	6

Excerpt From REVENUE PROCEDURE 87-57
1987-2 C.B. 687

Table 1.   General Depreciation System
            Applicable Depreciation Method: 200 or 150 Percent
            Declining Balance Switching to Straight Line
            Applicable Recovery Periods: 3, 5, 7, 10, 15, 20
                years
            Applicable Convention: Half-year

If the Recovery Year is:	and the Recovery Period is:					
	3-year	5-year	7-year	10-year	15-year	20-year
	the Depreciation Rate is:					
1	33.33	20.00	14.29	10.00	5.00	3.750
2	44.45	32.00	24.49	18.00	9.50	7.219
3	14.81	19.20	17.49	14.40	8.55	6.677
4	7.41	11.52	12.49	11.52	7.70	6.177
5		11.52	8.93	9.22	6.93	5.713
6		5.76	8.92	7.37	6.23	5.285
7			8.93	6.55	5.90	4.888
8			4.46	6.55	5.90	4.522
9				6.56	5.91	4.462
10				6.55	5.90	4.461
11				3.28	5.91	4.462
12					5.90	4.461
13					5.91	4.462
14					5.90	4.461
15					5.91	4.462
16					2.95	4.461
17						4.462
18						4.461
19						4.462
20						4.461
21						2.231

Authors' Note: Under Section 168(b)(2), 15-year and 20-year properties are subject to depreciation under the 150 percent declining balance method.

Table 2.   General Depreciation System
             Applicable Depreciation Method: 200 or 150 Percent
             Declining Balance Switching to Straight Line
             Applicable Recovery Periods: 3, 5, 7, 10, 15, 20
                years
             Applicable Convention: Mid-quarter (property placed
                in service in first quarter)

If the Recovery Year is:	and the Recovery Period is:					
	3-year	5-year	7-year	10-year	15-year	20-year
			the Depreciation Rate is:			
1	58.33	35.00	25.00	17.50	8.75	6.563
2	27.78	26.00	21.43	16.50	9.13	7.000
3	12.35	15.60	15.31	13.20	8.21	6.482
4	1.54	11.01	10.93	10.56	7.39	5.996
5		11.01	8.75	8.45	6.65	5.546
6		1.38	8.74	6.76	5.99	5.130
7			8.75	6.55	5.90	4.746
8			1.09	6.55	5.91	4.459
9				6.56	5.90	4.459
10				6.55	5.91	4.459
11				0.82	5.90	4.459
12					5.91	4.460
13					5.90	4.459
14					5.91	4.460
15					5.90	4.459
16					0.74	4.460
17						4.459
18						4.460
19						4.459
20						4.460
21						0.557

Table 6. General Depreciation System
Applicable Depreciation Method: Straight Line
Applicable Recovery Period: 27.5 years
Applicable Convention: Mid-month

If the Recovery Year is:	And the Month in the First Recovery Year the Property is Placed in Service is: the Depreciation Rate is:											
	1	2	3	4	5	6	7	8	9	10	11	12
1	3.485	3.182	2.879	2.576	2.273	1.970	1.667	1.364	1.061	0.758	0.455	0.152
2	3.636	3.636	3.636	3.636	3.636	3.636	3.636	3.636	3.636	3.636	3.636	3.636
3	3.636	3.636	3.636	3.636	3.636	3.636	3.636	3.636	3.636	3.636	3.636	3.636
4	3.636	3.636	3.636	3.636	3.636	3.636	3.636	3.636	3.636	3.636	3.636	3.636
5	3.636	3.636	3.636	3.636	3.636	3.636	3.636	3.636	3.636	3.636	3.636	3.636
6	3.636	3.636	3.636	3.636	3.636	3.636	3.636	3.636	3.636	3.636	3.636	3.636
7	3.636	3.636	3.636	3.636	3.636	3.636	3.636	3.636	3.636	3.636	3.636	3.636
8	3.636	3.636	3.636	3.636	3.636	3.636	3.636	3.636	3.636	3.636	3.636	3.636
9	3.637	3.637	3.636	3.636	3.636	3.637	3.636	3.636	3.636	3.636	3.636	3.636
10	3.636	3.636	3.636	3.636	3.636	3.636	3.636	3.636	3.636	3.636	3.636	3.636
11	3.636	3.636	3.636	3.637	3.636	3.636	3.637	3.637	3.637	3.637	3.637	3.637
12	3.637	3.637	3.637	3.636	3.637	3.637	3.636	3.636	3.636	3.637	3.637	3.636
13	3.636	3.636	3.636	3.637	3.636	3.636	3.637	3.637	3.637	3.636	3.636	3.637
14	3.637	3.637	3.637	3.636	3.637	3.637	3.636	3.636	3.636	3.637	3.637	3.636
15	3.636	3.636	3.636	3.637	3.636	3.636	3.637	3.637	3.637	3.636	3.636	3.637
16	3.637	3.637	3.637	3.636	3.637	3.637	3.636	3.636	3.636	3.637	3.637	3.636
17	3.636	3.636	3.636	3.637	3.636	3.636	3.637	3.637	3.637	3.636	3.636	3.637
18	3.637	3.637	3.637	3.636	3.637	3.637	3.636	3.636	3.636	3.637	3.637	3.636
19	3.636	3.636	3.636	3.637	3.636	3.636	3.637	3.637	3.637	3.636	3.636	3.637
20	3.637	3.637	3.637	3.636	3.637	3.637	3.636	3.636	3.636	3.637	3.637	3.636
21	3.636	3.636	3.636	3.637	3.636	3.636	3.637	3.637	3.637	3.636	3.636	3.637
22	3.637	3.637	3.637	3.636	3.637	3.637	3.636	3.636	3.636	3.637	3.637	3.636
23	3.636	3.637	3.636	3.637	3.636	3.636	3.637	3.637	3.637	3.636	3.636	3.637
24	3.637	3.637	3.637	3.636	3.637	3.637	3.636	3.636	3.636	3.637	3.637	3.636
25	3.636	3.636	3.636	3.637	3.636	3.636	3.637	3.637	3.637	3.636	3.636	3.637
26	3.637	3.637	3.637	3.636	3.637	3.637	3.636	3.636	3.636	3.637	3.637	3.636
27	3.636	3.636	3.636	3.636	3.636	3.636	3.637	3.637	3.637	3.636	3.636	3.637
28	1.970	2.273	2.576	2.879	3.182	3.485	3.636	3.636	3.636	3.636	3.636	3.636
29	0.000	0.000	0.000	0.000	0.000	0.000	0.152	0.455	0.758	1.061	1.364	1.667

The following table, from IRS Publication 946, "How to Depreciate Property," provides depreciation rates for nonresidential rental property subject to the 39-year recovery period under the Revenue Reconciliation Act of 1993:

Table A–7a. Nonresidential Real Property
Mid-Month Convention
Straight Line — 39 Years

Year	Month property placed in service											
	1	2	3	4	5	6	7	8	9	10	11	12
1	2.461	2.247	2.033	1.819	1.605	1.391	1.177	0.963	0.749	0.535	0.321	0.107
2-39	2.564	2.564	2.564	2.564	2.564	2.564	2.564	2.564	2.564	2.564	2.564	2.564
40	0.107	0.321	0.535	0.749	0.963	1.177	1.391	1.605	1.819	2.033	2.247	2.461

Chapter 15

LOSSES AND BAD DEBTS

Chapter 14 examined the depreciation deduction as a method by which the taxpayer is permitted to recover a capital expenditure. This Chapter focuses on the loss deduction and bad debt deduction rules of the Code. Although at first glance they may seem to have nothing in common with depreciation, they, too, may be regarded as statutory mechanisms that provide for the recovery of capital in qualifying circumstances. For example, business equipment purchased for $1,000 will have an adjusted basis of zero after depreciation deductions totaling $1,000 have been taken. Alternatively, assume that after $600 of depreciation deductions have been taken, reducing the adjusted basis to $400, the equipment is sold for $100, resulting in an allowable loss of $300. The loss of $300 allows the taxpayer to recover the part of its $1,000 investment that had not been recovered through depreciation deductions ($600) and the proceeds of the sale ($100).

§ 15.01 LOSSES

§ 165. Losses —

(a) **General rule — There shall be allowed as a deduction any loss sustained during the taxable year and not compensated for by insurance or otherwise.**

Section 165(a) authorizes a deduction for any uncompensated loss sustained during the year. However, Section 165(c) restricts the loss deduction for individuals to trade or business losses, losses in profit-seeking transactions, and casualty or theft losses. The deduction for casualty and theft losses with respect to personal use property is considered in detail in Chapter 24, in conjunction with other deductions allowed for personal expenditures. Note, however, a casualty or theft loss involving the taxpayer's business or investment property is governed by Section 165(c)(1) or (c)(2), and not by (c)(3). Thus, for example, assume Taxpayer's uninsured business vehicle is destroyed by fire. Despite the casualty nature of the resulting loss, the loss is within Section 165(c)(1) and is not subject to Section 165(c)(3) and the limitations imposed by Section 165(h), as would have been the case had the destruction occurred to Taxpayer's personal vehicle.

[A] The Business or Profit Requirement for Individuals

§ 165. Losses —

(c) **Limitations on losses of individuals — In the case of an individual, the deduction under subsection (a) shall be limited to —**

(1) **losses incurred in a trade or business;**

(2) **losses incurred in any transaction entered into for profit, though not**

connected with a trade or business. . . .

[1] Personal Losses Not Deductible

The business or profit requirement of Section 165(c)(1) and (c)(2) is, of course, consistent with one of the fundamental notions in the Code — namely, personal expenditures are generally not deductible. This same notion applies with respect to the depreciation deduction. To permit the deduction of a personal loss is functionally equivalent to permitting depreciation on personal-use property or authorizing a deduction for personal expenses generally. Section 165(c)(1) and (c)(2) are thus appropriate restrictions on the sweeping language of Section 165(a).

Section 165(c)(1) clearly echoes the "trade or business" language of Section 162(a), and activities that constitute a trade or business for Section 162 purposes do so also when the focus shifts to Section 165.[1] In many cases, an individual will be indifferent as to whether a deductible loss falls within Section 165(c)(1) or (c)(2), but in some circumstances it matters. For example, business losses may be deducted above the line,[2] whereas losses on profit-seeking transactions are below-the-line deductions unless they result from the sale or exchange or property.[3] Similarly, the net operating loss rules of Section 172 also favor business losses over investment or other nonbusiness losses in the computation of net operating loss carrybacks and carryforwards.

More frequently, however, the dividing line at issue in Section 165(c) litigation is not the line between business and profit-seeking activities, but the line between such activities, on the one side, and personal activities on the other. The language of Section 165(c)(2) recalls that of Section 212(2). Thus, where an expense with respect to property is deductible under Section 212, a loss on that property is generally allowed under Section 165(c)(2). Perhaps the most common example of a Section 165(c)(2) loss is the loss an investor incurs upon selling stock for less than he paid for it.

Example 1: Taxpayer buys XYZ stock for $100 and, later sells it for $80.

Analysis: Taxpayer has sustained a loss of $20. Since the loss was incurred in a transaction entered into for profit, the loss is allowed under Section 165(c)(2). It is possible that a loss allowable under Section 165(c) may be disallowed by another Code provision (e.g., Section 267 disallows losses on sales between related parties), or the deductibility may be postponed (e.g., Section 1211(b) limits the deductibility of capital losses).

Example 2: Taxpayer buys her personal residence for $500,000 and some years later, when it is still her residence, sells it for $450,000. Is the $50,000 loss allowed?

---

[1] See Chapter 12, *supra*, for a discussion of the term "trade or business."

[2] *See* I.R.C. § 62(a)(1).

[3] *See* I.R.C. § 62(a)(3).

Analysis: The loss has been sustained under Section 165(a), but it is nondeductible under Section 165(c), since it is not incurred in a trade or business or in a profit-seeking transaction, and it is not a casualty loss.

The denial of a deduction in Example 2 is appropriate because the loss is personal. Even if Taxpayer insists she was hoping to make a profit at the time she offered the home for sale and that she is thus in the same position as the unfortunate stock investor, the loss is nevertheless still nondeductible.[4] The principle involved here extends beyond personal residences. Section 165(c)(2) speaks of a "transaction entered into for profit"; it is not enough that at the time of sale a taxpayer was hoping to make a profit, since such a rule invites the virtual elimination of taxable income. The unlucky stock investor presumably had the requisite profit motive when he "entered into" the purchase of stock, and this distinguishes his situation from that of the residential homeowner. The fact that, prior to disposition, it may have become clear a loss was inevitable does not negate the transaction's having been entered into for profit.

The taxpayer's primary purpose in this regard will be controlling. In *Austen v. Commissioner*,[5] the Second Circuit stated that the "position for which petitioners contend [that simply having a profit motive satisfies the statute] would not provide a workable interpretation of Section 165. . . . The logical interrelation of Section 165 and Section 262 requires a decision as to which of the two motives was dominant, so that one or the other section can be applied." It is exceedingly doubtful that the profit-motive will be considered dominant when the taxpayer is making personal use of residential property. For example, in *Gevirtz v. Commissioner*,[6] the taxpayer bought land intending to build an apartment house on it, but instead (because other apartments were being built in the area) built and occupied for some years a large residence, capable of conversion to apartments. On later vacating the property, unsuccessfully trying to rent or sell it, and ultimately surrendering it to the mortgagee, she claimed a loss deduction. The court held that she had abandoned her original profit motive when she built and occupied the residence, that the possibility of future business use was "clearly subsidiary," and the deduction was denied.

[2] Conversion of Personal Use Property to Income Producing Property

The regulations provide that personal-use property may be converted into income-producing property so as to qualify for a Section 165(c)(2) deduction on disposition.[7] The question of whether a conversion has occurred is most apt to arise

---

[4] *See* Treas. Reg. § 1.165-9(a) ("Losses not allowed — A loss sustained on the sale of residential property purchased or constructed by the taxpayer for use as his personal residence and so used by him up to the time of the sale is not deductible under section 165(a).").

[5] 298 F.2d 583, 584 (2d Cir. 1962).

[6] 123 F.2d 707 (2d Cir. 1941).

[7] *See* Treas. Reg. § 1.165-9(b)(1) ("If property purchased or constructed by the taxpayer for use as his personal residence is, prior to its sale, rented or otherwise appropriated to income-producing purposes and is used for such purposes up to the time of its sale, a loss sustained on the sale of the property shall be allowed as a deduction under section 165(a).").

with regard to residences. Ordinarily, it is the rental of the vacated residence that brings about the conversion. Where the vacated residence is offered for rent, but not actually rented, prior to its sale, the conversion is deemed not to have taken place, and the loss is denied.[8] (Ironically, the Service concedes that the offer to rent a former residence is sufficient to satisfy the "held for the production of income" standard of Sections 167 and 212 and support deductions for depreciation and Section 212 expenses.)

The loss deduction is limited to the loss sustained after the property has been converted from personal to business or profit-seeking use. This principle is carried out by providing the basis for loss purposes is the adjusted basis of the property or the value of the property at the time it was converted to business use, whichever is lower.[9] The loss attributable to the period of personal use is thus nondeductible, consistent with the general principle expressed in Section 262. The subsequent business or profit-seeking loss is allowable.[10]

Likewise, where property is actually used at times for personal purposes and at other times for business or profit-seeking purposes, allocation of a loss between the (nondeductible) personal use and (deductible) business or profit-seeking use is required. For example, an allocation is necessary with respect to a loss realized on selling an automobile used partly for business and partly for personal purposes.

Apparently, no loss will be allowed if a conversion in the opposite direction occurs. If business property is converted to personal use, and a loss is thereafter realized, no deduction is allowable under Section 165(c)(1) or (c)(2).

> **Example:** Whitney paid $100,000 for a tract of land which she used for business purposes. When she terminated her business years later, she converted the land to personal use. The value of the land at the time was $90,000. Subsequently, she sold the land for $80,000.
>
> **Analysis:** Assuming that her adjusted basis in the land was $100,000, Whitney realized $20,000 of loss on the sale. None of this loss will be recognized under Section 165(c), not even the $10,000 loss attributable to the decline in value which occurred while she held the land for business purposes.

[B]   When Is a Loss Sustained?

The regulations provide that a loss "must be evidenced by closed and completed transactions, fixed by identifiable events."[11] A sale or exchange of property typically "fixes" the loss under Section 165, but just as mere appreciation in value does not constitute gross income, a mere decline in value is not a loss "sustained." For example, a deductible loss was not sustained by an air carrier when its routes,

---

[8] *See* Cowles v. Comm'r, T.C. Memo 1970-198.

[9] Treas. Reg. § 1.165-9(b)(2).

[10] See § 15.01[C][2], *infra*, for examples involving post conversion losses.

[11] Treas. Reg. § 1.165-1(b).

as a result of airline deregulation, declined substantially in value, but were not sold or abandoned as worthless.[12]

> **Example:** ABC stock, purchased for investment purposes for $10,000, declines in value to $500. May the shareholder claim a loss?

> **Analysis:** No loss has yet been sustained, so no loss is allowed under Section 165(c)(2). If the stock is subsequently sold for $500, the $9,500 loss is then sustained and becomes allowable.

As indicated, a loss may be sustained by the abandonment of an asset. But to establish abandonment for purposes of Section 165, the taxpayer must show both an intention to abandon property and an affirmative act of abandonment, an "identifiable event" that is observable to others and irrevocably cuts ties to the property, in contrast, for example, to the continued holding of an asset for possible future use or gain or to the mere non-use of an asset.[13]

> **Example:** In Year 1, Taxpayer purchases exclusive rights to a script for the remainder of its copyright period for purposes of producing a motion picture from the script. In Year 2, taxpayer decides that it will not produce a motion picture from the script and writes off the cost of the script for financial accounting purposes. Taxpayer nonetheless retains its rights to the script.

> **Analysis:** The decision not to produce the motion picture from the script and the write-off of its cost for financial accounting purposes do not constitute affirmative acts of abandonment. In addition, the retention of rights to the script indicate that the script is not worthless. Taxpayer may not deduct the cost of the script in Year 2 in the absence of showing an affirmative act of abandonment or the worthlessness of the script.

The obsolescence[14] and abandonment[15] of property may also give rise to a loss deduction.

> **Example:** Casey paid $25,000 for a piece of equipment for use in his business. Three years after he purchased the equipment, changes in the technology rendered the piece of equipment obsolete. At the time, Casey's adjusted basis in the equipment was $7,250 (Casey had claimed a total of $17,750 in depreciation deductions on the equipment). Casey discards the equipment. May Casey deduct the remaining basis in the equipment?

> **Analysis:** Casey will be entitled to a business loss deduction under Section 165(c)(1) in the amount of Casey's adjusted basis or unrecovered cost in the equipment, *i.e.*, $7,250. Thus, the loss deduction in combination with the prior depreciation deductions enabled Casey to "write off" the entire cost

---

[12] Rev. Rul. 84-145, 1984-2 C.B. 47.

[13] Rev. Rul. 2004-58, 2004-1 C.B. 1043. The example that follows in the text is based on Situation 1 in the Rev. Rul. 2004-58.

[14] See Treas. Reg. § 1.165-2, relating to obsolete nondepreciable property.

[15] See Treas. Reg. § 1.167(a)-8(a)(4), relating to abandonment of depreciable property.

of the equipment — a result which is appropriate in a tax system that taxes only net income.

[1] Worthless Securities

§ 165. Losses —

(g) Worthless securities —

(1) General rule — If any security which is capital asset becomes worthless during the taxable year, the loss resulting therefrom shall, for purposes of this subtitle, be treated as a loss from the sale or exchange, on the last day of the taxable year, of a capital asset.

(2) Security defined — For purposes of this subsection, the term "security" means —

(A) a share of stock in a corporation;

(B) a right to subscribe for, or to receive, a share of stock in a corporation; or

(C) a bond, debenture, note, or certificate, or other evidence of indebtedness, issued by a corporation or by a government or political subdivision thereof, with interest coupons or in registered form.

A loss is allowed for "securities," as defined by Section 165(g)(2), when they become "worthless." The regulations note that even an "extensive" shrinkage of value is not sufficient for this purpose.[16] Determining worthlessness can obviously be a difficult matter; the Supreme Court has said that worthlessness is determined not by the taxpayer's good faith subjective belief, but by an examination of all the facts and circumstances.[17] Disputes are bound to result not only as to the fact of worthlessness, but as to when it occurred. If the Commissioner asserts that worthlessness actually occurred in a year for which a refund claim is now barred by the statute of limitations, the consequences are harsh indeed. This problem, at least, has been eased considerably by Section 6511(d), which extends the normal three-year statute of limitations to seven years for refund claims based on Section 165(g).

[2] Theft Losses

§ 165. Losses —

(e) Theft losses — **For purposes of subsection (a), any loss arising from theft shall be treated as sustained during the taxable year in which the taxpayer discovers such loss.**

Theft losses are treated as sustained in the year the theft loss is discovered.[18]

---

[16] Treas. Reg. § 1.165-4(a).

[17] Boehm v. Comm'r, 326 U.S. 287 (1945).

[18] I.R.C. § 165(e).

Example: Bobby operates a back country guide service. A valuable rifle used by Bobby in this business was stolen sometime during the fall of 2012. Bobby did not discover the rifle's loss until the summer of 2013.

Analysis: Under Section 165(e), Bobby may not deduct the loss on the rifle in 2012, even by filing an amended return, but must deduct it in his return for 2013, the year he discovered the loss.

The Internal Revenue Service has stated that "theft" is a word of "general and broad connotation, covering any criminal appropriation of another's property. . . . [A theft is] a taking of property that was illegal under the law of the jurisdiction in which it occurred and was done with criminal intent."[19] A taxpayer must prove a theft loss occurred to claim a deduction, but need not show a conviction for the theft.

[C]   Amount of the Deduction

The amount of the loss deduction is limited by Section 165(b) to the adjusted basis of the property in question. The limitation is appropriate because the taxpayer is not required to treat as income any excess of fair market value over basis.

Example: Taxpayer sustains an uninsured loss to business or investment property that has a value of $100,000 and an adjusted basis of only $60,000.

Analysis: The deductible loss is only $60,000. The $40,000 in lost value was not included in taxpayer's income, and to allow a loss for the $40,000 would amount to a double tax benefit.

[1]   Reimbursement

To the extent a taxpayer receives insurance or other compensation, the loss is offset and the deduction reduced.[20]

Example: Assume the facts of the prior example except that Taxpayer carried some insurance on the property. Assume that the loss occurs and an insurance claim is filed in Year 1, and $40,000 of insurance proceeds are received in Year 2.

Analysis: The sustained loss occurs in Year 2 and must reflect the reimbursement received. The regulations state that, if there is a "reasonable prospect of recovery," the loss is not treated as sustained until the matter of reimbursement is determined with "reasonable certainty."[21] Assuming that $40,000 represents the full insurance recovery, Taxpayer's deductible loss will be $20,000, *i.e.*, the $40,000 in insurance proceeds will offset the $60,000 loss reducing the deduction to $20,000.

---

[19] Rev. Rul. 2009-9, 2009-1 C.B. 735.

[20] I.R.C. § 165(a).

[21] Treas. Reg. § 1.165-1(d)(2), (3).

[2] Post-Conversion Losses

As noted above, in the case of personal-use property, basis for loss purposes cannot exceed the lesser of basis or value at the time of conversion.[22]

Example 1: A car is purchased for $5,000 and used solely for personal purposes. No adjustment to its original basis of $5,000 is made since the car is not depreciable property under Sections 167 and 168. If the car is later converted to business use when its value is only $2,000, its basis for depreciation is $2,000 and its basis for loss purposes is $2,000 (reduced by allowable depreciation subsequent to the conversion).[23] In effect, a loss under Section 165 cannot exceed $2,000 without making the decline in value during the period of personal use deductible.

Example 2: A house is purchased for $100,000 in Year 1 for use as a personal residence. In Year 5, when the house is worth $80,000 (its basis is still $100,000), it is rented out and converted to income-producing purposes. Allowable depreciation is based on $80,000, the lesser of value or basis at conversion. If $10,000 total in depreciation is allowed in Years 5-10, and the house is sold for $65,000 in Year 11, the allowable loss is $5,000, calculated as follows. The amount realized is $65,000. The adjusted basis for loss purposes is $70,000, that is $80,000 (the lesser of basis or value at conversion) adjusted for the $10,000 in depreciation taken. The allowable loss is $5,000 ($70,000 adjusted basis less $65,000 realized).

Note that the basis discussed in the preceding examples is the basis for loss purposes only. For gain purposes, the normal basis rules are employed, not the "lesser of basis or value" rules. Thus, if the house in the last example had been sold for $150,000, there would be no loss. The gain would be computed on an adjusted basis of $90,000 (original basis of $100,000 minus $10,000 in depreciation), for a gain of $60,000.

If the house were sold for $80,000, no loss would be realized, because, as indicated in Example 2, the basis for loss purposes is $70,000; moreover, no gain would be realized either, because for gain purposes the basis is $90,000. In effect, where there are different bases for gain and for loss, a sale for an amount in between the two bases (here, in between $90,000 and $70,000) will result in neither gain nor loss being realized.

[D] Disallowed Losses

Losses otherwise allowable under Section 165 may be disallowed by other provisions of the Code. For example, Section 267(a)(1) disallows losses on "related party" sales or exchanges, and Section 1091 denies losses on "wash sales" of stock or securities. These provisions are considered in Chapter 27.

---

[22] Treas. Reg. § 165-9(b)(2), (c).

[23] Treas. Reg. § 1.167(g)-1.

§ 15.02　BAD DEBTS

§ 166.　**Bad debts** —

(a)　**General rule** —

(1)　**Wholly worthless debts** — There shall be allowed as a deduction any debt which becomes worthless within the taxable year.

(2)　**Partially worthless debts** — When satisfied that a debt is recoverable only in part the Secretary may allow such debt, in an amount not in excess of the part charged off within the taxable year, as a deduction. . . .

(e)　**Worthless securities** —

This section shall not apply to a debt which is evidenced by a security as defined in section 165(g)(2)(C).

Section 166 allows a deduction for debts that become worthless within the taxable year. Unlike Section 165(c), which provides special rules for losses sustained by individuals, Section 166 does not draw a distinction between corporate and individual taxpayers. It does, however, draw a line between business and nonbusiness bad debts, a matter addressed below. Note that, although a bad debt is essentially simply one type of loss, Congress has provided rules for bad debts that differ from the rules of Section 165. Also note that, where a debt is evidenced by a "security," the rules of Section 165 govern, and Section 166 does not apply.[24]

[A]　Bona Fide Debt Requirement

The provisions of Section 166 do not come into play unless a "bona fide debt" exists. There must be a debtor-creditor relationship based on a valid, enforceable obligation to pay a fixed or determinable sum of money.[25] A gift is not a debt. It is thus not surprising that family or related-party advances will be carefully scrutinized to determine whether or not bona fide debt was created. It will be presumed, subject to rebuttal, that, where the relationship is a close one, a gift and not a loan was intended.

[B]　Worthlessness

The debt must be a "bad" debt for a deduction to be allowable. Thus, for example, even when bona fide debt is present, forgiveness or cancellation of the debt may itself constitute a gift rather than evidence of worthlessness, and therefore be nondeductible. In some cases, of course, a debt may be canceled for business reasons. Again, no deduction is allowed by Section 166 if the debt was not worthless or partially worthless, but if the provisions of Section 162 are otherwise satisfied, a deduction would be allowable under that section.

"All pertinent evidence" with regard to the determination of worthlessness must be considered. Although factual disputes are inevitable, the regulations explicitly provide the taxpayer is not required to pursue legal action to establish

---

[24]　I.R.C. § 166(e).

[25]　Treas. Reg. § 1.166-1(c).

worthlessness.[26] Given the difficulty that may exist in determining the year worthlessness occurs, a seven-year statute of limitation for refund claims under Section 166 applies, as with worthless securities under Section 165(g).[27] Thus, even where the taxpayer has guessed wrong as to the year of worthlessness, there will ordinarily still be time to file a refund claim for the proper year.

[C] Business or Nonbusiness Debts

§ 166. Bad debts —

(d) Nonbusiness debts —

(1) General rule — In the case of a taxpayer other than a corporation —

(A) subsection (a) shall not apply to any nonbusiness debt; and

(B) where any nonbusiness debt becomes worthless within the taxable year, the loss resulting therefrom shall be considered a loss from the sale or exchange, during the taxable year, of a capital asset held for not more than 1 year.

(2) Nonbusiness debt defined — For purposes of paragraph (1), the term "nonbusiness debt" means a debt other than —

(A) a debt created or acquired (as the case may be) in connection with a trade or business of the taxpayer; or

(B) a debt the loss from the worthlessness of which is incurred in the taxpayer's trade or business.

Section 166(d) distinguishes between business and nonbusiness debts. Business debts are deductible under Section 166(a)(1) in the year they become wholly worthless. Moreover, partially worthless business debts are also deductible, under Section 166(a)(2), up to the amount charged off within the year. The business bad debt rules do not distinguish between individuals and corporations.

By contrast, nonbusiness bad debts are deductible only upon becoming wholly worthless. The Seventh Circuit, in *Buchanan v. U.S.*,[28] emphasized the importance of such total worthlessness, noting that, "if even a modest fraction of the [nonbusiness] debt can be recovered," the debt is not worthless for purposes of Section 166 and no deduction is available. The court also stated that bifurcating the debt into recoverable and nonrecoverable portions and allowing a deduction for the nonrecoverable portion would be inconsistent with the Section 166(d)(1)(B) requirement that the debt be completely worthless.

Nonbusiness debts, even if completely worthless, are deductible only as short term capital losses, rather than as ordinary losses as is the case with business bad debts.[29] The capital loss characterization is relatively disadvantageous because the deduction of capital losses is limited under Section 1211. In the case of an individual,

---

[26] Treas. Reg. § 1.166-2(a), (b).

[27] I.R.C. § 6511(d).

[28] 87 F.3d 197, 199 (7th Cir. 1996).

[29] I.R.C. § 166(d)(1).

capital losses in a given year are deductible only to the extent of the individual's capital gains plus an additional $3,000. In other words, although a taxpayer with capital gains can deduct capital losses up to the amount of his capital gains, capital losses are thereafter deductible only at the rate of $3,000 a year, and, thus, from a timing standpoint, the characterization rule of Section 166(d) can be quite harsh in some circumstances. The legislative history of the predecessor of Section 166(d), enacted in 1942, suggests the rationale for this limitation:

> The present law gives the same treatment to bad debts incurred in nonbusiness transactions as it allows to business bad debts. An example of a nonbusiness bad debt would be an unrepaid loan to a friend or relative. . . . This liberal allowance for nonbusiness bad debts has suffered considerable abuse through taxpayers making loans which they do not expect to be repaid.[30]

Apparently the congressional purpose behind Section 166(d) was to effect a compromise between outright disallowance and equal treatment with business debts. The Supreme Court has found that the provision was intended to place "nonbusiness investments in the form of loans on a footing with other nonbusiness investments."[31]

Section 166(d)(2) defines a nonbusiness debt as a debt other than one created or acquired in connection with the taxpayer's business, or other than one the loss from the worthlessness of which is incurred in the taxpayer's business. A context in which disputes commonly arise is that of the shareholder-employee who has made unrepaid advances to a closely held corporation. Is such a loan a business debt or a nonbusiness debt? In a leading case in this area, *Whipple v. Commissioner*,[32] the Supreme Court held that a controlling shareholder's organizational, promotional and managerial services to a corporation did not cause loans to the corporation to be classified as business debts:

> Petitioner must demonstrate that he is engaged in a trade or business, and lying at the heart of his claim is the issue upon which the lower courts have divided and which brought the case here: That where a taxpayer furnishes regular services to one or many corporations, an independent trade or business of the taxpayer has been shown. But . . . petitioner's claim must be rejected.

> Devoting one's time and energies to the affairs of a corporation is not of itself, and without more, a trade or business of the person so engaged. Though such activities may produce income, profit or gain in the form of dividends or enhancement in the value of an investment, this return is distinctive to the process of investing and is generated by the successful operation of the corporation's business as distinguished from the trade or business of the taxpayer himself. When the only return is that of an investor, the taxpayer has not satisfied his burden of demonstrating that he

---

[30] H. Rep. No. 2333, 77th Cong. 1st Sess. (1942); 1942-2 C.B. 372, 408.

[31] Putnam v. Comm'r, 352 U.S. 82, 92 (1956).

[32] 373 U.S. 193 (1963).

is engaged in a trade or business since investing is not a trade or business and the return to the taxpayer, though substantially the product of his services, legally arises not from his own trade or business but from that of the corporation. Even if the taxpayer demonstrates an independent trade or business of his own, care must be taken to distinguish bad debt losses arising from his own business and those actually arising from activities peculiar to an investor concerned with, and participating in, the conduct of the corporate business.

If full-time service to one corporation does not alone amount to a trade or business, which it does not, it is difficult to understand how the same service to many corporations would suffice. To be sure, the presence of more than one corporation might lend support to a finding that the taxpayer was engaged in a regular course of promoting corporations for a fee or commission, . . . or for a profit on their sale, . . . but in such cases there is compensation other than the normal investor's return, income received directly for his own services rather than indirectly through the corporate enterprise. . . . On the other hand, since the Tax Court found, and the petitioner does not dispute, that there was no intention here of developing the corporations as going businesses for sale to customers in the ordinary course, the case before us inexorably rests upon the claim that one who actively engages in serving his own corporations for the purpose of creating future income through those enterprises is in a trade or business. That argument is untenable . . . and we reject it. Absent substantial additional evidence, furnishing management and other services to corporations for a reward not different from that flowing to an investor in those corporations is not a trade or business. . . .[33]

An employee is engaged in business as an employee.[34] As a result, if an employee can demonstrate that a loan to one's employer is, in effect, required as a condition of employment to insure continued employment, the loan is a business debt arising out of the trade or business of being an employee.[35] The test of the regulations is that the loan must bear a proximate relationship to the taxpayer's trade or business.[36] When a loan is prompted by both investment and business reasons, as is often the case when the taxpayer is both shareholder and employee, the Supreme Court has held the business motive must be dominant for the debt to be characterized as a business debt.[37]

---

[33] *Id.* at 201–203.

[34] *See* I.R.C. § 62(a)(1).

[35] *See* Trent v. Comm'r, 291 F.2d 669 (2d Cir. 1961).

[36] Treas. Reg. § 1.166-5(b).

[37] *See* U.S. v. Generes, 405 U.S. 93 (1971).

[D] Amount Deductible

§ 166. Bad debts —

(b) Amount of deduction — For purposes of subsection (a), the basis for determining the amount of the deduction for any bad debt shall be the adjusted basis provided in section 1011 for determining the loss from the sale or other disposition of property.

The amount of a bad debt deduction is the debt's adjusted basis. This rule is self-evident in situations where the taxpayer has loaned money to the debtor.

> **Example 1:** Mary lends George $1,000. George repays none of the debt, which ultimately becomes totally worthless. Mary's adjusted basis in the debt is $1,000, and that will be the amount of her loss.

> **Example 2:** Mary lends George $1,000. George repays $200; the balance of the debt ultimately becomes worthless. Mary's adjusted basis in the debt is $800, and that will be the amount of her loss.

Suppose, however, a cash basis creditor cannot collect wages, rents, or other receivables owed to him. The regulations provide no bad debt deduction is allowed unless such amounts have been included in income, which would not be the case with the cash method taxpayer.[38] Thus, for example, a cash method landlord does not include unpaid rent in income, has no basis in the unpaid rent and is not entitled to a bad debt deduction if the rental obligation becomes worthless. Similarly, if a taxpayer performs services without compensation, the taxpayer's net worth is unchanged; if no income was recognized, no loss is appropriate and no deduction is allowed. If income was recognized, as with an accrual method taxpayer, a deduction is in order to reflect such recognized, but uncollected compensation. The same rule would apply to interest.

> **Example:** Assume unpaid interest of $100 has accrued on Mary's $1,000 loan to George. If Mary is a cash method taxpayer, her basis remains $1,000. If Mary is an accrual method taxpayer, and properly accrues the interest, her basis in the loan and unpaid interest increases to $1,100, reflecting the fact the interest has been included in her income.

[E] Guarantees

Losses arising out of loan guarantees are treated as losses from bad debts, and are classified as business or nonbusiness debts based on their connection with the taxpayer's trade or business.[39]

---

[38] Treas. Reg. § 1.166-1(e).

[39] *See generally* Treas. Reg. § 1.166-9.

§ 15.03 BAD DEBTS AND LOSSES: THE INTERPLAY BETWEEN SECTIONS 166 AND 165

Depending on the circumstances, taxpayers may seek to characterize a loss under Section 165 rather than under Section 166, and vice versa. Investment-related losses, for example, are subject to capital loss treatment if they fall under Section 166, whereas this is not necessarily the case under Section 165. By contrast, if the loss in question is a personal one, Section 165 denies a deduction (except for certain casualty and theft losses), whereas Section 166 at least allows a short-term capital loss. With respect to this latter point, note again the distinction Section 166 draws is between business and nonbusiness debts; although some commentators express varying degrees of reservation, the prevailing view is that personal bad debts are deductible, assuming the debt is bona fide, despite the absence of any business or profit-seeking motivation on the part of the lender. Note that this is inconsistent with the treatment of personal expenditures generally under Section 262. The Supreme Court has held Sections 165 and 166 are mutually exclusive, and that where by their terms both provisions are applicable in a given situation, Section 166 governs.[40]

---

[40] Spring City Foundry Co. v. Comm'r, 292 U.S. 182 (1934).

Chapter 16

TRAVEL EXPENSES

Few areas of the tax law contain as many rules as are to be found with respect to the deduction of meals, lodging and transportation expenses. Because these expenses often have significant personal expense elements, the Congress, Service and the courts have attempted to assure that only expenses predominantly business in nature are deducted. The result is a plethora of sometimes inconsistent rulings and decisions which often create arbitrary distinctions.

§ 16.01 COMMUTING

The choice of where one lives is generally personal. If one chose to do so, one could live nearer one's workplace and avoid the costs associated with a daily commute. Commuting costs are therefore appropriately viewed as personal in nature and nondeductible under Section 262.[1] In *Commissioner v. Flowers,*[2] the Supreme Court denied a deduction for travel expenses to a taxpayer who lived in Jackson, Mississippi, but whose principal place of employment was in Mobile, Alabama. The taxpayer was able to do much of his work at an office in Jackson and so spent most of his time there by his own choice. He did need to spend some time in Mobile, however, and sought to deduct the cost of trips from Jackson to Mobile and the cost of meals and lodging in Mobile. In denying the deduction, the Supreme Court stated that, for travel expenses to be deductible, they must not only be reasonable, necessary and incurred while away from home, they must also be "incurred in pursuit of business." According to the Court:

> [I]ncurred in pursuit of business . . . means that there must be a direct connection between the expenditure and the carrying on of the trade or business of the taxpayer or of his employer. Moreover, such an expenditure must be necessary or appropriate to the development and pursuit of the business or trade.

> The facts demonstrate clearly that the expenses were not incurred in the pursuit of the business of the taxpayer's employer, the railroad. Jackson was his regular home. Had his post of duty been in that city, the cost of maintaining his home there and of commuting or driving to work concededly would be non-deductible living and personal expenses lacking the necessary direct relation to the prosecution of the business. The character of such expenses is unaltered by the circumstance that the taxpayer's post of duty was in Mobile, thereby increasing the costs of transportation, food,

---

[1] *See* Treas. Reg. § 1.262-1(b)(5).

[2] 326 U.S. 465 (1946).

and lodging. Whether he maintained one abode or two, whether he traveled three blocks or three hundred miles to work, the nature of these expenditures remained the same.

The added costs in issue, moreover, were as unnecessary and inappropriate to the development of the railroad's business as were his personal and living costs in Jackson. They were incurred solely as the result of the taxpayer's desire to maintain a home in Jackson while working in Mobile, a factor irrelevant to the maintenance and prosecution of the railroad's legal business. The fact that he traveled frequently between the two cities and incurred extra living expenses in Mobile, while doing much of his work in Jackson, was occasioned solely by his personal propensities. The railroad gained nothing from his arrangement except the personal satisfaction of the taxpayer. The exigencies of business rather than the personal conveniences and necessities of the traveler must be the motivating factors. Such was not the case here.[3]

In other words, the taxpayer's expenses in traveling to and from Mobile constituted nondeductible commuting expenses.

In *Sanders v. Commissioner*,[4] the court disallowed deductions claimed by taxpayers for travel expenses between their work place at Vandenberg Air Force Base and the nearest community surrounding it where civilians such as the taxpayers could live. Civilians could not reside on the Air Force base. The Ninth Circuit quoted with approval the reasoning of the Tax Court: "There is no convincing way to distinguish the expenses here from those of suburban commuters. Petitioner's hardships are no different than those confronting the many taxpayers who cannot find suitable housing close to their urban place of employment and must daily commute to work. We see no reason why petitioners in the case at bar should receive more favored tax treatment than their urban counterparts who also cannot live near their worksites."[5]

The Service has taken the following positions regarding transportation to and from one's workplace:

(1) A taxpayer who works in two different locations on the same day for the same employer may deduct the cost of traveling from one work location to the other. "If at the end of his workday he goes home directly from his second place of employment, his trip would ordinarily be regarded as commuting and his transportation expenses would be nondeductible, at least in those situations where his transportation expenses in going from that location to his home do not exceed those from his headquarters office to his home."[6]

(2) "Where an employee having two separate employers is required to work on the same day at a different location within the same city for each

---

[3] *Id.* at 470–74.

[4] 439 F.2d 296 (9th Cir.), *cert. denied*, 404 U.S. 864 (1971).

[5] *Id.* at 299 (quoting 52 T.C. 964, 970 (1969)).

[6] Rev. Rul. 55-109, 1955-1 C.B. 261, 263.

of his employers, it is recognized that his transportation expenses in going from his first to his second place of employment are not incurred in discharging the duties of either job or in carrying on the business of either employer. . . . However, since both such positions constitute part of the employee's trade or business, local transportation expenses in getting from one place of employment to another constitute ordinary and necessary expenses incurred in carrying on his combined trade or business and in discharging his duties at both obligations during the same day."[7]

(3) "A taxpayer may deduct daily transportation expenses in going between the taxpayer's residence and a temporary work location outside the metropolitan area where the taxpayer lives and normally works."[8]

> **Example:** Maria, who owns her own investment advising business in Seattle, drove to Portland one day a week for three weeks to assess a start-up high technology company whose stock she is considering recommending to some of her clients. She drove from her home directly to Portland and returned the same day directly to her home in Seattle. Maria's principal place of business is her office in a downtown Seattle business complex. On days she drove to Portland, she never stopped at her office.

> **Analysis:** Given that Portland is a temporary work site, located outside the Seattle metropolitan area, Maria will be entitled to deduct the cost of her transportation to and from Portland.

(4) "If a taxpayer has one or more regular work locations away from the taxpayer's residence, the taxpayer may deduct daily transportation expenses incurred in going between the taxpayer's residence and a temporary work location in the same trade or business, regardless of distance."[9]

> **Example:** Assume Maria drove from her home directly to the home of a prospective client and, after conducting an initial interview with the client, drove to her office in downtown Seattle.

> **Analysis:** Maria will be allowed a deduction for the cost of her travel between her home and that of the prospective client under this rule. She should also be allowed a deduction for the cost of traveling from the client's home to her downtown office under the rule of paragraph (1) above.

(5) "If a taxpayer's residence is the taxpayer's principal place of business within the meaning of Section 280(c)(1)(A), the taxpayer may deduct daily transportation expenses incurred in going between the residence and another work location in the same trade or business, regardless of whether

---

[7] *Id.*

[8] Rev. Rul. 99-7, 1999-1 C.B. 361, 362. The ruling does not define the term "metropolitan area." *See* Bogue v. Commissioner, T.C. Memo 2011-164, rejecting a taxpayer's proposed definition and indicating that in applying the language "outside the metropolitan area" a court's focus should be on whether a work site is "unusually distant from the area where [a taxpayer] lives and normally works."

[9] *Id.*

the other work location is regular or temporary and regardless of the distance."[10]

Thus, if in the prior examples, Maria used her home as her principal place of business, her trips to visit prospective clients or to evaluate investment opportunities would be deductible notwithstanding the general rule against the deduction of commuting expenses. The costs of Maria's trips will not be considered commuting costs.

A taxpayer who performs work-related tasks while traveling from his residence to his principal place of work may be engaged in deductible Section 162(a) traveling rather than non-deductible commuting. In *Pollei v. Commissioner*,[11] two police captains were permitted to deduct the maintenance and operating costs of driving their personal cars between their homes and police headquarters, based on their being in an "on duty" status at such times. The Salt Lake City Police Department had ordered command-level officers, including the two captains in *Pollei*, to provide their own transportation during their tours of duty:

> By that same order, petitioners' tours of duty were extended to begin and end when the officers left for work or arrived home in their cars, rather than when they actually arrived at or left from police headquarters. [The Police Department] provided and installed necessary equipment in each officer's privately-owned vehicle to enable its use as an unmarked police car. Officers were required to notify the police dispatcher before leaving, and on arriving home, and were "on call" during their travel time to and from headquarters. While en route to headquarters or their homes, petitioners were expected to monitor the radio channels to be aware of the ongoing police activities, observe their subordinate officers in the field, patrol the streets, and respond to dispatcher calls for assistance. Petitioners were also required to call in any time they used the unmarked cars, whether they were on or off duty at the time. . . .

The Tax Court concluded that petitioners' responsibilities were no greater when in transit to and from headquarters than when petitioners used their unmarked vehicles for personal errands. However, the Tax Court's conclusion fails to acknowledge petitioners' supervisory roles and the [Police Department's] reliance on their daily drive to and from headquarters. By requiring petitioners' tour of duty to begin with their departure from and end upon their arrival at home, the [Department] was provided with a regular addition to the number of commanders supervising police activities. Petitioners' occasional or happenstance use of their unmarked cars on personal business while off-duty could not provide the [Department] with a similar expectation of a regular increment in its supervisory staff.

The IRS argues that allowing petitioners to claim these expenses will result in a deluge of claims for similar exceptions from taxpayers who may

---

[10] *Id.*

[11] 877 F.2d 838 (10th Cir. 1989).

routinely or even occasionally perform work-related tasks during their commute to work. It fears, for example, that an employee using a portable dictaphone or a car telephone while driving to work could claim deductions for commuting expenses under section 162(a). We view the facts and circumstances in this case as sufficiently unique to preclude that fear from becoming reality.

We think it unlikely that most employees could justifiably claim their performance of work-related tasks during their commute to their jobs as a condition of their employment. Rather, it is more likely that most employees perform these tasks voluntarily, perhaps for their convenience or to enhance their work record. Petitioners' performance of supervisory and patrol responsibilities as they drove to headquarters was mandated by the [Department] order, and petitioners were subject to discipline if they did not carry out those responsibilities. Petitioners had no other option but to drive their unmarked cars between their homes and headquarters. Use of public transportation was not a viable alternative for petitioners, who testified that they could not thereby monitor the police radio and respond to emergencies or dispatcher calls while traveling to and from headquarters. Petitioners' situation thus can be distinguished from cases in which a commuter's choice of residence location or personal convenience were cited as reasons for the disallowance of commuting expenses. . . .

When conditions of employment restrict an employee's discretion in typically personal choices such as meals eaten during working hours or mode of commuting to work, "that which may be a personal expense under some circumstances can when prescribed by company regulations, directives and conditions, lose its character as a personal expense and take on the color of a business expense."

Other factors limiting the potential number of successful claims under our holding today are the public service and safety aspects of petitioners' employment, factors reflected in the [Department's] orders directing petitioners mode of daily travel to and from headquarters. Most employees cannot legitimately claim a similar public service or safety component to their jobs, and so will be unable to justify the deduction of commuting expenses in reliance on our decision here.[12]

§ 16.02 OTHER TRANSPORTATION EXPENSES
Regulation § 1.162-2(b)(1).

If a taxpayer travels to a destination and while at such destination engages in both business and personal activities, traveling expenses to and from such destination are deductible only if the trip is related primarily to the taxpayer's trade or business. If the trip is primarily personal in nature, the traveling expenses to and from the destination are not deductible even though the taxpayer engages in business activities while at such destination. However,

---

[12] *Id.* at 839–42.

expenses while at the destination which are properly allocable to the taxpayer's trade or business are deductible even though the traveling expenses to and from the destination are not deductible.

Often, the characterization of one's transportation expenses is not simple. Assume an attorney was scheduled to take a deposition in a city located near a national park. The attorney decides to combine business and pleasure and following the deposition rents a car and spends three days fishing and hiking in the national park. If the attorney's primary purpose for the travel is business, she will be entitled to deduct the transportation costs which are business related. By contrast, if the trip is primarily personal in nature, the transportation expenses (and other traveling expenses) will not be deductible, although any expenses incurred while at the destination that are allocable to her trade or business are deductible.

The concern that transportation expenses often are heavily tainted with a personal flavor caused Congress to limit the amount which taxpayers could deduct when the mode of transportation is a cruise ship or some other form of luxury water transportation.[13] Specifically, no deduction is allowed for transportation by water to the extent such expenses exceed twice the per diem amounts (determined with reference to employees of the executive branch of the Federal government) for days of such transportation. As noted by the Staff of the Joint Committee on Taxation, "[t]axpayers who engage in luxury water travel ostensibly for business purposes may have chosen this means of travel for personal enjoyment over other reasonable alternatives that may better serve business purposes by being faster and less expensive. Also, the costs of luxury water travel may include elements of entertainment and meals (not separately charged) that are not present in other transportation."[14]

In addition to the limitation on luxury water transportation, Congress also added a provision denying a deduction for travel expenses when travel is considered by the taxpayer as a form of education.[15] For example, the high school Latin teacher who spends the summer in Rome is not allowed to deduct the travel expenses as Section 162 educational expenses.

§ 16.03 EXPENSES FOR MEALS AND LODGING WHILE IN TRAVEL STATUS

§ 162. Trade or business expenses.

(a) In General. There shall be allowed as a deduction all the ordinary and necessary expenses paid or incurred during the taxable year in carrying on any trade or business, including —

. . .

(2) traveling expenses (including amounts expended for meals and lodging other than amounts which are lavish or extravagant under the circumstances)

---

[13] *See* I.R.C. § 274(m)(1).

[14] Staff of the Joint Committee on Taxation, General Explanation of the Tax Reform Act of 1986, p. 62.

[15] *See* I.R.C. § 274(m)(2).

while away from home in the pursuit of a trade or business. . . .

Congress added the statutory predecessor to Section 162(a)(2) in 1921 to permit the entire amount of meal and lodging expenses to be deducted when taxpayer is "away from home." As will be discussed in Chapter 17, Section 274(n) now limits the deduction for meals to 50% of their cost. Prior to the 1921 congressional action, meals and lodging expenses incurred by a taxpayer while on a business trip were deductible only to the extent they exceeded the amount required for such purposes while the taxpayer was home.[16] In claiming deductions for meals and lodging under the pre-1921 law, taxpayers were required to provide a statement showing among other items: (1) the "number of members in taxpayer's family dependent upon him for support"; and (2) the "average monthly expense incident to meals and lodging for the entire family, including the taxpayer himself when at home." The difficulty in administering an excess-cost standard such as that contained in the prior law is obvious, and the Treasury Department itself asked Congress to amend Section 162 to allow taxpayers to deduct the entire amount of their meal and lodging expenses while traveling away from home on business.

With respect to meals, the Service long ago developed the so-called "overnight rule" or "sleep or rest rule," whereby a taxpayer traveling on business may deduct the cost of his meals only if his trip requires him to stop for sleep or rest. The rule was upheld by the Supreme Court in *United States. v. Correll*[17] as a reasonable interpretation of Section 162(a)(2). The Court reasoned that "[b]y so interpreting the statutory phrase ["away from home"] the Commissioner has achieved not only ease and certainty of application but also substantial fairness, for the sleep or rest rule places all one-day travelers on a similar tax footing, rather than discriminating against intracity travelers and commuters, who of course cannot deduct the cost of the meals they eat on the road." The Service ruled that railroad employees who have been authorized to stop performing their regular duties to get substantial sleep or rest prior to returning to their home terminals may deduct the costs of their meals and lodging.[18] The Service clarified the meaning of the "overnight rule" noting:

> . . . such absence need not be an entire 24-hour day or throughout the hours from dusk until dawn, but it must be of such duration or nature that the taxpayers cannot reasonably be expected to complete the round trip without being released from duty, or otherwise stopping . . . the performance of their regular duties, for sufficient time to obtain substantial sleep or rest.

> However, the Service does not consider the brief interval during which employees may stop, or be released from duty, for sufficient time to eat, but not to obtain substantial sleep or rest, as being an adequate rest period to satisfy the requirement for deducting the cost of meals on business trips completed within one day. Thus, amounts incurred and paid for such meals are not deductible.

---

[16] T.D. 3101, 3 C.B. 191.

[17] 389 U.S. 299 (1967).

[18] Rev. Rul. 75-170, 1975-1 C.B. 60.

The deduction for lodging recognizes that a taxpayer on a business trip incurs duplicate expenses in securing lodging when away from home on business while at the same time maintaining an apartment or home at his principal place of work. The deduction for lodging in the run of the mill business travel case generally is appropriate. A more difficult question regarding deductions for lodging can arise in cases where the taxpayer works in more than one location but doesn't incur duplicate lodging expenses. In *Glazer v. Commissioner,*[19] the taxpayer worked in the Albany, New York, office of his employer from January through June each year and in the New York City office of his employer from July through December each year. When Glazer moved from Albany to New York City, he vacated his Albany apartment, taking all his personal possessions with him. He claimed Albany as his home and sought to deduct his New York City living expenses under Section 162(a)(2). The Tax Court denied the deduction: "In the context of section 162(a)(2), the taxpayer must incur substantial continuing living expenses at a permanent place of residence. . . . Such requirement is in accord with the purpose underlying section 162(a)(2), *i.e.,* to ease the burden which falls upon the taxpayer who, because of the exigencies of his trade or business, must maintain two places of abode and thereby incur additional and duplicative living expenses."[20] The Tax Court concluded that New York City was his tax home during the time he lived there, and denied the deduction.

§ 16.04   WHERE IS THE TAXPAYER'S "HOME" FOR SECTION 162(a)(2) PURPOSES?

Surprisingly, the phrase "away from home" has never been interpreted by the Supreme Court, although the Court has had ample opportunity to consider it. Other federal courts and the Service have disagreed upon the phrase's meaning. The long-standing position of the Internal Revenue Service is that "home" within the meaning of Section 162(a)(2) is the taxpayer's principal place of business. If the taxpayer has more than one employer or works in more than one location, the principal place of business will be a factual determination.[21] Facts such as the amount of time the taxpayer spends working in a location and the amount of business activity generated in a given location will be relevant to the determination.

The Fifth Circuit decision in *Robertson v. Commissioner*[22] provides a good example of the application of the Service's position. In *Robertson*, the taxpayer, a justice of the Mississippi Supreme Court lived in Oxford, Mississippi even though the Mississippi Supreme Court is located in Jackson, Mississippi. Justice Robertson was a professor of law at the University of Mississippi in Oxford when he was appointed to the court. Following his appointment, he continued to live in Oxford and taught one course each semester at the law school. He spent four days each work week in Jackson, although he was only required to be in Jackson two days a week for court business. The judge did much of his judicial work at the law school

---

[19] T.C. Memo 1990-645.

[20] *Id.*

[21] Rev. Rul. 75-432, 1975-2 C.B. 60.

[22] 190 F.3d 392 (5th Cir. 1999).

library in Oxford. For his judicial service, Robertson received $75,000 per year as compared to the $15,000 per year he received for teaching at the law school. Affirming the Tax Court, the Fifth Circuit concluded that Jackson, Mississippi was Justice Robertson's home for purposes of Section 162. As a result, he could not deduct his travel expenses associated with his judicial work in Jackson. With reference to the word "home" in Section 162, the Fifth Circuit stated:

> The word "home" for purposes of Section 162 does not have its usual and ordinary meaning. This court has repeatedly recognized that the term "home" means the vicinity of the taxpayer's principal place of business and not where his personal residence is located. Thus, a taxpayer's "home" for purposes of Section 162 is that place where he performs his most important functions or spends most of his working time. If the taxpayer has two places of business or employment separated by considerable distances, the court applies an objective test [which] considers the length of time spent at each location, the degree of activity at each location and the relative proportion of the taxpayer's income derived from each location.[23]

Contrast the historic position of the Service and the Fifth Circuit regarding the meaning of the term "home" in Section 162(a)(2) with that of the Second Circuit, as reflected in its decision in *Rosenspan v. United States*.[24] In *Rosenspan*, the taxpayer, a traveling jewelry salesman, had no permanent residence, although he stored some of his personal belongings at his brother's home in Brooklyn and used his brother's address for purposes of voter registration, vehicle licensing and filing of tax returns. The taxpayer periodically visited the headquarters of the company in New York. Relying on the Service's historic position that "home" means principal place of business, the taxpayer argued that the company's headquarters in New York was his tax home and that therefore all of his sales trips were deductible. The Service, however, abandoned its historic definition of "home," and argued that the taxpayer's travel expenses during the year were not deductible because the taxpayer had no "home" to be "away from." The Second Circuit agreed with the Service that "home" should be its commonly understood meaning:

> When Congress uses such a nontechnical word in a tax statute, presumably it wants administrators and courts to read it in the way that ordinary people would understand, and not "to draw on some unexpressed spirit outside the bounds of the normal meaning of word. . . ." The construction which the Commissioner has long advocated not only violates this principle but is unnecessary for the protection of the revenue that he seeks. That purpose [the protection of revenues] is served, without any distortion of language, by the third condition laid down in *Flowers*, namely, "that there must be a direct connection between the expenditure and the carrying on of the trade or business of the taxpayer or of his employer" and that "such an expenditure must be necessary or appropriate to the development and pursuit of the business or trade."[25]

---

[23] *Id.* at 395.

[24] 438 F.2d 905 (2d Cir.), *cert. denied*, 404 U.S. 864 (1971).

[25] *Id.* at 911.

The Second Circuit's determination that "home" means "home" has the effect of placing an emphasis on the business necessity of incurring travel expenses.[26] As even the Second Circuit would apparently admit, the Service's historic definition of "home" and the Second Circuit's definition will likely produce the same results in almost all cases. *Rosenspan* may perhaps represent the exception.

Special treatment is accorded taxpayers engaged in temporary jobs. Generally, such a taxpayer will be considered to be in "travel status" and travel expenses paid or incurred in connection with the temporary assignment away from home are deductible.[27] In characterizing an assignment as "temporary" for purposes of this rule, the Service historically employed the so-called "one-year presumption." Under this presumption, assignments away from home of one year or less were generally considered temporary; assignments of over one year were presumed indefinite and thus not subject to the above deduction rule regarding temporary employment. The one-year presumption could be overcome if a taxpayer could demonstrate that he realistically expected the job to last less than two years and expected to return to his home when the job ended.[28]

In 1992, Congress amended Section 162(a) to provide that a "taxpayer shall not be treated as temporarily away from home during any period of employment if such period exceeds one year." Revenue Ruling 93-86[29] addresses the application of amended Section 162(a) in common fact scenarios. The ruling holds:

> . . . if employment away from home in a single location is realistically expected to last (and does in fact last for 1 year or less), the employment is temporary in the absence of facts and circumstances indicating otherwise. If employment away from home in a single location is realistically expected to last for more than 1 year or there is no realistic expectation that the employment will last for 1 year or less, the employment is indefinite, regardless of whether it actually exceeds 1 year. If employment away from home in a single location initially is realistically expected to last for 1 year or less, but at some later date the employment is realistically expected to exceed 1 year, that employment will be treated as temporary (in the absence of facts and circumstances indicating otherwise) until the date that the taxpayer's realistic expectation changes.

---

[26] Consistent with *Rosenspan*, the Tax Court in *Christy v. Comm'r*, T.C. Memo 1993-156, held that a taxpayer who was a caddie for professional golfers and traveled to tournaments throughout the United States was an itinerant worker without a tax home. Although the taxpayer maintained a room in his brother's condominium, he did not pay rent but paid only his share of utilities, phone bills and food. The Tax Court noted that, despite the taxpayer's personal ties to the area where his brother lived, the "majority of [his] living expenses . . . were incurred and paid where the [taxpayer] was physically present. The ratio of expenses paid on the road to the amount paid to [taxpayer's] brother in a best case scenarios is 30:1. [Taxpayer] has not proved that he incurred substantial living expenses at his alleged permanent place of residence." *See also* Henderson v. Comm'r, 143 F.3d 497 (9th Cir. 1998), denying travel deductions to a taxpayer who worked for a traveling ice show because he was, in effect, an itinerant and had no tax home for Section 162(a)(2) purposes.

[27] Peurifoy v. Comm'r, 358 U.S. 59 (1958).

[28] *See, e.g.*, Blankenship v. Comm'r, T.C. Memo 1979-336.

[29] 1993-2 C.B. 71.

With respect to the last part of the holding, Revenue Ruling 93-86 provides the following example. A taxpayer regularly employed in one location was assigned to a location some 250 miles away. The taxpayer reasonably expected this assignment away from home to last only nine months, after which time she would return home. After eight months, however, she was asked to remain for seven more months (for a total stay of 15 months). The Service concluded that taxpayer's employment away from home would be treated as temporary for the first eight months and as indefinite for the remaining seven months.

Ordinarily, seasonal employment is another form of temporary employment. Suppose an employee has two or more seasonal jobs on an ongoing basis. How should the expenses incurred by the employee be treated? Revenue Ruling 75-43 provides the following guidance:

> A seasonal job to which an employee regularly returns, year after year, is regarded as being permanent rather than temporary employment. For example, a railroad employee might habitually work eight or nine months each year transporting ore from the same terminal, maintaining a residence of the employee's family at or near such work location. During the winter, when the ore-hauling service is suspended, the same employee might also be employed for three or four months each year at another regular seasonal post of duty, taking up residence at or near such employment. The ordinary rule is that when an employee leaves one permanent job to accept another permanent job, such employee is regarded as abandoning the first job for the second, and the principal post of duty shifts from the old to the new place of employment. The employee in the above example, however, is not regarded as having abandoned the ore-hauling assignment during the period in which that service is suspended since the employee reasonably expects to return to it during the appropriate following season. The employee is conducting a trade or business each year at the same two recurring, seasonal places of employment, and under these circumstances the tax home does not shift during alternate seasons from one business location to the other, but remains stationary at the principal post of duty throughout the taxable year. In each case of this nature, a factual determination must be made in order to establish which of the seasonal posts of duty is the principal post of duty. Of course, the employee may only deduct the cost of the meals and lodging at the minor place of employment while duties there require such employee to remain away from the principal post of duty.[30]

Consider the following example:

Example: Taxpayer engages in a seasonal business in the Boston area. During the off-season, taxpayer breeds and races horses in central Florida. Taxpayer owns a home in Boston and a home in Florida. Taxpayer lives and works six months each year in Boston and six months each year in Florida. Taxpayer seeks to deduct his travel expenses, including meals and lodging, associated with his Florida business. Will Taxpayer be successful?

---

[30] Rev. Rul. 75-432, 1975-2 C.B. 60, 62.

Analysis: Apparently, the answer is "yes." These are essentially the facts of *Andrews v. Commissioner*.[31] The Commissioner argued the taxpayer had two tax homes, *i.e.*, his home in Boston and his home in Florida. As a result, he was never "away from home" and therefore could not deduct his travel expenses. The First Circuit concluded otherwise, holding that a taxpayer could only have one "home" for purposes of Section 162(a) and that duplicate living expenses incurred while on business at the other home ("the minor post of duty") were a cost of producing income and therefore deductible. The court in *Andrews* remanded the case for a determination of which of the two homes constituted the taxpayer's home. As noted by the court, in determining which home constituted the taxpayer's "home" for purposes of Section 162(a)(2), "the guiding policy must be that the taxpayer is reasonably expected to locate his 'home,' for tax purposes, at his 'major post of duty' so as to minimize the amount of business travel away from home that is required. . . ."

§ 16.05 OTHER CONSIDERATIONS

[A] Travel Expenses of Spouse

§ 274(m)(3). **Travel expenses of spouse, dependents, or others.**

No deduction shall be allowed under this chapter . . . for travel expenses paid or incurred with respect to a spouse, dependent, or other individual accompanying the taxpayer (or an officer of employee of the taxpayer) on business travel, unless

(A) the spouse, dependent, or other individual is an employee of the taxpayer,

(B) the travel of the spouse, dependent, or other individual is for a bona fide business purpose, and

(C) such expenses would otherwise be deductible by the spouse, dependent, or other individual.

Historically, a taxpayer could deduct the travel expenses of his spouse who accompanied him on a business trip if he could establish a bona fide business reason for her presence.[32] The expenses of a spouse had to be ordinary and necessary in connection with the business of the taxpayer. In 1993, however, Congress added Section 274(m)(3), severely restricting deductions for the travel expenses of a spouse, dependent or other person who accompanies a taxpayer on a business trip. Under this provision, a taxpayer may not deduct such expenses unless (1) the spouse, dependent, or other individual accompanying the taxpayer is a bona fide employee of the taxpayer; (2) the travel of the spouse, dependent or other individual is for a bona fide business purpose; and (3) the spouse, dependent or other individual could otherwise deduct the expense. One might argue that Section 274(m)(3) does not represent good tax policy as it negates deductions for costs which are

---

[31] 931 F.2d 132 (1st Cir. 1991).

[32] Treas. Reg. § 1.162-2(c).

reasonable in view of the circumstances of a business, *e.g.*, the presence of a non-employee spouse on a business trip may be critical to the success of the business effort. Nonetheless, the provision serves to negate abuses which have occurred historically with respect to travel deductions.

Employer-paid expenses for spousal travel, otherwise nondeductible to the employer under Section 274(m)(3), may be treated by the employer as deductible compensation to the employee pursuant to Section 274(e)(2); if not so treated, a nondeductible employer-paid expense is presumably a fringe benefit, the tax treatment of which to the employee is subject to the working condition fringe benefit rules of Section 132.[33]

[B]   Reimbursed Employee Expenses

Employers commonly reimburse their employees for travel expenses incurred for business purposes. An employee may claim a deduction under Section 162 for ordinary and necessary expenses, including travel expenses, incurred in his trade or business as an employee. However, such expenses may be deducted "above-the-line" only if they are reimbursed expenses satisfying the special rule of Section 62(c).[34] Unreimbursed employee expenses, or reimbursed expenses that do not satisfy the Section 62(c) rules are "below-the-line" deductions, subject to reduction under the 2%-floor rule of Section 67, and useful in any event only for taxpayers who itemize rather than take the standard deduction.

Qualifying reimbursement arrangements are labeled "accountable plans" by the regulations. Amounts paid to an employee under an accountable plan are excluded from gross income.[35] Since the reimbursement does not constitute income, the expense is not deductible; the result is a wash from the employee's standpoint. (For tax purposes, this is identical to including the reimbursement in gross income and permitting an above-the-line deduction for the expense. The approach of the regulations, however, makes things much simpler for the employee.) By contrast, amounts paid to an employee under a "nonaccountable plan" are included in gross income, and the expense is deductible only as a below-the-line, miscellaneous itemized deduction.[36]

The regulations require an accountable plan to satisfy a three-part test.[37] First, the reimbursement arrangement must provide reimbursements, advances or allowances only for deductible business expenses — the so-called "business connection" requirement.[38] Second, the expense must be properly substantiated.[39] "For example, with respect to travel away from home, [the regulation] requires that information sufficient to substantiate the amount, time, place and business

---

[33]   *See* Treas. Reg. § 1.132-5(t)(1). See generally Chapter 11, *supra*, for a discussion of fringe benefits.

[34]   I.R.C. § 62(a)(2)(A), (c).

[35]   Treas. Reg. § 1.62-2(c)(4).

[36]   Treas. Reg. § 1.62-2(c)(5).

[37]   Treas. Reg. § 1.62-2(c)(2)(i).

[38]   Treas. Reg. § 1.62-2(d)(1).

[39]   Treas. Reg. § 1.62-2(e)(1).

purpose of the expense must be submitted to the payor."[40] According to the regulations, however, qualifying arrangements for per diem allowances or mileage allowances for travel away from home may satisfy the substantiation requirement.[41] Third, the reimbursement arrangement must require the employee to return within a reasonable time any amount in excess of the substantiated expenses.[42] (If the employee nonetheless fails to do so, the excess amount is treated as paid under a nonaccountable plan and is thus includable in gross income.)[43] Again, special rules are provided by which arrangements for per diem allowances and mileage allowances for travel away from home may be deemed to satisfy this requirement.[44]

[C] Business-Related Meals

Meals may still qualify and be deductible as ordinary and necessary business expenses under Section 162(a) even when the taxpayer is not away from home. In such cases, the express provisions of Section 162(a)(2) and the other sections are thus inapplicable.[45] For example, if a taxpayer takes a client to lunch, the cost of the client's lunch, as well as the taxpayer's, is generally deductible as a business expense. The deductions for entertainment and business meals are considered in detail in Chapter 17, which also address the substantiation requirements for the deduction of meal expenses,[46] and the percentage limitation on the meal expense deduction.[47]

[D] Limitations on Foreign Travel

Generally, travel outside of the United States is subject to the same standards as domestic travel. For example, an American entrepreneur engaged in international business is entitled to deduct the travel expenses incurred in traveling to foreign countries if the travel is primarily related to his business. Where, however, the taxpayer travels outside the North American area to attend a business convention, seminar or similar meeting, Congress has imposed certain limitations. Specifically, the taxpayer must establish that it is reasonable for the convention, seminar or meeting to be held outside the North American area.[48] No deduction is allowed for costs incurred in attending conventions, seminars or meetings on cruise ships which have ports of call outside of the United States or its possessions, and a limitation of $2,000 per year is placed on deductions for expenses of conventions held on cruise ships which meet specified requirements.[49]

---

[40] Treas. Reg. § 1.62-2(e)(2).

[41] Treas. Reg. §§ 1.62-2(e)(2), 1.274-5T(g), (j).

[42] Treas. Reg. § 1.62-2(f)(1).

[43] Treas. Reg. § 1.62-2(c)(2), (3).

[44] Treas. Reg. § 1.62-2(f)(2).

[45] Treas. Reg. § 1.262-1(b)(5).

[46] I.R.C. § 274(a).

[47] I.R.C. § 274(n).

[48] I.R.C. § 274(h)(1).

[49] I.R.C. § 274(h)(2).

The North American area is defined as "the United States, its possessions, and the Trust Territories of the Pacific Islands, and Canada and Mexico."[50] In addition, there are specific reporting requirements.[51]

[E]   Relationship to Section 212

Travel expenses and meal expenses may be incurred in an income producing activity not rising to the level of a trade or business. While Section 212 and the regulations thereunder do not address the issue, it is clear from other provisions[52] that Congress intended meals and lodging expenses to be deductible under Section 212 subject to the same rules as meals and lodging expenses under Section 162. For example, in *Harris v. Commissioner*,[53] the court allowed a Section 212 deduction for travel expenses (including airplane fare, meals and lodging, local transportation costs and airport parking expenses) the taxpayer incurred in traveling from St. Louis to Charlotte, North Carolina to maintain certain lots he was holding for investment.

In 1986, however, the law was amended to deny a deduction under Section 212 for expenses allocable to a convention, seminar, or similar meeting.[54] Congress' specific concern was that taxpayers were using Section 212 to deduct expenses of investment seminars and tax shelter seminars which often were held in locations (including overseas locations) ideal for vacations and which were structured to provide time for extensive leisure activity. Travel expenses associated with business conventions and seminars, however, remain deductible under Section 162 subject to the specific rules discussed previously.

[F]   Substantiation Requirements

In addition to the specific requirements of Sections 162 and 212, taxpayers seeking to deduct transportation, meals, lodging or other travel and entertainment expenses must meet the substantiation requirements imposed by Section 274(d). These requirements are considered in Chapter 17.

---

[50] I.R.C. § 274(h)(3)(A).

[51] I.R.C. § 274(h)(5).

[52] *See, e.g.*, I.R.C. § 274(c), (d).

[53] T.C. Memo 1978-332.

[54] I.R.C. § 274(h)(7).

Chapter 17

ENTERTAINMENT AND BUSINESS MEALS

§ 274. Disallowance of certain entertainment, etc., expenses —

(a) Entertainment, amusement, or recreation —

(1) In general — No deduction otherwise allowable under this chapter shall be allowed for any item —

(A) Activity — With respect to an activity which is of a type generally considered to constitute entertainment, amusement, or recreation, unless the taxpayer establishes that the item was directly related to, or, in the case of an item directly preceding or following a substantial and bona fide business discussion (including business meetings at a convention or otherwise), that such item was associated with, the active conduct of the taxpayer's trade or business, or

(B) Facility — With respect to a facility used in connection with an activity referred to in subparagraph (A).

In the case of an item described in subparagraph (A), the deduction shall in no event exceed the portion of such item which meets the requirements of subparagraph (A).

(2) Special rules — For purposes of applying paragraph (1) —

(A) Dues or fees to any social, athletic, or sporting club or organization shall be treated as items with respect to facilities.

(B) An activity described in section 212 shall be treated as a trade or business.

(C) In the case of a club, paragraph (1)(B) shall apply unless the taxpayer establishes that the facility was used primarily for the furtherance of the taxpayer's trade or business and that the item was directly related to the active conduct of such trade or business.

(3) Denial of deduction for club dues — Notwithstanding the preceding provisions of this subsection, no deduction shall be allowed under this chapter for amounts paid or incurred for membership in any club organized for business, pleasure, recreation, or other social purpose.

§ 17.01 BUSINESS OR PLEASURE?

The problem of drawing the boundary line between business and personal expenses is a persistent, pervasive one in our tax system. The problem becomes particularly acute with regard to business-related entertainment expenses. It seems undeniable that, at least in some circumstances, entertainment activities provide a necessary "social lubricant," to borrow an expression from the Seventh

Circuit's opinion in *Moss v. Commissioner*,[1] and can be shown to be directly productive of business orders and profits. Section 162, it would seem, authorizes a deduction for such ordinary and necessary business expenses. But Section 262 denies a deduction for personal expenses, and most entertainment expenses, however intimate their connection to the taxpayer's business, also seem inherently personal.

Business entertainment is apt to consist of restaurant dining, parties, theater, ball games, cruises and the like, and most of the time there is likely to be some plausible business connection to the expenditures involved. The question then arises as to when, and to what extent, Section 162 prevails over Section 262. As a practical matter, of course, Congress is not likely to answer the question on a purely theoretical level. Practical considerations intrude, not to mention fairness and equity; expense-account living, and deductible wining and dining, for example, are practiced far more often by the highly-paid executive than the minimum wage worker. By contrast, many businesses argue their very survival depends on the deductibility of a significant portion of their goods or services, and business failure and unemployment is too high a price to pay for ending all entertainment-related deductions.

[A] Historical Background

Prior to 1962, the deduction of entertainment expenses was governed by the ordinary and necessary standard of Section 162. Under that standard it was relatively easy to deduct such expenses, even where the personal element appeared to loom quite large. In one well-known case, *Sanitary Farms Dairy, Inc. v. Commissioner*,[2] the cost to a dairy of sending its president and controlling shareholder and his wife, who were both experienced hunters, on an African big game hunt was held to be an ordinary and necessary business expense, since the hunt was intended to, and did in fact provide "extremely good advertising [for the dairy] at a relatively low cost." The court noted there was extensive newspaper coverage of the trip, films of the hunt were shown back home, and trophies from the hunt were displayed in the dairy's museum.

Moreover, the ease with which entertainment expenses could be deducted was exacerbated by the so-called "Cohan rule." In *Cohan v. Commissioner*,[3] Judge Learned Hand held that, where the taxpayer, the theatrical manager and producer George M. Cohan, had spent substantial sums on tax-deductible entertaining, but kept no account of them, it was error for the Board of Tax Appeals to allow no deduction at all; rather, the Board was directed to make on remand "as close an approximation as it can, bearing heavily if it chooses upon the taxpayer whose inexactitude is of his own making."[4] The *Cohan* rule thus inhibited administrative policing of entertainment expenses; it undoubtedly encouraged many taxpayers to inflate their expenses and to include quite marginal ones on their returns, trusting

---

[1] 758 F.2d 211 (7th Cir. 1985).

[2] 25 T.C. 463 (1955).

[3] 39 F.2d 540 (2d Cir. 1930).

[4] *Id.* at 544.

that approximation would produce acceptable results if they were audited, and reaping windfalls if they were not.

The perception that abuse was widespread and deep, and that personal expenses with little business connection were routinely being deducted, prompted proposals to completely disallow entertainment expenses. The congressional response was something considerably less than complete disallowance. The first step, in 1962, was the enactment of Section 274, which imposed in Section 274(a) requirements for entertainment expenses that were in addition to the ordinary and necessary rules of Section 162. In addition, Section 274(d) established substantiation requirements intended to overturn the *Cohan* rule in this area. Nonetheless, the substantiation requirements were not a problem for those willing to keep records, and the Section 274(a) requirements were easy to meet. The next major step, in 1978, was the amendment of Section 274(a) to deny any deduction for most entertainment facilities.

[B] Percentage Cutback for Meal and Entertainment Expenses

§ 274. Disallowance of certain entertainment, etc., expenses —

(n) Only 50 percent of meal and entertainment expenses allowed as deduction —

(1) In general — The amount allowable as a deduction under this chapter for —

(A) any expense for food or beverages, and

(B) any item with respect to an activity which is of a type generally considered to constitute entertainment, amusement, or recreation, or with respect to a facility used in connection with such activity,

shall not exceed 50 percent of the amount of such expense or item which would (but for this paragraph) be allowable as a deduction under this chapter.

(2) Exceptions — Paragraph (1) shall not apply to any expense if —

(A) such expense is described in paragraph (2), (3), (4), (7), (8), or (9) of subsection (e), [or]

(B) in the case of an expense for food or beverages, such expense is excludible from the gross income of the recipient under section 132 by reason of subsection (e) thereof (relating to de minimis fringes) . . . .

Further restrictions to Section 274 were added in 1986, disallowing a substantial percentage of otherwise allowable entertainment and meal expenses. The congressional concern with the personal element in business entertainment, and the 1986 response to it are described in the following excerpt:

. . . In general, prior law required some heightened showing of a business purpose for travel and entertainment costs, as well as stricter substantiation requirements than those applying generally to all business deductions; this approach is retained. . . . However, the prior-law approach failed to address a basic issue inherent in allowing deductions for many travel and entertainment expenditures — the fact that, even if reported accurately and having some connection with the taxpayer's business, such expenditures also convey substantial personal benefits to the recipients.

The Congress believed that prior law, by not focusing sufficiently on the personal-consumption element of deductible meal and entertainment expenses, unfairly permitted taxpayers who could arrange business settings for personal consumption to receive, in effect, a Federal tax subsidy for such consumption that was not available to other taxpayers. The taxpayers who benefit from deductibility tend to have relatively high incomes, and in some cases the consumption may bear only a loose relationship to business necessity. For example, when executives have dinner at an expensive restaurant following business discussions and then deduct the cost of the meal, the fact that there may be some bona fide business connection does not alter the imbalance between the treatment of those persons, who have effectively transferred a portion of the cost of their meal to the Federal Government, and other individuals, who cannot deduct the cost of their meals.

The significance of this imbalance is heightened by the fact that business travel and entertainment often may be more lavish than comparable activities in a nonbusiness setting. For example, meals at expensive restaurants and the most desirable tickets at sports events and the theatre are purchased to a significant degree by taxpayers who claim business deductions for these expenses. This disparity is highly visible, and has contributed to public perceptions that the tax system under prior law was unfair. Polls indicated that the public identified the full deductibility of normal personal expenses such as meals and entertainment tickets to be one of the most significant elements of disrespect for and dissatisfaction with the tax system.[5]

To reflect this personal element, and in lieu of including it in income, Congress has now generally limited the deduction for business meals and entertainment to 50% of the otherwise allowable amount.[6] However, the 50% cutback does not apply in a number of instances.[7]

[C] Business Meals and Entertainment Ticket Limitations

§ 274. Disallowance of certain entertainment, etc., expenses —

(k) Business meals —

(1) In general — No deduction shall be allowed under this chapter for the expense of any food or beverage unless —

(A) such expense is not lavish or extravagant under the circumstances,

---

[5] General Explanation to the Tax Reform Act of 1986, Jt. Comm. on Taxation, 99th Cong., 2d Sess., pp. 60–61.

[6] I.R.C. § 274(n)(1).

[7] I.R.C. § 274(n)(2).

and

(B) the taxpayer (or an employee of the taxpayer) is present at the furnishing of such food or beverages.

(2) Exceptions — Paragraph (1) shall not apply to —

(A) any expense described in paragraph (2),(3),(4),(7),(8), or (9) of subsection (e), and

(B) any other expense to the extent provided in regulations.

(l) Additional limitations on entertainment tickets —

(1) Entertainment tickets —

(A) In general — In determining the amount allowable as a deduction under this chapter for any ticket for any activity or facility described in subsection (d)(2), the amount taken into account shall not exceed the face value of such ticket.

(B) Exception for certain charitable sports events — Subparagraph (A) shall not apply to any ticket for any sports event —

(i) which is organized for the primary purpose of benefitting an organization which is described in section 501(c)(3) and exempt from tax under section 501(a),

(ii) all of the net proceeds of which are contributed to such organization, and

(iii) which utilizes volunteers for substantially all of the work performed in carrying out such event.

(2) Skyboxes, etc. — In the case of a skybox or other private luxury box leased for more than 1 event, the amount allowable as a deduction under this chapter with respect to such events shall not exceed the sum of the face value of non-luxury box seat tickets for the seats in such box covered by the lease. For purposes of the preceding sentence, 2 or more related leases shall be treated as 1 lease.

As noted previously, Section 274(n) generally limits the deduction for "any" food or beverage expense or entertainment expense to 50% of the otherwise allowable amount. There are additional special rules for business meals contained in Section 274(k): no deduction is allowed unless the meal is not lavish or extravagant, and the taxpayer or the taxpayer's employee is present. There is also a face-value limitation on most entertainment tickets.[8]

Since the 50% rule of Section 274(n) applies to the otherwise allowable expenses, other limitations should be applied first.

Example: If under Section 274(k) a $150 meal is lavish or extravagant to the extent of $50, only $100 is otherwise allowable, and the 50% limitation would result in a $50 deduction. (Taxes and tips relating to a meal or entertainment activity are included as part of its cost for purposes of

---

[8] *See* I.R.C. § 274(l)(1).

applying the 50% limitations; transportation cost to or from a business meal, however, is not subject to the reduction.)

The 50% limitation does not apply to employees who receive reimbursement from their employers, provided the employee accounts to the employer as required by Section 274(d).[9] It is the employer who is then subject to the 50% limitation of Section 274(n).

§ 17.02 ENTERTAINMENT ACTIVITIES

No deduction is permitted for any activity "of a type generally considered to constitute entertainment, amusement, or recreation" unless the taxpayer satisfies one of two tests: The expenditure must be either (1) "directly related to" the active conduct of the trade or business; or (2) "associated with" the active conduct of the trade or business and directly preceded or followed by a substantial and bona fide business discussion.[10] The regulations flesh all this out in considerable detail.

[A] "Directly Related" Entertainment

The chief purpose of the "directly related" standard is to prohibit deductions aimed merely at promoting goodwill.[11] Thus, in general, the "directly related" standard requires that the taxpayer reasonably anticipate some income or specific business benefit from the expense, actively engage in a business discussion, and be motivated principally by the business aspect of the business-entertainment combination. However, it is not necessary that more time be spent on business than on entertainment. There are alternative ways of satisfying the "directly related" standard: for example, the "clear business setting" test.[12] But note that if the taxpayers are not present or there are "substantial distractions" — such as at nightclubs, theaters, sporting events and cocktail parties — the expenditure is generally considered not to be directly related to the taxpayer's business.[13]

[B] "Associated with Entertainment"

The strictures of the "directly related to" statute are loosened considerably by the "associated with" standard. Under the latter, the taxpayer must have a "clear business purpose" for making the expenditure, but an intent to maintain business goodwill or obtain new business satisfies this requirement.[14] The substantial, bona fide business discussion that precedes or follows the entertainment must be for the purpose of obtaining income or other specific business benefit, and the business aspect must be the principal aspect of the combined business and entertainment;

---

[9] I.R.C. § 274(n)(2)(A), (e)(3).

[10] I.R.C. § 274(a)(1). The expediture must also meet the usual requirements for a Section 162 business deduction. A Section 212 income producing activity is treated as a trade or business for these purposes. I.R.C. § 274(a)(2)(B).

[11] Treas. Reg. § 1.274-2(c)(3).

[12] Treas. Reg. § 1.274-2(c)(4).

[13] Treas. Reg. § 1.274-2(c)(7).

[14] Treas. Reg. § 1.274-2(d)(2).

but it is not necessary that more time be spent on business than entertainment, nor must the business and entertainment necessarily take place on the same day. There is, of course, no requirement that any business be conducted during entertainment that is "associated with" the taxpayer's business. Moreover, entertainment expenses for spouses, both the host's and the guest's, are allowable.[15] In sum, although Section 274 has reduced the deductibility of entertainment activity expenses by 50%, it seems not to have too excessively narrowed the availability of the deduction.[16]

§ 17.03   ENTERTAINMENT FACILITIES

In the Revenue Act of 1978, Congress decided that, with respect to entertainment facilities, the potential for abuse was simply too great to continue allowing their use on a tax-deductible basis. Section 274 therefore generally denies any deductions for entertainment facilities.[17] Examples of possible entertainment facilities, as listed by the regulations, include hunting lodges, swimming pools, airplanes and vacation homes.[18] There is an exception to the rule of nondeductibility where the facility is a club that is used "primarily" for business purposes, *e.g.*, more than 50% business use,[19] and then only that portion "directly related to" the active conduct of the taxpayer's business is allowed.[20] In any event, no deduction is allowed for club dues, regardless of satisfaction of the primary use test.[21]

---

[15] Treas. Reg. § 1.274-2(d)(4).

[16] For example, see *Sullivan v. Comm'r*, T.C. Memo 1982-150. Edward Sullivan, the taxpayer, operated a service station known as Sully's DX Station in Chickasha, Oklahoma. Sully initially gave S&H Green Stamps to his customers but then decided he would attract more business by offering customers, many of whom were oil field workers, free beer. The issue, of course, was the deductibility of the beer in light of Section 274. The Tax Court held that Sully satisfied the rules for the deduction of entertainment expenses. Footnote 4 of the Tax Court decision is a memorable one:

> Petitioner's points are succinctly stated in his brief as follows:

> When I first opened my station business was very slow, as usual with a new business. Next I started using S&H Green Stamps to boost my sales. The majority of oil field workers (my customers) were single men who didn't have much time for licking stamps. I began giving beer. I know from past experience that "oilers" would much rather drink ice cold beer than lick stamps after a long hot day in the oil fields. . . . If I were to continue with Green Stamps I would have never increased my business. In 1977 my business was really strong until I got sick and had to sell out. I still feel good about it and I still have every receipt from every beer purchase as well as every Green Stamp purchase I ever made. Sir, I really don't feel in my heart how a small business man can be put down because he had an idea and made it work. . . .

> The force and truth of these statements are self-evident. We have no doubt that an oil worker, after a long, hard day in the field would much prefer to stop by Sully's Service Station for gas and a cold beer rather than go home licking S&H Green Stamps. Unlike the complex rule in *Shelly's* case — that nemesis of all first year law students of real property — the rule in Sully's case is simply that a small businessman who wants to obtain customers and sell more of his products can offer free beer to beer lovers. Stated differently, in exchange for purchasing gas, oil and other services, Sully said to his customers "This Bud's for you."

[17] I.R.C. § 274(a)(1)(B).

[18] Treas. Reg. § 1.274-2(e)(2).

[19] *See* Treas. Reg. § 1.274-2(e)(4)(iii).

[20] I.R.C. § 274(a)(2)(C).

[21] I.R.C. § 274(a)(3).

It is clear that otherwise allowable expenses for entertainment activities are not denied simply by reason of their association with an entertainment facility:

> For example, if a salesman took a customer hunting for a day at a commercial shooting preserve, the expenses of the hunt, such as hunting rights, dogs, a guide, etc., would be deductible provided that the current law requirements of substantiation, adequate records, ordinary and necessary, directly related, etc. are met. However, if the hunters stayed overnight at a hunting lodge on the shooting preserve, the cost attributable to the lodging would be nondeductible but expenses for any meals would be deductible if they satisfied the requirements of current law. The shooting preserve should provide the taxpayer with an allocation of charges attributable to the overnight lodging for the taxpayer and guests.[22]

It is nevertheless sometimes difficult to distinguish between a deductible entertainment activity and the nondeductible use of an entertainment facility. In *Harrigan Lumber Co. Inc., v. Commissioner,*[23] the Tax Court denied a deduction for annual lease payments for exclusive hunting rights on a ten-acre tract of land. The taxpayer used the hunting area, and a hunting lodge it built on the land, to entertain its business suppliers and customers. The Tax Court held that the hunting area was a "facility" and that the lease payments were "items with respect to a facility," although it conceded that:

> The distinction drawn by the Conference Report [to the Revenue Act of 1978] between entertainment activities within the meaning of section 274(a)(1)(A) and entertainment facilities within the meaning of section 274(a)(1)(B) is fuzzy at best. We discern from the examples and discussion in the legislative history, however, that a material difference between an entertainment activity that includes the use of real or personal property and an entertainment facility is whether the property used for the entertainment is occupied exclusively by the taxpayer for or during the recreation or entertainment. For example, use of a skybox at the stadium would not constitute exclusive occupancy of the sports stadium where the entertainment takes place.

> In this case, petitioner has exclusive right to use the hunting area for hunting, fishing and other recreation. Petitioner's exclusive lease of the hunting rights grants to petitioner, on prior notice, unfettered access to the hunting area. The hunting area is where the recreation takes place. During petitioner's recreation in the hunting area, petitioner has exclusive occupancy of the hunting area. Therefore, the hunting area is a facility used in connection with entertainment within the meaning of section 274(a)(1)(B).

> Petitioner argues, however, that the lease payments are expenditures for an intangible property right which is separate and apart from the real property to which the hunting rights are attached, and therefore, such expenditures are out-of-pocket expenses, which are deductible pursuant to

---

[22] General Explanation of the Revenue Act of 1978, Jt. Comm. on Taxation, 95th Cong., 2d sess., p. 207.

[23] 88 T.C. 1562 (1987), *aff'd,* 851 F.2d 362 (11th Cir. 1988).

section 1.274-2(e)(3)(iii)(a), Income Tax Regs. Petitioner argues further [based on the example from legislative history, quoted above, dealing with deductible hunting expenses] that hunting rights were considered specifically by Congress which decided that they were expenses of an activity and not expenses "with respect to" a facility.

In the above example the expenditures for the hunting rights, which are considered to be part of an activity and not "with respect to" a facility, are for the non-exclusive use of a commercial hunting preserve for one day. The taxpayer [in the example] has no control over the use of the property by others, no exclusive occupancy of the preserve for hunting and no right to access the property beyond the limited time permitted. The expenditure thus viewed relates more to the entertainment activity than to the entertainment facility. Where the taxpayer is, however, granted exclusive use of and unfettered access to the property, the character of the expenditure changes. Instead of being an expense incurred solely in connection with the particular activity, it becomes an expense for the continuing enjoyment of the property itself for the specified recreational purposes. In this case, petitioner's payments gave it continuing, unfettered access to the property and exclusive occupancy in order to hunt, fish and cook out. Moreover, these rights are meaningless apart from the hunting area to which they attach. Petitioner's payments were not made simply to acquire and hold "rights" but were made to enjoy the use of the property. Therefore, we reject petitioner's argument. The lease payments are an item "with respect to" a facility used in connection with entertainment within the meaning of section 274(a)(1)(B).[24]

Two concurring opinions declined to adopt the majority's formulation, but nonetheless held for the Commissioner, relying in whole or in part on the long-term nature of the lease. *Harrigan Lumber* was followed in *On Shore Quality Control Specialist, Inc. v. Commissioner*,[25] where the Tax Court disallowed the deduction of lease payments for use of a ranch for hunting purposes on the ground that the ranch was an entertainment facility. Under the taxpayer's lease arrangements, some friends and business acquaintances of the owner were also allowed to hunt on the ranch. The taxpayer thus argued that the ranch, under *Harrigan Lumber*, was not a "facility" with respect to the taxpayer because the lease was not an exclusive one. The *On Shore* court, however, concluded the exclusivity language in *Harrigan Lumber* referred to the right of the lessee to bar the general public from participation, not a limited number of persons covered by the lease, and it held that where the taxpayer "dominates" the hunting rights as in *On Shore*, the rights should be treated as exclusive ones, and the lease payments should be disallowed.

---

[24] *Id.* at 1566–68.

[25] T.C. Memo. 1996-95.

§ 17.04 SUBSTANTIATION REQUIREMENTS

§ 274. Disallowance of certain entertainment, etc., expenses —

(d) Substantiation required — No deduction or credit shall be allowed —

(2) for any item with respect to an activity which is of a type generally considered to constitute entertainment, amusement, or recreation, or with respect to a facility used in connection with such an activity. . . .

. . .

(4) with respect to any listed property (as defined in section 280F(d)(4)),

unless the taxpayer substantiates by adequate records or by sufficient evidence corroborating the taxpayer's own statement (A) the amount of such expense or other item, (B) the time and place of the travel, entertainment, amusement, recreation, or use of the facility or property, or the date and description of the gift, (C) the business purpose of the expense or other item, and (D) the business relationship to the taxpayer of persons entertained, using the facility or property, or receiving the gift. The Secretary may by regulations provide that some or all of the requirements of the preceding sentence shall not apply in the case of an expense which does not exceed an amount prescribed pursuant to such regulations.

Section 274(d) imposes special substantiation requirements on entertainment expenses, travel expenses, and other listed expenses. By the terms of the statute, the taxpayer is required to substantiate either by "adequate records" or "by sufficient evidence corroborating his own statement" the following: (1) the amount of the expense; (2) the time and place it was incurred; (3) the business purpose for the expense; and (4) the business relationship to the taxpayer of the persons entertained. The clear purpose of Section 274(d) is to reverse the *Cohan*[26] rule with regard to the listed types of expense. If substantiation is not provided, the deduction is disallowed even though it is otherwise properly deductible.

The "adequate records" requirement generally involves maintaining an account book, diary or similar record with entries made at or near the time of the expense, together with documentary evidence (bills and receipts) in support of the entries.[27] However, the documentary evidence aspect of the rule will be waived for expenditures of less than $75.[28] If the "adequate records" requirement is not met, the taxpayer must establish substantiation by his own statement, together with sufficient corroborative evidence; an uncorroborated statement will not support the deduction.[29]

The regulations provide exceptions to the general substantiation requirement in certain circumstances. Note, for example, that an employee "incurring" reimbursed

---

[26] *Cohan v. Commissioner*, 39 F.2d 540 (2d Cir. 1930), holding that where the taxpayer had kept inadequate records, the Board of Tax Appeals was required to make "as close an approximation as it can" of the allowable deductions. *See* § 17.01[A], *supra.*

[27] Treas. Reg. § 1.274-5T (c)(2).

[28] Treas. Reg. § 1.274-5(c)(2).

[29] Treas. Reg. § 1.274-5T(c)(3).

expenses does not have to report the reimbursement or the expenses, if he makes an "adequate accounting" to the employer.[30] No substantiation is required for certain per diem and mileage allowances.[31] In any case, however, excess reimbursements are reportable as income.

§ 17.05 EXCEPTIONS

§ 274. **Disallowance of certain entertainment, etc., expenses —**

(e) **Specific exceptions to application of subsection (a) — Subsection (a) shall not apply to —**

(1) **Food and beverages for employees — Expenses for food and beverages (and facilities used in connection therewith) furnished on the business premises of the taxpayer primarily for his employees.**

(2) **Expenses treated as compensation —**

(A) . . . **expenses for goods, services, and facilities, to the extent that the expenses are treated by the taxpayer, with respect to the recipient of the entertainment, amusement, or recreation, as compensation to an employee on the taxpayer's return of tax under this chapter and as wages to such employee for purposes of chapter 24 (relating to withholding of income tax at source on wages.) . . .**

(3) **Reimbursed expenses — Expenses paid or incurred by the taxpayer, in connection with the performance by him of services for another person (whether or not such other person is his employer), under a reimbursement or other expense allowance arrangements with such other person, but this paragraph shall apply —**

(A) **where the services are performed for an employer, only if the employer has not treated such expenses in the manner provided in paragraph (2), or**

(B) **where the services are performed for a person other than an employer, only if the taxpayer accounts (to the extent provided by subsection (d)) to such person. . . .**

Section 274(e) provides a number of exceptions to the basic rule of Section 274(a). Section 274(e)(2), for example, indicates that the disallowance rule does not apply to the extent the taxpayer's payment of an expense is treated as compensation to the recipient. Note, however, that substantiation is nonetheless required for Section 274(e) expenses, except to the extent waived by the Section 274(d) regulations themselves.

§ 17.06 BUSINESS MEALS

As discussed in previous Chapters, Section 162(a)(2) allows a deduction for one's own meals while away from home on business; Section 119 excludes from income meals furnished for the convenience of the employer; and Section 132 excludes

---

[30] Treas. Reg. § 1.274-5T(f)(2).

[31] Treas. Reg. § 1.274(d)-1. *See also* Treas. Reg. § 1.274-5T(j).

occasional supper money from income. Nevertheless, outside of safe harbors such as these, the proper tax treatment of one's own business meals remains somewhat controversial and uncertain; the matter is by no means squarely addressed by Section 274, despite the restrictions it places on meal expenditures generally.

The seminal case on the deductibility of one's own business meals is *Sutter v. Commissioner*.[32] Sutter, an industrial surgeon, sought to deduct, among other items, the cost of his own lunches at meetings of the local Chamber of Commerce and Hospital Council as well as a variety of business entertainment expenses. The Tax Court concluded that, despite the business context, the "cost of meals, entertainment, and similar items for one's self and one's dependents" (at least while not "away from home") is a personal expense and presumptively nondeductible. The presumption of nondeductibility, however, could be overcome by "clear and detailed evidence . . . that the expenditure in question was different from or in excess of that which would have been made for the taxpayer's personal purposes."[33]

Despite the burden that the *Sutter* rule places on the taxpayer, the Service recognized the administrative problems (for questionable amounts of revenue) its vigorous enforcement would entail, and long ago announced a more liberal policy. In Revenue Ruling 63-144,[34] which consists of a series of questions and answers on the deductibility of business expenditures for entertainment, travel, and gifts under Section 274, the Service posed and answered the following question:

Personal Portion of Business Meals

31. Question: Several of these questions and answers refer to the cost of the taxpayer entertaining a business customer at lunch or dinner. To what extent is the cost of the taxpayer's own meal deductible?

Answer: Judicial decisions under established law, applying the statutory rules that deductions are not allowed for personal expenses, hold that a taxpayer cannot obtain a deduction for the portion of his meal cost which does not exceed an amount he would normally spend on himself. The Service practice has been to apply this rule largely to abuse cases where taxpayers claim deductions for substantial amounts of personal living expenses. The Service does not intend to depart from this practice.

Note that this policy refers to business meals involving entertainment of a customer. The right to deduct the cost of one's own business meal may be particularly questioned when the meal involves only co-workers, partners, or other such colleagues, as opposed to meals involving entertainment of customers or clients. In other words, if co-workers talk business over lunch, may each of them deduct the lunch expense?

In *Moss v. Commissioner*[35] each member of a small law firm carried a tremendous litigation caseload and spent most of every working day in court. To

---

[32] 21 T.C. 170 (1953).

[33] *Id.* at 173.

[34] 1963-2 C.B. 129, 135.

[35] 758 F.2d 211 (7th Cir. 1985).

help manage their caseloads, they met each day for lunch, when the courts were in recess, at Café Angelo, where they discussed their cases and decided which lawyers would handle which court calls. Moss, one of the lawyers, sought to deduct his share of the lunch expense. The Seventh Circuit concluded the expense was nondeductible.

Although an argument can thus be made for disallowing any deduction for business meals, on the theory that people have to eat whether they work or not, the result would be excessive taxation of people who spend more money on business meals because they are business meals than they would spend on their meals if they were not working. . . . The law could require him to pay tax on the fair value of the meal to him; this would be (were it not for costs of administration) the economically correct solution. But the government does not attempt this difficult measurement; it once did, but gave up the attempt as not worth the cost. . . . The taxpayer is permitted to deduct the whole price, provided the expense is "different from or in excess of that which would have been made for the taxpayer's personal purposes" . . . . Because the law allows this generous deduction, which tempts people to have more (and costlier) business meals than are necessary, the Internal Revenue Service has every right to insist that the meal be shown to be a real business necessity. This condition is most easily satisfied when a client or customer or supplier or other outsider to the business is a guest. . . . It is undeniable that eating together fosters camaraderie and makes business dealings friendlier and easier. It thus reduces the costs of transacting business, for these costs include the frictions and the failures of communication that are produced by suspicion and mutual misunderstanding, by differences in tastes and manners, and by lack of rapport. A meeting with a client or customer in an office is therefore not a perfect substitute for a lunch with him in a restaurant. But it is different when all the participants in the meal are coworkers, as essentially was the case here. . . . They know each other well already; they don't need the social lubrication that a meal with an outsider provides — at least don't need it daily. If a large firm had a monthly lunch to allow partners to get to know associates, the expense of the meal might well be necessary, and would be allowed by the Internal Revenue Service. . . . It is all a matter of degree and circumstance (the expense of a testimonial dinner, for example, would be deductible on a morale-building rationale); and particularly of frequency. Daily — for a full year — is too often. . . . We may assume it was necessary for Moss's firm to meet daily to coordinate the work of the firm, and also, as the Tax Court found, that lunch was the most convenient time. But it does not follow that the expense of the lunch was a necessary business expense. The members of the firm had to eat somewhere, and the Café Angelo was both convenient and not too expensive. They do not claim to have incurred a greater daily lunch expense than they would have incurred if there had been no lunch meetings. Although it saved time to combine lunch with work, the meal itself was not an organic part of the meeting. . . . The case might be different if the location of the courts required the firm's members to eat each day either in a disagreeable restaurant, so that they derived less value from the meal than it cost them to buy it. . . . or in a restaurant too expensive for their personal tastes, so that, again, they would have gotten less value than the cash equivalent. But so far as appears, they picked the restaurant they liked most. . . .[36]

Moss v. Commissioner is not the only case that has presented the question of deducting meals involving co-workers. In *Sibla v. Commissioner* and *Cooper v. Commissioner*,[37] firemen were allowed to deduct their contributions to a fund for daily meals at the fire station, a contribution required by law whether or not they were able to eat the meal or be present at the station. However, in other cases, the taxpayer has not fared so well. For example, in *Wells v. Commissioner*,[38] the Tax Court denied a deduction to a county public defender for the costs of taking several staff members to lunch once a month, and of periodically taking two or three members and guests to dinner. In dictum, the court stated that occasional lunch meetings of a law firm of comparable size (over 33 attorneys) would be deductible; however, it held the costs to be not ordinary and necessary for the usual civil servant, such as the county public defender. In *Fenstermaker v. Commissioner*,[39] several executives of a company were reimbursed for up to 144 lunches per year, most of which were with fellow employees, though some were with outside consultants. Although company business was discussed at each meal, the reimbursements were included in income; no deduction was allowed for the expenditures on the ground that no showing had been made that the expenses exceeded what would have been incurred for personal purposes, and that only such excess would be deductible. In another case,[40] an employee sought to deduct the unreimbursed costs of (1) taking her employer's business customers to lunch and (2) providing periodic meals and parties to employees under her supervision so they would have higher morale. The Tax Court held that, to deduct business entertainment or meals under Sections 162 and 274, an employee "must show that the employer required or expected her to incur and to bear the expenses without reimbursement." The taxpayer satisfied this requirement as to the business customers, but not with respect to the co-workers.

[36] *Id.* at 212–14.

[37] 611 F.2d 1260 (9th Cir. 1980).

[38] T.C. Memo 1977-419.

[39] T.C. Memo 1978-210.

[40] Dunkelberger v. Comm'r, T.C. Memo 1992-723.

Chapter 18

EDUCATIONAL EXPENSES

§ 18.01 CATEGORIZATION OF EDUCATIONAL EXPENSES

In the early years of the Internal Revenue Code, the Service opposed allowance of a business deduction for an individual's education expenses as it regarded these expenses as inherently personal in nature, and opposed allowance of a deduction for them. The first case in which a court allowed a deduction for educational expenses, *Hill v. Commissioner*,[1] was decided in 1950. In *Hill*, the court held a teacher could deduct summer school expenses. The tax treatment of educational expenses continued to be governed by case law and rulings until 1958, when a comprehensive set of regulations was issued under Section 162. The 1958 regulations placed great emphasis on the "primary purpose" of the individual in incurring educational expenses. These regulations ultimately proved unsatisfactory and were replaced in 1967 by the current regulations, which rely on more objective criteria. This chapter considers the deductibility of education costs as business expenses under Section 162. In addition, at the end of this chapter, a variety of other tax incentives for non-business education expenses, including tax credits for higher education costs, are noted.

The deductibility of an educational expense may to some extent be seen as a matter of determining in which of three pigeonholes it properly belongs. An individual's educational expense may be purely personal, *e.g.*, a lover of fine foods takes a course in gourmet cooking, and the cost is therefore nondeductible. The expense, alternatively, may be indubitably business-related, *e.g.*, the student of gourmet cooking is the owner of a small restaurant, and he takes a class to maintain his skills and expand his repertoire. In these circumstances, the expense seems clearly ordinary and necessary under Section 162(a). Finally, the expense, although business-related, may be capital in nature and therefore nondeductible, *e.g.*, the student, a frustrated lawyer, takes a gourmet cooking class as one of a series of classes in a course of study leading to a certificate as a master chef, and an entree to a new career.

The utility of this personal-business-capital approach to educational expenses has its limits. For one thing, many educational expenses do not fit neatly within a single category, but have characteristics that overlap the boundary lines. For another, cases and rulings on occasion describe as "personal" what is more accurately labeled a capital expenditure. The cost of a law school education, for example, is hardly a "personal" expenditure equivalent to food, clothing, shelter, recreation and the like. In addition, the regulations permit deductions for educa

---

[1] 181 F.2d 906 (4th Cir. 1950).

tional expenses that "improve" skills as well as merely "maintain" them; this, of course, may simply be a bow to the inevitable, considering the daunting practical difficulties in trying to distinguish between maintenance and improvement in this context. Most importantly, however, an individual's educational expenses that are in the nature of capital expenditures are treated quite differently from the typical business-related capital expenditures. Instead of permitting the cost to be depreciated or amortized over time, or allowing the cost to be recovered on disposition or retirement, the expense is simply disallowed. Thus, for example, the cost of a law school education cannot be deducted over the life expectancy or working-life expectancy of the lawyer, nor is the cost allowed as a deduction upon the retirement or death of the lawyer. The regulations apparently take the position that such costs "constitute an inseparable aggregate of personal and capital expenditures."[2] Undoubtedly, such a rule eases the administration of educational expenses. Without it, for example, lawyers would surely also argue for amortization of college expenses because a bachelor's degree is a prerequisite for admission to law school.

The regulations dealing with educational expenses establish these rules: An individual may deduct educational expenses that either (1) maintain or improve skills required in his employment or trade or business, or (2) meet the express requirements of his employer, or applicable law, necessary to retain his established employment relationship, status, or rate of compensation.[3] However, an expense is nondeductible (even though it may satisfy the skill-maintenance or employer-requirement test) if it either (1) meets the minimum educational requirements for qualification in the taxpayer's employment or trade or business, or (2) qualifies the taxpayer for a new trade or business.[4] The taxpayer is thus required to avoid both of the two latter tests, while at the same time satisfying one of the two former tests.

§ 18.02   THE SKILL-MAINTENANCE OR EMPLOYER-REQUIREMENT TESTS

Assuming the expense is not disallowed under the minimum-educational-requirements or new-trade-or-business tests, an individual may deduct educational expenses that maintain or improve skills required in his employment or trade or business. The regulations provide that "refresher courses or courses dealing with current developments as well as academic or vocational courses" fall within this category.[5] Thus, the typical professional update seminars are routinely deductible to those in the field under the skill-maintenance test. An early example, prior to the issuance of the regulations, is found in *Coughlin v. Commissioner*,[6] allowing a deduction to a practicing tax attorney for the cost of attending the annual New York University Institute on Federal Taxation.

---

[2] Treas. Reg. § 1.162-5(b)(1).

[3] Treas. Reg. § 1.162-5(a).

[4] Treas. Reg. § 1.162-5(b)(2).

[5] Treas. Reg. § 1.162-5(c)(1).

[6] 203 F.2d 307 (2d Cir. 1953).

By contrast, a Chicago police detective was not permitted to deduct the cost of college studies consisting of a major in philosophy.[7] Although the police department "encouraged policemen to attend colleges and universities," and although a college education may "improve the job skills of all who avail themselves of it," the taxpayer failed to demonstrate a sufficient relationship between the education and the particular job skills required by a policeman so as to remove the expense from the realm of disallowed personal expenses. College courses are not necessarily classified as nondeductible, but these courses were "general and basically unrelated" to the taxpayer's duties as a policeman.[8] Similarly, educational expenses incurred by two public school science teachers in connection with a seminar held in Hawaii were ruled nondeductible for want of sufficient "connection" or "germaneness" to the taxpayer's job skills.[9]

Another issue that may arise in conjunction with the skill maintenance test is whether the taxpayer is carrying on a trade or business at the time the educational expense in question is incurred. In *Wassenaar v. Commissioner*,[10] a taxpayer who had a law degree, but had not practiced law, was not allowed to deduct the cost of obtaining his master of laws degree in taxation. In *Link v. Commissioner*,[11] the taxpayer lost his attempt to deduct the expenses incurred in obtaining a master's degree in business administration (MBA). The taxpayer in *Link* had commenced the two-year MBA program following graduation from college with a degree in operations research and three months' employment with Xerox Corporation as a market research analyst. The Tax Court's analysis was as follows:

> Implicit in both section 162 and the regulations is that the taxpayer must be established in a trade or business before any expenses are deductible. The question of whether petitioner was established in a trade or business is one of fact which we must discern from the evidence in this record. . . .

> There are a number of factors indicating that petitioner's employment at Xerox was merely a temporary hiatus in a continuing series of academic endeavors. [Among them] is the period of time of employment, both in absolute and relative terms. Petitioner worked only 3 months at Xerox before leaving to attend graduate school. While we decline to set a minimum period of time that one must be employed, such a short period of time is relevant evidence. In addition, viewing petitioner's post-high school activities as a continuum, he was employed in his field only 3 months out of a total of 6 years. Moreover, he effectively ceased employment when he returned to school. [During the two-year program, the taxpayer held part-time work at the university as a student research assistant and also held summer work and part-time work as a corporate intern, a job available only to MBA students.] The job at Xerox was but another summer position in an otherwise continuous pattern of schooling which petitioner decided he

---

[7]   Carroll v. Comm'r, 418 F.2d 91 (7th Cir. 1969).

[8]   *Id.* at 95.

[9]   Takahashi v. Comm'r, 87 T.C. 126 (1986).

[10]   72 T.C. 1195 (1979).

[11]   90 T.C. 460 (1988).

needed prior to establishing himself in a trade or business.[12]

A question related to those raised in *Wassenaar* and *Link* is whether a taxpayer, having clearly at one time carried on a trade or business, has abandoned or withdrawn from that trade or business when the educational expenses are incurred. The issue may arise when the taxpayer ceases working full-time in order to undertake full-time schooling. The position of the Internal Revenue Service[13] is that a suspension of employment for a year or less will ordinarily be considered temporary. The Tax Court, however, in approving as temporary a taxpayer's two-year suspension of employment to attend business school, commented: "There is no magic in a one-year limit. . ."[14] and noted that all the facts and circumstances should be considered in determining whether the suspension is temporary.

As an alternative to the skill-maintenance test, the taxpayer may deduct educational expenses that meet the express requirements of his employer or applicable law imposed as a condition to retention of his established employment relationship, status, or rate of compensation.[15] The employer-requirement test thus applies only with respect to "express requirements," and the regulations go on to impose additional limitations. The requirements must be imposed for a "bona fide business purpose." Moreover, only the "minimum education necessary" to retention of job, status, or pay will qualify; education beyond the minimum may, however, satisfy the skill maintenance test.

Hill v. Commissioner,[16] noted above, which predates the regulations, exemplifies satisfaction of the employer-requirement test. In order to renew her teaching certificate, a public school teacher was required by state regulation either to take college courses or pass an examination; she chose the former, and the cost of attending summer school to acquire the college credits was held deductible as an ordinary and necessary business expense. Public school teachers are among the main beneficiaries of the employer-requirement test, but other professions, such as law and medicine, are increasingly adopting mandatory continuing education requirements as a condition to retention of a license to practice.

§ 18.03 THE MINIMUM EDUCATIONAL REQUIREMENTS AND NEW TRADE OR BUSINESS TESTS

An individual may not deduct educational expenses required to meet the minimum educational requirements for qualification in his employment or trade or business.[17] However, once an individual has met those requirements, the expenses incurred to satisfy a subsequent change in the requirements will be deductible. The regulations point out that actually performing particular job duties does not establish that one has met the minimum educational requirements for qualification.

---

[12] *Id.* at 463–64.

[13] Rev. Rul. 68-591, 1968-2 C.B 73.

[14] Sherman v. Comm'r, T.C. Memo 1977-301.

[15] Treas. Reg. § 1.162-5(c)(2).

[16] 181 F.2d 906 (4th Cir. 1950).

[17] Treas. Reg. § 1.162-5(b)(2).

Details are provided on the applicability of the minimum-education rule to educational institutions, and the rule is illustrated by examples involving secondary and university teachers, and a law student hired by a law firm.[18]

Example 1: Tom, who holds a bachelor's degree, obtains temporary employment as an instructor at the School of Business at University Y and undertakes graduate courses as a candidate for a Ph.D. degree. Tom may become a faculty member only if he obtains his doctorate and may continue to hold a position as instructor only so long as he shows satisfactory progress towards obtaining this degree.

Analysis: The graduate courses taken by Tom constitute education required to meet the minimum education requirements for qualification in Tom's trade or business and, thus, the expenditures for such courses are not deductible.[19]

Example 2: Susan, who has completed two years of a normal three-year law school course leading to a Juris Doctor degree (J.D.), is hired by a law firm to do legal research and perform other functions on a full-time basis. As a condition to continued employment, Susan is required to obtain a J.D. and pass the state bar examination. Susan completes her law school education by attending night law school, and she takes a bar review course in order to prepare for the state bar examination.

Analysis: The law courses and bar review course constitute education required to meet the minimum educational requirements for qualification in Susan's trade or business and, thus, the expenditures for such courses are not deductible.[20]

An individual is also prohibited from deducting educational expenses that are "part of a program of study . . . which will lead to qualifying him in a new trade or business."[21] Note that this is an objective test. The fact that an individual may not intend to pursue the new trade or business, but may simply wish to improve his skills in his present employment, does not make the expenses deductible. If the education qualifies the individual for a new trade or business, no deduction is allowed. In a recent case denying an educational deduction to a 62-year-old Methodist minister who took courses at a local Catholic university and ultimately earned a bachelor's degree, the Tax Court reiterated its view that "it may be all but impossible for a taxpayer to establish that a bachelor's degree program does not qualify the taxpayer in a new trade or business."[22] The taxpayer took courses he deemed relevant to his ministry, including Introduction to Counseling, Internship in Ministry Practice, Death and Dying as a Life Cycle, Modern Social Problems, The Family, Community, Ethics in Human Services, Symphonic Choir, Basic Writing, and Writing Strategies. Applying the objective test of the regulations, the Tax

---

[18]   Treas. Reg. § 1.162-5(b)(2)(iii).

[19]   Treas. Reg. § 1.162-5(b)(2)(iii) Ex. 2.

[20]   Treas. Reg. § 1.165-5(b)(2)(iii) Ex. 3.

[21]   Treas. Reg. § 1.162-5(b)(3)(i).

[22]   Warren v. Comm'r, T.C. Memo 2003-175.

Court, in concluding that the degree program qualified taxpayer for a new trade or business, stated: "courses taken by the taxpayer provided him with a background in a variety of social issues that could have prepared him for employment with several, public agencies and private non-profit organizations outside of the ministry. Whether or not petitioner remains in the ministry is irrelevant."

Likewise, it appears clear that obtaining a law degree qualifies an individual for a new trade or business. Thus, an engineer or accountant cannot deduct the cost of obtaining a law degree, even if the study is mandated by his employer, and even if he intends to continue his nonlegal profession.[23] Similarly, in *Galligan v. Commissioner*,[24] the court held a law librarian could not deduct the expenses of a law school education although the court conceded that a legal education would be helpful to her in her work as a law librarian. As noted by the Tax Court:

> [B]y attending law school and obtaining her degree, Ms. Galligan became entitled to seek admission to the bar, as she did, and to enter the practice of law if she should choose. . . . [She apparently indicated that she did not intend to practice law.] Ms. Galligan's law school education was part of a program which qualified her for a new trade or business.

By contrast, taking one or more courses that are not part of a degree-granting course of study, that do not lead to qualification for a new trade or business, could be deductible under the skill-maintenance test.

The regulations also provide that a mere "change of duties" is not equivalent to a new trade or business if the new duties involve "the same general type of work" as the present employment. The challenge is thus to draw the line where the "new duties" move beyond the same general type of work to become a new trade or business. The line-drawing is done in a generous way for teachers; the regulations provide that all teaching and related duties involve the same general type of work. For example, not only is there no new trade or business involved when a teacher moves from elementary to secondary school, or from one subject matter to another, but, somewhat remarkably, a change from teacher to guidance counselor or to principal also involves no new trade or business.[25] For non-teachers, the regulations illustrate the distinction between the same general type of work and a new trade or business by providing that the cost to a psychiatrist of study and training in psychoanalysis is deductible.[26]

The Tax Court has applied what it described in *Glenn v. Commissioner*,[27] as a "commonsense approach" to determining when new titles or abilities constitute a new trade or business:

> [A] comparison [is] made between the types of tasks and activities which the taxpayer was qualified to perform before the acquisition of a particular title or degree, and those which he is qualified to perform afterwards. . . .

---

[23] Treas. Reg. § 1.162-5(b)(3)(ii) Ex. 2.

[24] T.C. Memo 2002-150, *aff'd*, 2003 U.S. App. LEXIS 7126 (8th Cir. 2003) (unpublished opinion).

[25] Treas. Reg. § 1.162-5(b)(3)(i).

[26] Treas. Reg. § 1.162-5(c)(3)(ii) Ex. 4.

[27] 62 T.C. 270, 275 (1974).

Where we have found such activities and abilities to be significantly different, we have disallowed an educational expense deduction, based on our finding that there had been qualifications for a new trade or business.

By way of examples, public accountants and certified public accountants were held in *Glenn v. Commissioner* to be in separate trades or businesses, as were fixed-wing airline pilots and helicopter pilots in *Lee v. Commissioner*.[28] In *Sharon v. Commissioner*,[29] the Tax Court, in a decision affirmed by the Ninth Circuit, held that a licensed New York attorney qualified for a new trade or business on obtaining his California license to practice law.

By contrast to cases involving the denial of deductions for educational expenses leading to a new trade or business, the Tax Court in *Allemeier v. Commissioner*[30] allowed a taxpayer to deduct his MBA tuition because the MBA did not qualify the taxpayer for a new trade or business. In reaching its conclusion, the Tax Court applied the "commonsense approach" of *Glenn v. Commissioner*, noted above, and compared the types of activities the taxpayer was qualified to perform before acquiring the MBA with those he was qualified to perform afterwards. Based on that comparison, the Tax Court found that the taxpayer's business did not change significantly after the taxpayer enrolled in the MBA program. (Compare *Allemeier* with *Link v. Commissioner*, discussed previously.) In addition, the Tax Court in *Allemeier* concluded that, because the MBA did not qualify Allemeier for a professional certification or license, his case was distinguishable from cases involving taxpayers embarking on a course of study that qualified them for a professional certification or license, e.g., cases involving law study leading to a law degree where the taxpayer performed many of the same activities following the law degree that taxpayer had performed before earning the degree.[31]

Consistent with its decision in *Allemeier v. Commissioner*, the Tax Court in *Singleton-Clarke v. Commissioner*,[32] held that a registered nurse who earned her MBA with a specialization in health care management could deduct the cost of the MBA education because she was already performing the tasks and activities of her trade or business before commencing the MBA program. Prior to pursuing the MBA, taxpayer had served for a number of years as a quality control coordinator at acute care hospitals and medical centers. After earning the degree, she was hired by another hospital as a performance management coordinator, a position comparable to the positions she had held prior to pursuing the MBA. The court, in finding for the taxpayer, noted:

> An MBA degree is different from a degree that serves as foundational qualification to attain a professional license. . . . An MBA is a more general course of study that does not lead to a professional license or certification. *Allemeier v. Commissioner*, T.C. Memo. 2005-207. This Court has had differing outcomes when deciding whether a taxpayer may deduct educa

---

[28] T.C. Memo. 1981-26.

[29] 66 T.C. 515 (1976), *aff'd*, 591 F.2d 1273 (9th Cir. 1978).

[30] T.C. Memo. 2005-207.

[31] See Treas. Reg. § 1. 162-5(b)(3)(ii), Ex. (2), and *Galligan v. Commissioner*, noted previously.

[32] T.C. Summary Op. 2009-182.

tion expenses related to pursing an MBA, depending on the facts and circumstances of each case. *The decisive factor generally is whether the taxpayer was already established in their trade or business.* [Emphasis added.]

§ 18.04 TRAVEL EXPENSES

§ 274.   Disallowance of certain entertainment, etc., expenses.

(m)   Additional limitations on travel expenses.

> . . .

(2)   Travel as form of education. No deduction shall be allowed under this chapter for expenses for travel as a form of education.

Section 274(m)(2) disallows any deduction for travel as a form of education. The legislative history suggests the skepticism Congress had concerning the educational travel deductions claimed by teachers and other taxpayers:

> The committee is concerned about deductions claimed for travel as a form of "education." The committee believes that any business purpose served by traveling for general educational purposes, in the absence of a specific need such as engaging in research which can only be performed at a particular facility, is at most indirect and insubstantial. By contrast, travel as a form of education may provide substantial personal benefits by permitting some individuals in particular professions to deduct the cost of a vacation, while most individuals must pay for vacation trips out of after-tax dollars, no matter how educationally stimulating the travel may be. Accordingly, the committee bill disallows deductions for travel that can be claimed only on the ground that the travel itself is "educational," but permits deductions for travel that is a necessary adjunct to engaging in an activity that gives rise to a business deduction relating to education.[33]

As the legislative history indicates, travel expenses, meals and lodging remain deductible where an individual travels away from home "primarily" to obtain education, the expenses of which are deductible.[34] The regulations employ a facts and circumstances test for determining the primary purpose of a trip, citing as an important factor the relative amounts of time spent in personal and educational activities. The regulations and the examples thereunder also provide that, even when the trip is not primarily personal, expenses properly allocable to personal activities may not be deducted; conversely, when the trip is primarily personal, the transportation costs are nondeductible, but meals and lodging allocable to the educational activity may still be deducted.

---

[33] H.R. Rep. 99-426, 99th Cong., 1st Sess., p. 122 (1985).

[34] *See* Treas. Reg. § 1.162-5(e)(1).

§ 18.05 EDUCATION TAX INCENTIVES

The cost of education, particularly higher education, has skyrocketed in recent years. In response to intense political pressure, Congress has created a host of tax incentives for higher education, prominent among them the Hope Scholarship Credit, the Lifetime Learning Credit, Coverdell Education Savings Accounts, and a deduction for certain interest paid on student loans.[35] In general, these tax incentives are aimed at higher education expenses that would not be deductible as business expenses under Section 162. They represent, in other words, a deliberate policy determination to provide tax incentives for expenditures that would typically be regarded, under the regulations, as "personal expenditures or . . . an insepa-rable aggregate of personal and capital expenditures."[36]

The Hope Scholarship Credit is a tax credit of up to $1,500 per student (plus inflation adjustments), for a maximum of two years, for the qualified tuition and related expenses of higher education.[37] The credit, which consists of 100% of the first $1,000 of qualifying expenses plus 50% of the next $1,000 of qualifying expenses, may be claimed for the qualifying expenses of the taxpayer, the taxpayer's spouse, and dependents. Among the restrictions and limitations on the Hope Credit are the following:

(1) Qualifying expenses are essentially tuition and required fees, except nonacademic fees.

(2) Eligible students are only those who are enrolled at least half-time in one of the first two years of postsecondary education in a program leading to a degree, certificate, or other recognized educational credential. Note that the credit is allowed for a maximum of two years, and not for years that begin after the student has completed the first two years of postsecondary education.[38]

(3) The credit is phased out for taxpayers with modified gross incomes between $40,000 and $50,000 (between $80,000 and $100,000 on joint returns).[39]

Congress has made a number of amendments to the Hope Scholarship Credit. The amended credit is now called the American Opportunity Tax Credit. For 2009 through 2017, the amendments, among other things, increase the amount of the Hope Scholarship Credit to a maximum of $2,500; make the credit available to the first four years of post-secondary education, rather than the first two; broaden qualifying expenses to include required course materials; make the credit partially

---

[35] Other education tax incentives include Section 127 (providing an exclusion for employer-provided educational assistance programs), Section 529 (providing for deferral of income earned on amounts placed in qualified state-authorized pre-paid tuition plans or college savings accounts) and Section 79(t) (eliminating the early withdrawal tax on withdrawals fomr IRAto pay certain higher education expenses).

[36] Treas. Reg. § 1.162-5(b)(1).

[37] I.R.C. § 25A(b).

[38] I.R.C. § 25A(b)(2).

[39] I.R.C. § 25A(b)(1), (d).

refundable; and significantly increase the adjusted gross income eligibility limits for the Hope credit.[40]

The Lifetime Learning Credit is a tax credit of up to $2,000 per taxpayer for the qualified tuition and related expenses of higher education.[41] The credit, which amounts to 20% of no more than $10,000 of qualifying expenses, may be claimed for the qualifying expenses of the taxpayer, the taxpayer's spouse, and dependents. The same phase-out rules, based on (inflation-adjusted) modified adjusted gross income, that apply to the Hope Credit also apply to the Lifetime Learning Credit.[42] (The increased income limits for the Hope Credit for 2009–2017, noted above, do not apply to the Lifetime Learning Credit.) The two credits are coordinated by a rule that prohibits taking both credits for the same student in the same year: the qualifying expenses of a student for whom a Hope Credit is allowed may not be taken into account for purposes of the Lifetime Learning Credit.[43]

> **Example:** Assume Taxpayer qualifies for both credits with respect to the educational expenses incurred on behalf of A, a dependent of Taxpayer. Assume A's educational qualifying educational expenses amount to $5,000. If Taxpayer claims the Hope Scholarship Credit based on the first $2,000 of A's qualifying expenses, Taxpayer may not claim any Lifetime Learning Credit with respect to A. In other words, a choice must be made between the two credits with respect to a given student's qualified education expenses.

It is, however, permissible to claim a Hope Credit on account of one student's qualifying expenses, and to claim a Lifetime Learning Credit on account of another student's qualifying expenses.

Aside from the amount of the credit, the Lifetime Learning Credit differs from the Hope Credit in several respects. First, as its name indicates, the Lifetime Learning Credit is not limited to a maximum number of years or to the first two years of higher education (as the Hope Credit was prior to the 2009 amendments). Graduate-level education, for example, may qualify for the credit. Second, there is no requirement under the Lifetime Learning Credit that a student be enrolled at least on a half-time basis in a degree-granting program; a single course at an eligible educational institution will suffice. Third, the Lifetime Learning Credit is calculated on a per taxpayer basis rather than on a per student basis, as with the Hope Credit. No matter how many eligible students there may be among the taxpayer and the taxpayer's spouse and dependents, the maximum credit remains $2,000. (Married taxpayers must file jointly to claim the credit.)[44] In any case, neither the Hope Credit nor the Lifetime Learning Credit may be allowed for any expense for which a deduction is allowed.[45]

---

[40] I.R.C. § 25A(i) (as amended by the American Taxpayer Relief Act of 2012).

[41] I.R.C. § 25A(c)(1).

[42] I.R.C. § 25A(d).

[43] I.R.C. § 25A(c)(2)(A).

[44] I.R.C. § 25A(g)(6)).

[45] I.R.C. § 25A(g)(5).

Coverdell Education Savings Accounts ("Coverdell Accounts") are trust accounts that may be created for any child under age 18 for the purpose of paying the child's qualified higher education expenses or qualified elementary and secondary education expenses.[46] Qualified education expenses include: expenses for tuition, fees, academic tutoring, special needs services in the case of special needs beneficiaries, books, supplies, computer equipment and other equipment; and expenses for room, board, uniforms and transportation.[47] Total contributions to one or more Coverdell Accounts for the benefit of any given child may not exceed $2,000 per year. Any individual can contribute to a child's Coverdell Account, up to the $2,000 maximum, except that for individuals with modified adjusted gross income between $95,000 and $110,000 (between $190,000 and $220,000 on joint returns), the $2,000 maximum is phased out. An individual with income above the upper limit thus cannot contribute to a Coverdell Account.[48] Contributions to a Coverdell Account are nondeductible. The tax advantages are that contributions in the account grow tax-free until withdrawal, and that the withdrawal itself will be tax-free to the extent it does not exceed the child's qualified higher education expenses for the year of withdrawal. (Withdrawals that exceed such expenses are generally subject to taxation, plus a 10% penalty tax, on that portion of the excess withdrawal that represents earnings on the contributions. Unused portions of Coverdell Accounts may be rolled over to other Coverdell Accounts of the child or members of the child's family.)[49]

Section 221(a) authorizes an above-the-line deduction for interest paid by a taxpayer on any qualified education loan. The maximum deduction is $2,500. The deduction is phased out for taxpayers with modified adjusted gross income between $50,000 and $65,000 (between $100,000 and $130,000 on joint returns). These modified adjusted gross income figures are subject to inflation adjustments. The deduction is available with respect to loans incurred by the taxpayer to pay for the cost of attendance for the taxpayer, the taxpayer's spouse, and the taxpayer's dependents at institutions of higher education while enrolled at least half-time in a program leading to a degree or other recognized educational credential.

A tax incentive for educational expenses, added by the 2001 Tax Act, is an above-the-line deduction for qualified higher education expenses.[50] In the case of a taxpayer whose adjusted gross income does not exceed $65,000 ($130,000 in the case of a joint return), up to $4,000 of qualified tuition and related expenses[51] may be deducted. If the taxpayer's adjusted gross income exceeds $65,000 but does not exceed $80,000 (in the case of joint returns, if adjusted gross income exceeds $130,000 but does not exceed $160,000), up to $2,000 of qualified tuition and expenses can be deducted.[52] Other taxpayers get no deduction. The deduction cannot be taken in the same year for the same student for whom a Hope Credit or

---

[46] I.R.C. § 530.

[47] I.R.C. § 530(b)(1).

[48] I.R.C. § 530(c).

[49] I.R.C. § 530(a), (d).

[50] I.R.C. § 222.

[51] I.R.C. § 222(d).

[52] I.R.C. § 222(b)(2).

Lifetime Learning Credit is claimed.[53] The Section 222 deduction is scheduled to sunset at the end of 2013.

---

[53] I.R.C. § 222(c)(2).

Chapter 19

OTHER DEDUCTIBLE PERSONAL EXPENSES

§ 19.01 MOVING EXPENSES

§ 82. Reimbursement for expenses of moving.

Except as provided in section 132(a)(6), there shall be included in gross income (as compensation for services) any amount received or accrued, directly or indirectly, by an individual as a payment for or reimbursement of expenses of moving from one residence to another residence which is attributable to employment or self-employment.

---

§ 132. Certain fringe benefits

(a) **Exclusion from gross income.** Gross income shall not include any fringe benefit which qualifies as a . . .

(6) qualified moving expense reimbursement.

. . .

(g) **Qualified moving expense reimbursement.** For purposes of this section, the term "qualified moving expense reimbursement" means any amount received (directly or indirectly) by an individual from an employer as a payment for (or a reimbursement of) expenses which would be deductible as moving expenses under section 217 if directly paid or incurred by the individual. Such term shall not include any payment for (or reimbursement of) an expense actually deducted by the individual in a prior taxable year.

---

§ 217. Moving Expenses.

(a) **Deduction allowed.** There shall be allowed as a deduction moving expenses paid or incurred during the taxable year in connection with the commencement of work by the taxpayer as an employee or as a self-employed individual at a new principal place of work.

(b) **Definition of moving expenses.**

(1) **In general.** For purposes of this section, the term "moving expenses" means only the reasonable expenses

(A) of moving household goods and personal effects from the former residence to the new residence, and

(B) of traveling (including lodging) from the former residence to the new place of residence.

Such term shall not include any expenses for meals.

(2)   Individuals other than taxpayer. In the case of any individual other than the taxpayer, expenses referred to in paragraph (1) shall be taken into account only if such individual has both the former residence and the new residence as his principal place of abode and is a member of the taxpayer's household.

(c)   Conditions for allowance. No deduction shall be allowed under this section unless —

(1) the taxpayer's new principal place of work —

(A) is at least 50 miles farther from his former residence than was his former principal place of work, or

(B) if he had no former principal place of work, is at least 50 miles from his former residence, and

(2) either —

(A) during the 12-month period immediately following his arrival in the general location of his new principal place of work, the taxpayer is a full-time employee, in such general location, during at least 39 weeks, or

(B) during the 24-month period immediately following his arrival in the general location of his new principal place of work, the taxpayer is a full-time employee or performs services as a self-employed individual on a full-time basis, in such general location, during at least 78 weeks, of which not less than 39 weeks are during the 12-month period referred to in subparagraph(A).

For purposes of paragraph (1), the distance between two points shall be the shortest of the more commonly traveled routes between such two points.

Prior to 1964, no deduction was allowed for employment-related moving expenses. Reimbursement for moving expenses incurred by an employee's relocation to a new job with the same employer was treated as nontaxable on the ground that the expenses were incurred primarily for the benefit of the employer. In 1964, Congress enacted both Sections 217 and 82, the former providing a deduction for certain moving expenses, and the latter requiring the inclusion in income of all reimbursements for moving expenses. Significant statutory changes, however, were made in 1993. First, the category of allowable moving expenses, described below, was narrowed considerably. In addition, an employer's payment or reimbursement of otherwise-deductible moving expenses — known as a "qualified moving expense reimbursement" — was made an excludable fringe benefit under Section 132.[1] Finally, Section 82 was amended to require inclusion in income of all reimbursements for moving expenses, except to the extent excluded by Section 132. Note, however, that Section 82 continues to operate independently of Section 217 to a considerable degree; a reimbursement is taxable, unless it constitutes a qualified moving expense reimbursement, regardless of whether the expense is allowable as a deduction under Section 217.

The legislative policy behind Section 217 has been expressed as follows:

---

[1] See I.R.C. § 132(a)(6), (g).

The mobility of labor is an important and necessary part of the nation's economy, since it reduces unemployment and increases productive capacity. It has been estimated that approximately one-half million employees are requested by their employers to move to new job locations each year. In addition, self-employed individuals relocate to find more attractive or useful employment. Substantial moving expenses often are incurred by taxpayers in connection with employment-related relocation, and these expenses may be regarded as a cost of earning income.[2]

Section 217 applies to the self-employed as well as to employees; it applies not only to those changing jobs with the same employer, but to persons entering the work force for the first time, to employees beginning work for a new employer, and to self-employed persons entering a new trade or business or moving to a new location.[3]

The preliminary requirement for a deductible moving expense is that it be incurred "in connection with the commencement of work."[4] Under the regulations,[5] the move must bear "a reasonable proximity both in time and place" to the new principal place of work, although the taxpayer need not have made arrangements for work prior to the move. The reasonable-proximity-in-time requirement is met if the moving expenses are incurred within one year of the commencement of work; those incurred after that one-year period may be held to lack the requisite proximity in time, depending on the circumstances of the case.

The statute also imposes two substantive, but mechanical requirements, one relating to minimum distance, and the other involving a minimum period of employment in the new location. First, the taxpayer's new principal place of work must be at least 50 miles farther from his former residence than was his former principal place of work.[6] In other words, if his commute to work would have increased at least 50 miles had he remained in his old residence, the distance test is met. Second, the taxpayer must be a full-time employee in the general location of the new principal place of work (though not necessarily with only one employer) for at least 39 weeks during the 12-month period immediately following the move. (Self-employed individuals must satisfy a full-time work test of 78 weeks within the 24-month period after the move, with at least 39 of the weeks in the first 12 months.)[7] The full-time employment requirement is waived in case of death, disability and certain involuntary separations from work.[8] The requirements, and their component parts, are detailed in the regulations. The 50-mile and 39-week requirements serve as a means of distinguishing moves of a purely personal nature from those necessitated by one's employment.

---

[2] General Explanation of the Tax Reform Act of 1969, Jt. Comm. on Taxation, 91st Cong., 2d Sess., p. 101 (1970).

[3] Treas. Reg. § 1.217-2(a)(3)(i). Compare Section 217 in this respect to Section 162.

[4] I.R.C. § 217(a).

[5] Treas. Reg. § 1.217-2(a)(3).

[6] I.R.C. § 217(c)(1).

[7] I.R.C. § 217(c)(2).

[8] I.R.C. § 217(d)(1).

The allowable moving expenses are set forth in Section 217(b): A deduction is allowed for the cost of transporting the taxpayer, other household members, and household belongings from the old residence to the new one, as well as for the reasonable cost of lodging en route.[9] Meal costs, however, do not qualify as moving expenses. All moving expenses are subject to a reasonableness requirement.[10]

Allowable moving expenses may be deducted to the extent they are not paid for or reimbursed by the taxpayer's employer. (Such payments or reimbursements are excluded from the employee's income as qualified moving expense reimbursements.)[11] If an employee deducts an allowable expense in one year, employer reimbursement received in a subsequent year is not excluded from income.[12] Moving expenses are deductible for the year in which they are paid or incurred (in accordance with the taxpayer's accounting method), rather than in the year in which the minimum period of employment requirement is satisfied. The taxpayer may elect to claim the deduction on the tax return for the year the expense was paid or incurred, provided it is possible to satisfy the employment requirement; if the requirement is, in fact, not met, the deducted amount constitutes income for the first year the requirement cannot be met.[13] (Similarly, it seems clear that an employer reimbursement initially excluded from income under Section 132(a)(6) would also constitute Section 82 income in the first year the employment requirement cannot be met.) Alternatively, the taxpayer who has not yet satisfied the employment requirement can instead forego taking the deduction in the original return, and file an amended return or claim for refund if the requirement is subsequently met.[14] The Section 217 deduction is an above-the-line deduction, thus placing on the same tax footing those individuals who are reimbursed by employers and those who are not.[15]

Note that a taxpayer takes inconsistent positions in claiming a deduction under Section 162 for travel expenses incurred away from home at a new principal place of work and in also claiming a deduction under Section 217 for moving expenses in connection with the commencement of work there. Which section actually governs depends on the facts and circumstances involved.[16] For Section 217 purposes, employment at the new principal place of work must be permanent or indefinite, rather than merely temporary, as is the case under Section 162(a)(2).[17]

---

[9] I.R.C. § 217(b)(1)(A), (b)(1)(B).

[10] I.R.C. § 217(a); Treas. Reg. § 1.217-2(b)(2).

[11] I.R.C. § 132(a)(6).

[12] I.R.C. § 132(g).

[13] I.R.C. § 217(d)(2), (d)(3).

[14] See Treas. Reg. § 1.217-2(d)(2).

[15] I.R.C. § 62(a)(15).

[16] Treas. Reg. § 1.217-2(c)(3)(iii). See also Treas. Reg. § 1.217-2(a)(1).

[17] Schweighardt v. Comm'r, 54 T.C. 1273 (1970). See also Goldman v. Comm'r, 497 F.2d 382 (6th Cir. 1974), disallowing a Section 217 deduction for the costs of moving taxpayer and his family back to their previous home, following a one-year temporary job elsewhere, in connection with which taxpayer had been allowed travel expenses under Section 162.

Example: Patricia accepts a teaching position at a law school located in the township of Blackacre, 1,500 miles from her current teaching location. She incurs the following moving expenses totaling $7,500 for which she is reimbursed in full by the law school:

(1) $5,000 to move her household belongings.

(2) $1,500, including $400 in meals and $600 in lodging, for Patricia, her husband and two minor children to drive across country to Blackacre at the time of their move.

(3) $1,000 in transportation, meals, and lodging for Patricia and her husband to travel to Blackacre prior to their move in order to locate and purchase a home after Patricia accepted the position.

What are the tax consequences to Patricia of these various expenditures and the reimbursement which she receives?

Analysis: Generally, Section 82 requires reimbursement for moving expenses be included in gross income. Section 132(a)(6), however, is an exception to this general rule and provides an exclusion for that amount of reimbursement which covers costs which would be deductible by the taxpayer under Section 217 if directly paid or incurred by the taxpayer. Assuming Patricia satisfies the reasonableness requirement and the time requirements of Section 217, the following expenses would be deductible by her[18] under Section 217:

(1) The $5,000 incurred for moving household belongings is deductible without limitation;[19]

(2) Except for the meal expenses,[20] the costs Patricia incurred in traveling from her former residence to the new residence in Blackacre are deductible.[21] Similarly, assuming the children and Patricia's husband are all members of Patricia's household and Patricia's former residence and the new residence is their principal place of abode, their travel expenses (other than meal expenses) are also deductible.[22]

(3) The $1,000 in travel expenses incurred by Patricia and her husband in traveling to Blackacre to locate a new home are not deductible. "[T]he deduction for traveling expenses from the former residence to the new place of residence is allowable for only one trip made by the taxpayer and members of his household. . . ."[23]

Thus, the sum of the amounts in (1) $5,000 and (2) $1,100, or a total of $6,100 of the $7,500 Patricia received in reimbursement from the law school will be

---

[18] Above the line, pursuant to Section 62(a)(15).

[19] I.R.C. § 217(b)(1)(A).

[20] I.R.C. § 217(b)(1).

[21] I.R.C. § 217(b)(1)(B).

[22] I.R.C. § 217(b)(2).

[23] Treas. Reg. § 1.217-2(b)(4).

excludable under Section 132(a)(6); the balance of $1,400 must be included in her gross income under Section 82. Of course, having received an exclusion for the $6,100 reimbursement received on account of deductible expenses, Patricia will not be entitled to claim any Section 217 deductions. If, however, Patricia did not receive the reimbursement from the law school until the year following the move, she would be entitled to claim an above-the-line deduction for items (1) and (2) (except for meal expenses) but would not get the benefit of an exclusion under Section 132(a)(6).[24]

§ 19.02 CHILD CARE EXPENSES

§ 21. Expenses for household and dependent care services necessary for gainful employment.

(a) Allowance of Credit —

(1) In General. — In the case of an individual for which there are one or more qualifying individuals (as defined in subsection(b)(1)), there shall be allowed as a credit against the tax imposed by this chapter for the taxable year an amount equal to the applicable percentage of the employment-related expenses (as defined in subsection (b)(2)) paid by such individual during the taxable year.

(2) Applicable Percentage Defined. — For purposes of paragraph (1), the term "applicable percentage" means 35 percent reduced (but not below 20 percent) by 1 percentage point for each $2,000 (or fraction thereof) by which the taxpayer's adjusted gross income for the taxable year exceeds $15,000.

(b) Definitions of Qualifying Individual and Employment-Related Expenses. — For purposes of this section —

(1) Qualifying Individual. — The term "qualifying individual" means —

(A) a dependent of the taxpayer (as defined in section 152(a)(1)) who has not attained age 13,

(B) a dependent of the taxpayer who is physically or mentally incapable of caring for himself or herself and who has the same principal place of abode as the taxpayer for more than one-half of such taxable year, or

(C) the spouse of the taxpayer, if the spouse is physically or mentally incapable of caring for himself or herself and who has the same principal place of abode as the taxpayer for more than one-half of such taxable year. . . .

(c) Dollar Limit on Amount Creditable. — The amount of the employment-related expenses incurred during any taxable year which may be taken into account under subsection (a) shall not exceed —

(1) $3,000 if there is 1 qualifying individual with respect to the taxpayer for such taxable year, or

(2) $6,000 if there are 2 or more qualifying individuals with respect to the taxpayer for such taxable year.

The amount determined under paragraph (1) and (2) (whichever is applicable)

---

[24] I.R.C. § 132(g).

shall be reduced by the aggregate amount excludable from gross income under section 129 for the taxable year.

In *Smith v. Commissioner*,[25] the Board of Tax Appeals determined that child care expenditures, in the absence of specific legislative authority, were personal in nature and could not be deducted even when incurred to enable parents to work. Although acknowledging that "certain disbursements normally personal may become deductible by reason of their intimate connection with an occupation carried on for profit," and that child care expenses "may in some indirect and tenuous degree relate to the circumstances of a profitable occupation," the Board was "not prepared to say that the care of children, like similar aspects of family and household life, is other than a personal concern."[26]

Specific legislative authority for a child care deduction was first enacted in 1954; the deduction, which was always limited in amount, although the limits were increased over the years, was repealed in 1976 in favor of the limited child care credit now found in Section 21.

Section 21 applies only if there are "employment-related expenses" and one or more "qualifying individuals."[27] The cost of qualifying services is limited to the taxpayer's earned income (and for a married couple, to the lesser of their two earned incomes), and in any case, such cost cannot exceed $6,000 (or $3,000, if there is only one dependent involved).[28] The tax credit allowed is 35% of this amount if the taxpayer's adjusted gross income is $15,000 or less; the credit declines to 20% as adjusted gross income increases.[29] (Since the credit percentage is reduced, but not below 20%, by one percentage point for each $2,000, or fraction thereof, of adjusted gross income in excess of $15,000, for taxpayers with adjusted gross income over $43,000 the credit percentage is 20%.) The maximum allowable credit is thus $1,050 for one dependent ($3,000 × 35%) and $2,100 for two or more ($6,000 × 35%). The credit is not refundable; thus, if the credit exceeds the tax liability, the excess credit is not allowed.

An example of the issues that have arisen in determining what constitutes employment-related expenses is found in *Zoltan v. Commissioner*,[30] where the Tax Court held that summer camp expenses incurred to assure the well-being and protection of a child while the taxpayer was gainfully employed qualified for the credit.[31] The *Zoltan* decision was distinguished in *Perry v. Commissioner*,[32] where a child care credit was denied for the cost of air travel for children to stay with their grandparents for school holidays, even though the cost of a babysitter for the holidays would have been greater. *Perry* noted that the bus transportation in *Zoltan*

---

[25] 40 B.T.A. 1038 (1939).

[26] *Id.* at 1039.

[27] I.R.C. § 21(b)(1), (b)(2).

[28] I.R.C. § 21(c), (d)(1).

[29] I.R.C. § 21(a)(2).

[30] 79 T.C. 490 (1982).

[31] Section 21 was amended in 1987, in response to cases like *Zoltan*, to provide that overnight camp expenses will not qualify as employment-related expenses.

[32] 92 T.C. 470 (1989).

was held to be part of the child care. The air travel in *Perry*, by contrast, was found to be preliminary to the care the grandparents were to provide, and thus constituted transportation expenses rather than child care.

Section 129 excludes from the gross income of an employee amounts paid or incurred by an employer pursuant to a dependent care assistance program. The exclusion cannot exceed $5,000. Section 129(e)(7) disallows a deduction or credit under any other Code section for any amount excluded from income by Section 129. Section 21(c) provides that the applicable dollar limit under that section is reduced by the aggregate amount excluded under Section 129. For example, a taxpayer with one qualifying individual who has $3,000 in otherwise eligible employment-related expenses, but who excludes $1,000 of dependent care assistance under Section 129, must reduce the dollar limit of eligible employment-related expenses to $2,000 for Section 21 credit purposes ($3,000 less the $1,000 excluded equals $2,000).

§ 19.03 LEGAL EXPENSES

Legal expenses may be deductible pursuant to Section 162 or Section 212 if they relate to a business or profit-seeking activity. To distinguish between deductible and nondeductible legal expenses, the Supreme Court, in *United States v. Gilmore*,[33] has applied an "origin-of-the-claim" test. If the origin of the claim litigated lies in a personal, as opposed to a business or profit-seeking transaction, the expenses are nondeductible.

> [T]he characterization, as "business" or "personal," of the litigation costs of resisting a claim depends on whether or not the claim *arises in connection with* the taxpayer's profit-seeking activities. It does not depend on the *consequences* that might result to a taxpayer's income-producing property from a failure to defeat the claim. . . .[34]

In *Gilmore*, the taxpayer argued that the legal expenses he incurred in connection with a divorce were deductible since they were incurred to protect from his wife's claims stockholdings critical to his business. The Court noted the characterization of costs incurred in fighting the wife's claims as business expenses depended upon whether the claims arose in connection with the taxpayer's business and not on the consequences which might result to taxpayer if he failed to defeat his wife's claims. The Court concluded the wife's claims to the stock arose entirely from their marital relationship and not from any income-producing activity. As a result, the costs incurred by the taxpayer in resisting the claims were not deductible.

The origin-of-the-claim test was also applied in a companion case to *Gilmore*, *United States v. Patrick*,[35] to deny a deduction for legal fees incident to a property settlement agreement involving transfers of stock, lease of real property, and creation of a trust for the benefit of the taxpayer's wife and children. Note, however, the regulations permit a deduction for fees and costs properly attributable to the

---

[33] 372 U.S. 39 (1963).

[34] *Id.* at 48.

[35] 372 U.S. 53 (1963).

production or collection of alimony, which is taxable income under Section 71.[36]

Legal expenses, even if business-related, are subject to the capital expenditures rule of Section 263.[37] In both the *Gilmore* and *Patrick* cases, the Supreme Court found it unnecessary to consider the Government's alternative arguments that the legal fees were capital expenditures. However, in subsequent litigation, the taxpayer in *Gilmore* was permitted to add the legal expenses incurred in the divorce to the basis of the property in question, on the theory that "defense of title" litigation expenses are capital expenditures, regardless of whether the litigation is primarily business or personal in character.[38]

Gilmore notes the "expenses of contesting tax liabilities" were made deductible by the addition of Section 212(3) to the Code which specifically allows a deduction for "all ordinary and necessary expenses paid or incurred during the taxable year . . . in connection with the determination, collection, or refund of any tax."[39]

Section 212(3) does not apply only in connection with the preparation of tax returns or where there are contested tax liabilities.[40] It is now generally accepted that Section 212(3) allows a deduction for tax planning advice as well. For example, in *Merians v. Commissioner*,[41] a divided Tax Court allowed a deduction for the portion of an estate planning fee it found allocable to tax advice.[42]

If a deduction is available for a portion of a legal fee, it is obviously incumbent upon a lawyer to provide the client with a statement allocating the fee between the deductible and nondeductible portions. As a practical matter, the allocation the lawyer makes is likely to be determinative in the ordinary case. There may be ethical issues involved when such an allocation is necessary and the lawyer's client is anxious to see the allocation weighted towards deductibility to the maximum extent possible.

---

[36] Treas. Reg. § 1.262-1(b)(7).

[37] See *Woodward v. Comm'r*, 397 U.S. 572 (1970), discussed in Chapter 13, *supra.*

[38] Gilmore v. U.S., 245 F. Supp. 383 (N.D. Cal. 1965).

[39] 372 U.S. at 48, n. 16. *See* Treas. Reg. § 1.212-1(l).

[40] *See* Treas. Reg. § 1.212-1(l).

[41] 60 T.C. 187 (1973).

[42] See also Rev. Rul. 72-545, 1972-2 C.B. 179, where the Service allowed deductions for tax advice in various situations incident to divorce, and Rev. Rul. 89-68, 1989-1 C.B. 82, allowing a deduction for legal fees incurred to obtain a ruling from the Service on the deductibility of certain medical expenses.

Chapter 20

HOBBY LOSSES

Losses incurred in carrying on personal hobbies clearly should not be, and are not, deductible. Losses incurred in carrying on a trade, business or in other profit-seeking activities are generally taken into account in determining a taxpayer's overall net income on which tax liability is based. The temptation to characterize a personal hobby and its associated expenses as business or profit-related is thus an obvious one, and Section 183 of the Code, which limits deductions attributable to activities "not engaged in for profit," is the congressional response.

§ 20.01 HISTORICAL DEVELOPMENT

Prior to the enactment of Section 183 in 1969, the Code contained a "hobby loss" provision (repealed as part of the 1969 changes) limiting the business losses an individual could use to offset other income to $50,000 per year; the limitation applied, however, only where business losses exceeded $50,000 a year for five consecutive years. This original hobby loss provision proved to have such limited applicability that Congress came to regard it as unsatisfactory. In fashioning a new hobby loss provision in 1969, Congress took a different tack:

> In addition to the [pre-1969] hobby loss provision, some court cases have provided another basis on which the loss can be denied; namely, that the activity carried on by the taxpayer from which the loss results is not a business but is merely a hobby. . . . [T]his basic principle provides a more effective and reasonable basis for distinguishing situations where taxpayers are not carrying on a business to realize a profit, but rather are merely attempting to utilize the losses from the operation to offset their other income.[1]

In the form proposed by the House of Representatives, Section 183 would have barred the deduction of losses resulting from activities carried on without a "reasonable expectation" of profit. The Senate, however, objected to this standard for distinguishing hobbies from business or profit-seeking activities:

> . . . [R]equiring a taxpayer to have a reasonable expectation of profit may cause losses to be disallowed in situations where an activity is being carried on as a business rather than as a hobby. Accordingly, [in the Senate bill] . . . the focus is to be on whether the activity is engaged in for profit rather than whether it is carried on with a reasonable expectation of profit. This will prevent the rule from being applicable to situations where many would consider that it is not reasonable to expect an activity to result in a

---

[1] S. Rep. No. 91-552, p. 103 (1969).

profit even though the evidence available indicates that the activity actually is engaged in for profit. For example, it might be argued that there was not a "reasonable" expectation of profit in the case of a bona fide inventor or a person who invests in a wildcat oil well. A similar argument might be made in the case of a poor person engaged in what appears to be an inefficient farming operation. . . . [T]his provision should not apply to these situations . . . if the activity actually is engaged in for profit.

. . . [I]n making the determination of whether an activity is not engaged in for profit, . . . an objective rather that a subjective approach is to be employed. Thus, although a reasonable expectation of profit is not to be required, the facts and circumstances (without regard to the taxpayer's subjective intent) would have to indicate that the taxpayer entered the activity, with the objective of making a profit. As previously indicated, a taxpayer who engaged in an activity in which there was a small chance of a large profit, such as a person who invested in a wildcat oil well or an inventor, could qualify under this test even though the expectation of profit might be considered unreasonable.[2]

The Senate's objections prevailed in the enactment of Section 183, and the regulations under the section clearly echo parts of the legislative history.[3]

§ 20.02 SECTION 183 ACTIVITIES

§ 183. Activities not engaged in for profit —

(a) **General rule — In the case of an activity engaged in by an individual or an S corporation, if such activity is not engaged in for profit, no deduction attributable to such activity shall be allowed under this chapter except as provided in this section.**

. . .

(c) **Activity not engaged in for profit defined — For purposes of this section, the term "activity not engaged in for profit" means any activity other than one with respect to which deductions are allowable for the taxable year under section 162 or under paragraph (1) or (2) of section 212.**

(d) **Presumption — If the gross income derived from an activity for 3 or more of the taxable years in the period of 5 consecutive taxable years which ends with the taxable year exceeds the deductions attributable to such activity (determined without regard to whether or not such activity is engaged in for profit), then, unless the Secretary establishes to the contrary, such activity shall be presumed for purposes of this chapter for such taxable year to be an activity engaged in for profit. In the case of an activity which consists in major part of the breeding, training, showing, or racing of horses, the preceding sentence shall be applied by substituting "2" for "3" and "7" for "5".**

The rules of Section 183 apply to an "activity not engaged in for profit." As a preliminary matter, it may be necessary to determine whether a given set of

---

[2] *Id.* at 103–04.

[3] *See* Treas. Reg. § 1.183-2(a).

undertakings or transactions constitutes only one, or more than one, activity and, in the latter case, to allocate income and expenses among activities.[4] Each activity must be tested separately as to whether it is an "activity not engaged in for profit." This critical phrase is central to the statute, and is defined by Section 183(c) to mean those activities which do not qualify for deductions under either Sections 162 or 212(1) or (2). In an effort to flesh out this statutory definition, the regulations provide a list of nine relevant factors, drawn from the case law on hobby losses, that "should normally be taken into account" in determining whether an activity *is* engaged in for profit:[5]

(1)   The manner in which the taxpayer carries on the activity;

(2)   The expertise of the taxpayer or the taxpayer's advisors;

(3)   The time and effort expended by the taxpayer in carrying on the activity;

(4)   The expectation that assets used in the activity may appreciate in value;

(5)   The success of the taxpayer in carrying on other similar or dissimilar activities;

(6)   The taxpayer's history of income or losses with respect to the activity;

(7)   The amount of occasional profits, if any, which are earned;

(8)   The financial status of the taxpayer; and

(9)   The elements of personal pleasure or recreation.

No one factor or number of factors is determinative, nor are the nine listed factors necessarily the only ones to be considered. Rather, the regulations employ an all-the-facts-and-circumstances test in each case, with "greater weight . . . given to objective facts than to the taxpayer's mere statement of his intent."[6]

For example, in *Antonides v. Commissioner*,[7] the court determined that a yacht chartering venture was an activity not engaged in for profit under Section 183. The court noted that based on a financial analysis of the cash flow from the yacht chartering venture, the taxpayer could not have anticipated making a profit on the operation within the foreseeable future, if ever. Nor could the taxpayer reasonably expect to make a profit as a result of the appreciation of the yacht. Although the taxpayers would have liked to have made a profit, the court concluded that, given all of the facts, the taxpayers were not actually motivated by the prospect of profit in acquiring the yacht.

The background to one well-known Section 183 case, *Dreicer v. Commissioner*,[8] was summarized as follows by an appellate court:

---

[4] *See generally* Treas. Reg. § 1.183-1(d).

[5] Treas. Reg. § 1.183-2(b).

[6] Treas. Reg. § 1.183-2(a).

[7] 893 F.2d 656 (4th Cir. 1990).

[8] 78 T.C. 642 (1982).

Dreicer, a citizen of the United States, maintains his residence in the Canary Islands, Spain, and engages heavily in global travel. He derives a substantial income as beneficiary of a family trust, and in the early 1950s, Dreicer began to focus his professional attention on the fields of tourism and dining. In 1955, he published *The Diner's Companion*, a compilation of his opinions on dining and on various restaurants throughout the world, but the book was a commercial failure. Undaunted, Dreicer conceived the idea of some day writing another book, this one to enshrine his reminiscence on a life dedicated to epicurism and travel. In preparation for this sybaritic swan song, he spent the next twenty years traveling about the world, staying in some of the finest hotels and dining in some of the best restaurants. The material he gathered was also to be utilized in lectures before travel organizations and public appearances on radio and television. By the mid-1970's, Dreicer had completed a rough draft of the second book — parts of which originally had appeared in *The Diner's Companion* — and titled it *My 27 Year Search for the Perfect Steak — Still Looking*. Two publishing houses to which he submitted a manuscript, however, returned it, and seemingly he abandoned all hope of publishing.

When Dreicer filed his federal income tax returns for 1972 and 1973, he claimed deductible losses of $21,795.76 and $28,022.05, respectively, for travel and other related business expenses. The Commissioner of Internal Revenue thereafter issued a notice of deficiency, disallowing the deductions on the ground that the losses arose from activities not pursued for profit, and the Tax Court agreed. The court disputed Dreicer's characterization of his professional self as a multi-media personality, finding instead that he was a writer-lecturer on tourism and dining. Having so defined his activity for Section 183 analysis, the court concluded that he had not entertained a bona fide expectation of profit for writing and lecturing, and on that account denied the deductions.[9]

The Circuit Court, concerned that "bona fide expectation of profit" was an incorrect Section 183 standard, remanded the case for a determination by the Tax Court of whether Dreicer had "an actual and honest objective of making a profit." The Tax Court on remand concluded that Dreicer failed to prove that he had such an objective.[10]

The Tax Court's decision in *Nissley v. Commissioner*[11] provides another good example of a court's application of the Section 183 factors. In that case, the taxpayers operated an Amway distributorship. (Amway is a supplier of household and personal use products. An Amway distributor makes money in part by selling the products to customers, but principally by recruiting others as distributors and receiving a bonus based on their sales and the sales of the distributors they in turn recruit.) The Tax Court noted that (1) the distributorship generated consistent and substantial losses; (2) the taxpayers failed to maintain a written business plan,

---

[9] Dreicer v. Comm'r, 665 F.2d 1292, 1294-5 (D.C. Cir. 1981.)

[10] 78 T.C. 642 (1982).

[11] T.C. Memo 2000-178.

budget, monthly expense reports, or break-even analyses; (3) the taxpayers lacked prior Amway-type experience, but had substantial income from other sources; and (4) the taxpayers derived personal pleasure from the Amway activities, including the opportunity to purchase at a discount Amway products for their personal use. Based on these factors, the court concluded that the taxpayers had not engaged in the Amway activity for profit.

By contrast, in *Weller v. Commissioner*,[12] the court, applying the nine nonexclusive factors of Regulation § 1.183-2(b) noted above, concluded that a former Boeing employee who created a limited liability company providing private glider flight instruction and glider plane rides was engaged in the glider activities for profit. The taxpayer in *Weller* purchased a high-performance glider with inherited money and secured the appropriate licenses and training to satisfy FAA requirements to operate as a glider flight instructor. He conducted the glider activities primarily on weekends from March through November, generally devoting all of his weekends during that period to glider activities. Taxpayer advertised his services through flyers placed in airports and aviation-related businesses as well advertisements placed in a flying publication. The Tax Court downplayed the significance of the fact taxpayer did not maintain thorough books and records for his glider activities beyond his flight logs. According to the court, the taxpayer's failure in this regard did not conclusively establish the lack of profit objective. "The purpose of maintaining books and records is more than to memorialize for tax purposes the existence of the subject transactions; it is to facilitate a means of periodically determining profitability and analyzing expenses such that proper cost saving measures might be implemented in a timely and efficient manner." In this regard, the court noted the taxpayer did review the expenses of his company and made adjustments to reduce expenses. Likewise the court rejected the notion that the taxpayer's enjoyment of flying demonstrated that the taxpayer's glider activity was not engaged in for profit. As the Tax Court noted, a business will not be turned into a hobby merely because the owner finds it pleasurable; suffering has never been a prerequisite to deductibility."[13]

It is not unusual for the judicial weighing process to include a reference to the taxpayer's "predominant purpose" with respect to the activity. In one case, for example, the Fourth Circuit commented:

> We note that the Tax Court [in the opinion below] required of the taxpayers a "predominant purpose and intention" of making a profit. The regulations provide that an activity will not be treated as not engaged in for profit merely because the taxpayer has purposes or motivation other than solely to make a profit, . . . § 1.183-2(b)(9), but that deductions are not allowable under sections 162 or 212 for activities carried on primarily as a sport or hobby, or for recreation . . . § 1.183-2(a). Our cases under section 162 have required only "the purpose of making a profit" . . . . We find nothing in section 183 or its legislative history changing this analysis or requiring this purpose to be predominant. . . . Section 183 requires simply

---

[12] T.C. Memo 2011-224.

[13] *Id. See also* Treas. Reg. § 1.183-2(b)(9).

that an activity be "engaged in for profit." The Senate report indicates only that under section 183 a taxpayer must have entered or continued an activity with "the objective of making a profit." We recognize, however, that under a related provision, section 166, the Supreme Court has required that a taxpayer have a "dominant business motivation" to avoid the less favorable tax treatment of nonbusiness bad debts, *United States v. Generes*, 405 U.S. 93, 103 (1972), and that other courts have required under sections 162 and 183 that a taxpayer have the "primary purpose" of making a profit. Whether or not a taxpayer must have the "primary" or "predominant" purpose of making a profit under sections 162, 183, or 212, we need not and do not decide [in the instant case.][14]

Section 183(d) creates a rebuttable presumption that the activity was engaged in for profit, with respect to a given year, if the activity was profitable (that is, if gross income exceeded deductions) for three years in the five-year period ending with the year in question. No inference to the contrary arises from a failure to establish the presumption.[15] If the presumption is not applicable, then the matter proceeds under the normal rule that the assessment of the Commissioner is presumptively correct and the taxpayer carries the burden of proving the assessment incorrect.

Section 280A of the Code also provides special rules for deductions relating to a "dwelling unit used by the taxpayer as a residence." This section will be discussed in the following chapter, addressing "dual-use" property generally. To avoid potential overlap problems, Section 183 does not apply to any dwelling unit for any year (or portion thereof) to which Section 280A applies, although such year nevertheless counts for purposes of the Section 183(d) presumption.[16]

Section 183 applies to individuals, "S corporations" (electing small business corporations),[17] and estates and trusts.[18] Case law has extended Section 183 to partnership activities as well.[19] With respect to corporations other than S corporations, no inference is to be drawn from Section 183 that any corporate activity is or is not a business or engaged in for profit.[20]

§ 20.03   DEDUCTIONS ALLOWABLE UNDER SECTION 183

§ 183.   Activities not engaged in for profit —

(b)   Deductions allowable — In the case of an activity not engaged in for profit to which subsection (a) applies, there shall be allowed —

(1) the deductions which would be allowable under this chapter for the taxable year without regard to whether or not such activity is engaged in for

---

[14] Faulconer v. Comm'r, 748 F.2d 890, 895–6, n. 10 (4th Cir. 1984).

[15] Treas. Reg. § 1.183-1(c)(1).

[16] I.R.C. § 280A(f)(3).

[17] *See* I.R.C. § 1361.

[18] Treas. Reg. § 1.183-1(a).

[19] *See, e.g.*, Brannen v. Comm'r, 78 T.C. 471 (1982), *aff'd*, 722 F.2d 695 (11th Cir. 1984).

[20] Treas. Reg. § 1.183-1(a).

profit, and

(2) a deduction equal to the amount of the deductions which would be allowable under this chapter for the taxable year only if such activity were engaged in for profit, but only to the extent that the gross income derived from such activity for the taxable year exceeds the deductions allowable by reason of paragraph (1).

Although sometimes described as a disallowance provision, Section 183 is actually a deduction-granting provision. If the activity in question constitutes a trade or business, or one engaged in for the production or collection of income or for the management, conservation or maintenance of property held for the production of income, deductions are allowable under Sections 162 or 212(1) or (2); in that case, Section 183 is simply not applicable. If, however, the taxpayer is engaged in an activity in which deductions are not allowed under Sections 162 or 212, Section 183 allows deductions as set forth in Section 183(b).

Section 183(b) establishes three categories of permitted deductions. Category 1 deductions are those, such as home mortgage interest under Section 163(h)(3) and state and local property taxes under Section 164, which are allowed to a taxpayer whether or not an activity is engaged in for profit. Pursuant to Section 183(b)(1), these deductions are allowed without regard to the income of the activity. Deductions attributable to the activity but which do not come within Category 1 are allowed only to the extent the gross income from the activity exceeds the total Category 1 deductions.[21] For example, assume an activity not engaged in for profit generates gross income of $1,000, and has Category 1 deductions of $1,100. Although Section 183(b)(1) allows all $1,100 to be deducted, no other deductions attributable to the activity could be taken. If, however, Category 1 deductions were only $700, up to $300 in additional deductions (i.e., non-Category 1 deductions) would be allowable under Section 183(b)(2). Section 183 thus adopts as a basic policy that deductions attributable to a not-engaged-in-for-profit activity should always be allowable at least to the extent of the income from the activity.

The Section 183 regulations divide into two separate, additional categories those deductions that do not fall within Category 1.[22] Category 2 deductions are those that do not result in a basis adjustment and that would otherwise be allowed if the activity were engaged in for profit; garden-variety Section 162 or 212 expenses fit in Category 2. Category 3 deductions are those, such as depreciation, that result in basis adjustments and that would be allowed if the activity were engaged in for profit. Category 2 deductions must be taken prior to Category 3 deductions. Category 3 deductions are thus allowed only to the extent the gross income from the activity exceeds the combined total of Category 1 and Category 2 deductions.

> **Example:** An activity not engaged in for profit generates $1,000 of gross income, and has expenses attributable to the activity of $500 for local property taxes, $400 for current wages paid, and $300 for depreciation.

---

[21] I.R.C. § 183(b)(2).

[22] Treas. Reg. § 1.183-1(b)(1)(ii), (iii).

Analysis: Under Section 183(b) and the regulations, deductions would be allowed for the full amount of the property taxes (as a Category 1 item), the full amount of the wages (a Category 2 item, allowed in full because Category 1 and 2 items do not exceed gross income from the activity), and for $100 of depreciation (a Category 3 item, limited to $100 so as not to exceed the gross income ceiling). In the event the activity used more than one depreciable asset, the regulations provide a formula for allocating the limited basis adjustment among multiple depreciable assets.[23]

---

[23] Treas. Reg. § 1.183-1(b)(2).

Chapter 21

HOME OFFICES, VACATION HOMES AND OTHER DUAL USE PROPERTY

The home office, the vacation home, the home computer and the business car all share in common the possibility of being used for both personal and business purposes. Separating the business or investment element from the personal element is challenging. In the context of mixed-use property, Congress, the courts and the Service have developed different rules to guide their decision-making.

§ 21.01 HOME OFFICE DEDUCTIONS

§ 280A. Disallowance of certain expenses in connection with business use of home, rental of vacation homes, etc.

(a) **General rule.** Except as otherwise provided in this section, in the case of a taxpayer who is an individual or an S corporation, no deduction otherwise allowable under this chapter shall be allowed with respect to the use of a dwelling unit which is used by the taxpayer during the taxpayer year as a residence.

(b) **Exception for interest, taxes, casualty losses, etc.** — Subsection (a) shall not apply to any deduction allowable to the taxpayer without regard to its connection with his trade or business (or with his income-producing activity).

(c) **Exceptions for certain business or rental use; limitation on deductions for such uses.** —

(1) **Certain business use.** Subsection (a) shall not apply to any item to the extent such item is allocable to a portion of the dwelling unit which is exclusively used on a regular basis —

(A) as the principal place of business for any trade or business of the taxpayer,

(B) as a place of business which is used by patients, clients, or customers in meeting or dealing with the taxpayer in the normal course of his trade or business, or

(C) in the case of a separate structure which is not attached to the dwelling unit, in connection with the taxpayer's trade or business.

In the case of an employee, the preceding sentence shall apply only if the exclusive use referred to in the preceding sentence is for the convenience of his employer. For purposes of subparagraph (A), the term "principal place of business" includes a place of business which is used by the taxpayer for the administrative or management activities of any trade or business of the taxpayer if there is no other fixed location of such trade or business where the taxpayer conducts substantial administrative or management activities of such trade or business.

. . .

(3) Rental use. Subsection (a) shall not apply to any item which is attributable to the rental of the dwelling unit or portion thereof determined after the application of subsection (e).

. . .

(5) Limitation on deductions. In the case of a use described in paragraph (1), (2) . . . and in the case of a use described in paragraph (3) where the dwelling unit is used by the taxpayer during the taxable year as a residence, the deductions allowed under this chapter for the taxable year by reasons of being attributed to such use shall not exceed the excess of —

(A) the gross income derived from such use for the taxable year, over

(B) the sum of —

(i) the deductions allocable to such use which are allowable under this chapter for the taxable year whether or not such unit (or portion thereof) was so used, and

(ii) the deductions allocable to the trade or business . . . in which such use occurs (but which are not allocable to such use) for such taxable year.

(d) Use as a residence. —

(1) in general. For purposes of this section, a taxpayer uses a dwelling unit during the taxable year as a residence if he uses such unit (or portion thereof) for personal purposes for a number of days which exceeds the greater of —

(A) 14 days, or

(B) 10 percent of the number of days during such year for which such unit is rented at a fair rental.

Congress in 1976 added Section 280A to provide objective criteria by which deductions for home offices (and vacation homes) could be evaluated. Note that Section 280A is listed among the disallowance provisions of the Code and that Section 280A(a) generally disallows deductions with respect to dwelling units used by the taxpayer during the taxable year as a residence.

[A] General Background — *Bodzin v. Commissioner*

Section 280A is best understood by considering the state of the law prior to 1976, as embodied in the facts of *Bodzin v. Commissioner*.[1] Stephen Bodzin was an attorney-adviser in the Office of the Chief Counsel of the Internal Revenue Service. His duties included working on public and private tax rulings as well as internal opinions addressing a variety of tax problems. The normal working hours for his job were 9:00 a.m. to 5:30 p.m. Bodzin, however, was a conscientious professional and often brought work home with him to the rented apartment in which he lived

---

[1] 60 T.C. 820 (1973).

with his wife and child. Bodzin's apartment included a study which he used as his home office. The study, an eight foot by twelve foot room, contained bookshelves with not only an assortment of tax works but also the personal libraries of both Bodzin and his wife. The room was furnished with a desk, chair, cabinets and lamps. Bodzin used the room to work on matters assigned him, to read about current tax developments, to work on the first draft of tax memoranda, to prepare for conferences associated with his work, and also to pay bills, reconcile his monthly bank statement and work on his stamp collection. While Bodzin was provided an office by the Government, he found that, given the distance between his apartment and place of work and his desire to spend time with his family, it was more convenient for him to work at home in the evenings and on weekends rather than return after work to his office.

Bodzin paid $2,100 to rent the apartment in 1967. He claimed $100 of that amount was attributable to the use of his study as a home office and deducted it as a business expense. The Commissioner disallowed the deduction; Bodzin petitioned the Tax Court for a redetermination of his tax. While $100 is not a significant amount, the Commissioner obviously regarded the matter, as did Judge Quealy, one of three dissenting Tax Court judges in the case, as "the nose of the camel."[2] Judge Quealy summarized the Commissioner's view of the matter when he noted: "It is common practice for lawyers, doctors, engineers, and other professionals who have any interest in attaining excellence in their profession, to read up on technical publications and other informative materials outside of their normal working hours. Such a practice hardly justifies claiming some part of the cost of the residence as a trade or business expense within the meaning of Section 162."[3]

The Commissioner's arguments were two: (1) an employee could not claim a home office deduction unless the home office were a condition of taxpayer's employment enabling the taxpayer to properly perform his employment duties; and (2) "where the work was done at home only as a matter of convenience in spite of adequate office facilities, the deduction is properly disallowed."[4]

The Tax Court majority rejected these standards and held "the applicable test for judging the deductibility of home office expenses is whether, like any other business expense, the maintenance of an office in the home is appropriate and helpful under all the circumstances."[5] The existence of employer-provided office space was not determinative of whether the home office was "appropriate and helpful." Applying the standard, the Tax Court majority concluded the Section 162 deduction claimed was appropriate and stated: "It makes no difference that the petitioner was not required to maintain a home office, that he wanted merely to do a good job, and that he liked his work. The expenses were 'necessary' because they were appropriate and helpful in the conduct of his business. They enabled him to keep a facility in his home wherein he could, and did, work. . . . They were

---

[2] *Id.* at 828.

[3] *Id.*

[4] *Id.* at 825.

[5] *Id.*

'ordinary,' and not capital, in nature."[6]

In his dissent, Judge Scott noted:

> Under the holding of the majority opinion, there would certainly be no professional person, and very few, if any, business people, who would not be entitled to deduct as a business expense some portion of the cost of rental of a home or the maintenance of a house since the great majority of such persons do professional reading and written work for themselves or their employers in their homes. In fact, this is probably true of the work they do unless their work is purely mechanical in nature. In my view it was never the intent of section 162 to change the personal expenditure of a taxpayer for a home for himself and his family into a business merely because the taxpayer is sufficiently interested in the work in which he engages to do some work in his home.[7]

Echoing the same thoughts was Judge Featherston, who in his dissent stressed the issue is whether the rental expenses were incurred in carrying on the taxpayer's trade or business. As he noted, nothing in the record indicated Bodzin would not have incurred the same rental expense even if he had done his overtime work at the office. This comment mirrored Judge Quealy's position that at a minimum the taxpayer should be required to establish "that the space claimed to have been devoted to this purpose in the residence of the taxpayer would not have been acquired except for such purpose."[8] Judge Featherston drew the following analogy:

> Surely the Commissioner would not be heard to claim petitioner received additional taxable income if he used his Internal Revenue Service office for such personal purposes as storing his golf clubs, keeping his umbrella or raincoat available for a rainy day, eating his lunch, taking personal telephone calls, etc. Such uses are merely incidental to the business use of the office. Similarly, petitioner's use of a room in his apartment for a few hours of overtime work each week is merely incidental to the purely personal purpose for which the rent was expended.[9]

The *Bodzin* story, however, did not end in the Tax Court. The Fourth Circuit, in a brief opinion, reversed the Tax Court noting "Bodzin did not use any part of his apartment as his place of business; like most lawyers and judges, he sometimes, by choice, did some of his reading and writing at home."[10] The court reasoned the deduction claimed by Bodzin was subject to the following language from Regulation Section 1.262-1(b)(3):

> Expenses of maintaining a household, including amounts paid for rent, water, utilities, domestic service, and the like, are not deductible. A taxpayer who rents a property for residential purposes, but incidentally conducts business there (his place of business being elsewhere) shall not

---

[6] *Id.* at 826.

[7] *Id.* at 827.

[8] *Id.* at 829.

[9] *Id.* at 827, 828.

[10] 509 F.2d 679, 681 (4th Cir. 1975).

deduct any part of the rent. If, however, he uses part of the house as his place of business, such portion of the rent and other similar expenses as is properly attributable to such place of business is deductible as a business expense.

Given its holding that no part of the apartment was used as Bodzin's place of business, the Fourth Circuit held it was unnecessary to decide whether the taxpayer's home office was appropriate and helpful in carrying on his business. Thus, it was unclear whether the Fourth Circuit in a dual use case would use the appropriate and helpful standard.

[B] Enactment of Section 280A

The Tax Court majority and dissenting opinions and the Fourth Circuit decision in *Bodzin* reflect well the differing views regarding the appropriate standard for home office deductions. In an effort to resolve the confusion in this area, Congress in the 1976 legislation rejected the "appropriate and helpful" standard and replaced it with more objective criteria. As noted by the Senate Finance Committee:

> With respect to the "appropriate and helpful" standard employed in the court decisions, the determination of the allowance of a deduction for these expenses is necessarily a subjective determination. In the absence of definitive controlling standards, the "appropriate and helpful" test increases the inherent administrative problems because both business and personal uses of the residence are involved and substantiation of the time used for each of these activities is clearly a subjective determination. In many cases the application of the appropriate and helpful test would appear to result in treating personal, living, and family expenses which are directly attributable to the home (and therefore not deductible) as ordinary and necessary business expenses, even though those expenses did not result in additional or incremental costs incurred as a result of the business use of the home.

With the enactment of Section 280A, taxpayers like Bodzin could avoid the disallowance of their home office expenses only if they met the Section 280A(c)(1) requirements. Note that Bodzin would be required to meet the following tests: (1) exclusivity; (2) regular use; (3) use of home office as principal place of business; and (4) "convenience of employer."[11] Obviously, Bodzin could not meet any of the standards. Had Section 280A existed at the time *Bodzin* was decided, the matter would have been easily resolved.

[C] Principal Place of Business

But this is not to say that Section 280A led to the easy resolution of all home office expense issues. The main occasion for litigation was the Section 280A(c)(1)(A) standard that the home office constitute the taxpayer's "principal place of business." In 1993, the Supreme Court, addressing conflicting standards in the

---

[11] I.R.C. § 280A(c)(1)(A)–(C).

lower courts, held in *Soliman v. Commissioner* that the principal place of business was the "most important or significant" place for the business, as determined by two primary considerations: "the relative importance of the activities performed at each business location and the time spent at each place."[12] Applying this test to Dr. Soliman, a self-employed anesthesiologist who spent most of his working time performing medical services at three hospitals, the Court held his home office was not the principal place of business, despite the fact that it was his only office and was essential to carrying on his medical practice. Rather, the actual treatment Dr. Soliman provided at the hospitals was "the essence of the professional service. . . , the most significant event in the professional transaction," thus rendering the home office less important than the hospitals from the standpoint of his business. The Court added the fact that more time was spent at the hospitals than at the home office further supported the determination that the home office was not the principal place of business. The *Soliman* tests were applied by the Ninth Circuit to hold a professional violinist was entitled to deduct expenses from the portion of her home used exclusively for musical practice.[13] The taxpayer performed regularly with a symphony and an orchestra, and also contracted with numerous studios to record music for movies. Since none of her employers provided a place to practice, she spent four to five hours a day practicing at home. The court found that application of *Soliman*'s relative-importance test yielded no definitive answer among her home office in which she practiced and the various concert halls and recording studios in which she performed. Accordingly, since the taxpayer spent far more time practicing at home than she did performing or recording, the court concluded *Soliman*'s time test tipped the balance in favor of finding her home office to be her principal place of business.

The congressional response to *Soliman* can be seen in the last sentence of Section 280A(c)(1). *Soliman* has been reversed, and a home office deduction deemed appropriate, for a place of business used for "administrative or management activities . . . , if there is no other fixed location of such trade or business where the taxpayer conducts substantial administrative or management activities. . . ." Of course, if this legislative definition of "principal place of business" does not apply in a given situation, the *Soliman* test will presumably continue to control.

> **Example:** Kevin is a self-employed contractor specializing in the construction of commercial buildings. Kevin's only office is his home office where he conducts all of his administrative work. Kevin, however, seldom meets clients at his home office; instead, he usually prefers to meet clients at the construction site or in the client's office. During the current year, Kevin spent about 80% of his time at two different construction sites and the balance of his time in his home office. May Kevin deduct his home office expenses?
>
> **Analysis:** As a self-employed contractor, Kevin may deduct expenses associated with his home office if he satisfies the requirements of Section

---

[12] 506 U.S. 168 (1993).

[13] Popov v. Commissioner, 246 F.3d 1190 (9th Cir. 2001). The case arose prior to the effective date of the amendment of Section 280A(c)(1), noted *infra*.

280A(c)(1). Kevin presumably satisfies the "exclusive use" and "regular basis" requirements. Because Kevin's home office is not a place where he meets clients and is not a separate structure, Kevin must establish it is his principal place of business. Section 280A does not define "principal place of business." The 1997 amendment to Section 280A(c)(1) does, however, provide that "principal place of business" includes a place where the administrative and management activities of a business take place if there is no other fixed business location where substantial administrative or management activities occur. Kevin should therefore be deemed to satisfy the principal place of business requirement.

[D] Convenience of Employer

Employees seeking to deduct home office expenses must also satisfy the "convenience of the employer" standard of Section 280A(c)(1), an issue that the Supreme Court did not need to address with the self-employed taxpayer in *Soliman.* In an earlier case, *Weissman v. Commissioner*,[14] the Second Circuit held a college professor was entitled to deduct the expenses of his home office, which he used for the scholarly research and writing required as a condition of his employment. The only office space provided by his employer was an office shared with several other professors. After holding that the home office, where he spent 80% of his working week, constituted the taxpayer's principal place of business, the court considered the convenience-of-the-employer requirement:

> . . . [I]t becomes clear that Professor Weissman has also satisfied the convenience-of-the-employer test. The cost of maintaining his home office was almost entirely additional to nondeductible personal living expenses because it was used exclusively for employment-related activities and because such use was necessary as a practical matter if Professor Weissman was faithfully to perform his employment duties. This practical necessity negates any claim that the office was used as a matter of personal convenience rather than for the convenience of the employer. . . . [H]ere the employer provided some space, *i.e.*, a shared office at the library. . . . [H]owever, . . . the relevant fact is that the employer provided no *suitable* space for engaging in necessary employment-related activities. Although City College has provided some space to Professor Weissman, it has not provided space in which he can effectively carry out his employment duties. The maintenance of a home office was not a personal preference of the employee; it spared the employer the cost of providing a suitable private office and thereby served the convenience of the employer.[15]

---

[14] 751 F.2d 512 (2d Cir. 1984).

[15] *Id.* at 516–17. However, it is doubtful that Professor Weissman would have satisfied the principal place of business test subsequently enunciated in *Soliman.*

[E]   Limitation on Amount of Deduction

Even if a taxpayer satisfies the business use requirements of Section 280A(c)(1), the amount of the deductions allowed for a home office is severely limited by Section 280A(c)(5). The gross income from *the use of the residence for trade or business purposes* is the ceiling for deductions. This ceiling is reduced by (1) those deductions (*e.g.*, the portion of real estate taxes or mortgage interest allocable to the home office) the taxpayer could claim regardless of whether the home office were used for trade or business purposes; and (2) those deductions (*e.g.*, secretarial expense, supplies, business telephone) attributable to the trade or business activity but which are not allocable to the dwelling unit itself. Expenditures which are not related to the use of the dwelling unit for business purposes, *e.g.*, expenditures for lawn care, are not taken into account in computing deductions allowable under Section 280A. The typical home office expenses are rent expense (as in *Bodzin*), depreciation, insurance, maintenance and utilities.

Consider the following example based on an example provided in Proposed Regulation Section 1.280A-2(i)(7):

> **Example:** Claire, a self-employed individual, uses an office in her home on a regular basis as a place of business for meeting with clients of her consulting service. She makes no other use of the office during the taxable year and uses no other premises for the consulting activity. Claire has a special telephone line for the office and occasionally employs secretarial assistance. She also has a gardener care for the lawn around her home during the year. Claire determines that 10% of the general expenses for the dwelling unit are allocable to the office. On the basis of the following figures, she determines that the sum of the allowable business deductions for the use of the office is $1,050 ($1,900 of gross income less $850 of expenditures not allocable to use of the unit):

Gross income from consulting services $1,900
less:

(a) *expenditures not allocable to use of unit* (Section 280A(c)(5)(B)(ii))

Expenses for secretary	$500
Business telephone	150
Supplies	200
Total	$850

(b) *always allowable deductions* (Section 280A(c)(5)(B)(i))

	Total	Allocable to Office
Mortgage interest	$5,000	$500[16]
Real estate taxes	2,000	200

---

[16] Prop. Treas. Reg. § 1.280A-2(i)(3) provides that:

> the taxpayer may determine the expenses allocable to the portion of the unit used for

(b) *always allowable deductions* (Section 280A(c)(5)(B)(i))

	Total	Allocable to Office
Total		$700

Sum of (a) and (b)		$1,550

Section 280A(c)(5) limit on further deductions:

Gross income of $1,900, less $1,550. . . . . $350

Thus, only $350 of Claire's other expenses may be deducted under Section 280A(c)(5). Assume that the share of the other expenses allocable to her home office were as follows:

	Total	Allocable to Office
Insurance	$600	$60
Utilities*	900	90
Lawn Care	500	0
Depreciation	3,200	320
Total Allocable to Office.		$470

* (not including residential telephone)

Note the amount of other deductions allocable to the unit exceeds the $350 limit. Prop. Treas. Reg. § 1.280A-2(i)(5) provides an ordering rule for claiming deductions and requires those deductions which do not cause an adjustment to basis be claimed first. Thus, the insurance and utility charges totaling $150 would be deductible first, leaving only $200 of the depreciation which may be deducted. The $120 of depreciation allocable to use of the unit which may not be deducted may be carried over to the succeeding tax year.[17]

The Internal Revenue Service has recently provided, as an alternative to the foregoing calculation, allocation and substantiation of actual expenses, an optional safe harbor for determining the amount of deductible expenses. Under the safe harbor method, a prescribed rate is multiplied by the square footage of the home office, not to exceed 300 square feet.[18]

---

business purposes by any method that is reasonable under the circumstances. If the rooms in the dwelling unit are of approximately equal size, the taxpayer may ordinarily allocate the general expenses for the unit according to the number of rooms used for the business purpose. The taxpayer may also allocate general expenses according to the percentage of the total floor space in the unit that is used for the business purpose. Expenses which are attributable only to certain portions of the unit, *e.g.*, repairs to kitchen fixtures, shall be allocated in full to those portions of the unit. Expenses which are not related to the use of the unit for business purposes, *e.g.*, expenditures for lawn care, are not taken into account for the purposes of Section 280A.

[17] I.R.C. § 280A(c)(5).

[18] Rev. Proc. 2013-13, 2013-6 I.R.B. 1. The initial prescribed rate, which may be updated from time to time, is $5.00, so the current maximum safe harbor allowance is $1,500 ($5.00 multiplied by 300 square feet).

§ 21.02   VACATION HOME DEDUCTIONS

§ 280A.   Disallowance of certain expenses in connection with business use of home, rental of vacation homes, etc.

(e)   Expenses attributable to rental. —

(1)   In general. — In any case where a taxpayer who is an individual . . . uses a dwelling unit for personal purposes of any day during the taxable year (whether or not he is treated under this section as using such unit as a residence), the amount deductible under this chapter with respect to expenses attributable to the rental of the unit (or portion thereof) for the taxable year shall not exceed an amount which bears the same relationship to such expenses as the number of days during each year that the unit (or portion thereof) is rented at a fair rental bears to the total number of days during such year that the unit (or portion thereof) is used.

(2)   Exception for deductions otherwise allowable. — This subsection shall not apply with respect to deductions which would be allowable under this chapter for the taxable year whether or not such unit (or portion thereof) was rented.

In 1976 Congress also addressed deductions taxpayers claimed for expenses associated with the rental of their vacation homes. By renting out the home for a portion of the year, even though personally using it for the remainder of the year, taxpayers attempted to claim deductions such as depreciation, maintenance and insurance deductions with respect to the vacation home on the basis that the rental of the home was a business or investment activity. The determination of whether a taxpayer rents property for the purpose of making a profit involves an examination of taxpayer's motive and the primary purpose for which the vacation home is held. Such a determination is largely subjective and extremely difficult to make. As in the case of home office deductions, Congress sought in Section 280A to provide objective criteria whereby the status of the rental of vacation homes could be determined and, in appropriate circumstances, deductions could be limited.

Section 280A limits the deductions a taxpayer may claim with respect to the rental of a dwelling unit if the taxpayer uses the dwelling unit for personal purposes for a period greater than 14 days or 10% of the number of the days during the year the vacation home is rented at a fair rental.[19] Deductions attributable to the rental may still be claimed,[20] but not in excess of the amount by which the gross income derived from the rental activity exceeds the deductions otherwise allowable without regard to such rental activity, e.g., mortgage interest and real estate taxes.[21] In *Bolton v. Commissioner*[22] the court held these "otherwise allowable expenses" must be ratably allocated to each day of the tax year, regardless of the use of the unit on

---

[19] *See* I.R.C. § 280A(d)(1). The rules of Section 280A(d)(2) define what constitutes personal use of a unit.

[20] I.R.C. § 280A(c)(3).

[21] I.R.C. § 280A(c)(5).

[22] 694 F.2d 556 (9th Cir. 1982).

any given day.[23] The portion of expenses (insurance, depreciation, utilities, etc.) allocable to rental activities is limited to an amount determined on the basis of the ratio of time the home is actually rented for a fair rental to the total time the vacation home is used during the taxable year for all purposes including rental.[24] Any rental expenses which are not deductible as a result of this limit may be carried forward to the succeeding taxable year.[25]

> **Example:** Cathy owns a lakeside cabin. During the current year, she spent 20 days at the cabin and rented the cabin at $100 per day (fair rental value) for 50 days. Cathy incurred the following expenses during the year with respect to the cabin:

Real estate taxes	$1,000
Interest on the cabin mortgage	6,000
Realtor's management fee	500
Utilities	500
Fire Insurance	500

Assume that annual depreciation on the cabin (computed pursuant to Section 168) would amount to $1,000 for the current year. How much, if any, of the above expenses may Cathy deduct for the year?

Analysis: First, it should be noted that Cathy is subject to the general disallowance rule of Section 280A(a) because she has used the cabin as a residence during the year for purposes of Section 280A, *i.e.*, she used the cabin for 20 days, which is longer than the greater of (a) 14 days or (b) 10% of the number of days during the year for which the cabin was rented (here 50 days). But Cathy also comes within the rental exception[26] to the Section 280A(a) general disallowance rule. Applying Section 280A(c)(5) and Section 280A(e) as interpreted by *Bolton*, the limitation on Cathy's deductions for utilities, fire insurance and depreciation is determined as follows:

> (A) the gross rental income for the taxable year less

> (B) the sum of

>> (i) the deductions allocable to the rental of the cabin which are allowable regardless of how the cabin is used (in this case that is the real estate tax and Section 163 interest deductions) and

>>> (ii) the deductions allocable to the business (rental activity) in which such use occurs but which are not allocable to such use for the current year (here there are no such deductions).

---

[23] *See* I.R.C. § 280A(e)(2).

[24] I.R.C. § 280A(e)(1).

[25] I.R.C. § 280A(c)(5).

[26] I.R.C. § 280A(c)(3).

Applying this formula to the facts of the example:[27]

Gross rental income:

Gross rental receipts (50 days at $100/day)	$5,000
Less management fee	500
Gross rental income	4,500
Less the allocable portion of the real estate taxes and mortgage interest	959

[Applying *Bolton*, 50/365 of $7,000 ($1,000 real estate tax plus $6,000 home mortgage interest) or $959 of real estate tax and interest expense is deemed allocable to the rental activity.]

Rental income in excess of the allocable real estate tax and interest	$3,541

Thus, the maximum amount of "other expenses" (in this case the allocable amounts of fire insurance, depreciation and utilities expense) which may be deducted by Cathy equals $3,541.

The other expenses are:

Utilities	$500
Fire insurance	500
Depreciation	1,000
Total	$2,000

The portion of these other expenses allocable to the rental is, according to Section 280A(e), a fraction of the expenses equal to 50/70, *i.e.*, the number of days the cabin was rented (50) to the total number of days the cabin was used (50 rent days plus 20 personal use days). 50/70 of $2,000 = $1,429. Thus, Cathy may deduct a total of $1,429 of the other expenses in addition to the $959 of real estate taxes and interest and the $500 management fee. If Cathy itemizes her deductions, she may also deduct the balance of the real estate taxes and interest or $6,041 ($7,000 less $959).

Note the effect of *Bolton* is to enable a taxpayer to claim a deduction for more "other expenses," *i.e.*, expenses other than interest or real estate taxes. If the 50/70 fraction had been used with respect to the real estate tax and interest instead of the 50/365 fraction, $4,286 of taxes and interest would have been allocable to the rental rather than $959. In turn this would have meant that the other expenses (fire insurance, utilities and depreciation) could only be deducted to the extent of $214, *i.e.*, gross rental of $4,500 less allocable interest and real estate tax of $4,286.

---

[27] *See* Prop. Treas. Reg. § 1.280A-3(d)(2).

§ 21.03   OTHER DUAL USE PROPERTY

[A]   Computers and Other "Listed Property"

The home computer has become a household item. Recognizing that taxpayers purchasing such equipment often use it for both personal and business reasons and might seek to convert nondeductible personal expenses into deductible business expenses, Congress in 1984 imposed limitations on deductions for computers and other "listed property."[28] "Listed property" means[29] (1) any passenger automobile, (2) any other property used as a means of transportation, (3) any property of a type generally used for purposes of entertainment, recreation, or amusement, (4) any computer or peripheral equipment, (5) any cellular telephone, and (6) any other property specified as such in the regulations.

Unless the business use percentage for the taxable year exceeds 50%, the taxpayer is required to use the alternative depreciation system of Section 168(g), and is thus limited to straight line depreciation on the property.[30] Furthermore, any deduction allowable as a result of a Section 179 election[31] to expense "listed property" is treated as a Section 168 depreciation deduction.[32] This in effect negates the use of Section 179 by taxpayers failing to meet the 50% standard. For example, if a taxpayer purchases an $8,000 computer which is used over 50% of the time for personal purposes, the taxpayer must use the alternative depreciation system and may not deduct any depreciation amount (including a Section 179 amount) in excess of the amount determined under Section 168(g).

> **Example:** Assume that Larry purchases a computer which he uses 40% of the time in his business as a freelance writer and 60% of the time for personal purposes. The computer cost Larry $3,000. How much depreciation may Larry deduct in the first year?

> **Analysis:** Larry is entitled to a $120 depreciation deduction determined as follows: Because Larry uses the computer for personal purposes more than 50% of the time, Larry must use the alternative depreciation system, *i.e.*, the straight line method over the class life (assume 5 years) of the computer. Larry may thus deduct 40% of the depreciation which is determined under the alternative system, for a total of $1,200 over the class life (*i.e.*, 0.40 × $3,000). On a straight line basis (taking into account the half year convention) Larry would be entitled to deduct $120 in the first year (40% of $3,000 [purchase price] × 20% [annual depreciation percentage under the straight line method with respect to property with a 5 year class life] × 0.5 [half year convention]).

---

[28] I.R.C. § 280F(b). A computer (and peripheral equipment) used exclusively at a regular business establishment and owned or leased by the person operating such establishment does not constitute "listed property."

[29] I.R.C. § 280F(d)(4)(A).

[30] I.R.C. § 280F(b)(2), (4).

[31] *See* Chapter 14, *supra*.

[32] I.R.C. § 280F(d)(1).

In addition, Congress has provided a special recapture rule[33] to address situations where, in a year following the year the "listed property" is placed in service, the taxpayer fails to meet the 50% use standard. Under this rule, excess depreciation claimed in the first year must be included in gross income in subsequent years. The necessity for this recapture rule is explained as follows by the Staff of the Joint Committee on Taxation:

> Congress was also concerned that some taxpayers acquired automobiles and other property very late in the taxable year and claimed a very high percentage of business use for that portion of the year. Business use in subsequent years would often be minimal. Taxpayers could nonetheless claim full ACRS deductions for that first year and not be subject to recapture by reason of greatly diminished business use in the subsequent years.[34]

Example 1: Cathy has her own private accounting practice which she operates out of a small building adjacent to her home. In August of Year 1, Cathy purchased a portable computer for $5,000 for use in her private accounting practice. Cathy, a calendar year taxpayer, estimates that 25% of the computer's use in Year 1 was related to her personal use in her home and the balance was related to her work in her private accounting practice in the building adjacent to her home. How will Cathy compute the Section 168 depreciation deductions on the computer for Year 1 assuming that she does not elect to expense the computer under Section 179?

Analysis: The portable computer is "listed property" under Section 280F(d)(4)(A)(iv). The computer does not fit within the exception of Section 280F(d)(4)(B) because Cathy does not use it "exclusively" at her office in the building adjacent to her home. However, Cathy's "qualified business use" of the property exceeds 50%. Under Section 280F(d)(6)(B) and Regulation Section 1.280F-6T(a)(1), her qualified business use is the 75% of the use in her private accounting practice.

Since Cathy's qualified business use exceeds 50%, she is not subject to the requirement of Section 280F(b)(2) relating to use of the alternative depreciation system. Her aggregate business/investment use for purposes of determining cost recovery deductions is 75%. Under Section 168, Cathy would be entitled to a Year 1 depreciation deduction of 20% of the $5,000, or $1,000. (Note that the half year convention is applicable to Year 1.) Seventy-five percent of this amount equals $750. Thus, Cathy can claim a $750 deduction under Section 168.

Example 2: Assume the same facts as in Example 1 and assume also that in Year 2, Cathy uses the portable computer only 40% of the time in her private accounting practice, and uses it 60% of the time for personal purposes in her home. What are the tax implications of this change in usage of the computer?

---

[33] I.R.C. § 280F(b)(2).

[34] General Explanation of the Revenue Provision of the Tax Reform Act of 1984, Staff of the Joint Committee on Taxation, H.R. 4170, 98th Cong., p. 560.

Analysis: In Year 2 Cathy no longer uses the computer "predominantly" in her private accounting business.[35] She is therefore subject to the special recapture rule of Section 280F(b)(2). In effect, Cathy will have to restore, by way of an income inclusion in Year 2, the difference between the depreciation she was allowed in Year 1 and the depreciation she would have been allowed had she computed the deprecation deduction under section 168(g) — the alternative depreciation system. Under that system, Cathy would be required to use the straight line method, assume a recovery period of 5 years (see Section 168(g)(3)(C)), and use the half year convention. Under Section 168(g), Cathy would have been entitled to depreciation on the computer equal to 0.75 ($1,000 × 0.5). [The straight line method over a five year period would normally produce $1,000 of depreciation each year. Because of the half year convention, however, there would only be $500 of depreciation available in Year 1. Since the computer is used for business purposes only 75% of the time, the depreciation deduction available would be 75% of $500.] The depreciation deduction for Year 1 is therefore $375. Because Cathy actually claimed $750 in depreciation deductions in Year 1, Cathy will be required to recapture $375 of that amount by including $375 in her income in Year 2. In Year 2 and subsequent years, Cathy would continue to use the alternative method of computing depreciation.

Employees are likewise limited in their ability to claim depreciation deductions on listed property, *e.g.*, home computers.[36] Thus, if the employee uses his own computer in connection with his employment, no depreciation deduction is available to the employee unless he can establish that use of the computer is "for the convenience of the employer and is required as a condition of his employment." As noted in the Conference Report:

> . . . [T]he terms "convenience of the employer" and "condition of employment" [are intended] to have the same meaning [in Section 280F(d)(3)] as [they do] with respect to the exclusion from gross income for lodging furnished to an employee. In order to satisfy the condition of employment requirement, the property must be required in order for the employee to properly perform the duties of his employment. This requirement is not satisfied merely by an employer's statement that the property is required as a condition of employment.[37]

It will thus be extremely difficult for an employee to claim a depreciation deduction with respect to a home computer or other "listed property" used in connection with his employment.

---

[35] I.R.C. § 280F(b)(3).

[36] I.R.C. § 280F(d)(3), (4).

[37] H. Rep. No. 98-861, p. 1027.

[B] Passenger Automobiles

Passenger automobiles are also treated as "listed property," and are therefore subject to the depreciation limitations described above. Thus, unless a taxpayer uses a passenger automobile more than 50% of the time for trade or business purposes, the taxpayer may not use the accelerated depreciation percentages provided by Section 168. Instead, the straight line method of depreciation, computed over a five-year period, must be used and no Section 179 election is available.

But Congress had a special concern for tax abuse potential it perceived to be associated with passenger automobiles:

> Congress believed that the investment incentives afforded by investment tax credit and accelerated cost recovery should be directed to encourage capital formation, rather than to subsidize the element of personal consumption associated with the use of very expensive automobiles. To the extent an automobile is required for [necessary business] transportation, the generally allowable tax benefits should be available. Beyond that point, however, the extra expense of a luxury automobile provides, in effect, a tax-free personal emolument which Congress believed should not qualify for tax credits or acceleration of depreciation deductions because such expenditures do not add significantly to the productivity which these incentives were designed to encourage.

> In addition, Congress was concerned . . . that some taxpayers had attempted to convert personal use to business use through a variety of arguments, such as . . . that signs, special paint, personalized license plates, or unique hood ornaments made the car a constant advertisement so that all use was business-related.[38]

To prevent, or at least reduce, this abuse, Congress limited the depreciation allowable with respect to a passenger automobile in the year it is placed in service and succeeding years. The original dollar limitations were as follows:[39]

Tax Year	Maximum Depreciation Allowed
First	$2,560
Second	$4,100
Third	$2,450
Each Succeeding Year	$1,475

These limits are adjusted for inflation for automobiles placed in service after 1988.[40]

---

[38] General Explanation of the Revenue Provision of the Tax Reform Act of 1984, Staff of the Joint Committee on Taxation, H.R. 4170, 98th Cong., p. 559.

[39] I.R.C. § 280F(a)(1)(A). When Section 280F(a) was enacted in 1984, its limitation on depreciation deductions was directed at so-called luxury automobiles — thus the title of the provision. But many non-luxury automobiles are now subject to the Section 280F depreciation limitations.

[40] I.R.C. § 280F(d)(7).

The limitations are applied after depreciation is computed under Section 168 and before the depreciation amount is reduced to reflect the portion of the automobile's use that is personal use.[41] The depreciation deduction determined after applying the statutory limitations is then further reduced by the proportion of the total use during that year that is personal use.[42] Consider the following examples:

Example 1: On July 1, Year 1, Marilyn purchases for $30,000 and places in service a passenger automobile which is 5-year recovery property under Section 168. The automobile is used exclusively in her business. Marilyn plans to use the accelerated depreciation percentages under Section 168.

Analysis: In Year 1, without the Section 280F(a)(1) limitation, her depreciation deduction under the half-year convention would be 20% of $30,000 or $6,000. Given Section 280F(a)(2), and disregarding inflation adjustments to the Section 280F(a)(1) limits, however, Marilyn is only allowed a depreciation deduction of $2,560.[43] If she continues to use the car exclusively in business during Years 2-5, her depreciation deductions will be $4,100, $2,450, $1,475, and $1,475, respectively. Marilyn will obviously not have recovered the entire cost of the car during the recovery period. She is therefore permitted to claim the excess as an expense for the first taxable year after the recovery period.[44] There is, however, a limitation placed even then on the amount which may be deducted in any post-recovery period year; it may not exceed $1,475.[45] Any excess is carried over to the next succeeding tax year, until the full cost is recovered.[46]

Example 2: Assume the same facts as in Example 1 except that Marilyn uses the automobile only 25% of the time in her business and 75% of the time for personal purposes.

Analysis: Because the business use does not exceed 50%, she may not use the accelerated depreciation percentages and is limited by Section 280F(b)(2) to the straight line method. Again disregarding inflation adjustments, Marilyn's maximum depreciation deduction for the year the property is placed in service is still $2,560[47] which is less than the maximum depreciation computed using Section 168(g), *i.e.*, 10% of $30,000 or $3,000 (note the use of the half-year convention). This maximum depreciation

---

[41] *See* I.R.C. § 280F(a)(2).

[42] General Explanation of the Revenue Provision of the Tax Reform Act of 1984, p. 561.

[43] Note that because Section 179 deductions are considered depreciation deductions under Section 168, the taxpayer would not be entitled to elect to take a Section 179 deduction. Under Section 280F, the use of the Section 179 election is available only under the following circumstances:

> (a) In the case of a passenger automobile, only if the 50% business use standard is satisfied and the amount of the I.R.C. § 168 depreciation deduction is less than the cap imposed by I.R.C. § 280F(a)(2). Considering how low that cap is, it is doubtful that taxpayers will benefit much from I.R.C. § 179 with respect to passenger automobiles which they purchase.

> (b) in the case of other listed property, only if the 50% business use standard is satisfied.

[44] I.R.C. § 280F(a)(1)(B).

[45] I.R.C. § 280F(a)(i)(B)(ii).

[46] I.R.C. § 280F(a)(1)(B)(i).

[47] I.R.C. § 280F(a)(1)(A)(i).

amount of $2,560 must now be allocated between the personal use and business use. Only 25% of $2,560 or $640 is deductible in the year the automobile is placed in service. Note, however, that for the purpose of computing depreciation deductions in subsequent years, Marilyn is treated as having been allowed a depreciation deduction in the prior year equal to that which would have been allowed if she had used the automobile exclusively for business purposes in the prior year.[48] Of course, the Section 280F(a)(1) limitation must be taken into consideration. Thus, for purposes of computing depreciation in subsequent years, Marilyn will be deemed to have been allowed $2,560 in depreciation in the year that the automobile was placed in service, rather than just the $640 actually allowed.[49]

Note: The examples above ignore the possible application of Section 168(k)(1), which provides 50% additional first year depreciation for certain property placed in service after 2007 and before 2015. For passenger automobiles, Section 168(k)(2)(F)(i) specifically provides that first year depreciation allowed under Section 280F(a)(1)(A) shall be increased by $8,000. Thus, instead of $2,560 in first year depreciation, taxpayers placing an automobile in service during this period will be entitled to a maximum first-year depreciation deduction of $10,560. (These dollar amounts disregard inflation adjustments.) Depreciation deductions for the second, third, and succeeding tax years remain unchanged.

§ 21.04   CONCLUSION

In sum, Congress, by means of Sections 280A and 280F, has attempted to prevent taxpayers in certain contexts from converting nondeductible personal expenses into deductible business or investment expenses. Such policing of the business/personal expense borders, however, has been accomplished only by adding considerable complexity to an already complex Code.

---

[48] I.R.C. § 280F(d)(2).

[49] *See* I.R.C. § 280F(d)(2); Temp. Treas. Reg. § 1.280F-4T(a)(1) and (2).

Chapter 22

THE INTEREST DEDUCTION

Prior to 1986, the interest taxpayers incurred on everything from gas to homes was generally deductible regardless of whether it had been incurred it in connection with a trade, business or investment activity or with personal consumption. In 1986, Congress significantly limited the deduction for personal interest, leaving, however, almost intact the most significant personal interest deduction — that for mortgages on one's personal residence. This chapter examines the interest deduction, focusing primarily on statutory limitations on the deduction as well as certain related timing rules. Some judicial limitations and additional statutory limitations of more general application are considered in Chapter 27.

§ 22.01 WHAT CONSTITUTES INTEREST?

A review of the case law and rulings reveals that the question — what is interest? — is not always easily answered. Consider, for example, the additional fees known as "points" a taxpayer pays when borrowing money from a bank or savings and loan to purchase a home.[1] The loan agreement may provide separate charges for all of the costs associated with the approval and processing of the loan, such as title report, preparation of documents, etc. The Service, considering such a situation,[2] ruled that the points constituted interest and reasoned that the points were based on the "economic factors that usually dictate an acceptable rate of interest."[3] The ruling provides the following instructive discussion on the nature of interest:

> For tax purposes, interest has been defined by the Supreme Court of the United States as the amount one has contracted to pay for the use of borrowed money, and as the compensation paid for the use or forbearance of money. See *Old Colony Railroad Co. v. Commissioner*, 284 U.S. 552 (1932). . . . A negotiated bonus or premium paid by a borrower to a lender in order to obtain a loan has been held to be interest for Federal income tax purposes. Likewise, overdraft charges are not interest.
>
> The payment or accrual of interest for tax purposes must be incidental to an unconditional and legally enforceable obligation of the taxpayer claiming the deduction. . . . There need not, however, be a legally enforce

---

[1] A "point" is equal to one percent of the amount of the loan, and is paid as a fee to the lender. For example, a charge of three points on a $100,000 loan would equal $3,000.

[2] Rev. Rul. 69-188, 1969-1 C.B. 54.

[3] The lender "considered the general availability of money, the character of the property offered as security, the degree of success that the borrower had enjoyed in his prior business activities, and the outcome of previous transactions between the borrower and his creditors." 1969-1 C.B. at 54.

able indebtedness already in existence when the payment of interest is made. It is sufficient that the payment be a "prerequisite to obtaining borrowed capital. . . ."

It is not necessary that the parties to a transaction label a payment made for the use of money as interest for it to be so treated. . . .

The method of computation also does not control its deductibility, so long as the amount in question is an ascertainable sum contracted for the use of borrowed money. . . . The fact that the amount paid . . . is a flat sum paid in addition to a stated annual interest rate does not preclude a deduction under section 163 of the Code.

To qualify as interest for tax purposes, the payment, by whatever name called, must be compensation for the use or forbearance of money per se and not a payment for specific services which the lender performs in connection with the borrower's account. For example, interest would not include separate charges made for investigating the prospective borrower and his security, closing costs of the loan and papers drawn in connection therewith or fees paid to a third party for servicing and collecting that particular loan. Also, even where service charges are not stated separately on the borrower's account, interest would not include amounts attributable to such services.[4]

Interest expense incurred in a trade or business would be deductible under Section 162 even if Section 163 did not exist. Many of the characterization questions regarding interest arise in business settings. For example, a common question is whether "loans" made by shareholders to their corporations are genuine debts or should be treated as shareholder contributions to capital. If treated as debts, the amounts repaid by the corporation to the shareholders with respect to the debt will constitute a combination of principal and interest, with the interest being deductible by the corporation. By contrast, if the "loan" is in substance a capital contribution, amounts paid to the shareholder are taxable dividends, rather than interest. Unlike interest, dividends paid to shareholders are not deductible by the corporation.

§ 22.02 DEDUCTION OF PERSONAL INTEREST

§ 163. Interest —

(a) **General rule** — There shall be allowed as a deduction all interest paid or accrued within the taxable year on indebtedness.. . .

(h) **Disallowance of deduction for personal interest** —

(1) **In general** — In the case of a taxpayer other than a corporation, no deduction shall be allowed under this chapter for personal interest paid or accrued during the taxable year.

(2) **Personal interest** — For purposes of this subsection, the term "personal interest" means any interest allowable as a deduction under this chapter other than —

---

[4] *Id.* at 55.

(A) interest paid or accrued on indebtedness properly allocable to a trade or business (other than the trade or business of performing services as an employee),

(B) any investment interest (within the meaning of subsection (d)),

(C) any interest which is taken into account under section 469 in computing income or loss from a passive activity of the taxpayer,

(D) any qualified residence interest (within the meaning of paragraph (3))

. . .

(F) any interest allowable as a deduction under section 221 (relating to interest on educational loans)

(3) Qualified residence interest — For purposes of this subsection —

(A) In general — The term "qualified residence interest" means any interest which is paid or accrued during the taxable year on —

(i) acquisition indebtedness with respect to any qualified residence of the taxpayer, or

(ii) home equity indebtedness with respect to any qualified residence of the taxpayer.

For purposes of the preceding sentence, the determination of whether any property is a qualified residence of the taxpayer shall be made as of the time the interest is accrued.

(B) Acquisition indebtedness —

(i) In general — The term "acquisition indebtedness" means any indebtedness which —

(I) is incurred in acquiring, constructing, or substantially improving any qualified residence of the taxpayer, and

(II) is secured by such residence.

Such term also includes any indebtedness secured by such residence resulting from the refinancing of indebtedness meeting the requirements of the preceding sentence (or this sentence); but only to the extent the amount of the indebtedness resulting from such refinancing does not exceed the amount of the refinanced indebtedness.

(ii) $1,000,000 Limitation — The aggregate amount treated as acquisition indebtedness for any period shall not exceed $1,000,000 ($500,000 in the case of a married individual filing a separate return).

(C) Home equity indebtedness —

(i) In general — The term "home equity indebtedness" means any indebtedness (other than acquisition indebtedness) secured by a qualified residence to the extent the aggregate amount of such indebtedness does not exceed —

(I) the fair market value of such qualified residence, reduced by

(II) the amount of acquisition indebtedness with respect to such residence.

(ii) Limitation — The aggregate amount treated as home equity indebtedness for any period shall not exceed $100,000 ($50,000 in the case of a separate return by a married individual).

Prior to 1986, taxpayers were entitled to deduct not only business and investment interest but also personal interest, such as interest on credit card balances. The allowance of a deduction for interest incurred in business and investment activities is appropriate in a system taxing only net income. The allowance of a deduction for personal interest, however, is an exception to the general rule that personal living expenses are not deductible.

In 1986, Congress significantly limited the deduction of "personal interest."[5] The Senate Report explained congressional rationale for this change as follows:

> Present law excludes or mismeasures income arising from the ownership of housing and other consumer durables. Investment in such goods allows consumers to avoid the tax that would apply if funds were invested in assets producing taxable income and to avoid the cost of renting these items, a cost which would not be deductible in computing tax liability. Thus, the tax system provides an incentive to invest in consumer durables rather than assets which produce taxable income and, therefore, an incentive to consume rather than save.

> Although the committee believes that it would not be advisable to subject to income tax imputed rental income with respect to consumer durables owned by the taxpayer, it does believe that it is appropriate and practical to address situations where consumer expenditures are financed by borrowing. By phasing out the present deductibility of consumer interest, the committee believes that it has eliminated from the present tax law significant disincentive to saving.[6]

The statute generally disallows the deduction of "personal interest,"[7] which is defined as any interest other than: (1) trade or business interest; (2) investment interest; (3) passive activity interest; (4) qualified residence interest; (5) certain interest on unpaid taxes; and (6) interest on educational loans pursuant to Section 221.[8]

[A] Trade or Business Interest

One exclusion from the definition of personal interest for purposes of the disallowance rule is "interest paid or accrued on indebtedness properly allocable to a trade or business (other than the trade or business of performing services as an

---

[5] I.R.C. § 163(h)(1).

[6] S. Rep. No. 99-313, 99th Cong., 2d Sess., p. 804 (1986).

[7] I.R.C. § 163(h)(1).

[8] I.R.C. § 163(h)(2).

employee).[9] Because our tax system seeks to tax only the net income of a business, it is appropriate that interest paid or incurred on account of a trade or business be deductible. What constitutes "interest paid or accrued on indebtedness properly allocable to a trade or business," however, has caused some controversy. In *Redlark v. Commissioner*,[10] the Tax Court held that interest paid by a taxpayer on a deficiency in Federal income tax arising out of adjustments caused by accounting errors in determining the income of an unincorporated business constituted deductible business interest. The Tax Court rejected the Commissioner's argument that the interest was personal interest in light of the regulations, which define personal interest to include interest "paid on underpayments of individual Federal, State, or local income taxes . . . regardless of the source of the income generating the tax liability."[11] According to the Tax Court, this temporary regulation, as applied to the circumstances presented in *Redlark*, "constitutes an impermissible reading of the statute. . . ."[12] However, an earlier decision by the Eighth Circuit in *Miller v. United States*,[13] had upheld the regulation as a reasonable interpretation of Section 163(h), and the Tax Court decision in *Redlark* itself was reversed by the Ninth Circuit.[14] According to the Ninth Circuit, "[the regulation reflects] a general policy . . . that personal income tax always constitutes a personal obligation so that deficiencies in meeting the obligation [are not allocable to taxpayer's business.]"[15] With other circuits following the Eighth and Ninth Circuits, the Tax Court in *Robinson v. Commissioner*[16] announced it would no longer follow its decision in *Redlark* and held the regulation in question to be a permissible construction of Section 163(h)(2)(A).

[B]   Qualified Residence Interest

"Qualified residence interest" is also excepted from the rule disallowing deduction of "personal interest,"[17] thus preserving the deduction for mortgage interest on personal residences.[18] Qualified residence interest is interest paid or accrued during the tax year on certain "acquisition indebtedness" and "home equity indebtedness" secured by the taxpayer's principal residence and on one other qualified residence.[19] "Acquisition indebtedness" is indebtedness (not in

---

[9] I.R.C. § 163(h)(2)(A).

[10] 106 T.C. 31 (1996).

[11] Treas. Reg. § 1.163-9T(b)(2)(i)(A).

[12] 106 T.C. at 47.

[13] 65 F.3d 687 (8th Cir. 1995).

[14] 141 F.3d 936 (9th Cir. 1998).

[15] *Id.* at 939.

[16] 119 T.C. 44 (2002).

[17] I.R.C. § 163(h)(2)(D).

[18] The home mortgage interest deduction is excepted from the 2% floor applying to miscellaneous deductions generally. I.R.C. § 67(b)(1).

[19] I.R.C. § 163(h)(3)(A). Section 163(h)(4)(A)(i) defines a qualified residence as "the principal residence (within the meaning of § 121) of the taxpayer" and "1 other residence of the taxpayer which is selected by the taxpayer for purposes of this subsection for the taxable year and which is used by the taxpayer as a residence (within the meaning of § 280A(d)(1))." For a dwelling unit to qualify as a

excess of $1,000,000) incurred in "acquiring, constructing, or substantially improving any qualified residence of the taxpayer." It also includes indebtedness resulting from the refinancing of acquisition indebtedness not in excess of the refinanced indebtedness.[20] "Home equity indebtedness" is indebtedness (other than acquisition indebtedness) secured by a qualified residence, e.g., a second mortgage. However, home equity indebtedness is limited to the excess of the fair market value of the qualified residence over the amount of acquisition indebtedness with respect to such residence. For purposes of the interest deduction, home equity indebtedness may not exceed $100,000.[21] Thus, the overall limit of indebtedness on a principal and second residence, the interest on which will be deductible, is $1,100,000.

The following examples demonstrate the application of the qualified residence interest rules:

> **Example 1:** Willa purchased a home 25 years ago for $50,000. The home is worth $300,000 today. Willa still owes $5,000 on the mortgage encumbering the home. May Willa deduct the interest on the $5,000 loan balance?
>
> **Analysis:** Willa may deduct whatever interest she pays each year on the outstanding mortgage. The $5,000 represents acquisition indebtedness.
>
> **Example 2:** Same facts as Example 1 except that Willa borrows an additional $75,000 to remodel her home and gives a second mortgage on the home to secure the loan. All $75,000 is used in the remodeling project. How much of the interest on the second mortgage may Willa deduct?
>
> **Analysis:** The additional $75,000 of debt will be considered acquisition indebtedness and Willa may deduct all interest paid with respect to that debt.
>
> **Example 3:** Assume the facts of Example 1 and assume also that Willa purchases a cabin on a lake located about 100 miles from her home. Willa uses the cabin on weekends during the fall, winter and spring and spends most of the summer at the cabin. Willa borrowed $250,000 from a local bank

---

residence pursuant to § 280A(d)(1), the taxpayer must use it for the greater of 14 days or 10 percent of the number of days during the taxable year for which the unit is rented at a fair rental price.§ 280A(d)(1). If the taxpayer, however, does not rent the dwelling unit at any time during a taxable year, the unit may be treated as a residence for the taxable year, notwithstanding § 280A(d)(1). § 163(h)(4)(A)(iii). A taxpayer may treat a residence that is "under construction" as a qualified residence for a period of up to 24 months if the residence becomes a qualified residence as of the time that the residence is ready for occupancy. Treas. Reg. § 1.163-10T(p)(5). *See* Rose v. Commissioner, T.C. Summ. Op. 2011-117. However, interest paid by a taxpayer with respect to a vacant lot which she and her husband owned and on which they camped yearly was not qualified residence interest within the meaning of § 163(h)(3) because the interest was not paid on a principal or second residence. See Garrison v. Commissioner, T.C. Memo. 1994-200, *aff'd without published opinion* 1995 U.S. App. Lexis 29726 (6th Cir. 1995).

[20] I.R.C. § 163(h)(3)(B). For example, if one borrows $100,000 to purchase a home and three years later refinances the $90,000 balance that is then owing on the home, the amount of the refinancing up to $90,000 will constitute acquisition indebtedness. If the refinancing were for $100,000 instead of just $90,000, the additional $10,000 would not be considered acquisition indebtedness unless it were used to improve the residence. If not used to improve the residence, it might nonetheless constitute "home equity indebtedness," the interest on which would also be deductible. See I.R.C. § 163(h)(3)(C).

[21] I.R.C. § 163(h)(3)(C).

to purchase the cabin which cost $300,000. Willa gave the bank a mortgage on the cabin to secure her repayment of the $250,000. May Willa deduct the interest she pays to the bank on the $250,000 loan?

Analysis: The $250,000 loan represents "acquisition indebtedness" under Section 163(h)(3)(B). There is a $1,000,000 limit on the amount of debt which will be treated as "acquisition indebtedness." The debt on the cabin combined with the debt on her residence in Example 1 amount to less than $1,000,000. The interest on both debts therefore constitutes "qualified residence interest." Willa may therefore deduct all of the interest on the cabin loan as well as on the loan described in Example 1.

Example 4: Same facts as Example 1 except that Willa borrows an additional $100,000, $70,000 of which is used to add a room to the home; the other $30,000 is used to assist her daughter get started in a business. How much of the interest on the $100,000 loan may Willa deduct?

Analysis: The $70,000 borrowed to add the room will be considered acquisition indebtedness, and Willa may deduct the interest paid with respect to that amount. The other $30,000 will be considered home equity indebtedness and, since it is both less than $100,000 and also less than the difference between the value of the home ($300,000) and the acquisition indebtedness totaling $75,000 (*i.e.*, $5,000 plus $70,000). Willa may deduct all of the interest paid on that amount.

Example 5: Same as Example 1 except Willa borrows $130,000 to purchase a Mercedes Benz and gives a second mortgage on her home to secure the loan. How much interest may she deduct on the $130,000 loan?

Analysis: $100,000 of the $130,000 will be considered home equity indebtedness, the interest on which is deductible; the other $30,000 will be considered personal indebtedness for which no deduction is allowed.

The Service has ruled that, given the statutory definitions of "acquisition indebtedness" and "home equity indebtedness" and the dollar limitations on both, a loan used to purchase a qualified residence may constitute acquisition indebtedness in part and home equity indebtedness in part.[22]

Example: In 2012, Taxpayer, an unmarried individual, purchased a principal residence for its fair market value of $1,500,000. Taxpayer paid $300,000 and financed the remainder by borrowing $1,200,000 through a loan secured by the residence. In 2012, Taxpayer paid the interest that accrued on the indebtedness during that year. Assume Taxpayer has no other debt secured by the residence.

Analysis: Taxpayer may deduct, as interest on acquisition indebtedness under Section 163(h)(3)(B), interest paid in 2012 on $1,000,000 of the $1,200,000 indebtedness used to acquire the principal residence. Taxpayer also may deduct, as interest on home equity indebtedness under Section 163(h)(3)(C), interest paid in 2012 on $100,000 of the remaining indebted

---

[22] Rev. Rul. 2010-25, 2010-2 C.B. 571.

ness of $200,000. The $200,000 of remaining indebtedness is secured by the qualified residence, is not acquisition indebtedness under Section 163(h)(3)(B), and does not exceed the fair market value of the residence reduced by the acquisition indebtedness secured by the residence. Thus, $100,000 of the $200,000 is treated as home equity indebtedness under Section 163(h)(3)(C).

As the Staff of the Joint Committee noted in its explanation of the changes made to Section 163 by the 1986 Act: "While Congress recognized that the imputed rental value of owner-occupied housing may be a significant source of untaxed income, the Congress nevertheless determined that encouraging home ownership is an important policy goal, achieved in part by providing a deduction for residential mortgage interest."[23] Although it is a valid concern of the government to encourage home ownership, it must be noted that there is no comparable tax break for individuals who cannot afford to own their own home and are forced to rent.

[C] Interest on Education Loans

In 1997, as part of a package of education tax incentives, Congress authorized the deduction of interest on education loans, a new category of deductible interest outside the confines of Section 163. Section 221 authorizes a limited deduction for interest paid by an individual on any "qualified education loan."[24] Qualified loans are essentially those incurred to pay higher education expenses (tuition, fees, room and board and related expenses) of the taxpayer, his or her spouse, or dependents.[25] Among other restrictions, the deduction is limited to $2,500 and is phased out for individuals with modified adjusted gross incomes from $50,000 to $65,000 ($100,000 to $130,000 on joint returns), amounts adjusted for inflation.[26] In addition, pursuant to Section 221(d)(1), the term "qualified education loan" does not include any indebtedness owed to a person related to the taxpayer within the meaning of Sections 267(b) and 707(b)(1). For example, if a taxpayer borrowed money from her parents to attend college, her indebtedness to her parents would not constitute a "qualified education loan."

§ 22.03 INVESTMENT INTEREST

§ 163. Interest —

(d) Limitation on investment interest —

(1) **In general — In the case of a taxpayer other than a corporation, the amount allowed as a deduction under this chapter for investment interest for**

---

[23] General Explanation of the Tax Reform Act of 1986, p. 263–64.

[24] I.R.C. § 221(a).

[25] I.R.C. § 221(e).

[26] I.R.C. § 221(b), (f). These phase-out ranges reflect changes made by the 2001 Tax Act. The current phase-out ranges for interest deductions on student loans (as well as other amendments to § 221 made in the 2001 act) were scheduled to expire at the end of 2012. The American Taxpayer Relief Act of 2012 made the act phase-out ranges (and other amendments by the 2001 act) permanent for tax years beginning after December 31, 2012.

any taxable year shall not exceed the net investment income of the taxpayer for the taxable year.

(2)   Carryforward of disallowed interest — The amount not allowed as a deduction for any taxable year by reason of paragraph (1) shall be treated as investment interest paid or accrued by the taxpayer in the succeeding taxable year.

(3)   Investment interest — For purposes of this subsection —

(A)   In general — The term "investment interest" means any interest allowable as a deduction under this chapter (determined without regard to paragraph (1)) which is paid or accrued on indebtedness properly allocable to property held for investment.

(B)   Exceptions — The term "investment interest" shall not include:

(i) any qualified residence interest (as defined in subsection (h)(3)), or

(ii) any interest which is taken into account under section 469 in computing income or loss from a passive activity of the taxpayer.

(4)   Net investment income — For purposes of this subsection —

(A)   In general — The term "net investment income" means the sum of —

(i) investment income, over

(ii) investment expenses.

(B)   Investment Income — The term "investment income" means the sum of —

(i) gross income from property held for investment (other than any gain taken into account under clause (ii)(I)),

(ii) the excess (if any) of —

(I) the net gain attributable to the disposition of property held for investment, over

(II) the net capital gain determined by only taking into account gains for losses from dispositions of property held for investment, plus

(iii) so much of the net capital gain referred to in clause (ii)(II) (or, if lesser, the net gain referred to in clause (ii)(I)) as the taxpayer elects to take into account under this clause.

Such term shall include qualified dividend income (as defined in Section 1(h)(11)(B)) only to the extent the taxpayer elects to treat such income as investment income for purposes of this subsection.

(C)   Investment expenses — The term "investment expenses" means the deductions allowed under this chapter (other than for interest) which are directly connected with the production of investment income.

Taxpayers engaged in investment activity often borrow to purchase investment assets which, initially at least, are not income producing. As a result, the interest on such borrowing, rather than offsetting income from the investment activity, offsets income from nonrelated activities, *e.g.*, one's professional compensation. Concerned about this ability that taxpayers had to insulate their unrelated income from tax, Congress in 1969 enacted Section 163(d), limiting the deduction of investment interest.

Until 1986, taxpayers were permitted under Section 163(d) to deduct investment interest to the extent of net investment income plus some specified dollar amount. In 1986, Congress strengthened the limitation by providing that investment interest for any taxable year could not be deducted in an amount greater than the taxpayer's net investment income. Investment interest is defined as interest "paid or accrued on indebtedness properly allocable to property held for investment."[27] Net investment income is the excess of investment income over investment expenses.[28] Investment income includes gross income from "property held for investment," *e.g.*, interest, dividends, royalties, annuities not attributable to a trade or business,[29] but generally investment income does not include net capital gain from the disposition of investment property.[30] (A taxpayer may, however, elect to include any amount of such net capital gain in computing investment income, but the price of such inclusion is an equivalent reduction in the net capital gain eligible for favorable capital gain rates.)[31] As discussed below, "qualified dividend income" as defined in Section 1(h)(11)(B) is treated in a manner similar to net capital gain. Investment income does not include income subject to the passive activity rules of Section 469.[32] Investment expenses are deductible expenses (other than interest and expenses taken into account under Section 469) which are directly connected with the production of investment income.[33]

> **Example:** A taxpayer has interest income of $2,000 and dividend income of $3,000, for total "investment income" of $5,000. The taxpayer has paid a fully-deductible $1,000 for investment advice related to dividend-producing stock, for a total of $1,000 in "investment expenses." What is the maximum investment interest the taxpayer may deduct this year?

> **Analysis:** The taxpayer's "net investment income" for the year is thus $4,000. If the taxpayer during the year has paid or incurred interest expenses on debt allocable to property held for investment, perhaps by borrowing money to purchase stock and paying interest on that borrowed money, such interest is deductible only to the extent of $4,000, the taxpayer's net investment income.[34] Note that the taxpayer must be able to allocate interest expenses in order to apply the rules of Section 163(d).[35]

---

[27] I.R.C. § 163(d)(3)(A).

[28] I.R.C. § 163(d)(4)(A).

[29] I.R.C. §§ 163(d)(5)(A), 469(e)(1).

[30] *See* I.R.C. § 163(d)(4)(B).

[31] *See* I.R.C. § 1(h). See Chapter 31, *infra*, for a discussion of capital gains.

[32] I.R.C. § 163(d)(4)(D). See Chapter 44, *infra*, for a discussion of the passive activity rules.

[33] I.R.C. § 163(d)(4)(C), (D).

[34] I.R.C. § 163(d)(1).

[35] See Treas. Reg. § 1.163-8T, which provides for allocation to be accomplished by tracing interest expenses to specific debt, and by tracing the debts to specific expenditures based on use of the debt proceeds. An interest expense allocated to an "investment expenditure" would thus continue investment

Congress amended Section 163(d)(4) in 2003 to provide that net investment income will include "qualified dividend income" (as defined in Section 1(h)(11)(B)) only to the extent the taxpayer agrees to forego the lower net capital gain rates (see Chapter 31) applicable to such dividends under Section 1(h)(11).[36] Thus, in the preceding example, the taxpayer could only include the $3,000 in dividend income in the calculation of her total investment income for Section 163(d) purposes if she agreed to forego the benefit of having the dividends taxed under Section 1(h)(11). If the taxpayer so agrees, her dividends will be subject to tax at ordinary income rates which are currently as high as 39.6%, depending on the taxpayer's tax bracket.

Investment interest expenses which, as a result of Section 163(d)(1), cannot be deducted in one taxable year may be carried forward to the succeeding taxable year.[37] Reversing its position regarding the amount of disallowed investment interest which may be carried forward, the Service ruled "the carryover of a taxpayer's disallowed investment interest to a succeeding taxable year under Section 163(d) is not limited by the taxpayer's taxable income for the taxable year in which the interest is paid or accrued."[38] Thus, a taxpayer will be entitled to use the interest deduction if and when the investment becomes profitable.

Presumably, the limitation on the deduction of investment interest will encourage taxpayers to consider the economic viability of investments and place less emphasis on tax advantages such as interest deductions. Taxpayers may not avoid the Section 163(d) limitation by claiming the interest expense is deductible under Section 212. As the Tax Court noted in *Malone v. Commissioner*,[39]"the limitation of Section 163(d) would be undermined if taxpayers could deduct under Section 212 interest which is not deductible under Section 163(d)."

§ 22.04 TIMING ISSUES AND LIMITATIONS

[A] Allocation of Prepaid Interest

§ 461. Methods of Accounting —

(g) Prepaid interest —

(1) In general — If the taxable income of the taxpayer is computed under the cash receipts and disbursements method of accounting, interest paid by the taxpayer which, under regulations prescribed by the Secretary, is properly allocable to any period —

(A) with respect to which the interest represents a charge for the use or forbearance of money, and

(B) which is after the close of the taxable year in which paid, shall be

---

interest subject to the Section 163(d) limitation rule.

[36] I.R.C. § 163(d)(4)(B). This provision has been made permanent by the American Taxpayer Relief Act of 2012.

[37] I.R.C. § 163(d)(2).

[38] Rev. Rul. 95-16, 1995-1 C.B. 9.

[39] T.C. Memo 1996-408.

charged to capital account and shall be treated as paid in the period to which so allocable.

(2)   Exception — This subsection shall not apply to points paid in respect of any indebtedness incurred in connection with the purchase or improvement of, and secured by, the principal residence of the taxpayer to the extent that, under regulations prescribed by the Secretary, such payment of points is an established business practice in the area in which such indebtedness is incurred, and the amount of such payment does not exceed the amount generally charged in such area.

Some statutory limitations on interest deductions relate to timing. Section 461(g)(1), for example, generally prevents a cash method taxpayer from claiming a current deduction for interest payments which compensate a lender for the use or forbearance of money in future years.[40] Rather, the taxpayer is permitted to deduct only the interest expense related to the current year; the balance may be deducted in the year(s) to which it relates. In effect, Section 461(g)(1) places the cash method taxpayer on the accrual method with respect to the deduction of prepaid interest.

Section 461(g)(2), however, provides an exception to this rule for qualifying "points" paid "in connection with the purchase or improvement of, and secured by, the [taxpayer's] principal residence." In *Huntsman v. Commissioner*,[41] the Tax Court, interpreting and applying this phrase, held that the taxpayers could not deduct currently the points they paid to refinance the debt on their personal residence. According to the Tax Court, the Section 461(g)(2) exception is limited to points "paid in respect of financing the actual purchase of a principal residence or financing improvements to such residence."[42] In refinancing transactions, by contrast, "the funds generated by the loans generally are used not to purchase or improve a principal residence but to pay off the loan that is already in existence and thereby lower the interest costs incurred or achieve some other financial goal not connected directly with home ownership."[43] In such refinancing circumstances, the exception in Section 461(g)(2) does not apply. The Tax Court noted that, if the points were otherwise deductible, they would be deductible ratably over the life of the loan.

The Eighth Circuit, however, reversed the Tax Court, concluding that Section 461(g)(2) merely requires that indebtedness be incurred "in connection with" the purchase or improvement of a taxpayer's residence. According to the court, a fair reading of the statute requires only that the indebtedness have an "association" or "relation" with the purchase of taxpayer's residence. Contrary to the Tax Court, a direct relationship between the indebtedness and the actual acquisition or improvement of the principal residence need not exist. Responding to the Tax Court's concern that the refinancing generally occurs because taxpayers wish to reduce their rate of interest or achieve some other financial objective, the Eighth Circuit stressed that those were not the circumstances in this case. Rather, the taxpayers

---

[40] The cash method taxpayer may generally deduct amounts when paid. The accrual method taxpayer, by contrast, may deduct amounts only when the "all events test" has been satisfied. *See* Treas. Reg. § 1.461-1(a)(2). See Chapters 28 and 29, *infra*, for a discussion of these two methods of accounting.

[41] 91 T.C. 917 (1988).

[42] *Id.* at 920.

[43] *Id.*

refinanced their debt in order to obtain permanent financing for the purchase of their home. The indebtedness being refinanced was short term indebtedness. (The Huntsmans had financed the purchase of their home by obtaining a three year loan with a balloon payment due at the end of three years.) According to the Eighth Circuit, this short term financing was merely an integrated step in the Huntsmans' efforts to secure permanent financing for the purchase of their home. Under these circumstances, the permanent mortgage obtained through the refinancing had sufficient connection with the purchase of the home to bring the Huntsmans' payment of points within the exception of Section 461(g)(2).[44]

Subsequently, the Service issued Revenue Procedure 94-27,[45] "to minimize possible disputes regarding the deductibility of points." To satisfy the Revenue Procedure so that the Service will treat the points as deductible by a cash method payer in the year paid, the points must (1) be appropriately designated on a Uniform Settlement Statement; (2) be computed as a percentage of the amount borrowed; (3) conform to local established business practice and not exceed the amount generally charged ("If amounts designated as points are paid in lieu of amounts ordinarily stated separately on the settlement statement [such as appraisal fees, inspection fees, title fees, attorneys' fees, and property taxes], those amounts are not deductible as points"); (4) be paid to acquire the taxpayer's principal residence (the Revenue Procedure is not satisfied if the points are paid to improve the principal residence, to purchase a residence not the principal residence, or to refinance a loan); and (5) be paid directly by the taxpayer out of funds not borrowed for this purpose as part of the overall transaction. (This may include points paid by the seller provided the taxpayer computes basis by subtracting seller-paid points from the purchase price of the residence.)

[B] Capitalization of Interest

Section 263A disallows a current deduction for interest incurred during the production period[46] on indebtedness directly or indirectly attributable to a taxpayer's production of certain real or tangible personal property for use in a trade or business or activity conducted for profit. Such interest must be added to the basis of the property and will be recovered through depreciation deductions or when the taxpayer sells or otherwise disposes of the property.

[C] Payment Issues

Aside from specific timing limitations, there are timing issues related to interest deductions involving the application of general accounting rules. For example, a cash method taxpayer may claim a deduction only when payment has been made.

Example 1: Needing cash for business purposes, Ben, a cash method taxpayer, borrows $10,000 from a bank, repayable the following year.

---

[44] 905 F.2d 1182 (8th Cir. 1990).

[45] 94-1 C.B. 613.

[46] The production period commences when production of property begins and ends when the property is ready to be placed in service or is ready to be held for sale. I.R.C. § 263A(f)(4)(B).

Pursuant to the terms of the loan agreement, however, the bank gives Ben only $9,000. The $1,000 difference between the amount Ben must repay and the amount he actually receives represents interest. Does the withholding of $1,000 by the bank constitute a payment by Ben enabling him to deduct the $1,000 in interest in the year he borrows the money?

Analysis: In general, the mere giving of a promissory note by a cash method taxpayer does not constitute a payment, even if the note is secured by collateral.[47] If Ben had borrowed $9,000 and given the lender two promissory notes due the following year — one for the principal amount of $9,000 and the other for interest in the amount of $1,000 — Ben's delivery of the $1,000 promissory note for interest would not constitute a payment of interest. The giving of the note is not a payment in cash or the equivalent of cash. Ben has not reduced his own funds in giving the note; indeed, if Ben never paid the note, he would have parted with nothing except his promise to pay.[48] The facts of the example differ from this alternative only in that there is one note and the loan on its face was for $10,000. In substance, however, Ben received only $9,000 of loan proceeds in each situation and agreed to pay $1,000 of interest. In both cases he would only be out of pocket the $1,000 interest in the year he paid the note(s). Ben therefore is not entitled to an interest deduction in the year he borrowed the funds.

Example 2: Amy, a cash method taxpayer, owes the First National Bank $5,000 interest on a business loan. Amy borrows $5,000 from the Last National Bank, immediately deposits the loan proceeds in her checking account at the First National Bank, and then delivers her check for $5,000 to the First National Bank in "payment" of the interest owing. Is Amy entitled to a deduction for the interest paid?

Analysis: Generally, "when a deductible payment is made with borrowed money, the deduction is not postponed until the year in which the borrowed money is repaid. Such expenses must be deducted in the year they are paid and not when the loans are repaid."[49] Thus, Amy will be treated as having paid the interest.

The result may be different, however, if the taxpayer borrows money from the same lender to make an interest payment that is due. In *Davison v. Commissioner*,[50] the taxpayer borrowed money from an insurance company. Two days before an interest payment was due, the insurance company transferred an amount equal to the interest payment to the taxpayer; the next day the taxpayer transferred that amount back to the insurance company as interest on the loan. In determining whether the taxpayer was entitled to an interest deduction, the Tax Court noted some "general principles" regarding interest deductions:

---

[47] Helvering v. Price, 309 U.S. 409 (1940).

[48] *See* Cleaver v. Comm'r, 158 F.2d 342 (7th Cir. 1946).

[49] Rev. Rul. 78-38, 1978-1 C.B. 67; Granan v. Comm'r, 55 T.C. 753, 755 (1971).

[50] 107 T.C. 35 (1996), *aff'd per curiam*, 141 F.3d 403 (2d Cir. 1998).

For cash basis taxpayers, payment must be made in cash or its equivalent. *Don E. Williams Co. v. Commissioner*, 429 U.S. 569, 577-578 (1977). . . . The delivery of a promissory not is not a cash equivalent but merely a promise to pay. *Helvering v. Price*, 309 U.S. 409, 413 (1940). . . . Where a lender withholds a borrower's interest payment from the loan proceeds, the borrower is considered to have paid interest with a note rather than with cash or its equivalent and, therefore, is not entitled to a deduction until the loan is repaid. . . . *Cleaver v. Commissioner*, 6 T.C. 452, 454, *aff'd*, 158 F.2d 342 (7th Cir. 1946). On the other hand, where a taxpayer discharges interest payable to one lender with funds obtained from a different lender, the interest on the first loan is considered paid when the funds are transferred to the first lender. . . .[51]

But in *Davison*, the interest was "paid" with funds obtained from the same lender to whom the interest was owed. In determining whether payment in fact has been made in these circumstances, the court imposed a two-part test:

The issue before us arises when a borrower borrows funds from a lender and immediately satisfies an interest obligation to the same lender. In order to determine whether interest has been paid or merely deferred, *it is first necessary to determine whether the borrowed funds were, in substance, the same funds used to satisfy the interest obligation.* Whether the relevant transactions were simultaneous, whether the borrower had other funds in his account to pay interest, whether the funds are traceable, and whether the borrower had any realistic choice to use the borrowed funds for any other purpose would all be relevant to this issue. Once it is determined that the borrowed funds were the same funds used to satisfy the interest obligation, the purpose of the loan plays a decisive role.

In light of the foregoing analysis, we hold that *a cash basis borrower is not entitled to an interest deduction where the funds used to satisfy the interest obligation were borrowed for that purpose from the same lender to whom the interest was owed.* This test is consistent with our traditional approach of characterizing transactions on a substance-over-form basis by looking at the economic realities of the transaction. . . . [T]here is no substantive difference between a situation where a borrower satisfies a current interest obligation by simply assuming a greater debt to the same lender and one where the borrower and lender exchange checks pursuant to a plan whose net result is identical to that in the first situation. In both situations, the borrower has simply increased his debt to the lender by the amount of interest. The effect of this is to postpone, rather than pay, the interest.[52]

This two-part test was satisfied in *Davison*, and the taxpayer was not permitted to deduct the interest payment made to the insurance company.

---

[51] *Id.* at 41.

[52] *Id.* at 32-33 (emphasis added).

Chapter 23

THE DEDUCTION FOR TAXES

In addition to the federal individual income taxes, Americans are also subject to a variety of state and local taxes. Some of these taxes are deductible for federal income tax purposes. This Chapter considers this special federal tax deduction.

§ 23.01 HISTORICAL BACKGROUND

The deduction for taxes has been a part of the Internal Revenue Code since its inception in 1913. The 1913 Tax Act provided: "In computing net income for the purpose of the normal tax, there shall be allowed as deductions . . . all national, State, county, school, and municipal taxes paid within the year, not including those assessed against local benefits." While the deduction for taxes has long been authorized, the specific content of the deduction provision has changed significantly over the years.

The most significant change occurred in 1964 when the provision was amended to read essentially as it does today. Prior to its amendment in 1964, Section 164, while in general allowing a deduction for taxes imposed by the United States, specifically disallowed a deduction for federal income taxes, FICA taxes on employees, federal estate and gift taxes and certain other federal taxes. In 1964, these disallowance provisions with respect to federal taxes were removed from Section 164 and became part of a new specific disallowance provision, Section 275.

§ 23.02 TAXES DEDUCTIBLE UNDER SECTION 164

§ 164. Taxes.

(a) General rule. Except as otherwise provided in this section, the following taxes shall be allowed as a deduction for the taxable year within which paid or accrued:

(1) State and local, and foreign, real property taxes.

(2) State and local personal property taxes.

(3) State and local, and foreign, income, war profits, and excess profits taxes.

. . .

In addition, there shall be allowed as a deduction, State and local, and foreign, taxes not described in the preceding sentence which are paid or accrued within the taxable year in carrying on a trade or business or an activity described in section 212 (relating to expenses for the production of income). Notwithstanding the preceding sentence, any tax (not described in the first sentence of this subsection) which is paid or accrued by the taxpayer in connection with an acquisition or disposition of property shall be treated as part of the cost of the acquired property or, in the case of a disposition, as a reduction in the amount realized on the disposition.

(b) Definitions and special rules. For purposes of this section —

(1) Personal property taxes. The term "personal property tax" means an ad valorem tax which is imposed on an annual basis in respect of personal property.

(2) State or local taxes. A state or local tax includes only a tax imposed by a State, a possession of the United States, or a political subdivision of any of the foregoing, or by the District of Columbia.

(3) Foreign taxes. A foreign tax includes only a tax imposed by the authority of a foreign country. . . .

(5) General Sales Taxes — For purposes of subsection (a)

(A) Election to deduct state and local sales taxes in lieu of state and local income taxes —

(i) In general. At the election of the taxpayer for the taxable year, subsection (a) shall be applied

(I) without regard to the reference to state and local income taxes, and

(II) as if state and local general sales taxes were referred to in a paragraph thereof. . . .

Section 164 specifically lists as deductible the following common taxes: state and local real property taxes; state and local personal property taxes; and state and local, and foreign, income taxes. In addition, under temporary legislation enacted in 2004 and subsequently extended, a taxpayer may make an annual election to deduct either state and local income taxes, or state and local general sales taxes, but not both. The election is provided in Section 164(b)(5).[1] To the extent that these taxes represent personal expenses (*e.g.*, state and local income taxes, or general sales taxes on items for personal use, or real property taxes on one's personal residence), Section 164 constitutes a significant exception to the general rule denying deduc

---

[1] This provision reflects the efforts of states that rely heavily upon sales taxes to have those taxes treated under the Code the same as state and local income taxes. The legislative history notes that the election is intended to provide "more equitable Federal tax treatment across States" and to bring about a "more neutral [Federal] effect on the types of taxes" that state and local governments decide to adopt. H.R. Rep. 108-548, pt. 1, 108th Cong., 2nd Sess. (2004). As originally enacted, the provision was effective only for 2004 and 2005, but Congress extended it thereafter through 2013. I.R.C. § 164(b)(5)(I). Without further extension, sales taxes will again become nondeductible for 2014 and later years — but further extension would not be unexpected.

A taxpayer who makes the election can deduct either sales taxes actually paid or an amount determined under tables published by the Internal Revenue Service. A taxpayer who uses the optional tables, based on the taxpayer's state of residence, filing status, adjusted gross income, and number of exemptions, can also deduct sales taxes paid on homes, motor vehicles, boats, and certain other items. To be deductible, a sales tax must be a general one, imposed at one rate with respect to a broad range of items, although exception is made for special rates on food, clothing, medical supplies and motor vehicles. I.R.C. § 164(b)(5)(B), (C), (H).

tions for personal and family living expenses.[2] Note that, if any of the taxes listed in Section 164 represent trade or business expenses or expenses incurred in an income producing activity, they would presumably be deductible under Sections 162 or 212 regardless of the existence of a specific reference to them in Section 164.[3]

The practical effect of Section 164, therefore, is to allow taxpayers a deduction for certain taxes paid or accrued outside of a trade or business or other income producing activity. Section 164 deductions are not subject to the 2% floor of Section 67.[4]

Individuals pay numerous taxes which are not deductible under Section 164, *e.g.*, federal income tax, Social Security tax, hotel taxes, gasoline taxes and highway tolls. In some cases, these taxes may be deductible as business expenses under Section 162 or expenses incurred in an income producing activity under Section 212.

§ 23.03 PARTY ELIGIBLE TO CLAIM THE DEDUCTION

Taxes are generally deductible only by the person upon whom they are imposed.[5] Thus, paying a tax deductible under Section 164(a) does not assure that the payor is entitled to a deduction. For example, a national bank, seeking to compete with state banks, elected to pay a state tax assessed against its depositors and requested no reimbursement from its depositors. The Service concluded the depositors received income in the amount of the taxes paid on their behalf and were also entitled to a deduction under Section 164(a). The bank was not entitled to a tax deduction under Section 164(a), but could deduct the tax payments paid as business expenses under Section 162(a).[6] Similarly, a taxpayer who gratuitously paid the tax liabilities of his partners and waived any right to contribution or reimbursement from them could not deduct his partners' share of the taxes which he paid.[7]

There are exceptions to the general rule that taxes are deductible only by the taxpayer on whom they are imposed. For example, as discussed *infra*, real property taxes must be apportioned between a buyer and a seller of real property regardless of which party is liable for the tax under state or local law. In some circumstances, moreover, it may not be entirely clear upon whom real property taxes are imposed. If real property is owned by several co-owners, one of the co-owners may pay and seek to deduct the entire real property tax. In *Powell v. Commissioner*,[8] the Tax Court concluded the taxpayer, co-owner of an undivided one-sixth interest in real

---

[2] *See* I.R.C. § 262.

[3] As trade or business expenses, they would be deductible above the line in computing adjusted gross income. If they were expenses incurred in an income producing activity, they would not be considered in computing adjusted gross income, unless allocable to rental or royalty income per Section 62(a)(4), but would instead be deductions taken below the line as itemized deductions in computing taxable income.

[4] I.R.C. § 67(b)(2).

[5] Treas. Reg. § 1.164-1.

[6] Rev. Rul. 69-497, 1969-2 C.B. 162.

[7] Farnsworth v. Comm'r, 270 F.2d 660 (3d Cir. 1959).

[8] T.C. Memo. 1967-32.

property, could deduct more than her one-sixth "share" of the property taxes she paid. The court reasoned:

> Then what does give a taxpayer the right to deduct real property taxes? Certainly if the tax is imposed on the owner of the property, or if the tax can mature into a personal liability of the owner upon nonpayment, the answer is clear. It is no less clear that any owner of real property, regardless of the fact or possibility of personal liability, has a legal right to protect his property interests by paying taxes justly due thereon. We see no reason why such a person should have any less right to the deduction of such taxes he pays. It seems to us that the proper test of whether or not a real property tax is deductible by the person who paid such tax is whether that person satisfied some personal liability or protected some personal right or beneficial interest in property. Respondent agrees that petitioner was the owner of a one-sixth undivided interest in the properties in question but claims that she had no personal liability for any more than one-sixth of the taxes levied on the whole property. Therefore, respondent maintains that petitioner was a mere volunteer with respect to her payment of the other five-sixths of the taxes due. But in taking this position the respondent has not considered whether petitioner was protecting a personal right or beneficial interest in property by her payment of those taxes. We think she was. That tenants in common each must have the right to occupy the whole property in common with their co-tenants is universally accepted. This petitioner was not entitled merely to occupy one-sixth of the property held in common with her brothers and sisters, but she was entitled to occupy the whole in common with them.

§ 23.04 SPECIAL PROBLEMS ASSOCIATED WITH THE DEDUCTION OF REAL PROPERTY TAXES AND ASSESSMENTS

[A] Real Property Assessments

§ 164. Taxes.

(c) Deduction denied in case of certain taxes. No deduction shall be allowed for the following taxes:

(1) Taxes assessed against local benefits of a kind tending to increase the value of the property assessed; but this paragraph shall not prevent the deduction of so much of such taxes as is properly allocable to maintenance or interest charges.

Local governments impose a variety of special assessments against property owners. Some of these assessments are for specific services rendered, *e.g.*, the collection and disposal of refuse; others are for improvements to specific areas within the jurisdiction, *e.g.*, special assessments for sidewalks or sewers; and some are for maintenance of existing improvements, retirement of debt, or payment of interest. To determine whether a taxpayer paying these assessments may treat them as real property taxes deductible under Section 164, the meaning of the term "tax" in Section 164 and the nature of the specific assessment must be considered.

A tax is an enforced contribution, exacted pursuant to legislative authority in the exercise of the taxing power, and imposed and collected for the purpose of raising revenue to be used for public or governmental purposes, and not as a payment for some special privilege granted or service rendered.[9] If, for example, a charge is levied by a local government for water and sewer services, such a charge is obviously not a tax at all, but simply a fee paid for services.[10] If a special assessment is levied to pay for local benefits which tend to increase the value of the property assessed, then, except to the extent that it is allocable to maintenance or interest charges, it is not deductible as a "tax" under Section 164.[11] For example, amounts imposed by a local government for benefits such as streets, sidewalks and other like improvements are not deductible when assessed only upon those properties that directly benefit from such improvements and when measured by the benefits each property receives.[12] Such assessments are to be distinguished from deductible real property taxes, which taxing authorities levy for the general welfare at a like rate against all property under their jurisdiction.

The denial of a deduction for amounts assessed against local benefits, however, does not strip such payments of tax significance. Subject to the Section 263 standard disallowing deductions for capital expenditures, such taxes are deductible under either Sections 162 or 212 if they are ordinary and necessary trade or business expenses or are incurred in an income producing activity. In the usual case where the assessment represents the cost of improvements in the nature of capital expenditures, the assessment may be added to the basis of the property subject to the assessment.[13]

[B] Apportionment of Real Property Taxes Between Buyer and Seller

§ 164. Taxes.

(d) Apportionment of taxes on real property between seller and purchaser.

(1) General rule. For purposes of subsection (a), if real property is sold during any real property tax year, then

(A) so much of the real property tax as is properly allocable to that part of such year which ends on the day before the date of the sale shall be treated as a tax imposed on the seller, and

(B) so much of such tax as is properly allocable to that part of such year which begins on the date of the sale shall be treated as a tax imposed on the purchaser.

(2) Special rules.

---

[9] Rev. Rul 79-180, 1979-1 C.B. 95.

[10] Rev. Rul. 79-201, 1979-1 C.B. 97.

[11] I.R.C. § 164(c)(1).

[12] Treas. Reg. § 1.164-4(a).

[13] I.R.C. § 1016(a)(1). *See* National Lumber v. Comm'r, 90 F.2d 216 (8th Cir. 1937).

(A) In the case of any sale of real property, if

(i) a taxpayer may not, by reason of his method of accounting, deduct any amount for taxes unless paid, and

(ii) the other party to the sale is (under the law imposing the real property tax) liable for the real property tax for the real property tax year,

then for purposes of subsection (a) the taxpayer shall be treated as having paid, on the date of the sale, so much of such tax as, under paragraph (1) of this subsection, is treated as imposed on the taxpayer. For purposes of the preceding sentence, if neither party is liable for the tax, then the party holding the property at the time the tax becomes a lien on the property shall be considered liable for the real property tax for the real property tax year.

(B) In the case of any sale of real property, if the taxpayer's taxable income for the taxable year during which the sale occurs is computed under an accrual method of accounting, and if no election under section 461(c) (relating to the accrual of real property taxes) applies, then, for purposes of subsection (a), that portion of such tax which

(i) is treated, under paragraph (1) of this subsection, as imposed on the taxpayer, and

(ii) may not, by reason of the taxpayer's method of accounting, be deducted by the taxpayer for any taxable year,

shall be treated as having accrued on the date of the sale.

When real property is sold, Section 164(d) provides that the portion of real property taxes allocable to that part of the "real property tax year" ending the day before the sale is treated as imposed on the seller; the portion allocable to that part of the real property tax year beginning on the day of the sale is treated as a tax imposed on the purchaser.[14]

The real property tax year is determined under local law and is the period to which the tax imposed relates.[15]

> **Example:** The real property tax year is a calendar year. Real property taxes for a given property for the real property tax year are $3,650. The real property is sold by Smith to Brown on March 1. Five hundred and ninety dollars ($590) of the tax, *i.e.*, 59/365 is treated as imposed on Smith and the remaining $3,060, *i.e.*, 306/365 is treated as imposed on Brown.

The apportionment cannot be reallocated by an agreement between the buyer and the seller, because the Code does not allow a deduction for a real property tax treated as imposed on another taxpayer.[16] For deduction purposes, it makes no difference whether the purchaser was reimbursed by the seller for the seller's "share" of the tax. The "real property tax year" and the date of the sale control the apportionment. For example, in one case, the purchaser of certain real property, in

---

[14] The sale of real property is generally considered to occur at the earlier of the transfer of legal title or the assumption of the benefits and burdens of ownership. Baird v. Comm'r, 68 T.C. 115 (1977).

[15] Treas. Reg. § 1.164-6(c).

[16] I.R.C. § 164(c)(2).

addition to paying the current year's real property taxes, also paid the real property taxes owing on the property for years prior to the purchase. The Tax Court held the purchaser was entitled to deduct only that portion of the taxes allocable to the time the purchaser owned the property; the remainder of the taxes, attributable to the period prior to the purchase, was added to the purchaser's basis in the property.[17]

Special rules govern when the apportioned tax is deductible. Subsequent Chapters address the cash and accounting methods of accounting and in turn the timing of deductions. As will be discussed in Chapter 28, cash method accounting rules generally permit a deduction only upon actual payment of the expense in question. However, if real property is sold and the *other party to the sale* is liable under local law for the tax for the real property tax year, a cash method buyer or seller is treated as having paid, on the sale date, the tax treated as imposed under the apportionment method described above.[18] If neither party is liable for the tax under local law, the party holding the property when the tax becomes a lien is considered liable for the tax.[19] The fact, however, that a taxpayer is considered liable for the tax does not mean such a taxpayer can deduct more than the apportioned share of the tax.[20]

The regulations provide that a cash method taxpayer who is not liable for the tax can elect to deduct the apportioned share either for the taxable year of the sale or, *if later*, for the year the tax is actually paid.[21] The regulations also provide that a cash basis seller *who is liable* for a real property tax that is not payable until after the sale date can elect to treat the seller's portion of the tax as paid on the sale date or in a later year when the tax is actually paid.[22] The liberal approach of the regulations on the timing of deductions makes it unnecessary for a seller to determine when a tax is later paid, given the option of treating the tax imposed on the seller as paid on the sale date. Conversely, even when the seller is liable under local law for a tax due after the sale date, and the buyer pays the tax, the regulations nevertheless give the seller the option of treating such payment as payment by the seller and taking the deduction at that time.

An accrual basis taxpayer may elect to accrue any real property tax, which is related to a definite time period, ratably over that period.[23] However, for accrual basis taxpayers who have not elected ratable accrual of their real property taxes and who would otherwise be unable to deduct the tax treated as imposed on them, the tax so imposed is treated as accruing on the date of the sale.[24]

---

[17] Riordan v. Comm'r, T.C. Memo 1978-194. See also *Casel v. Comm'r*, 79 T.C. 424 (1982), in which the court reaches a similar result with respect to back taxes paid by the purchaser of property at a foreclosure sale.

[18] I.R.C. § 164(d)(2)(A).

[19] *Id.*

[20] I.R.C. § 164(c)(2). *See* Pederson v. Comm'r, 46 T.C. 155 (1966).

[21] Treas. Reg. § 1.164-6(d)(1), (2).

[22] Treas. Reg. § 1.164-6(d)(1)(ii).

[23] I.R.C. § 461(c).

[24] I.R.C. § 164(d)(2)(B).

§ 23.05 PUBLIC POLICY CONSIDERATIONS

In his "Tax Proposals to the Congress for Fairness, Growth and Simplicity," President Reagan in 1985 proposed the repeal of the deduction for state and local taxes except for those taxes incurred in a trade or business or in a profit-seeking activity. His proposal noted:

> [T]he current deduction for state and local taxes disproportionately benefits high income taxpayers residing in high-tax States. The two-thirds of taxpayers who do not itemize deductions are not entitled to deduct State and local taxes, and even itemizing taxpayers receive relatively little benefit from the deduction unless they reside in high-tax States. Although the deduction for State and local taxes thus benefits a small minority of U.S. taxpayers, the cost of the deduction is borne by all taxpayers in the form of significantly higher marginal tax rates.
>
> . . .
>
> Some argue that the deductibility of State and local taxes is appropriate because individuals should not be "taxed on a tax." The argument is deficient for a number of reasons. First, it ignores the effect of State and local tax deductibility on the Federal income tax base. Deductibility not only reduces aggregate Federal income tax revenues, it shifts the burden of collecting those revenues from high-tax to low-tax States. Absent the ability to impose Federal income tax on amounts paid in State and local taxes, the Federal government loses the ability to control its own tax base and to insist that the burden of Federal income taxes be distributed evenly among the States.
>
> Second, the "tax on a tax" argument suggests that amounts paid in State or local taxes should be exempt from Federal taxation because they are involuntary and State or local taxpayers receive nothing in return for their payments. Neither suggestion is correct. State and local taxpayers have ultimate control over the taxes they pay through the electoral process and through their ability to locate in jurisdictions with amenable tax and fiscal policies. Moreover, State and local taxpayers receive important personal benefits in return for their taxes, such as public education, water and sewer services and municipal garbage removal. . . .
>
> The deduction for State and local taxes may also be regarded as providing a subsidy to State and local governments, which are likely to find it somewhat easier to raise revenue because of the deduction. . . . Even if a subsidy for State and local government spending were desired, provision of the subsidy through a deduction for State and local taxes is neither cost effective nor fair. On average, State and local governments gain less than fifty cents for every dollar of Federal revenue lost because of the deduction. Moreover, a deduction for State and local taxes provides a greater level of subsidy to high-income States and communities than to low-income States and communities. . . .

After considerable debate, Congress, in the 1986 Tax Reform Act, preserved the Section 164 deduction for most state and local taxes, but eliminated the deduction for state and local sales taxes. However, as noted previously, Congress, in 2004, restored a deduction for state and local sales taxes for taxpayers who elect to deduct such taxes in lieu of deducting state and local income taxes.[25]

---

[25] I.R.C. § 164(b)(5)(C).

Chapter 24

CASUALTY LOSSES

Section 165(c)(3) authorizes a deduction for an individual's uncompensated casualty and theft losses unconnected with a trade or business or with a transaction entered into for profit.[1]

§ 165. Losses —

(a)   General rule — There shall be allowed as a deduction any loss sustained during the taxable year and not compensated for by insurance or otherwise.

. . .

(c)   Limitation on losses of individuals — In the case of an individual, the deduction under subsection (a) shall be limited to —

. . .

(3) except as provided in subsection (h), losses of property not connected with a trade or business or a transaction entered into for profit, if such losses arise from fire, storm, shipwreck, or other casualty, or from theft. . . .

. . .

Section 262 bars a deduction for personal expenses. But for timing, the allowance of a deduction on the loss of property is the functional equivalent of allowing a deduction on acquisition of property or for depreciation associated with property. Strict consistency with Section 262 would thus argue for the nondeductibility of losses on personal-use property whether the loss is occasioned by casualty or otherwise. However, Section 165(c)(3), as limited by the rules of Section 165(h), suggests that Congress regards severe personal casualty losses as sufficiently different from life's ordinary losses and expenses, and as sufficiently related to one's wealth or ability to pay, so as to be taken into account in determining taxable income.

Each allowable casualty loss, however, is first subject to a $100 nondeductible floor; in addition, the net casualty loss for the year, determined after application of the $100 floor, is allowed only to the extent it exceeds 10% of the taxpayer's adjusted gross income.[2] Given the 10% nondeductible threshold, added to the Code in 1982, and the availability of insurance coverage for the more common significant risks, the average taxpayer will seldom be eligible to claim a casualty loss deduction.

---

[1] Individual casualty or theft losses that are business or profit-related do not fall under Section 165(c)(3); they are properly deductible under Section 165(c)(1) or (2). *See* Chapter 15, *supra*.

[2] I.R.C. § 165(h)(1), (2).

§ 24.01   DEFINITIONAL QUESTIONS

[A]   Casualty Losses

Most of the Section 165(c)(3) litigation has centered on the meaning of the word "casualty" in the statutory listing of "fire, storm, shipwreck, or other casualty" and theft as occasions for deduction of loss. Case law has limited qualifying casualties to those analogous to fire, storm, and shipwreck; the Service has insisted on an "identifiable event of a sudden, unexpected, and unusual nature." A sudden event is one that is "swift and precipitous and not gradual or progressive." An unexpected event is one that is "ordinarily unanticipated that occurs without the intent of the one who suffers the loss." An unusual event is one that is "extraordinary and nonrecurring, one that does not commonly occur during the activity in which the taxpayer was engaged when the destruction or damage occurred, and one that does not commonly occur in the ordinary course of day-to-day living of the taxpayer."[3] Such formulations are hardly free of ambiguity and elasticity, and differing interpretations of them can be expected.

> **Example 1:** Two diamond rings were lost when a woman, during an overnight stay in a hotel, took the rings off, wrapped them in tissue paper, and placed them on a table, all unbeknown to her husband, who by mistake flushed them down the toilet the next morning. Will a casualty loss be allowed?

> **Analysis:** A federal court has held that, under these circumstances, no casualty loss deduction would be allowed.[4] According to the court, the loss of the rings did not constitute a casualty. "It may be conceded that the loss of the rings was due to an unexpected and unusual cause and was not an intentional act on the taxpayer's part, but the loss lacks the element of suddenness. The primary cause of the loss was the placing of the rings in the . . . tissue. The loss was caused by a chain of events on the part of Mrs. Keenan and Mr. Keenan. There was no intervening sudden force, cause or occurrence which brought on the event such as would ever be present in a casualty arising from fires, storms or shipwreck, [*i.e.*, the types of casualties listed in Section 165(c)(3) with which the loss of the rings must be compared.]"[5] According to the court, the loss of the rings was not a loss of a similar kind or character to those types of loss, *i.e.*, fires, storm, shipwreck, identified in the statute. Therefore, no deduction under Section 165(c)(3) was allowable.

> **Example 2:** A woman placed her diamond ring in a glass of ammonia to soak, and her husband, not knowing the ring was in the glass, poured the contents of the glass down the kitchen sink and turned on the disposal, thereby damaging the ring. Does this loss qualify under the "other casualty" language of Section 165(c)(3)?

---

[3] Rev. Rul. 72-592, 1972-2 C.B. 101.

[4] Keenan v. Bowers, 91 F. Supp. 771 (E.D. S.C. 1950). [Note: This decision pre-dates the decisions discussed in the analyses to Examples 2 and 3.]

[5] *Id.* at 775.

Analysis: The Tax Court considered these facts in *Carpenter v. Commissioner*[6] and concluded that the loss resulted from a "casualty" as that term is used in Section 165(c)(3). The Court reasoned:

> We think the principle of *ejusdem generis* as now applied fulfills congressional intent in the use of the phrase "other casualty" in that it is being generally held that wherever force is applied to property which the owner-taxpayer is either unaware of because of the hidden nature of such application or is powerless to act to prevent the same because of the suddenness thereof or some other disability and damage results, he has suffered a loss which is, in that sense, like or similar to losses arising from the enumerated causes. Of course, we do not mean to say that one may wilfully and knowingly sit by and allow himself to be damaged in his property and still come within the statutory ambit of "other casualty." [The taxpayer] sustained a loss here under circumstances which it is true may be due to her or her husband's negligence, but this has no bearing upon the question whether an "other casualty" has occurred absent any wilfulness attributable thereto.[7]

As suggested by the quoted language, while it is clear that accidental losses can qualify as casualties within the meaning of Section 165(c)(3), no deduction will be allowed for damages resulting from a taxpayer's "willful act or willful negligence."[8]

Example 3: A diamond was lost from a taxpayer's diamond ring when her husband accidentally slammed the car door on her hand, breaking flanges that held the diamond in its setting. The taxpayer shook her hand, the uninsured diamond fell out, and was never found. May the taxpayer claim a casualty loss deduction for the diamond's value in the year it was lost?

Analysis: Yes, on identical facts the Tax Court in *White v. Commissioner*[9] held that the diamond was accidentally and irretrievably lost and had no value to the taxpayer after the loss. The loss resulted from an event that was (1) identifiable, (2) damaging to property, and (3) sudden, unexpected and unusual in nature. It therefore qualified as a "casualty" within the meaning of section 165(e)(3). The Service acquiesced in the decision.[10]

Forseeability or negligence (other than gross negligence) will not take an occurrence outside the ambit of "other casualty." In *Heyn v. Commissioner*,[11] a case involving a loss caused by landslide, the Tax Court noted:

> [F]orseeability may be a circumstance to be taken into account in determining whether a particular event is a casualty. But forseeability

---

[6] T.C. Memo. 1966-228.

[7] *Id.*

[8] *See, e.g.,* Treas. Reg. § 1.165-7(a)(3).

[9] 48 T.C. 430 (1967); Rev. Rul. 72-592, 1972-2 C.B. 101.

[10] Rev. Rul. 72-592, 1972-2 C.B. 101.

[11] 46 T.C. 302, 307–8 (1966).

alone is not conclusive. Meteorological forecasts may well forewarn a cautious property owner to take protective measures against an oncoming hurricane, but any ensuing losses may nevertheless be storm or casualty losses within the meaning of the law. Nor is negligence a decisive factor. Automobile accidents are perhaps the most familiar casualties today. Yet the owner of the damaged vehicle is not deprived of a casualty loss deduction merely because his negligence may have contributed to the mishap. . . .

We are unable to perceive any distinction between a casualty loss arising from an automobile collision and one resulting from a landslide. Certainly, in the absence of gross negligence, the mere fact that the automobile owner negligently failed to have faulty brake linings replaced or that he negligently took a calculated risk in driving with smooth tires would not deprive him of a casualty loss if his vehicle were damaged in an accident occurring as a result of either of those conditions. The accident would nonetheless qualify as a casualty, notwithstanding the owner's negligence or that the accident was the consequence of his having taken a calculated risk in respect of known hazards. And it seems clear to us that petitioner's position in respect of the landslide is no weaker.[12]

As noted above, Revenue Ruling 72-592 provides that "to be 'sudden' the event must be one that is swift and precipitous and not gradual or progressive." Consistent with that definition, the Service has ruled that, when a water heater bursts from rust and corrosion over a period of time, the damage to the water heater itself is not a casualty, but the resulting rust and water damage to rugs, carpet and drapes will qualify as a casualty loss under Section 165(c)(3).[13]

Perhaps the most interesting and contentious cases regarding "suddenness" are those addressing the impact of insects or disease. The Service has ruled that damage caused by termites to property does not constitute a casualty loss because it lacks the requisite "suddenness" comparable to fire, storm and shipwreck.[14] The ruling, reversing the Service's prior position allowing a deductible casualty loss for damage caused by termites up to 15 months after infiltration, stated that:

. . . [Termite] damage is the result of gradual deterioration through a steadily operating cause and is not the result of an identifiable event of a sudden, unusual or unexpected nature. Further, time elapsed between the incurrence of damage and its ultimate discovery is not a proper measure to determine whether the damage resulted from a casualty. Time of discovery of the damage, in some situations, may affect the extent of the damage, but this does not change the form or the nature of the event, the mode of its operation, or the character of the result. These characteristics are determinative when applying Section 165(c)(3) of the Code.[15]

---

[12] *Id.* at 307–8.

[13] Rev. Rul. 70-91, 1970-1 C.B. 37.

[14] Rev. Rul. 63-232, 1963-2 C.B. 97.

[15] *Id.*

By contrast, the Service has ruled that the loss from the death of 40 ornamental pine trees over a 5- to 10-day period, caused by a mass attack of southern pine beetles, was a casualty loss.[16] The ruling noted that, in addition to being sudden, the event was also "unusual and unexpected" since there had been no previous epidemic attacks in the area.

Compare Revenue Ruling 79-174 with *Maher v. Commissioner*.[17] *Maher* involved the death of ornamental palm trees following their infection by insects with lethal yellowing, a disease that kills palm trees in an average of 9 to 10 months. When the palm trees were infected and the disease became apparent, there was no treatment for, nor precautionary measures against, the disease. In denying a casualty loss deduction, the Tax Court reasoned the suddenness of the loss itself, not the suddenness of its onset, determines whether the suddenness requirement is met. The lapse of time from infection to the death of the trees indicated not a sudden loss, but a loss resulting from gradual deterioration. In affirming the Tax Court decision, the U.S. Court of Appeals for the Eleventh Circuit noted that disease has not been treated as falling within the "other casualty" category of Section 165(c)(3), acknowledging, however, that the line between diseases and other causes may be arbitrary.

Revenue Ruling 87-59[18] relied upon *Maher* in addressing whether a taxpayer could claim a casualty loss associated with the worthlessness of pine trees killed by southern pine beetles. As noted by the Service in the ruling:

> The killing of the pine trees by the southern pine beetles had no immediate effect on the usefulness of the timber because the beetles do not appreciably damage wood. The death of the trees, however, rendered them vulnerable to wood-destroying organisms that gradually caused the deterioration of the wood in the uncut trees and eventually rendered the timber worthless . . . . The entire process occurred over a 9-month period. Applying the reasoning in *Maher* to a situation involving trees grown for timber rather than ornamental use, the period of time from the precipitating event, the beetle attack, to the identifiable event that fixes the loss, the bulldozing and burning of worthless timber, determines the suddenness of the timber loss, and the period of 9 months over which the damage occurred is not sufficiently sudden to indicate a casualty loss.

The Tax Court and other courts have required a showing of physical damage in order to establish a "casualty loss."[19] For example, a district court denied a casualty loss deduction to taxpayers who claimed that, as a result of avalanche risk, they not only were restricted in the use of their home during winter months but also suffered a loss in the appraisal value of their home due to buyer resistance.[20]

---

[16] Rev. Rul. 79-174, 1979-1 C.B. 99.

[17] 76 T.C. 593 (1981), aff'd, 680 F.2d 91 (11th Cir. 1982).

[18] 1987-2 C.B. 59.

[19] Chamales v. Comm'r, T.C. Memo 2000-33 (rejecting taxpayers' argument that a decrease in property value caused by publicity associated with O.J. Simpson, who owned a nearby home, was deductible as a casualty loss). Cf. Finkbohner v. U.S., 788 F.2d 723 (11th Cir. 1986).

[20] Lund v. U.S., 2000-1 USTC ¶ 50,234 (D. Utah 2000).

[B] Theft Losses

With respect to theft losses, the regulations provide that "theft" includes, but is not necessarily limited to, larceny, embezzlement and robbery.[21] The Service has ruled the illegal taking of property, done with criminal intent, constitutes theft for purposes of Section 165(c)(3), even though the act may not fall within the statutory definition of "theft" under state law.[22]

> **Example:** A taxpayer gave a substantial amount of money and property to two fortunetellers in New York, who told him that they could improve his health and solve his problems. They did neither and the taxpayer never was able to recover his money and property from them. May the taxpayer claim a theft loss deduction under Section 165(c)(3)?

> **Analysis:** In a case based on these facts, the Commissioner argued that even though fortune telling is a crime in New York, it did not constitute theft. Specifically, the Commissioner emphasized that the taxpayer could not establish the elements of larceny. The Tax Court, rejecting this argument, and holding for the taxpayer noted: "Theft covers a broad field of illegality including 'any criminal appropriation of another's property to the use of the taker, particularly including theft by swindling, false pretenses, and any other form of guile.' "[23]

In claiming a deduction for theft losses, however, the taxpayer must prove a theft has occurred; a mere mysterious disappearance of property does not suffice.[24] By contrast, the taxpayer need not prove who stole the property in question. According to the court, in *Jacobson v. Commissioner*, it is sufficient that "the reasonable inferences from the evidence point to theft rather than mysterious disappearance."[25] In that case, taxpayer was held to be entitled to a theft loss where property she stored in a home she no longer occupied but had previously shared with her estranged husband was removed from the home without her knowledge or consent and never recovered.

§ 24.02 TIMING OF THE LOSS

§ 165. Losses —

(a) **General rule — There shall be allowed as a deduction any loss sustained during the taxable year and not compensated for by insurance or otherwise.**

. . .

(e) **Theft losses — For purposes of subsection (a), any loss arising from theft shall be treated as sustained during the taxable year in which the taxpayer discovers such loss.**

---

[21] Treas. Reg. § 1.165-8(d).

[22] Rev. Rul. 72-112, 1972-1 C.B. 60.

[23] Kreiner v. Comm'r, T.C. Memo 1990-587.

[24] *See, e.g.*, Allen v. Comm'r, 16 T.C. 163 (1951).

[25] 73 T.C. 610, 613 (1979).

A casualty loss is deductible in the year sustained, while a theft loss is deductible in the year discovered. If there exists a claim for reimbursement with a "reasonable prospect" for recovery, allowance of the loss awaits the resolution of the claim with "reasonable certainty."[26]

§ 24.03   AMOUNT OF THE LOSS

(h)   Treatment of casualty gains and losses —

(1) $100 limitation per casualty — Any loss of an individual described in subsection (c)(3) shall be allowed only to the extent that the amount of the loss to such individual arising from each casualty, or from each theft, exceeds $100.

(2) Net casualty loss allowed only to the extent it exceeds 10 percent of adjusted gross income —

(A)   In general — If the personal casualty losses for any taxable year exceed the personal casualty gains for such taxable year, such losses shall be allowed for the taxable year only to the extent of the sum of —

(i) the amount of the personal casualty gains for the taxable year, plus

(ii) so much of such excess as exceeds 10 percent of the adjusted gross income of the individual.

(B)   Special rule where personal casualty gains exceed personal casualty losses — If the personal casualty gains for any taxable year exceed the personal casualty losses for such taxable year —

(i) all such gains shall be treated as gains from sales or exchanges of capital assets, and

(ii) all such losses shall be treated as losses from sales or exchanges of capital assets.

(3)   Definitions of personal casualty gain and personal casualty loss — For purposes of this subsection

(A)   Personal casualty gain — The term "personal casualty gain" means the recognized gain from any involuntary conversion of property which is described in subsection (c)(3) arising from fire, storm, shipwreck, or other casualty, or from theft.

(B)   Personal casualty loss — the term "personal casualty loss" means any loss described in subsection (c)(3). For purposes of paragraph (2), the amount of any personal casualty loss shall be determined after the application of paragraph (1).

The amount of a casualty loss under Section 165(c)(3) is the lesser of (1) the adjusted basis of the property; and (2) the difference between the fair market value of the property beforehand and the fair market value afterwards — that is, the amount of the decline in value.[27] For purposes of theft losses, the value afterwards

---

[26] *See* Treas. Reg. §§ 1.165-1(d)(2), (3), 1.165-8(a)(2).

[27] Treas. Reg. § 1.165-7(b)(1).

is presumed to be zero, and the "lesser of" rule becomes simply the lesser of the adjusted basis or the fair market value of the property before the theft.[28]

> **Example 1:** A diamond ring, purchased for $1,000, increases in value to $3,000, and is then stolen. The amount of the theft loss is only $1,000, the basis of the ring.

> **Example 2:** The family car, purchased for $10,000, declines in value to $4,000 and is then damaged beyond repair in an accident. The basis may be $10,000, but the amount of the casualty loss cannot exceed the $4,000 value.

The rule is different with respect to business or investment property; if such property is totally destroyed by casualty (or lost by theft), and if the adjusted basis of such property exceeds the value of the property immediately before the casualty (or theft), the amount of the adjusted basis is the amount of the loss; the "lesser of" rule does not apply.[29]

> **Example:** A truck used in a taxpayer's business is stolen. The truck's value at the time of its theft was $20,000 and its adjusted basis was $15,000. The theft loss allowable would be $15,000. If the fair market value of the truck were $10,000, the theft loss would still be $15,000, i.e., the amount of the taxpayer's adjusted basis.

The amount of the loss must, of course, be reduced by any reimbursements received and, pursuant to Section 165(h)(1), further reduced by $100. (Note that the $100 nondeductible floor is applied to each casualty or each theft, rather than to each item destroyed or stolen in a single casualty or theft.)[30] Once the personal casualty and theft losses for the year have been determined, they will be deductible to the extent of any personal casualty gains for the year.[31] (A personal casualty gain would typically arise when the insurance proceeds received following a casualty or theft loss exceed the taxpayer's basis in the property in question. Assume, for example, some jewelry, purchased previously for $1,000, is now worth $2,000, and is insured for that amount. An insurance payment of $2,000 following the theft of the jewelry would produce a $1,000 casualty gain for the taxpayer.) If personal casualty losses exceed personal casualty gains for the year, the net casualty loss is deductible only to the extent it exceeds 10% of the taxpayer's adjusted gross income.[32]

> **Example 1:** In two separate incidents, a taxpayer whose adjusted gross income is $20,000 sustains personal casualty losses in the amounts of $1,700 and $800, and has no personal casualty gains.

> **Analysis:** The resulting Section 165(c)(3) deduction would be only $300, since the total losses of $2,500 must be reduced first by $200 ($100 per casualty), and then further reduced by $2,000, 10% of adjusted gross income. If the taxpayer's adjusted gross income were $23,000, no deduction

---

[28] Treas. Reg. § 1.165-8(c).

[29] Treas. Reg. § 1.165-7(b)(1).

[30] *See* Treas. Reg. § 1.165-7(b)(4)(ii).

[31] I.R.C. §§ 165(h)(4)(A), 1211(b).

[32] I.R.C. § 165(h)(2)(A).

would be allowed under Section 165(c) — 10% of the taxpayer's adjusted gross income equals $2,300 which, when combined with the $200 reduction under Section 165(h)(1), completely offsets the $2,500 of losses.

Example 2: During a given year, as the result of separate incidents, a taxpayer sustains personal casualty losses in the amounts of $3,700 and $4,000 and a personal casualty gain of $1,500. Taxpayer's adjusted gross income for the year is $50,000.

Analysis: Taxpayer's Section 165(c)(3) deduction is computed as follows. First, reduce the $7,700 of total casualty losses by $200 ($100 per casualty per Section 165(h)(1)) to $7,500. Next, compute the amount of the excess of the taxpayer's personal casualty losses over the taxpayer's personal casualty gains. That excess is $6,000 (i.e., $7,500 [personal casualty losses after the Section 165(h)(1) reduction] less $1,500 [the amount of the personal casualty gain]. Finally, compute the sum of (1) the taxpayer's personal casualty gains for the year ($1,500 in this example) and (2) so much of the $6,000 excess computed above that exceeds 10% of taxpayer's $50,000 adjusted gross income ($1,000 in this example, i.e., $6,000 less $5,000 (10% of $50,000). That sum — $2,500 — is the taxpayer's Section 165(c)(3) deduction for the year.

A casualty loss or gain is generally characterized as an "ordinary loss" or "ordinary gain" rather than as a "capital gain" or "capital loss." (Even if the property involved is a capital asset, the casualty or theft loss does not produce the "sale or exchange" required for capital gain or loss status.)[33] However, in the event personal casualty gains for the year exceed personal casualty losses, all such gains and losses are treated as capital gains and losses.[34] Capital gains and losses are discussed in detail in Chapter 31.

§ 24.04   INSURANCE COVERAGE

§ 165.   Losses —

(h)   Treatment of casualty gains and losses —

(4)   Special rules. —

(E)   Claim required to be filed in certain cases. — Any loss of an individual described in subsection (c)(3) to the extent covered by insurance shall be taken into account under this section only if the individual files a timely insurance claim with respect to such loss.

A casualty or theft loss, to the extent covered by insurance, may be taken into account only if a timely insurance claim is filed.[35] This provision overruled prior case law permitting a deduction where the taxpayer suffered a loss covered by insurance, but declined to file a claim for fear the insurance would be canceled.

---

[33] I.R.C. § 1222.

[34] I.R.C. § 165(h)(2)(B).

[35] I.R.C. § 165(h)(4)(E).

Insurance compensation for increased living expenses occasioned by casualty to one's personal residence is excluded from income.[36]

---

[36] I.R.C. § 123.

Chapter 25

MEDICAL EXPENSES

§ 213. Medical, dental, etc. expenses.

(a) Allowance of deduction. There shall be allowed as a deduction the expenses paid during the taxable year, not compensated for by insurance or otherwise, for medical care of the taxpayer, his spouse, or a dependent (as defined in section 152, determined without regard to subsections (b)(1), (b)(2), and (d)(1)(B) thereof), to the extent that such expenses exceed 10% of adjusted gross income.

(b) Limitation with respect to medicine and drugs. An amount paid during the taxable year for medicine or a drug shall be taken into account under subsection (a) only if such medicine or drug is a prescribed drug or is insulin.

. . .

(d) Definitions. — For purposes of this section —

(1) the term "medical care" means amounts paid —

(A) for the diagnosis, cure, mitigation, treatment, or prevention of disease, or for the purpose of affecting any structure or function of the body,

(B) for transportation primarily for and essential to medical care referred to in subparagraph (A),

(C) for qualified long-term care services. . . .

(D) for insurance . . . covering medical care referred to in subparagraphs (A) and (B) or for any qualified long-term care insurance contract . . . .

(2) Amounts paid for certain lodging away from home treated as paid for medical care. Amounts paid for lodging (not lavish or extravagant under the circumstances) while away from home primarily for and essential to medical care referred to in paragraph (1)(A) shall be treated as amounts paid for medical care if —

(A) the medical care referred to in paragraph (1)(A) is provided by a physician in a licensed hospital (or in a medical care facility which is related to, or the equivalent of, a licensed hospital), and

(B) there is not significant element of personal pleasure, recreation, or vacation in the travel away from home.

The amount taken into account under the preceding sentence shall not exceed $50 for each night for each individual.

§ 25.01   DEDUCTIBILITY OF MEDICAL EXPENSES

Section 213 provides a deduction for uncompensated medical expenses of the taxpayer and taxpayer's spouse and dependents to the extent the expenses exceed 10% of adjusted gross income.[1] The deduction is allowed only for expenses "actually paid" during the year.[2] Section 213 is an exception to the general rule of Section 262 prohibiting the deduction of personal expenses, but the exception is a limited one by virtue of the 10% nondeductible floor amount. The floor amount effectuates the congressional purpose of providing some relief to those individuals who sustain extraordinary unreimbursed medical expenses, but not to those whose medical expenses are judged to fall within more normal bounds. This limited provision is in contrast to the total statutory exclusions from income for employer-provided medical insurance premiums[3] and medical care expense reimbursement.[4]

The medical expense deduction has been part of the Code since 1942. As originally enacted, and for a number of years thereafter, the deduction was subject to varying maximum annual limitations, but these ceiling limitations have long since been removed.

[A]   Medicine and Drugs

At one time, expenditures for drugs and medicine were taken into account for purposes of the Section 213 deduction only to the extent such expenditures exceeded 1% of adjusted gross income. In 1984, this separate nondeductible amount for medicine and drugs was eliminated; at the same time, however, the category of qualifying medicine and drugs was considerably narrowed and now consists only of prescription drugs and insulin.[5] A "prescribed drug" means a drug or biological which requires a prescription of a physician for its use by an individual".[6]

> **Example 1:** Sara purchases birth control pills prescribed by a physician. May she deduct the cost of the prescription?
>
> **Analysis:** The Service ruled, long before the 1984 changes in Section 213, that a taxpayer may deduct the costs incurred in purchasing prescribed birth control pills.[7] The 1984 legislation narrows the scope of the medical expense deduction by eliminating a deduction for all but those drugs prescribed by an individual's physician as well as insulin. The birth control pills are deductible because they are a "prescribed drug."

---

[1] I.R.C. § 213(a). The 10% nondeductible floor takes effect for tax years beginning after December 31, 2012, except that for taxpayers 65 or older the nondeductible floor is 7.5% of adjusted gross income through 2016. From 1987 through 2012, the nondeductible floor percentaqge was 7.5% for all taxpayers.

[2] Treas. Reg. § 1.213-1(a)(1).

[3] I.R.C. § 106(a).

[4] I.R.C. § 105(b).

[5] I.R.C. § 213(b).

[6] I.R.C. § 213(d)(3).

[7] Rev. Rul. 73-200, 1973-1 C.B. 140.

Example 2: Kevin, as part of a New Year's resolution, begins a regimen of regular exercise, healthy eating, and use of a range of herbal treatments and vitamin supplements. The herbal treatments and vitamin supplements are all purchased "over the counter." May Kevin deduct their cost as medical expenses? What result if a doctor had prescribed the vitamins?

Analysis: No. The vitamins and herbal supplements are not prescribed drugs within the meaning of the statute and are therefore nondeductible. Even if a doctor had prescribed the vitamins, the cost would be nondeductible. Legislative history makes clear that only drugs that legally require a prescription constitute "prescribed" drugs.[8] Thus, for example, the Service has held that, where an individual with an injured leg was taking aspirin, a nonprescription drug, on the recommendation of his doctor, the cost was nondeductible pursuant to Section 213(b); however, the ruling also held the costs of nonprescription equipment and supplies, such as crutches, would be deductible if they otherwise constituted medical care expenses.[9]

[B] Counseling Costs

The deductibility of counseling costs has raised issues, some of which the Service and courts have directly addressed. For example, the Service has ruled that marriage counseling costs were not deductible where the counseling did not prevent or alleviate a physical or mental defect, but rather improved the taxpayer's marriage.[10] Similarly, payments for spiritual guidance or counseling have been held nondeductible.[11] By contrast, the Service has held the cost of treatment for sexual inadequacy and incompatibility is deductible.[12] In one case, amounts paid for Navajo healing ceremonies called "sings" were held deductible expenses for one suffering from cancer.[13]

It is not the licensing or the qualifications of the practitioner that are determinative, but the primary purpose of the treatment. If the treatment is one for the purpose of preventing or alleviating a physical defect, the expense is one for medical care. Marital counseling regarding whether and when to have children, for

---

[8] Pub. L. 97-248, 97th Cong., 2d Sess., Conf. Rep., p. 476.

[9] Rev. Rul. 2003-58, 2003-22 I.R.B. 959. By way of contrast, Revenue Ruling 2003-102, 2003-38 I.R.B. 559, holds that under Section 105(b), discussed in Chapter 10, reimbursements by an employer of amounts paid by an employee for medicine and drugs (such as antacid, allergy medicine, pain relievers, and cold medicines) purchased without a physician's prescription are excludable from the employee's income. "Amounts, however, paid by an employee for dietary supplements that are merely beneficial to the general health of the employee or the employee's spouse or dependents, are not reimbursable or excludable from gross income under § 105(b)." Revenue Ruling 2003-102 distinguished Revenue Ruling 2003-58 by noting that "Section 105(b) specifically refers to 'expenses incurred by the taxpayer for . . . medical care' as defined in § 213(d). There is no requirement in § 105(b) that the expense be allowed as a deduction for medical care under § 213(a) or that only medicine or drugs that require a physician's prescription be taken into account."

[10] Rev. Rul. 75-319, 1975-2 C.B. 88.

[11] Miller v. Comm'r, T.C. Memo 1980-136.

[12] Rev. Rul. 75-187, 1975-1 C.B. 92.

[13] Tso v. Comm'r, T.C. Memo, 1980-399.

example, seems clearly nondeductible on the ground that it is not for the prevention or alleviation of a physical or mental defect. The answer will presumably be the same with respect to counseling dealing with "anger" — that is, treating anger would not likely to be regarded as treating a physical or mental defect. Treatment for depression, however, will be regarded as treatment for the prevention or alleviation of a mental "defect" or illness. Deductibility would thus seem to turn on whether the counseling was undertaken "primarily" for the prevention or alleviation of a mental defect or illness.

> **Example 1:** Bill paid $5,000 to a stop-smoking clinic in an effort to quit his smoking habit. Bill was prompted to take this action because his new employer prohibits employees from smoking on the premises. May Bill deduct the cost of the clinic as a medical expense?

> **Analysis:** In Publication 502,[14] the Service states: "You can include in medical expenses amount you pay for a program to stop smoking. However, you cannot include in medical expenses amounts you pay for drugs that do not require a prescription, such as nicotine gum or patches, that are designed to help stop smoking."

> **Example 2:** Marty, who is seriously overweight, has suffered from hypertension and heart disease. At his doctor's direction, Marty has enrolled in a weight loss program and is incurring significant monthly costs. May Marty deduct the cost of the program as a medical expense? What if Marty were not suffering the problems indicated, but undertook the weight loss program merely for purposes of maintaining his general health?

> **Analysis:** When Marty undertakes the weight loss program at the direction of his physician as treatment for a specific disease, Marty may deduct the costs of the program as medical expenses.[15] By contrast, Marty may not deduct the costs of the weight loss program when Marty undertakes the program voluntarily as a means of maintaining his general health.

[C]   Capital Expenditures

The regulations provide that capital expenditures, ordinarily nondeductible, may constitute a deductible medical expense where the primary purpose of the expenditure is medical care of the taxpayer, spouse or dependent.[16] The regulation embraces noncontroversial items such as hearing aids, wheelchairs and crutches, but it has also been the subject of numerous taxpayer efforts, sometimes successful, to deduct the cost of such home improvements as swimming pools and various special equipment that seem to have nonmedical as well as medical uses. Note, however, that, where an improvement increases the value of property, the regulations limit the deduction to the amount by which the cost of the improvement

---

[14]   I.R.S. Publication 502, p. 14 (2012).

[15]   *Id.* at 15. Similarly, one assumes that a taxpayer who is directed by his physician to lose a large amount of weight may be entitled to deduct the costs of joining a health club assuming that under the circumstances that would represent a reasonable means of achieving the desired medical benefits.

[16]   Treas. Reg. § 1.213-1(e)(1)(iii).

exceeds the increase in value. If an improvement increases the value of one's home by an amount equal to its cost, the cost will be nondeductible, but it will increase the taxpayer's basis in the home.[17]

Example: Maureen pays $20,000 for the installation of a lap pool in Maureen's home on a doctor's recommendation that regular swimming exercise would be beneficial for Maureen's arthritis. May Maureen deduct the cost of the pool? Assume that the lap pool increased the value of Maureen's home by only $12,000.

Analysis: If the cost of the pool is viewed as a medical expense, Maureen's deduction would be limited to $8,000. As noted above, a capital expenditure that qualifies as a medical expense is deductible only to the extent that the expenditure exceeds the increase in the value of the related property, *i.e.*, Maureen's home in this example. The Service is likely to accept a lap pool or exercise pool, not suitable for general recreational use, as a medical expense, where the taxpayer's physician has prescribed swimming to alleviate a physical defect or condition. The Service is likely to look much more closely at the typical indoor swimming pool. If more than incidental recreational use is made of the pool, if swimming is only one of a number of ways in which the taxpayer could obtain necessary physical exercise, if public swimming pools are readily accessible and would do just as well as the private pool — if, in other words, the evidence points to a primary purpose for the pool other than medical care, the deduction is likely to be denied. Thus, in this example, it would make a difference if Maureen established that (1) swimming was the most beneficial form of exercise for Maureen's arthritis; (2) that the $20,000 spent on a lap pool in her home was a reasonable amount to expend to achieve the desired medical benefits; and (3) the in-house pool was the most practical means of Maureen having access to regular swimming opportunities throughout the year.[18]

[D] Meals and Lodging

The cost of hospital care, including meals and lodging, constitutes a medical expense, and the regulations provide that similar results obtain for other qualifying "institutions," including "special schools."[19] Outside the institutional setting, the Service regards the cost of foods and beverage, including special diets, as a nondeductible personal expense, except when such special foods supplement, rather than substitute for, a normal diet, and are taken solely to alleviate or treat an illness.[20] The Tax Court, however, has held that the cost of special foods taken as

---

[17] *Id.*

[18] Assuming that $12,000 of the cost of the lap pool must be capitalized by adding it to the basis of the Maureen's home, Maureen will not be allowed to deduct the $12,000 capitalized amount by depreciating the pool. Weary v. U.S., 510 F.2d 435 (10th Cir. 1975). The court reasoned that Section 213 only allows a deduction for "amounts paid" for medical care. Depreciation, according to the court, is not an "amount paid" for purposes of Section 213.

[19] Treas. Reg. § 1.213-1(e)(1)(v).

[20] Rev. Rul. 55-261, 1955-1 C.B. 307.

a substitute for a normal diet may be deductible to the extent it exceeds the cost of a normal diet.[21]

Food and lodging expenses incurred while away from home for medical care were initially deductible. However, in *Commissioner v. Bilder*,[22] the Supreme Court interpreted the 1954 enactment of current Section 213(d)(1)(B) to deny a deduction for meals and lodging expenses incurred in Florida by a taxpayer with a grave heart ailment whose doctor had advised him to spend the winter season in a warm climate. Section 213(d)(2), added in 1984, relaxes this rule of nondeductibility, to a limited extent, with respect to certain lodging costs. This section was interpreted and applied in *Polyak v. Commissioner*[23] where the Tax Court denied a medical expense deduction to a taxpayer who had moved to Florida for the winter to alleviate her chronic heart and lung ailments. The Tax Court noted that Section 213(d)(2) was intended to equalize the tax treatment of inpatient and outpatient care for taxpayers required to seek medical care away from home. Because Ms. Polyak did not go to Florida to seek medical attention and did not receive medical treatment in a licensed hospital or its equivalent, the requirements of Section 213(d)(2) were not met and no deduction was allowed.

[E]   Illegal Operations or Treatment

Under the regulations, amounts expended for "illegal operations or treatment" are not deductible,[24] and the term "medicine and drugs" includes only items that are "legally procured."[25] The Tax Court applied this provision to deny a deduction for the cost of procuring prostitutes for therapy.[26] The Service relied on the provision to deny a deduction for amounts paid to obtain and use marijuana for medical purposes — even with a physician's prescription, even when permitted under state law — where under federal laws the possession of marijuana is illegal.[27]

At the same time, however, the deductibility of medical care does not depend on licensing or other qualifications of the medical care provider. "Medical care" is determined by the nature of the services rendered, rather than the qualifications of the practitioner.[28] Nursing services, for example, need not be rendered by licensed or trained nurses to be deductible, but they must nonetheless be medical in nature, within the meaning of Section 213.

---

[21] Randolph v. Comm'r, 67 T.C. 481 (1976).

[22] 369 U.S. 499 (1962).

[23] 94 T.C. 337 (1990).

[24] Treas. Reg. § 1.213-1(e)(1)(ii).

[25] Treas. Reg. § 1.213-1(e)(2).

[26] Halby v. Commissioner, T.C. Memo. 2009–204.

[27] Rev. Rul. 97-9, 1997-9 I.R.B. 1.

[28] Rev. Rul. 63-91, 1963-1 C.B. 54.

[F]   Qualified Long-Term Care

In general, services rendered must be medical in nature, rather than household or personal services, to constitute medical care. However, in 1996 Congress provided that amounts paid for "qualified long-term care services" constitute medical care, although certain payments made to relatives for such services may not qualify.[29] Qualified long-term care services include not only diagnostic, therapeutic, treating, etc. services, but maintenance and care services as well, required by a chronically ill individual under a plan of care prescribed by a physician or certain other licensed professionals.[30] While the payment of medical insurance premiums ordinarily constitutes medical care under Section 213, only a limited amount of the premiums paid for long-term care insurance will qualify as medical care. For example, in the case of an individual who is 40 or younger, only $200 per year of premiums for long term care insurance will qualify for deduction while premiums up to $2,500 per year will be deductible by an individual who is more than 70 years old.[31]

[G]   Transportation Expenses

By statute, transportation expenses are deductible, if incurred "primarily for and essential to" medical care.[32] For example, car expenses, taxi fares, bus, railroad, and train fares incurred primarily for the rendition of medical services are allowable medical care expenses. "Transportation expenses of a parent who must go with a child who needs medical care" are deductible as are "transportation expenses of a nurse or other person who can give injections, medications, or other treatment required by a patient who is traveling to get medical care and is unable to travel alone." Also deductible are "transportation expenses for regular visits to see a mentally ill dependent if these visits are recommended as a part of [the dependent's] treatment."[33]

The statute does not specifically address the deductibility of the costs of meals and lodging incurred on the way to and from the site where the medical care is rendered; the deductibility of these items is open to question.[34] Prior to the enactment of that section, the Sixth Circuit, affirming a Tax Court decision, found such in-transit meals and lodging costs includable as "transportation" expenses.[35] The Service has not accepted this view. The enactment of Section 213(d)(2) may call into question the viability of the Sixth Circuit's rule.

---

[29]   I.R.C. § 213(d)(1)(C), (d)(11).

[30]   *See* I.R.C.§ 7702B(c).

[31]   I.R.C. § 213(d)(1)(D) (flush language), (d)(10). These amounts are indexed for annual adjustments.

[32]   I.R.C. § 213(d)(1)(B).

[33]   I.R.S. Publication 502, p. 14 (2011).

[34]   I.R.C. § 213(d)(2).

[35]   Montgomery v. Comm'r, 428 F.2d 243 (6th Cir. 1970).

§ 25.02   MEDICAL vs. PERSONAL EXPENSES

Section 213 has occasioned considerable litigation (which undoubtedly has been curtailed significantly by the higher nondeductible floor amount), primarily over the issue of whether the expense in question was a medical expense or a nondeductible personal expense. The statutory definition of "medical care" is a broad one. The usual medical expenditures will clearly qualify as amounts paid for "diagnosis, cure, mitigation, treatment, or prevention of disease, or for the purpose of affecting any structure or function of the body;"[36] as noted above, the definition also extends to medically related transportation costs,[37] qualified long-term care services,[38] and medical insurance,[39] and to certain lodging costs away from home for medical care.[40]

It is nonetheless inevitable that some expenditures, arguably motivated by medical concerns, also appear to address nonmedical needs and thus raise questions of deductibility. The regulations, on this point, flesh out the statute to some degree by providing that deductions shall be limited to expenses incurred "primarily" to prevent or alleviate physical or mental defects or illness, and will not extend to expenses that are "merely beneficial to . . . general health."[41] This guideline is useful, but it clearly leaves room for considerable debate. The Tax Court has interpreted the statute "as requiring a causal relationship in the form of a 'but for' test between a medical condition and the expenditures incurred in treating that condition, [requiring the taxpayer to prove] the expenditures were an essential element of the treatment and . . . would not have otherwise have been incurred for nonmedical reasons.[42]

Note that Section 213(d)(1)(A) is phrased disjunctively and also allows a deduction for amounts paid "for the purpose of affecting any structure or function of the body." The Service had therefore interpreted "medical care" to include elective procedures such as cosmetic surgery, *e.g.*, face-lift operations, removal of hair by electrolysis, etc., on the theory that these procedures affected a structure or function of the body.[43] In 1990, Congress, however, added Section 213(d)(9), which negates the deductibility of expenses incurred for cosmetic surgery and other similar procedures "unless the surgery or procedure is necessary to ameliorate a deformity arising from, or directly related to, a congenital abnormality, a personal injury resulting from an accident or trauma, or disfiguring disease." The legislative history indicates that the amount expended for insurance to cover the costs of cosmetic surgery of the nature described in Section 213(d)(9) will not be deductible, nor will reimbursement for such costs under a health plan provided by an employer

---

[36]   I.R.C. § 213(d)(1)(A).

[37]   I.R.C. § 213(d)(1)(B).

[38]   I.R.C. § 213(d)(1)(C).

[39]   I.R.C. § 213(d)(1)(D).

[40]   I.R.C. § 213(d)(2).

[41]   Treas. Reg. § 1.213-1(e)(1)(ii).

[42]   Magdalin v. Commissioner, T.C. Memo 2008–293, denying a deduction for certain expenses associated with fathering children through the use of unrelated gestational carriers.

[43]   Rev. Rul. 76-332, 1976-2 C.B. 81.

be excludable. Thus, the Service has held that amounts paid for breast reconstruction surgery following a mastectomy for cancer and amounts paid for vision correction surgery (laser eye surgery to correct myopia) are medical care expenses under Section 213(d) — such amounts, respectively, ameliorate a deformity directly related to a disease, and correct a bodily dysfunction; in contrast, amounts paid by individuals to whiten teeth discolored as a result of age are not medical care expenses under that section, but are instead expenses designed to improve appearance.[44] But the Tax Court has concluded that gender identity disorder was a disease for purposes of Section 213(d) and thus allowed a deduction for the costs of hormone therapy and sex reassignment surgery incurred by a taxpayer diagnosed with gender identity disorder.[45] The court, however, refused to allow a deduction for the taxpayer's breast augmentation surgery.

The Service holds the costs of a legal abortion, of in vitro fertilization (including temporary storage of eggs or sperm), of a legal sterilization or vasectomy and surgical reversals thereof are deductible.[46]

---

[44] Rev. Rul. 2003-57, 2003-22 I.R.B. 959.

[45] O'Donnabhain v. Commissioner, 134 T.C. 34 (2010).

[46] I.R.S. Publication 502, pp. 5, 8, 14–15 (2012).

Chapter 26

CHARITABLE DEDUCTIONS

§ 26.01 IN GENERAL

Charitable giving has tax-favored status. Although personal in nature, gifts to charities can be tax deductible. In allowing a deduction for charitable contributions, Congress seeks to encourage private support for a range of activities and organizations that "aid in the accomplishment of many social goals which our federal and local governments otherwise cannot or will not accomplish."[1] Rather than the government deciding which causes are worthy of support, the government uses the tax laws to encourage the taxpayers to make that decision. In effect, because of the charitable deduction, the taxpayer contributing to a charity makes the government a partner in supporting the charitable enterprise. For example, as a result of the charitable deduction, a taxpayer in a 35% tax bracket who has itemized deductions in excess of the standard deduction and contributes $1,000 to a religious organization will only be out-of-pocket $650. The other $350 received by the religious organization may be viewed as the government's contribution in the nature of foregone tax revenue. By assuming part of the cost of a charitable gift, the government encourages charitable giving.

§ 26.02 REQUIREMENTS FOR CHARITABLE DEDUCTIONS

§ 170. Charitable, etc., contributions and gifts —

(a) Allowance of deduction —

(1) General rule — There shall be allowed as a deduction any charitable contribution (as defined in subsection (c)) payment of which is made within the taxable year. A charitable contribution shall be allowable as a deduction only if verified under regulations prescribed by the Secretary.

The charitable deduction made its initial appearance in the tax code in 1917 as a relatively simple provision. In its entirety, the original provision read as follows:

[I]n computing net income in the case of a citizen or resident of the United States, . . . there shall be allowed as deductions . . . contributions or gifts actually made within the year to corporations or associations organized and operated exclusively for religious, charitable, scientific, or educational purposes, or to societies for the prevention of cruelty to children or animals, no part of the net income of which inures to the benefit of any private stockholder or individual, to an amount not in excess of

---

[1] Brinley v. Comm'r, 782 F.2d 1326, 1336 (5th Cir. 1986) (Hill, J., dissenting).

fifteen per centum of the taxpayer's taxable net income as computed without the benefit of this paragraph. Such contributions or gifts shall be allowable as deductions only if verified under rules and regulations prescribed by the Commissioner of the Internal Revenue, with the approval of the Secretary of the Treasury.

By contrast, the charitable deduction in its current form in Section 170 is a complex maze of rules limiting the deduction taxpayers may claim. The 1917 provision and the current provision, however, both impose similar requirements; *i.e.*, to be deductible a charitable transfer must:

(1)   be made to or for the use of a qualified recipient;

(2)   constitute a transfer of money or property made with no expectation of a return benefit;

(3)   actually be *paid* to the recipient within the taxable year for which the deduction is claimed;

(4)   not exceed certain percentage limitations; and

(5)   be substantiated by a contemporaneous written acknowledgment prepared by the donee organization and provided to the donor for any contribution of $250 or more (Section 170(f)(8)) or otherwise verified as required by regulations.

The determination of the amount of a charitable deduction depends on a variety of factors including: the nature of the contribution, *e.g.*, cash, tangible personal property, real property, intangible property, or services; the character of the property, *e.g.*, long or short-term capital gain property or ordinary income property; the recipient of the transfer, *e.g.*, a public charity or a private foundation; the use the recipient will make of the property, *e.g.*, immediate sale or use for tax exempt purposes; the form of the transfer, *e.g.*, outright or in trust; and the nature of the interest given, *e.g.*, undivided interest, future interest, etc.

[A] Who Is a Qualified Recipient?

§ 170. Charitable, etc., contributions and gifts —

(c) Charitable contribution defined — For purposes of this section, the term "charitable contribution" means a contribution or gift to or for the use of —

(1) A State, a possession of the United States, or any political subdivision of any of the foregoing, or the United States or the District of Columbia, but only if the contribution or gift is made for exclusively public purposes.

(2) A corporation, trust, or community chest, fund, or foundation —

(A) created or organized in the United States or in any possession thereof, or under the law of the United States, any State, the District of Columbia, or any possession of the United States;

(B) organized and operated exclusively for religious, charitable, scientific, literary, or educational purposes, or to foster national or international amateur sports competition (but only if no part of its activities involve the

provision of athletic facilities or equipment), or for the prevention of cruelty to children or animals;

(C) no part of the net earnings of which inures to the benefit of any private shareholder or individual; and

(D) which is not disqualified for tax exemption under section 501(c)(3) by reason of attempting to influence legislation, and which does not participate in, or intervene in (including the publishing or distributing of statements), any political campaign on behalf of (or in opposition to) any candidate for public office.

A contribution or gift by a corporation to a trust, chest, fund, or foundation shall be deductible by reason of this paragraph only if it is to be used within the United States or any of its possessions exclusively for purposes specified in subparagraph (B).

(3) A post or organization of war veterans, or an auxiliary unit or society of, or trust or foundation for, any such post or organization —

(A) organized in the United States or any of its possessions, and

(B) no part of the net earnings of which inures to the benefit of any private shareholder or individual.

(4) In the case of a contribution or gift by an individual, a domestic fraternal society, order, or association, operating under the lodge system, but only if such contribution or gift is to be used exclusively for religious, charitable, scientific, literary, or educational purposes, or for the prevention of cruelty to children or animals.

(5) A cemetery company owned and operated exclusively for the benefit of its members, or any corporation chartered solely for burial purposes as a cemetery corporation and not permitted by its charter to engage in any business not necessarily incident to that purpose, if such company or corporation is not operated for profit and no part of the net earnings of such company or corporation inures to the benefit of any private shareholder or individual.

For purposes of this section, the term "charitable contribution" also means an amount treated under subsection (g) as paid for the use of an organization described in paragraph (2), (3), or (4).

Section 170 allows a deduction for gifts or contributions to or for the use of a broad range of entities listed in Section 170(c). Among the entities listed are the United States, the states and political subdivisions thereof, as well as religious, charitable, scientific, literary or educational organizations. The Internal Revenue Service publishes a "Cumulative List of Organizations Described in Section 170(c)" to assist taxpayers in identifying organizations, contributions to which will be deductible.

The various requirements of Section 170 which must be met before an entity will qualify as an appropriate recipient of contributions reflect congressional concern that deductible contributions be limited to those which will be used for genuinely charitable purposes. Thus, for an organization to qualify as a Section 170(c) organization, it must be organized and operated exclusively for religious, charitable, or other specified purposes,[2] its net earnings cannot inure to the benefit of any private shareholder or individual,[3] and its lobbying and political activities must be limited.[4]

A review of the qualified recipients listed in Section 170(c) indicates that in no event will an individual be a qualified recipient. That limitation is appropriate since the charitable deduction is premised on the notion that amounts contributed to charity provide some societal benefit. A contribution benefitting only an individual is not a charitable contribution within the meaning of Section 170(c). For example, in *Tripp v. Commissioner*,[5] the Fifth Circuit denied a charitable deduction to a donor who specified that amounts he "contributed" to a college's scholarship fund were to be used for a particular individual. The college had not awarded any scholarships or other assistance to the student, and it simply credited the payments to the student's account as directed by the donor. That the college actually received the money from the donor was not itself enough to establish the gift as a charitable contribution to or for the use of a qualified recipient. Rather, the court held that the college was merely a conduit for, and not the intended beneficiary of, the gift. If, by contrast, Tripp's donation had been intended for a common scholarship pool to be distributed as the college determined, and Tripp had merely expressed a desire that the money be used for a specific student, a charitable deduction would have been appropriate.[6] Thus, while a contribution to a charitable organization, *e.g.*, a college, may ultimately benefit a particular individual, *e.g.*, the student who receives a scholarship, the organization and not the individual is the actual donee.

The decision in *Davis v. United States*,[7] presents an excellent example of the close questions courts have had to resolve with respect to the qualified recipient standard. The Supreme Court in *Davis* considered the appropriate interpretation of the statutory requirement that a gift purporting to be charitable must be given "to or for the use of" a qualified recipient. The taxpayers' sons served as full-time unpaid missionaries for two years for the Church of Jesus Christ of Latter-Day Saints. Consistent with Church practice, the taxpayers, as parents of the missionaries, provided the financial support necessary for their sons' missionary service, based on guidelines provided by the Church. The taxpayer-parents transferred funds to their sons' checking accounts, which the sons drew on as necessary during their missionary service. The parents subsequently claimed a charitable deduction on the basis that the transfers to their sons' accounts were charitable contributions "for the use of" the Church, or alternatively, that they were deductible as unreimbursed expenses incident to the rendering of services to a charitable organization.[8]

---

[2] I.R.C. § 170(c)(2)(B).

[3] I.R.C. § 170(c)(2)(C).

[4] I.R.C. § 170(c)(2)(D).

[5] 337 F.2d 432 (5th Cir. 1964).

[6] Peace v. Comm'r, 43 T.C. 1 (1964).

[7] 495 U.S. 472 (1990).

[8] *Cf.* Treas. Reg. § 1.170(A)-1(g).

The Supreme Court held for the government. Based on its review of the legislative and administrative history of Section 170, the Court concluded that a gift is "for the use of" a qualified organization "when it is held in a legally enforceable trust for the qualified organization or in a similar legal arrangement." The missionaries' checking accounts obviously did not meet this test. As for the alternative claim that the transferred funds were deductible as unreimbursed expenses for services rendered on behalf of the Church, the Court held that only the person rendering the services could claim the deduction for unreimbursed expenses. The parents could not claim the deduction because they had not rendered the services to the Church. Hence, the parents had not made a contribution "to or for the use of" the Church.

Consistent with the "to or for the use of" requirement in Section 170, as elaborated in *Davis*, a taxpayer who contributes cash or property to a trust for the benefit of a charitable organization is entitled to a charitable deduction.

[B]   What Is a "Contribution" or "Gift"?

In *Commissioner v. Duberstein*,[9] the Supreme Court, defining the term "gift" as used in Section 102, noted: "[a] gift in the statutory sense . . . proceeds from a detached and disinterested generosity, . . . out of affection, respect, admiration, charity or like impulses. And in this regard, the most critical consideration . . . is the transferor's 'intention.'" The *Duberstein* gift standard has generally been applied in determining whether a charitable contribution has been made.[10] Given this standard, a donor who expects to benefit directly from the transfer will generally not satisfy the Section 170 requirement of a "charitable contribution."

Consistent with the *Duberstein* analysis, Revenue Ruling 83-104,[11] provides: "A contribution for purposes of section 170 of the Code is a voluntary transfer of money or property that is made with no expectation of procuring a financial benefit commensurate with the amount of the transfer." That ruling examines six different situations in which parents contribute to an organization operating a private school attended by their child. According to that ruling, the determination of whether the contributions qualified as charitable contributions:

> . . . depends upon whether a reasonable person, taking all the facts and circumstances of the case into account, would conclude that enrollment in the school was in no manner contingent upon making the payment, that the payment was not made pursuant to a plan (whether express or implied) to convert nondeductible tuition into charitable contributions, and that receipt of the benefit was not otherwise dependent upon the making of the payment.

> In determining this issue, the presence of one or more of the following factors creates a presumption that the payment is not a charitable contribution: the existence of a contract under which a taxpayer agrees to

---

[9]   363 U.S. 278, 285 (1960).

[10]   *See, e.g.*, Allen v. U.S., 541 F.2d 786 (9th Cir. 1976).

[11]   1983-2 C.B. 46.

make a "contribution" and which contains provisions ensuring the admission of the taxpayer's child; a plan allowing taxpayers either to pay tuition or to make "contributions" in exchange for schooling; the earmarking of a contribution for the direct benefit of a particular individual; or the otherwise-unexplained denial of admission or readmission to a school of children of taxpayers who are financially able, but who do not contribute.

In other cases, although no single factor may be determinative, a combination of several factors may indicate that a payment is not a charitable contribution. In these cases, both economic and noneconomic pressures placed upon parents must be taken into account. The factors that the Service ordinarily will take into consideration, but will not limit itself to, are the following: (1) the absence of a significant tuition charge; (2) substantial or unusual pressure to contribute applied to parents of children attending a school; (3) contribution appeals made as part of the admission or enrollment process; (4) the absence of significant potential sources of revenue for operating the school other than contributions by parents of children attending the school; and (5) other factors suggesting that a contribution policy has been created as a means of avoiding the characterization of payments as tuition.[12]

Revenue Ruling 83-104 thus emphasizes the importance of the intention of the transferor and the circumstances surrounding the particular transfer.

In *Hernandez v. Commissioner*,[13] the U.S. Supreme Court denied a Section 170 charitable deduction for fees paid to the Church of Scientology for special auditing and training sessions. The Supreme Court noted: "[t]he legislative history of the 'contribution or gift' limitation, though sparse, reveals that Congress intended to differentiate between unrequited payments to qualified recipients and payments made to such recipients in return for goods or services. Only the former were deemed deductible. . . . [T]hese payments were part of a quintessential quid pro quo exchange: in return for their money, [taxpayers] received an identified benefit, namely, auditing and training sessions."[14]

While the taxpayers in *Hernandez* conceded that they expected to receive specific amounts of auditing and training for their payments, they argued that the quid pro quo analysis urged by the Service was inappropriate where the benefits received by the taxpayer are purely religious in nature. The Supreme Court rejected that argument, finding no support in Section 170 for that position and warning that its adoption would "raise problems of entanglement between church and state." If the taxpayer's position were adopted, the Court speculated that similar claims might be made by other taxpayers regarding services provided by church-supported schools and hospitals.

Where a contribution is made to a charitable organization partly in consideration for goods or services, the regulations provide the following test for deductibility,

---

[12] *Id.*

[13] 490 U.S. 680 (1989).

[14] *Id.* at 691.

drawn from *United States v. American Bar Endowment*:[15] the donor must both intend to make, and in fact make, a payment in excess of the fair market value of the goods or services. The charitable contribution is then limited to the amount of the payment that exceeds that value.[16] For this purpose, goods and services of insubstantial value may be disregarded.[17]Revenue Ruling 67-246,[18] provides examples of the application of a donor-benefit standard in connection with admission to or other participation in charitable fundraising activities such as charity balls, banquets, etc.:

Example 1: M Charity sponsors a symphony concert for the purpose of raising funds for M's charitable programs. M agrees to pay a fee calculated to reimburse the symphony for hall rental, musicians, salaries, advertising costs, and printing of tickets. Under the agreement, M is entitled to all receipts from ticket sales. M sells tickets to the concert charging $25 for balcony seats and $75 for orchestra seats. These prices approximate the established admission charges for concert performances by the symphony orchestra. The tickets to the concert and the advertising material promoting ticket sales emphasize that the concert is sponsored by, and is for the benefit of M Charity.

Analysis: Although taxpayers who acquire tickets to the concert may think they are making a charitable contribution to or for the benefit of M Charity, no part of the payments made is deductible as a charitable contribution for Federal income tax purposes. Since the payments approximate the established admission charge for similar events, there is no gift.

Example 2: The facts are the same as in Example 1, except M Charity desires to use the concert as an occasion for the solicitation of gifts. It indicates that fact in its advertising material promoting the event, and fixes the payments solicited in connection with each class of admission at $100 for orchestra seats and $40 for balcony seats. The advertising and the tickets clearly reflect the fact that the established admission charges for comparable performances by the symphony orchestra are $75 for orchestra seats and $25 for the balcony seats, and that only the excess of the solicited amounts paid in connection with admission to the concert over the established prices is a contribution to M.

Analysis: Under these circumstances a taxpayer who makes a payment of $200 and receives two orchestra seat tickets can show that his payment exceeds the established admission charge for similar tickets to comparable performances of the symphony orchestra by $50. The circumstances also confirm that that amount of the payment was solicited as, and intended to be, a gift to M Charity. The $50, therefore, is deductible as a charitable contribution.

---

[15] 477 U.S. 105 (1986).

[16] Treas. Reg. § 1.170A-1(h)(1), (2).

[17] *See* Rev. Proc. 90-12, 1990-1 C.B. 471; Treas. Reg. § 1.170A-1(h)(3), -13(f)(8), (9).

[18] 1967-2 C.B. 104.

Example 3: A taxpayer pays $25 for a balcony ticket to the concert described in Example 1. This taxpayer had no intention of using the ticket when he acquired it and he did not, in fact, attend the concert.

Analysis: No part of the taxpayer's $25 payment to M Charity is deductible as a charitable contribution. The mere fact that the ticket to the concert was not used does not entitle the taxpayer to any greater right to a deduction than if he did use it. The same result would follow if the taxpayer had made a gift to of the ticket to another individual. If the taxpayer desired to support M, but did not intend to use the ticket to the concert, he could have made a qualifying charitable contribution by making a $25 payment to M and refusing to accept the ticket to the concert.

Section 6115 requires that most Section 170(c) organizations, upon the receipt of a "quid pro quo contribution" in excess of $75, inform the donor that the deductible contribution is limited to the amount by which the donor's contribution to the charity exceeds the value of the goods or services provided to the donor by the charity. Section 6115(b) defines a "quid pro quo contribution as a payment made in consideration of goods or services provided by the payor to the donee organization." There is an exception for religious organizations where taxpayers receive religious benefits not sold in commercial transactions. The Code also restricts the amount of the deduction available for taxpayers who contribute to an institution of higher education and, as a result of their contributions, receive the right to purchase "tickets for seating at an athletic event in an athletic stadium of such institution."[19] Only 80% of the amount contributed under that circumstance will be treated as a charitable contribution. Obviously, any amount given for actual payment of tickets to sporting events will not be deductible. In addition, it is generally required as a condition of deductibility that the taxpayer substantiate, by contemporaneous written acknowledgment from the donee, any contribution of $250 or more.[20] In 2004, Congress added Section 170(f)(12) placing limits on the amount of the charitable deduction for contributions of motor vehicles with a claimed value of over $500. In general, if the charity sells a vehicle donated to it without making any significant use of the vehicle or materially improving it, the charitable deduction is limited to the gross proceeds from the sale.

[C]   Actual Payment Required

Section 170(a)(1) allows a deduction for a contribution the "payment of which is made within the taxable year." That language contrasts with the "paid or incurred" language of Section 162(a) or the "paid or accrued language" of Section 163. Unlike those sections, Section 170 imposes a specific timing rule with respect to charitable deductions. "Any charitable contribution as defined in section 170(c), *actually paid* during the taxable year is allowable as a deduction in computing taxable income *irrespective of the method of accounting employed or of the date on which the contribution is pledged.*"[21]

---

[19] I.R.C. § 170(l).

[20] I.R.C. § 170(f)(8) (added in 1993).

[21] Treas. Reg. § 1.170A-1(a) (emphasis added).

The regulations provide: "a contribution is made at the time delivery is effected. The unconditional delivery or mailing of a check which subsequently clears in due course will constitute an effective contribution on the date of delivery or mailing."[22]

Example: Marcella, a calendar year taxpayer, pledges $500 to X Charity on June 15; Marcella mails a check for $500 to X Charity on December 31; X Charity receives the check January 3 of the following year and the check is honored by Marcella's bank.

Analysis: Marcella's June 15 pledge does not entitle her to a charitable deduction.[23] The mailing of the check on December 31 does. If Marcella had not mailed the check until January 3 of the following year, she would not be entitled to a deduction in the year the pledge was made but would be entitled to a deduction in the year when the check was mailed.

A taxpayer, who makes a contribution to a charity by means of a charge to the taxpayer's bank credit card, may claim a charitable deduction in the year the charge is made. The taxpayer may not postpone the deduction until the taxpayer actually pays the indebtedness resulting from the charge.[24]

[D]   Limitation on Charitable Deductions

§ 170.   Charitable, etc., contributions and gifts —

(b)   Percentage limitations —

(1)   Individuals — In the case of an individual, the deduction provided in subsection (a) shall be limited as provided in the succeeding subparagraphs.

(A)   General rule — Any charitable contribution to —

(i) a church or a convention or association of churches.

(ii) an educational organization which normally maintains a regular faculty and curriculum and normally has a regularly enrolled body of pupils or students in attendance at the place where its educational activities are regularly carried on,

(iii) an organization the principal purpose or functions of which are the providing of medical or hospital care or medical education or medical research, if the organization is a hospital, or if the organization is a medical research organization directly engaged in the continuous active conduct of medical research in conjunction with a hospital, and during the calendar year in which the contribution is made such organization is committed to spend such contributions for such research before January 1 of the fifth calendar year which begins after the date such contribution is made.

(iv) an organization which normally receives a substantial part of its support (exclusive of income received in the exercise or performance by such organization of its charitable, educational, or other purpose or function constituting the basis for exemption under section 501(a)) from the United

[22]   Treas. Reg. § 1.170A-1(b).
[23]   Mann v. Comm'r, 35 F.2d 873 (D.C. Cir. 1929).
[24]   Rev. Rul. 78-38, 1978-1 C.B. 67.

States or any State of political subdivision thereof or from direct or indirect contributions from the general public, and which is organized and operated exclusively to receive, hold, invest, and administer property and to make expenditures to or for the benefit of a college or university which is an organization referred to in clause (ii) of this subparagraph and which is an agency or instrumentality of a State or political subdivision thereof, or which is owned or operated by a State or political subdivision thereof or by an agency or instrumentality of one or more States or political subdivisions.

      (v) a governmental unit referred to in subsection (c)(1),

      (vi) an organization referred to in subsection (c)(2) which normally receives a substantial part of its support (exclusive of income received in the exercise or performance by such organization of its charitable, educational, or other purpose or function constituting the basis for its exemption under section 501(a)) from a governmental unit referred to in subsection (c)(1) or from direct or indirect contributions from the general public,

      (vii) a private foundation described in subparagraph (E) or

      (viii) an organization described in section 509(a)(2) or (3),

shall be allowed to the extent that the aggregate of such contributions does not exceed 50 percent of the taxpayer's contribution base for the taxable year.

      (B)   Other contributions — Any charitable contribution other than a charitable contribution to which subparagraph (A) applies shall be allowed to the extent that the aggregate of such contributions does not exceed the lesser of —

      (i) 30 percent of the taxpayer's contribution base for the taxable year, or

      (ii) the excess of 50 percent of the taxpayer's contribution base for the taxable year over the amount of charitable contributions allowable under subparagraph (A) determined without regard to subparagraph (C).

If the aggregate of such contributions exceeds the limitation of the preceding sentence, such excess shall be treated (in a manner consistent with the rules of subsection (d)(1)) as a charitable contribution (to which subparagraph (A) does not apply) in each of the 5 succeeding taxable years in order of time.

      . . .

      (F)   Contribution base defined — For purposes of this section the term "contribution base" means adjusted gross income (computed without regard to any net operating loss carryback to the taxable year under section 172).

      (2)   Corporations — In the case of a corporation, the total deductions under subsection (a) for any taxable year shall not exceed 10 percent of the taxpayer's taxable income computed without regard to —

      (A) this section,

      (B) part VIII (except section 248),

      (C) any net operating loss carryback to the taxable year under section 172, and

(D) any capital loss carryback to the taxable year under section 1212(a)(1).

The charitable deduction is not unlimited. Specifically, Section 170(b) caps the amount which taxpayers may deduct in any one year as a percentage of a taxpayer's contribution base. "Contribution base" essentially means adjusted gross income.[25] The 1917 charitable deduction provision imposed a cap equal to 15% of the taxpayer's contribution base. In 1969, Congress increased the cap to as much as 50% of a taxpayer's contribution base, thereby further encouraging charitable giving. Lower caps are imposed on contributions to organizations not listed in Section 170(b)(1)(A).[26] In addition, Section 170(b)(1)(C) imposes lower caps on so-called "capital gains property." Charitable contributions by corporations are limited to 10% of the corporation's taxable income.[27] The existence of a cap prevents a person from avoiding income tax by giving all income to charity. Note, however, that charitable contributions not currently deductible because of the percentage limitation may be carried over for a five-year period.[28] As these caps indicate, the amount of the charitable deduction depends on the type of taxpayer, the nature of the property contributed, and the nature of the donee organization. Detailed examination of these limitations is beyond the scope of this book.

§ 26.03 CONTRIBUTION OF SERVICES

The value of the services contributed to a charity are not deductible.[29]

> **Example:** Assume Terry, a musician, agrees to provide a benefit concert for his church. Although Terry would normally charge $10,000 for such a concert, he does not charge the church anything. He may not deduct the $10,000.

Upon careful consideration, the rationale for this rule becomes clear. Assume Terry was paid $10,000 for his services and later gave the church $10,000 as a contribution. Obviously, he would have $10,000 of gross income as a result of the compensation he received for his services and would be entitled to claim a $10,000 charitable deduction (assuming the percentage limitation discussed previously was not applicable). If Terry simply refuses payment in lieu of making a cash contribution, he should be in no better tax position than if he had received payment and later contributed that amount to the church. He should therefore either include $10,000 in income and claim a $10,000 charitable deduction or report no income and claim no deduction.

While the regulation authorizes a deduction for certain unreimbursed expenses incurred in providing services to charitable organizations, such as transportation costs or the cost of a uniform,[30] the regulation is not applicable to payments made

---

[25] I.R.C. § 170(b)(1)(F).

[26] *See* I.R.C. § 170(b)(1)(B), (C), (D).

[27] I.R.C. § 170(b)(2).

[28] I.R.C. § 170(d)(1)(A).

[29] Treas. Reg. § 1.170A-1(g).

[30] *Id. See, e.g.*, Van Dusen v. Commissioner, 136 T.C. 515 (2011) (unreimbursed expenses incurred by

to cover expenses incurred incident to *another* taxpayer's services to charity.[31]

§ 26.04   CONTRIBUTION OF APPRECIATED PROPERTY

§ 170.   Charitable, etc., contributions and gifts —

(e)   Certain contributions of ordinary income and capital gain property —

    (1)   General rule — The amount of any charitable contribution of property otherwise taken into account under this section shall be reduced by the sum of —

      (A) the amount of gain which would not have been long-term capital gain if the property contributed had been sold by the taxpayer at its fair market value (determined at the time of such contribution), and

      (B) in the case of a charitable contribution —

        (i) of tangible personal property, if the use by the donee is unrelated to the purpose or function constituting the basis for its exemption under section 501 (or, in the case of a governmental unit, to any purpose or function described in subsection (c)),

        (ii) to or for the use of a private foundation (as defined in section 509(a)), other than a private foundation described in subsection (b)(1)(E), or

        (iii) of any patent, copyright (other than a copyright described in section 1221(a)(3) or 1231(b)(1)(C)), trademark, trade name, trade secret, know-how, software . . . or similar property, or applications or registrations of such property,

the amount of gain which would have been long-term capital gain if the property contributed had been sold by the taxpayer at its fair market value (determined at the time of such contribution).

Generally, if a taxpayer contributes property (other than cash) to a charitable organization, the amount of the contribution will be the fair market value of the property.[32] The donor is not required to include in income the appreciation inherent in the donated property, *i.e.*, the donation of the property does not constitute a realization event. In other words, the taxpayer is not subject to tax on the appreciation and yet is allowed to take the appreciated value of the property into account in computing the amount of the charitable deduction. The tax benefits to the donor should be obvious.

> **Example:** Charlotte owns stock valued at $10,000 and in which she has a $5,000 adjusted basis. Assume that Charlotte wishes to make a $10,000 contribution to a charity.

> **Analysis:** If she sells the stock for $10,000 and gives the proceeds to the charity, she will be entitled to a $10,000 charitable deduction but will have

---

a taxpayer in providing foster care for about 70 feral cats were deductible. The Tax Court found that, in taking care of the feral cats, the taxpayer was providing a service to a § 501(c)(3) organization specializing in the neutering of feral cats.)

[31] Davis v. U.S., 495 U.S. 472 (1990).

[32] Treas. Reg. § 1.170A-1(c)(1).

to report $5,000 of income. By contrast, if she contributes the stock to the charity, she may claim a $10,000 charitable deduction, but will not be required to include anything in income. If Charlotte is in a 35% tax bracket, she would save $1,750 in taxes (*i.e.*, $5,000 × 0.35) by donating the stock rather than first selling it and then donating the proceeds of the sale. [Note that this result is inconsistent with the result in the example in § 26.03 involving contributed services.] Of course, when the charity sells the stock for $10,000 it is not taxable on the $5,000 of gain inherent in the stock because the charity is tax exempt.

In 1969, Congress, in an effort "to put the heart back into giving," enacted § 170(e) placing certain limitations on the general rule allowing a charitable deduction for the fair market value of donated property. Congress has subsequently expanded the scope of the § 170(e) limitations. Under current § 170(e), in the case of gifts of appreciated property, the charitable deduction will equal the difference between the fair market value of the property and the amount of the gain which would not have been so-called "long-term capital gain" if the property had been sold at its fair market value. § 170(e)(1)(A). In effect, this provision generally allows the taxpayer a deduction only in the amount of the taxpayer's adjusted basis in ordinary income property (*e.g.*, inventory, artistic works produced by the taxpayer) and in property that upon sale would produce so-called "short term capital gain."

Even in the case of a charitable contribution of property that would have produced long-term capital gain if it had been sold, the charitable deduction must be reduced if: (a) the property is tangible personal property and the use by the donee is unrelated to the donee's tax exempt purpose or function or, as discussed below, the property is disposed of within three years of the contribution; (b) the property is contributed to certain types of private foundations; or (c) the property is intellectual property or taxidermy property as specified by the statute.[33] Again, with respect to contributions of the properties specified in the preceding sentence, the deduction will be reduced by the amount of long-term capital gain that would have resulted in a sale of the property at fair market value; the taxpayer is, in effect, allowed a charitable deduction equal only to the taxpayer's adjusted basis in the contributed property.

In 2004, Congress amended Section 170(e)(1)(B) by adding (B)(iii), thereby effectively limiting the deduction for contributions of patents or other intellectual property to the taxpayer's basis in the contributed property. In addition, Congress added Section 170(m) allowing an additional charitable deduction based on a specified percentage of certain income received or accrued by the charitable donee with respect to the contributed intellectual property. Congress added Section 170(e)(1)(B)(iii) because of its concern that taxpayers contributing intellectual property were taking advantage of the difficulties associated with valuing such property and were claiming excessive charitable contribution deductions based on erroneously inflated valuations. Charities thus received assets of questionable value while the taxpayer/donor received a significant but unjustified tax benefit. Congress sought to address this perceived abuse by limiting the taxpayer's charitable deduction to the taxpayer's adjusted basis in the property contributed. At the same

[33] I.R.C. § 170(e)(1)(B).

time, Congress recognized that some contributions of intellectual property are economically beneficial to the charity. To provide an economic incentive for a taxpayer to make such contributions, Congress added Section 170(m) allowing additional charitable deductions to the taxpayer in the future if the intellectual property contributed by the taxpayer generated income for the charitable organization. The details of Section 170(m) are beyond the scope of this book.

Although Chapter 31 addresses in detail the measurement of long and short term capital gain and the distinction between capital gain and ordinary income, a brief discussion of capital gain is necessary here to understand the limitations of Section 170(e). Preferential tax treatment applies to certain gains known as long-term capital gains. Section 1222(3) defines "long-term capital gain" as "the gains from the sale or exchange of a capital asset held for more than 1 year." "Short-term capital gain" is defined in Section 1222(1) as "gain from the sale or exchange of a capital asset held for not more than 1 year." Section 1221 defines "capital asset" and provides that items such as inventory, literary and artistic compositions held by a taxpayer who created them, and accounts receivable for services performed are not capital assets. By contrast, the shares of stock held by Charlotte in the example above constitute capital assets which, upon sale or exchange, will generate capital gain.

The following examples demonstrate the application of the Section 170(e) rules:

Example 1: Laura, a well-known artist, contributes one of her paintings valued at $10,000 to an art museum for its permanent collection.

Analysis: Pursuant to Section 1221(3)(A), the painting is not a capital asset. Disregarding any supplies used by Laura, her basis in the donated painting is $0. As a result, under Section 170(e)(1)(A), Laura will not be entitled to claim any charitable deduction (*i.e.*, she must reduce her charitable deduction ($10,000) by the amount of gain which would not have been long term capital gain if she had sold the painting ($10,000)). This result is the same as if Laura had donated her services.

Example 2: Mary contributed to her church a painting worth $10,000. Mary purchased the painting five years ago for $1,000. Because it has no use for the painting, the church intends to sell it at its annual auction.

Analysis: The painting is a capital asset.[34] Had Mary sold the painting for $10,000, she would have reported $9,000 of long term capital gain. Under Section 170(e)(1)(B), since the use of the painting is unrelated to the church's tax exempt purposes, Mary's charitable deduction would be limited to $1,000, *i.e.*, her deduction (which but for Section 170(e)(1)(B) would have been equal to $10,000 or the fair market value of the painting) would be reduced by $9,000, the long term capital gain inherent in the painting. Mary is thus limited to a deduction equal to her adjusted basis in the painting.

---

[34] Since Mary did not produce the painting herself, it does not lose "capital asset" status under Section 1221(3).

Example 3: Assume the facts of Example 2, except that Mary contributed the painting to City Museum for its permanent collection.

Analysis: The painting is a capital asset. Had Mary sold the painting for $10,000, she would have reported $9,000 of long term capital gain. Since the use to which the museum plans to put the painting is related to the purpose or function constituting the basis for the museum's charitable exemption, Mary's charitable deduction will not be limited by Section 170(e)(1)(B). She is entitled to claim a $10,000 charitable deduction and the long term capital gain inherent in the painting remains untaxed.

Section 170(e)(1)(B)(i)(II) limits a taxpayer's deduction for a contribution of tangible personal property to the taxpayer's adjusted basis in the property if, before the end of the taxable year in which the contribution is made, the donee organization disposes of the property, the property was identified by the donee organization as being for a use related to its exempt function, and the property had a fair market value of more than $5,000. In addition, under Section 170(e)(7), if the disposition of the property described above occurs in a year subsequent to the year of contribution but within three years of the contribution, the donor must include in income (in the year of disposition by the donee organization) an amount equal to the excess (if any) of the amount of the deduction the donor was allowed over the donor's basis in the property at the time of the contribution. The deduction limitation rules of both Sections 170(e)(1)(B)(i)(II) and 170(e)(7) are inapplicable if the donee organization makes the certification (described in Section 170(e)(7)(D)) indicating that the property contributed was either actually used by the donee for its exempt purpose or that its use for that purpose became impossible or infeasible. These provisions are obviously intended to prevent an end run around the deduction limitations imposed by Section 170(e).

§ 26.05   CONTRIBUTIONS OF PARTIAL INTERESTS IN PROPERTY

In contributing property to charity, taxpayers will often retain an interest in the property for themselves or for some other individual or noncharitable entity. Section 170(f)(3)(A) generally provides a charitable contribution of any interest in property consisting of less than the donor's entire interest will not be deductible. (Section 170(f)(2) provides special rules allowing certain transfers in trust to qualify for the charitable deduction. These complex rules are beyond the scope of this book.) Regulation § 1.170A-7(a)(1), for example, notes "a contribution of the right to use property which the donor owns, *e.g.*, a rent-free lease, shall be treated as a contribution of less than the taxpayer's entire interest in such property." Thus, if the owner of a commercial building were to give a charity the rent-free use of part of the building, the owner would not be entitled to a charitable deduction. The same result occurs if the owner rents the building to a charity at a below-market rate of rent.

If, however, a taxpayer's only interest in property is a partial interest, *e.g.*, the taxpayer owns only a remainder interest in a tract of land, the contribution of that property interest to a qualifying charity will entitle the taxpayer to a charitable deduction.[35] Of course, the taxpayer may not purposely divide and transfer property in order to create such an interest and thereby avoid Section 170(f)(3)(A). For example, assume a taxpayer desires to contribute to a charity an income interest in certain rental property she owns. If the taxpayer transfers the remainder interest in such property to her son and immediately thereafter contributes the income interest to the charity, the taxpayer will not be entitled to a charitable deduction for the contribution of the taxpayer's entire interest consisting of only the retained income interest.[36]

Section 170(f)(3)(B) sets forth a number of important exceptions to the general rule of Section 170(f)(3)(A). A taxpayer will be entitled to a charitable deduction for (1) a contribution of a remainder interest in a personal residence or farm; (2) contributions of undivided portions of the taxpayer's entire interest in property; and (3) a contribution of a qualified conservation easement.

An undivided portion of a donor's entire interest in property must consist of a fraction or percentage of each substantial interest or right owned by the donor in the property and must extend over the entire term of the donor's interest.[37]

> **Example 1:** Mike owns 100 acres of timber land in northwestern Montana. He contributes 50 acres to the University of Montana Foundation (a qualified charity). Mike will be entitled to a deduction based upon the fair market value of the 50 acres he transferred to the Foundation.
>
> **Example 2:** Assume the same facts as Example 1, except Mike transfers title to the 100 acres to himself and to the University of Montana Foundation as tenants in common. Mike will be entitled to a charitable deduction based on the fair market value of the undivided one-half interest in the land he contributed to the Foundation.

Undivided gifts of a portion of a donor's entire interest in property are not subject to Section 170(a)(3), which provides that a charitable contribution consisting of a future interest in tangible personal property shall be treated as made only when all intervening interests in, and rights to actual possession or enjoyment of, the property have expired or are held by persons other than the taxpayer or related parties. Regulation § 1.170A-5(a)(2) provides:

> Section 170(a)(3) [has] no application in respect of a transfer of an undivided present interest in property. For example, a contribution of an undivided one-quarter interest in a painting with respect to which the donee is entitled to possession during three months of each year shall be treated as made upon the receipt by the donee of a formally executed and acknowledged deed of gift. However, the period of initial possession by the donee may not be deferred in time for more than one year.

This regulation suggests, for example, that a taxpayer (other than the artist) owning a valuable painting could give an undivided one-third interest in the painting

---

[35] Treas. Reg. § 1.170A-7(a)(2)(i).

[36] *Id.*

[37] Treas. Reg. § 1.170A-7(b)(1)(i).

to an art museum specifying that the museum has the unrestricted right to the use and possession of the painting during four months of the year. Under these circumstances, it would appear the taxpayer should be entitled to a charitable deduction based on the fair market value of the undivided one-third interest in the painting contributed to the museum. Congres in 2006, however, added § 170(o) significantly changing the law with respect to gifts of undivided interests in tangible personal properly such as the artwork in the above example.

Section 170(o) has three important parts. First, that section requires that immediately before the contribution all interest in the item is owned (1) by the donor or (2) by the donor and the donee organization. § 170(o)(1)(A). Second, § 170(o)(2) provides that, for purposes of determining the deductible amount of each subsequent contribution of an interest in the same item (*e.g.*, the owner of the painting gives another one-third interest in the painting to the same art museum the next year), the fair market value of the item for purposes of computing the charitable deduction will be the lesser of (1) the value used for purposes of determining the charitable deduction for the initial one-third contribution; or (2) the fair market value of the item at the time of the subsequent contribution. For example, assume the painting in our example had a fair market value of $150,000 at the time of the initial contribution and that the one-third interest was valued at $50,000. Assume that, when the owner made a second contribution of a one-third interest, the painting had a fair market value of $210,000. Under § 170(o)(2), the painting would be considered to be worth only $150,000 for purposes of calculating the deduction allowable on the second contribution. Third, § 170(o)(3) provides a recapture rule whereby the failure of a donor who has made an initial fractional contribution to contribute all of the donor's remaining interest in the item to the same donee before the earlier of 10 years from the initial fractional contribution or the donor's death results in the loss of all deductions the donor has taken with respect to contributions of that item (the deductions are "recaptured"). The effect of recapture is that the donor would be required to report income in the amount of the deductions claimed. Recapture will also be triggered if the donee fails to take substantial physical possession of the item or fails to use the item for an exempt purpose. Taken together, the changes made in § 170(o) make fractional contributions of tangible personal property far less attractive.

As noted above, Section 170(f)(3)(B)(i) allows a charitable deduction for a non-trust transfer of a remainder interest in a personal residence or farm. The retained present interest may be either a life estate or a term of years.[38] The term "personal residence" includes a vacation home or second home, *i.e.*, any home used a personal residence.[39]

> **Example:** Ellen, who is single and has no children, transfers the remainder interest in her home to a local college, the campus of which is adjacent to Ellen's home. Ellen will be entitled to a charitable deduction for the fair market value of the remainder interest in Ellen's home.

---

[38] Treas. Reg. § 1.170A-7(b)(3), (4).

[39] Treas. Reg. § 1.170A-7(b)(3).

Qualified conservation easements likewise qualify for a charitable deduction under Section 170(f)(3)(B)(iii). Detailed rules regarding qualified conservation easements are to be found in Section 170(h) and the regulations. These rules are beyond the scope of this book.

§ 26.06   BARGAIN SALE TO CHARITY

§ 1011.   Adjusted basis for determining gain or loss —

(b)   Bargain sale to a charitable organization — If a deduction is allowable under section 170 (relating to charitable contributions) by reason of a sale, then the adjusted basis for determining the gain from such sale shall be that portion of the adjusted basis which bears the same ratio to the adjusted basis as the amount realized bears to the fair market value of the property.

If a taxpayer sells appreciated property to a charity at a bargain price, Congress has provided a special rule requiring the apportionment of the basis between the charitable contribution and the sale.[40] As a result, the taxpayer may have to recognize a gain on the sale.

> **Example 1:** A taxpayer sells property worth $100,000 to a charity for $25,000 and claims a charitable deduction for the difference. The taxpayer has a $40,000 adjusted basis in the property.

> **Analysis:** The taxpayer will not be entitled to claim a loss deduction on the sale portion.[41] The taxpayer must apportion the property's adjusted basis between the gift and the sale; the taxpayer's adjusted basis for purposes of the sale will equal $25,000/$100,000 × $40,000 = $10,000. The taxpayer will therefore recognize gain of $15,000 — that is, his amount realized on the sale is $25,000 and his adjusted basis for sale purposes is only $10,000, resulting in the gain of $15,000. His charitable deduction is $75,000.[42]

The contribution of property encumbered by debt may trigger unexpected gain under this special rule of Section 1011(b). The regulations provide:

> If property is transferred subject to an indebtedness, the amount of the indebtedness must be treated as an amount realized for purposes of determining whether there is a sale or exchange to which section 1011(b) and this section apply, even though the transferee does not agree to assume or pay the indebtedness.[43]

> **Example 2:** Same facts as in Example 1, except that the property, worth $100,000, is subject to a $25,000 debt. The taxpayer contributed the property to the charity, subject to the debt.

> **Analysis:** The amount realized would equal the $25,000 indebtedness to which the property is subject. As in Example 1, there would be a $25,000

---

[40] I.R.C. § 1011(b).

[41] See the discussion of part-gift/part-sale transactions in Chapter 4, *supra*.

[42] *See* Treas. Reg. § 1.1011-2(c), Ex. 1.

[43] Treas. Reg. § 1.1011-2(a)(3).

sale and a $75,000 charitable contribution. With respect to the sale, the adjusted basis would be again be $10,000, *i.e.*, 25,000/100,000, or ¼ of the $40,000 total adjusted basis. Accordingly, taxpayer would report gain of $15,000 and claim a $75,000 charitable deduction.

§ 26.07 SUBSTANTIATION

A donor who claims a deduction for a charitable contribution must maintain reliable written records regarding the contribution, regardless of the value or amount of such contribution. For a contribution of money, applicable record keeping requirements are satisfied only if the donor maintains as a record of the contribution a bank record or a written communication from the donee showing the name of the donee organization, the date of the contribution, and the amount of the contribution.[44] Thus, if a taxpayer puts a $20 bill in the collection basket at a church service, the taxpayer will not be allowed to claim a charitable deduction for the $20 unless the donor satisfies the requirement of Section 170(f)(17). The record-keeping requirements may not be satisfied by maintaining other written records. For a contribution of property other than money, the donor generally must maintain a receipt from the donee organization showing the name of the donee, the date and the location of the contribution, and a detailed description (but not the value) of the property.[45] However, a donor of property, other than money, need not obtain a receipt if circumstances make obtaining a receipt impracticable. Under such circumstances, the donor must maintain reliable written records regarding the contribution. The required content of such a record varies depending upon factors such as the type and value of property contributed.[46]

In addition to the foregoing recordkeeping requirements, additional substantiation requirements apply in the case of charitable contributions with a value of $250 or more. No charitable deduction is allowed for any contribution of $250 or more unless the taxpayer substantiates the contribution by a contemporaneous written acknowledgment of the contribution by the donee organization. Such acknowledgment must include the amount of cash and a description (but not value) of any property other than cash contributed, whether the donee provided any goods or services in consideration for the contribution, and a good faith estimate of the value of any such goods or services.[47] In general, if the total charitable deduction claimed for non-cash property is more than $500, the taxpayer must attach a completed Form 8283 (Noncash Charitable Contributions) to the taxpayer's return or the deduction is not allowed.[48] In general, taxpayers are required to obtain a qualified appraisal for donated property with a value of more than $5,000, and to attach an appraisal summary to the tax return.[49]

---

[44] I.R.C. § 170(f)(17).

[45] Treas. Reg. § 1.170A-13(b).

[46] *Id.*

[47] I.R.C. § 170(f)(8).

[48] I.R.C. § 170(0)(11).

[49] I.R.C. § 170(f)(11)(C).

Note that Section 170(f)(16)(A) denies a deduction for contributions of clothing or household items unless the clothing or household items are in "good used condition or better." A deduction may be allowed for a charitable contribution of a single item of clothing or a household item not in "good used condition or better" if the amount claimed for the item is more than $500 and the taxpayer includes with the taxpayer's return a qualified appraisal with respect to the property. Household items include furniture, furnishings, electronics, appliances, linens, and other similar items. Food, paintings, antiques, and other objects of art, jewelry and gems, and collections are excluded from the provision.[50]

---

[50] I.R.C. § 170(f)(16)(D).

Chapter 27

LIMITATIONS ON DEDUCTIONS

Each of the prior Chapters addressing specific deductions discussed both the requirements for and limitations on the deduction. The limitations imposed on the deductions often account for most of the complexity associated with a particular deduction section. These limitations serve the dual purposes of specifically defining the scope of the deduction and preventing abuse. This Chapter addresses additional important limitations on deductions.

§ 27.01 SECTION 267: LOSSES BETWEEN RELATED PARTIES

[A] Section 267(a)(1) Loss Rule

§ 267. **Losses, expenses, and interest with respect to transactions between related taxpayers.**

(a) **In General.**

(1) Deduction for losses disallowed. No deduction shall be allowed in respect of any loss from the sale or exchange of property, directly or indirectly, between persons specified in any of the paragraphs of subsection (b). . . .

. . .

(b) Relationships. The persons referred to in subsection (a) are:

(1) Members of a family, as defined in subsection (c)(4);

(2) An individual and a corporation more than 50% in value of the outstanding stock of which is owned, directly or indirectly, by or for such individual;

. . .

(c) Constructive ownership of stock. For purposes of determining, in applying subsection (b), the ownership of stock —

(1) Stock owned, directly or indirectly, by or for a corporation, partnership, estate, or trust shall be considered as being owned proportionately by or for its shareholders, partners, or beneficiaries;

(2) An individual shall be considered as owning the stock owned, directly or indirectly, by or for his family;

(3) An individual owning (otherwise than by the application of paragraph (2)) any stock in a corporation shall be considered as owning the stock owned, directly or indirectly, by or for his partner;

(4) The family of an individual shall include only his brothers and sisters (whether by the whole or half blood), spouse, ancestors and lineal descendants; and

(5) Stock constructively owned by a person by reason of the application of paragraph (1) shall for the purpose of applying paragraph (1), (2), or (3), be treated as actually owned by such person, but stock constructively owned by an individual by reason of the application of paragraph (2) or (3) shall not be treated as owned by him for the purpose of again applying either of such paragraphs in order to make another the constructive owner of such stock.

(d)   Amount of gain where loss previously disallowed. If

(1) in the case of a sale or exchange of property to the taxpayer a loss sustained by the transferor is not allowable to the transferor as a deduction by reason of subsection (a)(1) . . . ; and

(2) after December 31, 1953, the taxpayer sells or otherwise disposes of such property . . . at a gain,

then such gain shall be recognized only to the extent that it exceeds so much of such loss as is properly allocable to the property sold or otherwise disposed of by the taxpayer. . . .

To prevent the deduction of artificial losses, Congress enacted Section 267(a)(1), which denies a deduction for any loss incurred on the sale or exchange of property "directly or indirectly" between certain related persons. Section 267(b) provides a lengthy list of relationships which will trigger the disallowance rule.

> **Example 1:** Pete has a basis of $15,000 in certain stock having a fair market value of $10,000. If Pete sells the stock, he would realize and recognize $5,000 of loss, all of which he could use to offset gains he had realized earlier in the year on the sale of other stock. Because he believes the stock will increase in value during the coming year, Pete is not anxious to part with the stock. May Pete claim a $5,000 loss deduction if he sells the stock to his daughter for $10,000?
>
> **Analysis:** Initially, one must consider whether the specific requirements of Section 165, the applicable loss deduction provision, are satisfied. A threshold requirement of that section is that a loss exist. The regulations indicate that, to be deductible, "a loss must be evidenced by closed and completed transactions, fixed by identifiable events, and . . . actually sustained during the taxable year."[1] Furthermore, "only a bona fide loss is allowable. Substance and not mere form shall govern in determining a deductible loss."[2] It is questionable whether Pete's sale of stock to his daughter satisfies these requirements. Certainly, it is possible Pete may still have considerable practical control over the stock, thus raising serious doubts as to whether any loss has actually occurred. In any event, Section 267(b) identifies the father-daughter relationship as one which will negate

---

[1] Treas. Reg. § 1.165-1(b).

[2] *Id.*

the deduction of the loss incurred by the father on the sale of the stock.[3] Therefore the loss is not deductible.

Example 2: Subsequent to purchasing the stock from her father, the daughter sold the stock to an unrelated person for $12,000. What gain, if any, would she report? Could her father then claim the previously disallowed loss?

Analysis: Section 267(a)(1) does not provide that disallowed losses will be held in abeyance for future use of the seller; nor does it permit the purchaser to claim the seller's basis. In this example, therefore, the daughter's basis is a Section 1012 cost basis of $10,000. Section 267, however, does provide some relief in the form of Section 267(d), which provides that the daughter need only recognize gain to the extent that the gain exceeds the loss disallowed her father. Thus, while the daughter's realized gain on the sale is $2,000, none of that gain will be recognized because the gain does not exceed her father's loss of $5,000. In effect, Section 267(d) treats the daughter and father as one taxpayer by giving the daughter the benefit (but only to a limited extent) of the father's loss. The other $3,000 of loss incurred by the father, but disallowed under Section 267(a), disappears.

Section 267(a)(1) will generally negate the need for courts to consider whether a loss has actually occurred. However, in cases which do not involve the relationship between buyer and seller required by Section 267(a)(1), it will still be necessary for the courts, the Service and tax advisors to consider whether a loss has actually occurred. For example, in *Fender v. United States*,[4] the taxpayer-trusts realized substantial gain from the sale of certain stock. To offset this gain, the trustees sold some bonds which had declined substantially in value. The bonds were unrated and could not be sold in the public market. The purchaser of the bonds was a bank in which the trustee was a 40% shareholder. Forty-two days after the transfer of the bonds to the bank, the trusts repurchased the bonds for an amount even less than that which the bank had paid for the bonds. At the time of the repurchase, the trustee owned more than a 50% interest in the bank. Both the sale to the bank and the subsequent repurchase of the bonds were made at the fair market value of the bonds.

Agreeing with the Service's contention that no loss had been experienced by the trusts on the sale of the bonds to the bank, the court concluded the taxpayer-trusts had sufficient dominion over the bank through the stock ownership of the trustee to ensure that the apparent loss from the sale of the stock "could be recaptured through a repurchase of the bonds." Therefore, in selling the bonds, the trusts were not exposed to any real risk of loss. The court relied on *DuPont v. Commissioner*,[5] in which the Third Circuit concluded that no loss had occurred when two friends sold each other stock at a loss at the end of the year and repurchased the stock from one another at the start of the following year. Although both friends paid fair

---

[3] I.R.C. § 267(b)(1), (c)(4).

[4] 577 F.2d 934 (5th Cir. 1978).

[5] 118 F.2d 544 (3d Cir.), *cert. denied*, 314 U.S. 623 (1941).

market value for the stock purchased and no legal obligation to repurchase existed, the court nonetheless concluded sufficient dominion existed to assure repurchase and thus negate a bona fide sale.

McWilliams v. Commissioner[6] and *Miller v. Commissioner*[7] reflect some of the interpretation and application issues raised by taxpayers with reference to Section 267(a)(1). In *McWilliams*, the taxpayers, husband and wife, owned stock in their own names and the husband managed the independent estate of his wife. At various times, he ordered his broker to sell stock owned by his wife and to buy the same number of the same shares for his account at approximately the same price and vice-versa. The broker negotiated the sales through a stock exchange and the purchasers of the stock were thus never known. The stock that was repurchased by the broker for the account of either the husband or wife was represented by certificates different from the stock sold. The taxpayers filed separate tax returns and claimed the losses on these stock sales as deductions from gross income. The issue was whether the losses were subject to the limitation of Section 267(a)(1). Noting that Congress, in enacting Section 267(a)(1), was concerned about the bona fides of intra-family losses and that securities transactions were the most common vehicle for such losses, the Court rejected taxpayers' argument that Section 267(a)(1) is applicable only to sales made directly from one taxpayer to a related taxpayer or "mediately through some controlled intermediary." Rather, because of the "near-identity of economic interests" between related parties as defined in Section 267(b), the court concluded that "[i]t is a fair inference that even legally genuine intra-group transfers were not thought to result usually in economically genuine realizations of loss, and accordingly that Congress did not deem them to be appropriate occasions for the allowance of deductions."[8] By so interpreting Section 267(a)(1), the Court negated the possibility that related taxpayers could time their losses on investments while at the same time essentially continuing to hold the investments. The Court ruled that Section 267(a)(1) was applicable regardless of whether the transaction was consummated through the medium of a stock exchange. According to the Court, Congress' use of the language "directly or indirectly" was broad enough to encompass transactions like those in question where the stock was sold through an exchange to unknown purchasers and different certificates of stock in the same company were purchased.

Miller raised the issue of whether Section 267(a)(1) should be interpreted to include a "family hostility exception" where the related parties are hostile to one another, thereby rendering the sale equivalent to an arms length transaction. The taxpayer in that case sold stock and real estate to his brother with whom he had a strained relationship. He argued Section 267(b) merely created a rebuttable presumption and that the hostile relationship he had with his brother negated a finding that a family relationship existed between them within the meaning of Section 267(c)(4). The court, citing *McWilliams v. Commissioner,* found that Section 267 contains an "absolute prohibition" and "not a presumption against the allowance of losses on any sales between members of certain designated groups."

---

[6] 331 U.S. 694 (1947).

[7] 75 T.C. 182 (1980).

[8] 331 U.S. at 699.

According to the court, Congress sought to avoid the need for courts to have to look at the facts behind the sales, *i.e.* to determine whether a loss should be disallowed.

[B]   The Section 267(a)(2) Matching Requirement

§ 267. **Losses, expenses, and interest with respect to transactions between related taxpayers.**

(a) **In General.**

(2) **Matching of deduction and payee income item in the case of expenses and interest. If**

(A) **by reason of the method of accounting of the person to whom the payment is to be made, the amount thereof is not (unless paid) includible in the gross income of such person, and**

(B) **at the close of the taxable year of the taxpayer for which (but for this paragraph) the amount would be deductible under this chapter, both the taxpayer and the person to whom the payment is to be made are persons specified in any of the paragraphs of subsection (b),**

then any deduction allowable under this chapter in respect of such amount shall be allowable as of the day as of which such amount is includible in the gross income of the person to whom the payment is made (or, if later, as of the day on which it would be so allowable but for this paragraph). . . .

Certain Code provisions condition the deduction of expenses on the inclusion of related income. One such provision is Section 267(a)(2). Other similar, more sophisticated provisions are considered in Chapter 42.

As discussed in greater detail in Chapters 28 and 29, a cash method taxpayer generally reports income when it is received, not when it is earned; an accrual method taxpayer generally deducts an expense when it is incurred, not when it is paid.[9] It is the cash method taxpayer for whom payment is required in order to deduct the expense.[10] Thus, assume a cash method taxpayer renders deductible services to an accrual method taxpayer. The cash method taxpayer has no income in all likelihood until payment is made, but the accrual method taxpayer may well become entitled to a deduction once the services are rendered even though payment has not yet been made, and indeed may not be made for a substantial period of time. The concern underlying Section 267(a)(2) is that the different accounting methods make arrangements possible under which related parties can generate current deductions without current income. The mismatching potential is clear.

Section 267(a)(2) responds to this concern essentially by placing an accrual method taxpayer on the cash method of accounting with respect to the deduction of amounts owed to related cash method taxpayers. For example: John is a cash method taxpayer whose tax year is the calendar year. His father, Frank, operates

---

[9] Strictly speaking, income is included under the cash method when it is actually or constructively received. Treas. Reg. § 1.451–1(a). A deduction is allowed under the accrual method when all events have occurred that establish the fact of liability, the amount can be determined with reasonable accuracy, and economic performance has occurred. Treas. Reg. § 1.461–1(a)(2).

[10] Treas. Reg. § 1.461–1(a).

a business on the accrual method and calendar year. At the end of Year 1, Frank owes John $50,000 for services rendered to the business in Year 1. Under the accrual method, Frank would normally claim a $50,000 Section 162(a) deduction in Year 1. John, as a cash method taxpayer, would not be required to include anything in income until payment is actually (or constructively) received. However, because Frank and John are related parties under Section 267(a)(2)(B), Frank may not claim a $50,000 deduction in Year 1 for the amount owed to John. Rather, Frank will claim a deduction in the year in which John includes the $50,000 in income, i.e., presumably the year in which Frank pays John.

Consider another example. Under Section 267(b)(2), an individual and a corporation in which the individual is a more than 50% owner are related parties. As a result, if the individual, a cash method taxpayer, makes a loan to the accrual method corporation, Section 267(a)(2) denies an interest deduction to the corporation until the individual recognizes the corresponding interest income — that is, until the individual actually or constructively receives the interest from the corporation. Suppose an interest deduction is thus barred for one or more years because it is not paid. If in a later year the individual sells his interest in the corporation and the parties are no longer related, the question arises whether the corporation may now deduct the accrued but unpaid interest. The answer was "No" in *Ronald Moran Cadillac v. United States*.[11] The prior years' unpaid, accrued interest did not become deductible merely because the parties were no longer related. Rather, under Section 267(a)(2), an interest deduction barred because of the relationship in the year it accrued becomes deductible only when the interest is includible in the income of the cash method taxpayer — when it is paid. Interest that accrues after the parties are no longer related is, however, not subject to Section 267(a)(2).

[C] Other Matching Rules — Section 404(a)(5) and Section 83

It is worth noting at this point two other statutory matching rules that tie the payor's deduction of compensation to the payee's inclusion of the compensation in income. With respect to "nonqualified" plans deferring the receipt of compensation (generally, this is any arrangement that defers the receipt of compensation by the payee more than two and one-half months after the close of the payor's tax year),[12] Section 404(a)(5) provides that the payor may not claim a deduction until the payee includes the compensation in income. This rule could certainly impact the example given above, and deny a deduction until payment occurs, regardless of relationships. Note that Section 404(a)(5), unlike Section 267(a)(2), does not require that the parties be related.

Another matching rule, that of Section 83(h), is concerned with compensatory transfers of property subject to restrictions. As noted by the Staff of the Joint Committee on Taxation in its General Explanation of the Tax Reform Act of 1969,[13] Section 83

---

[11] 385 F.3d 1230 (9th Cir. 2004).

[12] Treas. Reg. § 1.404(b)-1T, Q&A-2.

[13] 91st Cong., 2d Sess., pp. 110–112 (1970).

provides that a person who receives a beneficial interest in property, such as stock, by reason of his performance of services must report as income in the taxable period in which received, the value of the property unless his interest in the property is subject to a substantial risk of forfeiture and is nontransferable. . . . If the property is subject to a substantial risk of forfeiture and is nontransferable, the employee is not required to recognize any income with respect to the property until his interest in the property either becomes transferable or no longer is subject to such risk. A substantial risk of forfeiture is considered to exist where the recipient's rights to the full enjoyment of the property are conditioned upon his future performance of substantial services.

Example: Kevin is employed by a publicly held corporation. As an incentive to keep Kevin as an employee, the company gives Kevin 100 shares of its common stock, but conditions the transfer on Kevin remaining in the service of the company for the next three years.

Analysis: Under Section 83(a), Kevin is not required to include the shares upon receipt because there is a substantial risk of forfeiture encumbering his right to the stock. (Assume that any transferee would also be subject to the risk of forfeiture and that therefore under Section 83 the stock is not considered to be transferable.) The risk of forfeiture will end after Kevin has worked for the company for three years, and Kevin will be required to include in income the value of the 100 shares at that time. Kevin's employer is entitled to a deduction under Section 162 for the value of the stock transferred, but Section 83(h) requires that there be a matching of income and deduction. Kevin's employer will be entitled to deduct the value of the stock only when Kevin is required to include the value in income.

§ 27.02　SECTION 265: EXPENSES RELATED TO TAX-EXEMPT INCOME

Section 265 prevents taxpayers from claiming double tax benefits as a result of tax-exempt income. Specifically, it disallows certain deductions allocable to such income.

[A]　Section 265(a)(1) General Rule

§ 265.　Expenses and interest relating to tax exempt income.

(a)　General Rule. No deduction shall be allowed for —

(1)　Expenses. Any amount otherwise allowable as a deduction which is allocable to one or more classes of income other than interest (whether or not any amount of income of that class or classes is received or accrued) wholly exempt from the taxes imposed by this subtitle, or any amount otherwise allowable under section 212 (relating to expenses for production of income) which is allocable to interest (whether or not any amount of such interest is received or accrued) wholly exempt from the taxes imposed by this subtitle.

Section 265(a)(1) disallows two categories of deductions: first, it disallows all deductions allocable to tax-exempt income, other than tax-exempt interest; second, it disallows Section 212 expenses allocable to tax-exempt interest.

The first category of deductions disallowed by Section 265(a)(1) includes deductions under Section 162 (trade or business expenses); Section 165 (losses); Section 212 (investment expenses); Sections 167 and 168 (depreciation expenses), etc. For example, in *Jones v. Commissioner*,[14] the taxpayer purchased for investment certain contingent remainder interests in two estates. To protect his investment in case the contingent remaindermen whose interests he purchased failed to survive the life tenants, the taxpayer purchased policies of life insurance on the remaindermen. The taxpayer sought to deduct the premiums paid on the policy. Because the proceeds from the life insurance policies would have been excluded from tax under Section 101, the court concluded the deduction for the premiums (otherwise allowable under Section 212) was disallowed under Section 265(a)(1). In a more recent case, no deduction was allowed for home mortgage interest and real property taxes allocable to a tax-exempt housing allowance received by an employee of the U.S. Immigration and Naturalization Service stationed abroad.[15] In another case, a physician, while a medical student, had received tax-exempt government scholarships that required her to perform future medical services in a "Health Manpower Shortage Area" to be designated by the government; the terms of the scholarships also provided that in the event she failed to perform the services she would repay three times the amount of the scholarships, plus interest. Some years after receiving the scholarships, the physician informed the government that she would not perform the services agreement. She entered into a repayment agreement with the government, and sought to deduct the repayment amounts as business expenses or business losses from her income as a physician. The repayments were held to be directly allocable to the exempt scholarship income, and thus nondeductible under Section 265(a)(1).[16]

In *Manocchio v. Commissioner*,[17] the Tax Court considered whether an otherwise allowable Section 162(a) deduction for expenses incurred in taking a flight training course would be disallowed by Section 265(a)(1) because the taxpayer received reimbursement for 90% of the costs under a special federal law providing veteran benefits. The reimbursement received by the taxpayer was tax-exempt under federal law. The taxpayer argued the reimbursed expenses were instead properly allocable to the taxable income that he derived from his employment as a pilot. He argued Section 265(a)(1) "was intended to apply only to expenses incurred in the *production* of exempt income, and should not be construed to apply to expenses which were merely paid *out of* exempt income."[18] The Tax Court disagreed, stating "we think the proximate one-for-one relationship between the

---

[14] 231 F.2d 655 (3d Cir. 1956).

[15] Induni v. Comm'r, 990 F.2d 53 (2d Cir. 1993), *aff'g* 98 T.C. 618 (1992). The Second Circuit held that the effect of Section 265(a)(6), exempting parsonage and military housing allowances from the operation of Section 265, was to bring deductions allocable to other tax-exempt housing allowances within the general disallowance rule of Section 265(a)(1).

[16] Stroud v. U.S., 906 F. Supp. 990 (D.S.C. 1995) (affirmed on this issue, but vacated in part and remanded on other grounds, by the Fourth Circuit in an unpublished opinion, 96-2 U.S.T.C. (CCH) ¶ 50,446 (4th Cir. 1996)).

[17] 78 T.C. 989, *aff'd*, 710 F.2d 1400 (9th Cir. 1983).

[18] *Id.* at 993.

reimbursement and the deduction overrides the underlying relationship between the deduction and the employment income, leaving the deduction 'directly allocable,' as that term is used in section 1.265-1(c), Income Tax Regs., solely to the reimbursement and to no other class of income."[19]

With respect to tax-exempt interest, Section 265(a)(1) disallows only Section 212 deductions allocable to such interest. Thus, other deductions, *e.g.*, Section 162 (trade or business) or Section 164 (state and local taxes), are not subject to the disallowance rule. As discussed below, interest deductions allocable to indebtedness to purchase or carry tax-exempt obligations are disallowed by Section 265(a)(2). Nevertheless, tax-exempt interest is accorded preferential treatment under Section 265, since only Sections 163 and 212 deductions allocable to it are disallowed whereas *all* deductions allocable to other types of tax-exempt income are disallowed by Section 265(a)(1). Classic examples of expenses subject to the disallowance rule are fees for safe-deposit boxes, investment advice and custodial care.

[B]   Section 265(a)(2): Tax-Exempt Interest

§ 265.   **Expenses and interest relating to tax exempt income.**

(a)   **General Rule. No deduction shall be allowed for —**

. . .

(2)   **Interest. — Interest on indebtedness incurred or continued to purchase or carry obligations the interest on which is wholly exempt from the taxes imposed by this subtitle.**

Section 265(a)(2) disallows interest expense deductions associated with the production of tax-exempt interest. Specifically, it disallows a deduction for "interest on indebtedness incurred to purchase or carry obligations the interest on which is wholly exempt from taxes. . . ." For example, while the interest generated by a municipal bond may be excludable under Section 103(a),[20] a taxpayer may not deduct any interest paid on money borrowed to purchase the municipal bonds. Note that it makes no difference the taxpayer never realizes tax-exempt interest income from the obligations; it is only necessary that the obligations would produce interest wholly exempt from tax.[21]

The Supreme Court, in *Denman v. Slayton*,[22] commented on the purpose of Section 265(a)(2) as follows:

> The manifest purpose of [Section 265(a)(2)] was to prevent the escape from taxation of income properly subject thereto by the purchase of exempt securities with borrowed money.

---

[19] *Id.* at 995. The Ninth Circuit, in affirming the Tax Court, never reached the Section 265(a)(1) issue. Rather, the appellate court concluded that the educational expenses were not deductible in any event under Section 162(a) because they were reimbursed.

[20] See the discussion of Section 103(a) in the Note on Miscellaneous Exclusions in Appendix A, *infra*.

[21] Rev. Proc. 72-18, 1972-1 C.B. 740.

[22] 282 U.S. 514 (1931).

Under the theory of the respondent, "A," with an income of $10,000 arising from non-exempt securities, by the simple expedient of purchasing exempt ones with borrowed funds and paying $10,000 interest thereon, would escape all taxation upon receipts from both sources. It was proper to make provision to prevent such a possibility.[23]

Application of Section 265(a)(2) can be difficult in cases where a taxpayer has not borrowed money specifically for the purpose of purchasing obligations producing tax-exempt interest. With respect to the determination of whether indebtedness was incurred to purchase or carry obligations producing tax-exempt income, the courts will consider all of the facts and the circumstances. The mere fact the taxpayer has incurred or continued a debt while holding tax-exempt obligations will not trigger the Section 265(a)(2) disallowance.[24]

Revenue Procedure 72-18[25] provides important guidance for determining when the disallowance rule of Section 265(a)(2) will be operative. The Revenue Procedure provides that "direct evidence of a purpose to carry tax-exempt obligations exists where tax-exempt obligations are used as collateral for indebtedness." Thus, where a taxpayer uses a portfolio of tax-exempt obligations as collateral for a business or personal loan, the interest on the loan will not be deductible.

However, if, for example, a taxpayer intending to invest in both tax-exempt bonds and real estate uses $50,000 of her savings to purchase the tax-exempt bonds and borrows $75,000 to purchase a piece of commercial property, the Revenue Procedure notes that:

> the purpose to purchase or carry tax-exempt obligations generally does not exist with respect to indebtedness incurred or continued by an individual in connection with the active conduct of a trade or business . . . unless it is determined that the borrowing was in excess of business needs. However, there is a rebuttable presumption that the purpose to carry tax-exempt obligations exists where the taxpayer reasonably could have foreseen at the time of purchasing the tax-exempt obligations that indebtedness probably would have to be incurred to meet future economic needs of the business of an ordinary, recurrent variety.

Thus, depending upon the specific facts, the interest on the $75,000 loan may be deductible.

The Revenue Procedure also provides a special rule for an individual taxpayer who, while owning tax-exempt obligations, incurs indebtedness to purchase goods or services for personal consumption or to purchase a home. According to the Revenue Procedure, Section 265(2) "will not apply to indebtedness of this type, because the purpose to purchase or carry tax-exempt obligations cannot reasonably be inferred where a personal purpose unrelated to the tax-exempt obligation

---

[23] *Id.* at 519–20.

[24] Wisconsin Cheesman, Inc. v. U.S., 388 F.2d 420 (7th Cir. 1968); Illinois Terminal Railroad v. U.S., 375 F.2d 1016 (Ct. Cl. 1967); Wynn v. U.S., 288 F. Supp. 797 (E.D. Pa. 1968), *aff'd,* 411 F.2d 614 (3d Cir. 1969).

[25] 1972-1 C.B. 740.

ordinarily dominates the transaction." Thus, for example, if a taxpayer who owns salable municipal bonds borrows money to purchase a home the interest on the home mortgage will not be subject to the limitation of Section 265(2).

The Revenue Procedure provides that, where a taxpayer holds tax exempt obligations and has outstanding indebtedness which is not directly connected with personal expenditures or incurred in the active conduct of a trade or business, there will be a rebuttable presumption that the taxpayer has a purpose to carry the tax-exempt obligations. According to the Revenue Procedure, this presumption may be overcome by establishing for example that (1) the tax-exempt obligations could not be sold at the time; (2) "the tax-exempt obligations could only have been liquidated with difficulty or at a loss"; or (3) an "investment advisor recommended that a prudent man should maintain a particular percentage of assets in tax-exempt obligations." The Revenue Procedure provides the following instructive example:

> **Example:** Taxpayer A, an individual, owns common stock listed on a national securities exchange, having an adjusted basis of $200,000; he owns rental property having an adjusted basis of $200,000; he has cash of $10,000; and he owns readily marketable municipal bonds [the interest on these is tax exempt] having an adjusted basis of $41,000. A borrows $100,000 to invest in a limited partnership interest in a real estate syndicate and pays $8,000 interest on the loan which he claims as an interest deduction for the taxable year. Under these facts and circumstances, there is a presumption that the $100,000 indebtedness incurred to finance A's portfolio investment is also incurred to carry A's existing investment in tax-exempt bonds since there are no additional facts or circumstances to rebut the presumption. Accordingly, a portion of the $8,000 interest payment will be disallowed under Section 265(2) of the Code.

[C] Allocation

In some circumstances, an expenditure may be indirectly allocable to both taxable and tax-exempt income. Only the *portion* of the expenditure allocable to the tax-exempt income is subject to Section 265. The regulations require that a "reasonable proportion" of the expenditure "in light of all the facts and circumstances" be allocated to the exempt income.[26] In the absence of other bases for allocation, the expense will be allocated to the taxable and tax-exempt income in the same proportions as the taxable and tax-exempt income bear to the total income received.[27]

§ 27.03 SECTION 1091: WASH SALES

§ 1091. **Loss from wash sales of stock or securities.**

(a) **Disallowance of loss deduction. In the case of any loss claimed to have been sustained from any sale or other disposition of shares of stock or securities where it appears that, within a period beginning 30 days before the**

---

[26] Treas. Reg. § 1.265-1(c).

[27] *See, e.g.,* Rev. Rul. 87-102, 1987-2 C.B. 78.

date of such sale or disposition and ending 30 days after such date, the taxpayer has acquired (by purchase or by an exchange on which the entire amount of gain or loss was recognized by law), or has entered into a contract or option so to acquire, substantially identical stock or securities, then no deduction shall be allowed under section 165 unless the taxpayer is a dealer in stock or securities and the loss is sustained in a transaction made in the ordinary course of such business. For purposes of this section, the term "stock or securities" shall, except as provided in regulations, include contracts or options to acquire or sell stock or securities.

. . .

(d)   Unadjusted basis in case of wash sale of stock. If the property consists of stock or securities the acquisition of which (or the contract or options to acquire which) resulted in the nondeductibility . . . of the loss from the sale or other disposition of substantially identical stock or securities, then the basis shall be the basis of the stock or securities so sold or disposed of, increased or decreased, as the case may be, by the difference, if any, between the price at which the property was acquired and the price at which such substantially identical stock or securities were sold or otherwise disposed of.

Another provision designed to prevent the deduction of artificial losses is Section 1091, which disallows losses on the sale or other disposition of stock or securities if the seller has acquired "substantially identical stock or securities" within a specified period. Specifically, Section 1091 disallows any loss realized on the sale of stock or securities if the seller acquires (or enters into a contract or option to acquire) substantially identical stock or securities within a period beginning thirty days before the date of the sale and ending thirty days after such a sale. There is thus a 61-day period during which acquisition of substantially identical stock or securities will result in disallowance of the loss realized on the sale.[28] These are referred to as "wash sales."

Unlike Section 267(a)(1), Section 1091 merely postpones, but does not permanently disallow, the loss realized. Deferral is accomplished through an adjustment to the basis of the stock or securities acquired during the 61-day period. The stock or securities will have a basis equal to the basis of the stock or securities sold, increased or decreased by the difference between the price at which the stock or securities were acquired and the price for which the loss stock or securities was sold.[29]

> **Example:** Mary owns 100 shares of stock in Primo Corporation. Mary paid $100 per share for the stock which has recently fallen in value to $75 per share. Mary would like to claim the $2,500 loss inherent in the stock but is also convinced that the Primo stock is currently selling at a bargain price. On December 5, Mary sells the stock on a stock exchange and on January 2 of the following year purchases an additional 100 shares of Primo stock for $80 per share.

---

[28] Except as otherwise provided in regulations, contracts or options to acquire or sell stock or securities are themselves "stock or securities." I.R.C. § 1091(a).

[29] I.R.C. § 1091(d).

Analysis: The $2,500 loss realized on the sale of the Primo stock will be disallowed by Section 1091; the basis of the stock purchased on January 2 will be $105 per share (the basis of the Primo stock sold ($100) plus the difference between what the stock was sold for per share ($75) and what Mary paid per share for the Primo stock purchased ($80)). The $25 per share loss inherent in the stock sold on December 5 is thus preserved. Because Mary's investment position really has not changed (except in the sense that she has added $5 per share to her investment in Primo) deferral of the loss is appropriate.

Note that Section 1091 is applicable only to losses; it does not apply to the sale of stock or securities at a gain, even if like stock or securities are purchased shortly before or after the sale. In addition, the disallowance rule of Section 1091 is triggered only if "substantially identical stock or securities" (or rights to acquire the same) are purchased within the 61-day period. The "substantially identical" standard significantly narrows the scope of Section 1091. For example, in Revenue Ruling 60-195,[30] the Service concluded that certain bonds issued by the same governmental body and having the same maturity date were nonetheless not "substantially identical" because the bonds had different interest rates. As noted by the Service, ". . . bonds are not 'substantially identical' if they are substantially different in any material feature, or because of differences in several material features considered together. Securities are substantially identical when the par value, interest yield, unit price and the security behind the obligation are the same."

§ 27.04 JUDICIAL LIMITATIONS ON INTEREST DEDUCTIONS

The interest deduction has often played a major role in tax-avoidance transactions. In combating tax avoidance, the courts have relied on a number of theories, including sham transaction, substance over form, and lack of a proper purpose. In one of the leading cases, *Knetsch v. United States*,[31] the taxpayer on December 11, 1953 purchased ten 30-year maturity deferred annuity savings bonds, each in the face amount of $400,000 and bearing interest at 2.5% compounded annually. The purchase price was $4,004,000. The taxpayer paid $4,000 in cash and for the balance gave a $4,000,000 nonrecourse note. "The notes bore 3.5% interest and were secured by the annuity bonds. The interest was payable in advance, and Knetsch on the same day prepaid the first year's interest, which was $140,000. Under the Table of Cash and Loan Values made part of the bonds, their cash or loan value at December 11, 1954, the end of the first contract year, was to be $4,100,000. The contract terms, however, permitted Knetsch to borrow any excess of this value above his indebtedness without waiting until December 11, 1954. Knetsch took advantage of this provision only five days after the purchase. On December 16, 1953, he received from the company $99,000 of the $100,000 excess over his $4,000,000 indebtedness, for which he gave his notes bearing 3.5% interest. This interest was also payable in

---

[30] 1960-1 C.B. 300.

[31] 364 U.S. 361 (1960).

advance and on the same day he prepaid the first year's interest of $3,465."[32] In his 1953 return, the taxpayer deducted $143,465 as interest paid on indebtedness. He followed this same pattern of prepaying interest, borrowing the cash value and deducting interest payments in each of the next two years. At the beginning of the fourth contract year, the taxpayer terminated the contract and received $1,000, the amount by which the cash value exceeded his indebtedness.

A review of the three years of the transaction indicated that the taxpayer had paid about $294,000 in interest and received back $203,000 in loans on the increase in cash surrender value. Thus, when the taxpayer terminated the insurance arrangement, he suffered an overall economic loss of $91,000 but the interest deductions claimed in 1953 and 1954 saved him approximately $233,000 in taxes.

The trial court concluded the transaction lacked commercial economic substance and was a sham. In its decision, the Supreme Court utilized the oft-quoted standard of *Gregory v. Helvering*:[33] "The legal right of a taxpayer to decrease the amount of what otherwise would be his taxes, or altogether avoid them, by means which the law permits, cannot be doubted. . . . But the question for determination is whether what was done, apart from the tax motive, was the thing which the statute intended."

The Court noted that, given the annual borrowing of cash values, Knetsch kept the cash value on which any annuity or insurance payments would be paid at the ridiculously low figure of $1,000; the monthly annuity of $90,171 which would be paid at the contract's maturity would therefore never occur. As stated by the Court: "Knetsch's transaction with the insurance company did 'not appreciably affect his beneficial interest except to reduce his tax' . . . for it is patent that there was nothing of substance to be realized by Knetsch from this transaction beyond a tax deduction. What he was ostensibly 'lent' back was in reality only the rebate of a substantial part of the so-called 'interest' payments." The Court viewed the $91,000 which was never returned to him as the insurance company's fee for "providing the facade of 'loans' whereby the taxpayer sought to reduce [his tax liability]." The Court characterized the transaction as a "sham."[34]

Knetsch does not provide much guidance for evaluating subsequent tax avoidance transactions. The above analysis of the Court establishes a broad economic substance test. Nonetheless, the case is regularly cited for the proposition that tax benefit alone is not enough to justify incurring of interest expense.

A factually interesting and instructive case that followed *Knetsch* is *Goldstein v. Commissioner*.[35] There, the taxpayer, a 70-year old housewife who lived with her husband on a meager pension, won over $140,000 in the Irish Sweepstakes. Her son, a C.P.A., together with an attorney, devised a scheme whereby the taxpayer could shelter a significant amount of her winnings from tax. Pursuant to the plan, the taxpayer borrowed almost a million dollars from two banks, used the proceeds to

---

[32] *Id.* at 363.

[33] 293 U.S. 465, 469 (1935).

[34] 363 U.S. at 366.

[35] 364 F.2d 734 (2d Cir.), *cert. denied*, 385 U.S. 1005 (1967).

purchase $500,000 of 0.5% U.S. Treasury notes and $500,000 1.5% U.S. Treasury notes, gave the Treasury notes to the banks as security, and prepaid over $81,000 in interest to the banks. The rate of interest on the bank loans exceeded the rate of interest paid on the Treasury notes. Although the taxpayer's son had projected a slight profit on the notes if they were held to maturity, the notes were sold before they matured and the taxpayer actually sustained an economic loss of over $25,000 because some notes were sold for less than the taxpayer had paid.

The Second Circuit rejected the Tax Court's holding that the transactions were a sham, finding instead that the loan arrangements were legitimate. The Second Circuit noted that the loans were made by independent financial institutions which possessed significant control over the future of the loan arrangements, the loan transactions did not immediately return the parties to the same position they had been in when they had started, and the taxpayer's notes were recourse notes.

The court, however, agreed with the Tax Court holding that the taxpayer's purpose in entering the transaction "was not to derive any economic gain or to improve [her] beneficial interest; but was solely an attempt to obtain an interest deduction as an offset to her sweepstake winnings."[36]

Because the interest rate which taxpayer was required to pay on the loans from the banks was higher than the interest rate on the Treasury notes, and because taxpayer had to pay her son and tax counsel $6,500 for their assistance, an economic loss was all but assured. The evidence indicated the taxpayer's son was aware of that fact and anticipated that the economic loss would be more than offset by the tax savings from the interest deductions. The court therefore rejected the taxpayer's argument that she entered into the transaction intending to make a profit. Citing *Knetsch v. U.S.*, the court held that Section 163(a) "does not permit a deduction for interest paid or accrued in loan arrangements [like the one before it] that can not with reason be said to have purpose, substance or utility apart from their anticipated tax consequences."[37] Discussing the Section 163(a) deduction, the court stated:

> [It] is fair to say that Section 163(a) is not entirely unlimited in its application and that such limits as there are stem from the Section's underlying notion that if an individual or corporation desires to engage in purposive activity, there is no reason why a taxpayer who borrows for that purpose should fare worse from an income tax standpoint than one who finances the venture with capital that otherwise would have been yielding income.
>
> In order fully to implement this Congressional policy of encouraging purposive activity to be financed through borrowing, Section 163(a) should be construed to permit the deductibility of interest when a taxpayer has borrowed funds and incurred an obligation to pay interest in order to engage in what with reason can be termed purposive activity, even though he decided to borrow in order to gain an interest deduction rather than to

---

[36] *Id.* at 738.

[37] 364 F.2d at 740.

finance the activity in some other way. In other words, the interest deduction should be permitted whenever it can be said that the taxpayer's desire to secure an interest deduction is only one of mixed motives that prompts the taxpayer to borrow funds; or, put a third way, the deduction is proper if there is some substance to the loan arrangement beyond the taxpayer's desire to secure the deduction. . . . [T]o allow a deduction for interest paid on funds borrowed for no purposive reason, other than the securing of a deduction from income, would frustrate Section 163(a)'s purpose; allowing it would encourage transactions that have no economic utility and that would not be engaged in but for the system of taxes imposed by Congress.[38]

Congress has now prohibited a cash method taxpayer from claiming a deduction for prepayments of interest allocable to years subsequent to the year of payment.[39] As a result, the schemes in both *Knetsch* and *Goldstein* have to a great extent now been negated by statute. Nevertheless, the sham doctrine applied in *Knetsch* and the "purposive activity" standard of *Goldstein* remain important weapons which the Commissioner may use to attack unwarranted deductions.

---

[38] *Id.* at 741.

[39] Section 461(g), noted in Chapter 22, *supra.*

Chapter 28

CASH METHOD ACCOUNTING

For the tax lawyer, correctly identifying an item as income or a deduction is not enough; knowing when that item must be reported as income or taken as a deduction is equally important. Successful tax planning requires in-depth understanding of the tax timing rules.

As discussed in Chapter 1, ours is an annual tax accounting system.[1] But knowing one must account to the government annually merely begins the fine tuning of the timing issue — instead of "when is something income" the issue becomes "in what tax year is something income." The answer is not as simple as one might expect.

Congress has provided different methods for determining the tax year an item is reportable as income or allowable as a deduction. The so-called "cash receipts and disbursements" method and "accrual" method are the most common. This Chapter examines the rules of the cash receipts and disbursements method (hereinafter the cash method) of accounting. The accrual method will be discussed in the next Chapter.

§ 28.01 INCOME UNDER THE CASH METHOD

[A] In General

Section 446(c)(1) authorizes the use of the cash method of accounting as long as it clearly reflects the taxpayer's income.[2] Because of its simplicity, most taxpayers, including almost all wage and salary earners, use the cash method. As suggested by its name, the cash method requires a taxpayer to report cash (and income in other forms) as received and to deduct expenses as they are paid. Receipt and disbursement or payment are thus the critical events. Although this method may seem simple, complex issues arise in its application.

The primary issues associated with the cash accounting method as applied to the timing of income arise in the application of three doctrines: constructive receipt, cash equivalency, and economic benefit. As demonstrated in the case law, the courts have often blurred the distinctions between these doctrines. Congress has recently sought to address some abuses not adequately addressed by court decisions and administrative rulings.

---

[1] I.R.C. § 441(a).

[2] *See* I.R.C. § 446(b).

[B] Constructive Receipt

Although, under the cash method, gains, profits, and other income are reported when received, generally a cash method taxpayer may not delay receipt of income and thereby reduce his taxes for a given year. "Generally, under the cash receipts and disbursements method in the computation of taxable income, all items which constitute gross income (whether in the form of cash, property, or services) are to be included for the taxable year in which actually or *constructively* received."[3]

Constructive receipt is explained:

> Income although not actually reduced to a taxpayer's possession is constructively received by him in the taxable year during which it is credited to his account, set apart for him, or otherwise made available so that he may draw upon it at any time, or so that he could have drawn upon it during the taxable year if notice of intention to withdraw had been given. However, income is not constructively received if the taxpayer's control of its receipt is subject to substantial limitations or restrictions.[4]

As discussed in more detail below, the doctrine of constructive receipt means that a taxpayer cannot turn his back on income or, more accurately, the cash method taxpayer who has control over his actual receipt of income made available to him must report it, regardless of whether he has actual physical possession of it.

> **Example 1:** Patrick is employed full time by a company and is paid monthly for his services. In an effort to reduce his 2012 taxes, Patrick, a cash method taxpayer, purposely waited until January 2, 2013 to pick up his December 2012 paycheck which was available to him on December 30. Has Patrick successfully deferred reporting the December 2012 wages until 2013?

> **Analysis:** No. By failing to pick up his December 2012 paycheck until January 2013, Patrick cannot thereby defer reporting his December wages for a full tax year. He will be deemed to be in constructive receipt of the paycheck on December 30, 2012.

> **Example 2:** On December 1, Tenant offers Landlord the monthly rent due that same day. May Landlord delay reporting the rental income by refusing the rent and asking Tenant to pay rent in January of the following tax year?

> **Analysis:** No. Just as the employee in Example 1 was deemed to be in constructive receipt of his paycheck when it was made available to him, so too Landlord will be considered to be in constructive receipt of the rent on the due date when Tenant offered to pay. Under these circumstances, Landlord controls receipt of the rental income. Landlord cannot turn his back on the income.

---

[3] Treas. Reg. § 1.446-1(c)(1)(i) (emphasis added).

[4] Treas. Reg. § 1.451-2(a).

[1] Specific Factors Affecting Application of Constructive Receipt Doctrine

Two requirements must be satisfied before the doctrine of constructive receipt is applicable: (1) the amount must be available to the taxpayer; and (2) the taxpayer's control over receipt must not be subject to substantial restrictions or limitations.[5] Considering these two closely related requirements together, the Tax Court noted in *Hornung v. Commissioner*,[6] that the "basis of constructive receipt is essentially unfettered control by the recipient over the date of actual receipt." As stated in *Baxter v. Commissioner*,[7] "[a]lthough the notion of constructive receipt blends a factual determination of what actually happened and a legal assessment of its significance, we have held that a finding of constructive receipt is a finding of fact. As such, it can be set aside only if clearly erroneous."

Given the factual focus of a constructive receipt determination, it is helpful to review the kinds of factors courts have considered significant in evaluating whether a taxpayer had "unfettered control over the date of actual receipt" of income.

[a] Distance

One factor has been the taxpayer's geographic proximity to the location where an item of income is being made available to the taxpayer. For example, in *Hornung v. Commissioner*,[8] Paul Hornung was informed by Sports Magazine on Sunday, December 31, that he had won a new Corvette for being named the most valuable player in the National Football League Championship game played that day in Green Bay, Wisconsin. The Corvette, however, was located at a New York dealership that was closed for the weekend. The court found that, under the circumstances, Hornung likely could not have taken possession of the car before January 1, and therefore did not have the kind of control necessary for constructive receipt.

The taxpayer in *Paul v. Commissioner*,[9] claimed he was in constructive receipt of lottery winnings in 1987, the year he won the New Jersey Lottery, and not in 1988, the year he received the check in payment of his lottery claim. Taxpayer mailed his lottery claim form to the New Jersey Lottery Commission in December 1987. He argued, however, that he could have driven 68 miles to Trenton, appeared in person before the Lottery Commission, and collected his winnings before the year end. The Tax Court in rejecting taxpayer's argument stated: "The fact that [taxpayer] would like the doctrine to apply to this case and that traveling 68 miles would not have been a burden to him is irrelevant; if such travel is necessary in order to prove entitlement to and obtain funds in a current taxable year, we consider the requirement a substantial limitation affecting unfettered control. Accordingly, we conclude that petitioner should have reported the lottery winnings

---

[5] Treas. Reg. § 1.451-2(a).

[6] 47 T.C. 428, 434 (1967).

[7] 816 F.2d 493, 494 (9th Cir. 1987).

[8] 47 T.C. 428, 434 (1967).

[9] T.C. Memo 1992-582.

in taxable year 1988." Similarly, in *Baxter v. Commissioner*,[10] the Ninth Circuit held a taxpayer could not be confronted with the choice of either driving 40 miles at year end to pick up a commission check or facing application of the constructive receipt doctrine.[11]

In *Ames v. Commissioner*,[12] the taxpayer, a CIA employee convicted of espionage for the Soviet Union, claimed he had constructively received income from the KGB in 1985, when it was allegedly set aside for him in the Soviet Union. The payments in question were actually received in the years 1989-1992. On the facts presented, the Tax Court concluded there was no constructive receipt:

> Assuming arguendo that some type of account was created and funds were segregated for petitioner, he did not have ready access to it, and certain conditions had to be met or had to occur before he could gain physical access to any funds. Petitioner had to contact the Soviets, using a complex arrangement of signal sites, to determine whether a "withdrawal" could be made. Next, the Soviets had to arrange to have the cash transferred into the United States and have it secretly left in a prearranged location for petitioner. There was no certainty that these conditions and steps could be accomplished under the existing circumstances, and the conditions represented substantial risks, limitations, and restrictions on petitioner's control of the funds, assuming they were even in existence and segregated for his exclusive benefit. There is no constructive receipt of income where delivery of the cash is not dependent solely upon the volition of the taxpayer. So long as the Soviets retained control over any funds or promised set-asides, there was no practical or legal way in which petitioner could compel payment. If the KGB had questioned petitioner's loyalty at any time before payment, there is no assurance that petitioner would have continued to receive cash deliveries or payments. So long as the Soviet Union retained the ability to withhold or control the funds, there was no constructive receipt.[13]

Generally, the date a check is received and not the date it is mailed determines the year of taxation. In Revenue Ruling 73-99,[14] the Service confirmed this, but noted that, if a taxpayer could have picked the check up before the year end, the taxpayer would be deemed in constructive receipt of the check. The Service in this ruling, however, failed to address the distance factor that proved determinative in both *Paul* and *Baxter*. It is not clear whether the courts in those cases would have applied the constructive receipt doctrine had the distance been short, *e.g.*, a few blocks or even a few miles.

---

[10] 816 F.2d 493 (9th Cir. 1987).

[11] *Cf.* McEuen v. Comm'r, 196 F.2d 127 (5th Cir. 1952).

[12] 112 T.C. 304 (1999).

[13] *Id.* at 313.

[14] 1973-1 C.B. 412.

[b]   Knowledge

In *Davis v. Commissioner*,[15] on December 31, 1974, the Postal Service attempted to deliver a certified letter containing a severance payment check to the taxpayer. The taxpayer, who did not expect to receive the check until sometime in the next year, was not home to sign the return receipt necessary to receive the letter. As a result, the taxpayer could not pick up the letter with the enclosed check until after January 1, 1975. In Revenue Ruling 76-3,[16] the Service concluded the taxpayer's absence from her home when delivery was attempted was not the kind of limitation or restriction that would negate constructive receipt. The Tax Court, however, disagreed and in *Davis* held that the taxpayer was not in constructive receipt because she did not know that the check was available to her in 1974.

[c]   Contractual Arrangements

A taxpayer is not considered in constructive receipt upon refusing a payment not yet due. For example, if a tenant on December 31 tenders payment of rent not due until January 1, and the landlord refuses the payment, the landlord is not in constructive receipt of the rent. While the refusal does constitute turning one's back on income, the Code does not require the landlord to forego contractual rights. If the rental payment is not due until January 1, the landlord should not be required to accept it before that time.[17]

[d]   Forfeitures or Other Penalties

Certain penalties and other restrictions may negate constructive receipt. For example, banks and savings and loan associations commonly impose a penalty if money is withdrawn from certain certificate accounts before maturity. Such a penalty on early withdrawal may constitute a sufficient restriction to negate constructive receipt. There will be no constructive receipt of interest on a certificate of deposit or other deposit arrangement "if an amount equal to three months' interest must be forfeited upon withdrawal or redemption before maturity" of deposit arrangements of one year or less.[18]

Revenue Ruling 80-300,[19] provides another example of a restriction the Service considered substantial enough to bar a finding of constructive receipt. In that ruling, key employees of a corporation received stock appreciation rights ("SARs") from the corporation. An employee could exercise — *i.e.*, cash in — SARs simply by giving written notification to the corporation. The employee would then receive a cash payment equal to the difference between the value of the corporation's stock at the date the SAR was exercised and the value of the stock at the date the SAR was granted. The Service found that the employee was not in constructive receipt of income as the stock appreciated in value, prior to exercise of the SAR, holding

---

[15] T.C. Memo 1978-12.

[16] 1976-1 C.B. 114.

[17] See, for example. Rev. Rul. 60-31, 1960-1 C.B. 174, discussed, *infra*.

[18] Treas. Reg. § 1.451-2(a)(2).

[19] 1980-2 C.B. 167.

that the "forfeiture of a valuable right" — in this case, "the right to benefit from further appreciation of stock . . . without risking any capital" — was "a substantial limitation that precludes constructive receipt of income." The ruling also held that the valuable right was lost and the limitation was removed once the employee exercised the SAR, and it was at that point that the employee recognized income.

[e]   Relationship of the Taxpayer to the Payor

Difficult constructive receipt questions often arise in the context of closely held corporations in which the owners are also the corporate employees and officers. If an officer-owner is not paid her salary during the year, will she nonetheless be deemed in constructive receipt of the salary because she has control over the corporation? As the Second Circuit confirmed in *Hyland v. Commissioner*,[20] in rejecting the taxpayer's effort to invoke the constructive receipt doctrine based on his 85% ownership interest in his corporation, if control of the corporation by the owner-officer were enough to establish constructive receipt of unpaid salaries, the distinction between shareholders and their corporation would be vitiated. "It would mean that in every close corporation, the corporate earnings are immediately constructively received by the controlling stockholder provided their withdrawal would not make the corporation insolvent. But the law ordinarily treats a corporation and its controlling shareholder as separate juristic persons and they are separately taxable."[21]

Before a shareholder-employee will be considered in constructive receipt of the salary owed her by her corporation, there must be some corporate action to set aside or otherwise make the salary available. In addition, the shareholder-employee must have some authority to draw a check to herself on the corporate accounts. In Revenue Ruling 72-317,[22] such facts, together with the fact that the corporation was able to make the salary payment, were sufficient to justify a finding of constructive receipt.

The Tax Court in *Hooper v. Commissioner*[23] found constructive receipt even though there were no book entries or corporate resolutions indicating the corporation had set funds aside or made them available to the taxpayers. In *Hooper*, the taxpayers for a number of years had rented certain real estate to their wholly-owned corporation. During the tax year in question, the taxpayers, acting as the board of directors of the corporation, decided the corporation would discontinue paying rent for the use of the taxpayers' real estate. A number of months later, following the discontinuance of the rental payments, the taxpayers transferred title to the real estate to the corporation. The issue before the Tax Court was whether the taxpayers were in constructive receipt of the rent which, but for the board's action in discontinuing payments, would have been paid to the taxpayers by the corporation for the period prior to the title transfer. The history

---

[20] 175 F.2d 422 (2d Cir. 1979).

[21] *Id.* at 424.

[22] 1972-1 C.B. 128.

[23] T.C. Memo 1995-108.

of rental payments, taxpayers' absolute control over the corporation, and the availability of sufficient corporate funds to pay rent convinced the court the taxpayers were in constructive receipt of the rents.

Consider a situation where a corporation, by resolution or in an employment contract, postpones until a future year payment of the salary of a controlling shareholder/employee. The corporate resolution may constitute a "substantial limitation or restriction"[24] thereby enabling the shareholder/employee to defer reporting income. It makes no difference that the employee, as the controlling shareholder, may modify the employment contract (or the corporate resolution) at will and has the power to withdraw corporate funds. In *Young Door Co. v. Commissioner*,[25] the Tax Court held that such a limitation in a corporate resolution with respect to bonus payments to controlling shareholders constituted a substantial restriction or limitation. In *Basila v. Commissioner*,[26] the Tax Court similarly concluded that a written employment contract specifying that a bonus would not be paid until the year following its computation prevented a controlling shareholder/employee from having an unrestricted right to demand payment of the bonus prior to the date set for payment.

As a rule of law, the constructive receipt doctrine may be employed by either the taxpayer or the Service. A taxpayer might want to argue constructive receipt due to a change in tax rates from one year to the next, or the running of the statute of limitations. That is precisely what occurred in *Hornung* and in *Ames* discussed above, *i.e.*, the taxpayers in those cases relied upon the constructive receipt doctrine in arguing that the income in question was reportable by them in an earlier tax year. Had they been successful, the statute of limitations would have prevented the government from collecting a tax on the income.

[2] Specific Exceptions to Constructive Receipt Rules

Various exceptions exist to the rule that one who has unfettered control over the receipt of income must report it. For example, although prizes are generally income, the Service has ruled that a taxpayer who refuses a prize is not required to report it as income.[27] Unlike the examples above, the taxpayer refusing the prize is not merely deferring receipt of income but foregoing forever the right to receive it.

Another exception is found in Section 125 with respect to "cafeteria plans" by which an employee may, in some instances, choose between receipt of cash or receipt of excludable fringe benefits. In effect, the employee faced with such a choice who chooses to receive excludable benefits in lieu of cash from his employer has turned his back on income. But for Section 125, which authorizes exclusion under those circumstances, the employee would arguably be in constructive receipt of income.

---

[24] *See* Treas. Reg. § 1.451-2(a).

[25] 40 T.C. 890 (1963).

[26] 36 T.C. 111 (1961).

[27] Rev. Rul. 57-374, 1957-2 C.B. 69.

[C] Cash Equivalency Doctrine

"[G]ross income includes income in any form, whether in money, property or services."[28] Assume Tom, a cash method taxpayer, performs services for Mary, who gives Tom one of the following items:

(1) an automobile worth $25,000;

(2) I.B.M stock worth $25,000;

(3) an I.B.M. bearer bond worth $25,000;

(4) a promissory note in which Mary agrees to pay Tom $25,000;

(5) a letter acknowledging Mary owes Tom $25,000 for services rendered; and

(6) an oral promise to pay Tom $25,000.

The "cash equivalency" doctrine determines which of the above items Tom must include in gross income.

Automobile and I.B.M. stock: If Tom received either the automobile or the I.B.M. stock, he would have reportable income in the year of receipt.[29] Both are property with clear value and appear to be bargained-for consideration.

I.B.M. bond: Although the I.B.M. bond merely represents I.B.M.'s promise to pay the bearer a sum certain on a specified date, it also appears to be bargained-for consideration, readily transferable, and should be included in income at its fair market value at the time of its receipt.[30]

Letter acknowledging debt: The same result will follow in the case of the letter acknowledging the debt. The letter merely evidences a debt; it doesn't constitute receipt of anything. Like the oral promise discussed below, the letter cannot be viewed as bargained-for consideration. It is not commonly traded and cannot be reduced to cash. Under these circumstances, deferral is appropriate. Like the oral promise, the letter establishes that Tom has an account receivable and nothing more. To the cash method taxpayer, an account receivable does not constitute income.

Oral promise: A fundamental difference between cash accounting and accrual accounting is that an accrual method taxpayer must include income when it is earned even if the taxpayer has received nothing, while a cash method taxpayer includes income only upon receipt. If, upon receipt of an oral promise to pay, a cash method taxpayer were required to report income, the distinction between cash and accrual accounting would be significantly blurred, if not entirely negated. Appropriately, therefore, Tom need not include anything in income merely because of Mary's oral promise. Taxation of the amount owed to Tom will be deferred until he actually or constructively receives payment.

---

[28] Treas. Reg. § 1.61-1(a).

[29] *See* Treas. Reg. § 1.61-1(a).

[30] *See* Treas. Reg. § 1.61-2(d)(4).

Mary's promissory note: Mary's promissory note presents a more difficult question. Mary's note is nothing more than a writing reflecting her promise to pay. By contrast, the I.B.M. note, discussed above, is apparently bargained-for-consideration and, unlike Mary's note, is readily transferable. With respect to the tax treatment of the receipt of property other than cash, and in particular with reference to the receipt of intangibles such as Mary's note, courts have invoked what is known as the "cash equivalency doctrine." Essentially, this doctrine embodies the notion that certain intangibles have so clear a value and are so readily marketable that a cash method taxpayer receiving them should not be entitled to defer reporting income. By contrast, other intangibles are not marketable and do not even have a clear "property" flavor. To require taxpayers to take these tangibles into account as gross income would obliterate the distinction between cash and accrual accounting.

In *Cowden v. Commissioner*,[31] the taxpayer leased oil and gas properties to Stanolind Oil Company in 1951. As part of the written contracts, Stanolind agreed to make "bonus" payments to the taxpayers in January 1952 and in January 1953. Late in 1951, and again, late in 1952, the taxpayers assigned the bonus payments to a bank for their face value, less relatively small discounts. The Commissioner argued the fair market value of the Stanolind obligations constituted a "cash equivalent," properly taxable as income to the taxpayers in 1951, when they were received. The Fifth Circuit, agreeing with the Commissioner, rejected the proposition that the cash equivalency doctrine required a negotiable instrument:

> A promissory note, negotiable in form, is not necessarily the equivalent of cash. Such an instrument may have been issued by a maker of doubtful solvency or for other reasons such paper might be denied a ready acceptance in the market place. We think the converse of this principle ought to be applicable. We are convinced that if a promise to pay of a solvent obligor is unconditional and assignable, not subject to set-offs, and is of a kind that is frequently transferred to lenders or investors at a discount not substantially greater than the generally prevailing premium for the use of money, such promise is the equivalent of cash and taxable in like manner as cash would have been taxable had it been received by the taxpayer rather than the obligation.[32]

Whether Mary's promissory note is a cash equivalent, and whether Tom, upon receipt of the note, would be required to include the note in gross income, depend upon several factors, including whether Mary was solvent at the time the note was made, and whether Mary's note is assignable and of a type frequently transferred.

Williams v. Commissioner,[33] examines these factors in addressing the tax treatment of the receipt of a written promise. In *Williams*, the taxpayer performed services for a client, who gave the taxpayer a promissory note payable approximately eight months later. The note was unsecured and bore no interest. At the time he gave the taxpayer the note, the client had no funds with which to pay it. On

---

[31] 289 F.2d 20 (5th Cir. 1961).

[32] *Id.* at 24.

[33] 28 T.C. 1000 (1957).

numerous occasions, the taxpayer tried unsuccessfully to sell the note to banks. The Service argued the taxpayer was required to include the note in income in the year received. The taxpayer contended he did not have to report the note until it was paid. The Tax Court held for the taxpayer, reasoning that the note had been given only as security for or as evidence of the indebtedness and not as payment. The mere change in form from an account payable to a note payable was insufficient to cause the realization of income by the taxpayer. In addition, considering the note bore no interest and was not marketable, the court held it had no fair market value.

The cash equivalency doctrine has generally been applied to negotiable notes and traditional securities; *Cowden* extends the doctrine beyond these usual limits. According to Revenue Ruling 68-606,[34] issued subsequent to *Cowden* and citing that case, a deferred-payment obligation that is "readily marketable and immediately convertible to cash" is properly includable in gross income on receipt under the cash method to the extent of its fair market value. The ruling held that the value of an installment bonus contract issued by an oil company was currently includable in the income of a cash method taxpayer since it was "freely transferable and readily saleable."

Checks are treated as cash equivalents. If a cash method taxpayer receives a check at year's end, the amount of that check must be included in gross income despite the inability of the recipient to cash it at that time. In *Kahler v. Commissioner*,[35] the taxpayer received a commission check for over $4,300 on December 31, 1946 after banking hours. The taxpayer cashed the check on January 2, 1947 at the drawee bank. The Tax Court concluded it made no difference that it was impossible to cash the check in 1946, noting: "where services are paid for other than by money, the amount to be included as income is the fair market value of [the property] taken in payment."[36] Quoting from *Estate of Spiegel*,[37] the court stated:

> It would seem to us unfortunate for the Tax Court to fail to recognize what has so frequently been suggested, that as a practical matter, in everyday personal and commercial usage, the transfer of funds by check is an accepted procedure. The parties almost without exception think and deal in terms of payment except in the unusual circumstance, not involved here, that the check is dishonored upon presentation, or that it was delivered in the first place subject to some condition or infirmity which intervenes between delivery and presentation.[38]

A concurring judge noted that merely because the taxpayer could not have cashed the check at a bank did not mean that he couldn't make some other use of the check in 1946. Thus, assuming the check is honored in due course and is not subject to some condition, a check received at year's end by a cash method taxpayer must be included in income just as though cash had been received.[39]

---

[34] 1968-2 C.B. 42.

[35] 18 T.C. 31 (1952).

[36] *Id.* at 34.

[37] 12 T.C. 524 (1949).

[38] *Id.* at 529.

[39] *See* Baxter v. Comm'r, 816 F.2d 493 (9th Cir. 1987).

If, however, a taxpayer receives a check on December 31 for services rendered and the check is post-dated to January 2, the post-dated check may be viewed as nothing more than a promise to make funds available on January 2.[40] In most cases a post-dated check will not satisfy the cash equivalency requirements and therefore its receipt will not require the taxpayer to report it as income.

[D] Economic Benefit Doctrine

The Supreme Court, in *Commissioner v. Smith*,[41] recognized that an economic or financial benefit conferred upon an employee as compensation is included in the concept of income. The Tax Court relied upon the economic benefit doctrine in *Sproull v. Commissioner*,[42] in finding that an amount irrevocably placed in trust for the benefit of an employee constituted income to the employee in that year, even though the money was not payable to the employee until subsequent years. The Tax Court emphasized the amount was fixed and irrevocably designated for the sole benefit of the employee.

Relying on *Sproull*, the Service ruled that a taxpayer had received a taxable economic benefit when his employer placed a bonus in escrow for him and required the escrowee to distribute the bonus to the taxpayer in installments over a five-year period.[43]

The economic benefit doctrine has been applied most often in the employee compensation context and with respect to prizes and awards held in escrow or trust-type arrangements. As noted by the Ninth Circuit in *Minor v. United States*:[44]

> Although taxation of deferred compensation plans is generally analyzed under the constructive receipt doctrine, . . . the economic benefit doctrine provides an alternate method of determining when a taxpayer receives taxable benefits. Under that doctrine, an employer's promise to pay deferred compensation in the future may itself constitute a taxable economic benefit if the current value of the employer's promise can be given an appraised value . . . . The economic benefit doctrine is applicable only if the employer's promise is capable of valuation . . . . A current economic benefit is capable of valuation where the employer makes a contribution to an employee's deferred compensation plan which is nonforfeitable, fully vested in the employee and secured against the employer's creditors by a trust arrangement.[45]

In Revenue Ruling 62-74,[46] a cash method taxpayer was awarded a cash prize in a contest. Pursuant to the contest terms, the contest sponsor placed the cash in a

---

[40] Griffin v. Comm'r, 49 T.C. 253 (1967).

[41] 324 U.S. 177 (1945).

[42] 16 T.C. 244, *aff'd*, 194 F.2d 541 (6th Cir. 1952).

[43] Rev. Rul. 60-31, 1960-1 C.B. 174, Ex. 4.

[44] 772 F.2d 1472 (9th Cir. 1985).

[45] *Id.* at 1474.

[46] 1962-1 C.B. 68.

noninterest-bearing escrow account with the amount to be paid to the taxpayer over a two-year period. The Service noted that the only difference between this case and *Sproull* was that in *Sproull* the taxpayer was entitled to the interest accruing on the corpus of the trust; in the contest case the taxpayer was entitled to no interest. Given this difference, the Service ruled that the taxpayer did not have to include the full amount of the cash deposit in income immediately, but only the current value of the payments. As the payments were received, the balance would be includable in income.

The economic benefit doctrine provides that "an individual should be taxed on any economic benefit conferred upon him, to the extent that the benefit has an ascertainable fair market value."[47] Thus, as suggested by Revenue Ruling 62-74, escrow arrangements provide a classic context for the application of the economic benefit doctrine. Where, for example, the purchase price of property is deposited in escrow for the benefit of a taxpayer/seller and is accessible only by the taxpayer and not by the depositor/purchaser or his creditors, the economic benefit doctrine should apply to treat the taxpayer/seller as having actually received the purchase price. If no interest is paid on the escrowed funds, the amount considered received by the taxpayer should be reduced to reflect the present value of the escrow amount.[48]

Some overlap exists between the economic benefit and cash equivalency doctrines. Undoubtedly, the cash equivalency doctrine, if broadly defined, would be adequate to address the arrangements such as the escrow arrangements discussed above. However, as indicated by *Cowden*, the cash equivalency doctrine has tended to be defined rather narrowly, with its primary application being found in the treatment of promissory notes. The economic benefit doctrine, by contrast, has a much broader scope. As such, it is appropriate to treat the economic benefit doctrine as separate from both the constructive receipt and cash equivalency doctrines.

[E] Deferred Compensation Arrangements

Because of the progressive tax rates, taxpayers have devised various methods for deferring compensation to years when they expect their income to be subject to tax at lower rates. Some deferral arrangements are specifically authorized by the Internal Revenue Code, *e.g.*, qualified pension and profit sharing plans. In general,

---

[47] Reed v. Comm'r, 723 F.2d 138 (1st Cir. 1983).

[48] In *Reed v. Commissioner*, 723 F.2d 138 (1st Cir. 1983), the court reached a contrary result. In *Reed*, a purchaser of stock in a closely held corporation deposited the purchase price for the stock in an escrow account on December 27, 1973. The escrowee was to hold the proceeds until January 3, 1974, at which time the proceeds were to be paid to the taxpayer/seller. There was no condition precedent to the disbursement of the escrowed funds other than the lapse of the seven days. The taxpayer/seller, who had specifically requested this arrangement in an effort to defer the gain from the sale from 1973 to 1974, was not entitled to any interest or investment income on the escrowed account. The First Circuit, in a questionable decision, concluded that the economic benefit doctrine was not applicable to this arrangement. The court based its decision in part on the fact that the taxpayer/seller did not receive any income from the escrowed funds. The First Circuit also concluded that the economic benefit doctrine was inapplicable because the taxpayer's rights under the escrow arrangement were not the equivalent of cash. This latter conclusion confuses the boundaries between the cash equivalency doctrine and the economic benefit doctrine.

these plans enable a taxpayer to defer compensation until retirement, when presumably most taxpayers are in a lower tax bracket and will therefore pay less tax when they receive the compensation they have deferred. Congressional authorization of these deferral arrangements serves a significant policy goal, *i.e.*, encouraging employees to save for their retirement years.

[1]   Non-Qualified Deferred Compensation Arrangements

In addition to deferral arrangements specifically authorized by the Code, so-called "nonqualified" deferred compensation arrangements or plans have also been common as part of executive compensation packages. An Internal Revenue Service audit guide[49] provides the following excellent tax analysis of nonqualified deferred compensation arrangements taking into account the doctrines of constructive receipt, cash equivalency, and economic benefit. Consider the following excerpt from that I.R.S. guide:

> A nonqualified deferred compensation plan is any elective or nonelective plan, agreement, method, or arrangement between an employer and an employee (or service recipient and service provider) to pay the employee compensation some time in the future. Nonqualified deferred compensation plans do not afford employers and employees the tax benefits associated with qualified plans because they do not satisfy all of the requirements of [Section 401(a)].

> Nonqualified deferred compensation plans include, for example, arrangements such as salary or bonus deferral arrangements whereby an employee is permitted to defer receipt of a portion of his or her salary or bonus that would otherwise be currently includible in gross income. These plans are typically unfunded, i.e., the employer has merely promised to pay the deferred compensation benefits in the future and the promise is not secured in any way. The employer may simply keep track of the benefit in a bookkeeping account, or it may voluntarily choose to invest in annuities, securities, or insurance arrangements to help fulfill its promise to pay the employee. Similarly, the employer may transfer amounts to a trust that remains a part of the employer's general assets, subject to the claims of the employer's creditors if the employer becomes insolvent, in order to help it keep its promise to the employee. To obtain the benefit of income tax deferral, it is important that the amounts are not set aside from the employer's creditors for the exclusive benefit of the employee. If amounts are set aside from the employer's creditors for the exclusive benefit of the employee, the employee may have currently includible compensation. [Note: As discussed below, the economic benefit doctrine would likely be applicable under these circumstances.]

> Nonqualified deferred compensation plans may be formal or informal, and they need not be in writing. While many plans are set forth in extensive detail, some are referenced by nothing more than a few provisions

---

[49] Market Segment Specialization Program Audit Guide for Nonqualified Deferred Compensation Plans (Apr. 13, 2005).

contained in an employment contract. In either event, the form of the arrangement is just as important as the way the plan is operated. That is, while the parties may have a valid nonqualified deferred compensation arrangement on paper, they may not operate the plan according to the plan's provisions. In such a circumstance, the efficacy of the arrangement is not dependent upon its form. . . .

Constructive Receipt Doctrine — Unfunded Plans

Establishing constructive receipt requires a determination that the taxpayer had control of the receipt of the deferred amounts and that such control was not subject to substantial limitations or restrictions. It is important to scrutinize all [deferred compensation] plan provisions relating to each type of distribution or access option. It also is imperative to consider how the plan has been operated regardless of the existence of provisions relating to types of distributions or other access options. Devices such as credit cards, debit cards, and checkbooks may be used to grant employees unfettered control of the receipt of the deferred amounts. Similarly, permitting employees to borrow against their deferred amounts achieves the same result. [Authors' note: If an employee has unfettered control over deferred amounts, then, despite whatever the specific provisions of the deferred compensation plan might state, the doctrine of constructive receipt will operate to defeat the deferral objectives of employees possessing such control.]

Economic Benefit — Funded Plans

Under the economic benefit doctrine, if an individual receives any economic or financial benefit or property as compensation for services, the value of the benefit or property is currently includible in the individual's gross income. More specifically, the doctrine requires an employee to include in current gross income, the value of assets that have been unconditionally and irrevocably transferred as compensation into a fund for the employee's sole benefit, if the employee has a nonforfeitable interest in the fund.

Section 83 codifies the economic benefit doctrine in the employment context by providing that if property is transferred to a person as compensation for services, the service provider will be taxed at the time of receipt of the property if the property is either transferable or not subject to a substantial risk of forfeiture. If the property is not transferable and subject to a substantial risk of forfeiture, no income tax is incurred until it is not subject to a substantial risk of forfeiture or the property becomes transferable.

For purposes of section 83, the term "property" includes real and personal property other than money or an unfunded and unsecured promise to pay money in the future. However, the term also includes a beneficial interest in assets, including money, that are transferred or set aside from claims of the creditors of the transferor, for example, in a trust or escrow account. Property is subject to a substantial risk of forfeiture if the individual's right to the property is conditioned on the future performance of substantial services or on the nonperformance of services. In addition, a substantial risk of forfeiture exists if the right to the property is subject to a condition other than the performance of services and there is a substantial possibility that the property will be forfeited if the condition does not occur.

Property is considered transferable if a person can transfer his or her interest in the property to anyone other than the transferor from whom the property was received. However, property is not considered transferable if the transferee's rights in the property are subject to a substantial risk of forfeiture.

[Cash Equivalency Doctrine]

The cash equivalency doctrine must also be considered when analyzing a nonqualified deferred compensation arrangement. Under the cash equivalency doctrine, if a promise to pay of a solvent obligor is unconditional and assignable, not subject to set-offs, and is of a kind that is frequently transferred to lenders or investors at a discount not substantially greater than the generally prevailing premium for the use of money, such promise is the equivalent of cash and taxable in like manner as cash would have been taxable had it been received by the taxpayer rather than the obligation. . . .

[2] Property Transfers Under Section 83

Section 83 provides, in general terms, that property transferred in connection with the performance of services is taxable to the extent that the fair market value of the property exceeds the amount (if any) paid for the property by the transferee. In many situations, the operation of Section 83 is obvious and unremarkable: when property is transferred, with no strings attached, as compensation for services, it is perfectly obvious that the recipient has compensation income equal to the value of the property; Section 83 is not needed to bring about this result — Section 61 itself would be sufficient.

But suppose there are some strings attached to the transfer. Suppose, for example, the recipient is the employee of the transferor, and the employee must return the property to the employer if the employee quits the job within the next three years. Section 83 was enacted to deal with this type of situation in particular: an employer-corporation's transfer to an employee shares of restricted corporate stock, requiring the employee to "earn out" the right to keep the stock by continuing to work for the employer for a certain length of time. If the employee remained for the requisite time, the stock became "nonforfeitable." If the employee quit before the requisite time had passed, the employee forfeited the stock back to the employer. Section 83, as noted, is far broader than this example, but the example does suggest a type of transfer Section 83 was intended to address.

The general rule adopted by the statute addresses both the timing and the amount of the income of the service-provider (such as an employee). If the property transferred is not subject to a substantial risk of forfeiture, compensation income is reported in the year of the transfer, and the amount of the compensation income is the fair market value of the property at the time of the transfer. If the property is subject to a substantial risk of forfeiture (and is not transferable), the compensation income is reported at the time the restriction lapses (that is, when the property ceases to be subject to the substantial risk of forfeiture); and the amount of the compensation income is the value of the property at the time the restriction lapses.[50] Similarly, the amount and timing of the employer's deduction is based upon the amount and timing of the service provider's income.[51]

There are a number of special rules and complications that this brief overview of Section 83 does not address. But at the core of Section 83 is the notion of nonforfeitability. Income arises when the property transferred is nonforfeitable. In that sense, Section 83 bears a close resemblance to the judicially developed economic benefit doctrine, as explained in an excerpt from the I.R.S. Audit Guide noted above:

> Section 83 codifies the economic benefit doctrine in the employment context by providing that if property is transferred to a person as compensation for services, the service provider will be taxed at the time of receipt of the property if the property is either transferable or not subject to a substantial risk of forfeiture. If the property is not transferable and subject to a substantial risk of forfeiture, no income tax is incurred until the property is not subject to a substantial risk of forfeiture or becomes transferable.
>
> For purposes of Section 83, the term "property" includes real and personal property other than money or an unfunded and unsecured promise to pay money in the future. However, the term also includes a beneficial interest in assets, including money, that are transferred or set aside from claims of the creditors of the transferor, for example, in a trust or escrow account.
>
> Property is subject to a substantial risk of forfeiture if the individual's right to the property is conditioned on the future performance of substantial services or on the nonperformance of services. In addition, a substantial risk of forfeiture exists if the right to the property is subject to a condition other than the performance of services and there is a substantial possibility that the property will be forfeited if the condition does not occur.
>
> Property is considered transferable if a person can transfer his or her interest in the property to anyone other than the transferor from whom the property was received. However, property is not considered transferable if the transferee's rights in the property are subject to a substantial risk of forfeiture.

---

[50] I.R.C. § 83(a).

[51] I.R.C. § 83(h).

[3] Section 409A and Revenue Ruling 60-31

Revenue Ruling 60-31[52] has long been the Service's most significant pronouncement discussing compensation deferral techniques. In that ruling, the Service made clear that it would respect deferred compensation arrangements (a) when the deferral was entered into prior to the commencement of services and (b) when the deferred amount was not secured in anyway, but merely constituted a promise to pay by the employer or other obligor. The ruling also indicated the Service would not inquire whether the payor would have been willing to enter into an agreement without deferral. While primarily focusing on the constructive receipt doctrine, the ruling also refers to the cash equivalency doctrine and the economic benefit doctrine.

In 2004, Congress enacted Section 409A to provide comprehensive statutory treatment of nonqualified deferred compensation arrangements. Section 409A essentially requires inclusion of all amounts deferred under a nonqualified plan, unless certain requirements are satisfied. Revenue Ruling 60-13, however, has continued viability after the enactment Section 409A and will have to be considered in conjunction with that provision. The ruling will be particularly important with respect to deferred compensation arrangements of independent contractors engaged in their own trade or business. As noted below, Section 409A will not apply to such independent contractors.

Between the issuance of Revenue Ruling 60-31 and the enactment of Section 409A, sophisticated planners developed a range of deferred compensation arrangements, typically for company executives, that Congress believed should not qualify for tax deferral. Specifically, Congress was aware of creative deferral arrangements that gave employees considerable security with respect to deferred amounts or provided employees with considerable control over deferred compensation. While, in general, such arrangements would negate deferral, planners devised methods that appeared to qualify for deferral when in fact they did not. For example, it was not uncommon for a nonqualified deferred compensation arrangement to be structured to allow an employee to change the terms of deferral or to receive a distribution of deferred amounts upon request subject to some minimal forfeiture provision (*i.e.*, a haircut provision). In sum, Congress was convinced greater policing of income deferral techniques was necessary. To that end, Congress enacted the specific rules found in Section 409A and outlined below.

While the specific details of § 409A are beyond the scope of this book, identification of a few of the salient features of that provision is appropriate. Section 409A provides in general that all amounts deferred under a nonqualified deferred compensation plan are currently includible in gross income to the extent not subject to a substantial risk of forfeiture and not previously included in gross income, unless certain requirements are satisfied.[53] Compensation is subject to a substantial risk of forfeiture if entitlement to the amount is conditioned on the performance of substantial future services by any person or the occurrence of a condition related to

---

[52] 1960-1 C.B. 174.

[53] I.R.C. § 409A(a)(1)(A).

a purpose of the compensation, and the possibility of forfeiture is substantial.[54] (Note how this general rule imports concepts from Section 83(a)). Among the requirements that must be satisfied if deferral is to be respected under § 409A are the following:

> (1) distributions of deferred compensation must be allowed only upon separation from service, death, a time specified in the plan, change in ownership of a corporation, occurrence of an unforeseeable emergency, or disability;[55]

> (2) except as provided by regulations, acceleration of benefits is prohibited;[56]

> (3) the election to defer compensation earned during the year must be made no later than the close of the preceding taxable year or at such other time as provided in the regulations;[57]

> (4) certain requirements must be met if the plan permits a delay in a payment or a change in the form of payment, *e.g.*, the plan requires that such election may not take effect until at least 12 months after the date on which the election is made.[58]

Note that the above requirements greatly limit the service provider's control over the timing of distributions of deferred compensation and the actual deferral of compensation itself.

In Notice 2005-1 noted above, the Service specified that Section 409A would not apply to arrangements between taxpayers all of whom use the accrual method of accounting. [The next chapter addresses the accrual method.] In addition, Section 409A also does not apply to arrangements between a service provider and a service recipient if (a) the service provider is actively engaged in the trade or business of providing substantial services, other than (I) as an employee or (II) as a director of a corporation; and (b) the service provider provides such services to two or more service recipients to which the service provider is not related and that are not related to one another.[59] Thus, deferred compensation arrangements with independent contractors will generally not be subject to Section 409A.

[F] Lottery Prizes

Section 451(h) allows states to offer prize winners the option of receiving in a single cash payment any lottery prize that otherwise is payable over at least ten years, provided the option is exercised within sixty days of the date of the taxpayer's entitlement to the prize. For example, if a taxpayer wins a state lottery

---

[54] I.R.C. § 409A(d)(4); 2005-1 C.B. 274, Notice 2005-1.

[55] I.R.C. § 409A(a)(2).

[56] I.R.C. § 409A(a)(3).

[57] I.R.C. § 409A(a)(4)(B). This requirement underscores congressional concern that deferral during or after the provision of services is generally inappropriate because the income has already been earned.

[58] I.R.C. § 409A(a)(4)(C).

[59] *See also* Treas. Reg. § 1.409A-1(f)(2).

that provides an option consistent with Section 451(h) and does not chose to receive the lottery prize in a single payment, the constructive receipt doctrine will not be applied to require inclusion of the entire prize in the year taxpayer wins. The economic benefit doctrine likewise will not be applicable because typically state lotteries do not provide an irrevocable set aside of funds for the benefit of the particular lottery winner. Rather, a state lottery typically purchases an annuity naming the lottery rather than the particular winner as the owner and beneficiary of the annuity. Likewise, the cash equivalence doctrine would not apply as it has not been established that prizes are frequently transferred to lenders or investors at a discount not substantially greater than the prevailing premium for the use of money.[60]

[G] Prepayments

Receipt is the critical event under the cash method. If a taxpayer is prepaid for services to be rendered, the taxpayer must report the prepayment received. For example, prepayments of rent are specifically required to be included in the year of receipt "regardless of the period covered or the method of accounting employed by the taxpayer."[61] Although prepayments received by a cash method taxpayer must be included in income when received, prepayments of deductible expenses by cash method taxpayers are not deductible in full.

§ 28.02   DEDUCTIONS UNDER THE CASH METHOD

[A] In General

Under the cash method, expenses are deductible when paid.[62] The rule is ordinarily straightforward in operation and produces the expected results. If, for example, Lawyer, a cash method, calendar year taxpayer, pays her December office rent on December 31 of the current year, Lawyer takes a current year Section 162 deduction; if Lawyer fails to make the payment until January 1 of the next year, the deduction is accordingly postponed until the year the payment is made. Suppose, however, Lawyer tenders the rent to Landlord on December 31, but Landlord rejects the rent and tells Lawyer to return with the rent on January 1 instead. If Landlord is a cash method taxpayer, the rent will be includable in Landlord's income on December 31 under the constructive receipt doctrine. However, Lawyer, who has not yet paid the rent, is not entitled to a December 31 deduction; there is no "constructive payment" doctrine. Deductions are allowed for payments only when "actually made," and for expenditures only "when paid." There is thus no counterpart on the deduction side to the constructive receipt doctrine with respect to income inclusion.

Some disagreement exists as to what constitutes "payment" of an expense. Clearly, payment has not occurred when the taxpayer transfers funds to his own

---

[60] *See* Private Letter Ruling 200031031.

[61] Treas. Reg. § 1.61-8(b).

[62] Treas. Reg. §§ 1.446-1(c)(1)(i), 1.461-1(a)(1).

agent. For example, a cash basis taxpayer may not deduct real estate taxes in the year paid into his mortgagee-bank's escrow account, but only when the mortgagee pays them to the taxing authority, since the mortgagee-bank is ordinarily treated as the agent of the taxpayer, not of the taxing authority.[63] Similarly, a cash method taxpayer's mere deposit of funds with a government agent as an offer in compromise of a disputed amount is not deductible when deposited; rather the deduction awaits acceptance of the offer.[64]

It is, of course, not necessary that payment be made in cash; payment can be made in property other than money. A $100 business expense paid with property worth $100 entitles the taxpayer to a $100 deduction. This transfer of property in satisfaction of a business expense may, however, generate taxable gain (or loss) to the taxpayer depending on the taxpayer's adjusted basis in the relinquished property and the nature of the property.[65]

Payment with borrowed funds constitutes payment for tax purposes.[66] (This may not be the case, however, if the funds are borrowed from the person to whom the taxpayer makes payment.) If a taxpayer pays an expense by check, payment takes place for tax purposes when the check is delivered, even though the taxpayer has the power to stop payment on the check, provided the check is unconditional and subsequently clears in due course.[67] Similarly, payment of an expense by a bank credit card is treated as payment at the time the charge is made, not when the taxpayer subsequently pays the bank. Revenue Ruling 78-39,[68] summarizes the foregoing rules in a situation in which the taxpayer uses a bank credit card to pay for medical expenses:

> In the instant case, when the cardholder used the bank credit card to pay the hospital for the medical expenses, the cardholder became indebted to a third party (the bank) in such a way that the cardholder could not prevent the hospital from receiving payment. The credit card draft received by the hospital from the cardholder could be deposited in the bank and credited to the hospital's account as if it were a check.

Since the cardholder's use of the credit card created the cardholder's own debt to a third party, the use of the bank credit card to pay a hospital for medical services is equivalent to use of borrowed funds to pay a medical expense. The general rule is that when a deductible payment is made with borrowed money, the deduction is not postponed until the year in which the borrowed money is repaid. Such expenses must be deducted in the year they are paid and not when the loans are repaid.[69]

---

[63] *See* Hradesky v. Comm'r, 65 T.C. 87 (1975), *aff'd*, 540 F.2d 821 (5th Cir. 1976).

[64] *See, e.g.*, Standard Brewing Co. v. Comm'r, 6 B.T.A. 980 (1927).

[65] *See* I.R.C. §§ 1001, 165(c).

[66] Granan v. Comm'r, 55 T.C. 753 (1971). *See* Chapter 22, *supra.*

[67] Treas. Reg. § 1.170A-1(b). The mailing of a check is regarded as the equivalent of delivery.

[68] 1978-1 C.B. 73.

[69] Granan v. Comm'r, 55 T.C. 753 (1971).

The issuance of one's own promissory note, however, has been held not to constitute payment. The taxpayer in *Helvering v. Price*[70] executed a guaranty agreement and secured note in favor of a bank, and subsequently, when the guaranty was called upon, gave the bank a second secured note, which it accepted as final payment of the original note given under the guaranty. The cash method taxpayer claimed a loss on the substitution of his note. The Supreme Court denied the loss noting there was no cash payment and the giving of the taxpayer's own note did not constitute payment. Although the note was secured, the Court held that the giving of collateral was not payment and did not convert a promise to pay into payment. A subsequent case, *Don E. Williams Co. v. Commissioner*,[71] involved an accrual method taxpayer and Section 404(a) of the Code, which allows a deduction for contributions "paid" by an employer to employee pension and profit-sharing plans. The Supreme Court held that the employer's delivery of its fully secured promissory demand notes did not entitle the employer to a deduction. Citing *Helvering v. Price*, the Court stated:

> [The reasoning of *Price*] is apparent: the note may never be paid, and if it is not paid, "the taxpayer has parted with nothing more than his promise to pay . . . ."

> The taxpayer argues that because its notes are acknowledged to have had value, it is entitled to a deduction equal to that value. It is suggested that such a note would qualify as income to a seller-recipient. Whatever the situation might be with respect to the recipient, the note, for the maker, even though fully secured, is still only his promise to pay. It does not in itself constitute an outlay of cash or other property. A similar argument was made in *Helvering v. Price*, . . . and was not availing for the taxpayer there . . . .

> The taxpayer suggests that the transaction equates with a payment of cash to the trustees followed by a loan, evidenced by the note in return, in the amount of the cash advanced. But . . . [w]hat took place here is clear, and income tax consequences follow accordingly. We do not indulge in speculating how the transaction might have been recast with a different tax result.

> Taxpayer heavily relies on the fact that three Courts of Appeals . . . have resolved the issue adversely to the Commissioner . . . .

> The three Courts of Appeals seemed to equate a promissory note with a check. The line between the two may be thin at times, but it is distinct. The promissory note, even when payable on demand and fully secured, is still, as its name implies, only a promise to pay, and does not represent the paying out or reduction of assets. A check, on the other hand, is a direction to the bank for immediate payment, is a medium of exchange, and has come to be treated for federal tax purposes as a conditional payment of cash. The factual difference is illustrated and revealed by taxpayer's own payment of

---

[70]   309 U.S. 409 (1939).

[71]   429 U.S. 569 (1977).

each promissory note with a check within a year after issuance.[72]

While payment of a deductible cost by check will generally entitle a taxpayer to a deduction in the year the check is delivered or mailed, a check under certain circumstances may be viewed as nothing more than a promissory note and therefore not entitle the taxpayer to a current deduction. For example, the taxpayer in *Blumeyer v. Commissioner*[73] owed money to North St. Louis Trust Co., (NSLT) under a guarantee agreement and on December 20, 1981, gave NSLT his check for $75,000. NSLT did not present the check for payment at the payor bank until the following January 22. Between December 20 and January 22, the taxpayer's bank account contained less than $6,000. On January 22, NSLT loaned taxpayer enough money to cover the check; petitioner authorized NSLT to wire the loan proceeds to his bank; and NSLT thereupon presented taxpayer's check for payment. Taxpayer sought a 1981 deduction on account of the delivery of his check to NSLT. The Tax Court held that the taxpayer was not entitled to a 1981 deduction. The court reasoned that the "payment" to NSLT was "a mere substitution of one note for another" because taxpayer did not acquire control over the borrowed funds and because the primary purpose of the loan from NSLT was to finance payment of the original guarantee to NSLT.[74] Furthermore, even if this were not a mere substitution of one note for another, no payment occurred in 1981 upon delivery of the check to NSLT. To apply the "relation back" doctrine under which payment is deemed to be paid on the date a check is delivered, the check must be delivered without conditions and be paid when presented in due course. Here, the court concluded that the delivery was conditioned upon NSLT's delay in cashing the check until the loan was made; moreover, the delay in presentment was not in the ordinary course of business, and thus presentment of the check did not occur in due course.

[B]   Cash Method Prepayments

All else being equal, when given a choice between paying now and paying later, most people will opt to pay later. But the Code is one of the reasons why all else is rarely equal. If a cash method taxpayer pays a deductible expense now rather than later, he may take an immediate tax deduction. Furthermore, if the value of the earlier tax deduction exceeds the "cost" of making the prepayment, then prepayment makes sense from an economic standpoint. Not surprisingly, the deductibility of prepayments is not unlimited. Suppose, for example, a cash method taxpayer purchases a building for use in trade or business. As discussed in Chapter 13, capital expenditures are not currently deductible. The fact that the cash method taxpayer has actually paid for the building does not change this result; the deduction timing rules of Section 461 are subject to the capital expenditure rules of Section 263. Thus, when an expenditure "results in the creation of an asset having a useful life which extends substantially beyond the close of the taxable year," as was obviously the case with respect to the building, a current deduction may be

---

[72] *Id.* at 577, 583.

[73] T.C. Memo 1992-647.

[74] See *Davison v. Comm'r*, 107 T.C. 35 (1996), discussed in Chapter 22, *supra.*

denied in whole or in part.[75]

Purchases of buildings and equipment, of course, present the easy cases.[76] The capitalization requirement applies to non-tangible assets as well. For example, in *Commissioner v. Boylston Market Association*,[77] the costs incurred in purchasing three years' fire insurance was held to be a capital expenditure. In addition, the Service has denied a full current deduction on "distortion of income" grounds for the cost of multi-year subscriptions to business and investment publications, nevertheless stating that the portion of the prepayment applicable to the first year generally will be deductible.[78] Previously, in *Grynberg v. Commissioner*,[79] the Tax Court applied a three-part test with respect to the deductibility of prepaid rentals: (1) the expenditure must constitute an actual payment rather than a deposit, (2) it must be made for a substantial business reason, and (3) it must cause no material distortion of income.

The Ninth Circuit presented a different approach in *Zaninovich v. Commissioner*.[80] In that case the taxpayers entered into a lease running from December 1, 1973 to November 30, 1974, and pursuant to the terms of the lease, the taxpayers paid the entire annual rental in December 1973. The taxpayers argued for deductibility of the entire payment; the Commissioner argued that only the one-twelfth applicable to December was currently deductible. In *Zaninovich*, a "one-year rule" was applied, and a rental payment covering a 12-month period was held currently deductible in full, even though 11 months of the rental period extended into the taxpayer's next tax year. Recall also that in *US Freightways Corp. v. Commissioner*, discussed briefly in Chapter 13, the court, in a case involving an accrual method taxpayer, adopted a similar one year rule with respect to payments for licenses and permits that were valid for a twelve month period extending across two tax years.

In view of cases like *Zaninivoch* and *US Freightways Corp.*, and in an effort to simplify administration both for the Service and for the taxpayer, the Treasury Department promulgated regulations under Section 263 (regarding capitalization) which provide a "12-month rule" which states that "a taxpayer is not required to capitalize amounts paid to create . . . any right or benefit for the taxpayer that does not extend beyond the earlier of (i) 12 months after the first date on which the taxpayer realizes the right or benefit; or (ii) the end of the taxable year following the taxable year in which the payment is made."[81] This "12-month rule" represents an exception to the general rule specified in the regulations which provides for the capitalization of prepaid expenses.[82] Applying that general rule, a regulation

---

[75] Treas. Reg. § 1.446-1(a)(1), (2).

[76] *See* Treas. Reg. § 1.263(a)-2(a).

[77] Comm'r v. Boylston Market Ass'n, 131 F.2d 966 (1st Cir. 1942).

[78] I.R. 86-169.

[79] 83 T.C. 255 (1984).

[80] 616 F.2d 429 (9th Cir. 1980).

[81] Treas. Reg. § 1.263(a)-4(f)(1).

[82] Treas. Reg. § 1.263(a)-4(d)(3)(i).

example[83] posits a three year prepayment of insurance premiums and concludes, much as did the court in *Boylston Market*, that the prepaid expense must be capitalized. Similarly, a second regulation example[84] considers a situation where a cash method taxpayer enters into a 24-month lease of office space and prepays the rental for that period. The example concludes that the prepayment must be capitalized. Contrast that example to *Zaninovich*.

By contrast to these examples requiring capitalization of prepaid expenses, the regulations provide a series of examples demonstrating the application of the "12-month rule" defined above.[85] In one example, the taxpayer, on December 1, 2005, pays a $10,000 insurance premium to obtain a property insurance policy with a one year term that begins on February 1, 2006. According to the regulation example, this prepayment expense must be capitalized and the "12-month rule" does not apply

> because the right or benefit attributable to the $10,000 payment extends beyond the end of the taxable year following the taxable year in which the payment is made. By contrast, if the one-year policy term had begun on December 15, 2005, the "12-month rule" . . . applies to the $10,000 payment because the right or benefit attributable to the payment neither extends more than 12 months beyond December 15, 2005 (the first date the benefit is realized by the taxpayer) nor beyond the end of the taxable year in which the payment is made.[86]

> **Example:** A cash method, calendar year taxpayer on December 31, 2012 makes an insurance payment due on January 10, 2013. Assume the insurance payment provides casualty coverage on taxpayer's business property for a twelve month period beginning on January 10, 2013. May the taxpayer deduct the insurance payment in 2012?

> **Analysis:** The "12-month rule" of the regulations is not applicable here because the right or benefit attributable to the premium payment extends beyond the end of the taxable year following the taxable year in which the payment is made.

There are other special rules relating to the deductibility of prepaid incidental supplies (deductible if taxable income clearly reflected)[87] or professional expenses (deductible if useful life is short).[88]

At one time, the prepayment of interest was such a prominent feature of many tax shelters, and such a source of taxpayer-Service disputes, that congressional intervention resulted. Section 461(g), enacted in 1976, provides that cash method taxpayers must treat prepaid interest as having been paid in the period to which it is properly allocable. The cash method taxpayer, in effect, is put on the accrual

---

[83] Treas. Reg. § 1.263(a)-4(d)(3)(ii) Ex. 1.

[84] Treas. Reg. § 1.263(a)-4(d)(3)(ii) Ex. 2.

[85] Treas. Reg. § 1.263(a)-4(f)(8).

[86] Treas. Reg. § 1.263(a)-4(f)(8) Exs. 1, 2.

[87] Treas. Reg. § 1.162-3.

[88] Treas. Reg. § 1.162-6.

method with respect to prepaid interest, with an exception allowed for "points" paid in connection with a principal residence.[89]

Prepaid expense questions are simply a manifestation of an inherent problem in cash method accounting. The chief virtue of the cash method is its simplicity, but the price of that simplicity is a certain tolerance of mismatching of income and expense. Income will not necessarily be received in the tax period earned, nor expenses paid in the tax period incurred, nor income and related expenses reported in the same tax period. Limiting the deductibility of certain prepaid expenses is one approach to fixing boundaries of tolerable mismatching. Another approach to addressing problems of cash method accounting is to forbid its use in certain circumstances. This approach is exemplified by Section 448: use of the cash method is prohibited for certain categories of taxpayers. Statutorily defined "tax shelters," as well as certain corporations and partnerships, simply may not compute taxable income under the cash method because the potential mismatching they may obtain is deemed unacceptable. In addition, the Regulations have long required that a taxpayer employ the accrual method for purchases and sales where use of an inventory is necessary.[90]

---

[89] I.R.C. § 461(g)(2).

[90] Treas. Reg. § 1.446-1(c)(2).

Chapter 29

ACCRUAL METHOD ACCOUNTING

Under the cash method of accounting, as discussed in the previous chapter, timing of income and deductions is determined by the actual or constructive receipt of the income item and actual payment of the deductible item. In general, under the accrual method, it is the earning of income, rather than the receipt of it, that is the critical event for inclusion purposes; and it is the fixing of the obligation to pay, not payment itself, that is the critical event for deduction purposes.

> **Example:** Laura Smith, a lawyer, provides legal advice to XYZ Corporation in December and that same month sends XYZ a bill for $1,000; XYZ pays the bill in January. For XYZ the legal fees represent an ordinary and necessary cost of doing business.

> **Analysis:** If Laura and XYZ are both cash method taxpayers, Laura will have $1,000 of income and XYZ will have a $1,000 deduction in January. However, if Laura and XYZ both use the accrual method of accounting, the answer is different. Accordingly, Laura must include the $1,000 in income in December and XYZ will be entitled to deduct the $1,000 expense in December.

§ 29.01 THE ALL EVENTS TEST

Section 451(a) provides that income is included in the year received, unless, under the taxpayer's accounting method, it is "properly accounted for as of a different period." Section 461 states that the amount of any allowable deduction "shall be taken for the taxable year which is the proper taxable year under the method of accounting used in computing taxable income." The regulations then flesh out these directions by providing that under the accrual method:

(1) an item of income is includable in gross income "when all the events have occurred which fix the right to such income and the amount thereof can be determined with reasonable accuracy."[1]

(2) an expense is deductible when all the events occur which establish the fact of liability, the amount can be determined with reasonable accuracy, and economic performance has occurred with respect to the liability.[2]

This formulation for accruing income and expense is commonly referred to as the "all events test." It originated in the Supreme Court decision in *United States v.*

---

[1] Treas. Reg. §§ 1.451-1(a)(1), 1.446-1(c)(1)(ii).

[2] Treas. Reg. §§ 1.461-1(a)(2), 1.446-1(c)(2).

Anderson,[3] where the court held that an accrual method taxpayer was required to deduct a tax on munitions profits in 1916, the year the munitions were sold and the tax was imposed, rather than in 1917, when the tax became due and was paid:

> Only a word need be said with reference to the contention that the tax upon munitions manufactured and sold in 1916 did not accrue until 1917. In a technical legal sense it may be argued that a tax does not accrue until it has been assessed and becomes due; but it is also true that in advance of the assessment of a tax, all the events may occur which fix the amount of the tax and determine the liability of the taxpayer to pay it. . . . In the economic and bookkeeping sense with which the statute and Treasury decision were concerned, the taxes had accrued.[4]

As indicated, *Anderson* involved the proper timing of an expense. The Supreme Court extended the all events test to the income side of the ledger in *Spring City Foundry Co. v. Commissioner*.[5] The accrual method taxpayer in that case sold some goods in 1920. Later that year, the purchaser filed a petition in bankruptcy and ultimately all that the taxpayer received were partial payments in 1922 and 1923. The Supreme Court held that the entire sales price nonetheless accrued in the year of the sale:

> Keeping accounts and making returns on the accrual basis, as distinguished from the cash basis, import that it is the *right* to receive and not the actual receipt that determines the inclusion of the amount in gross income. When the right to receive an amount becomes fixed, the right accrues. When a merchandizing concern makes sales, . . . a claim for the purchase price arises.[6]

The taxpayer was relegated to the bad debt provisions of the Code to account for the purchaser's failure to pay the full purchase price.

§ 29.02 ACCRUAL OF INCOME

[A] General Rules

For purposes of computing income, the accrual method focuses on "fixing" a right to income, and determining its amount with reasonable accuracy. Since Laura Smith, the lawyer in the example at the beginning of this Chapter, had a fixed right to the $1,000 of income in December, it is includable in her gross income at that time.

This example, however, is not intended to suggest that the fixing of a right to income is a process absolutely devoid of flexibility. The regulations state that a method in accord with generally accepted accounting principles, consistently used,

---

[3] 269 U.S. 422 (1926).

[4] *Id.* at 440-4.

[5] 292 U.S. 182 (1934).

[6] *Id.* at 184-85.

and consistent with the regulations, will be acceptable.[7] The same regulation goes on to provide, by way of example, that a manufacturer may account for a sale when an item is shipped, delivered, accepted, or when title passes. There is thus some flexibility in the determination of the time to accrue income on the sale of goods, if the determination is in accordance with the taxpayer's regular accounting method. Suppose, however, in a case involving a casual sale rather than a sale from inventory, an accrual method taxpayer enters into an executory contract for the sale of real estate in one year, but the transaction does not close and title does not pass until the following year. In *Lucas v. North Texas Lumber Co.*,[8] the Supreme Court held that the sales income was not properly accruable until the later year because no unconditional liability of the purchaser arose in the earlier year. *North Texas Lumber Co.*, however, should perhaps be viewed as addressing not only the issue of when a right to income is fixed under the all events test, but also the issue of when a sale is considered "closed" for tax purposes in order to compute gain or loss. More recently, the Tax Court held that gain accrued on the sale of real estate in the year the contract for deed was executed — not when the purchasers had made the required payments — because equitable title passed when the contract was executed, and for tax purposes, that was when the transaction closed.[9]

Income does not accrue until the amount can be determined with "reasonable accuracy." Note in this regard that the regulations provide for accrual on the basis of a "reasonable estimate," with the difference between the estimate and the exact amount accounted for in the year the latter is determined.[10] As with much else in life, of course, reasonableness may lie in the eye of the beholder. In *Continental Tie & Lumber Co. v. United States*,[11] for example, a taxpayer had a claim against the federal government for lost income, and Congress had passed a law authorizing awards in respect of such claims to be determined and made by a federal agency; the Court held that the right to the award was fixed by passage of the legislation, and that the amount of the award could reasonably be estimated on the basis of information in the taxpayer's possession.

[B]   Income Prior to Receipt: Accrual Issues

Suppose that an accrual method taxpayer has grave doubts about its ability to collect for services provided or goods sold. The Supreme Court required accrual on sale in *Spring City Foundry*, but there was no determination in that case that collectibility was doubtful at the time of the sale. Other courts and the Service, however, have recognized a limited exception to the general rule regarding accrual of income when sufficient doubt exists as to the collectibility of the income at the time the right to the income arises. For example, interest income was not accruable while "reasonable doubt" existed as to collectibility, but when collectibility was

---

[7] Treas. Reg. § 1.446-1(c)(1)(ii).

[8] 281 U.S. 11 (1930).

[9] Keith v. Comm'r, 115 T.C. 605 (2000).

[10] Treas. Reg. § 1.451-1(a)(l).

[11] 286 U.S. 290 (1932).

established, accrual was required.[12] In Revenue Ruling 80-361,[13] the Service held that interest income that was "uncollectible" at the time the right to it arose did not accrue; by contrast, where interest income was properly accrued, and subsequently became uncollectible, the taxpayer's remedy lay in the bad debt provisions of the Code rather than in the elimination of the proper accrual. The Tax Court held that a management fee was not accruable where the taxpayer was required to agree not to collect its fee as a condition for the debtor's obtaining a bank loan.[14]

Accrual of income for services rendered to the Cuban Government was not required, where collection was "at the mercy" of future Cuban administrations, and there was "real doubt and uncertainty" as to whether any amount would ever be paid.[15] By contrast, a judgment creditor of the United States was required to accrue an "acknowledged liability" of the United States, even though a congressional appropriation to pay the judgment did not occur until a later year.[16] Similarly, in *Georgia School-Book Depository, Inc. v. Commissioner*,[17] the court held that a company which served as a broker for textbooks to state schools in Georgia had to accrue the commission it earned at the time of the purchase of the books by the state even though the commission would be paid only when the state paid for the books purchased. Despite the fact that the fund which the state legislature had earmarked for the purchase of school books was insufficient at the time to pay for the books purchased and thus to pay the commissions owed the taxpayer, the court held that, given the assets of the state of Georgia and its record of fiscal probity, there was no reason to doubt that Georgia would ultimately pay for the books.[18]

Legal unenforceability of a claim does not necessarily bar accrual. In Revenue Ruling 83-106,[19] for example, the Service ruled that the owner of a gambling casino had to accrue gambling obligations owed by customers even though the obligations were not legally enforceable. The Service emphasized the owner's collection experience indicated that the owner had a reasonable expectancy of collecting on the obligations. In addition, in *Jones Lumber Co. v. Commissioner*,[20] the receipt of unassignable notes, with no ascertainable value, did not prevent accrual of the sales price, since the taxpayer did not establish reasonable doubt as to collectibility.

Finally, there is a special rule providing that a taxpayer need not accrue any portion of amounts to be received for the performance of services that, on the basis

---

[12] Clifton Mfg. Co. v. Comm'r, 137 F.2d 290 (4th Cir. 1943).

[13] 1980-2 C.B. 164.

[14] Commercial Solvents Corp. v. Comm'r, 42 T.C. 455 (1964) (acq.).

[15] Cuba Railroad Co. v. Comm'r, 9 T.C. 211 (1947) (acq.).

[16] Rev. Rul. 70-151, 1970-1 C.B. 116.

[17] 1 T.C. 463 (1943).

[18] See also *Koehring Co. v. United States*, 421 F.2d 715 (Ct. Cl. 1970), holding that accrual of royalty income was required, despite the debtor's financial problems, where there was "no real doubt" about the "ultimate receipt" of the royalties.

[19] 1983-2 C.B. 77.

[20] 404 F.2d 764 (6th Cir. 1968).

of experience, will not be collected.[21] The rule applies only if the taxpayer either (1) is performing services in one of several specified fields (health, law, engineering, architecture, accounting, actuarial science, performing arts, or consulting) or (2) does not exceed a $5,000,000 gross receipts test for any prior taxable year. The rule does not apply with respect to such service income that bears interest or a late charge. The five-year period preceding the current tax year (or, if less, the period the taxpayer has been in existence) will generally serve to determine the accruals that on the basis of experience will not be collected.[22]

Suppose the validity of the claim itself is contested. As the language of the all events test suggests, an unconditional right to income is necessary before the income is accrued. If the claim is disputed, income accrual awaits resolution of the dispute. For example, in Revenue Ruling 70-151,[23] accrual was required, not in the year taxpayer was awarded judgment against the United States, but in the following year when the government's petition for writ of certiorari was filed and denied.[24]

Timing questions concerning amounts held in escrow should be analyzed under the foregoing accrual principles. If the escrowed amount is not to be released until the taxpayer has rendered performance, then the taxpayer's right to the income is not yet fixed under the all events test, and accrual is not appropriate. Conversely, mere delay in ability to reach or apply amounts in escrow should not itself prevent accrual. Security or reserve accounts, often required by lenders or creditors, raise similar issues. In *Commissioner v. Hansen*,[25] an automobile dealer on the accrual method sold the commercial installment paper received from his customers to a finance company. The finance company paid most of the purchase price to the dealer and credited the remainder to a "dealer's reserve account" as security for the dealer and guarantee of the installment paper. The dealer argued that the withheld amount was not income until paid. The Supreme Court, however, held the dealer had to accrue the withheld amounts when they were entered on the finance company's books at the time of the sale, reasoning that it was at that time the dealer's right to receive them was fixed: That is, the amounts ultimately would either be paid to the dealer in cash, or would be used to satisfy his obligations to the finance company, and if the latter occurred, they would be as much "received" as if paid in cash.

Specific rules applicable to certain kinds of income should be noted. Interest income is treated as accruing as it is earned over the life of the loan. For example,

---

[21] I.R.C. § 448(d)(5).

[22] Treas. Reg. § 1.448–2(e), (f).

[23] 1970-1 C.B. 116.

[24] This accrual method rule must be distinguished from the claim of right doctrine. In *North American Oil v. Burnet*, 286 U.S. 417 (1932), discussed in Chapter 3, *supra*, entitlement to the 1916 earnings was in dispute throughout 1916, and regardless of accounting method, the taxpayer was not taxable then. However, the 1916 earnings were held taxable as of 1917, even though the dispute continued until 1922, because they were received in 1917 under a claim of right. While actual receipt is critical to the claim of right doctrine, it is the right to receive income which is at the heart of accrual accounting.

[25] 360 U.S. 446 (1959).

Revenue Ruling 74-607[26] states "performance occurs when the lender allows the borrower to use his money. When he has done this for one day, one day's performance has occurred and one day's interest accrues. . . ." However, accrual is not required with respect to income, including interest, that cannot be collected at the time "performance" occurs.[27]

The regulations tax dividend income to shareholders when it is "unqualifiedly made subject to their demands" and make no distinction between cash and accrual method taxpayers.[28] In effect, accrual method taxpayers are placed on the cash method with respect to dividend income, and ordinarily will be taxed on receipt of the dividend.

[C] Receipt Prior to Earning: Prepayments

As noted previously, the accrual method focuses on the fixing of the right to income. Income thus accrues as it is earned, through performance, even though payment follows some time later. Where payment has not been earned, however, but is instead received in advance of performance, the income is not properly accruable for financial accounting purposes. However, the same rule does not govern tax accounting. In a line of cases,[29] culminating in *Schlude v. Commissioner*,[30] the Supreme Court held that accrual method taxpayers were required to include advance payments in income. In *Schlude*, the taxpayers owned a dance studio offering dance lessons pursuant to certain contracts. The contracts required a down payment with installment payments thereafter and in some cases a down payment combined with a negotiable note for the balance owing under the

---

[26] 1974-2 C.B. 149.

[27] *See* Clifton Mfg. Co. v. Comm'r, 137 F.2d 290 (4th Cir. 1943); Rev. Rul 80-361, 1980-2 C.B. 164.

[28] Treas. Reg. § 1.301-1(b).

[29] *Schlude* is the final case in a famous trilogy of U.S. Supreme Court cases which also included *Automobile Club of Michigan v. Comm'r*, 353 U.S. 180, and *American Automobile Association v. U.S.*, 367 U.S. 687 (1961). In *Automobile Club of Michigan*, the Court rejected the taxpayer's effort to prorate club dues over the twelve month membership period. According to the Court, this method of accruing the dues was "artificial" since club services were performed only upon the demand of a club member. A member might never utilize any of the club's services despite paying a year's dues. *American Automobile Association* involved similar facts except the taxpayer demonstrated that statistically the organization performed services at approximately the same rate each month for its membership as a whole. Thus, the taxpayer argued its proration of dues reasonably matched the proportion of its yearly costs incurred each month in rendering services attributable to those dues. On this basis, the taxpayer attempted to distinguish *Automobile Club of Michigan* where no such statistical evidence was presented. The Court nonetheless rejected the taxpayer's argument noting that the federal fisc could not be funded using such statistics. Relying on its earlier decision in *Automobile Club of Michigan*, the Court concluded that AAA's accounting method was also "artificial" since the advance payments were for services which were to be performed only upon customer demand. Instead, the Court suggested the taxpayer would be required to report income on a contract-by-contract basis. Since under any given contract, services would only be provided on demand and thus might never be performed, inclusion of the membership fee must be occur in the year of receipt even though the payment covered dues for a period extending beyond the year of payment. The Court also noted that Congress had initially enacted a provision which would have permitted the taxpayer's method of accounting but subsequently reversed itself when it realized the method would have a "disastrous" impact on Government revenues. The Court noted that its policy was to defer to congressional procedures in the tax field.

[30] 372 U.S. 128 (1963).

contract. The taxpayers kept records on each student showing the numbers of hours taught together with the number of lessons remaining under the contract. At the end of each fiscal period, the student records were analyzed and the total number of hours taught during the period was multiplied by the rate per hour specified in the contract; the resulting figure was reported as earned income on the taxpayer's return. Likewise, the taxpayers reported income from lessons which had been canceled during the period but for which the student was required to pay.[31] The Court rejected the taxpayers' accrual method noting that it was vulnerable under Section 446(b) as not clearly reflecting income because the payments made in advance or currently due related to services which would only be provided if the customer demanded them. Since the services might never be provided and there were no fixed dates of performance, deferred reporting of amounts which were received or which were due was inappropriate. The Court therefore held that the taxpayers were required to report currently all cash receipts, negotiable notes received and contract installments due and payable. In effect, the Court's decision established the basis for the so-called "earliest of rule" of accrual accounting, i.e., "all the events that fix the right to receive income occur when (1) the payment is earned through performance, (2) payment is due the taxpayer, or (3) payment is received by the taxpayer, whichever happens earliest."[32]

Although *Schlude* might have appeared to slam the door on taxpayer efforts to defer the inclusion of prepayments in income, a few resourceful taxpayers and courts have occasionally found that a modest opening remains. *Artnell Co. v. Commissioner*[33] provides an excellent example. In *Artnell*, the taxpayer purchased all of the stock in Chicago White Sox, Inc., and immediately liquidated that corporation. At the time of the liquidation, the corporate balance sheets showed as "unearned income" proceeds from advance ticket sales for baseball games and revenues for related services such as season parking, broadcasting rights, etc. In filing an income tax return for Chicago White Sox, Inc., for the tax year ending with the date of the liquidation of the corporation, Artnell Co. did not include the deferred unearned income as gross income. Artnell argued that since this income related to future scheduled games to be played by the White Sox, those revenues were reportable in the year the games were played and not in the year the revenues were received. The Commissioner, in refusing to allow this deferral of income, relied on the *Schlude* line of cases. The Seventh Circuit, however, noted that in those cases the time and the extent of the performance of future services was uncertain. In *Artnell*, by contrast, the deferred income was allocable to White Sox games which were played on a fixed schedule. The court concluded that, in cases such as *Artnell*, where the time and extent of performance are certain and where income can be properly allocated to performance, deferral of income until

---

[31] The taxpayers' method may be viewed as tailored to avoid the problems raised in both *Automobile Club of Michigan* and *American Automobile Association* discussed in footnote 29, *supra*. The Court in *Schlude*, however, concluded that the method employed by taxpayer suffered from the same vice as that identified in the two earlier cases, *i.e.*, dance lessons were provided only upon demand and thus with respect to any contract some, none or all of the lessons might be rendered.

[32] Rev. Proc. 2004-34, 2004-1 C.B. 991.

[33] 400 F.2d 981 (7th Cir. 1968).

the year of performance will be found to reflect income clearly.[34] Nonetheless, such cases are exceptions; *Schlude* is the rule and it has been applied in numerous cases to hold prepaid income includable on receipt.

The most significant relief from the *Schlude* rule was provided by the Service, initially in Revenue Procedure 71-21, and subsequently in Revenue Procedure 2004-34,[35] which modified and superseded Revenue Procedure 71-21. Consider this common situation: An accrual method taxpayer provides services to a variety of clients, often over a period of many months. To assure payment, the taxpayer requires that all or a substantial portion of the total charges be paid before commencement of the services. Under the "earliest of" test, it is clear that the entire advance payment would be includable on receipt. Revenue Procedure 2004-34, however, modifies the "earliest of" test and authorizes a one-year deferral for advance payments covered by its terms, except to the extent that the taxpayer has included the advance payment in its revenues for financial accounting purposes — that is, by recognizing the payment in its "applicable financial statement."[36] To the extent of its inclusion in the taxpayer's applicable financial statement, the advance payment must be included in income in the year of receipt. If the taxpayer has no applicable financial statement, the advance payment must be included in income to the extent earned.

The Revenue Procedure applies to prepayments for services and for other specified items.[37] Prepayments for rent or interest, and certain other prepayments, are explicitly excluded from the scope of the Procedure.[38] In general terms, Revenue Procedure 2004-34 gives an option to the taxpayer receiving a covered advance payment: (1) include the full amount of the advance payment in income in the year of receipt (the "Full Inclusion Method"); or (2) include the advance payment in income in the year of receipt "to the extent recognized in revenues in its applicable financial statement," or, if the taxpayer has no applicable financial statement, "to the extent earned" in that year (the "Deferral Method"). Any portion of the advance payment not included in income in the year of receipt must be included in income in the next tax year.

Example: To draw upon an example given in Revenue Procedure 2004-34, assume Claire, an accrual method taxpayer, receives an advance payment

---

[34] The Tax Court, in *Tampa Bay Devil Rays, Inc. v. Comm'r*, T.C. Memo 2002-248, a case almost identical to *Artnell*, relied on *Artnell* in allowing the accrual method taxpayer to defer prepaid income. *See also* Boise Cascade Corp. v. U.S., 530 F.2d 1367 (Ct. Cl. 1976) (deferring until the following year prepaid income where services were to be performed at fixed dates or as expeditiously as possible); Morgan Guaranty Trust Co. of New York v. U.S., 585 F.2d 988 (Ct. Cl. 1978) (deferring until the following tax year *de minimis* amounts of prepaid interest).

[35] 2004-1 C.B. 991.

[36] An applicable financial statement is (1) a financial statement required to be filed with the Securities and Exchange Commission (SEC); (2) a certified audited financial statement by an independent CPA that is used for a "substantial non-tax purposes"; or (3) a financial statement, other than a tax return, required to be provided to the federal or state government or to a federal or state agency other than the SEC or IRS. See Rev. Proc. 2004-34, § 4.06, which also establishes a priority rule in the event there is more than one applicable financial statement.

[37] Rev. Proc. 2004-34, § 4.01(3).

[38] Rev. Proc. 2004-34, § 4.02.

of $120,000 for services under a 24-month contract that extends from November, Year 1, through October 31, Year 3. Claire provides 1/12 of the services in Year 1, 6/12 of the services in Year 2, and 5/12 of the services in Year 3. Claire recognizes the advance payment in those same proportions in her applicable financial statements for those years.

Analysis: Under the Full Inclusion method, Claire would include the entire advance payment in income in Year 1, the year of receipt. Under the Deferral Method (which Claire is permitted to use at her option), she would recognize 1/12 of the advance payment, or $10,000, in Year 1, since that is the amount included in revenues in her applicable financial statement. (If Claire had no applicable financial statement, then she would include 1/12, or $10,000, of the payment in income in Year 1, since that is the amount earned in Year 1.) However, under the Deferral Method, the remaining 11/12, or $110,000, of the advance payment must be included in income in Year 2, even though a lesser amount was both reflected in the Year 2 applicable financial statement and earned in Year 2, because the deferral of an advance payment is not permitted to extend beyond the tax year following the year of receipt.

Revenue Procedure 2004-34 represents a significant concession by the Commissioner intended, as was said earlier of Revenue Procedure 71-21, "to reconcile the tax and financial accounting treatment of [amounts received for services to be performed in the future] in a large proportion of [the] cases without permitting extended deferral in the time of including such payments in gross income." For taxpayers not falling within the "safe harbor" of Revenue Procedure 2004-34, an *Artnell*-type argument is apparently still available.

Schlude involved prepaid service income, but its principles have been applied to prepayments for goods. In *Hagen Advertising Displays, Inc. v. Commissioner*,[39] unconditional advance payments for goods, received prior to delivery, were held includable in income on receipt, on the authority of the *Schlude* line of cases. As in the services area, however, the government has since provided some relief from the rule. The regulations[40] permit the deferral of those advance payments for goods that meet the requirements therein detailed. Some legislative relief from the prepayment rule has also been enacted.[41]

One final point should be noted regarding prepayments. Deposits do not constitute income;[42] however, advance rentals are generally income on receipt regardless of the taxpayer's accounting method.[43] It is therefore necessary to distinguish between a deposit and a prepayment. The more restricted the taxpayer's use of the funds received, the more likely they are to be in the nature of a deposit.

---

[39] 407 F.2d 1105 (6th Cir. 1969).

[40] Treas. Reg. § 1.451-5.

[41] *See* I.R.C. §§ 455 (prepaid subscriptions), 456 (prepaid dues).

[42] *See* Chapter 3, *supra.*

[43] Treas. Reg. § 1.61-8(b).

§ 29.03 DEDUCTIONS UNDER THE ACCRUAL METHOD

[A] General Rules

As previously noted, under the accrual method an expense is deductible for the tax year in which "all the events have occurred which determine the fact of liability, the amount thereof can be determined with reasonable accuracy, and economic performance has occurred with respect to the liability."[44] By contrast to the cash method, under which payment of an expense is required for deductibility, deductions under the accrual method focus on establishing or "fixing" the "fact" of liability, and determining its amount with reasonable accuracy. Thus, in the example at the outset of this Chapter, XYZ's payment of the $1,000 legal fee to Laura is not the critical event for deduction purposes. Rather, the completion of the legal work by Laura and the setting of her fee will determine the appropriate timing of the deduction. Under the accrual method, there tends to be a "matching" of income with the expenses incurred in producing that income; this matching concept is at the heart of accrual method accounting.

A liability must be "fixed and certain," "unconditional," or "absolute" to satisfy the all events test. A liability contingent upon the occurrence of future events is not "fixed" for tax purposes. Most typically, perhaps, a liability accrues when the taxpayer receives performance from another — that is, when the taxpayer receives services or property, or the use of property, and his obligation to make payment is thereby established. Thus, as the Service noted in Revenue Ruling 98-39:[45]

> Generally, in a transaction where one taxpayer is accruing a liability to pay another taxpayer, the last event necessary to establish the fact of liability under the all events test of § 1.461-1(a)(2)(i) is the same event that fixes the right to receive income under the all events test of § 1.451-1(a). . . . In general, the event fixing the fact of liability pursuant to an agreement for services is performance of the services. . . .

More recently, in Revenue Ruling 2007-3,[46] the Service stated that "Generally . . . all the events have occurred that establish the fact of the liability when (1) the event fixing the liability, whether that be the required performance or other event, occurs, or (2) payment therefor is due, whichever happens earliest."

But not all liabilities are readily encompassed by these formulas. In *United States v. Hughes Properties*[47] the Supreme Court held that an accrual basis taxpayer, a casino operator, was entitled to deduct the amounts guaranteed for payments on "progressive" slot machines, even though the amounts had not yet been won at year's end by playing patrons. The Court emphasized that state regulations prohibited reduction of the jackpot without paying it out, and there was no evidence of tax avoidance by the taxpayer. The possibility that the jackpot might not be won if the casino went out of business, lost its license, or went into

---

[44] Treas. Reg. §§ 1.461-1(a)(2), 1.446-1(c)(1)(ii).

[45] 1998-2 C.B. 198.

[46] 2007-1 C.B. 350.

[47] 476 U.S. 593 (1986).

bankruptcy was regarded as simply a risk inherent in the accrual method which should not prevent accrual.[48] By contrast, in *United States v. General Dynamics Corporation*,[49] the Supreme Court distinguished *Hughes Properties* and held an accrual basis taxpayer could not deduct the reserve account it established for unpaid claims under its self-insured employee medical care plan. The Court reasoned that the last event necessary to fix liability was not the receipt of medical services by covered individuals, but their filing of proper claim forms. Since such filing had not occurred, no liability had yet accrued. Applying *General Dynamics* in *Chrysler Corporation v. Commissioner*,[50] the Tax Court held that the last event fixing the liability of Chrysler Corporation under its automobile warranties occurred no sooner than the filing of a claim for warranty service by a customer who purchased a Chrysler product from a Chrysler dealer or a claim for reimbursement by one of its dealers. The court rejected Chrysler's argument that its liability under the warranty was fixed upon the sale of its vehicles to its dealers.

Accrual of a liability turns on the fixing, not the payment of the liability, and therefore the financial condition of the taxpayer at the time of accrual generally will not bar a deduction. For example, the Service in one ruling allowed the full amount of interest accrued during the year to be deducted, although there was "no reasonable expectancy" that the taxpayer would pay the accrued interest in full; the ruling, however, distinguished the "doubt as to the payment" from a contingency that postpones accrual pending resolution of the contingency.[51] Similarly, where there was no "certainty" of an accrual method taxpayer's ability to pay, the Tax Court held a deduction was proper notwithstanding doubts as to the taxpayer's ultimate ability to pay.[52] By contrast, where a taxpayer during the pendency of a bankruptcy proceeding entered into an agreement with the United States Department of Energy and admitted to $30,000,000 in overcharges, the court disallowed the deduction for the Government's claim against the taxpayer because the taxpayer was unable to pay even a fraction of the amount. The court emphasized that to allow a deduction under the circumstances would not result in an accurate reflection of the taxpayer's income.[53]

[B]　Premature Accruals

Since deductions under the accrual method are based on the fixing of a liability, rather than its payment, an incentive is created for accrual basis taxpayers to exploit the distinction by attempting to fix a liability as soon as possible, while postponing its actual payment as long as possible. In these circumstances, a

---

[48] Section 461(h), discussed *infra*, did not apply to this case because the tax year in question preceded the effective date of Section 461(h). The Treasury, however, has issued Regulation § 1.461-4(g)(4), which provides: "if the liability of a taxpayer is to provide an award, prize, jackpot, or other similar payment to another person, economic performance occurs as payment is made to the person to which the liability is owed."

[49] 481 U.S. 239 (1987).

[50] T.C. Memo 2000-283, *aff'd*, 436 F.3d 644 (6th Cir. 2006).

[51] Rev. Rul. 70-367, 1970-2 C.B. 37.

[52] Cohen v. Comm'r, 21 T.C. 855 (1954) (acq.).

[53] Southwestern States Marketing Corp. v. U.S., 82 F.3d 413 (5th Cir. 1996).

liability to be paid tomorrow produces tax savings today. Indeed, taken to extremes, the present value of the tax deduction gained from accruing the liability can exceed the present value of the future payment — that is, the *current* tax savings obtained by the fixing of the liability, can be greater than the full cost of funding the liability today, if the liability need not actually be paid for a sufficiently long period of time. In any event, it is generally in the taxpayer's financial interest to assert that a particular liability has accrued for tax purposes at the earliest possible time.

Section 446(b) places an overarching, if ill-defined, limitation on any deductions that are part of an accrual method that "does not clearly reflect income." In *Mooney Aircraft, Inc. v. United States*,[54] which the court described as "yet another case in the continuing conflict between commercial accounting practice and the federal income tax," the accrual method taxpayer, an airplane manufacturer, issued with each airplane it manufactured and sold, an unconditional $1,000 "Mooney Bond," by which it promised to pay the bearer of the bond $1,000 when the corresponding airplane was permanently retired; 20 years or more could elapse between issuance of the bond and retirement of the airplane. The court agreed with the taxpayer that, upon issuance of the bond, the fact of liability was established, but it nonetheless upheld the Commissioner's refusal to allow a deduction upon issuance:

> The most salient feature in this case is the fact that many or possibly most of the expenses which taxpayer wishes to presently deduct will not actually be paid for 15, 20 or even 30 years (the taxpayer has not attempted to deny this). In no other case coming to our attention have we found anything even comparable to the time span involved in this case.
>
> In this case, the related expenditure is so distant from the time the money [from the sale of the plane] is received as to completely attenuate any relationship between the two. In what sense, is it an accurate reflection of income to regard it as an expense of doing business in the current year? We therefore find no difficulty in concluding that the Commissioner had a reasonable basis for disallowing the deduction as not clearly reflecting income.
>
> There is yet another reason why the time span is too long. The longer the time the less probable it becomes that the liability, though incurred, will ever in fact be paid.
>
> In the present case the taxpayer could in good faith use the monies it has received as capital to expand its business; if one day it became insolvent the expense might never be paid, yet the money would have been used as taxfree income. We repeat that because of the inordinate length of time involved in this case the Commissioner was clearly within his discretion in disallowing deduction of the "Mooney Bonds" as a *current* expense.[55]

---

[54] 420 F.2d 400 (5th Cir. 1969).

[55] *Id.* at 409, 410.

[C]   The Economic Performance Test: Section 461(h)

Prior to the enactment of Section 461(h) in 1984, there was considerable dispute as to whether the all events test permitted the taxpayer to deduct the estimated expenses of future performance. In *Schuessler v. Commissioner*,[56] for example, an accrual method taxpayer, engaged in the gas furnace business, sought to deduct a reserve account that represented his estimated cost of carrying out a guarantee, given to purchasers, to turn their new furnace on and off for each of the next five years. The Fifth Circuit held the sale of the furnace established a legal liability to turn the furnaces on and off for the next five years, and that the cost of doing so had been reasonably estimated and was therefore currently deductible. However, following *Schlude*, some commentators argued that *Schuessler*-type decisions were of dubious validity, on the ground that allowing the deductions of future costs could frequently achieve for taxpayers much the same result as the prohibited deferrals of prepaid income. The Internal Revenue Service, in any event, took the position that the all events test was not satisfied where the taxpayer had not yet rendered required performance.[57] For example, where an accrual method taxpayer installed oil and gas platforms pursuant to a lease with the federal government, and the taxpayer was contractually obligated to remove the platforms at the end of the lease, the Service held the cost of removal was not deductible until the removal services were actually performed.[58] By contrast, in *Ohio River Collieries Co. v. Commissioner*,[59] the Tax Court held an accrual basis taxpayer was entitled to deduct the reasonably estimated cost of reclaiming strip-mined land in the year it engaged in the strip-mining and, under local law, thereby incurred an obligation to reclaim the land. The Tax Court rejected the Commissioner's position that reclamation costs would be deductible only when the reclamation was performed. Taxpayer victories in *Ohio River Collieries* and other cases led to the enactment of Section 461(h), and the incorporation of the Service's economic performance standard into the Code.

§ 461(h).   Certain liabilities not incurred before economic performance.

(1)   In general. For purposes of this title, in determining whether an amount has been incurred with respect to any item during any taxable year, the all events test shall not be treated as met any earlier than when economic performance with respect to such item occurs.

(2)   Time when economic performance occurs. Except as provided in regulations prescribed by the Secretary, the time when economic performance occurs shall be determined under the following principles:

(A)   Services and property provided to the taxpayer. If the liability of the taxpayer arises out of —

---

[56]   230 F.2d 722 (5th Cir. 1956).

[57]   Section 461(h), discussed *infra*, adopts the economic performance requirement urged by the Service.

[58]   Rev. Rul. 80-182, 1980-2 C.B. 167. Regulation § 1.461-4(d)(7) Example 1 addresses the same factual scenario presented in Revenue Ruling 80-182 and reaches the same conclusion on the authority of Section 461(h).

[59]   77 T.C. 1369 (1981).

(i) the providing of services to the taxpayer by another person, economic performance occurs as such person provides such services,

(ii) the providing of property to the taxpayer by another person, economic performance occurs as the person provides such property, or

(iii) the use of property by the taxpayer, economic performance occurs as the taxpayer uses such property.

(B)   Services and property provided by the taxpayer. If the liability of the taxpayer requires the taxpayer to provide property or services, economic performance occurs as the taxpayer provides such property or services.

(C)   Workers compensation and tort liabilities of the taxpayer. If the liability of the taxpayer requires a payment to another person and

(i) arises under any workers compensation act, or

(ii) arises out of any tort, economic performance occurs as the payments to such persons are made. Subparagraphs (A) and (B) shall not apply to any liability described in the preceding sentence.

In 1984, Congress specifically adopted the Service's longstanding position that, for an amount to be deductible by an accrual method taxpayer, there must be current liability to pay that amount. In other words, the facts that the liability is fixed and the amount of the liability can be determined with reasonable accuracy are not enough to justify a current deduction; economic performance must also occur. Section 461(h)(1) specifically adds this economic performance requirement to the all events test, providing that "the all events test shall not be treated as met any earlier than when economic performance with respect to such item occurs." The legislative history for Section 461(h) states the following rationale for the economic performance test:

> Congress believed that the rules relating to the time of a deduction by a taxpayer using the accrual method of accounting should be changed to take into account the time value of money and the time the deduction is economically incurred. Recent court decisions in some cases permitted accrual method taxpayers to deduct currently expenses that were not yet economically incurred (i.e., that were attributable to activities to be performed or amounts to be paid in the future). Allowing a taxpayer to take deductions currently for an amount to be paid in the future overstates the true cost of the expense to the extent that the time value of money is not taken into account; the deduction is overstated by the amount by which the face value exceeds the present value of the expenses. The longer the period of time involved, the greater is the overstatement.[60]

Section 461(h)(2) establishes the following rules for determining when economic performance occurs:

> (1) If the liability arises as a result of another person providing services to the taxpayer, economic performance occurs as the services are pro

---

[60] General Explanation to the Tax Reform Act of 1984 prepared by the staff of the Joint Committee on Taxation, p. 260.

vided.[61] Thus, returning to the example at the beginning of this chapter, involving Laura's provision of deductible legal services to XYZ, economic performance occurred when Laura provided the legal services.

(2) If the liability results from the taxpayer's use of property, economic performance occurs "ratably over the period of time the taxpayer is entitled to the use of the property."[62] For example, when an owner of equipment rents the equipment to a taxpayer, economic performance occurs each day the taxpayer uses or is entitled to use the equipment.

(3) If the liability results from the taxpayer providing services or property, economic performance occurs as the taxpayer provides the service or the property.[63] For example, in *Ohio River Collieries*, discussed above, economic performance would occur as the strip-mined land was reclaimed.

Under a special rule with regard to workers' compensation and tort liabilities, economic performance occurs when payment is made.[64]

Example: Lucien, an accrual method taxpayer, owns a music store which sells musical instruments, including pianos. With each new piano sale, Lucien agrees to tune the piano annually free of charge to the purchaser for the first five years. Lucien estimates he will incur $100 of out-of-pocket expense on average over the five year period in fulfilling his obligation to each piano purchaser. In Year 1, Lucien sells 50 new pianos and thus estimates he will incur $5,000 in tuning expenses over the next five years. May he deduct the $5,000 in Year 1?

Analysis: Given the economic performance test of Section 461(h), the answer is clearly "No." Under Section 461(h)(2)(B), economic performance will only occur as Lucien actually provides the tuning service. Thus, even though Lucien may be able to satisfy the "all events test" as it existed prior to the enactment of Section 461(h), he cannot satisfy that test as it has been modified by Section 461(h).

[D] Recurring Item Exception to the Economic Performance Test

Section 461(h)(3) provides for recurring items a special exception under which a deduction is available even though economic performance has yet to occur. There are four statutory requirements which must be satisfied for this exception to apply:

(1) the all events test with respect to the item must be met during the taxable year without regard to the economic performance test;

---

[61] I.R.C. § 461(h)(2)(A)(i).

[62] I.R.C. § 461(h)(2)(A)(iii); Treas. Reg. § 1.461-4(d)(3).

[63] I.R.C. § 461(h)(2)(B).

[64] I.R.C. § 461(h)(2)(C).

(2) economic performance with respect to the item must occur within the shorter of:

(i) a reasonable period after the close of such taxable year;[65] or

(ii) 8½ months after the close of such taxable year;

(3) the item must be recurring in nature and the taxpayer must consistently treat items of such kind as incurred in the taxable year in which the requirements of (1) above are met, and

(4) either:

(i) the item is not a material item; or

(ii) the accrual of such item in the year in which the requirements of (1) above are met results in a more proper match against income than accruing the item in the taxable year when economic performance occurs.[66]

Example: Michael, an accrual method taxpayer, owns a small business that manufactures and sells widgets. Michael, a calendar year taxpayer timely files his tax return for each taxable year on the extended due date for the return (September 15 of the following taxable year). A dissatisfied purchaser may return the widget and receive a full refund. During Year 2, Michael's sales of widgets amounted to more than $750,000. In Year 3, 1,000 purchasers requested a refund of their $50 purchase price. Michael refunded $30,000 of the purchase price before September 15 of Year 3 and refunded the remaining $20,000 after such date but before the end of Year 3.

Analysis: Economic performance with respect to the refund amounts occurs when the refund is paid. Thus, but for recurring item exception, Michael would be required to take the refund into account (by way of a deduction or an adjustment to the gross receipts or cost of goods sold) in Year 3. If, however, all events have occurred that determine the fact of Michael's liability for the $30,000 refund and Michael has properly adopted the recurring item exception method of accounting, Michael will be entitled to deduct (or otherwise take into account) the $30,000 paid before September 15 of Year 3 in his tax return for Year for Year 2. Because economic performance (*i.e.*, payment) with respect to the remaining $20,000 occurs after September 15 of Year 3 (*i.e.*, more than 8½ months after the close of Year 2) that amount is not eligible for recurring item treatment. That amount is not incurred by Michael until Year 3 and therefore can't be taken into account in Year 2 (but would be deductible or otherwise allowable as an adjustment for Year 3).[67]

---

[65] Regulation § 1.461-5(b) interprets this to mean "the date the taxpayer files a timely (including extensions) return for that taxable year.

[66] I.R.C. § 461(h)(3).

[67] This example is based on Regulation § 1.461-5(e) Example 1.

[E]　Capitalization

If an accrued liability creates an asset with a useful life extending substantially beyond the taxable year, the liability must be capitalized.[68] Deductions under the accrual method, as under the cash method, are subject to Section 263, which prohibits the deduction of capital expenditures.[69]

As noted in prior chapters, in an effort to simplify administration for both the Service and the taxpayer, the Treasury has issued final regulations regarding capitalization of intangibles under Section 263 which provide a "12-month rule" to the effect that "a taxpayer is not required to capitalize amounts paid to create . . . any right or benefit for the taxpayer that does not extend beyond the earlier of (i) 12 months after the first date on which the taxpayer realizes the right or benefit; or (ii) the end of the taxable year following the taxable year in which the payment is made."[70] This 12-month rule represents an exception to the general rule specified in the regulations requiring the capitalization of prepaid expenses.[71]

If an accrual method taxpayer satisfies the "12-month rule," the taxpayer will not be allowed a deduction if the economic performance requirement of Section 461(h) has not been satisfied. The regulations specifically provide that the "12-month rule" will not affect "the determination of whether a liability is incurred during the taxable year, including the determination of whether economic performance has occurred with respect to the liability.[72] For example, if on December 15, an accrual method taxpayer prepays rent for January through June of the following year, no deduction would be available to the taxpayer (assuming the recurring item exception is inapplicable) because economic performance has not occurred, i.e., with regard to rent, economic performance occurs only as the taxpayer/renter is allowed to use the property.[73] The fact that the payment might otherwise come within the "12-month rule" does not change this result.[74]

[F]　Contested Liabilities

§ 461(f).　Contested liabilities.
If —

(1) the taxpayer contests an asserted liability,

(2) the taxpayer transfers money or other property to provide for the satisfaction of the asserted liability,

(3) the contest with respect to the asserted liability exists after the time of the transfer, and

(4) but for the fact that the asserted liability is contested, a deduction

---

[68]　Treas. Reg. § 1.461-1(a)(2).

[69]　*See* Chapter 13, *supra.*

[70]　Treas. Reg. § 1.263(a)-4(f)(1).

[71]　Treas. Reg. § 1.263(a)-4(d)(3)(i). See the discussion in Chapter 13, *supra.*

[72]　Treas. Reg. § 1.263(a)-4(f)(6).

[73]　Treas. Reg. § 1.461-4(d)(3).

[74]　Treas. Reg. § 1.263(a)-4(f)(8) Exs. 10 & 11.

would be allowed for the taxable year of the transfer (or for an earlier taxable year) determined after application of subjection (h),

then the deduction shall be allowed for the taxable year of the transfer.

In general, a contested liability cannot be deducted by an accrual method taxpayer because the contest, in effect, renders the liability contingent and prevents it from being "fixed" or "established." In *Dixie Pine Products Co. v. Commissioner*,[75] the Supreme Court held a taxpayer could not accrue a tax while contesting liability, and the Court suggested the proper date for accrual was when the liability was finally adjudicated. In *United States v. Consolidated Edison*,[76] the Court extended the *Dixie Pine* rule to deny accrual of a contested tax that was actually paid; accrual instead was to wait until the contest was finally determined. However, Section 461(f) overturns the *Consolidated Edison* decision and provides, in general, that payment of a contested liability accrues the liability and provides a current deduction in the year of payment. To be entitled to a deduction upon payment, the taxpayer must contest a liability, transfer money or other property in satisfaction thereof, continue the contest after the transfer, and be entitled to a deduction but for the contest. If a contested liability is not paid, it will not accrue until the contest is resolved. It is not necessary to institute litigation to have a contest, but the regulations do require a bona fide dispute.[77] A contest is settled when the parties reach agreement or the matter is finally adjudicated.[78]

Accrual during a contest requires that the taxpayer transfer money or other property in satisfaction of the liability. The regulation provides that the taxpayer must place the money or property beyond its control by transferring it to the person asserting the liability, to a court or public agency, or to a trustee or escrowee pursuant to written agreement between the taxpayer and the person asserting the liability, requiring delivery in accord with the outcome of the contest.[79] For example, a unilateral transfer to a bank as trustee has been held not to qualify.[80] In *Willamette Industries v. Commissioner*,[81] the court held the transfer requirement of Section 461(f)(2) was not satisfied by funding a settlement trust with a $20,000,000 letter of credit purchased from a bank for $85,000. The taxpayer was required to repay the bank for draws made on the letter of credit. Upon entry of final judgment against the taxpayer, the trust agreement directed the trustee to draw on the letter of credit for purposes of paying the plaintiffs. In rejecting the taxpayer's effort to deduct the $20,000,000 in the year when the trust was funded, the Tax Court concluded the taxpayer had merely "exchanged a contingent liability to the plaintiff for a contingent liability to the bank."[82] This arrangement was a

---

[75] 320 U.S. 516 (1944).

[76] 366 U.S. 380 (1961).

[77] Treas. Reg. § 1.461-2(b)(2).

[78] Treas. Reg. § 1.461-2(d).

[79] Treas. Reg. § 1.461-2(c)(1).

[80] Poirier & McLane Corp. v. Comm'r, 547 F.2d 161 (2d Cir. 1976); Rosenthal v. U.S., 11 Cl. Ct. 165 (1986).

[81] 92 T.C. 1166 (1989).

[82] *Id.* at 1182.

"type of legerdemain" that failed to satisfy the payment requirement of Section 461(f)(2).

Section 461(f) is applicable to cash method taxpayers as well as accrual method taxpayers, but its utility is essentially for the latter, since a cash method taxpayer may ordinarily deduct a liability upon payment even if the liability is contested.

§ 29.04   CHOICE OF ACCOUNTING METHODS

Section 446(c) provides that a taxpayer generally has the right to select the cash or accrual method, any other permitted method, or any permitted combination of methods. As a practical matter, however, most businesses of substantial size select the accrual method. A taxpayer engaged in more than one business may select a different accounting method for each business.[83] And a taxpayer may use one method for a business and another method for personal purposes.[84]

This freedom-of-choice is subject, however, to several general and specific limitations. The method of accounting chosen must be the one the taxpayer uses to compute income in keeping books.[85] A taxpayer who keeps no books or records will be deemed to have selected the cash method. As discussed above, the accounting method chosen is also subject to the overarching requirement of Section 446(b) that it clearly reflect the taxpayer's income. Thus, for example, the regulations provide that, as a permitted combination of methods, a taxpayer may account for purchases and sales on the accrual method, and other items of income and expense on the cash method. But the same regulations also provide that a taxpayer using the cash method for gross income purposes must also use it for expenses, and that use of the accrual method for business expenses requires use of the accrual method for gross income.[86] The taxpayer's method must also provide consistent treatment of income and deduction items from year to year.[87] In addition, once an accounting method is employed, it may not be changed without the Commissioner's consent.[88] Whether a change that is made constitutes a change in "the method of accounting" is often the threshold question. The Commissioner's consent to a change is typically conditioned on the taxpayer's agreeing to specified terms and adjustments.

Some specific limitations are applicable to certain taxpayers and activities. Section 448 prohibits use of the cash method by certain corporations and partnerships and by tax shelters.[89] In addition, the regulations provide that, in any case in which it is necessary to use an inventory, the accrual method is required with respect to purchases and sales.[90] Inventories are necessary if the production,

---

[83]   I.R.C. § 446(d).

[84]   Treas. Reg. § 1.446-1(c)(1)(iv)(b).

[85]   I.R.C. § 446(a).

[86]   Treas. Reg. § 1.446-1(c)(1)(iv)(a).

[87]   Treas. Reg. § 1.446-1(c)(2)(ii).

[88]   I.R.C. § 446(e).

[89]   I.R.C. § 448(a), (b).

[90]   Treas. Reg. § 1.446-1(c)(2)(i).

purchase or sale of merchandise is an income-producing factor.[91] Inventory accounting, and use of the accrual method for purchases and sales, is thus required for many business operations.[92] Finally, a number of Code provisions mandate special treatment for certain income and expense items in given circumstances.[93]

---

[91] Treas. Reg. § 1.471-1.

[92] In inventory accounting, gross profit or loss from sales in a given period is determined by subtracting the cost of goods sold from the gross sales proceeds. The cost of goods sold is in turn determined by adding together the cost of the opening inventory on hand at the commencement of the period and the cost of goods purchased during the period, and by then subtracting from that total the cost of the closing inventory on hand at the end of the period. *See* Note on Inventory Accounting in Appendix A, *infra*, for a further discussion of inventory accounting.

[93] *See, e.g.*, I.R.C. § 467.

Chapter 30

ANNUAL ACCOUNTING

Section 441 establishes the general rule that taxpayers are to make an annual accounting of their taxable income. Taxpayers are thus required to total income and expenses, gains and losses, on a yearly basis. In the main, such an annual accounting system seems administratively reasonable and also seems to produce tax results that fairly reflect one's ability to pay. Such, however, is not always the case. At times, the annual accounting system, in focusing on a twelve-month period, produces distorted measurements of taxable income, since the economic transactions on which income is based do not necessarily fit within a single taxable year. Income and expenses can fluctuate measurably; income can be bunched in one year, related expenses in another; a transaction seemingly done in one year may be undone in another. As a result, it sometimes appears that a transactional approach to measuring taxable income would be more accurate and fair, *i.e.*, that net profit or loss should be reported on a transaction by transaction basis rather than year by year. (Indeed, were it feasible, measuring taxable income on a lifetime basis would also be conceptually appealing.) However, the definitional and other administrative problems associated with transactional accounting would be daunting and, wholly apart from other concerns, are probably enough to prevent the wholesale adoption of transactional accounting in lieu of the present system. This chapter focuses on selected problems raised by the annual accounting system, and the responses to those problems.

§ 30.01 RESTORING AMOUNTS RECEIVED UNDER A CLAIM OF RIGHT

§ 1341. **Computation of tax where taxpayer restores substantial amount held under claim of right —**

(a) **General rule. — If —**

(1) an item was included in gross income for a prior taxable year (or years) because it appeared that the taxpayer had an unrestricted right to such item;

(2) a deduction is allowable for the taxable year because it was established after the close of such prior taxable year (or years) that the taxpayer did not have an unrestricted right to such item or to a portion of such item; and

(3) the amount of such deduction exceeds $3,000, then the tax imposed by this chapter for the taxable year shall be the lesser of the following:

(4) the tax for the taxable year computed with such deduction; or

(5) an amount equal to —

(A) the tax for the taxable year computed without such deduction,

minus

(B) the decrease in tax under this chapter (or the corresponding provisions of prior revenue laws) for the prior taxable year (or years) which would result solely from the exclusion of such item (or portion thereof) from gross income for such prior taxable year (or years).

As noted in Chapter 3, amounts received under a claim of right, without restriction as to disposition, constitute income. In *North American Oil v. Burnet*,[1] certain disputed funds, earned in 1916, were paid to the taxpayer in 1917. Although it was not until 1922 that the litigation involving the funds was finally terminated in the taxpayer's favor, the Supreme Court held the funds were nonetheless reportable as income in 1917 under the claim of right doctrine. If, however, the taxpayer in *North American Oil* had not been victorious, it would have been required to return the amount received and included in income under a claim of right. The tax system should and does take account of that restoration. The question is how it should be taken into account.

In *United States v. Lewis*,[2] The taxpayer received an improperly computed bonus in 1944, which he properly reported as income that year and repaid to his employer in 1946. The taxpayer sought a refund for overpayment of his 1944 taxes. Until repayment of the bonus in 1946, the taxpayer had claimed and used the bonus as his own. The government argued the repayment should be taken as a deduction in 1946 and a recomputation of the 1944 tax was not permissible. The Supreme Court agreed. The Supreme Court noted:

> Income taxes must be paid on income received (or accrued) during an annual accounting period. The "claim of right" interpretation of the tax laws has long been used to give finality to that period, and is now deeply rooted in the federal tax system. We see no reason why the Court should depart from this well-settled interpretation merely because it results in an advantage or disadvantage to a taxpayer.

What is at stake in the *Lewis*-type situation should be obvious. The *tax increase* resulting from including in income an amount received under a claim of right will not always be the same as the *tax savings* resulting from deducting its repayment in a later year. A taxpayer's marginal tax bracket can vary from year to year. A taxpayer will naturally prefer to deduct the restored funds when the tax savings thus produced exceeds the tax bite caused by inclusion in the earlier year. When the later year's tax savings are relatively small, a recomputation of the prior year's tax (and a refund of the excess tax paid) is preferable.

Congress responded to *Lewis* by enacting Section 1341. Rather than choose between deduction and recomputation, Congress fashioned a different remedy — a taxpayer who meets the requirements of Section 1341(a)(1)-(3) is directed to compute tax liability under the approach that produces the more favorable tax result.

---

[1] 286 U.S. 417 (1932).

[2] 340 U.S. 590 (1951).

Example 1: In Year 1, a taxpayer whose marginal tax rate is 25% properly included $10,000 in income received under a claim of right. Assume the taxpayer is required to repay the $10,000 in Year 3.

Analysis: The tax cost of inclusion in Year 1 is $2,500. If the taxpayer's marginal tax rate in Year 3 is 30%, the $10,000 deduction saves $3,000 in taxes — the deduction, in other words, is worth more than the tax cost of the original inclusion, and Section 1341(a) directs the taxpayer to deduct the repayment.

Example 2: Assume the facts of Example 1 except that the taxpayer is in a 20% marginal tax bracket in Year 3.

Analysis: In Year 3, a $10,000 deduction is worth only $2,000 to the taxpayer. The taxpayer's deduction of the $10,000 in Year 3 is thus worth less than the cost of including the $10,000 in Year 1. Section 1341(a) accordingly directs the taxpayer to forego the Year 3 deduction and instead to decrease his Year 3 tax liability by $2,500, the tax cost of the Year 1 inclusion.

Section 1341 does not, it should be stressed, provide for reopening the earlier year's tax return or for filing an amended return. What it directs instead (when it is more valuable than a deduction) is a tax decrease, in effect a tax credit, against the current year's tax liability in an amount equal to the added tax occasioned by the prior year's inclusion in income.[3] Essentially, the statute serves the function of an amended return without in fact authorizing one. This approach has a certain conceptual validity. Amended returns serve to correct errors and omissions in the original return, but the inclusion of income under a claim of right was in fact correct and appropriate, and not something rendered "erroneous" by virtue of subsequent events. Again, however, the tax decrease alternative is applied only when it produces a bigger tax savings than the deduction alternative.[4]

The requirements for applying Section 1341 should be noted carefully. First, relatively minor amounts are barred from Section 1341 treatment by a $3,000 threshold requirement.[5] Second, it is necessary that the restored item have been included in income for a prior year because it "appeared" the taxpayer had an unrestricted right to the income.[6] Third, it must be established in a subsequent year that the taxpayer did not have an unrestricted right to the income.[7] Fourth, the taxpayer must be entitled to a deduction because of the restoration of the item previously included in income.[8]

---

[3] I.R.C. § 1341(a)(5).

[4] *See* I.R.C. § 1341(a)(4).

[5] I.R.C. § 1341(a)(3).

[6] I.R.C. § 1341(a)(1).

[7] I.R.C. § 1341(a)(2).

[8] *Id.*

[A]   Appearance of a Right

It has been held, for example, that there is no "appearance" of an unrestricted right to income with respect to embezzled funds, and repayment is thus outside Section 1341.[9] The Service has also stated that the word "appeared" refers to "a semblance of an unrestricted right in the year received as distinguished from an unchallengeable right (which is more than an 'apparent' right) and from absolutely no right at all (which is less than an 'apparent' right). Whether the taxpayer had the semblance of an unrestricted right in the year of inclusion depends upon all the facts available at the end of such year."[10] The cited ruling thus holds that Section 1341(a) does not apply either to the repayment of funds received as the result of the taxpayer's "mere error," or to the repayment, "due to a subsequent event," of funds received under "absolute right." Instead, the ruling applies Section 1341(a) in one situation where, in the year of inclusion, the facts available to the taxpayer did not enable it to determine the proper amount of income, and in another situation where a regulatory agency with jurisdiction over the taxpayer retroactively changed a billing rate applicable to the year of inclusion. Suffice it to say that distinguishing among the appearance of a right, the lesser "no right," and the greater "unchallengeable right," may occasionally become problematic.

One court's response to all this is instructive. In *Dominion Resources v. United States*,[11] the taxpayer, a public utility, successfully sought to apply Section 1341 to customer refunds made (pursuant to requirements of its regulatory authorities) in 1991, when tax rates were lower than they had been when funds were collected in earlier years. The Fourth Circuit refused to adopt the Service's argument that the taxpayer could not avail itself of Section 1341 where it had an "actual" rather than merely an "apparent" right to the income it received in the earlier years.

> All that § 1341(a)(1) requires is that "an item be included in gross income for a prior taxable year (or years) because it appeared that the taxpayer had an unrestricted right to such item." Things very often "appear" to be what they "actually" are. As a matter of plain meaning, the word "appeared" generally does not, as the IRS urges, imply only false appearance, and generally does not exclude an appearance that happens to be true.[12]

According to the court, "The IRS's cramped construction of Section 1341 simply does not find adequate support in the plain language of the statute, its legislative history, or the case law interpreting it. Accordingly, we must reject that construction." The Fourth Circuit instead cited with favor the Tax Court's formulation of an "appropriate, workable" interpretation of Section 1341 — namely, a requirement that the taxpayer's lack of an unrestricted right to the income in question "must arise out of the circumstances, terms and conditions of the original payment of such

---

[9] See, for example, Rev. Rul. 65-254,1965-2 C.B. 50, relegating the individual taxpayer to a Section 165(c)(2) deduction instead. *See also* Kraft v. U.S., 991 F.2d 292 (6th Cir. 1993).

[10] Rev. Rul. 68-153, 1968-1 C.B. 371, 373.

[11] 219 F.3d 359 (4th Cir. 2000).

[12] *Id.* at 364.

item to the taxpayer."[13] The Fourth Circuit concluded that the taxpayer satisfied this formulation and was entitled to apply Section 1341 to its refunds to its customers.

[B] No Unrestricted Right

As noted earlier, Section 1341(a)(2) requires that the taxpayer establish in a later year that he did not have an unrestricted right to the amount received in the prior year. Thus, voluntary repayments may not come within Section 1341.

Several cases reflect the uncertain boundaries of this requirement. For example, in *Pike v. Commissioner*,[14] the taxpayer, an attorney who represented life insurance companies, sold at a profit some stock in one of the companies. His right to retain the profits was disputed, and he subsequently paid the profits to the company, not because he admitted liability or was compelled to do so, but because he feared controversy over the matter would endanger his professional career. Holding the taxpayer had failed to establish that he was not entitled to retain the profits, as required by Section 1341(a)(2), the Tax Court also held the payment was allowable as a Section 162 deduction.[15]

By contrast, in *Barrett v. Commissioner*,[16] the Tax Court held the taxpayer, a stockbroker, was entitled to a credit under Section 1341(a)(5) for amounts paid in 1984 to settle civil suits arising out of his purchase and sale of certain stock options in 1981. The 1981 sale of the options had generated a short-term capital gain of some $187,000, which the taxpayer reported, but had also led to the civil suits and the institution of civil proceedings by the Securities and Exchange Commission (SEC) to revoke taxpayer's brokerage license. The taxpayer maintained his innocence, but settled the suits by repaying part of the profits from the sale; the SEC administrative proceedings were then dropped as well. In applying Section 1341(a)(5), the court rejected as "ludicrous" the Commissioner's argument that the repayment was voluntary, and held that the good faith, arm's length settlement of the dispute had the same effect as a judgment in establishing the fact and amount of taxpayer's legal obligation for repayment and establishing that he did not have an "unrestricted right" to that amount when he received it. *Pike* was held distinguishable on its facts.

The *Barrett* approach, however, was rejected by a district court in *Parks v. United States*.[17] In that case, the taxpayer sold his business at a profit and reported the income. He subsequently settled fraud-related litigation arising out of the sale, made repayment, and sought to apply Section 1341 to the repayment. In denying the taxpayer's motion for summary judgment in reliance upon *Barrett*, the district court held the settlement did not eliminate the government's opportunity to demonstrate, if such were the case, that the previously-reported income had been

---

[13] *Id.* at 367 (*citing* Pahl v. Comm'r, 67 T.C. 286, 290 (1976)).

[14] 44 T.C. 787 (1985) (acq.).

[15] See Chapter 12, *supra*, regarding the deduction of voluntary payments as "ordinary and necessary" business expenses under Section 162.

[16] 96 T.C. 713 (1991) (nonacq.).

[17] 945 F. Supp. 865 (W.D. Pa. 1996).

obtained by fraud, and that Section 1341 would therefore be inapplicable to the repayment on the grounds the taxpayer had not "appeared to have an unrestricted right" to the income, as required by Section 1341(a)(1). According to *Parks*, to refuse to look behind the settlement agreement where there are allegations of intentional wrongdoing could effectively read Section 1341(a)(1) out of the statute.

In addition, the *Barrett* case was distinguished in *Wang v. Commissioner*,[18] where the taxpayer, an intern for a brokerage house, sold insider information. The Securities and Exchange Commission initiated civil and criminal proceedings against the taxpayer, who settled the civil action by payment of $125,000 to a restitution fund. The Tax Court rejected the taxpayer's effort to apply Section 1341 to the payment, on the ground that the statute did not apply where, as here, there was no claim of right, or the appearance thereof, to the illegal funds the taxpayer received. *Barrett* was distinguished on the basis that its focus had been on whether the taxpayer's repayment was voluntary, not on whether the income had been received under claim of right or on whether the taxpayer appeared to have an unrestricted right to income.

§ 30.02   THE TAX BENEFIT RULE

§ 111.   Recovery of tax benefit items —

(a)   Deductions — Gross income does not include income attributable to the recovery during the taxable year of any amount deducted in any prior taxable year to the extent such amount did not reduce the amount of tax imposed by this chapter.

The preceding section dealt with the repayment of amounts previously included in income. Suppose, conversely, the taxpayer recovers an amount deducted in a prior year. To take a common example, suppose the taxpayer properly takes a bad debt deduction in one year, and in a later year receives payment on the supposed bad debt. The annual accounting system does not permit the reopening of a prior year's tax return to take account of events occurring in later years. The judicially-developed tax benefit rule, however, requires the amount received in payment of the bad debt to be included in income in the current year. There are, in fact, two aspects to the tax benefit rule when a taxpayer recovers a previously deducted amount.

Under the "inclusionary aspect" of the tax benefit rule, the recovery constitutes gross income: the deduction gave rise to a tax benefit that, in light of later events, turned out to be unwarranted, and the taxpayer in effect gives back the tax benefit by including the recovered amount in income. It is likely, of course, that the taxpayer's marginal tax brackets in the year of deduction and year of recovery will differ, and consequently the tax saved by the prior year's deduction will not be precisely equal to the tax increase caused by the subsequent inclusion. The tax benefit rule does not attempt to take account of such differences. It provides no "best-of-both-worlds" equivalent to Section 1341. The recovered amount simply constitutes income in the year of recovery.

---

[18]   T.C. Memo. 1998-389.

There is, however, a second aspect to the tax benefit rule, and this "exclusionary aspect" has been codified in Section 111. To the extent a previously deducted amount did not produce a tax savings, its recovery will not constitute income.[19] In effect, if the deduction produces no tax benefit, recovery of the deducted amount produces no income.

> **Example 1:** Taxpayer in Year 1 properly takes a $10,000 business bad debt deduction, and in Year 3 the debt is paid in full. Assume Taxpayer in Year 1 had $50,000 of taxable income prior to taking the bad debt deduction. What are the tax consequences in Year 3?
>
> **Analysis:** The entire $10,000 deduction produced a tax benefit in Year 1, and all $10,000 recovered in Year 3 constitutes gross income under the inclusionary aspect of the tax benefit rule.[20]
>
> **Example 2:** Assume the facts of Example 1 except that Taxpayer's taxable income in Year 1, prior to taking the $10,000 bad debt deduction, had been zero.
>
> **Analysis:** In these circumstances, the subsequent recovery is excluded from income under the exclusionary aspect of the tax benefit rule, since the deduction produced no tax savings. (A critical assumption in this example is that the net loss in Year 1 did not carryover to some other year and produce a tax savings in that year.)[21]
>
> **Example 3:** Assume the facts of Example 1 except that Taxpayer's taxable income, prior to the deduction, had been $6,000 instead of zero.
>
> **Analysis:** Six thousand dollars of the $10,000 deduction would have reduced Taxpayer's tax liability in Year 1. The remaining $4,000 portion of the deduction that produced no tax savings in Year 1 (or in any other year, we are assuming) would be excluded from income on "recovery" of the $10,000 debt.

The tax benefit rule, in its inclusionary and exclusionary aspects, thus represents an attempt to put a taxpayer in approximately (not exactly, given changes in marginal tax rates from year to year) the same position as if only the "proper" amount had been deducted originally.

Perhaps the most common context for application of the tax benefit rule involves the refund of previously deducted state income tax.

> **Example 1:** Assume in Year 1 Taxpayer's standard deduction is $3,000. In addition, assume Taxpayer's itemized deductions total $3,400, including $1,000 on account of state income tax. (Also assume the Section 68 overall limitation on itemized deductions does not apply.) Since allowable deductions are $3,400, Taxpayer elects to itemize rather than take the $3,000

---

[19] I.R.C. § 111(a).

[20] Since the tax tables most taxpayers use to compute tax liability move in $50 steps or brackets, it may be argued that some minor portion of the deduction — less than $50 — falls entirely within the final $50 bracket, produces no tax savings and is thus excludable. We will ignore this *de minimis* amount.

[21] See § 30.03, *infra*, regarding net operating losses.

standard deduction. Assume in Year 2 Taxpayer receives a $500 state income tax refund on the Year 1 taxes. How should the taxpayer treat the $500 refund?

Analysis: All $500 is income *unless* part of it is excluded by Section 111(a). Taxpayer's itemized deductions would have totaled only $2,900 had the "extra" $500 in state income taxes not been deducted, but Taxpayer would nonetheless have effectively received $3,000 in deductions through the standard deduction. In effect, given the $3,000 standard deduction that Taxpayer would receive at a minimum, part of the state income taxes paid produced no tax benefit. The part producing no tax benefit is the amount necessary to bring the itemized deductions up to the amount of standard deduction.

In this example, with $2,400 in other itemized deductions, the first $600 in the state income taxes produced no tax benefit. The remaining $400 exceeded the standard deduction and did produce a tax benefit. Thus, the first $400 of the state income tax refund constitutes income; any refund in excess of $400 is excluded from income by Section 111(a).

Example 2: Assume the facts of Example 1, except Taxpayer's other itemized deductions exceeded the standard deduction amount.

Analysis: Now the entire state income tax deduction of $1,000, not just a portion of it, would have produced a tax benefit. Accordingly, any refund would be included in income in its entirety.

Section 111(a) excludes those recovered amounts that, when deducted, did not reduce tax. At one time, what Section 111(a) excluded were those recovered amounts that had not reduced taxable income when deducted. The distinction between "reducing tax" and "reducing taxable income" is important in some instances. For example, if a taxpayer is subject to the alternative minimum tax,[22] a deduction may reduce taxable income but may not ultimately reduce tax liability. Thus, Section 111(a) appropriately keys the exclusion to tax reduction, not taxable income. Nonetheless, it is clear from the legislative history of the current version of Section 111(a) that the simplified procedure described above may be followed for individual taxpayers receiving refunds of state and local income taxes. Such taxpayers may simply compare (1) the amount of the refund, with (2) the amount by which the prior year's itemized deductions (determined after the application of Section 68) exceeded the standard deduction. The lesser of these two amounts is included in income.[23] In Revenue Ruling 92-91,[24] a similar rule was applied with

---

[22] *See* Chapter 44, *infra.*

[23] See the Explanation of Technical Corrections to the Tax Reform Act of 1984 and Other Recent Tax Legislation, Jt. Comm. on Taxation (1987), p.74. See also Revenue Ruling 93-75, 1993-2 C.B. 63, which states the simplified procedure as follows: A refund of previously-deducted state income tax is included in income to the extent "the taxpayer's itemized deductions in the prior year (after the application section 68 of the Code)" exceed "the deductions the taxpayer would have claimed ([*i.e.,*] the greater of (1) the itemized deductions after the application of section 68, or (2) the standard deduction) had the taxpayer paid the proper amount of state income tax in the prior year" and thus received no refund.

[24] 1992-2 C.B. 49.

respect to a refund of a home mortgage interest overcharge. The taxpayer's deduction, upon payment in good faith of the amount erroneously asserted by the lender to be due, was held to be proper. The lender's refund of the interest overcharge in the following year was held includable in income under the tax benefit rule; and since the amount of the reimbursement was less than the amount by which the prior year's itemized deductions exceeded the standard deduction, the reimbursement was fully includable in income.

The tax benefit principle — that the restoration or refund of previously deducted amounts constitutes income — is pervasive in tax law. It is codified, for example, in Section 104(a), where the general rule, excluding compensation for personal physical injuries or physical sickness from income, is not extended to amounts attributable to previously deducted medical expenses. As a further example, Section 461(f) allows a deduction for contested liabilities upon payment. The regulations, in an illustration of tax benefit principles, provide that the subsequent refund of a contested, deducted amount is includable in income, subject to the exclusionary rule of Section 111.[25]

[A]   The "Fundamental Inconsistency" Test

In *Hillsboro National Bank v. Commissioner*,[26] a state property tax on bank shares was refunded to shareholders of the bank although the property tax had originally been paid by the bank itself. The bank had properly taken a deduction for the payment under Section 164(e), and when refund of the property tax was subsequently made directly to the shareholders, the Service sought to charge the bank with income under the tax benefit rule.

In analyzing the applicability of the tax benefit rule, the Supreme Court rejected the idea that a "recovery" by the party charged with the income is always necessary to invoke the rule. Rather, said the Court,

> The basic purpose of the tax benefit rule is to achieve rough transactional parity in tax . . . and to protect the Government and the taxpayer from the adverse effects of reporting a transaction on the basis of assumptions that an event in a subsequent year proves to have been erroneous. Such an event, unforseen at the time of an earlier deduction, may in many cases require the application of the tax benefit rule. We do not, however, agree that this consequence invariably follows. Not every unforseen event will require the taxpayer to report income in the amount of his earlier deduction. On the contrary, the tax benefit rule will "cancel out" an earlier deduction only when a careful examination shows that the later event is indeed fundamentally inconsistent with the premise on which the deduction was initially based. That is, if that event had occurred within the same taxable year, it would have foreclosed the deduction. In some cases, a subsequent recovery by the taxpayer will be the only event that would be fundamentally inconsistent with the provision granting the deduction. In such a case, only actual recovery by the taxpayer would justify application

---

[25] Treas. Reg. § 1.461-2(a)(3).

[26] 460 U.S. 370 (1983).

of the tax benefit rule. For example, if a calendar-year taxpayer made a rental payment on December 15 for a 30-day lease deductible in the current year . . . the tax benefit rule would not require the recognition of income if the leased premises were destroyed by fire on January 10. The resulting inability of the taxpayer to occupy the building would be an event not fundamentally inconsistent with his prior deduction as an ordinary and necessary business expense. . . . The loss is attributable to the business and therefore is consistent with the deduction of the rental payment as an ordinary and necessary business expense. On the other hand, had the premises not burned and, in January, the taxpayer decided to use them to house his family rather than to continue the operation of his business, he would have converted the leasehold to personal use. This would be an event fundamentally inconsistent with the business use on which the deduction was based. In the case of the fire, only if the lessor — by virtue of some provision in the lease — had refunded the rental payment would the taxpayer be required under the tax benefit rule to recognize income on the subsequent destruction of the building. In other words, the subsequent recovery of the previously deducted rental payment would be the only event inconsistent with the provision allowing the deduction. It therefore is evident that the tax benefit rule must be applied on a case-by-case basis. A court must consider the facts and circumstances of each case in light of the purpose and function of the provisions granting the deductions.[27]

In *Hillsboro* itself, the Court found no fundamental inconsistency between the bank's deduction and the state's repayment to shareholders:

> We conclude that the purpose of Sec. 164(e) was to provide relief for corporations making these payments, and the focus of Congress was on the act of payment rather than on the ultimate use of the funds by the state. As long as the payment itself was not negated by a refund to the corporation, the change in character of the funds in the hands of the state does not require the corporation to recognize income, and we reverse the judgment below.[28]

[B]   Erroneous Original Deduction

Another issue that may arise under the tax benefit rule occurs when the deduction the taxpayer takes in the prior year is erroneous. Does the tax benefit rule apply to a subsequent refund, or is the Commissioner's remedy limited to challenging the erroneous deduction within the time period of the statute of limitations? The Ninth Circuit in *Unvert v. Commissioner*[29] rejected the so-called erroneous deduction exception to the tax benefit rule and instead, affirming the Tax Court, held the refund was taxable under the tax benefit rule. The appellate court noted that the Tax Court approach had been to hold that "Unvert had a duty of consistency and was estopped from contending that the deduction he had

---

[27]   *Id.* at 383–5.

[28]   *Id.* at 394–5.

[29]   656 F.2d 483 (9th Cir. 1981).

previously claimed was improper"; the Ninth Circuit, however, found it unnecessary to consider the estoppel theory and affirmed simply "on the basis that the erroneous deduction exception should be rejected."[30] To the same effect in rejecting the erroneous deduction exception, and applying the tax benefit rule "regardless of the propriety of the original deduction," is *Hughes & Luce v. Commissioner*,[31] holding that a law firm must include in income client reimbursements for expenses the firm had previously paid and deducted, but which the firm later conceded should have been treated as nondeductible loans to the clients.

§ 30.03 NET OPERATING LOSSES

§ 172. Net operating loss deduction —

(a) Deduction allowed — There shall be allowed as a deduction for the taxable year an amount equal to the aggregate of (1) the net operating loss carryovers to such year, plus (2) the net operating loss carrybacks to such year. For purposes of this subtitle, the term "net operating loss deduction" means the deduction allowed by this subsection.

(b) Net operating loss carrybacks and carryovers —

(1) Years to which loss may be carried —

(A) General rule — Except as otherwise provided in this paragraph, a net operating loss for any taxable year —

(i) shall be a net operating loss carryback to each of the 2 taxable years preceding the taxable year of such loss, and

(ii) shall be a net operating loss carryover to each of the 20 taxable years following the taxable year of the loss.

(c) Net operating loss defined — For purposes of this section, the term "net operating loss" means the excess of the deductions allowed by this chapter over the gross income. Such excess shall be computed with the modifications specified in subsection (d).

(d) Modifications — The modifications referred to in this section are as follows:

(1) Net operating loss deduction — No net operating loss deduction shall be allowed.

(2) Capital gains and losses of taxpayers other than corporations — In the case of a taxpayer other than a corporation —

(A) the amount deductible on account of losses from sales or exchanges of capital assets shall not exceed the amount includable on account of gains from sales or exchanges of capital assets; and

(B) the exclusion provided by section 1202 shall not be allowed.

(3) Deduction for personal exemptions — No deduction shall be allowed

---

[30] *Id.* at 485.

[31] 70 F.3d 16, 21 (5th Cir. 1995).

under section 151 (relating to personal exemptions). No deduction in lieu of any such deduction shall be allowed.

(4) **Nonbusiness deductions of taxpayers other than corporations — In the case of a taxpayer other than a corporation, the deductions allowable by this chapter which are not attributable to a taxpayer's trade or business shall be allowed only to the extent of the amount of the gross income not derived from such trade or business.**

The rather cursory treatment given here to the topic of net operating losses belies its real-world significance. The harshness of the annual accounting rule is exemplified by the Supreme Court's decision in *Burnet v. Sanford & Brooks Co.*[32] In three out of four years between 1913 and 1916, the taxpayer had a loss on its operations under a government contract; in one of the four years, the contract had produced income. In the aggregate, however, the four years' results were a net loss of some $176,000. The taxpayer successfully sued to recover the net loss, and in 1920 the taxpayer received payment of the $176,000 plus interest. The Commissioner sought to tax the $176,000 recovery; the taxpayer objected that no tax was due because the transaction as a whole had generated no profit to it. On the basis of the annual accounting system of taxation, the Court held for the government:

> But [taxpayer] insists that, if the sum which it recovered is the income defined by the statute, still it is not income, taxation of which without apportionment is permitted by the Sixteenth Amendment, since the particular transaction from which it was derived did not result in any net gain or profit. But we do not think the amendment is to be so narrowly construed. A taxpayer may be in receipt of net income in one year and not in another. The net result of the two years, if combined in a single taxable period, might still be a loss; but it has never been supposed that that fact would relieve him from a tax on the first, or that it affords any reason for postponing the assessment of the tax until the end of a lifetime, or for some other indefinite period, to ascertain more precisely whether the final outcome of the period, or of a given transaction, will be a gain or a loss.

> The Sixteenth Amendment was adopted to enable the government to raise revenue by taxation. It is the essence of any system of taxation that it should produce revenue ascertainable, and payable to the government, at regular intervals. Only by such a system is it practicable to produce a regular flow of income and apply methods of accounting, assessment, and collection capable of practical operation. It is not suggested that there has ever been any general scheme for taxing income on any other basis. The computation of income annually as the net result of all transactions within the year was familiar practice, and taxes upon income so arrived at were not unknown, before the Sixteenth Amendment. . . . It is not to be supposed that the amendment did not contemplate that Congress might make income so ascertained the basis of a scheme of taxation such as had been in actual operation within the United States before its adoption. While, conceivably, a different system might be devised by which the tax could be assessed, wholly or in part, on the basis of the finally ascertained results of particular

---

[32] 282 U.S. 359 (1931).

transaction, Congress is not required by the amendment to adopt such a system in preference to the more familiar method, even if it were practicable. It would not necessarily obviate the kind of inequalities of which respondent complains. If losses from particular transactions were to be set off against gains in others, there would still be the practical necessity of computing the tax on the basis of annual or other fixed taxable periods, which might result in the taxpayer being required to pay a tax on income in one period exceeded by net losses in another.[33]

Section 172 of the Code, the forerunner of which was first enacted in 1918, is the principal form of relief from the *Burnet v. Sanford & Brooks Co.* rule. In broad outline, Section 172 provides that a loss in one year may be used to offset income in another year so that the loss is not wasted. Generally speaking, the loss is ordinarily carried back two years (through the filing of amended returns for those years) and carried forward twenty years until it has been fully absorbed, and thus it is very likely that a net business loss will eventually be deducted by an ultimately profitable business. For example, a net operating loss in Year 3 would first be applied against Year 1 taxable income. If there were insufficient Year 1 taxable income to absorb the loss, the unused portion of the loss would be carried to Year 2. If Year 2 income did not fully absorb the loss, the unused portion would be carried forward to Year 4, Year 5, etc., until fully absorbed.[34] A taxpayer, however, may elect, with respect to a given year's net operating loss, to dispense with the entire two-year carryback period, and carry the loss forward only.[35]

Example: Assume a Year 3 net operating loss of $100,000. Assume taxable income of $20,000 each in prior Years 1 and 2, and in subsequent Year 4. How should the taxpayer treat the Year 3 loss?

Analysis: The $100,000 loss is first carried back to Year 1, where it fully offsets the $20,000 in income; Year 1 taxable income is thus reduced to zero, and the taxpayer will file an amended Year 1 tax return to this effect, and obtain a tax refund. $80,000 of loss is then carried to Year 2, where it fully absorbs the $20,000 of income and results in the filing of another amended tax return. The unused loss of $60,000 is carried forward to Year 4, where $20,000 more is absorbed. This leaves $40,000 of unused loss to carry forward to Year 5; if Year 5 income is $50,000 the $40,000 of loss is fully absorbed and effectively results in a Year 5 taxable income of $10,000.

This summary of Section 172 has ignored its sometimes fearsome complexities. Section 172(c) defines net operating loss simply enough as the excess of deductions allowed over gross income, computed as modified by Section 172(d). In general, the losses that may be carried back and forward are business losses, rather than personal losses. (Capital losses, which will be discussed in Chapter 31, have a separate carryover provision.)[36] Personal exemptions, for example, do not enter into the computation of a net operating loss, and unused personal exemptions may not

---

[33] *Id.* at 364–6.

[34] I.R.C. § 172(b)(1)(A), (2).

[35] I.R.C. § 172(b)(3).

[36] I.R.C. §§ 1212, 172(d)(2).

be carried over to other years.[37] Furthermore, nonbusiness deductions of individuals are allowable in computing a net operating loss only to the extent of nonbusiness income.[38] An individual thus, in general, computes a net operating loss as follows: Add together (1) business deductions and (2) nonbusiness deductions to the extent they do not exceed nonbusiness income. From this total, subtract the taxpayer's gross income. The balance, if any, constitutes the individual taxpayer's net operating loss.

---

[37] I.R.C. § 172(d)(3).
[38] I.R.C. § 172(d)(4).

Chapter 31

CAPITAL GAINS AND LOSSES

§ 31.01 HISTORICAL OVERVIEW

This chapter sets forth the special set of rules applicable to capital gains and losses.

Section 31.01 of this chapter traces the history of the tax preference given to long term capital gains — a preference that has varied considerably in its details over the years — and the history of the concomitant limitation on the deductibility of capital losses. This historical overview concludes by summarizing the principle arguments made in support of the preferential treatment for long term capital gains.

Section 31.02 describes, with numerous examples, the extraordinarily complicated statutory provision — Section 1(h) of the Code — that carries out the current preference given to long term capital gains. Technically, as § 31.02 discusses, the preference requires that the taxpayer have a "net capital gain" for the year; and each of the components of net capital gain (namely, "28% rate gain"; "unrecaptured Section 1250 gain"; and "adjusted net capital gain") has its own separate preferential rates. (Indeed, one of the components, adjusted net capital gain, itself has alternative preferential rates.) Section 31.02 also discusses the preference given to "qualified dividend income." Section 31.02 concludes with a summary of an additional aspect of the complexity of Code Section 1(h), the necessity and importance of determining how to attribute capital losses to particular components of net capital gain.

Following this extensive review of the capital gains preference, Section 31.03 describes, with several examples, the limitation on the deductibility of capital losses under current law, the negative aspect of the special treatment given capital gains and losses.

To have a capital gain or a capital loss one must have a capital asset. Section 31.04 thus sets out, in some detail, the statutory definition of a capital asset, as well as the principal statutory exclusions from the definition, and the changing judicial gloss on the definition.

By definition, a capital gain or loss arises out of the "sale or exchange" of a capital asset. Section 31.05 thus explores the sale-or-exchange requirement; it notes case law clarifications of the meaning of a sale or exchange, and also notes some instances where Congress has dispensed with the need for an actual sale or exchange by treating certain events as constructive sales or exchanges.

Section 31.06 discusses the so-called "*Arrowsmith* rule," a judicial doctrine under which the characterization of a gain or a loss may be based on the characterization of a related gain or loss in a prior year.

Finally, Section 31.07 briefly notes that a capital gain or loss is characterized as long term or short term based on its holding period — that is, on whether or not the asset was held for more than one year before its sale or exchange.

[A]   Preferential Treatment for Long Term Capital Gain

While today it is clear that a profit realized on the sale of assets like stock is income, it required a Supreme Court decision to establish that principle. In *Merchants' Loan and Trust Company v. Smietanka*,[1] the taxpayer argued that the increase in value of stock when realized through a sale or other disposition did not constitute "income" within the meaning of the Sixteenth Amendment. According to the taxpayer, " 'income' as used in the Sixteenth Amendment . . . does not include the gain from capital realized by a single isolated sale of property but that only the profits realized from sales by one engaged in buying and selling as a business — a merchant, a real estate agent, or broker — constitute income which may be taxed." Rejecting that argument, the Court noted the taxpayer's construction "would, in large measure, defeat the purpose of the [Sixteenth] Amendment." Contrary to the taxpayer's position, the appreciation on the stock was income subject to tax when the appreciation was realized through the sale of the stock.[2]

Congress, however, in the same year as the Court's decision in *Merchants Land and Trust Company*, acknowledged that special tax treatment for the gain recognized on the disposition of certain assets was justified. In the Revenue Act of 1921, Congress provided preferential tax treatment for the gains (referred to as "capital gains") from the sale or exchange of a class of assets Congress characterized as "capital assets." The Act defined a "capital asset" as "property acquired and held by the taxpayer for profit or investment for more than two years (whether or not connected with his trade or business), but does not include . . . stock in trade of the taxpayer or other property of a kind which would properly be included in the inventory of the taxpayer if on hand at the close of the taxable year." While tax rates on all other income ranged as high as 58%, the Act limited the tax which could be imposed on capital gains to 12.5%.[3]

In the 1921 Revenue Act, Congress limited the preferential tax treatment to gains from assets which had been held "for more than two years." The length of the holding period required for capital asset designation suggests one of the major reasons justifying capital gain treatment, *i.e.*, to tax capital gains like all other income would be harsh, considering the gain often represents appreciation accruing over a number of years. The gain inherent in an asset is not reportable as

---

[1]   255 U.S. 509 (1921).

[2]   *Id.* at 520–1.

[3]   Specifically, the Revenue Act of 1921 provided that, in computing his tax, a taxpayer would segregate all capital gains (gains from the sale or exchange of capital assets), capital losses (losses from the sale or exchange of capital assets) and capital deductions (allowable deductions allocable to items of capital gain). The excess of the capital gains over the sum of the capital losses and capital deductions constituted "capital net gain." At the election of the taxpayer, the taxpayer's tax would be computed by adding the 12.5% of the capital net gain to the tax computed on the taxpayer's ordinary net income (*i.e.*, net income excluding all items of capital gain, capital loss and capital deduction).

income until it has been "realized." Thus, even though an asset may appreciate at a steady rate over a number of years, the appreciation will generally not be taxed as income until the asset is sold or exchanged. As a result, gain accruing over the years is bunched into one tax year for purposes of taxation. By providing preferential treatment to such gains, Congress sought to mitigate this bunching problem.[4] The two-year holding period, included in the definition of "capital asset" in the 1921 Act, assured that gains generated over a short term would not be tax-preferred. Beginning with the 1938 Revenue Act, tax-preferred capital gains were referred to as "long term capital gains" while gains without tax preference were denominated "short term capital gains."

Congressional concern regarding the bunching problem is best exemplified in the refinements made to the capital gain structure in the 1934 Revenue Act. The 1934 Act introduced a sliding scale approach to capital gain preferential treatment based on the holding period of capital assets. It provided that 100% of the gain or loss recognized upon the sale or exchange of a capital asset was to be taken into account in computing net income if the capital asset had been held for a year or less; the percentage of recognized gain or loss decreased in steps as the holding period lengthened, down to 30% if the asset was held more than 10 years. This sliding scale method, however, was short-lived. In the 1938 Revenue Act, Congress shortened the holding period required for preferential capital gains treatment to eighteen months. The 1942 Revenue Act further shortened the long term holding period requirement to six months. The six-month holding period requirement for long term capital gains existed from 1942 through 1976 and again from 1984 through 1986.[5] For 1988 and following years, only the gains (and losses) from the sale or exchange of capital assets held for more than one year will be long term and therefore eligible for preferential treatment. As discussed below, Congress in 1997 provided even greater preferential treatment for the gains resulting from the sale or exchange of certain capital assets held for more than eighteen months. This eighteen month holding period, however, was quickly changed to the current twelve month period.

Congress has not only varied the holding period necessary for preferential treatment, it has also varied the nature and the amount of the preference itself. The Revenue Act of 1921 limited the tax on capital gain to 12.5%; by contrast, the Revenue Act of 1942 provided that only 50% of long term gain (and long term loss) would be taken into account in computing net income. Thus, under the 1942 Act, the rate of tax applicable to capital gains depended on the specific rate bracket of the taxpayer. Beginning with the Revenue Act of 1951, the preference for capital gains took the form of a deduction from gross income equal to 50% of the net capital gain, a term defined as "the excess of the net long-term capital gain for the taxable year over the net short-term capital loss for such year."[6] The 50%

---

[4] The bunching problem is a function of the rule that appreciation on property is not taxed as income until the appreciation is realized through an event like a sale or an exchange. If one were taxed each year on the increase in the value of one's property during the year, the bunching problem would not exist.

[5] The holding period for long term capital gains was increased to nine months for 1977 and then to one year for the period 1978 through June 22, 1984.

[6] I.R.C. § 1222(11).

deduction was increased in 1978 to 60% and remained at that level until the repeal of the preference in 1986 as part of a major tax act which reduced the top individual income tax rates from 50% to 28%.[7] With this significant reduction in tax rates, Congress concluded there was no continuing need to provide a reduced rate of tax for net capital gains. The legislative history of the 1986 Tax Reform Act explained:

> The committee believes that, as a result of the reduction of individual tax rates on such forms of capital income as business profits, interest, dividends, and short term capital gains, the need to provide a reduced rate for net capital gain is eliminated. This will result in a tremendous amount of simplification for many taxpayers since their tax will no longer depend upon the characterization of income as ordinary or capital gain. In addition, this will eliminate any requirement that capital assets be held by the taxpayer for any extended period of time . . . in order to obtain favorable treatment. This will result in greater willingness to invest in assets that are freely traded (e.g., stocks).[8]

The ink was not dry on the 1986 legislation, however, before many taxpayers and their advisors began complaining that the elimination of any preference for capital gains meant Congress had, in effect, increased the tax on capital gains. Those taxpayers were correct. Considering that prior to the 1986 Act there was a 60% above the line deduction for net capital gain and a maximum rate of tax of 50%, net capital gains were subject to a maximum tax rate of 20%. For example, if a taxpayer realized $1,000 of long term capital gain on the sale of stock, only $400 of that gain would be taxable as a result of the 60% deduction and that $400 could not be taxed at a rate greater than 50%. The taxpayer in this scenario pre-1986 Act would thus not pay a tax greater than $200 on the sale of the stock. After the 1986 Act, however, the same taxpayer could be subject to a tax as high as $280 (28% of $1,000).

Since 1986, restoration of a preference for long term capital gain has been a subject of continual debate within Congress. When it increased maximum individual rates from 28% to 31% in 1990 and from 31% to 39.6% in 1993, Congress retained the maximum rate (established in 1986) of 28% on net capital gain. By retaining the 28% maximum rate on net capital gain, Congress reintroduced into the Code a modest preference for long term capital gains. That level of preference did not satisfy the advocates of capital gain preferential treatment. In the 1997 Act, Congress established a new preferential treatment structure for net capital gain. The most prominent feature of that new structure was a 20% maximum rate on certain long term capital gains, a rate that was initially retained when phased-in reductions in maximum individual rates were enacted in 2001 tax legislation, but was subsequently lowered to 15% in 2003, until restored to 20% for high-income taxpayers effective in 2013.[9]

---

[7] The deduction was an above the line deduction, i.e., it was a deduction taken in computing adjusted gross income. I.R.C. § 62(4) (repealed by the 1986 Tax Reform Act).

[8] Tax Reform Act of 1986, Senate Finance Committee Report on H.R. 3838, 99th Cong., 2d Sess., p. 169 (1986).

[9] I.R.C. § 1(h).

To encourage investors to fund new ventures and small businesses, Congress in 1993 added an exclusion from gross income of 50% of the gain from the sale or exchange of "qualified small business stock" held for more than five years.[10] This provision was retained as a part of the new preferential rate structure for capital gains. (The exclusion has been raised to 100% on a temporary basis, effective for stock acquired after September 27, 2010 and before January 1, 2014.) In general, gain eligible for this special benefit is limited to the greater of: (1) ten times the taxpayer's basis in the stock or (2) $10,000,000 of gain from the disposition of the stock.[11]"Qualified small business stock" is stock of a Subchapter C corporation issued after August 10, 1993.[12] The stock must be that of a qualified small business (in general, a corporation with gross assets not greater than $50 million at the time of the issuance of the stock); and must be acquired by the taxpayer at its original issuance.[13] The section contains numerous requirements and limitations which significantly narrow the kind of stock eligible for this special preferential treatment.

[B] Limitation on the Deduction of Capital Losses

While providing preferential treatment for capital gain in the Revenue Act of 1921, Congress did not provide any corresponding limitation on the deduction of capital losses. In the Revenue Act of 1924, Congress rectified this situation. As noted by a member of the House Ways and Means Committee:

> [T]he injustice to the Government is too obvious to require much comment. The taxpayer may refrain from taking his profits, or, if he does take them, pays but a 12.5 percent tax, whereas he is at liberty at any time to take advantage of any losses that may have been incurred and avail himself of a full deduction from his income. When we consider that the rate on the larger incomes runs as high as 58 percent, it can readily be realized how great the advantage is. The Government can collect but 12.5 percent of a gain, but it is compelled to lighten the burden of the taxpayer to the extent of 58 percent of his losses. Take, for example, the case of a man with an income of $350,000 a year. Assume that in 1917 he bought year 1917 5,000 shares of stock at $100 par, and that he sells those shares in 1922 for $600,000, showing a profit of $100,000. By reason of this transaction, he would pay, in addition to the tax on his regular income, $12,500 to the Government. But assume that instead of selling this stock at a profit, he sold it in 1922 at a loss of $100,000. He would then be entitled to deduct the $100,000 from his income of $350,000, and the loss to the government by reason of that deduction would be $58,000. Is there any further argument needed?[14]

---

[10] I.R.C. § 1202.

[11] I.R.C. § 1202(b)(1).

[12] I.R.C. § 1202(c)(1).

[13] I.R.C. § 1202(d)(1).

[14] Report of the Committee on Ways and Means on H. R. 13770, H. Rep. No. 1388, 67th Cong., 4th Sess. (1923).

Just as the 1924 Revenue Act provided that the maximum tax on capital gains could not exceed 12.5%, the Act also provided that a taxpayer's tax liability (computed without considering capital gains and losses) could not be reduced by more than 12.5% of the "capital net loss" (the excess of the sum of the capital losses plus the capital deductions over the total amount of capital gain). Beginning with the Revenue Act of 1934, capital losses could be deducted only to the extent of capital gains; up to $2,000 of any excess of capital losses over gains could also be deducted. Any capital losses not deductible because of the limitation were carried over to the following year or years until used. As discussed in some detail below, similar limitations on the deductibility of capital losses continue to exist, except that the excess capital loss deduction has been raised to $3,000.

[C] Justification for Preferential Capital Gain Treatment

Before considering the current preferential treatment structure which has emerged through congressional action in 1997 and 1998, it will be instructive to consider the kinds of arguments pro and con which have been made and continue to be made in the debates regarding the creation and retention of a capital gain preference. Proponents of preferential capital gain treatment justify such treatment on a number of theories in addition to the bunching theory described previously. First, some supporters contend the gain realized on the sale or exchange of a capital asset is often largely due to inflation and does not represent any real increase in the value of the asset. A reduced rate of tax on capital gains therefore negates, at least to some extent, imposition of tax on such illusory gains.

Second, proponents argue the mobility of capital could be impaired if capital gains were taxed like any other income. Knowing the gain from the sale or exchange of a capital asset would be taxed like compensation or any other income, taxpayers might retain appreciated assets simply to avoid the tax burden. Taxpayers might continue to hold appreciated assets until death so as to take advantage of the stepped-up basis accorded property acquired from a decedent.[15] Many believe that this so-called "lock-in" effect could seriously harm the economy.

Third, proponents of preferential treatment argue that taxing capital gains at the same rate as other income is a disincentive to savings. By contrast, when capital gains are given preferential tax treatment, people are encouraged to save (by investing in stock, etc.), thus increasing the capital available for business investment. The availability of investment funds for capital formation is particularly critical to new and small businesses. Furthermore, additional business investment results in greater productivity and a correspondingly higher standard of living. Denial of preferential capital gain treatment would therefore significantly hinder economic growth.

While the arguments advanced for preferential capital gain treatment are legion, there are strong arguments opposing preferential treatment. One of the primary arguments against preferential treatment is that such treatment creates the need for complex statutory provisions designed to prevent taxpayers from converting ordinary income into capital gain. Furthermore, the existence of

---

[15] *See* I.R.C. § 1014(a).

preferential capital gain treatment requires the courts and the Service to determine whether in a particular case a gain is a capital gain or ordinary income. Indeed, a considerable body of case law and rulings has developed over time addressing the issue of what constituted a capital gain.

In addition, critics of preferential capital gain treatment argue that the problems identified by proponents of such treatment could be better addressed through other means. For example, inflation concerns could be addressed by means of periodically adjusting the basis of property to account for inflation; and bunching problems could be addressed through an income averaging mechanism. Indeed, with the shortening of the holding period for long term capital gain treatment to one year, the argument that preferential capital gain treatment was justified because of bunching was rendered almost meaningless with respect to assets held for only the minimum period required for long term capital gain treatment.

§ 31.02   CURRENT LAW: SECTION 1(h)

[A]   Maximum Rates on Long Term Capital Gain Under the Current Law

§ 1222.   Other terms relating to capital gains and losses.

For purposes of this subtitle —

(1)   Short-term capital gain. — The term "short-term capital gain" [STCG] means gain from the sale or exchange of a capital asset held for not more than 1 year, if and to the extent such gain is taken into account in computing gross income.

(2)   Short-term capital loss. The term "short-term capital loss" [STCL] means loss from the sale or exchange of a capital asset held for not more than 1 year, if and to the extent that such loss is taken into account in computing taxable income.

(3)   Long-term capital gain. The term "long-term capital gain" [LTCG] means gain from the sale or exchange of a capital asset held for more than 1 year, if and to the extent such gain is taken into account in computing gross income.

(4)   Long-term capital loss. The term "long-term capital loss" [LTCL] means loss from the sale or exchange of a capital asset held for more than 1 year, if and to the extent that such loss is taken into account in computing taxable income.

(5)   Net short-term capital gain. The term "net short-term capital gain" [NSTCG] means the excess of short-term capital gains for the taxable year over the short-term capital losses for such year.

(6)   Net short-term capital loss. The term "net short-term capital loss" [NSTCL] means the excess of short-term capital losses for the taxable year over the short term capital gains for such year.

(7)   Net long-term capital gain. The term "net long-term capital gain"

[NLTCG] means the excess of long-term capital gains for the taxable year over the long-term capital losses for such year.

(8)   Net long-term capital loss. The term "net long-term capital loss" [NLTCL] means the excess of the long-term capital losses for the taxable year over the long-term capital gains for such year.

. . .

(11)   Net capital gain. The term "net capital gain" [NCG] means the excess of the net long-term capital gain [NLTCG] for the taxable year over the net short-term capital loss [NSTCL] for such year. [NLTCG − NSTCL = NCG]

Current Section 1(h) provides a lower tax rate for certain capital gains. The preferential rates of Section 1(h) apply only when the taxpayer has "net capital gain," which is defined as the excess of the net long-term capital gain for the taxable year over the net short-term capital loss for such year.[16] Accordingly, preferential treatment exists only for long term capital gains. Technically, preferential treatment exists only when the taxpayer's long term gains exceed the sum of taxpayer's long term capital losses and net short term capital loss. *Short term capital gains are accorded no preference and are therefore subject to tax at ordinary income rates as high as 39.6%.*

Example 1: Short Term Capital Gain Only. Assume John sold stock for $50,000. John's basis in the stock was $40,000 and John had held the stock for 10 months. Assume this was John's only sale or exchange during the year and John had no "qualified dividend income" (*see* § 31.02[B][4]).

Analysis: John has $10,000 of STCG. John has no net capital gain. (Applying the formula NLTCG − NSTCL = NCG, it is obvious there is $0 NLTCG and $0 NSTCL and therefore $0 NCG.) Therefore, John is not entitled to any preferential treatment on the gain from the stock sale. If John were in a 39.6% tax bracket, he would be required to pay $3,960 in federal tax on the stock gain.

Example 2: Long Term Capital Gain Only. Assume the same facts as Example 1 except that John held the stock for 2 years.

Analysis: Under these circumstances, John has a net capital gain of $10,000 (NLTCG of $10,000 less NSTCL of $0 = $10,000). Under Section 1(h), even if John were in the 39.6% bracket, his federal tax on the stock gain would be taxed at a preferential rate — in this case under current law at a rate of 20% for a tax of $2,000 on the stock gain. (However, the maximum rate in lower brackets would be 15%, or a maximum tax of $1,500 on the stock gain, as discussed *infra.*

Example 3: Long Term Capital Gain and Short Term Capital Gain. Assume the facts of Example 2 except that John also had a short term capital gain of $10,000.

---

[16]   I.R.C. § 1222(11). "Qualified dividend income" is also a component of net capital gain and is subject to preferential tax treatment. I.R.C. § 1(h)(11). Qualified dividend income is discussed at § 31.02[B][4].

Analysis: John's net capital gain is still $10,000 (NLTCG of $10,000 less NSTCL of $0 = $10,000). Assuming that John were in the 39.6% bracket, John would pay a tax of $2,000 (0.2 × $10,000) on the long term capital gain and would pay a tax of $3,690 on the short term capital gain.

Example 4: Long Term Capital Gain and Long Term Capital Loss. Assume the facts of Example 2 except that John also had a long term capital loss of $10,000.

Analysis: John has no net capital gain (NLTCG of $0 less NSTCL of $0 = $0).

Prior to the enactment of the 1997 Act, net capital gain was taxed at a maximum rate of 28%. Under pre-1997 law, the only taxpayer who benefitted from the preferential capital gain treatment was a taxpayer in a rate bracket higher than 28%. Taxpayers in rate brackets of 28% or below would pay the same rate of tax on their net capital gain as they would on ordinary income.[17]

In amending Section 1(h) in 1997 to provide increased preferential treatment for certain classes of long term capital gain, Congress dramatically changed the rate structure applicable to net capital gains but did not change any of the definitions in Section 1222. Thus, for example, "long term capital gain" is still defined as the "gain from the sale or exchange of a capital asset held for more than 1 year. . . ."

[B] The Components of Net Capital Gain: 28-Percent Rate Gain; Unrecaptured Section 1250 Gain; and Adjusted Net Capital Gain

Section 1(h) sets forth the preferential treatment accorded long term capital gains. Unfortunately, the provision is one of the most dense provisions in the Internal Revenue Code. Rather than setting the specific language of the provision out as part of this Chapter, this Chapter provides a detailed analysis of the provision which illuminates the primary features of the capital gain preferential treatment structure.

Under current Section 1(h), the maximum capital gain rate on net capital gain (or more to the point, on long term capital gains) will vary depending upon the nature of the assets giving rise to the long term capital gains. In no event, however, will the maximum rate of tax on any long term capital gains exceed 28%. To compute the tax on a taxpayer's net capital gain, one must first determine the extent, if any, to which net capital gain is made up of either "28-percent rate gain" (taxed at a maximum tax rate of 28%) or "unrecaptured section 1250 gain" (taxed at a maximum tax rate of 25%). Any net capital gain remaining after those two categories of gain have been separated from net capital gain is referred to as "adjusted net capital gain."[18] "Adjusted net capital gain" is subject to the greatest

---

[17] Of course, it still made a difference to these taxpayers whether their gains were capital or ordinary gains. See, for example, the Section 1211 limitation on capital losses.

[18] I.R.C. § 1(h)(4).

preferential treatment, *i.e.*, a maximum tax rate of 15% or 20%, depending on bracket the taxpayer is in.

In the discussion that follows concerning the maximum rate of tax on the various groups or components of net capital gain, an initial assumption is made, for the sake of simplicity, *that there are no long term or short term capital losses or qualified dividend income to be taken into account in computing net capital gain.* Thus, our focus will be solely on the long term capital gains that are reflected in net capital gain.

[1]   28-Percent Rate Gain: Collectibles Gain and Section 1202 Gain

As the name suggests, that part, *if any*, of a taxpayer's net capital gain characterized as 28-percent rate gain will be taxed at a maximum rate of 28%. This category of long term capital gain is subject to preferential treatment only if the taxpayer is in a tax bracket higher than 28%. Thus, for example, if a taxpayer is in the 15% bracket, that taxpayer's 28-percent rate gain would be subject to tax at 15% just as in the case of taxpayer's ordinary income. In general, "28-percent rate gain" is the sum of: (1) collectibles gain[19] (*i.e.*, gain from the sale or exchange of any rug or antique, metal, gem, stamp or coin, work of art or other collectible[20] which is a capital asset held for more than one year) and (2) Section 1202 gain,[21] which, in general, is 50% of the gain from the sale or exchange of certain stock described in Section 1202.

> **Example: 28-Percent Rate Gain.** Mary is a taxpayer in the 35% tax bracket. During the current year, she realizes $5,000 long term capital gain on the sale of some antique furniture which she had received as a wedding gift from her grandmother and $10,000 in long term capital gain for a work of art Mary had held for three years. Assume these are Mary's only capital gain/loss transactions during the year.
>
> **Analysis:** Mary has a net capital gain of $15,000. The gains from the sales of both the antique furniture and the work of art are 28-percent rate gain because they constitute "collectibles gain."[22] Mary will thus be subject to capital gains tax at a rate of 28% on the $15,000 of net capital gain. She will be subject to tax at a 35% rate on the balance of her taxable income. If Mary were in the 15% bracket, Mary would pay capital gains tax at a rate of 15% on the sale of the furniture and the art work. Mary thus will get preferential treatment only to the extent that she is in a bracket greater than 28% when she sells the art or the furniture.

---

[19] I.R.C. § 1(h)(6).

[20] As defined by Section 408(m).

[21] As defined in Section 1(h)(8).

[22] As defined in Section 1(h)(6).

[2] Unrecaptured Section 1250 Gain — 25% Rate

Net capital gain to the extent of so-called "unrecaptured Section 1250 gain" is subject to a maximum rate of tax of 25%.[23] In general, unrecaptured Section 1250 gain is the long term capital gain attributable to depreciation allowed with respect to real estate (*e.g.,* buildings) held for more than one year.[24] The following simple example will demonstrate the nature of this category of gain.

> **Example: Unrecaptured Section 1250 Gain.** Assume Anna, a taxpayer in the 35% bracket, sold a commercial building for $100,000. Anna had paid $100,000 for the building 10 years ago and had been allowed straight-line depreciation deductions aggregating $25,000 on the building during the period in which she held the building for use in her business. Thus, Anna's adjusted basis in the building at the time of the sale was $75,000. Assume the sale of the building was Anna's only disposition of property during the year.

> **Analysis:** Under Section 1001, Anna's recognized gain on the sale of the building is $25,000. Assume the gain is characterized as long term capital gain under Section 1231 (discussed in Chapter 32). The only reason that Anna had any gain on the property was because she had claimed $25,000 in depreciation over time and had to make a downward adjustment to her basis in the building to reflect that depreciation. That adjustment in basis resulted in the $25,000 of gain on the sale of the property. Thus, all $25,000 of gain is the result of depreciation deductions claimed by Anna and the gain is characterized as unrecaptured Section 1250 gain.[25] Given the assumption the sale of the building was Anna's only property disposition during the year, Anna's net capital gain is $25,000. Because all of the net capital gain is unrecaptured Section 1250 gain, Anna is subject to a maximum rate of tax on this gain of 25%.

[3] Adjusted Net Capital Gain: 20%, 15% and 0% Rates

Net capital gain reduced by a taxpayer's 28-percent rate gain and unrecaptured Section 1250 gain equals adjusted net capital gain.[26] Adjusted net capital gain is subject to a maximum tax rate of 20% for taxpayers in the highest tax bracket of 39.6%; for taxpayers in the 28%, 33%, or 35% brackets the adjusted net capital rate is 15%.[27] Unlike 28-percent rate gain or unrecaptured Section 1250 gain, adjusted net capital gain is accorded further preferential treatment if the taxpayer is in a 10% or 15% bracket. In that case, the rate of tax on the adjusted net capital gain is

---

[23] I.R.C. § 1(h)(1)(E).

[24] I.R.C. § 1(h)(7). This book does not address in detail unrecaptured Section 1250 gain although Chapter 33, *infra,* will address in some detail the concept of depreciation recapture.

[25] The concept of "recapture" is addressed in Chapter 33, *infra.*

[26] I.R.C. § 1(h)(4).

[27] I.R.C. § 1(h)(1)(C)(D). Tax legislation in 2003 reduced the maximum rate on adjusted net capital gain from 20% to 15% through 2008. The 15% rate was extended temporarily through 1912, when it was made permanent for most taxpayers, but restored to 20% for those taxpayers in the 39.6% bracket.

zero.[28] A classic example of a transaction which will produce this category of gain would be the sale of stock held by the taxpayer for more than one year.

Example 1: Adjusted Net Capital Gain Taxed at 15% Rate. Jeff and Kathy, married taxpayers filing jointly, are in the 35% tax bracket. During 2013, Jeff and Kathy realized $10,000 in long term capital gain as a result of their sale of certain stock held for more than one year. Jeff and Kathy had no other capital gain/loss transactions during the year.

Analysis: The couple's net capital gain is thus $10,000. Since Jeff and Kathy had no 28-percent rate gain or unrecaptured Section 1250 gain as defined previously, their adjusted net capital gain is $10,000 (*i.e.*, adjusted net capital gain equals net capital gain in this example). Jeff and Kathy will therefore pay tax at the rate of 15% on their $10,000 of net capital gain and will be subject to a marginal tax rate of 35% on all of their other income. If Jeff and Kathy were in the 39.6% bracket, the tax on the $10,000 of net capital gain would be 20% of $10,000, or $2,000.

Example 2: Adjusted Net Capital Gain Taxed at 0% in 2008 and in Part at 15%. In 2013, Jeff and Kathy, married taxpayers filing jointly, have $66,000 of taxable income made up of $36,000 of ordinary income and $30,000 of long term capital gain from the sale of Microsoft stock held for more than one year. (Assume Jeff and Kathy have no deductions or exemptions.) Assume for purposes of this example, that, for taxpayers filing joint returns, the first $40,000 of taxable income is taxed at 10% or 15% and amounts of taxable income in excess of $40,000 but less than $100,000 are taxed at 28%.

Analysis: The taxpayers have a net capital gain of $30,000. None of this $30,000 of gain constitutes either 28-percent rate gain or unrecaptured Section 1250 gain. Jeff and Kathy thus have adjusted net capital gain of $30,000. Section 1(h) will result in their tax liability being computed as follows: First, the excess of their taxable income ($66,000 over the net capital gain ($30,000) or $36,000 (the ordinary income) will be taxed at the regular rate, *i.e.*, 10% or 15%. Because these brackets cover taxable income up to $40,000, there will be $4,000 of the net capital gain which, but for the special rules of Section 1(h) would be taxable at 15%.[29] Since all of the net capital gain constitutes adjusted net capital gain, this $4,000 will be taxed not at 15%, but at 0%. The remaining $26,000 of net capital gain (which here is the remaining amount of adjusted net capital gain) will be taxed at 15% instead of 28%.[30]

While the above examples have addressed situations in which net capital gain was comprised solely of long term capital gains characterized as 28-percent rate gain or

---

[28] I.R.C. § 1(h)(1)(B). 2003 tax legislation reduced the rate in question here from 10% to 5%, and to 0% in 2008, and 2006 legislation extended the zero rate from 2008 to 2010. The rate was extended through 2012 by legislation in 2010. The 0% rate became permanent in 2013.

[29] I.R.C. § 1(h)(1)(B).

[30] I.R.C. § 1(h)(1)(C). Note the taxpayers' income level is well below the 39.6% bracket, which triggers the 20% rate on adjusted net capital I.R.C. § 1(h)(1)(D).

solely of long term capital gains which would constitute adjusted net capital gain, it is easy to imagine situations where taxpayer will have a net capital gain which includes a combination of the various components described above. Consider the following example:

> **Example: Mixture of Short Term Capital Gain, 28-Percent Rate Gain and Adjusted Net Capital Gain.** Fred is in the 35% tax bracket. During 2013, Fred has short term capital gain of $10,000 from the sale of A stock held for less than one year, $10,000 of long term capital gain from the sale of a work of art held for a number of years, and $10,000 of long term capital gain from the sale of C stock held for more than one year. Fred has no other capital gain/loss transactions during the year.

> **Analysis:** Fred's net capital gain will be $20,000 (*i.e.*, NLTCG ($20,000) − NSTCL ($0) = $20,000). (Note that in this example, Fred's short term capital gain has no impact on the determination of net capital gain.) Fred's net capital gain will be taxed as follows: the $10,000 of 28-percent rate gain, *i.e.*, the gain on the sale of the work of art, will be taxed at 28% and the remaining net capital gain (*i.e.*, the adjusted net capital gain), which results from the sale of the C stock, will be taxed at 15%. The remaining taxable income of Fred, including the short term capital gain, will be subject to a marginal tax rate of 35%. If Fred were in the 39.6% bracket, the answer would be the same, except the gain on the C stock would be taxed at 20%, with the remaining taxable income subject to a marginal tax rate of 39.6%.

Note: If the taxpayer's marginal tax rate is 39.6%, but the amount of the taxable income in that bracket is less than the taxpayer's adjusted net capital gain, the adjusted net capital gain taxed at 20% will be the amount otherwise taxed at 39.6%. The remaining adjusted net capital gain will be taxed at 15%.

[4]   Adjusted Net Capital Gain: Qualified Dividend Income

Starting with 2003 tax legislation, "qualified dividend income" is treated as part of adjusted net capital gain and thus taxed at the 20%, 15% or 0% rates applicable to such gain. The 2003 legislation represented a major shift in the historic tax treatment of dividends, which were previously taxed at the rates applicable to ordinary income, rather than at capital gain rates. The change was justified by the claim that it would lower the cost of capital and lead to economic growth and job creation.

Qualified dividend income consists of dividends from U.S. corporations (with some exceptions) and from certain foreign corporations.[31] The favorable tax treatment of this income is accomplished by including it in computing net capital gain and, more specifically, by including it in the computation of adjusted net capital gain.[32]

> **Example 1: Qualified Dividend Income, With Additional Net Capital Gain.** Assume in 2013 Laura has $10,000 long-term capital gain from the

---

[31]   I.R.C. § 1(h)(11)(B).

[32]   I.R.C. § 1(h)(3), (11)(A).

sale of stock; $5,000 long-term capital gain from the sale of a collectible; and $3,000 of qualified dividend income. Net capital gain, as determined without regard to the dividend, is $15,000; the dividend income increases the net capital gain to $18,000. *See* Section 1(h)(11)(A). The adjusted net capital gain is determined by subtracting the 28-percent rate gain, here the collectibles gain, from net capital gain (as determined without regard to the dividend income), and by adding the qualified dividend income. *See* Section 1(h)(3). Thus, the adjusted net capital gain in this example is $13,000 — that is, $15,000 net capital gain, excluding dividend income; less $5,000 28-percent rate gain; plus $3,000 dividend income. The dividend income is thus effectively taxed at the 20%, 15% or 0% rate applicable to adjusted net capital gain.

Two questions: Why do Section 1(h)(3) and Section 1(h)(11) require that, as a preliminary matter, net capital gain and adjusted net capital gain be determined without regard to qualified dividend income? Why is the qualified dividend income added only after the preliminary determination has been made? Consider the following example.

Example 2: Qualified Dividend Income, With No Additional Net Capital Gain. Change the facts of Example 1 so that the stock sale produces a long-term capital loss, rather than a gain, to go along with the $5,000 collectibles gain and the $3,000 dividend income. The capital loss here exceeds the total of the collectibles gain and the dividend income. If there were no preliminary determination of net capital gain under Section 1(h)(11), there would be no net capital gain at all, and no adjusted net capital gain to be taxed at 20%, 15% or less. But, by first determining net capital gain without regard to qualified dividend income, the special tax rate on dividend income is preserved. Thus, net capital gain, considering only the $10,000 stock loss and the $5,000 collectibles gain, is zero (not negative $5,000). Adding the dividend income to zero then produces net capital gain of $3,000. Similar calculations under Section 1(h)(3) produce an adjusted net capital gain of $3,000, taxable at 20%, 15% or less pursuant to Section 1(h)(C) or (D). In this manner, the qualified dividend income is assured of taxation at these preferential rates even where there otherwise is no net capital gain (indeed, there is otherwise a capital loss) for the taxpayer.

[C]   Attribution of Capital Losses Included in the Computation of Net Capital Gain

Having considered the maximum tax rates applicable to various types of long term gain included in a taxpayer's net capital gain, it is now necessary to focus briefly on the impact of capital losses which are taken into account in computing net capital gain. Specifically, it is necessary to consider how the Code attributes capital loss to the various components of net capital gain. (At the outset, it must be noted that, in the net capital gain computation, short term capital losses are offset initially against short term capital gain and it is only the excess short term capital losses which must be attributed to one of the categories of long term capital gain.)

Example: During the current year, Elizabeth, who is taxed in the 39.6% bracket, has $5,000 of short term capital gain from the sale of stock and $10,000 short term capital loss from the sale of stock. In addition, Elizabeth has $15,000 of long term capital gain from the sale of stock held for more than one year.

Analysis: Elizabeth's net capital gain is $10,000. [Taxpayer's NLTCG is $15,000; the taxpayer's NSTCL is $5,000 (*i.e.*, $10,000 STCL − $5,000 STCG = $5,000). Therefore, NLTCG ($15,000) less NSTCL ($5,000) equals $10,000 NCG.] Since there is in this example only one category of long term capital gain, the net short term capital loss of $5,000 is of necessity attributed to that category.

Note in the above example, that, where a taxpayer has a short term capital loss the existence of short term capital gain will have the effect of increasing the amount of net capital gain. Thus, if there were no short term capital gain, the net capital gain would have been $5,000 (*i.e.*, NLTCG ($15,000) − NSTCL ($10,000) = $5,000).

It is now necessary to consider how long term capital losses and net short term capital losses will be attributed among multiple categories of the long term capital gains which are taken into account in computing net capital gain. As is demonstrated below, that attribution will make a significant difference considering that the long term capital gains included in net capital gain are subject to tax at varying rates. The applicable rules are very pro-taxpayer, and may be summarized as follows:

(1) *Short-term capital losses.* Short-term capital losses are first applied to reduce short-term capital gains. Any net short-term capital loss is then applied to reduce any net gain in the 28-percent rate gain category; then to reduce any unrecaptured Section 1250 gain; and finally, to reduce any adjusted net capital gain.

(2) *Long-term capital losses.* Long-term capital losses are first applied against long-term capital gains in the same category — *e.g.*, collectibles losses are applied against collectibles gain; losses in the "20%/15% group" — *i.e.*, losses on property not in the 28-percent rate gain category or the unrecaptured Section 1250 gain category — are applied against gains from such property. Any net loss in the 28-percent rate gain category is applied to reduce the unrecaptured Section 1250 gain, and then to reduce the adjusted net capital gain category. Any net loss in the "20%/15% group" first reduces gain in the 28-percent rate gain category, then reduces unrecaptured Section 1250 gain.

Example 1: Allocating a Net Short Term Capital Loss Among Multiple Categories of Long Term Capital Gain. Assume a 39.6% bracket taxpayer has a total of $15,000 of long term capital gain in 2013. That gain represents the aggregate of $9,000 of long term capital gain from the sale of stock held for more than one year and $6,000 of long term capital gain from the sale of antiques held for many years. Assume also that the taxpayer has a $5,000 net short term capital loss for the year.

Analysis: The taxpayer's net capital gain equals $10,000 (*i.e.*, NLTCG ($15,000) − NSTCL ($5,000) = $10,000). Included in the computation of net capital gain are some long term capital gains which would be subject to a maximum tax of 20% and some long term capital gains ("collectibles gain") which would be subject to a maximum tax of 28%. To which of these gains will the $5,000 of net short term capital loss be allocated? Section 1(h)(5) clearly provides that net short term capital loss under these circumstances will be applied first to the 28-percent rate gain and only to the extent that the amount of 28-percent rate gain is less than the net short term capital loss will the net short term capital loss be attributable to the gain from the sale of stock held for more than one year. In other words, under Section 1(h), the 28-percent rate gain will be $6,000 less the $5,000 NSTCL or $1,000. In turn, the adjusted net capital gain will be $9,000 (*i.e.*, adjusted net capital gain equals net capital gain ($10,000) less 28-percent rate gain ($1,000)). This treatment of the net short term capital gain, of course, is very favorable to the taxpayer as it maximizes the amount of long term gain which will be taxed at the 20% rate.

Example 2: Allocating Collectibles (Long Term Capital) Loss Among Multiple Categories of Long Term Capital Gain. Assume the same facts as Example 1 except that, instead of a $5,000 net short term capital loss, the taxpayer has a $5,000 long term capital loss as a result of the sale of a work of art held for more than one year.

Analysis: Once again, the taxpayer's net capital gain will be $10,000 (*i.e.*, NLTCG will be the excess of LTCG ($15,000) over LTCL ($5,000) or $10,000 and NSTCL will be $0. Thus, NCG = $10,000). The issue is to which category of long term capital gain will the $5,000 of long term capital loss be attributed. Not surprisingly, Section 1(h)(5) requires the $5,000 of LTCL be allocated to the 28-percent rate gain since it is a collectibles loss, *i.e.*, a loss from the kind of property which would have given rise to 28-percent rate gain.[33] Thus, the 28-percent rate gain in this example will again be $1,000 (*i.e.*, $6,000 LTCG from the sale of the antiques less $5,000 of LTCL from the sale of the work of art). In turn, the adjusted net capital gain will be $9,000 just as before ($10,000 NCG less $1,000 28-percent rate gain). So, the taxpayer will pay tax at the rate of 28% on $1,000 of net capital gain and 20% on the remaining $9,000 of the net capital gain.

Example 3: Allocating Other Long Term Capital Loss Among Multiple Categories of Long Term Capital Gain. Assume the same facts as in Example 2 except that the $5,000 long term capital loss is a result of the sale of stock held for more than one year.

Analysis: Again, net capital gain will be $10,000. Here, however, the $5,000 of long term capital loss will not be attributed to the 28-percent rate gain since the loss in this case did not arise from the sale of assets which would have produced 28-percent rate gain. Thus, the 28-percent rate gain will equal $6,000. In turn, adjusted net capital gain will equal $4,000 (*i.e.*, NCG

---

[33] I.R.C. § 1(h)(6).

of $10,000 less $6,000 of 28-percent rate gain). The taxpayer will therefore be subject to a tax of 28% on $6,000 of the net capital gain and a tax of 15% on the remaining $4,000 of net capital gain.

As this brief overview of the attribution of capital losses suggests, the attribution rules are generally quite favorable to the taxpayers. Suffice it to say, the combination of the varying rates of tax on long term capital gain and the attribution of capital losses to the various classes of long term capital gain make Section 1(h) unwieldy and adds significant complexity to this already complex characterization area.

§ 31.03   CURRENT LAW: APPLICATION OF THE SECTION 1211(b) LIMITATION ON THE DEDUCTION OF CAPITAL LOSSES

§ 1211.   Limitation on capital losses.

(b)   Other taxpayers. In the case of a taxpayer other than a corporation, losses from sales or exchange of capital assets shall be allowed only to the extent of the gains from such sales or exchanges, plus (if such losses exceed such gains) the lower of —

(1) $3,000 ($1,500 in the case of a married individual filing a separate return), or

(2) the excess of such losses over such gains.

---

§ 1212(b).   Loss carryovers — other taxpayers.

(1)   In general. If a taxpayer other than a corporation has a net capital loss for any taxable year —

(A) the excess of the net short-term capital loss over the net long-term capital gain for such year shall be a short-term capital loss in the succeeding taxable year, and

(B) the excess of the net long-term capital loss over the net short-term capital gain for such year shall be a long-term capital loss in the succeeding taxable year.

(2)   Treatment of amounts allowed under section 1211(b)(1) or (2).

(A)   In general. For purposes of determining the excess referred to in subparagraph (A) or (B) of paragraph (1), there shall be treated as a short-term capital gain in the taxable year an amount equal to the lesser of —

(i) the amount allowed for the taxable year under paragraph (1) or (2) of section 1211(b), or

(ii) the adjusted taxable income for such taxable year.

Throughout its tinkering with the preference for long term capital gain, Congress has retained the limitation on the deduction of capital losses. Section 1211(b) specifically provides that capital losses may be deducted dollar for dollar to the extent of capital gains. For purposes of the Section 1211 limitation, it makes no difference whether the capital gains and losses are long term or short term. For example, a dollar of short term capital loss will offset one dollar of long term capital gain. To the extent capital losses exceed capital gains, up to $3,000 of the excess may be deducted. In effect, a taxpayer may use capital losses (whether long term or short term) to offset on a dollar for dollar basis up to $3,000 of ordinary income in a given tax year. Capital losses which a taxpayer could not deduct because of the Section 1211(b) limitation may be carried over to the next tax year.[34]

The following examples illustrate the application of Sections 1211(b) and 1212(b) while also demonstrating the overall mechanics of the capital gain and loss structure of the Code.

> **Example 1:** Assume in the current year Tom has a salary of $75,000 and recognizes from various sales of corporate stock $5,000 of long term capital gain, $1,000 of short term capital gain, and $8,000 of long term capital loss from the sale of stock held for 15 months.
>
> **Analysis:** Section 61(a)(3) specifies that gains derived from dealings in property constitute gross income. Therefore, Tom's gross income for the current year is $81,000. Tom does not have a "net capital gain" on these facts. When a taxpayer's aggregate capital losses (both short term and long term) equal or exceed taxpayers aggregate capital gains (both long term and short term), there is no possibility of net capital gain (apart from qualified dividend income). However, as discussed below, Tom will be permitted to deduct all $8,000 of his capital loss.

To begin with, note that the loss is allowable under Section 165(c)(2) as a loss on a transaction entered into for profit. However, capital losses may be deducted only to the extent provided in Sections 1211 and 1212.[35] There are two parts to the Section 1211(b) limitation. Capital losses may be deducted to the extent of:

(1)   capital gains (this part of Section 1211(b) will be referred to hereinafter as the capital gain offset rule);

PLUS

(2)   up to $3,000 of any capital losses in excess of capital gains may be deducted against ordinary income[36] (this part of Section 1211(b) will be referred to hereinafter as the ordinary income offset rule).

Note that Section 1211 is not a deduction granting provision. Rather, Section 1211 serves only to limit the deduction of losses which are deductible under other provisions of the Code. In this case, the loss on the stock is deductible under Section 165(c)(2); Section 1211(b) represents only a potential limitation on the amount of the deduction which may be claimed in the current year. Here, the total capital loss ($8,000) exceeds the total capital gains ($6,000) by $2,000. Under the capital gain offset rule of Section 1211(b), Tom may deduct $6,000 of the capital loss (*i.e.*, an amount of loss equal to the capital gains); under the ordinary income offset rule of

---

[34] I.R.C. § 1212(b).

[35] I.R.C. § 165(f).

[36] I.R.C. § 1211(b)(1), (2).

Section 1211(b), Tom may deduct the $2,000 of excess capital loss as well since that amount is less than the $3,000 ceiling. Thus, Tom in this example will be allowed to deduct his entire capital loss. Section 62(a)(3) provides that the $8,000 in deductible capital loss will be deducted "above the line" in computing adjusted gross income. Assuming that Tom had no other above the line deductions, Tom's adjusted gross income would be $73,000 (*i.e.*, $81,000 less $8,000).

As demonstrated by this Example, Section 1211(b) permits long term capital losses to offset dollar for dollar both short term capital gains and long term capital gains. Similarly, short term capital losses will offset dollar for dollar short term as well as long term capital gains.

Example 2: Assume the same facts as Example 1 except that Tom also recognized $3,000 of short term capital loss from the sale of other investment property.

Analysis: Tom's gross income is still $81,000. Tom has a total of $11,000 in capital losses ($8,000 long term capital loss and $3,000 short term capital loss). Section 165(c)(2) authorizes a deduction for these losses subject to the Section 1211(b) limitation. Based on Example 1, Tom's Section 165(c)(2) deduction for the capital losses recognized will be limited by Section 1211(b) to $9,000: Tom may deduct (1) the capital losses to the extent of capital gains (thus, $6,000 of the capital losses are deductible under the capital gain offset portion of Section 1211(b)) plus (2) up to $3,000 of the excess of the capital losses over capital gains (here, $3,000 of capital losses are deductible under the ordinary income offset portion of Section 1211(b)). Tom's adjusted gross income will therefore be $72,000 ($81,000 less $9,000). Tom has thus deducted a total of $9,000 of the $11,000 of capital losses. (As in Example 1, Tom has no net capital gain.)

Suppose Tom had qualified dividend income. Would that permit him to deduct currently a greater amount of his net capital losses? Is the dividend income, which is taxable at capital gains rates, treated as capital gain income for purposes of determining the dollar limitation on deductible capital losses? The answer to both of these questions is "No." Qualified dividend income is not a capital gain because it is not gain from the sale or exchange of a capital asset. *See* Section 1222(1), (3). Accordingly, it is not part of the Section 1211(b) calculation on deducting capital losses. Thus, even if Tom had qualified dividend income, the answer in Example 2 does not change. He can currently deduct only $9,000 of capital losses.

The $2,000 of capital loss which, because of Section 1211, may not be deducted currently will be carried over to the next year pursuant to the rules of Section 1212(b).

Under Section 1212(b)(1), the capital losses carried over will retain their long term or short term status and will be deemed to have been incurred in the carryover year. For example, if the $11,000 of capital losses realized by Tom in the current year had all been long term capital losses, the $2,000 of carryover losses would be long term capital losses. By contrast, had Tom's losses all been short term capital losses, the $2,000 carryover losses would retain their character as short term capital losses. Losses disallowed under Section 1211(b) will be carried over from year to year indefinitely until they are utilized to offset capital gains or ordinary income. Capital losses unused at a taxpayer's death simply disappear.

In Example 2 above, Tom had a long term capital loss of $8,000 and a short term capital loss of $3,000 or a total of $11,000 in capital losses. Only $9,000 of these losses were deductible currently. Under the capital gain offset part of Section 1211(b), Tom was allowed to deduct capital losses to the extent of capital gains. Because Tom had $6,000 of capital gain, Tom was entitled to deduct $6,000 of capital loss. In addition, Tom was permitted under the ordinary income offset part of Section 1211(b)(1) and (2) to deduct an additional $3,000 of the capital losses.

Section 1212(b) specifies which of these losses were deducted and which were carried over. First, note that it applies when the taxpayer other than a corporation has a "net capital loss," a term defined as capital losses in excess of those allowed under Section 1211.[37] Thus, in Example 2, Tom has a net capital loss, and the Section 1212(b) carryover rules will apply. Next, note that Section 1212(b) in effect establishes two rules for determining which losses were deducted and therefore which losses remain to be carried over:

Rule 1: In applying the capital gain offset portion of Section 1211(b), short term capital losses will be netted first against short term capital gains, and long term losses will be netted first against long term gains. If short term losses exceed short term capital gains, the excess (or net) short term capital losses will then be netted against excess (or net) long term capital gains, if any. Similarly, if long term capital losses exceed long term capital gains, the excess (or net) long term capital losses will be netted against the excess (or net) short term capital gains, if any.

Rule 2: Short term capital losses, if any, will be deemed to have been deducted first in the ordinary income offset part of Section 1211(b). That is accomplished by the "special rule" of Section 1212(b)(2) which generally provides that the amount allowed under the ordinary income offset rule of Section 1211(b) shall be treated as short-term capital gain in that year for purposes of applying Rule 1 above. (However, where the taxpayer has a "negative taxable income," the amount treated as a short-term gain may be less than the amount allowed as a Section 1211(b) offset. This has the effect of enhancing the amount of the carryover and preventing a "wasting" of the Section 1211(b) offset in negative taxable income situations.) In other words, it is just as though the taxpayer, rather than offsetting ordinary income, were offsetting short term capital gain. Thus, in this Example, since the ordinary income offset amounts to $3,000, it is as if Tom had $4,000 of short term capital gain, rather than only $1,000. For purposes of determining the capital loss carryover, we must assume that we have $5,000 of long term capital gain and $4,000 of short term capital gain.

Applying Rule 1, $5,000 of the long term capital loss will offset the $5,000 long term capital gain. Tom then has $3,000 net long term capital loss, *i.e.*, the excess of the long term capital loss over the long term capital gain. Next, the $3,000 of short term capital loss will be netted against the $4,000 of deemed short term capital gain.

---

[37] I.R.C. § 1222(10).

All $3,000 of the short term capital loss is consumed and Tom is left with a net short term capital gain of $1,000 (*i.e.*, excess of the short term capital gain over the short term capital losses). Tom now has $3,000 of net long term capital loss and $1,000 of net short term capital gain. These are netted against each other under Section 1212(b)(1)(B) leaving $2,000 of long term capital loss to be carried over to the following year. For purposes of allocating long term capital losses among multiple categories of long term capital gain, as discussed previously, the long term losses carryover under Section 1212(b)(1)(B) will be allocated to the 28-percent rate gain.

§ 31.04 DEFINITION OF CAPITAL ASSET

§ 1221. Capital asset defined.

(a) In general. For purposes of this subtitle, the term "capital asset" means property held by the taxpayer (whether or not connected with his trade or business) but does not include —

(1) stock in trade of the taxpayer or other property of a kind which would properly be included in the inventory of the taxpayer if on hand at the close of the taxable year, or property held by the taxpayer primarily for sale to customers in the ordinary course of his trade or business;

(2) property, used in his trade or business, of a character which is subject to the allowance for depreciation provided in section 167, or real property used in his trade or business;

(3) a copyright, a literary, musical, or artistic composition, a letter or memorandum, or similar property, held by —

(A) a taxpayer whose personal efforts created such property,

(B) in the case of a letter, memorandum, or similar property, a taxpayer for whom such property was prepared or produced, or

(C) a taxpayer in whose hands the basis of such property is determined, for purposes of determining gain from a sale or exchange, in whole or part by reference to the basis of such property in the hands of a taxpayer described in subparagraph (A) or (B);

(4) accounts or notes receivable acquired in the ordinary course of trade or business for services rendered or from the sale of property described in paragraph (1);

(5) a publication of the United States Government (including the Congressional Record) which is received from the United States Government or any agency thereof, other than by purchase at the price at which it is offered for sale to the public, and which is held by —

(A) a taxpayer who so received such publication, or

(B) a taxpayer in whose hands the basis of such publication is determined for purposes of determining gain from a sale or exchange, in whole or in part by reference to the basis of such publication in the hands of a taxpayer described in subparagraph (A);

. . .

(8) supplies of a type regularly used or consumed by the taxpayer in the

ordinary course of a trade or business of the taxpayer.

(b)   Definition and special rules.

. . .

(3)   Sale or exchange of self-created musical works — At the election of the taxpayer, paragraphs (1) and (3) of subsection (a) shall not apply to musical compositions or copyrights in musical works sold or exchanged by a taxpayer described in subsection (a)(3).

The Revenue Act of 1924 defined "capital asset" as "property acquired and held by the taxpayer for more than two years (whether or not connected with his trade or business), but does not include stock in trade of the taxpayer or other property of a kind which would properly be included in the inventory of the taxpayer if on hand at the close of the taxable year, or property held by the taxpayer primarily for sale in the course of his trade or business."[38] Under the 1924 Revenue Act, essentially all property, including personal use property, constituted capital assets unless the assets could be classified as inventory-type assets. Since then, Congress has added a number of other exceptions to the definition of capital asset in Section 1221. While the statutory definition of capital asset appears remarkably broad, it is clear Congress intended capital gain treatment to be an exception and not the rule. The courts have tended to construe "capital asset" narrowly, thus significantly limiting taxpayers' opportunities to claim preferential capital gain treatment.

[A]   Section 1221(a)(1): Inventory, Stock in Trade and Property Held Primarily for Sale to Customers in the Ordinary Course of the Taxpayer's Trade or Business

The denial of capital asset status (and therefore preferential capital gain treatment) to inventory-type items is consistent with the congressional purpose underlying preferential capital gain treatment. As the Supreme Court noted in *Corn Products Refining Co. v. Commissioner*:[39]

Congress intended that profits and losses arising from the everyday operation of business be considered as ordinary income or loss rather than capital gain or loss. The preferential treatment [historically provided gains from the sale or exchange of capital assets] applies to transactions in property which are not the normal source of business income. It was intended "to relieve the taxpayer from . . . excessive tax burdens on gains resulting from a conversion of capital investments, and to remove the deterrent effect of those burdens on such conversions. . . ."[40]

---

[38] The predecessor to the 1924 Revenue Act, the 1921 Revenue Act, denied capital asset status to "property held for the personal use or consumption of the taxpayer or his family" and specifically required that property be "acquired and held by the taxpayer for profit or investment." The 1924 Act and all subsequent tax law, however, have accorded capital asset status to personal use property. *See* I.R.C. § 1221.

[39] 350 U.S. 46 (1955).

[40] *Id.* at 52.

Because gains derived from the sale or exchange of inventory-type assets undoubtedly constitute ordinary business income, Section 1221(a)(1) was drafted to encompass a wide range of everyday business income. Clearly, there is considerable overlap among the three categories of property listed in Section 1221(a)(1). For example, "inventory" could be properly characterized as "property held by the taxpayer primarily for sale to customers in the ordinary course of his trade or business." At the same time each category includes property which may not be included in either of the other categories. For example, tracts of land held by a dealer in real property may not be viewed as either "inventory" or "stock in trade"; likewise raw materials used in the production of a product, while clearly inventory, may not be said to be "property held by the taxpayer primarily for sale to customers in the ordinary course of his trade or business."

Generally, few problems are encountered identifying the inventory or stock in trade of a taxpayer. The most troublesome questions involving Section 1221(a)(1) have focused on the interpretation of the words "property held by the taxpayer primarily for sale to customers in the ordinary course of his trade or business." The interpretation of the words "primarily for sale" in Section 1221(a)(1) was the focus of the Supreme Court's decision in *Malat v. Riddell*.[41] There, the taxpayer was a member of a joint venture which had acquired property with the intent to develop it commercially or to sell it at a profit. Unable to secure the necessary financing for development, the joint venture sold the property. The taxpayer claimed capital gain treatment for his share of the gain, but the Service argued that the gain was ordinary income. The Service reasoned the word "primarily for sale" in Section 1221(a)(1) required only that the taxpayer's purpose to sell be "substantial." The Court rejected that interpretation noting:

> The purpose of the statutory provision with which we deal is to differentiate between the "profits and losses arising from the everyday operation of a business" on the one hand . . . and "the realization of appreciation in value accrued over a substantial period of time" on the other. . . . A literal reading of the statute is consistent with this legislative purpose. We hold that, as used in Section 1221(a)(1), "primarily" means "of first importance" or principally.[42]

In a number of cases following *Malat v. Riddell*, the courts have found that, rather than a dual purpose, the taxpayer's purpose had changed so that the taxpayer's sole purpose in holding the property was to sell it.

The gains from sales of subdivided real estate historically raised some of the more difficult and interesting questions regarding the interpretation of the Section 1221(a)(1) language "primarily for sale to customers in the ordinary course of his trade or business." Consider the following scenario: A farmer owned a large tract of land bordering a town. As the town grew, the farmer's land became more valuable for subdivision purposes than for farming purposes. The farmer subdivided, improved and sold the land. The Tax Court in *Bynum v. Commissioner*,[43]

---

[41] 383 U.S. 569 (1966).

[42] *Id.* at 572.

[43] 46 T.C. 295 (1966).

addressing this kind of case, concluded the property fell within Section 1221(a)(1) as being primarily held for sale to customers in the ordinary course of business and that the gain was therefore ordinary income. The *Bynum* court emphasized as important factors in its decision the number of lots which the taxpayers created, the improvements they made to the lots, and the taxpayers' promotional and selling activities. The Fifth Circuit, in *Biedenharn Realty Co., Inc. v. U.S.*,[44] while acknowledging that "individual factors have varying weights and magnitudes, depending on the facts of the case," considered the following factors in determining the character of gains from the sale of subdivided land: frequency and substantiality of sales; improvements made to the land; taxpayer's solicitation and advertising efforts; and utilization of real estate brokers and agents. Of these factors, the frequency and substantiality of sales was the most important.[45]

[B] Section 1221(a)(2): Property Used in the Taxpayer's Trade or Business

Section 1221(a)(2) excludes from capital asset status property used in the taxpayer's trade or business that is either depreciable property or real property. Nonetheless, Section 1221(a)(2) property held for more than a year is accorded special treatment by Section 1231, which in effect provides quasi-capital asset status to such property. Sections 1231 and 1221(a)(2) are addressed in detail in the next chapter, so at this point it is sufficient merely to note the Section 1221(a)(2) exclusion for real or depreciable property used in the taxpayer's trade or business.

[C] Section 1221(a)(3): Copyrights, Literary, Musical, or Artistic Compositions, Etc.

Prior to 1950, amateur composers, artists and authors who sold their works at a gain could characterize their gain as capital. Because their gain was comparable to personal service income, the capital gain characterization was inconsistent with the principle that ordinary business income was not eligible for preferential treatment. In the Revenue Act of 1950, Congress specifically provided that a "copyright, literary, musical, or artistic composition; or similar property" was not a capital asset if held by a taxpayer whose personal efforts created the property or by a taxpayer whose basis in the property was determined[46] in whole or in part by reference to the basis of the property in the hands of a person whose efforts created the property. The provision, codified as Section 1221(a)(3), was expanded in 1969 to include letters, memoranda and similar property.[47] However, in 2006, Congress provided a special tax break for the sale or exchange of self-created

---

[44] 526 F.2d 409 (5th Cir. 1976).

[45] To reduce the volume of litigation regarding gains from subdivided land, Congress in 1954 enacted Section 1237. This provision enables taxpayers to avoid the Section 1221(a)(1) characterization if certain conditions are met. The provision, however, is likely too narrow and complex to provide much solace to most taxpayers.

[46] Tax legislation of 2001 added the phrase "other than by reason of section 1022."

[47] The primary purposes of the 1969 amendment was to prevent taxpayers from claiming substantial charitable deductions when they donated their papers, etc. to a library or other charitable organization. See Section 170(e), discussed in Chapter 26, *supra*.

musical works. Section 1221(b)(3) provides that a taxpayer may elect to have Section 1221(a)(1) and (a)(3) not apply to sales or exchanges of taxpayer-created musical compositions or copyrights in musical works. In effect, by providing that the inventory exclusion of Section 1221(a)(1) and the copyright and musical composition exclusion of Section 1221(a)(3) shall not apply, the sale of self-created musical works will receive capital gains treatment, rather than ordinary income treatment, at the election of the taxpayer.[48]

[D] Section 1221(a)(4): Accounts Receivable for Services Rendered or Inventory-Type Assets Sold

In some respects, in denying capital asset status to accounts receivable for services rendered or for inventory-type assets sold, Section 1221(a)(4) states the obvious. Amounts received by a service provider or by one selling inventory-type assets are clearly normal business income and should be treated as ordinary income. Likewise, where a cash method taxpayer has an account receivable as a result of providing services or selling inventory, any gain recognized from the sale of that account receivable should be ordinary income. Section 1221(a)(4) insures that result by denying capital asset status to such accounts.

In contrast to a cash method taxpayer, an accrual method taxpayer has already included in income the amount represented by the account receivable. As a result, the accrual method taxpayer has a basis in the account receivable equal to the amount included in income. If the accrual method taxpayer sells her account receivable, she will often receive an amount less than her basis in the account and will therefore have a loss deductible under Section 165(c)(1). By denying capital asset status to the account receivable, Section 1221(a)(4) insures that the loss will be ordinary. Considering the limitation on the deductibility of capital losses, this result is favorable to the accrual method taxpayer. Of course, in the rare case where the account receivable is sold by the accrual method taxpayer for an amount in excess of basis, the taxpayer will have ordinary income.

[E] Section 1221(a)(5): Certain Publications of the U.S. Government

Section 1221(a)(5) is important primarily because of the limit it places on charitable deductions for gifts of government publications to public libraries, universities, etc. By denying capital asset status to U.S. Government publications (including the Congressional Record) when acquired other than by purchase at the price the publication is offered for sale to the public, Section 1221(a)(5), in conjunction with Section 170(e)(1), assures that the taxpayer contributing the publications will not be entitled to a charitable deduction in excess of the taxpayer's basis in the publications. Section 1221(a)(5) is applicable only if the publications described above are held by the taxpayer who received the publication or by a taxpayer whose basis in the publication is determined by reference to the basis of

---

[48] For charitable deduction purposes, however, a taxpayer will be limited to a deduction equal to the taxpayer's basis, rather than the fair market value of the self-created work. I.R.C. § 170(e)(1)(A), as amended in 2006.

the publication in the hands of a taxpayer who received the publication. For example, government publications received by a Congressman free of charge are not capital assets and, if sold, will generate ordinary income to the Congressman. More importantly, however, if these publications are contributed to a charitable organization, Section 170(e)(1) will deny a charitable deduction. Likewise, if the Congressman first gives the publications to a family member, who then contributes them to charity, no charitable deduction will be allowed.[49]

[F] Section 1221(a)(8): Supplies Used or Consumed in the Taxpayer's Trade or Business

Section 1221(a)(8), enacted in 1999, excludes from capital asset status supplies of a type regularly used or consumed by the taxpayer in the ordinary course of trade or business. This type of asset can be thought of as so close to inventory (excluded from the definition of capital asset by Section 1221(a)(1)) that capital asset characterization is likewise appropriate for it as well.[50]

[G] Judicially Established Limits on Capital Asset Definition

Drawing the line between assets which should be characterized as capital assets and those which should not has on occasion proven difficult for the courts. Superficially at least, certain assets seem to be capital assets within the meaning of Section 1221. On closer examination, however, courts have found that to accord those assets capital asset status would frustrate congressional purpose. For example, in the seminal case of *Corn Products Refining Co. v. Commissioner*,[51] a manufacturer of products made from grain corn sought to protect itself from sharp increases in raw corn prices by buying "corn futures" (contracts for future delivery of raw corn at a set price) whenever the price was favorable. The taxpayer took delivery on the futures contracts when necessary to its operations, and it sold the remaining contracts if no shortages of raw corn developed. Over the two tax years in question, the taxpayer made a profit on the sales of the contracts; it contended that the contracts were capital assets, generating capital gains and losses on their sales. The Supreme Court, noting that the taxpayer's purchases of futures contracts had been found to "constitute an integral part of its manufacturing business," held to the contrary:

> Admittedly, petitioner's corn futures do not come within the literal language of the exclusions set out in section [1221]. They were not stock in trade, actual inventory, property held for sale to customers or depreciable property used in a trade or business. But the capital-asset provision of Section [1221] must not be so broadly applied as to defeat rather than further the purpose of Congress. Congress intended that profits and losses

---

[49] *See* I.R.C. § 1221(a)(5)(B).

[50] Congress in 1999 added two additional categories to the six discussed above, *i.e.*, commodities derivative financial instruments held by a commodities derivatives dealer, and certain hedging transactions. I.R.C. § 1221(a)(6), (7). These topics are outside the scope of this text.

[51] 350 U.S. 46 (1955).

arising from the everyday operation of a business be considered as ordinary income or loss rather than capital gain or loss. The preferential treatment provided by Section [1221] applies to transactions in property which are not the normal source of business income. Since this section is an exception from the normal tax requirements of the Internal Revenue Code, the definition of a capital asset must be narrowly applied and its exclusions interpreted broadly. This is necessary to effectuate the basic congressional purpose. This Court has always construed narrowly the term "capital assets" in Section [1221].[52]

The *Corn Products* decision thus added a gloss to Section 1221 with which taxpayers and courts have since had to struggle.

Following *Corn Products*, the courts decided numerous cases involving stock or securities, which, as with the futures contracts in *Corn Products*, assured their holders of a source of supply. In many cases the stock or securities were also held for investment purposes. Where such dual purposes existed, a taxpayer realizing a gain on the sale of stock or securities found it advantageous to emphasize an investment purpose with respect to the stock or securities thereby hoping to assure capital gain treatment. By contrast, if a loss were realized on the sale of the stock or securities, the taxpayer, relying on *Corn Products*, would argue that the primary purpose for holding the stock or securities had been for business reasons and that the loss therefore was an ordinary loss. Ironically, while the Service won in *Corn Products*, taxpayers subsequently used the doctrine established in that case to avoid the characterization of stock losses as capital losses. Partly to minimize the potential whipsawing of the government, the Tax Court eventually held in *W.W. Windle Company v. Commissioner*,[53] that "stock purchased with a substantial investment purpose is a capital asset even if there is a more substantial business motive for the purchase," and that a subsequent abandonment of the investment motive was irrelevant. The Service accepted this result in Revenue Ruling 78-94,[54] and thus, prior to 1988, the taxpayer's motivation in purchasing an asset could be critical to the determination of whether it was a capital asset. However, in *Arkansas Best Corp. v. Commissioner*,[55] the Supreme Court concluded capital stock held by a taxpayer was a capital asset notwithstanding the taxpayer's argument that it had acquired the stock for business purposes. The Court rejected the motivation test in *Arkansas Best*, noting it was not statutorily founded and could lead to abuse, *e.g.*, taxpayers could argue they had an investment purpose for holding stock sold at a gain thereby claiming preferential capital gain treatment and they had a business purpose for holding stock sold at a loss and thereby claim ordinary loss treatment. According to the Court, stock is "most naturally viewed as a capital asset" and does not fall within any of the categories of property excluded from capital asset status by Section 1221. The Court characterized *Corn Products* as simply "a broad reading of the inventory exclusion of Section 1221."

---

[52] *Id.* at 51–52.

[53] 65 T.C. 694, 712 (1976).

[54] 1978-1, C.B. 58.

[55] 485 U.S. 212 (1988).

Although the taxpayer in *Arkansas Best* argued the stock in question had been purchased for business purposes, it was clear the stock was not purchased to assure a source of supply. The Supreme Court's decision in *Arkansas Best* nevertheless appears to foreclose the argument that a loss upon the sale of stock purchased to ensure a source of supply is an ordinary loss. In *Cenex, Inc. v. United States*,[56] the taxpayer sold petroleum products and, to assure a source of supply of refined petroleum products, acquired stock in a corporation that operated an oil refinery. That stock subsequently became worthless and the taxpayer claimed an ordinary loss, arguing the stock qualified for the Section 1221 inventory exclusion as an "inventory substitute . . . purchased in order to obtain a supply of petroleum products, which are actual inventory in its business." The Federal Circuit denied the claim, finding in the aftermath of *Arkansas Best* that surrogates or substitutes for inventory "must bear a close relationship to actual inventory and can do so if they are closely related to the taxpayer's inventory-purchase system." The corn futures in *Corn Products* satisfied this test because they were redeemable for corn and because the cost of inventory was directly related to the cost of the corn futures — gains and losses on futures were the same as gains and losses on actual inventory would have been. In contrast, the stock in *Cenex* was not redeemable for inventory, nor related in value to the value of the petroleum products — in sum, it was simply not closely related to its inventory-purchase system. The source of supply doctrine itself, according to the court, is "incompatible with *Arkansas Best*" and hence not a basis on which to treat the stock as an ordinary asset.[57]

In another post-*Arkansas Best* case, the Fifth Circuit, in *Azar Nut Company v. Commissioner*,[58] considered the meaning of the Section 1221(a)(2) language "used in [the taxpayer's] trade or business." As part of the employment package it offered a high level executive, Azar Nut Company agreed to purchase the executive's residence at fair market value whenever the executive's employment with the taxpayer was terminated. Azar Nut subsequently fired the executive, purchased the

---

[56] 156 F.3d 1377 (Fed. Cir. 1998).

[57] As a result of questions that arose following the Supreme Court's decision in *Arkansas Best*, the Service issued regulations in 1994 addressing the characterization of gains and losses from so-called hedging transactions. In these regulations, the Service abandoned its earlier position that gain or loss realized in the context of many common business hedging transactions was capital rather than ordinary in nature. Treas. Reg. § 1.1221-2(a)(1) provided that "the term capital asset does not include property that is part of a hedging transaction . . ." Treas. Reg. § 1.1221-2(b)(1) defined a hedging transaction as a transaction entered into by a taxpayer in the normal course of the taxpayer's business primarily to reduce the risk of price changes or currency fluctuations with respect to "ordinary property." The risk being reduced must relate to "ordinary property," i.e., property the sale or exchange of which could not produce capital gain or capital loss regardless of the taxpayer's holding period when the sale or exchange occurs. Treas. Reg. § 1.1221-2(c)(5). The regulations were intended to negate claims that losses on corporate stock (e.g., stock purportedly held to ensure a source of supply) were ordinary. The holding of stock would not be a hedging transaction even if the stock were held "to . . . ensure the availability of goods." T.D. 8555, 1994-33 I.R.B. 9. Treas. Reg. § 1.1221-2(e)(1) imposed a requirement that the taxpayer identify a transaction as a hedging transaction "before the close of the day on which the taxpayer enters into the transaction." These regulations provided some certainty in an otherwise gray area and benefitted taxpayers who realized losses from hedging transactions. In 1999, Congress amended Section 1221 to add certain hedging transactions as a statutory exclusion from capital asset treatment. I.R.C. § 1221(a)(7).

[58] 931 F.2d 314 (5th Cir. 1991), *aff'g*, 94 T.C. 455.

residence pursuant to the agreement, and ultimately sold it at a substantial loss. The company claimed an ordinary loss deduction, arguing the residence was not a capital asset because it was "used in" its trade or business. The Fifth Circuit observed that "Azar argues that this 'used in' exception includes any asset acquired by a taxpayer under the terms of a contract or similar agreement that is an integral part of the taxpayer's business, even if the asset never plays a role in business operations after its acquisition." But the court rejected this reasoning:

> Azar's interpretations of the "used in" exception essentially excludes from capital asset treatment any asset purchased with a "business purpose," as that term was used under the *Corn Products* Doctrine. . . . The Supreme Court recently renounced the *Corn Products* Doctrine in *Arkansas Best Corporation v. Commissioner* . . . , holding that business purpose is irrelevant to determining whether an asset falls within the general definition of "capital asset." Azar urges us to consider business purpose in analyzing the "used in" exception. We conclude that the plain language of Section 1221(a)(2) precludes consideration of business purpose in all but the most exceptional circumstances. The words "used in" clearly require ordinary asset treatment for properties that, once acquired, play a role in the taxpayer's business operations. Those words do not suggest that an asset may be excepted from capital-asset treatment simply because the asset is acquired with a business purpose. To qualify under the "used in" exception, an asset must be "used in" the taxpayer's business, and an asset that has no meaningful association with the taxpayer's business operations after it is acquired cannot reasonably fall within the plain words of the statute.[59]

Wholly apart from *Corn Products/Arkansas Best* issues, the courts have also been required to characterize payments received by taxpayers who have sold their right to collect future income. The seminal case in this regard is *Hort v. Commissioner*[60] holding that consideration received by a landlord for cancellation of a lease constituted ordinary income and not capital gain. According to the Court, the cancellation of the lease was nothing more than the relinquishment of the right to receive a stream of future rental payments. The payment received for the cancellation was merely a substitute for the payment of rent. Just as the rent would have been ordinary income, the substitute for it, *i.e.*, the payment for cancellation of the lease, is also ordinary income. A more recent case applying *Hort* principles involved a taxpayer who won a state lottery prize entitling him to receive annual payments for the next 20 years and who then later sold a portion of several future annual payments in return for a single lump-sum payment.[61] The taxpayer claimed the lump-sum payment constituted capital gain. The Tax Court disagreed, holding that the lump-sum payment was merely the discounted value of future ordinary income, not payment for an increase in the value of income-producing property, and

---

[59] *Id.* at 316-17.

[60] 313 U.S. 28 (1941).

[61] Davis v. Comm'r, 119 T.C. 1 (2002); *see also* U.S. v. Maginnis, 356 F.3d 1179 (9th Cir. 2004); Lattera v. Comm'r, 437 F.3d 399 (3d Cir. 2006); Watkins v. Comm'r, 447 F.3d 1269 (10th Cir. 2006); Womack v. Comm'r, 510 F.3d 1295 (11th Cir. 2007); Prebola v. Comm'r, 482 F.3d 610 (2d Cir. 2007).

further holding that the right to future annual payments was not a capital asset within Section 1221. Accordingly, the lump-sum payment was ordinary income.

§ 31.05   THE SALE OR EXCHANGE REQUIREMENT

Pursuant to Section 1222, only gains or losses resulting from the "sale or exchange" of capital assets will be treated as capital gains and losses. As noted in *Freeland v. Commissioner*,[62] "Congress intended the words 'sale or exchange' to have a broad meaning, not to be limited to the standard transfer of property by one person to another in exchange for a stated consideration in money or money's worth."

In the common case, it will be easy to determine whether the sale or exchange requirement has been satisfied. Under certain circumstances, however, more difficult questions may arise. For example, in *Kenan v. Commissioner*,[63] the court concluded that the satisfaction of a bequest with appreciated property constituted a sale or exchange for purposes of Section 1222. As a result, capital gain treatment was appropriate. According to the court, the term "exchange" "does not necessarily have the connotation of a bilateral agreement which may be said to attach to the word "sale."

Similarly, in *Yarbro v. Commissioner*,[64] the issue before the court was "whether an individual taxpayer's loss resulting from the abandonment of unimproved real estate subject to a nonrecourse mortgage exceeding the market value is an ordinary loss or a capital loss." Concluding the loss was capital, the court relied upon a number of earlier decisions in rejecting the taxpayer's contention that the abandonment here did not constitute a sale or an exchange. *Yarbro* noted that in *Helvering v. Nebraska Bridge Supply & Lumber Co.*,[65] the Supreme Court had held a tax forfeiture sale constituted a "sale or an exchange," and in *Helvering v. Hammel*,[66] the Supreme Court had held an involuntary foreclosure sale of real estate satisfied the "sale or exchange" requirement, thus resulting in capital loss rather than ordinary loss. *Yarbro* also noted that in *Freeland v. Commissioner*,[67] an owner's conveyance of land to a mortgagee by a quitclaim deed had constituted a "sale or exchange." According to the *Yarbro* court,

> [T]he abandonment followed by the mortgagee's foreclosure . . . is the functional equivalent of the foreclosure sale in *Hammel*, the tax forfeiture in *Nebraska Bridge Supply*, and the quitclaim in lieu of foreclosure in . . . *Freeland*. In all these transactions, the taxpayer-owner is relieved of his obligation to repay the debt and is relieved of title to the property. Because the mortgagee is legally entitled to recover the property in any of these

---

[62]   74 T.C. 970, 980 (1980).

[63]   114 F.2d 217 (2d Cir. 1940).

[64]   737 F.2d 479 (5th Cir. 1984).

[65]   312 U.S. 666 (1941).

[66]   311 U.S. 504 (1941).

[67]   74 T.C. 970 (1980). In *Freeland*, the nonrecourse indebtedness encumbering the property exceeded the fair market value of the property.

cases, the fact that out of prudence he concludes he must go through foreclosure proceedings to formalize his interest in the land is not a rational basis for altering the character of the gain or loss realized by the taxpayer on the transaction. The differences in these transactions is not a difference in substance, but only in form. . . . [W]here the taxpayer would be eligible for capital gains treatment upon the sale of property had it appreciated in value, he should not be allowed to avoid the limitations on deductions for capital losses by using an artfully timed abandonment rather than a sale, voluntary reconveyance, or foreclosure.[68]

While technically Section 1222 requires a particular type of disposition before there will be capital gain or capital loss, Congress has in many cases negated the need for a sale or an exchange. For example, if any security which is a capital asset becomes worthless, the loss resulting shall be treated as a loss from the sale or exchange of a capital asset.[69] Another significant provision provides that amounts received on the retirement of a debt instrument shall be treated as received in exchange for that instrument.[70] Similarly, sale or exchange treatment applies on the cancellation, lapse, expiration or other termination of certain property rights or obligations.[71] Congress has also provided sale or exchange treatment in cases involving involuntary conversions which would traditionally not be considered sales or exchanges.[72]

§ 31.06 THE *ARROWSMITH* RULE: CHARACTERIZATION OF CERTAIN GAINS OR LOSSES DEPENDENT ON PRIOR TAX TREATMENT OF RELATED GAINS OR LOSSES

When a corporation liquidates, the shareholders are required to report the gain (or loss), if any, on the receipt of their share of liquidation proceeds. The gain or loss recognized by the shareholder is treated as gain or loss from an exchange of their stock. Thus, because the stock will generally be a capital asset in the hands of a shareholder, the gain or loss on receipt of the liquidation proceeds will be capital gain or capital loss. Subsequent to the liquidation, however, the shareholders may be held liable for unpaid debts of the corporation. A shareholder who is required to make payment to a creditor of the liquidated corporation is entitled to claim a loss deduction. The Supreme Court has held that, even though the payment of the corporate debt does not constitute a sale or an exchange, the payment can generate a capital loss. In *Arrowsmith v. Commissioner*,[73] the taxpayers had received partial distributions in 1937-39 and a final liquidating distribution in 1940, which they properly reported as capital gains; in 1944, they were required to pay a judgment

---

[68] 737 F.2d at 485-86.

[69] I.R.C. § 165(g)(1).

[70] I.R.C. § 1271(a).

[71] I.R.C. § 1234A.

[72] I.R.C. § 1231 (discussed in Chapter 32, *infra*). *See also* I.R.C. §§ 1235, 1241.

[73] 344 U.S. 6 (1952).

against the corporation, which they sought to classify as an ordinary business loss. The Supreme Court held that the loss was capital:

> It is not . . . denied that had this judgment been paid after liquidation, but during the year 1940, the losses would have been properly treated as capital ones. For payment during 1940 would simply have reduced the amount of capital gains taxpayers received during that year.

> It is contended, however, that this payment which would have been a capital transaction in 1940 was transformed into an ordinary business transaction in 1944 because of the well-established principle that each taxable year is a separate unit for tax accounting purposes. But the principle is not breached by considering all the 1937-1944 liquidation transaction events in order properly to classify the nature of the 1944 loss for tax purposes. Such an examination is not an attempt to reopen and readjust the 1937 to 1940 tax returns, an action that would be inconsistent with the annual tax accounting principle.[74]

The Supreme Court a number of years later relied on the so-called *Arrowsmith* rule in deciding *United States v. Skelly Oil Co.*[75] As that case demonstrates, the *Arrowsmith* rule is much broader than just a gain/loss characterization rule. In *Skelly Oil*, the taxpayer refunded approximately $505,000 to certain customers for overcharges on the sale of natural gas in prior years. The taxpayer had included the refunded amount in gross income as part of its total receipts from the sale of natural gas. In the year when it refunded the $505,000, the taxpayer sought to deduct that amount on the theory that, when a taxpayer is required to restore amounts previously included in income under the claim-of-right doctrine, the taxpayer is entitled to a deduction.[76]

However, in the year the taxpayer had included the $505,000 overcharge in gross income, the taxpayer had also claimed a Section 613 depletion deduction equal to 27.5% of the taxpayer's gross income from receipts from oil and gas wells. Thus, during the same year in which taxpayer included in gross income the $505,000 which taxpayer later refunded, the taxpayer was allowed to deduct 27.5% of that amount. The taxpayer's taxable income for that year was therefore increased by a net of only $366,000 as a result of the inclusion of the $505,000 in income. Given that fact, the Service argued that the refund of the half million dollars should generate only a $366,000 deduction. Agreeing with the Service, the Supreme Court noted that:

> [T]he annual accounting concept does not require us to close our eyes to what happened in prior years. For instance, it is well settled that the prior year may be examined to determine whether the repayment gives rise to a regular loss or a capital loss. *Arrowsmith v. Commissioner* . . . . The rationale for the *Arrowsmith* rule is easy to see; if money was taxed at a special lower rate when received, the taxpayer would be accorded an unfair tax windfall if repayments were generally deductible from receipts taxable

---

[74] *Id.* at 8–9.

[75] 394 U.S. 678 (1969).

[76] See Chapter 3, *supra*, and the discussion of *North American Oil Consolidated v. Burnet*, 286 U.S. 417 (1932).

at the higher rate applicable to ordinary income. The Court in *Arrowsmith* was unwilling to infer that Congress intended such a result.

> This case is really no different. . . . In essence, oil and gas producers are taxed on only 72.5% of their "gross income from the property" whenever they claim percentage depletion. The remainder of their oil and gas receipts is in reality tax exempt. We cannot believe that Congress intended to give taxpayers a deduction for refunding money that was not taxed when received. . . . Accordingly *Arrowsmith* teaches that the full amount of the repayment cannot, in the circumstances of this case, be allowed as a deduction.[77]

As *Skelly Oil* and the facts of *Arrowsmith* itself indicate, the *Arrowsmith* rule should not be overlooked. For purposes of this Chapter, the import of *Arrowsmith* should be clear: gains or losses generated as a result of a transaction covering more than one year may be characterized as capital gains or losses even though technically the sale or exchange requirement does not appear to be met.

§ 31.07 HOLDING PERIOD

Under current law, property must be held for more than one year before its sale or exchange if there is to be long term capital gain or loss. Only long term capital gains are entitled to the preferential treatment accorded by Section 1(h). However, the limitation on deductibility of capital losses does not depend on the long or short term nature of the loss. The holding period of assets is also implicated in provisions like Section 170(e), which limits the charitable deduction allowable on gifts of appreciated property.

In some circumstances, Section 1223 allows the "tacking" of holding periods. For example, if a taxpayer receives property by gift, the taxpayer/donee's holding period will include the donor's holding period.[78] Similarly, if a taxpayer exchanges Land A for Land B in an exchange qualifying for like kind exchange treatment under Section 1031 (discussed in Chapter 38), the taxpayer's holding period in Land B will include the period during which the taxpayer held Land A.[79]

---

[77] 394 U.S. at 684-85.

[78] I.R.C. § 1223(2).

[79] I.R.C. § 1223(1).

Chapter 32

QUASI-CAPITAL ASSETS: SECTION 1231

At the risk of slighting important details and qualifications, one might summarize Section 1231 by stating that its primary purpose is to provide special, favorable tax treatment to the sale, exchange or involuntary conversion of real or depreciable property used in the taxpayer's trade or business. Recall that under Section 1221(a)(2) such property is excluded from the definition of "capital asset." But for Section 1231, any gain or loss recognized on the disposition of such property would necessarily be ordinary gain or loss. Under Section 1231, however, a recognized gain on the sale, exchange or involuntary conversion of such property may be characterized as capital gain (hence, the term "quasi-capital asset"), while a recognized loss may remain characterized as an ordinary loss. This capital-gain/ordinary-loss set of alternatives gives taxpayers the "best of both worlds."

Although the enactment in 1938 of the predecessor of Section 1221(a)(2) provided ordinary loss treatment to taxpayers holding depreciable trade or business property that had declined in value, it simultaneously eliminated capital gain treatment for those taxpayers holding depreciable property that had increased in value. (The reference to real property in Section 1221(a)(2) was not added until 1942.) The enactment of the predecessor of Section 1231 in 1942 drew its impetus from the wartime conditions. Congress concluded it was inappropriate to tax at high ordinary income rates the gains from sales to the government of vessels used in the taxpayer's business or gains resulting from the receipt of insurance proceeds in excess of the basis of property destroyed in the course of the ongoing war. As enacted, however, the statute applied to dispositions well beyond those that were war-related. Section 1231 remains in the Code today long after the specific wartime conditions that prompted it had passed.

§ 32.01 IDENTIFYING SECTION 1231 GAINS AND LOSSES

§ 1231. **Property used in the trade or business and involuntary conversions —**

(a) **General rule —**

(1) **Gains exceed losses. — If —**

(A) the section 1231 gains for any taxable year, exceed

(B) the section 1231 losses for such taxable year,

such gains and losses shall be treated as long-term capital gains or losses, as the case may be.

(2) **Gains do not exceed losses. — If —**

(A) the section 1231 gains for any taxable year, do not exceed

(B) the section 1231 losses for such taxable year,

such gains and losses shall not be treated as gains and losses from sales or exchanges of capital assets.

(3)   Section 1231 gains and losses. — For purposes of this subsection —

(A)   Section 1231 gain. — The term "section 1231 gain" means —

(i) any recognized gain on the sale or exchange of property used in the trade or business, and

(ii) any recognized gain from the compulsory or involuntary conversion (as a result of destruction in whole or in part, theft or seizure, or an exercise of the power of requisition or condemnation or the threat or imminence thereof) into other property or money of —

(I) property used in the trade or business, or

(II) any capital asset which is held for more than 1 year and is held in connection with a trade or business or a transaction entered into for profit.

(B)   Section 1231 loss. — The term "section 1231 loss" means any recognized loss from a sale or exchange or conversion described in subparagraph (A).

(4)   Special rules. — For purposes of this subsection —

(A) In determining under this subsection whether gains exceed losses —

(i) the section 1231 gains shall be included only if and to the extent taken into account in computing gross income, and

(ii) the section 1231 losses shall be included only if and to the extent taken into account in computing taxable income, except that section 1211 shall not apply.

(B) Losses (including losses not compensated for by insurance or otherwise) on the destruction, in whole or in part, theft or seizure, or requisition or condemnation of —

(i) property used in the trade or business, or

(ii) capital assets which are held for more than 1 year and are held in connection with a trade or business or a transaction entered into for profit,

shall be treated as losses from a compulsory or involuntary conversion.

(C) In the case of any involuntary conversion (subject to the provisions of this subsection but for this sentence) arising from fire, storm, shipwreck, or other casualty, or from theft, of any —

(i) property used in the trade or business, or

(ii) any capital asset which is held for more than 1 year and is held in connection with a trade or business or a transaction entered into for profit,

this subsection shall not apply to such conversion (whether resulting in gain or loss) if during the taxable year the recognized losses from such conversions exceed the recognized gains from such conversions.

(b)   **Definition of property used in the trade or business. — For purposes of this section —**

(1)   **General rule. — The term "property used in the trade or business" means property used in the trade or business, of a character which is subject to the allowance for depreciation provided in section 167, held for more than 1 year, and real property used in the trade or business, held for more than 1 year, which is not —**

(A)   **property of a kind which would properly be includible in the inventory of the taxpayer if on hand at the close of the taxable year,**

(B)   **property held by the taxpayer primarily for sale to customers in the ordinary course of his trade of business,**

(C)   **a copyright, a literary, musical, or artistic composition, a letter or memorandum, or similar property, held by taxpayer described in paragraph (3) of section 1221(a), or**

(D)   **a publication of the United States Government (including the Congressional Record) which is received from the United States Government, or any agency thereof, other than by purchase at the price at which it is offered for sale to the public, and which is held by a taxpayer described in paragraph (5) of section 1221(a).**

The initial step in applying Section 1231 is the identification of those gains and losses that are subject to its provisions. Section 1231 gains and losses are generated by two categories of transactions. First, Section 1231 gains and losses result from "the sale or exchange of property used in the trade or business."[1] Note the general definition in Section 1231(b)(1), reprinted above, of the term "property used in the trade or business." Consider the following aspects of the general definition:

(1) The property must be depreciable or real property used in the trade or business. Thus, this definition embraces property excluded from capital asset classification under Section 1221(a)(2).[2]

(2) The property must have been held more than one year. Section 1231(a)(3)(A)(ii)(II) also imposes a "more than one year" holding period requirement applicable to other property covered by § 1231. *Thus, there is no such thing as a short-term § 1231 transaction.*

(3) Property described in Section 1221(a)(1), (3) or (5) is explicitly excluded from the definition in Section 1231(b)(1). Property described in Section 1221(a)(4) is excluded from the definition by the requirement that such property be depreciable. Thus, by way of example, because inventory is not depreciable, it will not constitute "property used in the trade or business," and will thus continue to generate ordinary income or loss on disposition.

[Gains or losses from capital assets disposed of by sale or exchange are not covered by Section 1231. As discussed below, when a capital asset is sold or exchanged,

---

[1]   I.R.C. § 1231(a)(3)(A)(i).

[2]   Certain timber, coal, iron ore, livestock, and unharvested crops are included specially within the definition. I.R.C. § 1231(b)(2), (3), (4).

capital gain and loss treatment is provided by Section 1221.]

Second, Section 1231 gains and losses also arise from the involuntary or compulsory conversion of two types of property: (1) the now-familiar "property used in the trade or business," and (2) capital assets held for more than one year in connection with a trade or business or a transaction entered into for profit.[3] [Note also that Section 165(h)(2)(B), discussed in Chapter 24, addresses the characterization of gains and losses from the involuntary conversion of capital assets held for other than business or profit-seeking purposes, and therefore Section 1231 need not address those gains or losses.] By making the gains and losses from involuntary conversions subject to Section 1231, Congress afforded the possibility of long-term capital gain (and long-term capital loss) treatment which otherwise would be unavailable since involuntary conversions generally do not constitute sales or exchanges as required by Section 1222. (Condemnations, however, have historically been accorded sale or exchange treatment. Note that condemnation gains and losses do not enter the Preliminary Hotchpot discussed below, but are instead considered only in the Principal Hotchpot analysis also discussed below.)

As noted above, the phrase "property used in the trade or business" excludes property "held by the taxpayer primarily for sale to customers in the ordinary course of business." Definitional questions concerning this exclusion may arise under Section 1231, as they have with the identical language in Section 1221(a)(1). For example, in *International Shoe Machine Corp. v. United States*,[4] the taxpayer's main source of income was from the leasing of shoe machinery; only a small portion of the taxpayer's income resulted from sales of the machinery. The taxpayer argued the gain recognized on the sale of the shoe machinery was Section 1231 gain from the sale of "property used in the trade or business." Consequently, the taxpayer claimed capital gain treatment. Notwithstanding the taxpayer's argument, the Court concluded that, because the selling of the machinery was "an accepted and predictable, albeit small" part of the taxpayer's business, the machinery constituted property held primarily for sale to customers in the ordinary course of business and was not within Section 1231. Any gain resulting from the sale was therefore ordinary income.

In sum, in determining whether a taxpayer's recognized gains or losses are Section 1231 gains or losses and thus subject to the Section 1231 rules, one must consider both the event that triggers the gain or loss and the nature of the property involved. For example, the gain or loss recognized on the sale or exchange of a piece of depreciable equipment held by the taxpayer for more than a year and used in the taxpayer's business will be Section 1231 gain or loss as would the gain or loss from the involuntary conversion of that equipment. By contrast, the gain or loss from the sale or exchange of a capital asset held for more than one year, *e.g.*, stock, would not be a Section 1231 gain or loss. Of course, in the latter situation, there is no need for Section 1231 — the taxpayer's gain or loss will be long-term capital gain or loss under the general definitions provided in Section 1222.

---

[3] I.R.C. § 1231(a)(3)(A)(ii).

[4] 491 F.2d 157 (1st Cir. 1974).

§ 32.02 THE HOTCHPOT ANALYSIS

Once a taxpayer has identified all of her Section 1231 gains and losses for the year, Section 1231(a)(1) and (2) require that the taxpayer compare the total Section 1231 gains to the total Section 1231 losses. Pursuant to the general rules of Section 1231(a)(1) and (2), if the taxpayer's Section 1231 gains exceed her Section 1231 losses, all of the Section 1231 gains will be characterized as long-term capital gains and all of the Section 1231 losses will be characterized as long-term capital losses. By contrast, if the taxpayer's Section 1231 gains do not exceed the taxpayer's Section 1231 losses, the gains and losses will not be treated as gains or losses from the sale of capital assets, i.e., the gains or losses will be ordinary. This gain/loss comparison has been referred to as the "hotchpot" analysis, *i.e.*, all of the Section 1231 gains and losses are combined in a hotchpot for purposes of characterization.

Section 1231(a)(1) and (2) as described above establishes the general rule which we will refer to as the "Principal Hotchpot Analysis." As a result of amendments made in 1969, however, a subset of the Section 1231 gains and losses must first be analyzed pursuant to what we refer to as the "Preliminary Hotchpot Analysis." [The Preliminary Hotchpot is sometimes referred to in the literature as the "firepot" because Section 1231 losses resulting from the destruction of property by fire are the most common Section 1231 items subject to the "Preliminary Hotchpot Analysis."]

Section 1231(a)(4)(C) provides the statutory base for the Preliminary Hotchpot Analysis. It provides that Section 1231 gains and losses resulting from certain involuntary conversions will not be subject to characterization under Section 1231 — they will not enter the Principal Hotchpot and will thus be ignored for Section 1231 purposes — if the total of such losses exceeds the total of such gains. In that event, this subset of Section 1231 gains and losses will be characterized outside of Section 1231 and, as a result, will necessarily be ordinary gains and losses. If, however, the Section 1231 losses included in the Preliminary Hotchpot do not exceed the Section 1231 gains included in that hotchpot, this subset of Section 1231 gains and losses is simply lumped with the other Section 1231 gains and losses in the Principal Hotchpot and will be subject to the general rules of Section 1231(a)(1) and (2) discussed *infra*.

With regard to the Principal Hotchpot, note that, while the Preliminary Hotchpot rules are applicable only to Section 1231 gains and losses arising out of certain involuntary conversions, the Principal Hotchpot rules apply to all of a taxpayer's Section 1231 gains and losses, except, of course, for those that are disregarded as a result of the operation of Section 1231(a)(4)(C) [the Preliminary Hotchpot rule]. As noted at the outset of this Overview, once a taxpayer has determined the Section 1231 gains and losses that enter the Principal Hotchpot, the taxpayer then compares the total Section 1231 gains in the Principal Hotchpot to the total Section 1231 losses in the Principal Hotchpot. (Note the special rule of Section 1231(a)(4)(A) directing that the capital loss limitation provisions of Section 1211 should be disregarded in determining whether Section 1231 gains exceed Section 1231 losses.) A net positive number in the Principal Hotchpot renders all of the gains and losses long-term capital gains and losses; a net negative number (or gains exactly equal to losses) renders all gains and losses ordinary.

Consider the following examples and the analysis of each:

Example 1: During the current year, Taxpayer realizes an uninsured $10,000 loss from a fire that destroyed depreciable personal property used in Taxpayer's trade or business for more than one year. Taxpayer also recognized a $5,000 gain from an insurance recovery resulting from the destruction by fire of depreciable real property used in Taxpayer's trade or business for the last few years.[5]

Analysis: First, determine whether the gain and the loss are described in Section 1231(a)(3). They clearly are. Then determine whether they arise from transactions described in Section 1231(a)(4)(C). The fire loss and the fire gain are both the result of involuntary conversions described in that provision and are related to the types of property referred to in the provision. Therefore, both the gain and the loss enter the Preliminary Hotchpot. Since the loss exceeds the gain, Section 1231(a)(4)(C) makes Section 1231(a) inapplicable. The gain and the loss will therefore be characterized as "ordinary," *i.e.*, Taxpayer will deduct the loss as an ordinary loss under Section 165(a), and will report the gain as ordinary income under Section 61(a)(3). [The loss is ordinary because depreciable personal property used in the trade or business is not a capital asset per Section 1221(a)(2). The gain from the insurance recovery is not a capital gain because there is no sale or exchange and the asset is not a capital asset; the gain is therefore ordinary gain.]

Example 2: Assume the same facts as in Example 1, except the gain from the fire insurance proceeds is $15,000 instead of $5,000.

Analysis: The insurance gain in the Preliminary Hotchpot now exceeds the fire loss. Remember that Section 1231(a)(4)(C) (the Preliminary Hotchpot rule) only applies if the losses included in the Preliminary Hotchpot exceed the gains included in the Preliminary Hotchpot. As a result, Section 1231(a)(4)(C) is inapplicable and therefore both the insurance gain and the fire loss will be characterized using the Principal Hotchpot analysis. Applying Section 1231(a)(1), because the insurance gain exceeds the fire loss, the insurance gain will be characterized as a long-term capital gain and the fire loss will be a long-term capital loss.

Example 3: Same as Example 1, except, instead of Taxpayer realizing $5,000 gain from an insurance recovery, Taxpayer realized it from the sale of land held for use in Taxpayer's business for more than one year.

Analysis: As in Example 1, Taxpayer's $10,000 fire loss is included in the Preliminary Hotchpot. The gain from the sale of the land, however, would not be included because a sale is not an event described in Section 1231(a)(4)(C). Thus, the fire loss is the only Section 1231 item included in the Preliminary Hotchpot and, as a result, the loss will be characterized outside of Section 1231 and will be an ordinary loss. By contrast, the $5,000

---

[5] Assume Sections 1245 and 1250 (discussed in Chapter 33) are inapplicable. Assume also that Taxpayer has no other gains or losses for the year.

gain is the only Section 1231 item included in the Principal Hotchpot and will, therefore, be characterized as long-term capital gain under Section 1231(a)(1). Note how the interaction between Section 1231(a)(4)(C) and Section 1231(a)(1) in this example provided Taxpayer with "the best of both worlds," i.e., Taxpayer's fire loss was characterized as an ordinary loss and Taxpayer's gain on the sale of the land was characterized as long-term capital gain. Were Section 1231(a)(4)(C) not in the Code, both the fire loss and the land sale gain would have been included in the Principal Hotchpot. Because the fire loss exceeded the land sale gain, Section 1231(a)(2) would have applied and the fire loss would have been an ordinary loss and the land sale gain would have been an ordinary gain.

Example 4: Same as Example 1, except Taxpayer also realized a loss of $5,000 on the sale of her home.

Analysis: The loss on the home sale is not allowed.[6] Since it is not a "recognized" loss, it is not a "Section 1231 loss." Remember Section 1231 is not a deduction-granting provision; rather it characterizes certain gains and losses otherwise recognized under the Code. (One could, of course, further note that the sale of a capital asset — the home — is not a transaction covered by Section 1231.) Thus, the analysis of Example 1 is unchanged.

Example 5: Same as Example 1, except Taxpayer also recognized a loss of $10,000 from the condemnation of land used in her business. The land was held for more than one year.

Analysis: Since the Preliminary Hotchpot does not apply to condemnation gains and losses, the condemnation loss will be characterized pursuant to the Principal Hotchpot rules. The analysis of Example 1 remains unchanged with regard to the insurance gain and the fire loss — both will be ordinary. Since the condemnation loss is the only Section 1231 item included in the Principal Hotchpot, Section 1231(a)(2) provides it will not be treated as a loss from the sale or exchange of a capital asset. Therefore, the condemnation loss will be ordinary.

§ 32.03   RECAPTURE OF NET ORDINARY LOSSES: SECTION 1231(c)

§ 1231. Property used in the trade or business and involuntary conversions —

(c) Recapture of net ordinary losses

(1) **In general. — The net section 1231 gain for any taxable year shall be treated as ordinary income to the extent such gain does not exceed the non-recaptured net section 1231 losses.**

(2) **Non-recaptured net section 1231 losses. — For purposes of this subsection, the term "non-recaptured net section 1231 losses" means the excess**

---

[6] Treas. Reg. § 1.165–9(1).

of —

(A) the aggregate amount of the net section 1231 losses for the most 5 recent preceding taxable years beginning after December 31, 1981, over

(B) the portion of such losses taken into account under paragraph (1) for such preceding taxable years.

(3)   Net section 1231 gain. — For purposes of this subsection, the term "net section 1231 gain" means the excess of —

(A) the section 1231 gains, over

(B) the section 1231 losses.

(4)   Net section 1231 loss. — For purposes of this subsection, the term "net section 1231 loss" means the excess of —

(A) the section 1231 losses over,

(B) the section 1231 gains.

(5)   Special rules. — For purposes of determining the amount of the net section 1231 gain or loss for any taxable year, the rules of paragraph (4) of subsection (a) shall apply.

The preceding discussion has assumed that Section 1231(c) was not applicable. Section 1231(c) is described as a "recapture" provision, discussed more fully in Chapter 33. The problem Section 1231(c) addresses can be illustrated with the following examples.

Example 1: Assume Taxpayer owns and is prepared to sell some land and a truck. Both the land and truck have been used in Taxpayer's business and have been held for more than one year. The land is worth $100,000 and has a basis of $75,000; the truck is worth $5,000 and has a basis of $10,000. Assume Taxpayer sells the land and the truck in the same year.

Analysis: The land and the truck are both property used in Taxpayer's trade or business within the meaning of Section 1231(b). Thus, the $25,000 gain on the land and the $5,000 loss on the truck will be included in Taxpayer's principal hotchpot. Assuming the sales of the land and the truck are the only Section 1231 transactions during the year, the gain will be long-term capital gain and the loss will be long-term capital loss.[7]

Example 2: Assume the facts of Example 1, except Taxpayer sells the truck in Year 1 and the land in Year 2.

Analysis: Disregarding Section 1231(c), the loss on the truck, as the only Section 1231 item in Year 1, would be characterized as ordinary; likewise, the gain on the sale of the land, as the only Section 1231 item in Year 2, would be characterized as long-term capital gain. This result is one Taxpayer would likely prefer. In the absence of Section 1231(c), taxpayers could pick and choose the year of disposal of their Section 1231 assets, thereby maximizing, as suggested by the example, the likelihood of

---

[7] I.R.C. § 1231(a)(1).

long-term capital gain treatment for Section 1231 gains and ordinary loss treatment for Section 1231 losses. Section 1231(c) attempts to curtail these tax planning possibilities. Applying Section 1231(c) to the facts of this Example, the $5,000 loss on the truck will be characterized in Year 1 as a "net Section 1231 loss." If in any of the next five years Taxpayer has a "net Section 1231 gain," the first $5,000 of it (which would otherwise have been long-term capital gain under the Principal Hotchpot) is converted to ordinary income. Thus, if the land is sold in Year 2, as in the example, producing in the year of sale a net Section 1231 gain of $25,000, Section 1231(c) requires that $5,000 of the gain be treated as ordinary income; only the remaining $20,000 of the net Section 1231 gain will be long-term capital gain. The effect of Section 1231(c) in this example is to limit Taxpayer's long-term capital gain to $20,000, which equals the "net" long-term capital gain Taxpayer would have had on selling both the land and the truck in the same year.

In any year Section 1231(c) requires some of the net Section 1231 gains to be characterized as ordinary income, a question arises as to which Section 1231 gains will be so characterized. For example, assume that in 2013 a taxpayer entered into two transactions — the sale of a commercial building on which the taxpayer had claimed depreciation deductions and the sale of a tract of unimproved land used in taxpayer's business. Assume that the taxpayer recognized a gain of $10,000 on each of these transactions and that both of the $10,000 gains would be characterized as long-term capital gains but for Section 1231(c). The $10,000 of gain from the sale of the commercial building constitutes "unrecaptured Section 1250 gain" taxable under Section 1(h) at a maximum rate of 25%, whereas the sale of the land produces long-term capital gain taxable at a maximum rate of either 15% or 20% as discussed in Chapter 31.[8] Finally, assume that as a result of the application of Section 1231(c), $10,000 of the Section 1231 gain must be recharacterized as ordinary income. Which gain will be so characterized — the gain from the sale of the building, or the gain from the sale of the land? According to the Code, the issue is to be resolved by the Secretary of the Treasury in either forms or regulations.[9] In Notice 97-59,[10] the Service provided that:

> If a portion of the taxpayer's net section 1231 gain for the year is recharacterized as ordinary income under section 1231(c), the gain so recharacterized consists first of any net section 1231 gain in the 28-percent group [28 percent rate gain], then any section 1231 gain in the 25-percent group [unrecaptured section 1250 gain], and finally any net section 1231 gain [adjusted net capital gain].

Thus, in this example, the $10,000 gain which Section 1231(c) treats as ordinary income will be the $10,000 of gain from the sale of the commercial property, i.e., the "unrecaptured section 1250 gain." None of the $10,000 of gain from the sale of the

---

[8] As discussed in Chapter 31, the American Taxpayer Relief Act of 2012 permanently extended the 15% maximum tax on most long-term capital gains. For certain "high income individuals," however, the Act increased the tax on most long-term capital gains to 20%.

[9] I.R.C. § 1(h)(8).

[10] 1997-2 C.B. 309.

land will be recharacterized as ordinary income. Instead, the gain from the land sale will be long-term capital gain taxed at a maximum rate of 15% or 20%.

Returning to Example 2, at the outset of this discussion of Section 1231(c) recapture, assume that Taxpayer sells the land, instead of the truck, in Year 1. The result is a long-term capital gain of $25,000 under Section 1231(a)(1). (It is also a net Section 1231 gain under Section 1231(c), but we are assuming that this was Taxpayer's first Section 1231 transaction, and thus there are no net Section 1231 losses from any of the five prior years to worry about.) Now Taxpayer sells the truck in a subsequent year. The result is a $5,000 ordinary loss under Section 1231(a)(2); Section 1231(c) does not require re-opening the Year 1 transaction and recharacterizing the gain, nor does it require that the ordinary loss be converted to long-term capital loss to match long-term capital gain generated in Year 1. So, in a sense, the tax game can still be played if one follows the right order. Congress apparently regarded it as sufficient that Taxpayer (following the sale of the truck) in this latter example has $5,000 of "non-recaptured net Section 1231 losses" that will cause $5,000 of any net Section 1231 gain in the next five years to be converted into ordinary income.

Chapter 33

DEPRECIATION RECAPTURE

Perhaps the best way to understand the concept of depreciation recapture is to consider an example involving personal property (as opposed to real property). Assume Taxpayer purchases some depreciable equipment for use in her business. The allowable depreciation deductions Taxpayer takes on the equipment will reduce Taxpayer's adjusted basis in the equipment.[1] For example, if Taxpayer purchased the equipment for $100 and properly took depreciation deductions of $30, she would have an adjusted basis of $70 in the equipment. If Taxpayer now sells the equipment for $80, she realizes and recognizes a gain of $10. In substance, the gain of $10 results from Taxpayer's having taken depreciation deductions that turned out to be $10 in excess of the $20 decline in the value of the equipment (from $100 to $80). This "excess" depreciation of $10 (excess only in the sense that it was greater than the decline in value; the example assumes that the depreciation taken was proper) is "recaptured" in the form of gain of $10 on the sale of the equipment. Taxpayer is, in effect, forced to give back the "excess" deduction of $10 by recognizing income of $10. This result is achieved through the basis mechanism of Section 1016 and the amount-realized-minus-adjusted-basis formula of Section 1001.

What is the character of that income of $10? Under Section 1221(a)(2), the equipment is not a capital asset, but pursuant to Section 1231, the gain might be characterized as capital gain. However, this gain resulted solely from the taking of depreciation deductions, not from any appreciation in the value of the equipment. The depreciation deductions reduced Taxpayer's ordinary income during the years depreciation was taken. This "excess" depreciation of $10 meant that Taxpayer's ordinary income was $10 less than it otherwise would have been. True, Taxpayer recognized $10 of income on the sale, but that $10 might be long term capital gain through Section 1231. If ordinary income is taxed at a higher rate than capital gains, then the "excess" depreciation saves more in taxes than is produced by its "recapture" in the year the equipment is sold. That result did not seem quite right to Congress, and the Section 1245 depreciation recapture provisions were enacted in 1962 as a result. Section 1245 adopts a simple remedy: the recognized recapture income is to be characterized as ordinary income.[2] Gain on the disposition of "Section 1245 property"[3] that is due to depreciation deductions, rather than economic appreciation in value, is not eligible for capital gain treatment. To that extent, Section 1231 is superseded.

---

[1] I.R.C. § 1016(a)(2).

[2] I.R.C. § 1245(a)(1).

[3] This term is defined in Section 1245(a)(3). For our purposes assume that "Section 1245 property" consists of depreciable personal property.

The tax law thus comes full circle as regards characterization. Under Section 1221(a)(2), the $10 gain on the sale of the equipment in our example would be characterized as ordinary income. Under Section 1231, the gain may be characterized as long term capital gain. Section 1245, however, has the final word: to the extent Section 1245 applies to the gain, the gain is ordinary income.

There is one additional aspect of the depreciation recapture provisions worth noting at this point. They are primarily characterization provisions. They are also, however, recognition provisions, and in some circumstances they will require recognition of income at a time earlier than would otherwise be the case.[4]

§ 33.01   SECTION 1245 RECAPTURE

§ 1245.   Gains from Dispositions of Certain Depreciable Property.

(a)   General rule.

(1)   Ordinary income. Except as otherwise provided in this section, if section 1245 property is disposed of the amount by which the lower of

(A) the recomputed basis of the property, or

(B)

(i) in the case of a sale, exchange, or involuntary conversion, the amount realized, or (ii) in the case of any other disposition, the fair market value of such property,

exceeds the adjusted basis of such property shall be treated as ordinary income. Such gain shall be recognized notwithstanding any other provision of this subtitle.

(2)   Recomputed basis. For purposes of this section,

(A)   In general. The term "recomputed basis" means, with respect to any property, its adjusted basis recomputed by adding thereto all adjustments reflected in such adjusted basis on account of deductions (whether in respect of the same or other property) allowed or allowable to the taxpayer or to any other person for depreciation or amortization.

. . .

(C)   Certain deductions treated as amortization. Any deduction allowable under section 179 . . . shall be treated as if it were a deduction allowable for amortization.

(3)   Section 1245 property. For purposes of this section, the term "section 1245 property" means any property which is or has been property of a character subject to the allowance for depreciation provided in section 167 and is either

(A) personal property,

. . .

(b)   Exceptions and limitations.

---

[4] See Section 453(i) in Chapter 40, *infra*.

(1) **Gifts.** Subsection (a) shall not apply to a disposition by gift.

(2) **Transfers at death.** Except as provided in section 691 (relating to income in respect of a decedent), subsection (a) shall not apply to a transfer at death.

. . .

(d) **Application of section.** This section shall apply notwithstanding any other provision of this subtitle.

Section 1245 provides that recognized gain on the disposition of "Section 1245 property" shall be included in income as ordinary income to the extent of depreciation deductions taken with respect to the property. As a general proposition, Section 1245 applies to depreciable personal property, while Section 1250 (discussed below) applies to depreciable real property. The definition of Section 1245 property, however, is not in fact limited to depreciable personal property but includes specified types of real property.[5] Moreover, the term "personal property" encompasses both tangible and intangible personal property.[6] Note that the statutory definition of "Section 1245 property" includes property that is or has been of depreciable character.[7] By way of illustration, the regulations point out that if father uses an automobile in his business — thus qualifying it as Section 1245 property — and then gives the automobile to his son as a gift for his son's personal use, the automobile is Section 1245 property in the hands of the son, even though the automobile is no longer depreciable given the son's personal use of it.[8]

What Section 1245 aims to recapture as ordinary income is the gain on disposition that represents depreciation deductions, as opposed to the gain that reflects an increase in the property's value. Section 1245(a)(1) accomplishes this result, when Section 1245 property is disposed of at a gain, by labeling as ordinary income the difference between adjusted basis and the lesser of (1) the "recomputed basis" and (2) the amount realized (or the fair market value, if the disposition is not a sale, exchange, or involuntary conversion). "Recomputed basis" is essentially the basis that results from adding the adjusted basis and the depreciation or amortization previously taken.[9] As a practical matter, recomputed basis is thus generally the taxpayer's original basis in the property. However, recomputed basis means adding to the adjusted basis "all adjustments reflected in such adjusted basis on account of deductions (whether in respect of the same or other property)" on account of depreciation or amortization.[10] For example, if the taxpayer acquired the property by gift, the taxpayer's basis under Section 1015 may reflect depreciation deductions taken by the donor, which would enter into the computation of recomputed basis when the taxpayer disposed of the property. Thus, in this situation, the Section 1245 ordinary income "taint" attached to the property while

---

[5] I.R.C. § 1245(a)(3).

[6] I.R.C. § 1245(a)(3); Treas. Reg. § 1.1245-3(b).

[7] I.R.C. § 1245(a)(3).

[8] Treas. Reg. § 1245–3(a)(3)

[9] Section 179 deductions are treated as amortization deductions for this purpose. I.R.C. § 1245(a)(2)(A), (C).

[10] I.R.C. § 1245(a)(2)(A).

in the hands of the donor continues to attach to the property in the hands of the donee. By way of contrast, the taint does not carry over to property acquired in an arm's length purchase. In this case, the purchaser's basis is based on the cost of the property, and does not reflect any adjustments on account of depreciation that may have been taken while in the hands of the previous owner.

Example 1: A taxpayer paid $100,000 for a heavy duty truck to be used in her business. After claiming $40,000 in Section 168 depreciation deductions on the truck, the taxpayer sold the truck for $75,000. What are the tax consequences of the sale to the taxpayer?

Analysis: Under Section 1016, the taxpayer's adjusted basis in the truck was $60,000 at the time of the sale, i.e., $100,000 less the $40,000 in depreciation deductions. Taxpayer's gain on the truck is therefore $15,000 (amount realized of $75,000 less the adjusted basis of $60,000). But for Section 1245, the gain on the truck would have been Section 1231 gain and would likely have been characterized as long term capital gain. Section 1245, however, trumps Section 1231.[11] The taxpayer's "recomputed basis" is $100,000, i.e., the adjusted basis of $60,000 plus the $40,000 in depreciation deductions allowed with respect to the truck.[12] The amount realized, however, was only $75,000, which is less than the recomputed basis. As a result, Section 1245(a)(1) characterizes as ordinary income "only" the $15,000 difference between the amount realized and the adjusted basis. Obviously, since the total realized gain in this example is $15,000, the Section 1245(a)(1) formula cannot sensibly produce a result that treats more than $15,000 as ordinary income.

Example 2: Assume the facts of Example 1 except the truck was sold for $105,000 instead of $75,000. What are the tax consequences of the sale?

Analysis: The taxpayer's gain realized is $45,000 (amount realized of $105,000 less adjusted basis of $60,000). Nonetheless, the taxpayer's recomputed basis, as in Example 1, is $100,000. That amount, however, is less than the amount realized of $105,000. As a result, the amount which Section 1245(a)(1) treats as ordinary income is $40,000 — the difference between the recomputed basis and the taxpayer's adjusted basis in the truck. Section 1245 does not characterize the remaining $5,000 of realized gain. Instead, Section 1231 will characterize the remaining gain which presumably will be characterized as long term capital gain.[13] In effect, during the period in which taxpayer owned the truck, the truck increased in value by $5,000 even though the taxpayer was allowed $40,000 in depreciation deductions during the period. Section 1245 requires that the $40,000 of depreciation be "recaptured" as ordinary income, but permits the economic gain of $5,000 to enter the Section 1231 hotchpot.

---

[11] Treas. Reg. § 1.1245-6(a).

[12] I.R.C. § 1245(a)(2)(A).

[13] Treas. Reg. § 1.1245-6(a).

Example 3: Assume the facts of Example 1 except the taxpayer, instead of selling the truck, gave it to her son as a gift. The son used the truck for one year for personal purposes and then sold the truck for $70,000. What are the tax consequences to the taxpayer and the taxpayer's son?

Analysis: The taxpayer's gift of the truck will not result in any income to the taxpayer. While Section 1245(a)(1) states that the Section 1245 income will "be recognized notwithstanding any other provision of this subtitle," Section 1245(b)(1) specifically provides that Section 1245(a) will not apply to a disposition by gift. The gift, however, will not negate the Section 1245 taint associated with truck; the son will take the truck with a Section 1015 adjusted basis ($60,000 in this case) and the Section 1245 taint will also pass to the son. Thus, when the son sells the truck for $70,000, the son's recomputed basis, according to Section 1245(a)(2), will be $100,000, *i.e.*, the $60,000 adjusted basis of the son to which is added back the $40,000 of depreciation which was allowed to the taxpayer/donor. Since the son's amount realized of $70,000 is less than the recomputed basis, it will be used to determine the amount of ordinary income on the sale by the son. Thus, the son's ordinary income will be $10,000, *i.e.*, the difference between the amount realized of $70,000 and the son's adjusted basis in the truck of $60,000.

Note that Section 1245 does not apply to losses.[14] This is consistent with the rationale for the statute which is to prevent taxpayers from converting ordinary income into capital gain. The inapplicability to losses follows from the literal language of the statute.[15]

Also note the striking scope of the statute. Section 1245 recapture may result whenever Section 1245 property is "disposed of," whether by sale, exchange, involuntary conversion or "other disposition." Moreover, if Section 1245(a)(1) characterizes gain as ordinary income, the gain is recognized — and Section 1245 applies — "notwithstanding any other provision of this subtitle."[16] Any escape from the recognition and characterization rule of Section 1245(a)(1) must be found within Section 1245 itself. Section 1245(b) in fact provides a number of exceptions. For the most part, what the exceptions have in common is that they involve dispositions in which the basis of the property transferred carries over (in whole or in part) to the transferee. See Example 3 above. The "recapture potential" is thus preserved in the hands of the transferee,[17] and to the extent it is preserved, the application of Section 1245(a)(1) is postponed.

---

[14] Treas. Reg. § 1.1245-1(d).

[15] I.R.C. § 1245(a)(1).

[16] I.R.C. § 1245(a)(1), (d).

[17] I.R.C. § 1245(a)(2)(A).

§ 33.02 SECTION 179 RECAPTURE

§ 179(d)(10). Recapture in certain cases.

The Secretary shall, by regulations, provide for recapturing the benefit under any deduction allowable under subsection (a) with respect to any property which is not used predominantly in a trade or business at any time.

As noted, Section 1245 is at least potentially applicable to any disposition of Section 1245 property. The Service has, however, ruled that the conversion of an automobile from business use to personal use is not a "disposition" of the automobile.[18] However, a conversion to personal use may entail no adverse tax consequences. Section 179 expensing of assets, discussed in Chapter 14 on depreciation, provides its own version of recapture.[19] If property with respect to which a Section 179 deduction was taken is converted to personal use — specifically, if such property is not used predominantly in a trade or business at any time — the taxpayer must give up the "benefit" of the Section 179 deduction. The Section 179 "benefit" is the difference between the deduction taken under Section 179 and the deduction that would have been allowed under Section 168 (had Section 179 not been elected) for the period of business use involved.[20] If Section 179 recapture applies, the taxpayer appropriately receives a basis increase to reflect the income which has been charged. Also note that Section 179 recapture is inapplicable when Section 1245 recapture applies.[21]

> **Example:** Sandi paid $50,000 for a truck she used in her business. In the year that Sandi placed the truck in service in her business, Sandi appropriately claimed a Section 179 deduction of $20,000 and a Section 168 depreciation deduction of $6,000. (The truck is five year property and Sandi is entitled to a Section 168 depreciation deduction in Year 1 of 20% of the unadjusted basis of $30,000 ($50,000 − $20,000 Section 179 deduction)). [This example disregards any possible application of Section 168(k).] The following year when the truck was worth $50,000, Sandi converted the truck to personal use. Three years later, Sandi sold the truck for $35,000.

> **Analysis:** Sandi's conversion of the truck to personal use in Year 2 is not a "disposition" of the truck under Section 1245(a)(1). While Section 1245 does not apply at the time of the conversion, Section 179(d)(10) does. The benefit to be recaptured under Section 179 is the excess deduction taken under Sections 179 and 168 combined over the Section 168 deductions which would have been allowed if no election had been made under Section 179. In addition to the $20,000 Section 179 deduction, Sandi will have been allowed depreciation deductions totaling $10,800 (*i.e.*, $6,000 in Year 1 and $4,800 in Year 2). Note that, in the year of the conversion, Sandi would nonetheless be entitled to one-half year's depreciation [*i.e.*, 0.5 (0.32 × 30,000)]. Thus, Sandi will have claimed a total of $30,800 in Sections 168 and 179 deductions. Had Sandi not elected Section 179 expensing, she would have

---

[18] Rev. Rul. 69-487, 1969-2 C.B. 165.

[19] I.R.C. § 179(d)(10).

[20] *See* Treas. Reg. § 1.179-1(e)(1), (5).

[21] Treas. Reg. § 1.179-1(e)(3).

been entitled to depreciation deductions under Section 168 using an unadjusted basis of $50,000 rather than $30,000. In that case, her depreciation deduction would have been $10,000 in Year 1 ($50,000 × 0.20) and $8,000 [*i.e.*, 0.5 ($50,000 × 0.32)] in Year 2 for a total of $18,000 in Section 168 deductions. The difference between the deductions actually allowed — $30,800 — and the Section 168 deductions which would have been allowed had no Section 179 election been made — $18,000 — equals $12,800. That amount is recaptured as ordinary income by Section 179.[22] In turn, Sandi's basis in the property, which was $19,200 (*i.e.*, $50,000 − $30,800 in Section 179 and Section 168 deductions) is increased by the $12,800 of recaptured income and will thus be $32,000. When Sandi sells the truck for $35,000, Sandi recognizes $3,000 of gain. Since the truck is personal property which had been depreciable, it is Section 1245 property and Section 1245(a) will apply to characterize the $3,000 of gain as ordinary income. [Sandi's recomputed basis will be $50,000, *i.e.*, $32,000 plus the $18,000 in depreciation deductions allowed. The amount realized of $35,000 is less than the recomputed basis and therefore under Section 1245(a) it is the amount realized — $35,000 — from which one subtracts the adjusted basis — $32,000 — to arrive at the amount of ordinary income — $3,000.]

§ 33.03   SECTION 1250 RECAPTURE

§ 1250.   Gain from dispositions of certain depreciable realty.

(a)   **General rule. Except as otherwise provided in this section —**

(1) **Additional depreciation after December 31, 1975.**

(A)   **In general. If section 1250 property is disposed of after December 31, 1975, then the applicable percentage of the lower of**

(i) **that portion of the additional depreciation (as defined in subsection (b)(1) or (4) attributable to periods after December 31, 1975, in respect of the property, or**

(ii) **the excess of the amount realized (in the case of a sale, exchange, or involuntary conversion), or the fair market value of such property (in the case of any other disposition), over the adjusted basis of such property,**

shall be treated as gain which is ordinary income. Such gain shall be recognized notwithstanding any other provision of this subtitle.

(B)   **Applicable percentage. For purposes of subparagraph (A), the term "applicable percentage" means —**

   . . .

(v) **in the case of all other section 1250 property, 100%.**

---

[22] The same answer ($12,800) is obtained by comparing the Section 179 deduction ($20,000) with the Section 168 deduction that would have been deductible with respect to that same $20,000. The Year 1 deduction on $20,000 is 0.20, or $4,000; the Year 2 deduction on $20,000 is 0.5 ($20,000 × 0.32), or $3,200. The total of the two years is $7,200, which is $12,800 less than the $20,000 taken under Section 179. This is the approach of the Regulations, but note that either approach provides the same answer.

(b)   Additional depreciation defined. — For purposes of this section

(1)   In general. The term "additional depreciation" means, in the case of any property, the depreciation adjustments in respect of such property; except that, in the case of property held more than one year, it means such adjustments only to the extent that they exceed the amount of the depreciation adjustments which would have resulted if such adjustments had been determined for each taxable year under the straight line method of adjustment.

. . .

(3)   Depreciation adjustments. The term "depreciation adjustments" means in respect of any property, all adjustments attributable to periods after December 31, 1963, reflected in the adjusted basis of such property on account of deductions (whether in respect of the same or other property) allowed or allowable to the taxpayer or to any other person for exhaustion, wear and tear, obsolescence, or amortization. . . .

. . .

(c)   Section 1250 property. For purposes of this section, the term "section 1250 property" means any real property (other than section 1245 property . . .) which is or has been property of a character subject to the allowance for depreciation provided in section 167.

The recapture rules of Section 1250, first enacted in 1964, are considerably looser than those of its 1962 predecessor, Section 1245. Section 1250 applies to depreciable real property, except for the limited categories of real property included within Section 1245.[23] However, when Section 1250 property is disposed of at a gain, the depreciation subject to recapture and characterization as ordinary income is, in general, only the depreciation taken in excess of straight line depreciation, what is statutorily labeled "additional depreciation."[24] Consider again the example used at the outset of this chapter — property is purchased for $100 and sold for $80 after $30 in depreciation has been taken. Assume now, however, that the property in question is real property, such as a building. If the $30 in depreciation were taken on a straight line basis, the "additional depreciation" would be zero; none of the gain of $10 ($80 amount realized, $70 adjusted basis) would be characterized by Section 1250; it would presumably all be characterized under Sections 1231 and 1221(a)(2). Suppose, however, that the $30 of depreciation were taken under an accelerated method, and that only $25 in depreciation would have been taken under a straight line method up to the time of disposition. The "additional depreciation" taken would equal $5, and that $5 would be characterized as ordinary income.[25] Since the taxpayer's total gain was $10, the remaining gain of $5 would be eligible for Section 1231 treatment.

Under current law, in effect since 1986, depreciation on real property must be taken on a straight line basis. In general, therefore, there can be no "additional depreciation" on real property acquired after 1986, and Section 1250 thus threatens to become mere surplusage. Note, however, that if Section 1250 property is not held

---

[23]   I.R.C. § 1250(c).

[24]   I.R.C. § 1250(a)(1)(A), (b)(1).

[25]   I.R.C. § 1250(a)(1)(A).

more than a year, all depreciation taken is additional depreciation.[26] Also note the special tax rate applicable to "unrecaptured Section 1250 gain" discussed below.

§ 33.04   UNRECAPTURED SECTION 1250 GAIN

As discussed in Chapter 31, long term capital gain is accorded preferential treatment. Under Section 1(h), that preferential treatment depends on the nature of the asset sold or exchanged. The maximum rate of tax on "unrecaptured Section 1250 gain" is 25%.[27] Thus, unrecaptured Section 1250 gain is accorded more favorable treatment than, for example, the long term capital gain resulting from the sale of collectibles which is taxed at a maximum rate of 28%. By contrast, the tax treatment of unrecaptured Section 1250 gain is not as favorable as, for example, the long term capital gain resulting from the sale of stock held for more than one year, which is taxed at a maximum rate of 15% or 20%.

"Unrecaptured Section 1250 gain" is the long term capital gain from Section 1250 property attributable to depreciation deductions allowed to the taxpayer and not otherwise recaptured as ordinary income.[28] Consider the following example:

Example: Martin spent $500,000 on the construction of a commercial building on leased land. Martin used the property in his business for a number of years and then sold the property for $550,000. Using the straight line method, Martin properly claimed a total of $200,000 in depreciation deductions over the period during which he used the building. Martin's adjusted basis in the building was thus $300,000 at the time of the sale. Martin realized $250,000 in gain on the sale.[29]

Analysis: Considering that the building was sold for only $50,000 more than Martin originally paid for the building, one may properly conclude that only $50,000 of the $250,000 of realized gain is attributable to economic appreciation. The remaining $200,000 of the gain represents the depreciation deductions allowed to Martin. In effect, Section 1001 requires Martin to include as part of his gain all of the depreciation deductions claimed since there was no actual economic depreciation on the property. (This analysis, of course, disregards inflation.) The character of the $250,000 gain would be determined under Section 1231. (As explained below, none of the gain would be characterized under Section 1250.) Assuming that the sale of the building was Martin's only Section 1231 transaction during the year, the $250,000 would constitute long term capital gain. Were the property in this example "Section 1245 property" instead of "Section 1250 property," $200,000 of the $250,000 of gain would have been recaptured as ordinary income and Martin would have characterized only the remaining $50,000 of gain under Section 1231. In other words, all of the depreciation would have been "recaptured" as ordinary income. However, under Section 1250, the

---

[26] I.R.C. § 1250(b)(1).

[27] I.R.C. § 1(h)(1)(D).

[28] I.R.C. § 1(h)(7).

[29] I.R.C. § 1001.

gain on the Section 1250 property in this example would be recaptured as ordinary income only to the extent of the depreciation taken by Martin in excess of the depreciation which would have been allowable under the straight line method. Because Martin used the straight line method of depreciation with respect to the building, none of the gain would be characterized as ordinary income under Section 1250. The $200,000 of gain attributable to the depreciation deductions claimed by Martin therefore constitutes unrecaptured Section 1250 gain, *i.e.*, the gain of $200,000 is attributable to depreciation deductions on Section 1250 property, is presumably characterized by Section 1231 as long term capital gain, and is not otherwise recaptured as ordinary income. This $200,000 of gain would be subject to a maximum rate of tax of 25%. The other $50,000 of gain would be subject to a maximum rate of tax of 15% or 20%.

As the above example suggests, any time a taxpayer sells at a gain real property which the taxpayer has depreciated, the taxpayer must determine how much of the gain constitut1es unrecaptured Section 1250 gain.

It may be well at this point to revisit the special exclusion rules under Section 121 related to gain from the sale of a principal residence.[30] The exclusion rule is not applicable to gain attributable to depreciation allowed with respect to the residence.[31] A common context in which a taxpayer will claim depreciation deductions on a residence is in conjunction with a home office.[32] The long term gain attributable to depreciation allowed with respect to a principal residence will be characterized as unrecaptured Section 1250 gain and will be subject to tax at a maximum rate of 25%.

> **Example:** Susan, a single taxpayer, realized a gain of $250,000 on the sale of her principal residence. Assume she had owned and used the residence for ten years at the time of the sale, and had been allowed depreciation deductions of $30,000 on account of a business office she maintained in the home.

> **Analysis:** As a result of Section 121(d)(6), $30,000 of her $250,000 gain will not be excludable under Section 121(a) but would be subject to tax, presumably at a 25% rate as unrecaptured Section 1250 income. The remaining $220,000 of her gain on the sale would be excludable under Section 121(a), assuming she met the requirements specified in that provision.

§ 33.05 SECTION 1239 ORDINARY INCOME

Section 1239 is a special characterization rule, not really a recapture-of-depreciation rule in the same sense as Sections 1245 and 1250. But it is worth noting here both to fill out the historical record and to point out its relationship to Sections 1245 and 1250. Section 1239 substantially predates Sections 1245 and 1250. It mandates that any gain recognized on a sale or exchange of depreciable property

---

[30] See Chapter 6, *supra*, for a detailed discussion of Section 121.

[31] I.R.C. § 121(d)(6).

[32] *See* Chapter 21, *supra*.

between certain related parties (such as a taxpayer and a corporation in which the taxpayer's ownership exceeds 50%)[33] be characterized as ordinary income; none of the recognized gain, in other words, is eligible for capital gain treatment under Section 1231. Section 1239 is thus at once narrower and broader than Sections 1245 and 1250. It is narrower in the sense that it applies only with respect to related party transactions; Sections 1245 and 1250, of course, have no such limitation. It is broader in the sense that it characterizes all recognized gain as ordinary income. By contrast, Sections 1245 and 1250 characterize as ordinary income all or part of the depreciation deductions taken; they do not characterize as ordinary income the gain that reflects appreciation in value.

Example 1: Assume a taxpayer purchases a piece of equipment for $100,000, uses the equipment in her business claiming a total of $40,000 in depreciation deductions on the equipment, and then ultimately sells the equipment for $110,000 to her wholly owned corporation. Assume the corporation intends to use the equipment in its business and that the equipment will therefore be depreciable by the corporation. What are the tax consequences to the taxpayer on the sale of the equipment to her corporation?

Analysis: The taxpayer and the corporation are related persons within the meaning of Section 1239.[34] Because the equipment in the hands of the corporation will be depreciable under Section 167 (the equipment is a wasting asset and the corporation intends to use the equipment in its business), all of the gain realized on the sale will be ordinary income. Here, there is $50,000 of gain realized on the sale by the taxpayer, *i.e.*, amount realized of $110,000 less $60,000 adjusted basis. Thus, there is $50,000 of ordinary income recognized by the taxpayer. Note, however, that the equipment in this example is also Section 1245 property. Technically, Section 1245 would also be applicable. Under Section 1245, the taxpayer's recomputed basis would be $100,000 (*i.e.*, the adjusted basis of $60,000 plus the $40,000 in depreciation deductions). The difference between the recomputed basis and the adjusted basis is $40,000 and Section 1245 would characterize that amount of the $50,000 gain as ordinary income; the remaining $10,000 of gain (representing economic gain on the equipment) would be characterized as Section 1231 gain and would likely be long term capital gain. Section 1239, however, will control and all $50,000 of gain will be characterized as ordinary income.

Example 2: Assume the same facts as in Example 1 except the property is a building rather than a piece of equipment. What will the tax consequences be to the taxpayer on the sale of the building to the corporation?

---

[33] See Section 1239(b) and (c) for the principal related party transactions covered by the statute. They include transactions between a person and "controlled entities" with respect to the person; between a taxpayer and a trust in which the taxpayer or taxpayer's spouse is a non-remote beneficiary; and between an executor of an estate and a beneficiary, except for transfers to satisfy a pecuniary bequest.

[34] I.R.C. § 1239(b)(1), (c)(1)(A).

Analysis: The results under Section 1239 will be the same, *i.e.*, the taxpayer will realize $50,000 of gain all of which will be characterized as ordinary income. Note, however, that the building is also Section 1250 property. Under Section 1250, the ordinary income amount would have been only the amount of "additional depreciation," *i.e.*, the difference between accelerated depreciation deductions and deductions allowable to the taxpayer with respect to the building under the straight line method. As noted above, after 1986 there will be no "additional depreciation" and therefore none of the $50,000 of gain realized would have been characterized as ordinary income under Section 1250. Again, however, Section 1239 controls and will require the taxpayer to report $50,000 of ordinary income.

Compare Examples 1 and 2. Note that, in the absence of Section 1239, $40,000 of the $50,000 would have been ordinary income in Example 1; Section 1239 had the effect of increasing the amount of ordinary income from $40,000 to $50,000. By contrast, in the absence of Section 1239 all $50,000 of the gain on the sale of building would have been Section 1231 gain and likely long term capital gain since there would have been no Section 1250 recapture. With the application of Section 1239, however, all $50,000 of the gain on the building will be treated as ordinary income. Comparing Examples 1 and 2, it is clear that the impact of Section 1239 is much greater with respect to Section 1250 property than with respect to Section 1245 property.

The impetus for the enactment of Section 1239 was the differential between the tax rates on ordinary income and capital gains. An individual could, for instance, depreciate high value business property to a very low basis, then sell it to her wholly owned corporation, and (prior to the enactment of Section 1239) pay only capital gains tax on the sale as a result of the operation of Section 1231. The corporation could then depreciate the property all over again from its new high basis purchase price. In effect, the property is "redepreciated," providing depreciation deductions to the corporation to offset its ordinary income, at the price of a capital gains tax to the individual taxpayer. Given a tax rate differential, the tax saved by the corporation exceeds the tax paid by the individual, although the parties are in essence a single economic unit. Section 1239 blocked this arrangement by taxing the seller's gain at ordinary income rates.

Since Sections 1245 and 1250 apply to many more transactions than does Section 1239, Section 1239 declined in importance after the enactment of those provisions. It still, however, remains a trap for the unwary, since it can characterize as ordinary income gain that Sections 1245 and 1250 may not reach.

§ 33.06 OTHER RECAPTURE PROVISIONS

As noted in Chapter 32, Section 1231(c) relates to recapture of net ordinary losses. As a result of Section 1231(c), gain that may have escaped Sections 1245 and 1250 and was preliminarily classified as long term capital gain under Section 1231(a)(1), can nonetheless wind up as ordinary income.

In addition to the principal recapture provisions of Sections 1245 and 1250, the Code contains a number of other recapture provisions which are of limited applicability and beyond the scope of this text.[35]

---

[35] *See, e.g.,* I.R.C. §§ 1252, 1254, 1255.

Chapter 34

ASSIGNMENT OF INCOME

To this point in this book, the focus has been on the "what question," the "when question," and the "character question." The book first examined what items are included in an individual's gross income, what expenditures should be reflected as deductions from income in arriving at the individual's taxable income, and when the items of income and deduction should be included or deducted. Matters of characterization — capital gains and losses, ordinary income and loss, and their significance — were then discussed. Now, however, the focus shifts to assignment of income and a new question, the "who question" — who is the proper taxpayer to be charged with the income or expenditure at issue?

In general, the taxpayer who receives income is the taxpayer taxed on it. Indeed, in the usual case, there is simply no other taxpayer on the scene to whom the income could plausibly be attributed, and hence no real alternative exists in any event. On occasion, however, there are two or more candidates for taxation, and a question this situation poses is whether the person receiving the income will be the person taxed on it. The assignment of income doctrine developed principally to answer this question in the numerous settings in which it arises.

§ 34.01 THE PROGRESSIVE RATE STRUCTURE

The "who question" is significant because of the Code's progressive tax rate structure.[1] Since the "tax cost" of a dollar of income depends on the rate at which it is taxed, there is an obvious tax savings to taxpayers (and a corresponding tax loss to the Treasury) in shifting income from a higher-bracket taxpayer to a lower-bracket taxpayer. Thus, a worthwhile tax benefit may be achieved within a family unit if a family member whose income will be taxed at 39.6% can successfully shift some of her income to another family member whose income is taxed in the 15% bracket. If the taxpayers involved regard themselves as essentially a single economic unit, they may well be indifferent as to who actually receives the income, and concerned instead with who will be taxed on it. The value of income-shifting is decreased as tax rates are compressed. To eliminate the value of income-shifting, one must assure that a dollar of income will be taxed identically, no matter which taxpayer bears the tax. This could be accomplished by adopting a system that taxed gross income — not necessarily net income, since the availability of deductions, and hence the effective rate of tax, could vary among taxpayers — and taxed the gross income at a flat rate, from the first dollar to the last. Alternatively, a system could be designed that taxed the income of the group, not the individual, so that income shifts within the group would be meaningless. The joint return, of course, achieves

---

[1] *See* I.R.C. § 1.

precisely this result for husband and wife. When they file a joint return they are taxed on their "group" income and, with certain exceptions, income-shifting between them is pointless. In general, however, our tax system taxes individuals, not groups, and taxes them at progressive rates on net income.

§ 34.02   DEVELOPMENT OF RULES LIMITING INCOME-SHIFTING

Disparities in tax rates made it necessary to develop rules to answer the who-shall-be-taxed question. This "who" question is the most common issue in the assignment of income area. Assignment of income issues, however, can also arise with just one taxpayer. Because tax rate disparity often drives tax planning where two or more taxpayers are involved, it becomes apparent that very similar issues can arise where rate disparity opportunities confront the individual taxpayer. The annual accounting principle provides one such set of opportunities. If, for whatever reason, the same income will be taxed at a higher rate next year than this year, there is an incentive to find a way to "accelerate" future income into the present tax period, and it may become necessary, for tax purposes, to determine whether and when the taxpayer has realized the income.

Another type of assignment of income issue arises with respect to a topic addressed in Chapter 31, the character of the income in question. As noted in that Chapter, capital gain income is subject to tax at a rate considerably lower than that of ordinary income. The rate disparity, of course, encourages creative taxpayers to try to convert ordinary income into capital gains. Taxpayers may seek to have income characterized as capital gain rather than ordinary income to take advantage of the preferential rate of tax on capital gain and also to increase the amount of capital loss they may deduct. Under Section 1211, the amount of capital loss currently deductible depends in part on the amount of capital gain currently reportable.

In answering the "who" question, two general rules should be kept in mind. First, income is taxed to the taxpayer who controls the earning of the income. The Supreme Court decisions in *Lucas v. Earl*,[2] and *Helvering v. Eubank*,[3] provide the foundation for this rule.

In *Lucas v. Earl*, the taxpayer and his wife entered into a contract providing, among other things, that the earnings of either one would be received and owned as joint tenants. (The contract was entered into in 1901 — prior to the imposition of the modern individual income tax — and was presumed valid and enforceable under state law.) Twenty years later, when there was an income tax, but as yet no joint return, the taxpayer sought to have his salary taxed half to himself and half to his wife pursuant to the contract. The Supreme Court refused, holding the taxpayer earned the salary and would be taxed on it.

> But this case is not to be decided by attenuated subtleties. It turns on the import and reasonable construction of the taxing act. There is no doubt

---

[2]   281 U.S. 111 (1930).

[3]   311 U.S. 122 (1940).

that the statute could tax salaries to those who earned them and provide that the tax could not be escaped by anticipatory arrangements and contracts however skillfully devised to prevent the salary when paid from vesting even for a second in the man who earned it. That seems to us the import of the statute before us and we think that no distinction can be taken according to the motives leading to the arrangement by which the fruits are attributed to a different tree from that on which they grew.[4]

The taxpayer in *Eubank*, a life insurance agent, was entitled to receive a commission when policy holders renewed the policies the taxpayer had previously sold to them. The taxpayer later assigned to a trust his right to the renewal commissions. Thus, when policy holders paid the renewal premiums on policies the taxpayers had sold, the life insurance company paid the renewal commission to the trust rather than to the taxpayer. The Supreme Court concluded the renewal commissions were nonetheless taxable to the taxpayer in the year paid to the trust.

Thus, whether the taxpayer assigns his right to income for services before performing the services (*Lucas v. Earl*) or after performing the services (*Helvering v. Eubank*), the taxpayer, and not the assignee, is taxed on the income when it is paid.

> **Example:** A high-bracket employee directs his employer to pay his wages, or to pay other taxable benefits, directly to his low-bracket child. Will this shifting of income be respected?

> **Analysis:** No. The income will be taxed to the employee, the one who earned the income. The employee will be deemed to have made a gift of the income to the child. The child may exclude the gift under Section 102.

The second general rule is that income from property is taxed to the one who owns the property and thus controls the income generated by the property. In *Helvering v. Horst*,[5] the taxpayer owned negotiable bonds. The right to interest was represented by interest coupons that could be detached from the bonds. Shortly before interest was due on the bonds, the taxpayer gave the interest coupons (but not the bonds) to his son. Later that same year, the son collected the interest payments when the coupons came due. The Supreme Court held the taxpayer, not the son, was taxable on the interest.

> **Example:** A landlord directs that rent from a building she owns be paid to her child. Will this shift of rental income be respected?

> **Analysis:** No. The landlord owns the building and controls the earning of the income and will therefore be taxed on the income. The child will be treated as receiving an excludable gift.

As these examples illustrate, to use receipt as the criterion for determining who is the appropriate taxpayer would invite widespread manipulation of the progressive rate structure. The search is rather for the true earner of the income, and it is to that taxpayer the income will be attributed.

---

[4] 281 U.S. at 114, 115.

[5] 311 U.S. 112 (1940).

It is possible, however, for the taxpayer who owns property to sell his "right" to future income from the property.

> **Example:** Taxpayer owns a dividend-paying stock. To take advantage of the deductibility of a substantial expense incurred this year, Taxpayer would like to accelerate income into the current year. Because the accumulated income will be offset by the expense, Taxpayer can in effect receive the income tax-free. Accordingly, Taxpayer assigns to Child a fixed dollar amount of future stock dividends, and directs the corporation to pay all future dividends to Child until the dollar amount is reached. Child pays Taxpayer the present value of the future dividends. (Because of the regular dividend-paying history of the corporation, the present value of the future dividends can be accurately determined.)

> **Analysis:** According to the Sixth Circuit in *Stranahan v. Commissioner*,[6] the dividends, when paid to Child, are taxed to Child. The court found the transaction to be "economically realistic, with substance." The "good and sufficient consideration" distinguished it from the gratuitous transfer in *Helvering v. Horst*; the absence of any intent or effect to avoid or escape recognition of the dividends — the dividend income was instead accelerated — distinguished it from the *Lucas v. Earl* line of cases.

§ 34.03   COMMUNITY PROPERTY

Community property laws can impact the operation of the general rule discussed above, attributing service income to the true earner of that income. Under community property laws, earnings during marriage are deemed the property of the husband-wife community and not the property of the spouse performing the services generating the earnings. In *Poe v. Seaborn*,[7] the Supreme Court held that, under the community property laws of the State of Washington, each of the spouses was taxable on half of his or her own earnings and on half of his or her spouse's earnings. It also noted that state law determines the rights of persons with regard to income or property, and federal law determines the federal tax consequences of those rights. The effect of *Poe v. Seaborn* is to permit spouses to split their income. As a result, a married couple's tax liability could vary significantly depending on whether the couple lived in a community property jurisdiction or a common law jurisdiction. To negate this unfairness, Congress in the 1948 authorized married couples to file joint returns.

Notwithstanding the congressional action in 1948, the rule of *Poe v. Seaborn* remains viable and the splitting of income in community property jurisdictions can still have some important tax consequences. For example, because, pursuant to *Poe v. Seaborn*, federal tax law generally respects state property law characterizations and definitions, the IRS has taken the position that registered domestic partners and spouses in same-sex marriages in California must, for federal income tax purposes, each report one-half of his or her community income whether received in

---

[6]   472 F.2d 867 (6th Cir. 1973).

[7]   282 U.S. 101 (1930).

the form of compensation for personal services or income from property.[8] Likewise, where pension benefits earned through the employment of one spouse during the marriage are community property, and where a divorce decree requires the employee-spouse to pay half the monthly pension benefits to the nonemployee-spouse as her share of community property, the employee spouse and the nonemployee spouse will each be taxable on half the pension benefits.[9]

§ 34.04   APPLICATION OF THE ASSIGNMENT OF INCOME RULES

The Ninth Circuit decision in *Kochansky v. Commissioner*,[10] provides a classic example of the application of the principles enunciated in *Lucas v. Earl* and *Helvering v. Eubank*. In *Kochansky*, the taxpayer, as part of a divorce settlement, agreed to pay to his wife a portion of any contingent fee to which he became entitled as a result of representing a client in a medical malpractice suit. After the divorce, the malpractice suit was favorably settled and the taxpayer received the contingent fee. Despite the fact that taxpayer, as required by the terms of the divorce settlement, distributed a portion of the fee to his ex-wife, the Commissioner contended the taxpayer was taxable on the entire fee. Agreeing with the Commissioner and the Tax Court, the Ninth Circuit held the case was controlled by *Lucas v. Earl*. Income is taxable to the person who earns the income and an anticipatory assignment of personal service income will not serve to shift the tax liability for that income. In *Kochansky*, the contingent fee represented compensation to the taxpayer for services he rendered. The taxpayer, after the divorce settlement, continued to render services to the client and controlled the personal services that produced the fee. Taxpayer transferred only a right to receive a portion of the income to his wife. Applying the tree-fruit metaphor of *Lucas v. Earl*, the Ninth Circuit noted the taxpayer had transferred only the fruit. The fact the fee was contingent did not render the fee something other than compensation for taxpayer's professional services.

The shifting of income from services and property can occur in a variety of contexts that are anything but straight-forward. For example, in *Commissioner v. Giannini*,[11] the taxpayer, the president of a corporation, informed the corporation's board of directors that he would refuse to accept any income from the corporation for his services during the remainder of the year and urged the corporation to use the money for some worthwhile cause. The corporation contributed the compensation otherwise payable to the taxpayer to the University of California. The Service argued that, even though the taxpayer had not actually received the income, the taxpayer had, in effect, directed the disposition of the income and therefore was taxable on it. Taxpayer argued: "A person has the right to refuse property proffered to him, and if he does so, absolutely and unconditionally, his refusal amounts to a renunciation of the proffered property, which, legally, is an abandonment of right to

---

[8] Chief Counsel Advice 201021050 (May 5, 2010).

[9] Eatinger v. Commissioner, T.C. Memo. 1990-310.

[10] 92 F.3d 957 (9th Cir. 1996).

[11] 129 F.2d 638 (9th Cir. 1942).

the property without a transfer of such right to another. Property which is renounced (*i.e.*, abandoned) cannot be 'diverted' or 'assigned' by the renouncer, and cannot be taxed upon the theory that it was received."[12] The court nonetheless held for the taxpayer, noting the taxpayer did not direct the corporation to give the money to any specific organization. Indeed, ". . . the corporation could have kept the money. All arrangements with the University of California regarding the donation . . . were made by the corporation, the taxpayer participating therein only as an officer of the corporation."[13]

Addressing a more common situation, the Service, in Revenue Ruling 66-167,[14] ruled that, because a taxpayer serving as the executor of an estate effectively communicated his intention to serve without compensation, he did not have to report as income the fees or commissions he would otherwise have had a right to receive under state law. According to the ruling, the requisite intention to serve on a gratuitous basis will ordinarily be deemed to have been adequately manifested if, within six months after his initial appointment, the executor or administrator of an estate supplies one or more of the decedent's principal devisees or heirs with a formal waiver of any right to compensation for his services.

Sometimes, the incidence of taxation turns on agency law. For example, in Revenue Ruling 74-581,[15] law school clinical faculty who were appointed to represent indigent defendants through the school's clinical programs, were required by the school to turn over to it any amounts they received for such representation. According to the Service, the faculty members were "working solely as agents of the law school" and were not taxable on the amounts thus received and paid over to the law school. By contrast, in Revenue Ruling 84-13,[16] a psychologist in private practice was required, pursuant to vows of poverty and obedience taken as a member of a religious order, to obtain the order's permission to establish the practice and to turn over to the order amounts received from the practice. The psychologist selected the clients, established the fees, maintained the records and paid the expenses; the order conducted an annual review of the psychologist's budget but did not engage in the provision of psychology services or control the details of the work or the means and method to accomplish it. Based on these facts, the ruling concluded that the amounts received by the psychologist were earned in an individual capacity, not as an agent of the order, and were taxable to the psychologist despite the vow of poverty.

The distinction between income from services and income from property is blurred when services result in the creation of property.

Example 1: Assume a professional author writes a short story and transfers the copyright to her son. Given the author's reputation, numerous

---

[12] *Id.* at 640.

[13] *Id.* at 640-41.

[14] 1966-1 C.B. 20.

[15] 1974-2 C.B. 25.

[16] 1984-1 C.B. 21.

magazines are willing to purchase the story. Shortly after receiving the copyright, the son sells the story to a publisher. Has the author successfully shifted the income?

Analysis: The Service might argue that the income from the story represents personal service income which the author could not shift to her son. By contrast, the son will surely argue that the copyright represents property, the author's transfer of which effectively shifted the income. As the Ninth Circuit noted in *Siegel v. United States*,[17] "the line between earned income and income from property is not always marked with dazzling clarity." In such a case, the copyright would be treated as property and the amounts received by the son upon the sale of the story to a publisher would constitute income to the son and not to the author.[18]

Example 2: Assume the author in Example 1 had contracted with a publisher to write the short story. Upon completing the story, the author made a gift of the manuscript and copyright to her son, who in turn transferred the copyright to the publisher and collected the income. What result?

Analysis: Using the fruit-tree metaphor of *Lucas v. Earl*, the owner of the tree would generally be taxed on the fruit of the tree. Thus, one might assume the author's child, as owner of the manuscript and copyright, would be taxed on the amount received from the publisher. If, however, the fruit hanging on the tree at the time of the tree's transfer is ripe, the transferor, by transferring the tree, may not be able to avoid being taxed on the income. In this example, the author will likely be taxed on the amounts received by the child from the publisher since the author had already arranged for the purchase of the story and had presumably negotiated the price. The child would be treated as receiving an excludable gift from the author.

If a publicly held corporation declares a stock dividend payable to holders of stock on the record date, a gratuitous transfer of stock by a shareholder on the record date will not successfully deflect the dividend income to the donee.[19] By contrast, where the controlling shareholder in a closely held corporation transferred preferred stock in the corporation to a charity after a dividend had been declared, but a few days before the record date, the Fifth Circuit held the dividend income was not taxable to the donor.[20] The court cited Regulation Section 1.61-9(c) in support of the distinction between declaration and record dates and found that the assignment of income doctrine was not applicable to the transaction. The court noted:

---

[17] 464 F.2d 891 (1973).

[18] Rev. Rul. 54-599, 1954-2 C.B. 52. *Compare* Wodehouse v. Comm'r, 177 F.2d 881 (2d Cir. 1949), *with* Wodehouse v. Comm'r, 178 F.2d 987 (4th Cir. 1949).

[19] Bishop v. Shaughnessy, 195 F.2d 683 (2d Cir. 1962).

[20] Caruth v. U.S., 865 F.2d 644 (5th Cir. 1989).

When a taxpayer gives away earnings derived from an income-producing asset, the crucial question is whether the asset itself, or merely the income from it, has been transferred. If the taxpayer gives away the entire asset, with accrued earnings, the assignment of income doctrine does not apply. . . .

The IRS, however, . . . urges that we hold [the donor] taxable upon the dividend because here the fruit was exceptionally ripe. . . . We fail to see why the ripeness of the fruit matters, so long as the entire tree is transplanted before the fruit is harvested. . . .

We believe that, at bottom, the IRS mistakes the character of the asset donated. The IRS wishes to treat the [preferred stock] as a mere conduit for [the controlling shareholder's] earnings, rather than as a source of those earnings. . . .

At the risk of mixing metaphors, the preferred stock was the tree that grew the fruit, rather than merely a crate for conveying the fruit.[21]

The "ripened fruit" issue is addressed in other contexts as well. The taxpayer in *Salvatore v. Commissioner*[22] inherited her husband's gas station, which her children operated for several years after his death. An opportunity arose to sell the property for a substantial profit, the taxpayer and the children agreed the sale was in the family's best interest, and the taxpayer thereupon executed an agreement to sell the property to a major oil company. Shortly thereafter, before the sale closed, taxpayer conveyed a half-interest in the property to her children as a gift. On closing, taxpayer and her children conveyed their respective interests to the buyer in return for its payment to them of the purchase price. Taxpayer reported only half the gain on the sale. The Commissioner argued all of the gain was taxable to her, and the Tax Court agreed:

The only question is whether petitioner is taxable on all or only one-half of the gain realized from the sale of the service station property. This issue must be resolved in accordance with the following principle stated by the Supreme Court in *Commissioner v. Court Holding Co.*, 324 U.S. 331, 334 (1945):

The incidence of taxation depends upon the substance of a transaction. The tax consequences which arise from gains from a sale of property are not finally to be determined solely by the means employed to transfer legal title. Rather, the transaction must be viewed as a whole, and each step, from the commencement or negotiations to the consummation of the sale, is relevant. *A sale by one person cannot be transformed for tax purposes into a sale by another by using the latter as a conduit through which to pass title.* To permit the true nature of a transaction to be disguised by mere formalisms, which exist solely to alter tax liabilities, would seriously

---

[21] *Id.* at 648-50.

[22] T.C. Memo, 1970-30.

impair the effective administration of the tax policies of Congress. [Emphasis added.]

Petitioner's subsequent conveyance, unsupported by consideration, of an undivided one-half interest in the property to her children — all of whom were fully aware of her prior agreement to sell the property — was merely an intermediate step in the transfer of legal title from petitioner to Texaco; petitioner's children were only "conduit[s] through which to pass title." That petitioner's conveyance to the children may have been a bona fide completed gift prior to the transfer of title to Texaco, as she contends, is immaterial in determining the income tax consequences of sale, for the form of a transaction cannot be permitted to prevail over its substance. In substance, petitioner made an anticipatory assignment to her children of one-half of the income from the sale of the property.[23]

As is illustrated by the above cases, the law on assignment of income has been developed primarily by the courts, although there are some specific areas now controlled by statute and regulation.[24] In addition, there are also instances of congressional concessions in the assignment of income area. The joint return, as noted, taxes income to husband and wife as if each had earned half of it, regardless of who actually earned it.

§ 34.05 THE KIDDIE TAX

§ 1(g). **Certain unearned income of minor children taxed as if parent's income.**

(1) **In general. In the case of any child to whom this subsection applies, the tax imposed by [I.R.C. § 1] shall be equal to the greater of —**

(A) **the tax imposed by this section without regard to this subsection, or**

(B) **the sum of**

(i) **the tax which would be imposed by this section if the taxable income of such child for the taxable year were reduced by the net unearned income of such child, plus**

(ii) **such child's share of the allocable parental tax.**

(2) **Child to whom subsection applies. This subsection shall apply to any child for any taxable year if —**

(A) **such child —**

(i) **has not attained age 18 before the close of the taxable year, or**

(ii) **(I) has attained age 18 before the close of the taxable year and meets the age requirements of section 152(c)(3) (determined without regard to subparagraph (B) thereof), and**

---

[23] *Id.* (emphasis added).

[24] *See, e.g.,* I.R.C. § 704(e) (family partnerships); § 1366(e) (a special type of corporation known as an "S corporation"); § 482 (two or more businesses under common control); § 1(g) (the "kiddie tax").

(II) whose earned income (as defined in section 911(d)(2)) for such taxable year does not exceed one-half of the amount of the individual's support (within the meaning of section 152(c)(1)(D) after the application of section 152(f)(5) (without regard to subparagraph (A) thereof)) for such taxable year

(B) either parent of such child is alive at the close of the taxable year, and

(C) such child does not file a joint return for the taxable year.

(3)   Allocable parental tax. For purposes of this subsection —

(A)   In general. The term "allocable parental tax" means the excess of —

(i) the tax which would be imposed by [I.R.C. § 1] on the parent's taxable income if such income included the net unearned income of all children of the parent to whom this subsection applies, over

(ii) the tax imposed by this section on the parent without regard to this subsection.

For purposes of clause (i), net unearned income of all children of the parent shall not be taken into account in computing any exclusion, deduction, or credit of the parent.

(B)   Child's share. A child's share of any allocable parental tax of a parent shall be equal to an amount which bears the same ratio to the total allocable parental tax as the child's net unearned income bears to the aggregate net unearned income of all children of such parent to whom this subsection applies.

. . .

(4)   Net unearned income. For purposes of this subsection —

(A)   In general. The term "net unearned income" means the excess of —

(i) the portion of the adjusted gross income for the taxable year which is not attributable to earned income (as defined in section 911(d)(2)), over

(ii) the sum of —

(I) the amount in effect for the taxable year under section 63(c)(5)(A) (relating to limitation on standard deduction in the case of certain dependents), plus

(II) The greater of the amount described in subclause (I) or, if the child itemizes his deductions for the taxable year, the amount of the itemized deductions allowed by this chapter for the taxable year which are directly connected with the production of the portion of adjusted gross income referred to in clause (i).

(B)   Limitation based on taxable income. The amount of the net unearned income for any taxable year shall not exceed the individual's taxable income for such taxable year.

. . .

(7)   Election to claim certain unearned income of child on parent's return.

(A)   In general. If —

(i) any child to whom this subsection applies has gross income for the taxable year only from interest and dividends (including Alaska Permanent Fund dividends),

(ii) such gross income is more than the amount described in paragraph (4)(A)(ii)(I) and less than 10 times the amount so described,

(iii) no estimated tax payments for such year are made in the name and TIN of such child, and no amount has been deducted and withheld under section 3406, and

(iv) the parent of such child (as determined under paragraph (5)) elects the application of subparagraph (B).

such child shall be treated (other than [for] purposes of this paragraph) as having no gross income for such year and shall not be required to file a return under section 6012.

(B)   Income included on parent's return. In the case of a parent making the election under this paragraph —

(i) the gross income of each child to whom such election applies (to the extent the gross income of such child exceeds twice the amount described in paragraph (4)(A)(ii)(I)) shall be included in such parent's gross income for the taxable year,

(ii) the tax imposed by this section for such year with respect to such parent shall be the amount equal to the sum of —

(I) the amount determined under this section after the application of clause (i), plus

(II) for each such child, 10 percent of the lesser of the amount described in paragraph (4)(A)(ii)(I) or the excess of the gross income of such child over the amount so described, and

(iii) any interest which is an item of tax preference under section 57(a)(5) of the child shall be treated as an item of tax preference of such parent (and not of such child).

As one would expect, income-shifting is particularly tempting in family situations. When a parent shifts income to a child, the income remains in the family unit. If the income shift results in a lower tax payment, the family unit has more after-tax income than it otherwise would have had.

Intrafamily shifting of compensation income was largely controlled historically by cases like *Lucas v. Earl* and *Helvering v. Eubank*. However, Congress was concerned that an unsatisfactory level of income deflection continued to exist as a result of intrafamily transfers of income-producing property.

The so-called "kiddie tax"[25] substantially eliminates the benefits of income-shifting to a child subject to the tax (hereinafter referred to as a "covered child"). Prior to the enactment of the kiddie tax in 1986, a favorite technique for reducing the aggregate tax liability of a family was to spread income-producing assets among the various members of the family. Minor children were generally subject to the same income tax rules as adults, so parental transfers of assets to their children —

---

[25] I.R.C. § 1(g).

who were presumably in a lower tax bracket than the parents — effectively reduced the family tax bill. Disputes could arise about whether ownership had in fact been transferred, but if the transfer were properly carried out, the income from the property would be taxed to the child. Congress came to regard this income-splitting technique as a manipulation of the progressive rate structure, and a form of tax avoidance that should be restricted.

The approach taken by Congress is to tax the "net unearned income" of a covered child at the top marginal tax rate of his or her parents (unless, of course, the child is in a higher bracket). The net unearned income is still taxed to the child, not to the parents, but it is taxed to the child as if it were additional parental taxable income. Subsection 1(g), however, casts a net that reaches far beyond the income-shifting technique just described, since it applies to all the net unearned income of a covered child, regardless of the source of the income.[26] Earned income basically consists of personal services income.[27] Unearned income includes not only the income attributable to property transfers from parents, but also those from other relatives, friends or strangers as well. Moreover, as the regulations point out, the section applies to unearned income attributable to assets acquired with the child's own earned income, such as interest on bank deposits attributable to a child's newspaper route earnings.[28] The decision to expand the reach of the section beyond parent-child or other intrafamily transfers was presumably based on the administrative difficulties that would have been encountered with a provision dependent on the source of the income-producing asset.

At the same time, note the limitations on the scope of Section 1(g). Section 1(g) applies to a child who is under the age of 18.[29] In addition, as a result of 2007 amendments to Section 1(g), the kiddie tax also applies to a child if (1) the child has attained the age of 18 by the end of the tax year but is not yet 19 or the child is a full-time student under the age of 24[30] **and** (2) the child's earned income does not exceed one-half of the amount of the child's support.[31] Under no circumstance will the kiddie tax apply unless the child has at least one living parent, and it does not apply to a married child who files a joint return.[32] Given the above limitations regarding children covered by the kiddie tax, income shifting remains viable for a transferor's children, dependents and relatives whose age or circumstances negate the application of the kiddie tax to them. Moreover, the definition of net unearned income — the income subject to tax at the parental tax rate — permits a limited amount of unearned income of a covered child to be taxed at that child's tax rate instead of the parental rate.

The rules of Section 1(g) are complemented by special provisions relating to the standard deduction and personal exemption. First, Section 151(d)(2) provides that,

---

[26] Temp. Treas. Reg. § 1.1(i)-1T, Q&A-8.

[27] I.R.C. § 911(d)(2).

[28] Temp. Treas. Reg. § 1.1(i)-1T, Q&A-8, Ex. (5).

[29] I.R.C. § 1(g)(2)(A)(i).

[30] I.R.C. §§ 1(g)(2)(A)(i)(I), 152(c)(3).

[31] I.R.C. § 1(g)(2)(A)(ii)(II).

[32] I.R.C. § 1(g)(2)(B), (C).

if a dependency deduction with respect to an individual is allowable to another taxpayer, that individual may not claim a personal exemption on his or her own tax return. Second, under Section 63(c)(5) that individual's standard deduction may not exceed the greater of an inflation-adjusted $500 or the sum of $250 and such individual's earned income. (Of course, it also may not exceed the basic standard deduction.) Thus, a covered child who is allowable as a dependent on the return of one or both parents will find that on her own return she may not claim the personal exemption or the basic standard deduction, but will instead take the limited standard deduction.

Assuming Section 1(g) applies, the tax imposed on the child is the greater of two amounts:

(1) The tax imposed without regard to Section 1(g) (this would be the greater amount when the child is in a higher tax bracket than the parents); or

(2) The sum of: (a) the normal tax that would be imposed if the child's taxable income were reduced by net unearned income, and (b) the child's share of the "allocable parental tax."[33]

"Net unearned income" is essentially unearned income, minus the sum of two amounts: (1) the special standard deduction of Section 63(c)(5)(A) (hereinafter referred to as the "limited standard deduction"), as noted above; and (2) a second Section 63(c)(5)(A) deduction, or the allowable itemized deductions directly connected with the unearned income, whichever is greater.[34] On the assumption that such itemized deductions will rarely exceed the limited standard deduction, net unearned income will ordinarily equal the child's unearned income, minus twice the limited standard deduction. (Net unearned income, in any event, cannot exceed taxable income.)[35] For example, if a child under 18 has unearned income of $5,000, net unearned income will likely be $3,100, i.e., $5,000 − 2($950) = $3,100 (assuming the limited standard deduction is $950). If, however, allowable itemized deductions directly connected with the unearned income were $1,000, then net unearned income would be $3,050 — that is, $5,000 minus the sum of $950 plus $1,000.

Example: Junior, who is 15 years old and lives with both parents, earned $2,000 picking beans and berries during the summer of Year 1. He deposited the money in a savings account where it earned $100 interest in Year 1. In addition, Junior had income of $700 in Year 1 from a trust established by his grandmother under which he is the beneficiary. Assum

---

[33] I.R.C. § 1(g)(1). The Service has made clear that not only the tax itself, but any penalties or interest imposed for failure to file the return or to pay the tax, are imposed on the child. Notice 89-7, Q&A-4, 1989-1 C.B. 627. "Generally, a child who can be claimed as a dependent on another taxpayer's return must file an income tax return if (i) all of the child's income is earned income (such as wages) totaling more than the basic standard deduction amount . . . or (ii) the child has unearned income (such as interest or dividends) and his other total income (earned or unearned) is more than $500 [inflation-adjusted]." Q&A-1. See I.R.C. § 6013(a). The Service has promised to be aware of the "special communicative difficulties" involved in dealing with a child about tax liability. Id., Q&A-7.

[34] I.R.C. § 1(g)(4)(A).

[35] I.R.C. § 1(g)(4)(B).

ing Junior has no itemized deductions, does the kiddie tax apply to Junior in Year 1? Assume the limited standard deduction under Section 63(c)(5)(A), adjusted for inflation, is $950.

Analysis: Junior is 15 at the close of Year 1 and has at least one living parent. According to Section 1(g), he is thus (potentially at least) a "child to whom [Section1(g)] applies." No kiddie tax can be imposed unless his unearned income exceeds twice the limited standard deduction, assumed here to be $950.[36] Thus, no kiddie tax can be imposed unless Junior's unearned income exceeds $1,900. Here it does not because Junior only has $800 in unearned income, *i.e,* $700 of trust income and $100 of interest income. Note that the interest income, although traceable to Junior's earned income (*i.e.,* the $2,000 from picking berries), is nonetheless unearned income. By contrast, if the trust income had been $2,500 instead of $700, Junior's unearned income would then have totaled $2,600 (trust income of $2,500 plus interest income of $100). Net unearned income would thus be $700 — that is, the $2,600 unearned income less $1,900, and the kiddie tax would apply. (The $1,900 reduction represents the $950 limited standard deduction amount, plus the greater of (a) another $950 or (b) the itemized deductions directly connected with the unearned income — here, zero.)[37]

The "allocable parental tax" is the tax generated by taxing at the parental marginal rate all of the net unearned income of all children of the parent to whom Section 1(g) applies.[38] The statute requires the tax under Section 1 be computed on the parent's taxable income assuming that it includes the child's net unearned income as defined above. From this figure is subtracted the tax that would be imposed on the parent's taxable income without the inclusion of the child's unearned income. The difference is the tax on the child's income which the child must pay.

Example: Assume Junior in the previous example has gross income of $2,600, all of it from interest. Assume also that Junior has no deductions and the limited standard deduction is $950.

Analysis: Junior's net unearned income as explained above would be $700. Assume the parents' taxable income is $500,000 and the tax on that amount would be $175,000. Assume the tax on $500,700 of taxable income (*i.e.,* the parents' taxable income combined with Junior's net unearned income of $700) would be $175,245. The difference between the two figures is $245. This is Junior's tax liability on the $700 of net unearned income. In effect, $700 of Junior's income is being taxed at a 35% rate. Junior, of course, is also subject to tax on the other $1,900 of income. Assuming Junior is claimed by his parents as a dependent, Junior will not be allowed a personal exemption to offset this other income and, as noted on these facts, will be limited to a standard deduction of $950 under Section 63(c)(5)(A). Junior will thus also pay a tax on taxable income of $950 (i.e., $1,900 less the

---

[36] Temp. Treas. Reg. § 1.1(I)-1T, Q&A-1.

[37] I.R.C. § 1(g)(4)(ii); Temp. Treas. Reg. § 1.1(I)-1TQ&A-6.

[38] I.R.C. § 1(g)(3)(A)(i).

limited standard deduction of $950). Assuming a 10% rate of tax, Junior's tax liability on the $950 will be $95. As indicated by Section 1(g)(1), Junior's total tax on the $2,600 of income will be a combination of the "allocable parental tax — $245 — and the tax computed on Junior's taxable income reduced by Junior's net unearned income — $95. Thus, Junior's total tax on the $2,600 is $340 or an effective rate of tax of about 13%.

Where there is more than one child subject to the provisions of Section 1(g), the allocable parental tax must be shared among the children. The allocable parental tax will be shared among the children on the basis of each child's proportionate share of the aggregate net unearned income of all of the parent's children to whom Section 1(g) applies.[39]

Example: Assume Brother (under 18) has $4,000 of net unearned income and Sister (also under 18) has $1,000 of net unearned income. Assume this total net unearned income of $5,000, taxed at the marginal parental rate, generates tax liability of $2,000. How much of this tax is attributable to Brother?

Analysis: Since Brother's net unearned income of $4,000 is 80% of the total net unearned income, his "share" of the allocable parental tax of $2,000 is equal to 80%, or $1,600.

Where the parents of a covered child are not married, or if married, file separate returns, Section 1(g)(5) provides special rules for determining which parent's taxable income is to be taken into account. If the child's parents file a joint return, or if the parent whose taxable income is to be taken into account files a joint return with a spouse not the child's parent, the total taxable income shown on the joint return is the parental income for kiddie tax purposes.[40]

Finally, there is a "parental election" under which parents in certain circumstances may elect to include unearned income of a minor child in the parental return.[41] To qualify for the parental election, the minor child's gross income must be only from interest and dividends and, in addition, must be more than the limited standard deduction of Section 63(c)(5)(A) but less than ten times that amount.[42] If the parental election is made, the child is treated as having no gross income for the taxable year and will not be required to file a tax return.[43] The parent in turn will include in income the child's gross income to the extent it exceeds twice the limited standard deduction of Section 63(c)(5)(A). The tax payable by the parents will be calculated based on such inclusion plus an additional tax equal to the lesser of 10% of the Section 63(c)(5)(A) amount or the excess of the child's gross income over the Section 63(c)(5)(A) amount.

Example: Assume Junior's parents, who are in the 35% tax bracket, establish a trust for Junior who is 12 years old and who would be in a 10%

---

[39] I.R.C. § 1(g)(3)(B).

[40] Temp. Treas. Reg. § 1.1(i)-1T, Q&A-10, Q&A-13.

[41] I.R.C. § 1(g)(7).

[42] I.R.C. § 1(g)(7)(A)(i), (ii).

[43] I.R.C. § 1(g)(7) (flush language).

tax bracket. The trust earns $5,000 of interest income taxable to Junior. Junior has no other income. Assume the parents make the election under Section 1(g)(7), and the limited standard deduction is $950.

Analysis: Because Junior has no income other than interest, Junior's parents may make the election and will include $3,100 of Junior's income in their gross income — $3,100 is the excess of Junior's gross income over twice the limited standard deduction of $950. The parents' tax will be the sum of (1) the tax computed on their income plus the $3,100 identified in this paragraph; and (2) the lesser of $95 (i.e., 10% of the limited standard deduction of $950), or $405 (10% of $4,050, where $4,050 is the excess of Junior's gross income [$5,000] over the limited standard deduction). Thus, in this case, Junior's parents will add $95 to their tax liability as a result of the computation in (2) above. Junior will be treated as having no gross income for the year and will not be required to file a return for the year.

Chapter 35

BELOW MARKET LOANS

§ 35.01 HISTORY: PRE-SECTION 7872

[A] Early IRS Attempts at Taxation

The history of taxation of interest-free or below-market loans is the story of IRS failure, persistence and ultimate success. That history begins in the Tax Court with *Dean v. Commissioner*,[1] decided almost fifty years after the enactment of the first post-Sixteenth Amendment income tax legislation. In *Dean*, the Service claimed the taxpayers had understated their income by failing to report the economic benefit they derived from over two million dollars of interest-free loans they received from their family corporation. The Service argued the interest-free loans received by the Deans generated taxable income, just as a shareholder's rent-free use of corporate property does.[2] Rejecting the Service's argument, the court noted that, if instead of receiving the rent-free use of corporate property, the shareholders actually paid rent, they could not deduct the rent if their use of the property were personal.[3] By contrast, if the shareholders borrowed *money* and agreed to pay interest, they could deduct the interest paid on the loan regardless of their use of the loan proceeds.[4] The Tax Court concluded: "We have heretofore given full force to interest-free loans for tax purposes, holding that they result in no interest deduction for the borrower . . . nor interest to the lender. We think it to be equally true that an interest-free loan results in no taxable gain to the borrower."[5]

The Service's challenge to interest-free loans was not without merit. As both a concurring opinion and a dissenting opinion noted, the Tax Court's holding that interest-free loans did not generate taxable income was overly broad. According to the dissent, "[I]t is difficult to believe that the interest-free loan in excess of $2 million . . . by a personal holding company to its majority stockholder . . . did not result in any economic benefit to the borrower." Both the concurrence and dissent indicated that the majority's reliance on the Section 163(a) interest deduction as a basis for distinguishing interest-free loans from rent-free use of corporate

---

[1] 35 T.C. 1083 (1961) (nonacq.).

[2] *See, e.g.,* Frueauff v. Comm'r, 30 B.T.A. 449 (1934).

[3] I.R.C. § 262.

[4] I.R.C. § 163(a). *Dean,* of course, was decided well before the enactment of Section 163(h), disallowing deductions for most personal interest except for a few limited types of personal interest including qualifying home mortgage interest and interest on educational loans.

[5] 35 T.C. at 1090.

property was misplaced since, under certain circumstances, a Section 163(a) deduction would be disallowed. For example, if the proceeds of a loan were used to purchase tax-exempt municipal bonds, a deduction for the loan interest would be disallowed under Section 265(a)(2).[6]

In its most important income tax decision following *Dean*, the Tax Court, in *Greenspun v. Commissioner,*[7] explained its reasoning in *Dean* as follows:

> [H]olding that no income was realized . . . in *Dean* . . . we reasoned that had the taxpayers borrowed the funds on interest-bearing notes, their payment of interest would have been fully deductible under Section 163. Underlying this reasoning was the idea that, economically speaking, an interest-free loan from a corporation to its shareholder or employee is in substance no different from the making of a loan on which interest is charged accompanied by an increase in dividends or compensation in an amount equal to the interest charged. Consequently, to give effect to the economic reality of the situation, we attempted in *Dean* to equalize the tax treatment of the two loan transactions.[8]

The court then provided the following example:

> [A]ssume that A, an employee of X Co., received as his only form of compensation an interest-free loan from X Co. in the amount of $20,000 for a period of 1 year. Further assume the prevailing interest rate at the time was 5 percent or $1,000 a year. The economic effect of this transaction is the same as if X Co. had charged A interest at 5 percent on the $20,000 loan, and, at the same time, paid him a salary of $1,000 which A in turn used to pay the interest. Assuming no other facts, in the second hypothetical, A would have gross income from his salary of $1,000 and an interest deduction of $1,000 or taxable income of $0. Consistent with this result, in the first hypothetical involving the interest-free loan, A's taxable income under our holding in *Dean* would be $0.[9]

In *Greenspun*, the Tax Court, in effect, acknowledged that (1) an interest-free loan does generate *gross* income; and (2) the gross income generated is completely offset by an assumed interest deduction. Recognizing the *Dean* dissenters were correct in noting that under certain circumstances the interest deduction would not

---

[6] In reaching its conclusion that an interest-free loan does not generate taxable income, the Tax Court appeared to suggest that interest-free loans could be ignored altogether for tax purposes. Thus, apparently, the economic benefit conferred by an interest-free loan would not have to be reflected in gross income. This analysis distorted the computation of gross income, and in turn resulted in an understatement of adjusted gross income. Adjusted gross income is significant for various purposes, *e.g.*, determining the amount of the deductible medical expenses and deductible charitable contributions. *See* I.R.C. §§ 213(a), 170(b)(1)(F).

[7] 72 T.C. 931 (1979), *aff'd*, 670 F.2d 123 (9th Cir. 1982). *Greenspun* involved a below-market loan, *i.e.*, interest at a rate less than the market rate was charged on the loan between Howard Hughes, the lender, and the editor and publisher of the *Las Vegas Sun*, a Las Vegas daily newspaper. According to the Service, the difference between a market rate of interest and the actual interest charged constituted gross income to the borrower.

[8] *Id.* at 948, 949.

[9] *Id.*

be available (*e.g.*, if the loan proceeds were used to purchase tax-free municipal bonds, thus triggering the interest deduction disallowance rule of Section 265), the Tax Court in *Greenspun* stated that "[w]hen and if we are confronted with such a case, we will decide at that time whether *Dean* is applicable, and if so, whether we shall continue to adhere to our decision in *Dean*."[10]

Judge Nims, dissenting in *Greenspun*, raised a cautionary note regarding the court's reasoning that the borrower would have a constructive interest deduction which would offset the gross income from the interest free loan. "If this approach is pursued, the Court may expect to be eventually confronted with a case in which the Commissioner asserts imputed interest income to the lender — a quid pro quo for the constructive deduction allowed the borrower. One can easily visualize this occurring, for example in the stockholder-controlled corporation context."[11] The Commissioner never did seek to charge the lender with income; as discussed below, the Congress in the 1984 Tax Reform Act did.

[B] Gift Tax Consequences of Interest-Free Loans

Shortly after its loss in *Dean*, the Service found itself again before a court challenging interest-free loans; in *Johnson v. Commissioner*,[12] however, its attack changed. According to the Service, the taxpayers in *Johnson* had made a taxable gift to their children to whom they had made substantial interest-free loans repayable on demand. Rejecting the Service's imputation-of-interest argument, the *Johnson* court noted Congress was the proper body to change the long-standing position that interest-free loans were not taxable. *Johnson* represented the first time in the then 34-year history of the gift tax in which the Service had sought to tax interest-free loans as gifts.

[C] Post *Dean/Johnson* History

In addition to its failure to address the taxation of interest-free loans until the early 1960s, the Service also failed to respond timely to the decisions in *Dean* and *Johnson*. Indicative of an ambivalence regarding the taxation of interest-free loans, the Service waited 12 years before it announced its non-acquiescence in *Dean*.[13] The Service waited seven years to announce that it would not follow *Johnson*.[14]

---

[10] *Id.* at 950.

[11] *Id.* at 957-58.

[12] 254 F. Supp. 73 (N.D. Tex. 1966).

[13] 1973-2 C.B. 4.

[14] Rev. Rul. 73-61, 1973-1 C.B. 408. In this ruling, the Service provided means for determining the gift element of both demand and term loans. In the case of term loans, the Service provided that accepted actuarial methods should be used to compute the gift value of the loan at the time that it was made. A term loan involves only one reportable gift, *i.e.*, the value of the interest-free use of the money for the term of the loan. By contrast, the value of the gift element of a demand loan is the value of the use of the money for such portion of the year as the donor permits the donee to use the money. Thus, at the end of each year a demand loan is outstanding, the value of the gift for that year must be determined. If the demand loan is outstanding for five years, there would be a separate gift calculated for each of those years.

Finally, more than a decade after the *Dean* decision, the Service began aggressively asserting the taxability of interest-free loans. The Service consistently lost. The Service's persistence, however, finally bore fruit in *Dickman v. Commissioner.*[15] At issue in that case was whether taxable gifts resulted when a lender made interest-free demand loans to a relative and to a closely held corporation. The Eleventh Circuit rejected the Tax Court's view that such loans did not generate gift tax liability and held that interest-free loans are subject to the gift tax whether they are made for a fixed term or are made on a demand basis.[16] The appellate court reasoned the use of money constitutes a property interest, and that whenever one transfers property for less than full consideration, a taxable gift has been made. The Eleventh Circuit noted that, for gift tax purposes, the lender had no deduction which would offset the gift comparable to the interest deduction a borrower could use to offset the income generated by an interest-free loan.

The Supreme Court agreed with the Eleventh Circuit, noting "[t]he right to use money is plainly a valuable right, readily measurable by reference to current interest rates; the vast banking industry is positive evidence of this reality."[17] In holding that interest-free loans generated taxable gifts, the Court recognized the income-shifting potential of such loans: "A substantial no-interest loan from parent to child creates significant tax benefits for the lender quite apart from the economic advantages to the borrower. This is especially so when an individual in a high income tax bracket transfers income producing property to an individual in a lower income tax bracket, thereby reducing the taxable income of the high-bracket taxpayer at the expense, ultimately, of all other taxpayers and the Government."[18] The taxpayer argued unsuccessfully that to elevate interest-free loans to the status of taxable gifts would cause "a loan of the proverbial cup of sugar to a neighbor or a loan of lunch money to a colleague" or any number of intrafamily transfers to constitute taxable gifts. The Court rejected that argument, stating it did not believe the focus of the Service to be on such matters. "When the Government levies a gift tax on routine neighborly or familial gifts, there will be time enough to deal with such a case."[19]

The Service was quick to act on *Dickman* and issued Announcement 84-60,[20] providing guidelines for computing the gift value of interest free loans. According to the Announcement, the value of the gift element of demand loans was to be determined by multiplying the "average outstanding loan balance" for a period by the lesser of either the statutory interest rates on refunds and deficiencies or the annual average rate for three month Treasury bills. Consistent with the Court's analysis in *Dickman,* the Announcement was limited in scope to those interest-free loans to which the reasoning of *Dickman* would apply. Specifically, the Announcement provided that, if the value of the gift were less than the annual gift

---

[15] 465 U.S. 330 (1984).

[16] 690 F.2d 812 (11th Cir. 1982).

[17] 465 U.S. at 337–38.

[18] *Id.* at 339.

[19] *Id.* at 341.

[20] 1984-23 I.R.B. 58.

exclusion, no gift had to be reported.[21] In addition, married couples could make interest-free loans of up to $100,000 without incurring any gift tax.

§ 35.02 RATIONALE FOR SECTION 7872

In rejecting the Service's position regarding the income taxation of interest-free loans, many courts had stressed that the taxation of these loans was more appropriately a matter for congressional action. Congress finally addressed interest-free loans in the 1984 Tax Reform Act. As a review of Section 7872 and the discussion which follows indicates, the tax treatment for interest-free loans fashioned by Congress reflects both gift and income tax notions developed in the earlier case law. For example, Judge Nims in *Greenspun* speculated that treating the borrower as having constructively paid interest might later result in the lender being deemed to have constructively received an interest payment. That is precisely how Congress chose to analyze interest-free loans. Likewise, Section 7872 reflects the gift treatment accorded certain interest-free loans by the Supreme Court in *Dickman* and by the Service in Announcement 84-60.

The rationale for Section 7872 provided by the Staff of the Joint Committee reflects this congressional reliance on various theories advanced in the pre-1984 income and gift cases. In particular, Congress was concerned about the income-shifting potential of interest-free loans the Supreme Court had identified in *Dickman.*

Under prior law, loans between family members (and other similar loans) were being used to avoid the assignment of income rules and the grantor trust rules. A below-market loan to a family member, for example, generally involves a gratuitous transfer of the right to use the proceeds of the borrowing until repayment is demanded (in the case of a demand loan) or until the end of the term of the loan (in the case of a term loan). If the lender had assigned the income from the proceeds to the borrower instead of lending the proceeds to the borrower, the assignment of income doctrine would have taxed the lender (and not the borrower) on the income. . . .

In addition, loans from corporations to shareholders were being used to avoid rules requiring the taxation of corporate income at the corporate level. A below-market loan from a corporation to a shareholder is the economic equivalent of a loan by the corporation to the shareholder requiring the payment of interest at a market rate, and a distribution by the corporation to the shareholder with respect to its stock equal to the amount of interest required to be paid under the terms of the loan. If a transaction were structured as a distribution and a loan, the borrower would have dividend income and an offsetting interest deduction. The lender would have interest income. Under prior law, if the transaction was structured as a below-market loan, the lender avoided including in income the interest that would have been paid by the borrower. As a result the lender was in the same economic position as it would have been if it had

---

[21] Section 2503(b) generally provides a $10,000 exclusion, indexed for inflation, for gifts made during a year to any person. For 2013, the exclusion is $14,000.

deducted amounts distributed as dividends to shareholders.

Finally, loans to persons providing services were being used to avoid rules requiring the payment of employment taxes and rules restricting the deductibility of interest in certain situations by the person providing the services. A below-market loan to a person providing services is the economic equivalent of a loan requiring the payment of interest at a market rate, and a payment in the nature of compensation equal to the amount of interest required to be paid under the terms of the loan. Under prior law, a transaction structured as a loan and a payment in the nature of compensation often did not result in any tax consequences for either the lender or the borrower because each would have offsetting income and deductions. However, there were a number of situations in which the payment of compensation and a loan requiring the payment of interest at a market rate did not offset. For example, if a taxpayer used the proceeds of an arm's-length loan to invest in tax-exempt obligations, the deduction for interest paid on the loan would be disallowed under section 265. Similarly, if a term loan extended beyond the taxable year in which it was made, income and deductions did not offset because the compensation income was includible in the year the loan was made. In such circumstances, substantial tax advantages could have been derived by structuring the transaction as a below-market loan.[22]

§ 35.03   OPERATION OF SECTION 7872

Section 7872 applies to "below-market loans," defined as loans with respect to which either no interest, or an interest rate lower than the "applicable Federal rate" of interest, is charged.[23] Note the word "loan" is to be interpreted broadly for purposes of Section 7872.[24] Below-market loans are categorized according to their repayment requirements as either term loans or demand loans. A demand loan is payable in full at any time upon the demand of the lender.[25] A term loan is any loan which is not a demand loan, *i.e.,* it is payable at a specified time.[26] The "applicable Federal rate" refers to rates on marketable obligations of the United States, and depends on the maturity of the given obligation. Thus, the applicable Federal rate for term loans is the applicable Federal rate (compounded semiannually) as of the loan date for a government obligation having approximately the same maturity as the loan.[27] The applicable Federal rate for demand loans is the "Federal short-term rate in effect under section 1274(d) for the period of which the amount of forgone interest is being determined, compounded semiannually."[28]

---

[22] General Explanation of the Revenue Provisions of the Deficit Reduction Act of 1984, Staff of the Joint Committee on Taxation, 98th Cong., pp. 527–528.

[23] I.R.C. § 7872(e)(1).

[24] Prop. Treas. Reg. § 1.7872-2(a)(1).

[25] I.R.C. § 7872(f)(5).

[26] I.R.C. § 7872(f)(6).

[27] I.R.C. § 7872(f)(2)(A).

[28] I.R.C. § 7872(f)(2)(B).

Section 7872 applies to term or demand loans in one of the following categories:

(1) Gift loans, *i.e.*, below-market loans in which the forgone interest is in the nature of a gift.[29] The loans in *Johnson* and *Dickman* would have qualified as "gift loans."

(2) Corporation-shareholder loans, *i.e.*, below-market loans directly or indirectly between a corporation and its shareholders.[30] The loans in *Dean* would have been included in this category.

(3) Compensation-related loans, *i.e.*, below-market loans directly or indirectly between an employer (or party for whom an independent contractor provides services) and an employee (or independent contractor).[31] *Greenspun* involved this type of loan. In some instances, the recipient of a below-market corporate loan might be both a shareholder and an employee. If the corporation is a publicly held corporation and the shareholder/employee owns more than 0.5% of the voting power of voting stock, the loan will be treated as a corporation-shareholder loan; if the corporation is not publicly held and the shareholder/employee owns more than 5% of the voting power of voting stock, the loan will also be treated as corporation-shareholder loan.[32]

(4) Tax-avoidance loans, *i.e.*, a below-market loan which has as one of the principal purposes of the interest arrangements the avoidance of any Federal tax.[33] The proposed regulations state the forbidden purpose is present if a principal factor in structuring a transaction as a below-market loan, rather than a loan at market rates plus a payment by lender to borrower, is to reduce the tax liability of lender or borrower.[34]

(5) "Significant-effect" loans, *i.e.*, certain below-market loans, to be determined by regulations,[35] where the interest arrangements have a significant effect on any Federal tax liability of the lender or borrower.[36]

Note the potential scope of these latter two categories, a scope somewhat narrowed by regulatory exemptions.[37]

As explained by the Staff of the Joint Committee on Taxation, "[l]oans that are subject to [Section 7872] . . . are recharacterized as an arm's-length transaction in

---

[29] I.R.C. § 7872(f)(3).

[30] I.R.C. § 7872(c)(1)(C).

[31] I.R.C. § 7872(c)(1)(B).

[32] Proposed Regulation § 1.7872-4(d)(2) describes these and other circumstances in which such a loan will be presumed to be a corporate-shareholder loan, rather than compensation-related.

[33] I.R.C. § 7872(c)(1)(D).

[34] Prop. Treas. Reg. § 1.7872-4(e)(1).

[35] The proposed regulations simply "reserve" significant-effect loans for future definition. Prop. Treas. Reg. § 1.7872-4(f).

[36] I.R.C. § 7872(c)(1)(E).

[37] Proposed Regulation § 1.7872-5T exempts various loans from the rules of Section 7872, including obligations of the U.S., loans under life insurance contracts, etc.

which the lender made a loan to the borrower in exchange for a note requiring the payment of interest at the applicable federal rate. This rule results in the parties being treated as if: (1) The borrower paid interest to the lender that may be deductible to the borrower and is included in income by the lender; and (2) the lender (a) made a gift subject to the gift tax (in the case of a gratuitous transaction), or (b) paid a dividend or made a capital contribution (in the case of a loan between a corporation and a shareholder), or (c) paid compensation (in the case of a loan to a person providing services). . . ."[38] Below-market loans under the statute are characterized as "economically equivalent to loans bearing interest at the applicable Federal rate, coupled with a payment by the lender to the borrower sufficient to fund" the interest payment.[39]

[A]   Treatment of Term Loans Other Than Term Gift Loans

§ 7872(b).   Treatment of [term loans other than term gift loans].

(1)   In general. For purposes of this title, in the case of any below-market loan to which this section applies and to which subsection (a)(1) does not apply [note that § 7872(a)(1) applies only to gift loans and demand loans], the lender shall be treated as having transferred on the date the loan was made . . . and the borrower shall be treated as having received on such date, cash in an amount equal to the excess of

(A) the amount loaned, over

(B) the present value of all payments which are required to be made under the terms of the loan.

(2)   Obligation treated as having original issue discount. For purposes of this title —

(A)   In general. Any below-market loan to which paragraph (1) applies shall be treated as having original issue discount in an amount equal to the excess described in paragraph (1).

(B)   Amount in addition to other original issue discount. Any original issue discount which a loan is treated as having by reason of subparagraph (A) shall be in addition to any other original issue discount on such loan (determined without regard to subparagraph (A)).

The timing of the various deemed transfers and their amounts depend on whether the loan is characterized as (1) a term loan other than a term gift loan or (2) or a demand loan or a term gift loan.[40] In the case of a term loan other than a term gift loan, a two-step process must be followed in evaluating the tax consequences to the lender and the borrower. First, "the lender is treated as transferring to the borrower and the borrower is treated as receiving from the lender an amount equal to the excess of the amount of the loan over the present value of all principal and interest payments due under the loan. This transfer is treated as occurring on

---

[38] Joint Committee Report to the Deficit Reduction Act of 1984, p. 528.

[39] Prop. Treas. Reg. § 1.7872-1(a).

[40] I.R.C. § 7872(a), (b).

the date the loan is made."[41] As a result of this first step, the lender may have a deduction for payments deemed made to the borrower and the borrower may have income resulting from the deemed receipt. For purposes of this chapter, "present value" can be described as the value today of a sum of money to be received in the future. The amount of "discount," *i.e.*, the difference between today's present value and the amount to be paid or received in the future, depends on the assumed interest rate and the length of the period involved.

The following example demonstrates the application of the first step in evaluating the tax consequences of term loans (other than term gift loans).

Example: An employer wishes to reward an employee for particularly good work during the year. Rather than giving that employee an outright bonus, the employer gives the employee an interest-free loan of $50,000, repayable in three years.

Analysis: Under Section 7872, the present value of a $50,000 payment required to be made three years hence must be determined. Assume that, if $38,000 were placed today in a bank account paying the applicable Federal rate of interest compounded semiannually, the balance in the account would be $50,000 at the end of three years. Thus, $38,000 is the Section 7872 present value of the $50,000 payment the employee must make to the employer in three years. Applying Section 7872(b)(1), the employer would be treated as having given to the employee $12,000 in compensation at the time the loan was made (*i.e.*, the difference between the $50,000 the employee currently received and the $38,000 *present* value of the $50,000 repayment three years later.) Therefore, assuming such additional compensation is reasonable, the employer will deduct the $12,000 under Section 162 as an ordinary and necessary business expense. At the same time, the employee is deemed to have received compensation valued at $12,000 and must include that amount in gross income in the year the loan was received.

Section 7872(b)(2) provides the second step of this two-step process, under which "an amount equal to the excess of the amount of the loan [$50,000, in this example] over the present value of the payments due under the loan [$38,000, in this example] is treated as original issue discount.[42] As a result, the borrower is treated as transferring to the lender, and the lender is treated as receiving from the borrower, interest income at a constant rate over the life of the loan. The interest the borrower is treated as paying is [generally] deductible to the same extent as interest actually paid by the borrower."[43] In the example above, the employee would be deemed to

---

[41] Joint Committee Report to the Deficit Reduction Act of 1984, p. 532.

[42] Original issue discount is discussed in detail in Chapter 42, *infra*. Essentially, "original issue discount" refers to the difference between the issue price of an obligation and the price to be paid at maturity. For example, assume a corporation issues a bond as evidence of its indebtedness. Assume also that the bond was issued in exchange for $9,000, and, under the terms of the bond, $20,000 will be paid to the bearer at maturity. There is $11,000 of original issue discount inherent in the bond. Original issue discount represents interest which must be reported by the lender in the above example and which is generally deductible by the borrower-corporation. Rather than waiting until maturity of the loan, the lender and borrower must account for this interest element throughout the period of the loan.

[43] Joint Committee Report to the Deficit Reduction Act of 1984, p. 532.

be paying interest of $12,000 over three years to the lender. The lender would have $12,000 interest income over three years, and the employee might be able to deduct this deemed interest payment over the three years, subject to Section 163(h) and any other provisions disallowing deduction of interest.

[B] Demand Loans and Term Gift Loans

§ 7872(a).   Treatment of gift loans and demand loans.

(1)   In general. For purposes of this title, in the case of any below-market loan to which this section applies and which is a gift loan or a demand loan, the forgone interest shall be treated as —

(A) transferred from the lender to the borrower, and

(B) retransferred by the borrower to the lender as interest.

(2)   Time when transfers made. Except as otherwise provided in regulations prescribed by the Secretary, any forgone interest attributable to periods during any calendar year shall be treated as transferred (and retransferred) under paragraph (1) on the last day of such calendar year.

The Joint Committee Report to the Deficit Reduction Act of 1984 explains the operation of Section 7872(a) demand loans and gift loans as follows:

> In the case of a demand loan, the lender is treated as transferring to the borrower, and the borrower is treated as receiving from the lender, an amount equal to the foregone interest on an annual basis. . . . In the case of a term gift loan, the lender is treated as transferring to the borrower, and the borrower is treated as receiving from the lender, an amount equal to the excess of the amount of the loan over the present value of all principal and interest payments due under the loan.

> In addition, in the case of a demand loan or a term gift loan, the borrower is treated as transferring to the lender, and the lender is treated as receiving from the borrower, an amount equal to the [forgone] interest on an annual basis. This foregone interest is included in income by the lender and deductible by the borrower to the same extent as interest actually due on the loan from the borrower. . . . [U]nder the provisions generally applicable to term loans, an original issue discount analysis is required to determine the timing and amount of the deemed transfers by the borrower to the lender. By treating gift loans as demand loans for these purposes, such analysis is avoided.

The income tax effects of a term gift loan may be illustrated by an example based in legislative history.[44] Assume that, on January 1, P, a calendar year taxpayer, makes a $200,000 gift loan to S, a calendar year taxpayer, for two years at five percent simple interest payable annually. S is thus required to pay P $10,000 interest each year. Assume this is a below market loan because the applicable Federal rate is higher than five percent; further assume the present value of all payments to be made by S — the interest payments and the principal repayment —

---

[44] Joint Committee Report to the Deficit Reduction Act of 1984, pp. 532–33.

is $175,240. P is thus treated as making a transfer to S of $24,760 ($200,000 less $175,240) as a gift, excludable as such from S's income and nondeductible by P.[45] In addition, however, S is treated as retransferring to P each year an amount equal to the difference between the interest actually paid by S (here, $10,000) and the interest that would be payable if interest were paid annually on $200,000 at the applicable Federal rate, compounded semiannually; assume that amount would be $24,720. Thus, the amount treated as retransferred by S to P each year as interest is $14,720 (*i.e.,* the excess of interest computed at the applicable Federal rate (compounded semiannually) over interest actually payable on the loan). This amount, which would be included in income by the lender P and, subject to the rules governing the deductibility of interest, deductible by the borrower S, would be in addition to the $10,000 actually due each year under the terms of the loan.[46]

Note that, for income tax purposes, a term gift loan is treated as though it were a demand loan except for purposes of the gift tax provisions of the Code.[47] Thus, as indicated by the example, the amount of the gift deemed made is the difference between the principal amount of the loan and the present value of all payments which must be made on the loan.[48] If, in the example above, the loan had been a demand gift loan, there would have been no need to make a separate calculation of the gift amount. Rather, the amount of the gift deemed to be made by P to S would have equaled the forgone interest for the year.[49] For example, if applying the applicable Federal interest rate, the interest for one year on $200,000 would have amounted to $24,720 and S actually was only required to pay $10,000 interest that year, there would be $14,720 of forgone interest on the demand loan for the first loan year. That amount would have represented the amount of the gift from P to S for that year as well as the amount of the deemed transfer from S to P. The gift from P to S and the deemed transfer from S to P would both be presumed to have occurred on the last day of the taxable year.[50] Assuming the loan were outstanding for the next year, another gift in the same amount would be deemed made by P to S, and S would be deemed to have retransferred as interest that same amount to P. P, of course, could not deduct the gift of $14,720 she is deemed to have made to S in each of the years the loan was outstanding; S would exclude the gifts from income.[51] Assuming no disallowance rules[52] were applicable, S would be entitled to deduct as interest the amounts deemed retransferred to P on the last day of each calendar year.

Note that if, in the above demand loan example, the relationship had been an employer/employee relationship rather than a donor/donee relationship, the $14,720 deemed transfer from P to S would have been characterized as compensation

---

[45] The deemed transfer of $24,760 is a gift by P for gift tax purposes as well, and may create gift tax or estate tax liability for P; but such transfer tax issues are beyond the scope of this book.

[46] Joint Committee Report to the Deficit Reduction Act of 1984, pp. 532–33.

[47] *See* I.R.C. § 7872(d)(2).

[48] I.R.C. § 7872(b)(1).

[49] I.R.C. § 7872(a)(1)(A).

[50] I.R.C. § 7872(a)(2).

[51] I.R.C. § 102(a).

[52] *E.g.,* I.R.C. §§ 163(h), 265(a)(2), 163(d).

potentially currently deductible by P and clearly includible by S. The amount deemed retransferred by S to P would have the same consequences to both parties as described in the gift demand loan case described above.

Finally, if P were a corporation and S a shareholder and this were a corporation-shareholder loan, P would be deemed to have paid a dividend of $14,720 to S in each year the loan was outstanding. P would not be entitled to deduct the dividend and S would be required to include it in income. The tax consequences of the deemed retransfer of the forgone interest amount by S to P would be the same as in the gift demand loan example — i.e., interest income to P and an interest expense to S, deductible subject to disallowance rules.[53]

[C] Exceptions to the Basic Operating Rules

Section 7872 provides exceptions to the general rules described above. Two *de minimis* exceptions exist. The first is a $10,000 exception relating to gift loans, compensation-related loans, and corporation-shareholder loans. Essentially, as long as the outstanding amount of gift loans between borrower and lender does not exceed $10,000, Section 7872 does not apply to such loans. This exception, however, will not apply to any gift loan directly attributable to the purchase or carrying of income-producing assets.[54] This limit on the exception is consistent with the general purpose of Section 7872 described previously, i.e., to prevent avoidance of the assignment of income rules. This same $10,000 *de minimis* exception is also applicable to compensation-related loans and corporation-shareholder loans. This *de minimis* rule does not apply, however, if a principal purpose of the interest arrangement is avoidance of any Federal tax.[55]

The second exception is a $100,000 exception applicable in the case of a gift loan directly between individuals. Provided the aggregate outstanding loans from lender to borrower do not exceed $100,000, the amount considered as retransferred by the borrower to the lender as of the close of any calendar year shall not exceed the borrower's net investment income.[56] Moreover, if the borrower's net investment income is less than $1,000, the deemed retransfer is zero. However, if a principal purpose of the arrangement is tax avoidance, the $100,000 exception is inapplicable.[57]"Net investment income" has the same definition as under Section 163(d). As the legislative history notes:

> Thus, the term [net investment income] generally means the excess of investment income over investment expense. The term "investment income" generally means (1) the gross income from interest, dividends, rents and royalties, (2) the net short-term capital gain attributable to the disposition of property held for investment, and (3) any amounts treated

---

[53] For cases applying these rules in the corporate-shareholder setting, see *KTA Tator, Inc. v. Comm'r*, 108 T.C. 100 (1997) (interest income to corporation; no deduction for deemed distribution to shareholder) and *Mason v. Comm'r*, T.C. Memo 1997-352 (imputed dividend income to shareholders).

[54] I.R.C. § 7872(c)(2).

[55] I.R.C. § 7872(c)(3).

[56] I.R.C. § 7872(d)(1).

[57] I.R.C. § 7872(d)(1)(B).

under section 1245 . . . but only to the extent such income, gain and amounts are not derived from the conduct of a trade or business. The term "investment expense" generally means the deductions allowable under sections 162, 164(a)(1) or (2), 166, 167, 171, 212 or 611 directly connected with the production of income.

In addition, if a borrower has less than $1,000 of net investment income for the year, such borrower's net investment income for the year is deemed to be zero. Thus, if the aggregate outstanding amount of loans from the lender to the borrower does not exceed $100,000 on any day during a year, and the borrower has less than $1,000 of net investment income for the year, no amount is treated as retransferred by the borrower to the lender for such year.[58]

The $100,000 exception enables parents to provide large interest-free loans to their children to assist them in purchasing a home, or paying for education, travel, or other personal expenses. If the children have no investment income in excess of $1,000, there will be no tax consequences to the parent or child. Such interest-free arrangements were not the focus of congressional concern in enacting Section 7872.[59]

Example: On January 1, Year 1, Alice lends her son, Robert, $50,000 to enable him to make a downpayment on his home. The loan is a demand loan and is interest free. It is the only outstanding below-market loan from Alice to Robert. Assume the applicable federal rate is 10%, Robert has $2,000 in investment income in Year 1, and Robert makes no payments on the loan in Year 1. What tax consequences to Robert and to Alice?

Analysis: The loan is a gift loan subject to the below-market loan rules discussed above. Under Section 7872(a)(1), the forgone interest is treated as transferred from Alice to Robert as a gift and retransferred from Robert to Alice as interest. The forgone interest for the year January 1 to December 31, Year 1 is $5,125, determined as follows: The interest accrued over the first six month period using a 10% applicable Federal rate is $2,500 ($50,000 × 10% × ½); for the second six month period, the interest accrued is $2,625 ($52,500 × 10% × ½). Thus, normally, Alice would be deemed at year end to have made a gift of $5,125 ($2,500 plus $2,625) to Robert, and Robert would be deemed at the same time to have made an interest payment (potentially deductible under Section 163(h) as home mortgage interest if all formalities are met) of $5,125 to Alice (who would have to

---

[58] Joint Committee Report to the Deficit Reduction Act of 1984, p. 536; I.R.C. § 7872(d)(1)(D), (E)(ii).

[59] A number of other exemptions from I.R.C. § 7872 have been provided by regulation on the ground that "the interest arrangements do not have a significant effect" on tax liability. Temp. Treas. Reg. § 1. 7872-5T(a)(1). The exemptions, however, are lost if the loan is a tax-avoidance loan. Among the exemptions are those for certain loans made available to the general public and for government-subsidized loans. Temp. Treas. Reg. § 1.7872-5T(b)(1), (5). Also exempt are loans taxpayer establishes have no significant effect on tax liability, based on all the facts and circumstances, including "whether items of income and deduction generated by the loan offset each other . . . , the amount of such items . . . , the cost to the taxpayers of complying with . . . section 7872 . . . and any non-tax reasons for . . . [the] below-market loan. . . ." Temp. Treas. Reg. § 1.7872-5T(b)(14), (c)(3).

include that amount in her gross income). The special exception of Section 7872(d)(1), however, is applicable because this is a gift loan between individuals not exceeding $100,000. Thus, Robert will be deemed to have retransferred interest to Alice in an amount not greater than Robert's investment income — in this case $2,000. Alice will have to report $2,000 of interest income and Robert may potentially deduct $2,000 of home mortgage interest.

Chapter 36

TAX CONSEQUENCES OF DIVORCE

This chapter discusses the tax consequences of divorce and separation. Various issues arise in such a situation, such as the treatment of property transfers between spouses and former spouses incident to divorce,[1] personal exemptions for dependent children of divorced parents, and the proper filing status of parents following separation or divorce. Many of the issues raised in this chapter are of the "who-is-the-proper-taxpayer" variety. The tax burden that was borne, prior to divorce, within a single economic unit, must now be allocated between taxpayers with generally adverse interests. This chapter addresses the rules involved in the allocation.

§ 36.01 ALIMONY: GENERAL REQUIREMENTS

§ 71. Alimony and separate maintenance payments.

  (a)   General rule. Gross income includes amounts received as alimony or separate maintenance payments.

  (b)   Alimony or separate maintenance payments defined. For purposes of this section —

  (1)   In general. The term "alimony or separate maintenance payment" means any payment in cash if —

  (A) such payment is received by (or on behalf of) a spouse under a divorce or separation instrument,

  (B) the divorce or separation instrument does not designate such payment as a payment which is not includible in gross income under this section and not allowable as a deduction under section 215,

  (C) in the case of an individual legally separated from his spouse under a decree of divorce or of separate maintenance, the payee spouse and the payor spouse are not members of the same household at the time such payment is made, and

  (D) there is no liability to make any such payment for any period after the death of the payee spouse and there is no liability to make any payment (in cash or property) as a substitute for such payments after the death of the payee spouse.

---

§ 215. Alimony, etc., payments.

---

[1] These are nontaxable events under the special "nonrecognition" rule of Section 1041.

(a) General rule. In the case of an individual, there shall be allowed as a deduction an amount equal to the alimony or separate maintenance payments paid during such individual's taxable year.

In 1917, in the absence of any statute specifically addressing taxation of alimony, the Supreme Court held that alimony payments to a divorced wife did not constitute income.[2] For the next 25 years, alimony remained nontaxable to the recipient and nondeductible to the payor. In 1942, finding that the nondeductibility of alimony, in conjunction with high wartime tax rates, created an excessive tax burden on the payor, Congress reversed the rules and enacted the forerunners of present Sections 71 and 215. Under Section 71(a) and Section 61(a)(8), amounts received as "alimony or separate maintenance payments" are specifically includible in gross income. Section 215 provides an above-the-line deduction for such payments "actually paid," essentially mandating the cash method for deduction purposes.[3]

In 1984, Congress revised and, in most respects, simplified the rules governing the tax consequences of divorce and separation. Alimony payments remained includible to the recipient and deductible by the payor, but the definition of alimony was changed substantially. The 1984 Act eliminated prior law requirements that alimony payments be "periodic" and that they be made in discharge of a legal obligation of support arising out of the marital or family relationship.[4] Under current law, a payment must meet the following requirements to constitute alimony:

(1) *The payment must be in cash.*[5] Payments in the form of property or services do not qualify as alimony, and a controversial matter under prior law — the proper characterization of a property transfer as either alimony or property settlement — is effectively neutralized by the cash-only requirement.

(2) *The payment must be received by "or on behalf of" the spouse (or former spouse).*[6] Thus, cash payments to third parties may in some circumstances qualify as alimony.[7] For example, a mortgage payment, made by one spouse with respect to property owned by the other spouse, may be deductible as alimony.[8]

(3) *The payment must be made "under a divorce or separation instrument."*[9] When the alimony provisions were first enacted in 1942, the joint return was not part of the Code. To restrict income-splitting techniques between husband and wife, the only payments qualifying as alimony were those made under a decree of divorce or separate maintenance, or a written instrument incident to such a decree.[10] The joint return, enacted in 1948, eliminated the incentive for income-shifting between husband and wife, and thus also eliminated the reason for so limiting the availability

---

[2] Gould v. Gould, 245 U.S. 151 (1917).

[3] I.R.C. §§ 62(a)(10), 215(a); Treas. Reg. § 1.215-1(a).

[4] Temp. Treas. Reg. § 1.71-1T(a), Q&A-3.

[5] I.R.C. § 71(b)(1).

[6] I.R.C. § 71(b)(1)(A).

[7] Temp. Treas. Reg. § 1.71-1T(a), Q&A-6.

[8] In this regard, see Revenue Ruling 67-420, 1967-2 C. B. 63, issued under pre-1984 law.

[9] I.R.C. § 71(b)(1)(A), (2).

[10] Now Section 71(b)(2)(A).

of the alimony deduction. In 1954, Congress accordingly broadened the alimony definition to encompass payments under a written separation agreement of the parties, whether or not divorce follows, and also payments under a support decree.[11] The requirement for a "divorce or separation instrument" is thus easily satisfied in the ordinary case.

Payments made under an oral agreement, not reduced to writing, however, do not qualify. Thus, in *Ewell v. Commissioner*,[12] the Tax Court rejected the taxpayer's argument that an oral agreement with his former spouse constituted part of a written agreement. In addition, the court rejected the taxpayer's contention that "a written list of expenses his former spouse gave him, the letters exchanged by the attorneys, and notations [taxpayer] made on checks he issued, considered together, constitute[d] a written separation agreement." The court stressed that an "agreement requires mutual assent or a meeting of the minds." As the court noted, "[l]etters which do not show that there was a meeting of the minds are not a written separation agreement under section 71(b)(2)." Similarly, notations on a check do not establish an agreement between the parties.

(4) *The divorce or separation instrument must not designate the cash payment as one that is excludable from the gross income of the recipient and nondeductible to the payor.*[13] This provision gives the parties the flexibility to deny Section 71 and Section 215 treatment to otherwise qualifying payments.[14] Absent such a provision, cash payments intended to be part of a property settlement agreement would be taxed as alimony. Of course, even if the payments are in fact in the nature of spousal support, the parties have the ability to designate non-alimony treatment for them.

(5) *If the spouses are legally separated under a decree of divorce or separate maintenance, they must not be members of the same household at the time the payment is made.*[15] If the parties are not legally separated, payments under a written separation agreement[16] or a support decree[17] may constitute alimony even though the parties are members of the same household.[18] Presumably, the "same household" prohibition reflects a congressional concern that spouses who may go through "tax divorces" to avoid the so-called "marriage penalty"[19] but continue to

---

[11] *See* I.R.C. § 71(b)(2)(B), (C).

[12] T.C. Memo 1996-253. Compare *Leventhal v. Comm'r*, T.C. Memo 2000-92, holding that letters signed by the attorneys representing each of the parties to a divoce constituted a written separation agreement.

[13] I.R.C. § 71(b)(1)(B).

[14] See Temporary Regulation § 1.71-1T(b), Q&A-8, for the details of such designation.

[15] I.R.C. § 71(b)(1)(C).

[16] I.R.C. § 71(b)(2)(B).

[17] I.R.C. § 71(b)(2)(C).

[18] Temp. Treas. Reg. § 1.71-1T(b), Q&A-9.

[19] *See* Boyter v. Commissioner, 74 T.C. 989 (1980). The "marriage penalty" refers to the fact that where both spouses are employed, their joint tax liability may be greater than their tax liability in the aggregate would have been if they filed as unmarried individuals. In the 2001 Tax Act, Congress took the first steps in eliminating the marriage penalty problem by increasing the basic standard deduction for married taxpayers over a 5-year period, starting in 2005, so as to be twice the amount for unmarried individuals; and by widening the 15% tax bracket for married taxpayers filing joint returns over a 4-year

live together, should be treated the same as never-married individuals living together, and should not be allowed to engage in income-shifting between themselves.

(6) *The payor spouse must have no obligation to make payments for any period after the death of the payee spouse.*[20] This rule is a reflection of an underlying congressional policy that alimony is in the nature of spousal support, and that the alimony inclusion and deduction provisions should generally be restricted to support-type payments. Payments continuing beyond the death of the payee spouse smack of property settlement arrangements, for which no deduction is allowed (and no inclusion required).[21] Expressed another way, where the payor spouse is required to transfer a portion of his or her income to a spouse or former spouse, it is appropriate that the transferred income is, in essence, ultimately taxed, through Sections 71 and 215, to the payee spouse, not the payor. By contrast, where the transfer is part of a property division, *i.e.*, a transfer of property as opposed to income, the rationale no longer exists for shifting the tax burden that arose out of the payor's income. Sections 71 and 215, of course, do not impose any tracing requirement with respect to cash payments, but payments that may be required for periods after the payee's death are in effect deemed to lack this implicitly-required spousal support element or potential. The statute is satisfied if such post-death liability is barred pursuant to local law. Thus, either the language of the divorce decree itself or conditions imposed by state law can satisfy the requirement of Section 71(b)(1)(D).

In determining whether payments satisfy Section 71(b)(1)(D), courts have conducted a two-part inquiry. First, courts have looked for an unambiguous condition terminating the payments; that condition may be found either in the plain language of the divorce decree itself or as imposed by operation of state law. Second, where there is no unambiguous termination condition in either the divorce decree or state law, courts have independently evaluated "the language of the decree" as a whole to determine whether the payments in question satisfy Section 71(b)(1)(D). If neither part is satisfied, the payments do not constitute alimony.[22]

---

period, starting in 2005, so as to be twice the size of the tax bracket for unmarried individuals. The 2003 Tax Act increased the basic standard deduction to twice that for unmarried individuals for 2003 and 2004 and for those same years also widened the 15% bracket for married taxpayer's filing jointly so as to be twice the size of that bracket for unmarried individuals. The Working Families Tax Relief Act of 2004 made the 2003 increase in the standard deduction and the 2003 widening of the 15% bracket effective for taxable years 2005-2010. This marriage penalty relief was made permanent by the American Taxpayer Relief Act of 2012.

[20] I.R.C. § 71(b)(1)(D).

[21] H.R. Rep. No. 98-432, Part II, p. 1496 states: "In order to prevent the deduction of amounts which are in effect transfers of property unrelated to the support needs of the recipient, the bill provides that a payment qualifies as alimony only if the payor . . . has no liability to make any such payment for any period following the death of the payee spouse."

[22] Hoover v. Commissioner, 102 F.3d 842 (6th Cir. 1996). Where "state family law is ambiguous as to the termination of payments upon the death of the payee, a federal court will not engage in complex, subjective inquiries under state law; rather the court will read the divorce instrument and make its own determination based on the language of the document." *Hoover*, at 846. *See also* Johanson v. Commissioner. 541 F.3d 973 (9th Cir. 2008).

In *Webb v. Commissioner*,[23] the Tax Court applied the section to deny alimony characterization to a cash payment the taxpayer made to his ex-wife pursuant to the terms of their separation agreement. Under that agreement, the taxpayer specifically agreed to pay his ex-wife a lump-sum amount of $200,000 and an additional $15,000 to enable her to purchase an automobile. In another part of the agreement entitled "Maintenance," he agreed to pay her $40,000 per year for five years. These maintenance payments were to cease on the death of either party. Simultaneously with the execution of the agreement, the taxpayer paid his ex-wife the $215,000 and claimed a Section 215 alimony deduction; she excluded the payment. The Tax Court concluded that the $215,000 payment did not constitute alimony because it created a liability which would not have terminated with the ex-wife's death. According to the court, were she to have died before the taxpayer paid her the $215,000, her estate could have enforced his obligation to pay, and such an obligation to pay does not comport with the requirements for alimony under Section 71. That the payment was actually made simultaneously with the execution of the agreement did not change the result: "To conclude otherwise would cause any cash payment made simultaneously with the issuance of a decree or the execution of an agreement necessarily to be treated as alimony even though the provisions of the decree or agreement clearly reveal that the payments were lump sum payments for purposes other than support or maintenance."[24]

Stedman v. Commissioner[25] presents a situation much more common than that presented in *Webb*. In *Stedman*, the divorce court ordered the taxpayer to pay his ex-spouse's attorney fees, which amounted to more than $100,000. The court ordered that these fees be paid in monthly installments out of the taxpayer's Civil Service Retirement System benefits. Taxpayer claimed a Section 215 deduction for the monthly payments he made pursuant to the court order. The Tax Court concluded the payments were not deductible because they did not satisfy the requirement of Section 71(b)(1)(D) and thus did not constitute alimony. The court reasoned that, because neither the court order nor applicable state law provided for the termination of the monthly payments upon the death of the ex-spouse, the taxpayer could be required to continue to make the attorney fee payments if his ex-spouse died before those payments had been made in full. Presumably, in view of *Webb*, the court would have reached the same conclusion if the taxpayer had been ordered to pay the attorney fees in a lump sum. As in *Webb*, the taxpayer's ex-spouse might die before the lump sum payment was made. Because, in that circumstance, the attorney fees would be payable even after the death of the ex-spouse, it could not satisfy the requirement of Section 71(b)(1)(D).

In *Okerson v. Commissioner*,[26] the taxpayer was ordered to pay alimony to his former wife over a period of approximately 10 years. Although the decree provided that the alimony payments would terminate upon her death, it also provided that any remaining installments were to be paid for the education of the children of the parties. Similarly, the taxpayer was ordered to make further alimony payments over

---

[23] T.C. Memo 1990-540.

[24] *Id.*

[25] T.C. Memo. 2008-239.

[26] 123 T.C. 258 (2004).

several years to his former wife's lawyer, on behalf of his former wife and on account of her legal fees. These alimony payments would also terminate upon her death, but in that event any remaining installments were to be paid directly to the lawyer. The Tax Court held that both sets of alimony payments violated the "substitution payment" provision of Section 71(b)(1)(D), which requires that there not only be no liability to make payments after the death of the payee spouse, but also that there be no liability to make any other payment as a substitute therefor. The potential obligations that arose in the event of the former wife's death — payments for the children's education and the payments to be made directly to the lawyer — were held to be prohibited substitute payments, and accordingly the payments in the decree designated as alimony failed to qualify as alimony.

§ 36.02 CHILD SUPPORT

§ 71(c). Payments to support children.

(1) In general. Subsection (a) shall not apply to that part of any payment which the terms of the divorce or separation instrument fix (in terms of an amount of money or a part of the payment) as a sum which is payable for the support of children of the payor spouse.

(2) Treatment of certain reductions related to contingencies involving child. For purposes of paragraph (1), if any amount specified in the instrument will be reduced —

(A) on the happening of a contingency specified in the instrument related to a child (such as attaining a specified age, marrying, dying, leaving school, or a similar contingency), or

(B) at a time which can clearly be associated with a contingency of a kind specified in subparagraph (A),

an amount equal to the amount of such reduction will be treated as an amount fixed as payable for the support of children of the payor spouse.

In addition to satisfying the requirements described above, a cash payment must also avoid classification as child support in order to qualify as alimony.[27] Child support payments, of course, merely reflect pre-existing parental support responsibilities for which the Code grants no deduction, except through the Section 151 dependency exemption; the continuing parent-child relationship, unlike the marital relationship, is not terminated by the divorce decree. Thus, a payment "fixed" as child support by the divorce or separation instrument is not alimony.[28] Prior to 1984, the Supreme Court, in *Commissioner v. Lester*,[29] held that a written separation agreement providing for specified reductions in the payments to the payee spouse as each of the spouses' children marries, dies or becomes emancipated did not "fix" the amount of the specified reductions as child support. A payment that clearly seemed to constitute child support might thus have received alimony treatment. The 1984 Act, however, deliberately reversed the *Lester* decision by treating certain

---

[27] I.R.C. § 71(c).

[28] I.R.C. § 71(c)(1).

[29] 366 U.S. 299 (1961).

reductions in payments as amounts fixed for child support.[30] Thus, for example, where a divorce decree provided that a taxpayer's "alimony" payments of $150 per week to his ex-wife were to "continue to her death, remarriage or until the youngest child reaches 18 years, whichever first occurs," and thereafter cease, the Tax Court held the payments did not constitute alimony.[31] The legislative reversal is consistent with the policy decision that spouses should be able to deny alimony status to payments that would otherwise qualify,[32] but not create alimony out of payments that manifest too clearly a purpose other than spousal support.[33]

The regulations identify two situations in which payments will be presumed to be reduced at a time clearly associated with the happening of a contingency related to a child of the payor.[34] The first situation is where payments are to be reduced not more than 6 months before or after the date the child is to attain the age 18, 21, or the local age of majority. The second situation is where the payments are to be reduced on two or more occasions which occur not more than one year before or after a different child of the payor spouse attains a certain age between the ages of 18 and 24. The presumption in the two situations "may be rebutted . . . by showing that the time at which the payments are to be reduced was determined independently of any contingencies relating to the children of the payor."[35]

> **Example 1:** Assume Frank and Maureen have two children, Patrick, who was 14 years old on February 1, Year 1; and Katie, who was 13 years old on September 15, Year 1. Their written agreement provides that the parents will have joint custody of the children who will reside with Maureen, and also provides that Frank will pay Maureen $1,500 per month as alimony beginning in Year 1. The alimony payments, however, are to cease at the end of Year 4.
>
> **Analysis:** If alimony ceases at the end of Year 4, there is a "first situation" problem because Patrick will be 17 years 11 months old at that time. Thus, the alimony will be reduced within 6 months of Patrick attaining age 18. Therefore, the $1,500 alimony per month will be presumed to be for the payment of child support unless Frank can present evidence to rebut the presumption.
>
> **Example 2:** Same facts as in Example 1 except the alimony will cease at the end of Year 6.
>
> **Analysis:** Again, there is a "first situation" problem because Katie will be 18 years 3.5 months old at the time alimony ceases. The regulation, however, provides that "the presumption in [situation 1] will be rebutted conclusively if the reduction is a complete cessation of alimony or separate maintenance payments during the sixth post separation year . . . or upon

---

[30] I.R.C. § 71(c)(2).

[31] Fosberg v. Comm'r, T.C. Memo. 1992-713.

[32] *See* I.R.C. § 71(b)(1)(B).

[33] *See, e.g.,* I.R.C. § 71(b)(1)(D), (c), (f).

[34] Temp. Treas. Reg. § 1.71-1T(c), Q&A-18.

[35] *Id.*

the expiration of a 72-month period."[36] The "six post-separation years" are the "six consecutive calendar years beginning with the first calendar year in which the payor pays to the payee an alimony or separate maintenance payment."[37] Thus, the presumption is conclusively rebutted in this example and the $1,500 monthly payments will be treated as alimony.

Example 3: Same facts as Example 1 except that alimony payments are reduced to $1,000 per month at the end of Year 4 and cease at the end of Year 6.

Analysis: The reduction of alimony by $1,000 in Year 4 will create the same "first situation" problem discussed in Example 1. $1,000 of the monthly alimony payments will be presumed to be fixed for child support and therefore will not constitute alimony. There is also a "second situation" problem presented in this case because of the cessation of alimony in Year 6. Patrick will be 17 years 11 months old at the end of Year 4 when the first reduction occurs; Katie will be 18 years 3.5 months old when the alimony ceases at the end of Year 6. Thus, reductions in payment have occurred on two occasions not more than one year before or after a different child of Maureen attains the age of 18 (or any other age between 18 years and 18 years 11 months.) Thus, the reductions presumptively constitute child support payments. Note that the conclusive rebuttal rule applied in Example 2 is not applicable in a "second situation" scenario such as this one. As reflected in this example, the characterization of payments as either alimony or child support can be controlled by careful drafting of the divorce settlement agreements.

§ 36.03 EXCESS FRONT-LOADING

§ 71(f). Recomputation where excess front-loading of alimony payments —

(1) **In general. If there are excess alimony payments —**

(A) the payor spouse shall include the amount of such excess payments in gross income for the payor spouse's taxable year beginning in the 3rd post-separation year, and

(B) the payee spouse shall be allowed a deduction in computing adjusted gross income for the amount of such excess payments for the payee's taxable year beginning in the 3rd post-separation year.

(2) **Excess alimony payments.** For purposes of this subsection, the term "excess alimony payments" means the sum of —

(A) the excess payments for the 1st post-separation year, and

(B) the excess payments for the 2nd post-separation year.

(3) **Excess payments for 1st post-separation year.** For purposes of this subsection, the amount of the excess payments for the 1st post-separation year

---

[36] *Id.*

[37] Temp. Treas. Reg. § 1.71-1 T(c), Q&A-21.

is the excess (if any) of —

(A) the amount of the alimony or separate maintenance payments paid by the payor spouse during the 1st post-separation year, over

(B) the sum of —

(i) the average of —

(I) the alimony or separate maintenance payments paid by the payor spouse during the 2nd post-separation year, reduced by the excess payments for the 2nd post-separation year, and

(II) the alimony or separate maintenance payments paid by the spouse during the 3rd post-separation year plus

(ii) $15,000.

(4)   Excess payments for 2nd post-separation year. for purposes of this subsection, the amount of the excess payments for the 2nd post-separation year is —

(A) the amount of the alimony or separate maintenance payments paid by the payor spouse during the 2nd post-separation year, over

(B) the sum of —

(i) the amount of the alimony or separate maintenance payments paid by the payor spouse during the 3rd post-separation year, plus

(ii) $15,000.

. . .

(6)   Post-separation years. For purposes of this subsection, the term "1st post-separation year" means the 1st calendar year in which the payor spouse paid to the payee spouse alimony or separate maintenance payments to which this section applies. The 2nd and 3rd post-separation years shall be the 1st and 2nd succeeding calendar years, respectively.

Cash payments not fixed as child support and complying with the rules previously discussed constitute alimony, includible in the payee's income and deductible to the payor. These rules by themselves leave open the possibility that several years' worth of alimony might be compressed into a single year or two, in order to obtain several years' tax deductions all at once. The rules also leave open the prospect that cash payments could be taxed as alimony even when they are in substance part of a property settlement, part of a division of marital assets, and bear no relationship to spousal support.[38] As a practical matter, property settlements tend to be characterized by relatively large payments over a relatively short period of time — perhaps simply a single lump-sum payment. To limit these payment manipulations, the drafters of the 1984 Act created the excess front-loading rules of Section 71(f) as part of their attempt "to define alimony in a way that would conform to general notions of what type of payments constitute alimony as distinguished from property settlements and to prevent the deduction of large,

---

[38] The spouses could elect non-alimony treatment under Section 71(b)(1)(B) for such payments, but presumably would not do so where alimony treatment would result in a lower combined tax liability.

one-time lump-sum property settlements."[39]

Section 71(f) is basically a recapture provision. Payments characterized as "excess alimony payments," having been included by the payee and deducted by the payor in a prior year, are "recaptured" in the subsequent year. The tax treatment is then reversed: the excess amount is deductible by the payee and includible by the payor. The payor, who is the real target of Section 71(f), is forced to "give back" the excess deduction — excess in the sense that, retroactively, Section 71(f) determines that to some extent the prior alimony treatment was not warranted. Rather than reopen and adjust the tax returns of the payor and payee for the year of payment, however, the give-back occurs in the year the determination of the excess is made. (The tax benefit rule operates in somewhat similar fashion; the payor spouse is giving back in a later year the tax benefit of a prior year. The payee spouse, by contrast, receives a later-year deduction on account of the prior-year excess included in income.)

Under Section 71(f), recapture of excess alimony payments can take place in one year only — the "3rd post-separation year," a term defined in Section 71(f)(6). Recapture cannot occur in any other year.[40]"Excess alimony payments," if any, are determined based on alimony payments in three years — the 1st, 2nd, and 3rd post-separation years. In other words, based on the alimony paid in these three years, it may be determined in year three that excess alimony was paid in years one and two. If so, that excess is recaptured in year three. In 1986, the Joint Committee on Taxation summarized the rule as follows:

> [T]he front-loading alimony rules of Section 71(f) [are designed] to better conform to the current trend of state divorce law to require short term support payments on a theory of "rehabilitative alimony." Under the Act, if the alimony payments in the first year exceed the average payments in the second and third year by more than $15,000, the excess amounts are recaptured in the third year by requiring the payor to include the excess in income and allowing the payee who previously included the alimony in income a deduction for that amount in computing adjusted gross income. A similar rule applies to the extent the payments in the second exceed the payments in the third year by more than $15,000. This rule is intended to prevent persons whose divorce occurs near the end of the year from making a deductible property settlement in the beginning of the next year. Recapture is not required if either party dies or if the payee spouse remarries by the end of the calendar year which is two years after the payments began and payments cease by reason of that event. Also the rule does not apply to temporary support payments (described in sec. 71(b)(2)(C)) or to payments which fluctuate as a result of a continuing liability to pay, for at least three years, a fixed portion or portions of income from the earnings of a business, property or services. The portions of the payor's income which are payable to the payee spouse under this exception

---

[39] General Explanation of the Revenue Provisions of the Tax Reform Act of 1984, Jt. Comm. on Taxation, p. 714.

[40] I.R.C. § 71(f)(1).

may vary as the payor's income varies, so long as the percentages are themselves fixed in the instrument.[41]

As the statutory formula indicates, the recapture rule will not apply if the payments do not decrease by more than $15,000 each year during the three year period. In effect, Congress has created a safe harbor which presumably renders the recapture rule inapplicable to the great majority of alimony awards.

Example 1: Richard makes alimony payments totaling $150,000 to his ex-wife, Helen, in 2011, the first post-separation year. Richard makes no payments in 2012 and 2013. In 2011, Richard deducted the $150,000 he paid in alimony and Helen included the $150,000 in alimony she received. Will any of the alimony payments made by Richard be recaptured?

Analysis: The excess alimony payment for 2012, the second post-separation year, is $0 as there were no alimony payments in 2012. The excess alimony payments for 2011, the first post-separation year, were $135,000, *i.e.*, the excess of the alimony paid in 2011 ($150,000) over the sum of (1) the average of the alimony paid in second and third post-separation years ($0); and (2) $135,000 ($150,000 − $15,000 = $135,000.) Richard must report $135,000 in his income for 2013 as excess alimony payments and Helen may deduct $135,000 from her income in that year.

Example 2: Richard makes alimony payments of $75,000 to his ex-wife, Helen, in 2011, the first post-separation year. In 2012, he pays $50,000 and in 2013, he pays $25,000. Richard deducts the alimony paid and Helen includes in gross income the alimony she received from Richard. Will any of the alimony payments be recaptured?

Analysis: In 2013, $37,500 is recaptured and reported in Richard's gross income and that same amount is deductible by Helen in computing her adjusted gross income. Excess payments in 2012, the second post-separation year, amount to $10,000, *i.e.*, the amount of alimony paid in 2012 ($50,000) less (a) the sum of the alimony paid in 2013 ($25,000) and (b) $15,000. Excess payments in 2011, the first post-separation year, amount to $27,500. The latter figure is arrived at by first computing the average of:

(a) $40,000 — the payments made in the second post-separation year ($50,000) less the excess payment of $10,000 determined above; and

(b) $25,000 — the payments made in the third post separation year.

The average is $32,500, *i.e.*, $65,000/2. Pursuant to Section 71(f)(3), that average is increased by $15,000 and the resulting total of $47,500 is then subtracted from the payments made in the first post-separation year ($75,000) to arrive at the excess payments ($27,500) for the first post-separation year. The sum of the excess payments for the first-post

---

[41] Explanation to the Technical Corrections Provisions of the Tax Reform Act of 1986, Jt. Comm. on Taxation, pp. 118-19. The 1986 Act modified the more complex front-loading alimony rules originally enacted in 1984.

separation year — $27,500 — and the excess payments for the second post-separation year — $10,000 — equals $37,500 and is the amount which Richard must report as income in 2013 and which Helen may deduct.

This recapture rule generally prevents a type of rate arbitrage which former spouses might attempt if one former spouse were in a high tax bracket and the other were in a low tax bracket. Despite the rule, however, taxpayers can nonetheless have alimony treatment for what is in essence a property settlement by simply varying the payments from year to year by no more than $15,000 or by backloading the payments. Of course, the other requirements under Section 71(b) would have to be satisfied, *e.g.*, the payments could not continue after the death of the payee spouse.

Example 3: Assume Richard in Example 2 made alimony payments to Helen in the amount of (a) $50,000 each year; or (b) $60,000 in 2011, $50,000 in 2012, and $40,000 in 2013; or (c) $25,000 in 2011, $50,000 in 2012 and $75,000 in 2013. Would Richard be required to recapture any of the alimony in these various alternatives?

Analysis: In each of these alternatives, as in Examples 1 and 2, Richard would pay a total of $150,000 to Helen over the three-year period. Unlike Examples 1 and 2, however, in each of the alternatives in this example, no recapture income would be reportable by Richard. In (a) the alimony amount remains static and there is thus no front loading, which is what Section 71(f) addresses. In (b), while the payments in 2011 are greater than the payments in 2012 or 2013, the difference from year to year is less than $15,000 — a variance that is permissible under the Section 71(f) formula. In (c) the alimony is backloaded which is permissible — Section 71(f) only addresses front-loading situations.

While the payee has the benefit of an above-the-line deduction in the third post-separation year, this relief will prove illusory if the payee does not have sufficient gross income in that year to enable the payee to utilize fully the deduction. Thus, in Example 1 above, Helen will be entitled to a $135,000 deduction in the third post-separation year. To the extent that Helen does not have at least $135,000 of gross income in that year, the deduction is wasted and the alimony is taxed twice, *i.e.*, Helen will have reported the alimony as income in the first post-separation year and Richard will have been required to report $135,000 of income in the third post-separation year. Helen cannot carry the deduction forward into subsequent years. She must either use it in 2013 or lose it.

Despite the recapture rule, some taxpayers may nonetheless find it worthwhile to front-load alimony and thereby trigger recapture in the third post-separation year.

Example 4: Assume the facts of Example 1 but also assume Richard is in a 35% tax bracket in 2011 but can order his affairs so that he will be in the 25% bracket in 2013.

Analysis: Richard will have had the advantage of a $150,000 deduction when he was in a 35% tax bracket and will have to include $135,000 as a result of the recapture rule when he is in a 25% bracket. The deduction in

2011 of the $135,000 recaptured in 2013 saved Richard $47,250 in taxes while the inclusion of the $35,000 in 2013 costs Richard $33,750.

§ 36.04　ALIMONY TRUSTS

If a divorced or separated spouse (the husband, let us assume) establishes and funds a trust, the income from which is to be paid to the other spouse, Section 682 taxes to the wife, the trust beneficiary, the income from this so-called alimony trust, income which would otherwise be taxable to the husband, under general rules relating to taxation of trust income. No deduction shall be allowed to the husband on account of the trust income taxed to the wife, an appropriate denial because the income in question was never taxed to the husband.[42]

§ 36.05　DEPENDENCY EXEMPTION

§ 151(a).　Allowance of deductions.
In the case of an individual, the exemptions provided by this section shall be allowed as deductions in computing taxable income.

. . .

(c)　Additional exemptions for dependents. An exemption of the exemption amount for each individual who is a dependent (as defined in section 152) of the taxpayer for the taxable year.

(d)　Exemption amount. For purposes of this section —

(1)　In general. Except as otherwise provided in this subsection, the term "exemption amount" means $2,000 [adjusted for inflation]

---

§ 152.　Dependent Defined.

(a)　In general. For purposes of this subtitle, the term "dependent means —

(1) a qualifying child, or

(2) a qualifying relative.

. . .

(c)　Qualifying child. —
For purposes of this section —

(1)　In general. — The term "qualifying child" means, with respect to any taxpayer for any taxable year, an individual —

(A) who bears a relationship to the taxpayer described in paragraph (2),

(B) who has the same principal place of abode as the taxpayer for more than one-half of such taxable year,

(C) who meets the age requirements of paragraph (3), and

(D) who has provided over one-half of such individual's own support for

---

[42] I.R.C. § 215(d).

the calendar year in which the taxable year of the taxpayer begins.

(2)   Relationship. — For purposes of paragraph (1)(A), an individual bears a relationship to the taxpayer described in this paragraph if such individual is —

(A) a child of the taxpayer or a descendant of such child, or

(B) a brother, sister, stepbrother, or stepsister of the taxpayer or a descendent of any such relative.

(3)   Age requirements. —

(A)   In general. — For purposes of paragraph (1)(C), an individual meets the requirements of this paragraph if such individual —

(i) has not attained the age of 19 as of the close of the calendar year in which the taxable year of the taxpayer begins, or

(ii) is a student who has not attained the age of 24 as of the close of such calendar year.

(B)   Special rule for disabled. — In the case of an individual who is permanently and totally disabled (as defined in section 22(e)(3)) at any time during such calendar year, the requirements of subparagraph (A) shall be treated as met with respect to such individual.

(4)   Special rule relating to 2 or more claiming qualified child. —

(A)   In general. — Except as provided in subparagraph (B), if (but for this paragraph) an individual may be and is claimed as a qualifying child by 2 or more taxpayers for a taxable year beginning in the same calendar year, such individual shall be treated as the qualifying child of the taxpayer who is —

(i) a parent of the individual, or

(ii) if clause (i) does not apply, the taxpayer with the highest adjusted gross income for such taxable year.

(B)   More than 1 parent claiming qualified child. — If the parents claiming any qualified child do not file a joint return together, such child shall be treated as the qualifying child of —

(i) the parent with whom the child resided for the longest period of time during the taxable year, or

(ii) if the child resides with both parents for the same amount of time during such taxable year, the parent with the highest adjusted gross income.

(d)   Qualifying relative. —

For purposes of this section —

(1)   In general. — The term "qualifying relative" means, with respect to any taxpayer for any taxable year, an individual —

(A) who bears a relationship to the taxpayer described in paragraph (2),

(B) whose gross income for the calendar year in which such taxable year begins is less than the exemption amount (as defined in section 151(d)),

(C) with respect to whom the taxpayer provides over one-half of the individual's support for the calendar year in which such taxable year begins, and

(D) who is not a qualifying child of such taxpayer or of any other taxpayer for any taxable year beginning in the calendar year in which such taxable year begins.

(2)   Relationship. — For purposes of paragraph (1)(A), an individual bears a relationship to the taxpayer described in this paragraph if such individual is any of the following with respect to the taxpayer:

(A) A child or a descendant of a child.

(B) A brother, sister, stepbrother, or stepsister.

(C) The father or mother, or an ancestor of either.

(D) A stepfather or stepmother.

(E) A son or daughter of a brother or sister of the taxpayer.

(F) A brother or sister of the father or mother of the taxpayer.

(G)   A   son-in-law,   daughter-in-law,   father-in-law,   mother-in-law, brother-in-law, or sister-in-law.

(H) An individual (other than an individual who at any time during the taxable year was the spouse, determined without regard to section 7703, of the taxpayer) who, for the taxable year of the taxpayer, has the same principal place of abode as the taxpayer and is a member of the taxpayer's household.

(e)   Special Rule for Divorced Parents, Etc. —

(1)   In   general. — Notwithstanding   subsection   (c)(1)(B),   (c)(4),   or (d)(1)(C), if —

(A) a child receives over one-half of the child's support during the calendar year from the child's parents,

(i) who are divorced or legally separated under a decree of divorce or separate maintenance,

(ii) who are separated under a written separation agreement, or

(iii) who live apart at all times during the last 6 months of the calendar year, and —

(B) such child is in the custody of 1 or both of the child's parents for more than one-half of the calendar year, such child shall be treated as being the qualifying child or qualifying relative of the noncustodial parent for a calendar year if the requirements described in paragraph (2) or (3) are met.

(2)   Exception where custodial parent releases claim to exemption for the year. — For purposes of paragraph (1), the requirements described in this paragraph are met with respect to any calendar year if —

(A) the custodial parent signs a written declaration (in such manner and form as the Secretary may by regulations prescribe) that such custodial parent will not claim such child as a dependent for any taxable year beginning in such calendar year, and

(B) the noncustodial parent attaches such written declaration to the noncustodial parent's return for the taxable year beginning during such calendar year.

. . .

(4) **Custodial parent and noncustodial parent.** — For purposes of this subsection —

(A) **Custodial parent.** — The term "custodial parent" means the parent having custody for the greater portion of the calendar year.

(B) **Noncustodial parent.** — The term "noncustodial parent" means the parent who is not the custodial parent.

In the case of a child of divorced or separated parents, the child will ordinarily be a dependent of the custodial parent, as a "qualifying child" of that parent, or, in other words, the parent having custody of the child for the greater part of the year will ordinarily be entitled to the dependency exemption.[43] In 2008 the Treasury finalized regulations providing detailed guidance regarding determination of the "custodial parent" and "noncustodial parent." In general, "the custodial parent is the parent with whom the child resides for the greater number of nights during the calendar year, and the noncustodial parent is the parent who is not the custodial · parent. . . . [A] child resides with a parent for a night if the child sleeps (i) at the residence of that parent (whether or not the parent is present); or (ii) in the company of the parent, when the child does not sleep at a parent's residence (for example, the parent and child are on vacation together)."[44] The regulations address a number of special circumstances, including situations where a parent works at night.[45] The regulations also provide that if a child is in the custody of one or both parents for more than one-half of the calendar year, and the child resides with each parent an equal number of nights during the calendar year, the parent "with the higher adjusted gross income for the calendar year is treated as the custodial parent."[46]

Prior to the amendment of Section 152(e) in 1984, there was a special rule under which the noncustodial parent could be entitled to the exemption if he or she provided, or was treated as providing, more support to the child than was provided by the custodial parent. As a result of this special rule, it was not uncommon that both the custodial and noncustodial parent, based on support provided, claimed the dependency exemption. Prior law thus could foster uncertainty, put each parent to the test of measuring and documenting the support provided, and involve the Service in what was essentially a parental dispute. The aim of the 1984 amendments to Section 152(e) was to put an end to these uncertainties and disputes.

---

[43] I.R.C. § 152(a)(1), (c)(1)(B), (c)(4)(B); Temp. Treas. Reg. § 1.152-4T(a), Q&A-1. A "qualifying child" must also meet certain age limits, and must not have provided over one-half of his or her own support for the year. I.R.C. § 152(b)(1)(C), (D), (b)(3). A tie-breaker based on highest adjusted gross income is provided where the child has resided with both parents for the same amount of time. I.R.C. § 152(b)(4). *See* Notice 2006-86, 2006-41 I.R.B. 1.

[44] Treas. Reg. § 1.152-4(d).

[45] Treas. Reg. § 1.152-4(d)(5).

[46] Treas. Reg. § 1.152-4(d)(4).

Under the current version of Section 152, the custodial parent receives the exemption even though the noncustodial parent may have provided more support than the custodial parent.[47] The noncustodial parent is ordinarily allowed the exemption only if the custodial parent has released the claim to the exemption in writing.[48] The release can be permanent or cover one or more years, and a copy must be attached to the noncustodial parent's tax return for each year the exemption is sought.[49] Certain threshold requirements must be met for the release to be effective: the parents must be divorced or separated under a decree or written agreement or live apart for the last six months of the year; they must provide more than half of the child's support, and they must have custody of the child for over half the year.[50] But as long as those requirements are met, the dependency exemption may thus be allocated to the noncustodial parent by agreement of the parents, which provides some additional tax flexibility to them. Other exceptions to the general rule awarding the dependency exemption to the custodial parent are provided for "multiple support agreements" and certain pre-1985 decrees or agreements.[51] As a practical matter, of course, there is usually no question as to parental entitlement to the exemption, and Section 152 provides the rules for determining which parent can claim it. For the noncustodial parent to claim the exemption, however, it is essential that the written declaration be obtained. A provision in the divorce decree awarding the dependency exemption to the noncustodial parent will not suffice.[52]

§ 36.06 FILING STATUS

The filing status of divorced or separated parents has tax significance. For example, the tax rates for heads of household are significantly lower than those for unmarried individuals (other than surviving spouses and heads of household).[53] Generally, an unmarried parent, not a surviving spouse, who maintains a home that satisfies a principal-place-of-abode test for a qualifying child of the individual or for certain other dependents or relatives, will be entitled to "head of household" status.[54] A custodial parent who has head of household status does not lose it, and the noncustodial parent does not achieve it, by virtue of the release of the claim to the dependency exemption under Section 152(e). (Note also that a custodial parent who releases the claim may also remain eligible for the child and dependent care credit and earned income credit.)[55] As to whether an individual is "not married" at

---

[47] I.R.C. § 152(e)(1).

[48] I.R.C. § 152(e)(2).

[49] Temp. Treas. Reg. § 1.152-4T.

[50] I.R.C. § 152(e)(1).

[51] I.R.C. § 152(e)(3), (5).

[52] See, e.g., Curello v. Comm'r, T.C. Summ. Op. 2005-23, noting that "State courts by their decisions cannot determine issues of Federal tax law," and the "language in a divorce decree purportedly giving a taxpayer the right to an exemption does not entitle the taxpayer to the exemption if the signature requirement of § 152(e) is not met."

[53] I.R.C. § 1(b), (c).

[54] I.R.C. § 2(b).

[55] I.R.C. §§ 21(e)(5), 32(c)(1)(A).

the close of the tax year, as required for head of household status, see the provisions relating to marital status in Sections 2(b)(2), 2(c), and 7703(6).

§ 36.07 PROPERTY TRANSFERS

§ 1041.   Transfers of property between spouses or incident to divorce.

(a) General rule. No gain or loss shall be recognized on a transfer of property from an individual to (or in trust for the benefit of)—

(1) a spouse, or

(2) a former spouse, but only if the transfer is incident to the divorce.

(b) Transfer treated as gift; transferee has transferor's basis. In the case of any transfer of property described in subsection (a)—

(1) for purposes of this subtitle, the property shall be treated as acquired by the transferee by gift, and

(2) the basis of the transferee in the property shall be the adjusted basis of the transferor.

(c) Incident to divorce. For purposes of subsection (a)(2), a transfer of property is incident to the divorce if such transfer —

(1) occurs within 1 year after the date on which the marriage ceases, or

(2) is related to the cessation of the marriage.

In *United States v. Davis*,[56] the Supreme Court held a taxpayer's transfer of appreciated property to his former wife, pursuant to their property settlement agreement, in return for her release of her marital rights produced recognized taxable gain to the transferor-husband. The transferee-wife, in turn, took a fair market value basis in the property.[57]

In one sense, the *Davis* result was unremarkable. The transfer of appreciated property in satisfaction of an obligation ordinarily is a taxable event to the transferor, and *Davis* could be seen as an application of that principle. However, the *Davis* rule had its critics. For one thing, the tax treatment of the transferor appeared harsh; the gain charged to the transferor seemed to be phantom gain. The tax consequences of the divorce, moreover, could vary according to the form of property ownership. For example, in contrast to the *Davis* result when appreciated property owned by one spouse was transferred to the other, no taxable gain resulted where the parties equally divided community property, or where jointly-held property was partitioned.

In addition, the *Davis* rule presented both a trap for taxpayers unaware of the tax consequence of their transfers, and also an enforcement problem for the government — transferors with recognized gain might overlook or decline to report

---

[56] 370 U.S. 65 (1962).

[57] Moreover, subsequent to *Davis*, the Service ruled that the release of marital rights in return for property resulted in no realized gain or loss to the releasing spouse. Rev. Rul. 67-221, 1967-2 C.B. 63. The Service apparently viewed the spouse as having a basis in her marital rights equal to the fair market value of those rights.

the gain, whereas transferees could properly take a fair market value basis in the transferred property. The predictable consequences were confusion and litigation, followed by efforts by a number of states to tailor their divorce and property laws so as to make property transfers on divorce nontaxable.[58] Essentially, divorce was simply regarded by many as an inappropriate occasion to tax the built-up gain in property that was, after all, not being transferred outside the two-spouse community.

One of the important changes wrought by the 1984 Act, therefore, was the legislative reversal of *Davis* by the enactment of Section 1041. Under Section 1041, no gain or loss is recognized on a property transfer between spouses or incident to divorce. The transfer instead is treated as a gift, with the transferee taking the transferor's basis.[59] The significance of Section 1041 thus extends well beyond the divorce tax area. It applies not only to transfers "incident to divorce" but to any transfer of property between spouses, whether in the form of a gift, or a sale or exchange at arm's length.[60] (Special rules apply where the transferee spouse is a nonresident alien, or where there is a transfer in trust of property with liabilities in excess of basis.[61]) Section 1041 reflects a congressional policy that transfers between spouses are, in effect, transfers within a single economic unit, and accordingly, should not be taxed; this policy is then extended to encompass transfers incident to divorce as well, as part of an effort to keep tax laws "as unintrusive as possible with respect to relations between spouses."[62]

Notwithstanding the effort, the tax laws, of course, do intrude on relations between divorcing spouses. Property transfers incident to divorce may be nontaxable, but they carry with them significant tax consequences. Since neither gain nor loss is recognized, and the transferor's basis carries over to the transferee, the parties effectively determine who bears the *future* tax burden in appreciated property, and who receives the *future* tax benefit on property with a value less than its basis, when they decide how their separately-owned and jointly-owned property is divided. For example, two items of property may each be worth $1,000, but if one has a basis of $100 and the other a basis of $2,000, their "values" are potentially quite different. Likewise, both properties may be worth the same amount and have the same basis but one asset if sold may give rise to long term capital gain and the other asset if sold may result in ordinary income, *e.g.*, a Section 1245 asset.

> **Example 1:** Frank and Maureen jointly own some ABC stock (fair market value of $30,000, adjusted basis of $45,000) and a parcel of land (fair market value of $60,000, basis of $20,000 and currently subject to a $30,000 mortgage). Pursuant to their divorce decree, Frank transfers to Maureen his interest in the land, subject to the mortgage, and Maureen transfers to Frank her interest in the ABC stock. Three years later, Frank sells the

---

[58] *See generally* H.R. Rep. 98-432, 98th Cong., 2d Sess., p. 1491.

[59] I.R.C. § 1041(a), (b). Temp. Treas. Reg. § 1.1041–1T(d), Q&A-10, –11.

[60] Temp. Treas. Reg. § 1.1041–1T(a), Q&A-2. Special rules apply where the transferee spouse is a nonresident alien, or where there is a transfer in trust of property with liabilities in excess of basis. § 1041(d)(3).

[61] I.R.C. § 1041(d), (e)

[62] H.R. Rep. 98-432, 98th Cong., 2d Sess., pp. 1491–2.

ABC stock for $40,000, and Maureen sells the land for $10,000 in cash, but subject to the $30,000 mortgage. What are the tax consequences to Maureen and Frank?

Analysis: No gain or loss will be recognized by Frank and Maureen on the transfers pursuant to the divorce. The nonrecognition rule of Section 1041 is applicable even if the transferred property is subject to liabilities which exceed the adjusted basis of the property as in this case.[63] As a result of the transfer, Frank's basis in the ABC stock is $45,000, *i.e.*, Section 1041(b)(2) provides that the basis shall be the adjusted basis of the transferor. The fact that the adjusted basis of the stock is greater than its value makes no difference.[64] (Compare this basis rule to that of Section 1015 which negates the transfer of built-in loss in a gift situation.) When Frank sells the ABC stock for $40,000, he will be entitled to claim a $5,000 capital loss deduction subject to the limitations of Section 1211(b).[65]

Using the same analysis, Maureen will have a $20,000 basis in the land. She will have a $20,000 gain on the land when she sells it for $10,000 cash and the purchaser takes it subject to the $30,000 mortgage (her amount realized will be $40,000).

Example 2: Assume the facts of Example 1 except, instead of transferring to Maureen his interest in the land, Frank pays Maureen $15,000 for her interest in the ABC stock and $15,000 for her interest in the land. Frank later sells the stock for $40,000 and the land for $10,000 subject to the $30,000 mortgage. What are the tax consequences to Maureen and Frank?

Analysis: Even though Frank may regard the transactions with Maureen as sales, they are subject to the rules of Section 1041 and Frank will therefore be treated as acquiring Maureen's interests in the stock and land by gift. Thus, Frank will have a $45,000 basis in the stock and will have a $20,000 basis in the land. When he sells the stock, he will have a $5,000 loss; when he sells the land he will have $20,000 of gain just as Maureen did in Example 1.[66]

Example 3: Pursuant to their divorce decree, Frank transferred to Maureen ownership of a truck which he had purchased for $30,000 and used in his business for a number of years. Frank had completely depreciated the truck and thus had a $0 adjusted basis in the truck. At the time of the transfer, the truck was valued at $15,000. Maureen used the truck for personal purposes for one year and then sold the truck for $12,000. What are the tax consequences to Maureen and Frank?

---

[63] Treas. Reg. § 1.1041-1TQ&A 12.

[64] Treas. Reg. § 1.1041-1TQ&A 11.

[65] I.R.C. §§ 165(c)(2), 165(f), 1211(b).

[66] See *Godlewski v. Comm'r*, 90 T.C. 200 (1988), holding that even though a taxpayer paid cash for a one-half interest in certain property, Section 1041 does not provide for a cost basis but rather for a carryover basis, *i.e.*, the "purchaser" takes the same basis that the transferor/seller had in the property.

> **Analysis:** Frank will have no gain on the transfer of the truck. Maureen will take a $0 basis in the truck. When she sells the truck for $12,000, she will recognize $12,000 of gain. Because the truck is Section 1245 property, *i.e.*, tangible personal property which has been subject to depreciation, Maureen will be required to report all $12,000 of gain as ordinary income. In other words, the Section 1245 taint carried over to Maureen.[67]

Consider another example, drawn from the temporary regulations, involving liabilities:

> **Example 4:** Assume Frank owns a vacant lot with a basis of $5,000 and a fair market value of $20,000. In contemplation of divorce, Frank borrows $15,000, using the property as security for the loan. Incident to divorce, Frank transfers the property to Maureen subject to the liability.

> **Analysis:** Even though the liability exceeds Frank's basis in the property, he recognizes no gain on the transfer pursuant to Section 1041(a), and Maureen takes a basis in the property of only $5,000 under Section 1041(b).[68]

Section 1041(c) defines "incident to divorce" as encompassing transfers occurring within one year after the date on which the marriage ceases or transfers that are related to the cessation of the marriage. In providing this definition, Congress clearly recognized that some property transfers associated with a divorce may occur some time after the divorce has taken place. There may be a myriad of reasons why property could not be transferred by the spouses contemporaneously with the divorce, *e.g.*, title problems. Note that any transfer between ex-spouses occurring within one year after a divorce will be treated as "incident to the divorce" and therefore subject to Section 1041 even though the transfer is unrelated to the divorce. The regulations provide guidance regarding the meaning of "related to the cessation of the marriage" as used in Section 1041(c):

> A transfer of property is treated as related to the cessation of the marriage if the transfer is pursuant to a divorce or separation instrument . . . and the transfer occurs not more than 6 years after the date on which the marriage ceases. Any transfer not pursuant to a divorce or separation instrument and any transfer occurring more than 6 years after the cessation of the marriage is presumed to be not related to the cessation of the marriage. This presumption may be rebutted only by showing that the transfer was made to effect the division of property owned by the former spouses at the time of the cessation of the marriage.[69]

> **Example:** Assume a divorce decree requires Frank to transfer to Maureen one-half of the assets of a business they jointly owned. The transfer does not occur immediately because the parties engage in a protracted action

---

[67] See Chapter 33, *supra*, regarding depreciation recapture.

[68] Temp. Treas. Reg. § 1.1041-1T(d), QTemp. Treas. Reg. § 1.1041-1T(d), Q&A-12.

[69] Treas. Reg. § 1.1041-1T, Q&A-7.

regarding the valuation of the property. The assets are finally transferred to Maureen five years after the divorce decree is entered. Will the transfer qualify under Section 1041?

Analysis: The transfer of assets under these circumstances will qualify for Section 1041 nonrecognition as being "related to the cessation of the marriage." If the transfer had occurred more than six years after the entry of the divorce decree, Section 1041 would still apply given the language of the regulation.

If a transfer of property by one ex-spouse to another falls outside of Section 1041, the *Davis* rule discussed above should apply.

The statute, broad as it is, does have its limits. For example, it encompasses property transfers, but not transfers of services.[70]

Although the Service at one time indicated that Section 1041 did "not shield from recognition income that is ordinarily recognized upon the assignment of that income to another taxpayer,"[71] it has since concluded that Section 1041 generally overrides assignment of income principles that would normally attribute the income generated by property to the owner of the property.[72]

The temporary regulations under Section 1041 also provide that, in some circumstances, a transfer of property "on behalf of a spouse" to a third party may qualify under Section 1041.[73] The regulation identifies qualifying transfers to third parties as those where the transfer is required by the divorce or separation instrument or is made pursuant to written request of (or written consent or ratification by) the non-transferring spouse.[74] When the regulation applies, the transfer on behalf of a spouse is recharacterized as (1) a transfer from the transferring spouse to the nontransferring spouse, followed by (2) a transfer by the non-transferring spouse to the third party.

In addition, regulations applying Section 1041 address property transfers in the specialized context of corporate redemptions of stock.[75] Under well established corporate tax law, if Shareholder A has a "primary and unconditional" obligation to purchase the stock of Shareholder B, and, if in lieu of such purchase, the corporation instead redeems the stock of Shareholder B, the corporation's redemption of B's stock will be treated as a "constructive distribution" to A, typically resulting in dividend income to Shareholder A.[76] Suppose, however, Shareholder A and Shareholder B are husband and wife and own all of the stock of the corporation in question. Incident to their divorce, the corporation redeems the stock of

---

[70] Temp. Treas. Reg. § 1.1041-1T(a), Q&A-4.

[71] Rev. Rul. 87-112, 1987-2 C.B. 207.

[72] Rev. Rul. 2002-22, 2002-1 C.B. 849.

[73] *See* § 1.1041-1T, Q&A-9. Qualifying transfers are those where the transfer to a third party is required by the divorce or separation instrument or is made pursuant to the written request of the non-transferring spouse.

[74] Temp. Treas. Reg. § 1041–1T(c), Q&A-9.

[75] Treas. Reg. § 1.1041-2.

[76] Treas. Reg. § 1.1041-2(a)(2); Rev. Rul. 69-608, 1969-2 C.B. 42.

Shareholder B. If the form of the transaction is respected, the redemption is a taxable event for Shareholder B. By contrast, if the corporation's redemption of the stock tendered by Shareholder B is treated as a transfer "on behalf of" Shareholder A, B will be deemed to have transferred the stock to Shareholder A in a nontaxable Section 1041 transfer, and Shareholder A will have a taxable event, *i.e.*, a "constructive distribution" from the corporation.[77] Any property received by Shareholder B from the corporation in respect of the redeemed stock will be deemed transferred by the corporation to Shareholder A in redemption of Shareholder A's stock and then transferred from Shareholder A to Shareholder B.[78]

Prior to the promulgation of the regulations discussed above, a question that had arisen in several cases — and had produced inconsistent answers — was: What standard should be applied to determine whether Shareholder B's transfer of stock to the corporation in redemption should be treated as a transfer on behalf of Shareholder A?[79] The regulations essentially apply the "primary and unconditional obligation" standard (the "applicable tax law") from corporate tax law to resolve the issue, *i.e.*, if the corporation's redemption of Shareholder B's stock satisfies a primary and unconditional obligation of Shareholder A to purchase the stock, Shareholder B will be treated as engaging in a nontaxable Section 1041 exchange, and Shareholder A will have a constructive distribution from the corporation. Consistent with the policy of providing flexibility in structuring property transfers during marriage and incident to divorce, the regulations include a special rule allowing the parties, by means of a written agreement or in the divorce or separation instrument, to designate whether the redemption will be taxable to the redeeming shareholder-spouse or the nonredeeming shareholder-spouse. In effect, the parties by agreement or decree may elect to apply or not apply the rule drawn from corporate tax law. But, in the absence of agreement or decree, the corporate tax law standard of "primary and unconditional obligation" will govern.[80]

§ 36.08 SPECIAL RULES REGARDING PERSONAL RESIDENCE — SECTION 121

§ 121(d)(3).   Property owned by spouse or former spouse.
For purposes of this section —

(A) **Property transferred to individual from spouse or former spouse.** In the case of an individual holding property transferred to such individual in a transaction described in section 1041(a), the period such individual owns such property shall include the period the transferor owned the property.

(B) **Property used by former spouse pursuant to divorce decree, etc.** Solely for purposes of this section, an individual shall be treated as using property as such individual's principal residence during any period of ownership while such individual's spouse or former spouse is granted use of the property under

---

[77] Treas. Reg. § 1.1041-2(a)(2), (b)(2).

[78] *Id.*

[79] *See, e.g.*, Arnes v. U.S., 981 F.2d 456 (9th Cir. 1992); Arnes v. Comm'r, 102 T.C. 522 (1994); Read v. Comm'r, 114 T.C. 14 (2000).

[80] Treas. Reg. § 1.1041-2(c).

a divorce or separation instrument (as defined in section 71(b)(2)).

As discussed in detail in Chapter 6, Section 121 allows a taxpayer to exclude up to $250,000 of gain on the sale of a principal residence. A married couple filing a joint return may exclude up to $500,000 of gain. To qualify for the exclusion, a taxpayer, during the five year period ending on the date of the sale or exchange, must have owned and used the property as the taxpayer's principal residence for periods aggregating at least two years. Where spouses file a joint return and seek to take advantage of the $500,000 exclusion, only one spouse must meet the ownership requirement; both spouses, however, must meet the use requirement.

In enacting Section 121, Congress provided two special rules applicable to circumstances commonly encountered in divorces. First, Congress provided that, where property is transferred to an individual in a transaction qualifying under Section 1041, the period of ownership of that individual for purposes of Section 121 will include the period the transferor owned the property.[81]

> **Example 1:** Assume Annie and George divorce and agree that, as part of their property settlement, Annie will transfer to George the title to the home in which they had lived for a number of years. Assume also that title to the home was in Annie's name alone, and George sells the home within one year of the divorce. Will George be entitled to the benefit of the Section 121 exclusion?
>
> **Analysis:** But for Section 121(d)(3)(A), George would not have owned the home long enough to satisfy the two year ownership requirement of Section 121. Given Section 121(d)(3)(A), however, George will be deemed to have owned the home during the period when title to the home was in Annie's name alone as well as during the period title was in his name. As a result, George will be entitled to exclude up to $250,000 of gain from the sale as long as George satisfies the other requirements of Section 121, including the use requirement.

The second special rule is specifically applicable to situations where a taxpayer continues to have an ownership interest in a residence but does not live in the residence because, pursuant to a divorce or separation instrument, the taxpayer's spouse or former spouse is granted the use of the residence. Under these circumstances, the taxpayer will be treated as using the residence while the residence is used by the taxpayer's spouse or former spouse.

> **Example 2:** Assume Jeff and Susan divorce and, pursuant to their divorce decree, Susan is entitled to live in the home (owned as tenants in common by Jeff and Susan) until their youngest child attains the age of 18. Assume that six years later their youngest child attains the age of 18, and Susan used the home as her principal residence throughout the six year period. Consistent with the terms of the divorce decree, Jeff and Susan then sell the home and divide the proceeds. Will Jeff be entitled to the benefit of the Section 121 exclusion?

---

[81] I.R.C. § 121(d)(3)(A); Treas. Reg. § 1.121-4(b)(1).

Analysis: Given Section 121(d)(3)(B), Jeff will be deemed to have satisfied the use requirement of Section 121. Assuming Jeff meets all of the other requirements of Section 121, Jeff will be entitled to claim an exclusion of up to $250,000 for the gain attributable to his share of the residence. Susan will also be entitled to the Section 121 exclusion for her share of the gain assuming she satisfies the Section 121 requirements.[82]

§ 36.09   LEGAL EXPENSES

Section 212 allows taxpayers to deduct expenses incurred in producing income and in seeking tax advice. Like Section 162 (allowing a deduction for expenses incurred in carrying on a trade or business), Section 212 is subject to the general rule of Section 262 denying deductions for personal, living, and family expenses. Under the origin-of-the-claim test, legal expenses in connection with a divorce will generally be nondeductible personal expenses; however, subject to the 2% floor rule of Section 67, the cost of tax planning advice is generally regarded as deductible under Section 212, as are the legal expenses attributable to amounts includible in income as alimony.[83]

The leading case in this area is *U.S. v. Gilmore*,[84] In that case, the taxpayer sought to deduct those legal expenses he incurred in his divorce resisting his wife's claims to a share of stock in three corporations in which he was not only the controlling stockholder but also president and managing officer. Taxpayer argued the legal expenses were "business" expenses because they were incurred by him to protect his livelihood as well as his investment. The Court emphasized that in characterizing expenses as "business" or "personal" the focus must be on the origin of the claim with respect to which the expenses were incurred rather than on the potential consequences, *e.g.*, loss of income producing or business property, which would result if the claim were successful. The Court concluded the wife's claims "stemmed entirely from the marital relationship, and not, under any tenable view of things, from income-producing activity." Therefore, no deduction was allowable under Section 212.

---

[82] Treas. Reg. § 1.121-4(b)(2).

[83] *See* Treas. Reg. § 1.262-1(b)(7).

[84] 372 U.S. 39 (1963).

Chapter 37

EFFECT OF DEBT ON BASIS AND AMOUNT REALIZED

Chapter 4 provided an introduction to the concepts of "basis," "adjusted basis," and "amount realized" and the relationship of these concepts to one another, especially where recourse liabilities were involved. Subsequent chapters, *e.g.*, Chapter 14 on depreciation, addressed Code provisions with regard to the application of which these concepts played significant roles. This chapter will further develop the relationship between debt, especially nonrecourse debt, and basis and amount realized.

§ 37.01 *CRANE v. COMMISSIONER*

Crane v. Commissioner[1] is a seminal decision addressing debt, basis, and amount realized. In *Crane*, the taxpayer inherited property encumbered by considerable nonrecourse debt. The taxpayer claimed depreciation deductions based on the fair market value of the property at the time of decedent's death. Later, she sold the property for a small amount of cash and the purchaser took the property subject to the outstanding nonrecourse liabilities. At issue was the amount of gain realized on the sale. The first question the Supreme Court addressed was the taxpayer's basis in the property when she inherited it. Under Section 1014(a), the basis of inherited property acquired from a decedent is equal to the fair market value of the "property" at the date of the decedent's death. The taxpayer contended the basis of the property should have been its fair market value at the decedent's death less the debt encumbering the property. The Commissioner argued, and the Supreme Court agreed, that the fair market value of the property at a decedent's death was its value without any adjustment for outstanding liabilities, including nonrecourse liabilities.

The Court then considered the "amount realized" upon taxpayer's sale of the property and concluded the nonrecourse liabilities taken subject to by the purchaser must be considered part of taxpayer's amount realized. The Court reasoned that, if the debt encumbering the property had been recourse, the taxpayer would have had to treat the purchaser's assumption of that debt as a benefit constituting part of the taxpayer's amount realized. The fact the outstanding debt in *Crane* was nonrecourse made no difference.

Based on *Crane*, two general rules could be stated:

(1)   Liabilities, whether recourse or nonrecourse, a taxpayer assumes, takes
        subject to, or otherwise incurs in the acquisition of property are included

---

[1] 331 U.S. 1 (1947).

in a taxpayer's basis; and

(2)   Liabilities of a seller, whether recourse or nonrecourse, assumed or taken subject to by a purchaser, are included in the seller's amount realized.

In concluding that a seller must include in her amount realized any nonrecourse liability taken subject to by a buyer, the *Crane* court reasoned that "a mortgagor, not personally liable on [a] debt, who sells the property subject to the mortgage and for additional consideration, realizes a benefit in the amount of the mortgage as well as the boot."[2] This statement was qualified, however, by footnote 37 of the opinion stating "Obviously, if the value of property is less than the amount of the mortgage, a mortgagor who is not personally liable cannot realize a benefit equal to the mortgage. Consequently, a different problem might be encountered where a mortgagor abandoned the property or transferred it subject to the mortgage without receiving boot. That is not this case." Footnote 37, probably the most famous footnote in tax history, thus raised a question that remained unresolved until addressed by the Supreme Court in *Commissioner v. Tufts*.[3]

§ 37.02   *COMMISSIONER v. TUFTS*

Footnote 37 was subject to differing interpretations by the courts. The Third Circuit, in *Millar v. Commissioner*,[4] rejected the taxpayer's argument that, as a result of the *Crane* footnote, a seller did not have to include in amount realized the entire amount of nonrecourse indebtedness if that indebtedness exceeded the fair market value of the property. The *Millar* court emphasized that to allow taxpayers to include nonrecourse indebtedness in the basis of property enabled taxpayers to claim large depreciation deductions. To prevent taxpayers from realizing, in effect, a double deduction, a seller had to include in the amount realized the entire amount of any nonrecourse indebtedness encumbering the property sold. With respect to footnote 37, the court noted:

> Footnote 37, if taken literally, might furnish support for the taxpayers' argument that the Supreme Court carved out an exception in the *Crane* holding in circumstances where the value of the property surrendered or exchanged is less than the value of the nonrecourse obligation which is satisfied. However, this Court declines to accept a literal reading of that footnote. . . . [I]t must be remembered that the footnote in *Crane* was *dictum*. Furthermore, the footnote was but a postulate or hypothetical set of facts not before the Court . . . involving a clearly different time and clearly different legal circumstances. . . .[5]

Judge Friendly echoed these same concerns in *Estate of Levine v. Commissioner*,[6] a Second Circuit decision.

---

[2] *Id.* at 14. The additional consideration is referred to as "boot."

[3] 461 U.S. 300 (1983).

[4] 577 F.2d 212 (3d Cir.), *cert. denied*, 439 U.S. 1046 (1978).

[5] *Id.* at 215.

[6] 634 F.2d 12 (2d Cir. 1980).

If nonrecourse mortgages contribute to the basis of property, then they must be included in the amount realized on sale. Any other course would render the concept of basis nonsensical by permitting sellers of mortgaged property to register large tax losses, stemming from an inflated basis and a diminished realization of gain. It would also permit depreciation deductions in excess of a property holder's real investment which could never be subsequently recaptured.[7]

The Fifth Circuit, in its *Tufts* decision,[8] subsequently reversed by the Supreme Court, rejected these concerns. The Fifth Circuit reasoned as follows:

There is an even more compelling reason why the fact that a taxpayer has previously enjoyed the benefit of large depreciation deductions is insufficient to justify an expansion of the definition of amount realized. We see, looking to the Internal Revenue Code, that Congress has already in fact accounted for those previous deductions. According to the Code, "gain" from the sale or other disposition of property is computed by subtracting the "adjusted basis" from the "amount realized. . . ." The "adjusted basis" is the cost of the property adjusted to reflect the depreciation, depletion, and other costs chargeable against the property. Thus, any tax benefits that the taxpayer may have received in the form of prior deductions have already been factored into the gain equation through adjustments to basis. Since those deductions have been accounted for through adjustments to basis, it follows logically that they cannot also support an expansion of the definition of amount realized. To account for those deductions twice in the same equation by expanding the definition of amount realized as well as adjusting basis downward would, we think, be taxing the taxpayer twice on the same component of gain. The Commissioner's reliance on a theory of tax benefit, then, is misplaced. The Code clearly provides for a "recapture" of the prior deductions, but not through its definition of amount realized.[9]

The Fifth Circuit also took exception to the *Crane* court's economic benefit theory:

This economic benefit theory is, we think, seriously flawed in that it is premised on the notion that "an owner of property, mortgaged at a figure less than that at which the property will sell, must and will treat the conditions of the mortgage exactly as if they were his personal obligations." We admit that we initially succumbed to the facile appeal of that notion, but on reflection we are convinced that it rings true only so long as the taxpayer actually wants to keep the property. If the taxpayer decides, for any reason whatsoever, that he no longer wants the burdens and responsibilities that accompany ownership, he can transfer the property to a third party with absolutely no regard to that party's willingness or ability to meet the mortgage obligations, yet rest assured that his other assets cannot be reached. We agree with Professor Bittker:

---

[7] *Id.* at 15.

[8] 651 F.2d 1058 (5th Cir. 1981).

[9] *Id.* at 1060–61.

Relief from a nonrecourse debt is not an economic benefit if it can be obtained only by giving up the mortgaged property. It is analogous to the relief one obtains from local real property taxes by disposing of the property. Like nonrecourse debt, the taxes must be paid to retain the property; but no one would suggest that the disposition of unprofitable property produces an economic benefit equal to the present value of the taxes that will not be paid in the future. Bittker, *Tax Shelters, Nonrecourse Debt, and the Crane Case*, 33 Tax L. Rev. 277, 282 (1978).

We do not deny that Mrs. Crane received *some* benefit: a purchaser had to pay off the mortgage or at least be willing to take the property subject to the mortgage before Mrs. Crane could pocket her $2,500 in equity. We do, however, seriously question whether the full amount of nonrecourse debt is an accurate measure of that benefit.[10]

The conflicting views of the Fifth and Third Circuits were the focus of the Supreme Court's decision in *Tufts*. In *Tufts*, a partnership borrowed $1.85 million on a nonrecourse basis to fund the construction of an apartment complex. The partnership's initial basis in the complex was thus $1.85 million. Because of an economic downturn in the area, the partnership was unable to make payments on the nonrecourse debt forcing the partners to sell the apartment complex to an unrelated third party who took the property subject to the nonrecourse liability. The third party purchaser, who obviously intended to attempt to renegotiate the debt with the lender, paid the partners only a negligible amount for their interest in the complex. Prior to the sale, the partnership had claimed a total of $400,000 in depreciation deductions and thus had a $1,450,000 adjusted basis in the complex. The fair market value of the complex at the time of its sale was $1,400,000 and the outstanding nonrecourse debt remained at $1,850,000. The partners therefore claimed a loss of $50,000, *i.e.*, the difference between the adjusted basis of the complex — $1,450,000 — and its fair market value of $1,400,000. The partners' position, of course, appeared too good to be true. After all, they had invested nothing[11] and had had the benefit of depreciation deductions amounting to $400,000. The Service challenged the taxpayers, arguing that the amount realized on the sale was equal to $1,850,000, the amount of the outstanding nonrecourse debt. [We are disregarding the negligible amount the purchaser paid to the partners.] As a result, rather than a loss, the Service argued that the partnership had a gain of $400,000 (Amount realized of $1,850,000 less adjusted basis of $1,450,000). This gain, of course, would exactly equal the amount of the depreciation deductions the partners had claimed but for which they had made no investment. The Tax Court, relying on the Third Circuit's *Millar* decision, agreed with the Service and upheld the deficiencies it asserted against the partners. The Fifth Circuit reversed the Tax Court on the basis of the reasoning set forth above.

In view of the conflicting views reflected in the Fifth Circuit's *Tufts* decision and the Third Circuit's decision in *Millar*, the Supreme Court granted certiorari in

---

[10] *Id.* at 1062–63.

[11] The partners had actually invested a very small amount of money. Rather than complicate matters, however, we have chosen to ignore the insignificant investment of the partners.

Tufts. The Supreme Court ultimately reversed the Fifth Circuit and held the entire amount of nonrecourse indebtedness had to be included in the partners' amount realized. The Court refused the opportunity to overrule *Crane* and instead held the *Crane* standard was equally applicable to situations where the unpaid amount of a nonrecourse liability exceeded the value of the property transferred. According to the Court, *Crane* did not rest on the theory of economic benefit; rather, *Crane* stands for the proposition that a nonrecourse mortgage will be treated as a true loan, *i.e.*, as a recourse obligation.

> Because no difference between recourse and nonrecourse obligations is recognized in calculating basis, *Crane* teaches that the Commissioner may ignore the nonrecourse nature of the obligation in determining the amount realized upon disposition of the encumbered property. He thus may include in the amount realized the amount of the nonrecourse mortgage assumed by the purchaser. The rationale for this treatment is that the original inclusion of the amount of the mortgage in basis rested on the assumption that the mortgagor incurred an obligation to repay. Moreover, this treatment balances the fact that the mortgagor originally received the proceeds of the nonrecourse loan tax-free on the same assumption. Unless the outstanding amount of the mortgage is deemed to be realized, the mortgagor effectively will have received untaxed income at the time the loan was extended and will have received an unwarranted increase in the basis of his property.[12]

Tufts thus stands for the proposition that, on a taxable disposition of property, a taxpayer's amount realized includes the amount of nonrecourse liabilities which the party acquiring the property takes the property subject to, even if the liabilities exceed the fair market value of the property.

The Service resisted the application of *Tufts* in *Allan v. Commissioner.*[13] The taxpayers in *Allan* had defaulted on their obligations under a nonrecourse mortgage encumbering their real property, and the mortgagee paid the property taxes as they came due and also charged the taxpayers for interest payments on the mortgage, adding the amounts to the mortgage principal as nonrecourse advances. The accrual-basis taxpayers, who deducted the taxes and interest as they accrued,[14] ultimately transferred the property to the mortgagee in lieu of foreclosure; they included the entire debt, which greatly exceeded the value of the property, in their amount realized. The Commissioner agreed that *Tufts* mandated such treatment with respect to the original principal balance, and conceded on appeal that *Tufts* also governed the advances for property taxes. However, the Commissioner objected throughout to the inclusion of the accrued interest in the amount realized,

---

[12] 461 U.S. at 309, 310. Note how Section 7701(g) incorporates the *Tufts* holding. Compare Treas. Reg. § 1.1001–2.

[13] (8th Cir. 1988), *aff'g* 86 T.C. 655.

[14] The tax years in question were prior to the enactment of Section 461(h), imposing an economic performance requirement as part of the "all events test" for accrual method taxpayers. See Chapter 29, *supra*, for a detailed discussion of Section 461(h). See Regulation § 1.461-4(g)(6) regarding economic performance and tax liabilities.

categorizing the interest as an "unpaid expense." According to the court, the Commissioner argued

> that "unpaid" expenses do not fall within the ambit of *Tufts*, and should therefore be considered separately. The Commissioner concluded that if these amounts were not included in amount realized, they were properly recognized as ordinary income under the "tax benefit rule," because the discharge of the liabilities was "fundamentally inconsistent" with the prior deductions. In essence, the Commissioner did not wish to allow appellees to receive a deduction at ordinary income rates, and then recognize the discharge of the obligation upon which the deductions were based at capital gains rate.[15]

Affirming the Tax Court, the Eighth Circuit, however, concluded the advances for interest, like the advances for taxes, constituted "a legitimate debt obligation, *i.e.*, a true loan" and that there was "no distinction in economic substance in this instance between borrowing from a third party to make the interest payments to [the mortgagee] or borrowing that money from [the mortgagee]."[16] Accordingly, the court held the entire amount of the nonrecourse debt was part of the amount realized on disposition of the property and, as a result, application of the tax benefit rule was precluded.[17]

In *Aizawa v. Commissioner*,[18] the Tax Court considered the application of *Tufts* in a situation where the taxpayer continued to be liable on a *recourse* debt following a foreclosure sale of the property secured by the debt. Specifically, the taxpayer remained liable for that part of the recourse debt not satisfied by the proceeds of the foreclosure sale. For purposes of determining gain or loss on the foreclosure sale, the court concluded the amount realized equaled the proceeds of the foreclosure sale.

> **Example:** Emily purchased Blackacre for $100,000, borrowing the full purchase price on a recourse basis. When Blackacre increased in value to $300,000, Emily refinanced the property, borrowing an additional $75,000 and executing a new recourse note in the total amount of $175,000. Emily used the $75,000 proceeds for personal purposes unrelated to Blackacre. As a result of an extended drought, the value of the property fell precipitously. Emily defaulted on the $175,000 mortgage encumbering the property and the property was sold at a foreclosure sale for its fair market value of $125,000. A deficiency judgment in the amount of $50,000 was entered against Emily. Emily's adjusted basis in Blackacre was $100,000, *i.e.*, the same amount that she had originally paid for the property. What are the tax consequences to Emily of the foreclosure sale?

---

[15]   856 F.2d at 1172.

[16]   *Id.* at 1174.

[17]   The Tax Court later relied upon *Allan* in holding that a taxpayer may deduct interest which had accrued on a nonrecourse mortgage, was outstanding at the time of a foreclosure sale and was included, together with the principal amount of the mortgage, in the taxpayer's amount realized on the foreclosure sale. Catalano v. Comm'r, T.C. Memo 2000-82, *rev'd on other grounds*, 279 F.3d 682 (9th Cir. 2002).

[18]   99 T.C. 197 (1992).

Analysis: According to *Aizawa*, the amount realized by Emily is $125,000 and not the $175,000 balance of the recourse mortgage. Emily will thus have $25,000 of gain to report (*i.e.*, amount realized of $125,000 less adjusted basis of $100,000). If Emily fails to pay the remaining $50,000 and that debt is forgiven, Emily may have cancellation of indebtedness income in that amount. Obviously, if Emily pays the deficiency judgment there will be no further tax consequences.

The Tax Court in *Webb v. Commissioner*[19] applied the reasoning of *Aizawa* in concluding a taxpayer incurred a loss upon the foreclosure of a recourse mortgage. The court rejected the Commissioner's position that *Aizawa* was distinguishable because the fair market value of the property in *Webb* exceeded the foreclosure price. The court noted the taxpayer, like the taxpayer in *Aizawa*, was subject to a deficiency judgment after the foreclosure sale. As a result, the amount realized on the foreclosure sale was only the amount received at public auction. This amount was significantly less than the adjusted basis in the property, thus resulting in a realized and recognized loss.

§ 37.03   NONRECOURSE BORROWING AND THE SECTION 108 INSOLVENCY EXCLUSION

The Service, in Revenue Ruling 92-53,[20] considered the impact of excess nonrecourse indebtedness, *i.e.*, nonrecourse debt in excess of the fair market value of property securing the debt, on the determination of insolvency for purposes of the Section 108 insolvency exclusion.[21] In that ruling, the Service concluded

> [t]he amount by which a nonrecourse debt exceeds the fair market value of the property securing the debt is taken into account in determining whether, and to what extent, a taxpayer is insolvent within the meaning of section 108(d)(3) of the Code, but only to the extent that the excess nonrecourse debt is discharged.

The Service reasoned that, to ensure the fresh start intended by Section 108,

> the amount by which a nonrecourse debt exceeds the fair market value of the property securing the debt should be treated as a liability in determining insolvency for purposes of section 108 of the Code to the extent that the excess nonrecourse debt is discharged. Otherwise, the discharge could give rise to a current tax when the taxpayer lacks the ability to pay that tax. Nonrecourse debt should also be treated as a liability in determining insolvency under section 108 to the extent of the fair market value of the property securing the debt.
>
> However, excess nonrecourse debt that is not discharged does not have a similar effect on a taxpayer's ability to pay a current tax resulting from

---

[19] T.C. Memo 1995-486.

[20] 1992-2 C.B. 48.

[21] See Chapter 9, *supra*, for a detailed discussion of income from the discharge of indebtedness and the insolvency exclusion.

the discharge of another debt (whether recourse or nonrecourse). That excess nonrecourse debt should not be treated as a liability in determining insolvency for purposes of section 108 of the Code.[22]

Example: Assume a taxpayer owed a local bank $500,000 on a nonrecourse loan secured by real property which had fallen in value to $400,000. The taxpayer's only other assets had an aggregate fair market value of $100,000 and the taxpayer was personally liable on other indebtedness in the amount of $50,000. The bank agreed to modify the terms of the nonrecourse loan by reducing the principal amount owing by $75,000.

Analysis: Pursuant to Revenue Ruling 92-53, the taxpayer's indebtedness for purposes of the Section 108(a)(1)(B) exclusion will be the sum of:

(1) $50,000 — the outstanding recourse indebtedness;

(2) $400,000 — the portion of the nonrecourse debt equal to the fair market value of the property securing the debt;

(3) $75,000 — the amount of the excess nonrecourse indebtedness (the excess of the total nonrecourse debt of $500,000 over the $400,000 fair market value of the real estate or $100,000) which is discharged.

Thus, the taxpayer, prior to the discharge, is deemed for Section 108 purposes to have total debt of $525,000. That debt exceeds the fair market value of the taxpayer's property ($400,000 + $100,000 = $500,000) by $25,000 and the taxpayer is considered insolvent to that extent. As a result, $25,000 of the $75,000 of discharged indebtedness will be excluded from gross income.

§ 37.04   NONRECOURSE BORROWING AND APPRECIATED PROPERTY

When the owner of appreciated property, with an adjusted basis far below market value, borrows against the increased equity in the property, the owner does not recognize gain, even if the loan proceeds are used for a totally unrelated purpose.

This rule was announced by the Second Circuit in *Woodsam Associates, Inc. v. Commissioner*.[23] In *Woodsam Associates*, Mrs. Woods had purchased certain improved real property in New York City. Subsequent to the purchase, she borrowed on a nonrecourse basis an amount in excess of her adjusted basis in the property. She later contributed the property to Woodsam Associates, Inc., receiving stock in exchange. Woodsam Associates ultimately disposed of the property at a foreclosure sale. Because Mrs. Woods' exchange of the property for stock in the corporation was nontaxable, Woodsam Associates took the same basis in the property as that of Mrs. Woods.[24] Woodsam Associates, Inc., however, contended

---

[22] 1992-2 C.B. at 49.

[23] 198 F.2d 357 (2d Cir. 1952).

[24] I.R.C. § 362.

that when Mrs. Woods borrowed against the property on a nonrecourse basis, she recognized gain to the extent of the difference between the amount of the indebtedness and her adjusted basis in the property. If the corporation were correct in its analysis, Mrs. Woods' basis in the property would have been increased by the amount of gain she was required to report as a result of the borrowing. In turn, the corporation would have received the property with a stepped-up basis, and ultimately realized a lesser gain on the foreclosure sale.

The Second Circuit rejected this argument, noting that a mortgagee, even in the case of a nonrecourse loan, was in effect nothing more than a preferred creditor. Mrs. Woods, by borrowing against her equity, had not disposed of the property but rather had merely augmented the indebtedness outstanding against the property.

> Mrs. Woods was the owner of this property in the same sense after the execution of this mortgage that she was before. As pointed out in our decision in the *Crane* case . . . "the lien of a mortgage does not make the mortgagee a co-tenant; the mortgagor is the owner for all purposes. . . . He has all the income from the property; he manages it; he may sell it; any increase in its value goes to him; any decrease falls on him, until the value goes below the amount of the lien." Realization of gain was, therefore, postponed for taxation until there was a final disposition of the property at the time of the foreclosure sale. Therefore, Mrs. Wood's borrowing did not change the basis for the computation of gain or loss.[25]

Even though the taxpayer did not prevail in *Woodsam Associates*, the decision is obviously favorable to taxpayers who have considerable equity in property with a low adjusted basis. It enables them to withdraw (via nonrecourse borrowing) from the property an amount far greater than they invested and yet not be deemed to have "realized" gain. Nevertheless, the result is consistent with *Crane's* treatment of nonrecourse debt as recourse debt for purposes of computing basis and amount realized.

> **Example 1:** Bernie purchased a commercial building for $500,000 in 1990. Bernie used $100,000 of his own cash to purchase the building and borrowed the balance of the purchase price from a local bank on a nonrecourse basis. The current balance owing on this indebtedness, which is secured by a first mortgage on the building, is $75,000. Because of an upturn in business activity in the area in which the building is located, the building currently has a fair market value of $1,000,000. Given the large equity he has in the property, Bernie refinances the building and borrows $500,000 on a nonrecourse basis. $75,000 of the new borrowing is used to pay the balance owing on the old mortgage and the other $425,000 is used by Bernie to invest in a business venture unrelated to the commercial building. Assume Bernie's adjusted basis in the building is $225,000.[26] Does the new borrowing (1) generate additional basis for Bernie in the building or (2) represent a realization event resulting in gain recognition?

---

[25] 198 F.2d at 359.

[26] This example assumes that Bernie has claimed $275,000 in depreciation deductions since purchasing the property.

Analysis: Since the new loan is not used to improve the building but rather is used in an unrelated venture, the loan does not result in any adjustment of the building's basis.[27] Even that part of the loan used to repay the balance on the original indebtedness does not result in an upward adjustment of the basis. Consistent with the *Crane* teaching, Bernie's original basis of $500,000 in the property reflected not only the $100,000 of his own cash used to purchase the property but also the $400,000 he had borrowed for that purpose. In other words, Bernie had already received credit for making the additional $400,000 investment.

Whether the new nonrecourse loan of $500,000 constitutes a realization event may appear to be a difficult question. After all, Bernie now has no personal obligation to repay this debt. He can do whatever he chooses to do with the $500,000 in loan proceeds he received. Nevertheless, Bernie, as a nonrecourse borrower, is treated like one who borrows on a recourse basis and is obligated to repay the borrowed funds. There is no realized and recognized gain to the extent of the difference between the amount of the loan ($500,000) and his adjusted basis in that mortgaged property ($225,000). If, instead of borrowing $500,000, Bernie had sold the building for $500,000 (with the purchaser paying Bernie $425,000 in cash and taking subject to the $75,000 mortgage), Bernie would have had to report $275,000 in gain.

Example 2: Same facts as above. If Bernie sells the building a year later for $1,100,000 and the purchaser pays Bernie $600,000 in cash and takes the building subject to the $500,000 mortgage, what will Bernie's amount realized be?

Analysis: *Woodsam Associates* indicated that the gain the taxpayer sought to have triggered upon the borrowing by Mrs. Woods was "postponed for taxation until the time of the foreclosure sale."[28] Accordingly, Bernie's amount realized is $1,100,000, *i.e.*, the sum of $600,000 in cash and the $500,000 in debt taken subject to by the purchaser. Assuming for the sake of simplicity that Bernie still has a $225,000 adjusted basis in the property, he will recognize gain of $875,000. To check this result, consider the following analysis:

> *Amount Contributed by Bernie:* $425,000 cash, *i.e.*, $100,000 down payment plus $325,000 subsequently paid out of pocket to retire the initial mortgage.

> *Amount of Benefits Received by Bernie:* $275,000 in depreciation deductions; $425,000 net proceeds of the refinancing (*i.e.*, $500,000 less $75,000 withheld to pay the balance of the original indebtedness owing by Bernie); and $600,000, the amount paid to Bernie by the purchaser. Total benefits received by Bernie: $1,300,000.

---

[27] *See* I.R.C. § 1016.

[28] 198 F.2d at 359.

Subtracting Bernie's total contributions ($425,000) from his total benefits ($1,300,000), Bernie has $875,000 of gain.

§ 37.05   IMPACT OF CONTINGENT LIABILITIES

The rule that nonrecourse liabilities incurred on the acquisition of property are includable in basis created an opportunity for abuse. At no risk to themselves, taxpayers could agree to pay inflated prices for depreciable property and finance their purchase by giving the seller a nonrecourse note. If respected, this arrangement would enable the taxpayer to claim a basis in the acquired property equal to the inflated purchase price. As a result, the taxpayer could claim greater depreciation deductions than would be available had the property been purchased at its fair market value. In addition, the taxpayer could claim an interest deduction with respect to the outstanding indebtedness. Likewise, from the standpoint of the seller, little risk was entailed. The seller, if a cash method taxpayer, could report the sale of the property on an installment basis and thus report gain only if and when paid.[29]

In *Estate of Franklin*,[30] the Ninth Circuit addressed just such abuses. In that case, the taxpayers purchased a motel, making a payment characterized as "prepaid interest" at closing and agreeing to pay the balance under an installment contract providing for annual payments as well as a balloon payment after ten years. The purchase was combined with a leaseback of the property to the sellers. The lease payments approximated the annual installment payments the purchasers were required to make. As a consequence, no cash, other than the prepaid interest, would cross between the taxpayers and the sellers until the balloon payment was due. Because of the leaseback, taxpayers never had physical possession of the property. The court concluded that the purchase price the taxpayers agreed to pay for the motel far exceeded its fair market value and therefore the taxpayers could not be expected to make the investment in the property represented by the nonrecourse debt. As a result, the court ignored the nonrecourse debt for purposes of depreciation and interest deductions. Revenue Ruling 77-110,[31] issued in the aftermath of *Estate of Franklin*, also treats nonrecourse indebtedness under similar circumstances as too contingent to be considered for purposes of basis and the computation of interest and depreciation deductions, and allows inclusion in basis only that portion of the purchase price that was paid in cash.[32]

With respect to *Estate of Franklin*, one might argue the Ninth Circuit erred in failing to hold the taxpayers had a basis at least equal to the fair market value of the property. However, the court apparently believed the liability was so great in relation to the fair market value of the property that it was unlikely any investment

---

[29] See Chapter 40, *infra*, for a detailed discussion of the installment method of accounting. Essentially, this method of accounting permits a seller to report the gain realized on the sale when payments are actually received.

[30]   544 F.2d 1045 (9th Cir. 1976).

[31]   1977-1 C.B. 58.

[32] As discussed in Chapter 43, *infra*, Congress has now directly addressed the problem of nonrecourse debt through the "at risk" rules of Section 465, which place limits on the allowable deductions attributable to nonrecourse debt.

would ever be made. Indeed, unless the property substantially appreciated, the taxpayer almost assuredly would not make any further payments on the property. Where liability is so contingent and where the tax avoidance motive seems so clear, refusal to accord tax significance to the liability seems appropriate.[33]

Although *Tufts* requires nonrecourse debt to be included in the amount realized on the disposition of property even though the debt exceeds the fair market value of the property, *Tufts* is not inconsistent with *Estate of Franklin*. Because they are factually distinguishable, the two cases announce rules which may coexist. In *Estate of Franklin*, the debt incurred exceeded the fair market value of the property securing its payment, thus justifying the court's refusal to acknowledge it as a true debt for tax purposes. By contrast, in *Tufts*, the original debt did not exceed the value of the property; it was thus not contingent debt in the *Estate of Franklin* sense. Given the *Crane* rationale that nonrecourse debt is to be treated as recourse debt, the investors in *Tufts* appropriately claimed interest deductions with respect to the debt and included the debt in the basis of the property, thereby generating substantial depreciation deductions. In effect, for tax purposes, the taxpayers received advance credit for an investment they had not yet made. These tax benefits, as well as the exclusion of the loan proceeds from income, were justified on the premise that the investors would make the investment represented by the nonrecourse debt, *i.e.*, they would repay the loan. Upon disposition, when it was clear there was no longer a possibility the debt would be repaid (or the investment made), it was appropriate to require the balance of the indebtedness to be taken into income by including it in the amount realized.

---

[33] In *Pleasant Summit Land Corporation v. Comm'r*, 863 F.2d 263 (3d Cir. 1988), *cert. denied*, 493 U.S. 901 (1989), the Third Circuit took an approach different from that of the Ninth Circuit in *Estate of Franklin*. The Third Circuit stated that it is appropriate "to disregard only the portion of nonrecourse debt in excess of the fair market value of the property when it was acquired for purposes of calculations of the depreciation and interest deductions and to regard the nonrecourse debt as genuine indebtedness to the extent it is not disregarded." The Second Circuit in *Lebowitz v. Comm'r*, 917 F.2d 1314 (2d Cir. 1990), the Fifth Circuit in *Lukens v. Comm'r*, 945 F.2d 92 (5th Cir. 1991), and the Court of Federal Claims in *Bergstrom v. U.S.*, 37 Fed. Cl. 164 (1996), have rejected the Third Circuit's position and followed the Ninth Circuit's position as reflected in *Estate of Franklin*.

Chapter 38

LIKE KIND EXCHANGES

§ 1031. Exchange of property held for productive use or investment.

(a) Nonrecognition of gain or loss from exchange solely in kind.

(1) In general. No gain or loss shall be recognized on the exchange of property held for productive use in a trade or business or for investment if such property is exchanged solely for property of a like kind which is to be held either for productive use in a trade or business or for investment.

(2) Exception. This subsection shall not apply to any exchange of

(A) stock in trade or other property held primarily for sale,

(B) stocks, bonds, or notes,

(C) other securities or evidences of indebtedness or interest,

(D) interests in a partnership,

(E) certificates of trust or beneficial interests, or

(F) choses in action.

Gains or losses *realized* on the sale or exchange of property must generally be *recognized*.[1] Under Section 1031 of the Code, however, no gain or loss is recognized when property held for productive use in a trade or business or for investment is exchanged solely for property of "like kind" to be held for productive use in a trade or business or for investment. This *nonrecognition* rule embodied in Section 1031(a)(1) has been part of the Code since its enactment in the Revenue Act of 1921.

Section 1031(a)(2) lists six exceptions to this nonrecognition rule. The exception for stock in trade or other property held primarily for sale was part of the original 1921 legislation. (Compare the wording of this exception with that of Section 1221(a)(1), excluding certain property from the definition of a capital asset.) There are additional exceptions for exchanges of stocks, bonds, notes, choses in action, certificates of trust or beneficial interest, or other securities or evidences of indebtedness or interest. Congress added these exceptions in 1923 largely to curb the abuse by brokers and investment houses that had established "exchange departments" to exchange appreciated securities for their customers without recognition of gain, while selling for cash and recognizing losses on those securities that had declined in value. Finally, the exception for interests in a partnership was added in response to several court decisions holding that, at least in certain circumstances, an exchange of an interest in one partnership for an interest in

---

[1] I.R.C. § 1001(c).

another partnership could qualify under Section 1031.[2] Congress, however, accepted the position of the Service that partnership interests were investment interests similar to those already excluded from Section 1031 and thus not appropriate candidates for nonrecognition treatment.

§ 38.01   CONTINUITY OF INTEREST

For tax purposes, an exchange is typically equivalent to cashing in one's investment in the property exchanged. The nonrecognition rule of Section 1031, however, is premised primarily on the notion that the property received in a like kind exchange is simply a continuation of the taxpayer's investment in a modified form. Since the investment is in substance a continuing one, the taxpayer has only technically, but not effectively, "realized" gain or loss, and the exchange is thus regarded as an inappropriate time to levy a tax or permit a deduction. In 1934, when Congress considered and rejected repeal of the predecessor of Section 1031, it expressed concern that elimination of the nonrecognition rule would place a "severe handicap" on "legitimate exchanges," leaving taxpayers with paper gains on exchanges, but without cash to pay the tax on the gains. The courts have emphasized this congressional concern and the underlying continuity of investment principle in their application of Section 1031. A secondary justification for Section 1031 has been the supposed administrative difficulty in valuing the property received in like kind exchanges.

The congressional justifications for nonrecognition, and for exclusions from nonrecognition, are reflected in the 1934 House Ways and Means Committee report rejecting repeal of the predecessor of Section 1031:

> The law has provided for 12 years that gain or loss is recognized on exchanges of property having a fair market value, such as stocks, bonds, and negotiable instruments; on exchanges of property held primarily for sale; or on exchanges of one kind of property for another kind of property; but not on other exchanges of property solely for property of like kind. In other words, profit or loss is recognized in the case of exchanges of notes or securities, which are essentially like money; or in the case of stock in trade; or in case the taxpayer exchanges the property comprising his original investment for a different kind of property; but, if the taxpayer's money is still tied up in the same kind of property as that in which it was originally invested, he is not allowed to compute and deduct his theoretical loss on the exchange, nor is he charged with a tax upon his theoretical profit. The calculation of the profit or loss is deferred until it is realized in cash, marketable securities, or other property not of the same kind having a fair market value.

> The Treasury Department states that its experience indicates that this provision does not in fact result in tax avoidance. If all exchanges were made taxable, it would be necessary to evaluate the property received in exchange in thousands of horse trades and similar barter transactions each

---

[2] Meyer v. Comm'r, 58 T.C. 311 (1972), *aff'd per curiam*, 503 F.2d 556 (9th Cir. 1974).

year, and for the time being, at least, claims for theoretical losses would probably exceed any profits which could be established. The committee does not believe that the net revenue which could thereby be collected, particularly in these years, would justify the additional administrative expense. Consequently, the exchange provisions have not been changed.[3]

§ 38.02 THE LIKE KIND REQUIREMENT

According to the regulations, "like kind" refers to the nature or character of property, or its kind or class, not to its grade or quality.[4] The regulations give a strikingly broad interpretation of "like kind" to real property, making it immaterial whether real estate is improved or unimproved for Section 1031 purposes, and providing as examples of qualifying transactions an exchange of city real estate for a ranch or farm, an exchange of a 30-year leasehold in real estate for real estate, and an exchange of improved real estate for unimproved real estate.[5] Provided the property interest in question constitutes an interest in real property, the cases and rulings have followed this liberal approach, applying Section 1031 to such exchanges as the exchange of remainder interests in two parcels of farm land,[6] a tenancy in common interest in land for 100% ownership of a portion thereof,[7] a leasehold in a building for a sublease in another part of the building,[8] the exchange of a leasehold interest (until exhaustion of the deposit) in a producing oil lease constituting real property for an improved ranch,[9] an undivided interest in mineral rights in certain land for an undivided interest in improved realty,[10] golf club property for property subject to 99-year condominium leases,[11] and perpetual water rights recognized under local law as real property for a fee interest in land (although the right to a specified amount of water does not qualify).[12] A 30-year leasehold is like kind to a fee interest according to the regulations, and for this purpose, optional renewal periods are added to the initial term of the lease.[13]

Historically, a much narrower approach was taken with respect to exchanges of personal property. Prior to the promulgation of additional regulations in 1991, there were only two examples provided by the regulations of like kind exchanges of personal property — a business truck for a new business truck, and a passenger automobile used in business for a new passenger automobile to be used in business

---

[3] H. Rep. 704, 73d Cong., 2d Session, p. 13.

[4] Treas. Reg. § 1.1031(a)-1(b).

[5] Treas. Reg. § 1.1031(a)-1(c).

[6] Rev. Rul. 78-4, 1978-1 C.B. 256.

[7] Rev. Rul. 73-476, 1973-2 C.B. 300.

[8] Rev. Rul. 75-515, 1975-2 C.B. 466.

[9] Rev. Rul. 68-331, 1968-1 C.B. 352.

[10] Comm'r v. Crichton, 122 F.2d 181 (5th Cir. 1941).

[11] Koch v. Comm'r, 71 T.C. 54 (1978).

[12] Rev. Rul. 55-749, 1955-2 C.B. 295. Compare *Weichens v. U.S.*, 228 F. Supp. 2d (D. Ariz. 2002), where the court held the exchange of a 50-year water right for a fee simple interest in farmland did not qualify as a like kind transaction, even though the water right constituted an interest in real property.

[13] Rev. Rul. 78-72, 1978-1 C.B. 258.

— and they hardly stretched the statutory language. In addition to these limited examples, case law and Treasury rulings also provided examples of like kind exchanges of personal property. For example, like kind treatment has been extended to an exchange of gold bullion for "bullion-type" gold coins whose fair market value greatly exceeds the face amount,[14] but gold bullion and silver bullion are not like kind,[15] nor are U.S. currency and foreign currency,[16] nor are Swiss francs and U.S. collector-type gold coins.[17] Exchanges of baseball player contracts are within Section 1031.[18]

Regulations issued in 1991 provide considerably more guidance regarding exchanges of personal property.[19] Under these regulations, the like kind requirement is satisfied if *depreciable tangible* personal property is exchanged for property *either* of a like kind *or* of a "like class." Depreciable tangible personal property is of like class to other depreciable tangible personal property if both properties are within the same "General Asset Class."[20] There are thirteen General Business Asset Classes, drawn from Revenue Procedure 87-56 (discussed in Chapter 14 on depreciation), and described in the regulations. For example, office furniture, fixtures and equipment are all within the same General Business Asset Class.[21]

Depreciable tangible personal properties are also of like class if within the same "Product Class."[22] Property within a Product Class consists of depreciable tangible personal property listed in a six-digit product class within certain sectors of the North American Industry Classification System.[23] Such properties are within the same Product Class if listed under the same six-digit class in the product code. The General Business Asset Classes and product codes will be modified from time to time.[24]

If the personal property in question is nondepreciable or intangible, it may be eligible for like kind treatment based upon all the facts and circumstances. No like classes are provided for these properties. Thus, such personal properties qualify only if "like kind" to one another.[25] With respect to intangible personal property, the regulations state, by way of example, that an exchange of copyrights on two novels is a like kind exchange, but not an exchange of a copyright on a novel and a copyright on a song.[26] The goodwill or going concern value of one business is not like

---

[14] Rev. Rul. 82-96, 1982-1 C.B. 113.

[15] Rev. Rul. 82-166, 1982-2 C.B. 190.

[16] Rev. Rul. 74-7, 1974-1 C.B. 198.

[17] California Federal Life Ins. Co. v. Comm'r, 79 T.C. 197 (1981), *aff'd*, 680 F.2d 85 (9th Cir. 1982).

[18] Rev. Rul. 71-137, 1971-1 C.B. 104.

[19] *See* Treas. Reg. § 1.1031(a)-2.

[20] Treas. Reg. § 1.1031(a)-2(b)(1).

[21] Treas. Reg. § 1.1031(a)-2(b)(2).

[22] Treas. Reg. § 1.1031(a)-2(b)(1).

[23] *See* Treas. Reg. § 1.1031(a)-2(b)(3).

[24] Treas. Reg. § 1.1031(a)-2(b)(4).

[25] Treas. Reg. § 1.1031(a)-2(c)(1).

[26] Treas. Reg. § 1.1031(a)-2(c)(3) Exs. 1, 2.

kind to the goodwill or going concern value of another business.[27]

The transfer of multiple assets creates special problems with respect to the like kind requirement. The Service, in Revenue Ruling 57-365,[28] ruled the noninventory assets of two telephone companies, including both real and personal property, were like kind, and hence held the exchange of all the assets except inventory and securities of one company for similar assets of another company was within Section 1031. The Service has clarified Revenue Ruling 57-365 and ruled a transfer of assets of similar businesses cannot be treated as the transfer of a single property for another single property — that is, it is not to be analyzed as a "business for business" exchange, but must be analyzed in terms of the underlying assets.[29] It is now essential to analyze multiple asset exchanges with reference to the regulations issued in 1991.[30]

On occasion, an exchange may fail to qualify for nonrecognition on the ground that the property given up or received constitutes payment of income. For example, in one ruling the receipt of real estate in exchange for a lease on various properties was held to constitute advance rent to the taxpayer and not to be within Section 1031.[31]

§ 38.03   THE HOLDING REQUIREMENTS

Section 1031(a) requires the property exchanged be property "held for productive use in a trade or business or for investment" and the property acquired be property "to be held either for productive use in a trade or business or for investment."[32] The statutory language obviously excludes personal-use property from the scope of Section 1031. Thus, the exchange of a piece of residential real estate used as rental for another piece of residential real estate to be used as the taxpayer's personal residence does not satisfy the "to be held" requirement. Many taxpayers who have vacation homes and second homes have sought to treat those homes as investment property, thereby affording them the possibility of a Section 1031 exchange. The Service has issued a safe harbor procedure under which it will not challenge whether a dwelling unit qualifies as Section 1031 property.[33]

The applicability of Section 1031 to one party to an exchange does not depend on its applicability to other parties. For example, if Smith exchanges rental real estate

---

[27] Treas. Reg. § 1.1031(a)-2(c)(2).

[28] 1957-2 C.B. 521.

[29] Rev. Rul. 89-121, 1989-2 C.B. 203.

[30] The regulations provide detailed and complex guidance on the tax consequences of multiple asset exchanges under Section 1031. While Section 1031 is generally applied on an asset-by-asset basis, the regulations create an exception to this general rule in the case of an exchange of multiple properties. The regulations attempt to create from one multiple asset exchange a series of like kind exchanges. The regulations provide five detailed examples to assist in resolving multiple asset exchange problems. Treas. Reg. § 1.1031(j)-1(d) Ex. 1–5.

[31] Rev. Rul. 66-209, 1966-2 C.B. 299.

[32] Compare those requirements with the "property used in a trade or business" language of Sections 1221(2) and 1231.

[33] Rev. Proc. 2008-16, 2008-1 C.B. 547.

for Jones' personal residence, which Smith will hold for rental purposes, Section 1031 is applicable to Smith even though on these facts it cannot apply to Jones.

The statute is phrased in the disjunctive, and the regulations make clear that an exchange of trade or business property for investment property, or vice versa, if the properties are otherwise like kind, may qualify for nonrecognition.[34] If, for example, land held for investment purposes is exchanged for business realty, the exchange falls within Section 1031.

Section 1031 imposes two holding requirements, *i.e.*, the property given up in the exchange must be "held" for productive use in a trade or business or for investment and the property received in the exchange is "to be held" for either productive use in a trade or business or for investment purposes. Assume, for example, a taxpayer purchases a residence the taxpayer holds for rental purposes. Six months later, the taxpayer exchanges the residence for another residence the taxpayer also intends to hold for rental purposes. Alternatively, assume the residence given up had been held for a long period of time, but the residence acquired on the exchange is itself promptly disposed of. Whether Section 1031 applies in either case may be academic. If property is acquired at a cost basis equal to its fair market value, and promptly exchanged, there is likely to be little or no gain or loss to recognize even if Section 1031 does not apply to the exchange; conversely, if property acquired in an exchange is promptly sold for cash, it may not matter whether the exchange was itself a recognition event if the same total gain or loss is recognized on the exchange and sale combined.

The answer, however, will not always be academic. Although the words of the statute may clearly disqualify many exchanges associated with brief holding periods, other exchanges may raise troublesome issues. Section 1031 has been applied where the taxpayer exchanged real property and then promptly transferred the real property received to a two-person partnership in return for a general interest in the partnership; the property received was regarded as held for investment on the ground its contribution to the partnership was a mere change in form, not a liquidation of the investment.[35] Similarly, in *Bolker v. Commissioner*,[36] the court held a taxpayer satisfied the holding requirement when he received property in a liquidating distribution from a corporation and immediately exchanged that property for other like kind property. The court stated:

> We hold that if a taxpayer owns property which he does not intend to liquidate or to use for personal pursuits, he is "holding" that property "for productive use in trade or business or for investment" within the meaning of section 1031(a). Under this formulation, the intent to exchange property for like-kind property satisfies the holding requirement, because it is not an intent to liquidate the investment or to use it for personal pursuits.[37]

---

[34] Treas. Reg. § 1.1031(a)-1(a)(1).

[35] Magneson v. Comm'r, 753 F.2d 1490 (9th Cir. 1985), *aff'g* 81 T.C. 767 (1983).

[36] 760 F.2d 1039 (9th Cir. 1985).

[37] *Id.* at 1045.

An exchange may not qualify under Section 1031 where the intent at the time of the exchange is to make a charitable contribution of the property received,[38] or to give the property received to one's children;[39] but the absence of prearrangement or concrete plans at the time of the exchange may mean that a subsequent gift of the property received does not take the prior exchange out of Section 1031.[40]

Section 1031 was amended in 1989 to impose a two-year holding period on exchanges between related persons.[41] As noted, specific holding periods are not otherwise provided in Section 1031. The amendments are obviously aimed at restraining the taxpayer — for two years, at least — from effectively cashing out business or investment property through a related party, while using Section 1031 to obtain nonrecognition. The holding period requirement applies with respect to both the property received by the taxpayer and the property transferred by the taxpayer to the related person.[42] A number of exceptions are provided, including one for non-tax-avoidance transfers.[43] If the holding requirements are not satisfied, the gain or loss that was not recognized on the exchange is reported in the year the subsequent, disqualifying transfer occurs.[44]

Example: Last year, Kurt exchanged an undeveloped lot in City A for a tract of land owned by his son. Kurt's adjusted basis in the lot is $10,000 and the lot's fair market value is $250,000. The son's land had a value of $250,000 and the son, who had recently purchased the land, had an adjusted basis in the land of $225,000. Assume both Kurt and his son qualified for Section 1031 nonrecognition on the exchange (assume, e.g., that each of them held for investment purposes the property relinquished and each will hold for investment purposes the property acquired. Assume also that this year the son sold the lot acquired in the exchange for $250,000. What are the tax consequences of the exchange and ultimate sale by the son?

Analysis: But for Section 1031(a), Kurt would be required to report $240,000 in gain on the exchange, *i.e.*, the difference between the value of the land he received from his son ($250,000) and Kurt's adjusted basis in the lot ($10,000). In addition, if Section 1031 were inapplicable, Kurt would have taken a fair market value basis of $250,000 in the land received from his son. *See Philadelphia Park Amusement Co. v. United States* in Chapter 4. Instead, assuming Section 1031 is applicable, Kurt will recognize no gain and, as discussed below, will take a $10,000 basis in the land received from his son.[45]

---

[38] Lindsley v. Comm'r, T.C. Memo 1983-729.

[39] Click v. Comm'r, 78 T.C. 225 (1982).

[40] Wagensen v. Comm'r, 74 T.C. 653 (1980).

[41] I.R.C. § 1031(f), (g).

[42] I.R.C. § 1031(f)(1)(C).

[43] I.R.C. § 1031(f)(2).

[44] I.R.C. § 1031(f)(1).

[45] I.R.C. § 1031(d).

If Section 1031 applies, the son likewise will not report any gain and will take a basis of $225,000 in the lot received from Kurt.[46] When the son sells the lot for $250,000, he will then recognize the $25,000 of gain previously deferred under Section 1031. But for section 1031(f), no other gain would have to be reported at the time. In effect, it would be just as if Kurt had exchanged his basis in the lot ($10,000) for his son's basis in the land ($225,000) thereby enabling the family unit of Kurt and his son to sell Kurt's lot for $250,000 in cash and recognize only $25,000 of gain rather than the $240,000 of gain Kurt would have reported had Kurt, instead of exchanging the lot for his son's land, simply sold the lot himself for $250,000 in cash.

Section 1031(f) prevents this swapping of basis between related parties. Under these circumstances, Section 1031(f)(1) denies nonrecognition treatment to both Kurt and his son on the exchange. In effect, last year's exchange of properties between Kurt and his son will be treated, retroactively, as a taxable exchange because of the son's sale of the lot this year. Thus, on Kurt's exchange of the lot for his son's land, Kurt will be required to report $240,000 of gain — that is, all the gain inherent in the lot. Similarly, on his exchange of the land for Kurt's lot, the son will be required to report the $25,000 of gain inherent in his land at the time. Both would then take a fair market value basis of $250,000 in the property each had acquired. Again, see *Philadelphia Amusement Park Co. v. United States* in Chapter 4. Therefore, when the son sold for $250,000 the lot he had received from Kurt, there would be no additional gain to report.

Note that, despite these consequences, Kurt and his son do not file amended returns reporting these gains for the year of the exchange. Section 1031(f)(1) provides that the gain Kurt and his son must recognize by reason of the application of that section will not be taken into account for tax purposes until the date on which the son's sale of the lot occurred. Since that sale occurred this year, Kurt and his son would report their gain on this year's tax returns.

To address more sophisticated arrangements, Congress enacted Section 1031(f)(4) specifically making Section 1031 inapplicable to any exchange that is part of a transaction (or series of transactions) structured to avoid the purposes of Section 1031(f). The Service applied Section 1031(f)(4) in Revenue Ruling 2002-83[47] to disallow the benefit of Section 1031(a) nonrecognition treatment to a taxpayer (A) under the following circumstances:

Individual A owns real property (Property 1) with a fair market value of $150x and an adjusted basis of $50x. Individual B owns real property (Property 2) with a fair market value of $150x and an adjusted basis of $150x. Both Property 1 and Property 2 are held for investment within the meaning of Section 1031(a). A and B are related persons within the meaning of Section 267(b). C, an individual unrelated to A and B, wishes to acquire Property 1 from A. A enters into an agreement for the transfer of

---

[46] I.R.C. § 1031(d).

[47] 2002-2 C.B. 927.

Property 1 and Property 2 with B, C, and a qualified intermediary [a person or entity employed to help facilitate a like-kind exchange; see the discussion, *infra*]. The qualified intermediary is unrelated to A and B. Pursuant to their agreement, on January 6, 2003, A transfers Property 1 to the qualified intermediary who transfers Property 1 to C for $150x. On January 13, 2003, the qualified intermediary acquires Property 2 from B, pays B the $150x sales proceeds from the qualified intermediary's sale of Property 1, and transfers Property 2 to A.

According to the ruling, the above arrangement is comparable to a situation where A and B engaged in a like-kind exchange by which A transferred Property 1 to B in exchange for B's transfer of Property 2 to A. If B sold Property 1 to C within two years of the exchange, Section 1031(f) would deny A nonrecognition treatment. Similarly, the ruling concludes that Section 1031(f) will deny A nonrecognition treatment in the circumstances described in the ruling. In an analogous situation, the Tax Court applied Section 1031(f)(4) to deny nonrecognition treatment.[48]

§ 38.04   "SOLELY" FOR LIKE KIND PROPERTY: THE PRESENCE OF "BOOT"

§ 1031.   Exchange of property held for productive use or investment.

(b)   Gain from exchanges not solely in kind. If an exchange would be within the provisions of subsection (a) . . . if it were not for the fact that the property received in exchange consists not only of property permitted by such provisions to be received without the recognition of gain, but also of other property or money, then the gain, if any, to the recipient shall be recognized, but in an amount not in excess of the sum of such money and the fair market value of such other property.

(c)   Loss from exchanges not solely in kind. If an exchange would be within the provisions of subsection (a) . . . if it were not for the fact that the property received in exchange consists not only of property permitted by such provisions to be received without the recognition of gain or loss, but also of other property or money, then no loss from the exchange shall be recognized.

Section 1031 would be of little utility if qualifying exchanges could consist only of like kind properties of equal value. The like kind properties transferred in a Section 1031 exchange are almost invariably unequal in value and at least one of the parties will have to transfer cash or non-like kind property ("boot") to even up the exchange. The party giving, but not receiving, cash or other nonqualifying property, remains within the language of Section 1031(a) since he receives solely like kind property for the property he gives up; the cash or other nonqualifying property he conveys will be reflected in the basis of the property acquired, a matter discussed below. By contrast, the party receiving cash or other nonqualifying property is not receiving "solely" like kind property. Section 1031, however, does not disqualify this exchange, but requires recognition of gain on the like kind property to the extent of the boot received (*but not in excess of gain realized*). Recognition of loss on like kind property, however, is prohibited.

---

[48]   Teruya Brothers, Ltd. v. Commissioner, 124 T.C. 45, aff'd, 580 F.3d 1038 (9th Cir. 2009).

Example: Assume Taxpayer exchanges property worth $50,000, with an adjusted basis of $20,000, for like kind property worth $40,000 and cash of $10,000. What are the tax consequences to Taxpayer?

Analysis: Taxpayer will realize gain of $30,000 on the exchange. Under Section 1031(b), however, only $10,000 of the realized gain will be recognized. However, if the property exchanged had a basis of $80,000 instead of $20,000, none of the $30,000 realized loss would be recognized.

The nonrecognition rules of Section 1031 are addressed only to gain or loss inherent in the like kind property in the transaction. Gain or loss on non-like kind property is not governed by Section 1031, and such gain or loss is recognized under the general rule of Section 1001(c). Thus, the party giving nonqualifying property in an exchange recognizes gain or loss to the extent of the difference between the value received and the adjusted basis of the property given up.

Example: Assume Taxpayer exchanges land worth $500,000 with an adjusted basis of $200,000 and a piece of business equipment worth $50,000 with an adjusted basis of $100,000 for a parcel of real estate worth $550,000. Assuming Taxpayer meets the holding requirements of Section 1031, will any gain or loss be recognized on the exchange?

Analysis: While the gain inherent in Taxpayer's land will not be recognized, the loss of $50,000 incurred on the exchange of the nonqualifying property, *i.e.*, the business equipment, will be recognized (assuming the requirements of Section 165 are satisfied). In effect, Taxpayer is exchanging equipment worth $50,000 for $50,000 worth of real estate. Because the equipment and the real estate are not like kind properties, Section 1031 is inapplicable to that part of the exchange. The loss will therefore be recognized. By contrast, Taxpayer is viewed as exchanging $500,000 of land for $500,000 of real estate — a like kind exchange entitling Taxpayer to nonrecognition treatment with respect to the gain realized on this part of the exchange.

§ 38.05   TREATMENT OF LIABILITIES

It is common for one or more of the properties in a like kind exchange to be transferred subject to a liability, or for one party to the exchange to assume a liability of another party. Such liability relief is treated under Section 1031 as money received by the taxpayer relieved of the liability.[49] Liability relief is thus a form of boot. If Taxpayer A transfers land worth $500,000, but subject to a mortgage of $100,000, to Taxpayer B in return for land worth $400,000, Taxpayer A is treated as having received $100,000 in cash. (Taxpayer B will be given credit in basis as if she had paid $100,000 in cash to A.)

To this point, the treatment of liabilities may seem a simple matter. However, if both properties in a like kind exchange are transferred subject to liabilities, the matter is more complicated. Assume Taxpayer A transfers land worth $500,000, subject to a mortgage of $300,000; Taxpayer B transfers land worth $300,000,

---

[49] I.R.C. § 1031(d) (last sentence).

subject to a mortgage of $100,000. According to the regulations, only the *net* liability relief constitutes money received.[50] Thus, A is treated as receiving $200,000 in cash; B is treated as receiving none.

One further complication remains. Suppose instead A's land was worth $400,000 instead of $500,000. A therefore pays B $100,000 in cash to equalize the transaction. The same regulation provides that "money received" is now present on both sides: B has $100,000 of money received in the form of the cash; A has $200,000 of net liability relief which is generally treated as money received. But in computing A's "money received," one must first offset the net liability relief by the $100,000 in cash A paid to B; A's "money received" is thus only $100,000. The rationale for this regulation is apparently that A, instead of paying the cash to B, could have used the cash to pay down the liability encumbering the property A was transferring to B. In turn, this would have reduced the liability relief A has as a result of the exchange and thus the amount of money A is deemed to have received under Section 1031(d). Two rules are therefore apparent: (1) cash received always counts as "money received"; and (2) *net* liability relief, *reduced* by any cash paid, also constitutes "money received."

§ 38.06 BASIS CALCULATIONS

§ 1031. Exchange of property held for productive use or investment.

(d) Basis. If property was acquired on an exchange described in this section, . . . then the basis shall be the same as that of the property exchanged, decreased in the amount of any money received by the taxpayer and increased in the amount of gain or decreased in the amount of loss to the taxpayer that was recognized on such exchange. If the property so acquired consisted in part of the type of property permitted by this section, . . . to be received without the recognition of gain or loss, and in part of other property, the basis provided in this subsection shall be allocated between the properties (other than money) received, and for the purpose of the allocation there shall be assigned to such other property an amount equivalent to its fair market value at the date of the exchange. For purposes of this section, . . . where as part of the consideration to the taxpayer another party to the exchange assumed a liability of the taxpayer or acquired from the taxpayer property subject to a liability, such assumption or acquisition (in the amount of the liability) shall be considered as money received by the taxpayer on the exchange.

Section 1031, in common with other nonrecognition provisions of the Code, defers the recognition of gain or loss rather than permanently excluding gain or disallowing loss. The unrecognized gain or loss is preserved, through the basis mechanism, in the like kind property received. Since non-like kind property constitutes boot, such property winds up with a fair market value basis in the recipient's hands. In effect, the taxpayer is treated as having purchased the non-like kind property.[51]

---

[50] Treas. Reg. § 1.1031(d)-2 Ex. 2.

[51] See the discussion of *Philadelphia Park Amusement Co. v. U.S.* in Chapter 4, *supra.*

The mechanics of the basis calculation with respect to like kind property are set forth in the first sentence of Section 1031(d). Unrecognized gain or loss is preserved by using as a starting point the total bases of all the properties given up. This "substituted basis" is adjusted up or down for gain or loss recognized on the transaction (as noted above, loss may be recognized when nonqualifying property is transferred as part of the exchange), and is also decreased by "money received." Although not specified in the statute, the examples in the regulations properly provide that (1) liability relief is treated as money received, thus decreasing basis; (2) liabilities taken on are treated as money paid; and (3) money paid increases basis. (It may be somewhat confusing to see that, for basis computation purposes, the regulations increase basis by total liabilities taken on and by total cash paid, then decrease basis by total liability relief and by total cash received. By contrast, in determining "money received" for *gain recognition* purposes, it was only the *net* liability relief (reduced by any cash paid) not the total liability relief, that counted. It may ease the confusion to realize that the basis answers remain precisely the same if the upward and downward adjustments are done based on a netting of liabilities.) Where non-like kind property (known as "boot") is received, basis is first allocated to the non-like kind property to the extent of its fair market value, thus preserving in the like kind property, consistent with the general rule of Section 1031(a), the unrecognized gain or loss.

When money is received, or liability relief occurs, or loss is recognized, the taxpayer is in effect receiving a partial return of investment, and it is appropriate to reduce basis to reflect that fact. When money is paid, or liabilities are taken on, or gain is recognized, the taxpayer is in effect increasing investment, and it is appropriate to increase basis as a result. A single event may of course have offsetting effects. For example, $10 in cash received decreases basis since it is money received, but if it also triggers $10 of recognized gain, it increases basis by the same amount, so that the net effect is to leave basis unchanged. The non-like kind property received should have a fair market value basis. The like kind property received should have a basis that preserves the unrecognized gain or loss in the property given up. Section 1031(d) and the regulations thereunder provide the formula: the basis of the like kind property received equals (1) the *adjusted basis* of all like kind and non-like kind property given up; (2) *plus* any gain recognized, liability taken on, or cash paid; (3) *minus* any loss recognized, liability shed, or cash received; (4) with the resulting total basis *allocated* first to non-like kind property received to the extent of its fair market value; and (5) with the *remaining* basis constituting the basis of the like kind property.

> **Example 1:** Elizabeth owns a parcel of land worth $500,000 which is subject to a mortgage of $100,000. Elizabeth's adjusted basis in the land is $100,000. Elizabeth exchanges the land for another parcel of land owned by Caroline. Caroline's land is worth $400,000 and Caroline has a $200,000 basis in the land. Assume the transaction qualifies as a like kind exchange from the standpoint of both Elizabeth and Caroline. What are the tax consequences to the parties?
>
> **Analysis:** First, consider Elizabeth's situation. Elizabeth's amount realized is $500,000, *i.e.*, $400,000 of land plus $100,000 of liability relief. Elizabeth's adjusted basis is $100,000. Elizabeth's realized gain is thus $400,000.

Elizabeth must recognize $100,000 of that realized gain because Elizabeth is deemed to have received $100,000 of boot, *i.e.*, the liability relief is treated as money received (Section 1031(d) last sentence). Elizabeth thus has $100,000 of recognized gain (presumably long term capital gain); $300,000 of Elizabeth's realized gain is not recognized. Elizabeth's basis in the $400,000 parcel of land acquired from Caroline equals $100,000, *i.e.*,

Basis of relinquished land ..	$100,000
less the liability relief	($100,000)
plus the gain recognized . . .	$100,000
Basis of acquired land	$100,000

This basis preserves the $300,000 of gain realized by Elizabeth which was not recognized as a result of the application of Section 1031.

Now consider Caroline's tax consequences. Caroline's amount realized is $500,000; Caroline's adjusted basis is $300,000, *i.e.*, the sum of the $200,000 basis of land relinquished and the $100,000 of liabilities taken on. Caroline's gain realized is $200,000. None of this gain will be recognized. Caroline's basis in the $500,000 parcel of land acquired from Elizabeth will be $300,000 determined as follows:

Basis of relinquished land ..	$200,000
plus liabilities assumed	$100,000
less cash received	0
plus gain recognized	0
less loss recognized	0
Basis of acquired land	$300,000

This basis preserves the $200,000 of gain realized which was not recognized.

Example 2: Assume the same facts as Example 1 except Caroline's land is worth $600,000 but is subject to a $200,000 mortgage. What are the tax consequences to each of the parties?

Analysis: First, consider Elizabeth's tax consequences. Elizabeth's gain realized is determined as follows:

Fair market value of land received	$600,000
plus liabilities encumbering Elizabeth's land . . .	$100,000
Total consideration received by Elizabeth	$700,000
Less:	
Elizabeth's adjusted basis in land	$100,000
Liabilities encumbering Caroline's land	$200,000
Total	($300,000)
Gain Realized	$400,000

Elizabeth is giving up land encumbered by a $100,000 liability and is receiving land subject to $200,000 of liability. Thus, Elizabeth experiences no net liability relief. Therefore, Elizabeth is not deemed to have received any boot. Thus, none of the $400,000 of gain realized is recognized.

Elizabeth's basis in the land received from Caroline will be determined as follows:

Adjusted basis of land transferred	$100,000
Liabilities encumbering Caroline's land	$200,000
Total	$300,000
less: liabilities encumbering Elizabeth's land . . .	($100,000)
plus: gain recognized	$0
Elizabeth's basis	$200,000

This basis will preserve the $400,000 gain realized that was not recognized.

Now consider Caroline's tax consequences. Caroline's gain realized is determined as follows:

Fair market value of land received	$500,000
plus liabilities encumbering Caroline's land	$200,000
Total consideration received by Caroline	$700,000
Less:	
Caroline's adjusted basis in land	$200,000
Liabilities encumbering Elizabeth's land	$100,000
Total	($300,000)
Gain Realized	$400,000

Caroline is giving up land encumbered by a $200,000 liability and is receiving land subject to $100,000 of liability. Thus, Caroline experiences net liability relief of $100,000. Therefore, Caroline is deemed to have received boot in the amount of $100,000. Thus, $100,000 of the $400,000 of gain realized is recognized.

Caroline's basis in the land received from Elizabeth will be determined as follows:

Adjusted basis of land transferred	$200,000
Liabilities encumbering Elizabeth's land	$100,000
Total	$300,000
Less: liabilities encumbering Elizabeth's land . .	($200,000)
Plus: gain recognized	$100,000
Caroline's basis	$200,000

This basis will preserve the $300,000 gain realized that was not recognized.

Example 3: Assume the facts of Example 2 except Caroline's land is encumbered by $300,000 rather than $200,000 of liability. As a result, Caroline will give Elizabeth $100,000 in cash in addition to Caroline's land. What are the tax consequences to the parties?

Analysis: First, consider Elizabeth's tax consequences. Elizabeth's gain realized is determined as follows:

Fair market value of land received	$600,000
plus cash received	$100,000
plus liabilities encumbering Elizabeth's land	$100,000
Total consideration received by Elizabeth	$800,000
Less:	
Elizabeth's adjusted basis in land	$100,000
Liabilities encumbering Caroline's land	$300,000
Total	($400,000)
Gain Realized	$400,000

Elizabeth is giving up land encumbered by a $100,000 liability and is receiving land subject to $300,000 of liability. Thus, Elizabeth experiences no net liability relief. Therefore, Elizabeth is not deemed to have received any boot as a result of liability relief. Elizabeth has, however, also received $100,000 in cash. Elizabeth must therefore recognize $100,000 of the $400,000 of gain realized.

Elizabeth's basis in the land received from Caroline will be determined as follows:

Adjusted basis of land transferred	$100,000
Liabilities encumbering Caroline's land	$300,000
Total	$400,000
less: liabilities encumbering Elizabeth's land	($100,000)
less: cash received	($100,000)
plus: gain recognized	$100,000
Elizabeth's basis	$300,000

This basis will preserve the $300,000 gain realized that was not recognized.

Now consider Caroline's tax consequences. Caroline's gain realized is determined as follows:

Fair market value of land received	$500,000
plus liabilities encumbering Caroline's land	$300,000
Total consideration received by Caroline	$800,000
Less:	
Caroline's adjusted basis in land	$200,000
Cash given to Elizabeth	$100,000
Liabilities encumbering Elizabeth's land	$100,000

Total .... ($400,000)

Gain Realized $400,000

For purposes of Section 1031(b), the amount of "other property or money", *i.e.*, boot, received by Caroline is $100,000 (*i.e.*, consideration received by Caroline in the form of a transfer subject to a liability of $300,000 is offset by consideration given in the form of a receipt of property subject to a $100,000 liability and by the $100,000 cash paid by Caroline to Elizabeth.) As noted in the regulations, "Although consideration received in the form of cash or other property is not offset by consideration given in the form of an assumption of liabilities or a receipt of property subject to a liability, consideration given in the form of cash or other property is offset against consideration received in the form of an assumption of liabilities or a transfer of property subject to a liability."[52] Therefore, under Section 1031(b), Caroline recognizes $100,000 of the $400,000 gain realized.

Caroline's basis in the land received from Elizabeth be determined as follows:

Adjusted basis of land transferred $200,000

Cash given to Elizabeth $100,000

Liabilities encumbering Elizabeth's land $100,000

Total $400,000

less: liabilities encumbering Elizabeth's land ... ($300,000)

plus: gain recognized $100,000

Caroline's basis $200,000

This basis will preserve the $300,000 gain realized that was not recognized.

§ 38.07   THE RELATIONSHIP BETWEEN § 267(a)(1) AND § 1031

The preservation of unrecognized loss in cases where exchanges occur between related persons, as defined in Section 267(b), may result in what appears to be inconsistency between Section 1031 and Section 267(a)(1). Assume Taxpayer gives to his daughter a tract of land worth $100,000 and with an adjusted basis of $120,000 in exchange for $20,000 in cash and a piece of real estate worth $80,000. Assume also that, except with respect to the receipt of the cash, Taxpayer meets the holding and like kind requirements of Section 1031. Under Section 1031(c), even though Taxpayer is receiving boot, no loss can be recognized by Taxpayer. Section 1031(d), however, preserves Taxpayer's loss in the basis of the real estate received by Taxpayer from his daughter. Thus, under Section 1031(d), Taxpayer would take a basis of $100,000 in the real estate (*i.e.*, $120,000 basis in the land relinquished less $20,000 cash received). If Taxpayer later sold the real estate for $100,000, Taxpayer would recognize $20,000 of loss.

---

[52] Treas. Reg. § 1.1031(d)-2 Ex. 2.

Compare those results to the results if Section 1031 did not exist and the same exchange took place. Under those circumstances, Section 267(a)(1) would disallow Taxpayer's $20,000 loss on the taxable exchange. Given *Philadelphia Park Amusement Co.*, Taxpayer would take a fair market value basis of $80,000 in the real estate received from his daughter. His daughter would likewise take a fair market basis in the tract of land received from her father. The $20,000 loss that inhered in Taxpayer's tract of land would simply disappear. Note, however, that Section 267(d) might provide some relief to the Taxpayer/daughter family unit if the daughter were later to sell the tract of land at a gain. Revenue Ruling 72-151[53] confirms that Section 1031(d) controls in a situation like that presented in the above example.

§ 38.08   SALE OR EXCHANGE?

Former Regulation Section 1.1002-1(d) described an exchange as, ordinarily, "a reciprocal transfer of property, as distinguished from a transfer of property for a money consideration only." Suppose, for example, a taxpayer "sells" qualifying property for cash to a buyer, and then by prearrangement immediately "purchases" qualifying like kind property from the same person. If the transaction is in substance an exchange rather than a sale and purchase, the provisions of Section 1031 will govern. The Service has applied this principle to a situation in which a taxpayer sold used business equipment to a dealer under one contract, and purchased new like kind equipment from the same dealer under a separate contract; despite the separate contracts, the two transactions were "reciprocal and mutually dependent" and were treated as a trade-in exchange rather than a sale and purchase.[54] The same exchange-in-substance rule has also been extended to cover a case where the sale of old trucks was made by the parent corporation and the purchase of the new trucks (from the same manufacturer) was made by the parent's subsidiary corporation.[55] As a result, the taxpayer was not allowed to deduct the loss incurred on the old trucks.

The Service, however, has not always been successful in advancing this rule. For example, in *Bell Lines, Inc. v. U.S.*,[56] the taxpayer purchased new trucks from one manufacturer and, with the assistance of the manufacturer, sold taxpayer's old trucks to an independent used truck dealership. Unknown to the taxpayer was the fact that the manufacturer had made an agreement with the used truck dealership whereby the dealership agreed to purchase taxpayer's trucks. Under the agreement, the dealership would attempt to sell the old trucks purchased from the taxpayer and would be allowed to keep any profits from the sale. If, however, the dealership sustained losses on the sale, the manufacturer of the new trucks agreed to assume those losses. Obviously, had the taxpayer merely traded-in the old trucks for new trucks Section 1031 would have been applicable and no gain would have been recognized by the taxpayer. Of course, the taxpayer would have taken a basis in the new trucks which was considerably less than the purchase price of the new

---

[53] 1972-1 c.b. 224.

[54] Rev. Rul. 61-119, 1961-1 C.B. 395.

[55] Redwing Carriers, Inc. v. Tomlinson, 399 F.2d 652 (5th Cir. 1968).

[56] 480 F.2d 710 (4th Cir. 1973).

trucks. In turn, the depreciation deductions available to the taxpayer with respect to the new trucks would be greatly diminished. This basis question was the focus of concern in *Bell Lines*. The court rejected the Service's argument that, in effect, the taxpayer had exchanged the old trucks for the new trucks. According to the court, the purchase of the new trucks and the sale of the old trucks were not mutually dependent and, from the taxpayer's standpoint, were separate transactions with unrelated parties. The court therefore concluded that an exchange triggering Section 1031 had not occurred. In another case,[57] a taxpayer initially contracted to exchange unimproved land for improved land, but when the other party failed to make certain improvements on time, the taxpayer sold his land for cash to the other party, and three months later (when the improvements had been completed) purchased the improved land. The court held a sale and purchase took place rather than an exchange.

Another context in which the sale-or-exchange issue can arise involves the sale and leaseback of real estate. If the lease (with optional extensions) runs 30 years or more, the leasehold and a fee interest will be treated as like kind.[58] If a taxpayer "sells" real property for cash but at a loss, and simultaneously enters into a long-term lease of the property, the Service's view is that Section 1031 bars the loss. This view was upheld in a case involving a sale of real property for cash and a 95-year leasehold in the property, where the lease had a capital value — that is, where the lease was worth more than the rent to be paid.[59] In other cases, where the sale was at full value and the lease at fair rental, and the lease had no capital value, the loss on the sale has been allowed.[60]

§ 38.09   THREE-WAY EXCHANGES AND DEFERRED EXCHANGES

Often an exchange cannot be effected with just two parties. Consider the following example: Amy is interested in disposing of her ranch and acquiring a farm owned by Claire. Because there is considerable gain inherent in Amy's property, she would prefer to exchange her ranch for Claire's farm. Unfortunately, Claire is not interested in an exchange but wants cash. Meanwhile, Brendan offers to purchase Amy's ranch for cash. Instead of accepting Brendan's offer, Amy proposes that Brendan purchase Claire's farm and then exchange that farm for Amy's ranch. Brendan agrees to accommodate Amy and the transaction proceeds pursuant to Amy's proposal. The *simultaneous* exchange of Amy's ranch for the farm acquired by Brendan occurs. A three-way exchange such as this can qualify for Section 1031 treatment, even though Amy could have sold the ranch for cash to Brendan.[61] Similarly, if Amy, Brendan, and Claire had engaged in a round-robin exchange under which Amy transferred her ranch to Brendan, Brendan transferred real

---

[57] Swaim v. U.S., 651 F.2d 1066 (5th Cir. 1981).

[58] Treas. Reg. § 1.1031(a)-1(c).

[59] *Century Electric Co. v. Comm'r*, 192 F.2d 155 (8th Cir. 1951).

[60] *See* Jordan Marsh Co. v. Comm'r, 269 F.2d 453 (2d Cir. 1959); Leslie Co. v. Comm'r, 64 T.C. 247 (1975) (nonacq.), *aff'd*, 539 F.2d 943 (3d Cir. 1976).

[61] *See, e.g.*, Rev. Rul. 77-297, 1977-2 C.B. 304.

property to Claire, and Claire transferred the farm to Amy, Section 1031 would apply to each party satisfying the holding requirements, provided the properties are like kind.[62] It is thus not necessary to receive the like kind property from the same person to whom one has transferred property.

In Revenue Ruling 90-34,[63] the Service concluded that a similar rule was applicable in "2-way" exchanges. In that ruling, X and Y enter into a contract requiring X to transfer Blackacre to Y, and Y agrees to acquire and transfer to X like kind property identified by X which is of comparable value to Blackacre. In the event X does not identify such property in a timely manner, Y agrees to pay X cash for Blackacre. If X identifies the replacement property and Y arranges for the property to be transferred to X without Y ever holding title to the property, the ruling concludes that an exchange qualifying under Section 1031 has occurred. This ruling has particular importance in view of the concern that a party in Y's position might have with respect to possible environmental liabilities which may be associated with the replacement property identified by X and which may be attributable to anyone in the chain of title. In other words, Y is willing to arrange for the acquisition of replacement property in order to accommodate X's desire to qualify for Section 1031 exchange treatment but does not wish to ever actually hold title to the replacement properties. The regulations essentially adopt the position of this ruling.[64]

The receipt of cash in return for one's property, even if the proceeds are immediately invested in like kind property, is fatal to Section 1031 treatment. For example, had Amy sold her ranch to Brendan and five minutes later used the sale proceeds to purchase Claire's farm, Amy would not be entitled to Section 1031 treatment. As originally described, the transaction resulted in Amy's securing Section 1031 treatment as a result of Brendan's willingness to purchase Claire's farm. Problems may arise if Brendan is unable or unwilling to take title to Claire's property. The regulations authorize the use of a "qualified intermediary" in a *simultaneous* exchange such as that described in the example.[65] Amy may therefore hire someone to serve as an accommodator, *i.e.*, to acquire Claire's farm using Brendan's money and to transfer the farm to Amy and Amy's ranch to Brendan.

Unlike the simultaneous exchange described in the example above, taxpayers often are confronted with situations where they have a buyer for their property but would prefer to have the benefit of Section 1031 treatment. Section 1031 does not require that the exchange of properties be simultaneous. Assume in the above example that Amy did not know of the availability of Claire's farm at the time that Brendan offered to purchase Amy's ranch for cash. Amy can still utilize Section 1031 if she agrees to transfer the ranch immediately to Brendan in exchange for Brendan's promise to purchase and transfer to Amy like kind properties to be designated by Amy within a given period of time.

---

[62] Rev. Rul. 57-244, 1957-1 C.B. 247.

[63] 1990-1 C.B.154.

[64] Treas. Reg. § 1.1031(k)-1(g)(4)(iv).

[65] Treas. Reg. § 1.1031(b)-2. See the discussion, *infra*, regarding qualified intermediaries.

In the first case to provide any detailed discussion of this issue, the court in *Starker v. United States*[66] held that a taxpayer was entitled to Section 1031 treatment on the ultimate receipt of like kind property even though the property to be received had not been identified at the time of the transfer of the property given up, and even though the taxpayer had reserved the right for up to five years to designate the property or properties to be received or to receive cash in whole or in part instead. Congress and the Treasury were not enamored with *Starker* or the indefinite deferral arrangements that decision sanctioned. They viewed such arrangements as creating serious administrative problems for the Service, expanding Section 1031 beyond congressional intent, and bearing sufficient resemblance to a sale to be taxed as one. In 1984, Congress responded to *Starker* by enacting Section 1031(a)(3), requiring the taxpayer to identify replacement property within 45 days of the transfer of the relinquished property and to receive the replacement property no later than 180 days after the transfer or the due date (including extensions) of the taxpayer's tax return for the year of the transfer, whichever is earlier.

The regulations on deferred exchanges require that a written, unambiguous designation of "replacement property" — that is, the property to be received on a deferred exchange — be made and delivered within the 45-day "identification period."[67] Because of a number of contingencies which may render the replacement property unacceptable to the taxpayer, *e.g.*, zoning, title, or environmental problems, the regulations permit the taxpayer to identify alternate property under the "3-property rule," the "200-percent rule," or the "95-percent rule." Under these rules, a taxpayer may identify three replacement properties of any value (the 3-property rule), or alternatively, any number of replacement properties that in the aggregate do not exceed twice the value of the property relinquished (the 200-percent rule).[68] The receipt of incidental property, *e.g.*, furniture transferred with an apartment building, will not cause taxpayer to fail the 3-property rule.[69] As a general rule, if the taxpayer identifies too much property, the taxpayer will be treated as having identified *no* property and therefore will not be entitled to the benefit of Section 1031 nonrecognition.

However, despite the failure to satisfy either the 3-property rule or the 200-percent rule, the taxpayer will nevertheless qualify for Section 1031 treatment if the taxpayer actually receives "identified replacement property the fair market value of which is at least 95 percent of the aggregate fair market value of all identified replacement property (the '95-percent rule')."[70] The 95 percent rule may be helpful in situations where properties are subject to debt. Assume, for example, the taxpayer wishes to exchange property worth $100,000 that is not subject to debt. By the end of the identification period, the taxpayer has identified four replacement properties, each with a value of $100,000, subject to a $75,000 mortgage. In these circumstances, since the taxpayer identified four properties that

---

[66] 602 F.2d 1341 (9th Cir. 1979).

[67] Treas. Reg. § 1.1031(k)-1(b), (c).

[68] *See* Treas. Reg. § 1.1031(k)-1(c)(4)(i).

[69] Treas. Reg. § 1.1031(k)-1(c)(5).

[70] *See* Treas. Reg. § 1.1031(k)-1(c)(4)(ii)(B).

in the aggregate have a fair market value that is 400 percent of the property relinquished, the taxpayer fails to satisfy either the three-property rule or the 200-percent rule, and will ordinarily be deemed to have identified no replacement property. However, if prior to the end of the exchange period, the taxpayer receives all four of the identified properties, he will be deemed to have satisfied the identification requirements of the regulation, because the properties received will have a value of at least 95 percent (in this case, 100 percent) of the properties identified. (Fair market value of identified property is determined on the earlier of the date received or the last day of the exchange period.)

The regulations provide that replacement property is received within the "exchange period" — the period designated in Section 1031(a)(3)(B), not in excess of 180 days — if the replacement property received is "substantially the same property as identified."[71] Property being produced may qualify as like kind property. For example, real property may be exchanged for real property that is to be improved. For purposes of the "substantially the same property" test, real property to be produced need not be completed on or before the date the property is received. However, "the property received will be considered to be substantially the same property as identified only if, had production been completed on or before the date the taxpayer receives the replacement property, the property received would have been considered to be substantially the same property as identified."[72]

The regulations also provide several "safe harbors" that permit taxpayers to use security or guarantee arrangements, qualified escrow accounts, qualified intermediaries, and interest and growth factors as part of deferred exchanges.[73] The taxpayer who uses a safe harbor will not be in actual or constructive receipt of money or other property on account of such use. Actual or constructive receipt of money or other property, prior to completion of the exchange, can obviously trigger recognition of gain or loss, potentially to the full extent of the realized gain or loss.[74] A taxpayer thus ignores the safe harbors at its peril.

The most important of these safe harbors is the "qualified intermediary" safe harbor. Simply stated, this safe harbor authorizes a taxpayer to utilize the services of a person or entity[75] to acquire and transfer properties, thereby accommodating the exchange. According to the regulations, the qualified intermediary will not be considered an agent of the taxpayer for purposes of Section 1031. Consider again the example involving Amy, Brendan, and Claire. Assume that Brendan is unwilling to purchase and transfer to Amy property Amy might identify. Under this safe harbor, Amy could hire an intermediary who would sell Amy's ranch to Brendan, use the sale proceeds to acquire the property designated by Amy (in this case Claire's farm), and transfer Claire's farm to Amy. The fact the intermediary was technically an agent of Amy would not make any difference. Thus, the qualified intermediary safe harbor in effect allows an agent of Amy to sell Amy's ranch to Brendan for cash

---

[71] Treas. Reg. § 1.1031(k)-1(d)(1).

[72] Treas. Reg. § 1.1031(k)-1(e)(3)(iii).

[73] *See* Treas. Reg. § 1.1031(k)-1(g).

[74] Treas. Reg. § 1.1031(k)-1(f)(2).

[75] The person may not be a "disqualified person" within the meaning of Regulation § 1.1031(k)-1(k).

without jeopardizing the availability of Section 1031 treatment for Amy.

The intermediary must act as a true conduit, that is, the intermediary must acquire the relinquished property from the taxpayer and transfer it, and also acquire the replacement property and transfer it to the taxpayer.[76] As noted previously, however, the regulations permit direct deeding, thus enabling the intermediary to remain outside of the chain of title.[77] The regulations impose a number of requirements that must be satisfied for the intermediary safe harbor and the other safe harbors to be operative.[78]

§ 38.10   REVERSE *STARKER* EXCHANGES

So-called "reverse *Starker* exchanges" are exchanges where the replacement property is acquired before the relinquished property is transferred. For example, assume Anna places a tract of commercial land on the market. Jenna is interested in acquiring Anna's land but wishes to engage in a like kind exchange. Anna, however, wants cash for her land. Pursuant to Revenue Procedure 2000-37,[79] Jenna may arrange for an exchange accommodator to acquire Anna's land using money provided by Jenna or borrowed from a third party. Jenna in turn will identify the property that she will transfer to the accommodator in exchange for Anna's land. The exchange accommodator will then sell the property received from Jenna and use the proceeds to repay Jenna or any third party who provided the accommodator to acquire Anna's land. Note that Regulation § 1.1031(k)-1 does not apply to "reverse *Starker* transactions."

§ 38.11   EXCHANGES QUALIFYING FOR BOTH § 121 AND § 1031

As discussed in detail in Chapter 6, Section 121 provides an exclusion for gain realized on the sale or exchange of a principal residence if, among other conditions, a taxpayer has owned and used the property as her principal residence for periods aggregating two years in the five year period preceding the date of the sale or the exchange. Thus, a taxpayer may qualify for the exclusion under Section 121 even though, at the time of the disposition of the property, the taxpayer is holding the property for business or investment purposes. This in turn raises the possibility that Section 1031 may also be applicable if there is an exchange of the property for other like kind property. Consider the following examples of situations where both Section 121 and Section 1031 would be applicable to an exchange:

Example 1: John and Mary, husband and wife, purchased a home in River City in 2000. They used the home as their principal residence until 2008 when they moved into a senior residence. At the time of their move in 2008, they converted their River City home to rental use. In 2010, they exchanged

---

[76]   Treas. Reg. § 1.1031(k)-l(g)(4)(iii)(B).

[77]   *See* Treas. Reg. § 1.1031(k)-l(g)(4)(iv),(v).

[78]   *See, e.g.*, Treas. Reg. § 1.1031(k)-1(g)(6).

[79]   2000-2 C.B. 308.

the home for another rental unit. Under these circumstances, the exchange is potentially subject to both Sections 121 and 1031.

Example 2: Assume the same facts as Example 1 except John and Mary never converted the home to a rental but rather lived in it until the 2010 exchange. During the time of their ownership of the home, however, they used one-third of the home for business purposes and two-thirds of the home as their principal residence. Again, they should be entitled to use both Section 121 and Section 1031 on the exchange.

With the limited exception of Section 121(d)(10) (discussed *infra*), neither Section 121 nor Section 1031 addresses the application of both provisions to a single exchange of property. Rev. Proc. 2005-14[80] acknowledges that both provisions may be applicable in a single exchange and provides important guidance as to how to apply the two provisions under those circumstances.

Utilizing as a model the rules of Section 121(d)(5)(B), which addresses the interrelationship of Sections 121 and 1033 (discussed in the next chapter), Rev. Proc. 2005-14 provides the following rules for applying Sections 121 and 1031 to the same transaction:

a. Section 121 must be applied to gain realized before applying Section 1031.

b. Under Section 121(d)(6), the Section 121 exclusion does not apply to gain attributable to depreciation deductions for periods after May 6, 1997 claimed with respect to the business or investment portion of a residence. However, Section 1031 may apply to such gain.

c. In applying Section 1031, cash or other non-like kind property (boot) received in exchange for the property used in the taxpayer's trade or business or held for investment (the relinquished business property) is taken into account only to the extent the boot exceeds the gain excluded under Section 121 with respect to the relinquished business property.

d. In determining the basis of the property received in the exchange to be used in taxpayer's trade or business or held for investment (the replacement property), any gain excluded under Section 121 is treated as gain recognized by the taxpayer. Thus, under Section 1031(d), the basis of the replacement business property is increased by any gain attributable to the relinquished business property that is excluded under Section 121.

Consider the following example:

Example: John and Mary purchased a large older home near State University in 1990. They paid $150,000 for the home. The home was their principal residence until 2008 at which time they moved to a senior residence. Immediately prior to moving, John and Mary invested $50,000 to convert their University-area home into an executive rental. Early in 2010,

---

[80] 2005-1 C.B. 528.

when the home was worth $900,000, they exchanged it for a four-plex apartment building in River City (the four-plex had an appraised fair market value of $500,000) and $400,000 in cash. Assume John and Mary had claimed a total of $15,000 of depreciation on the University-area home and had an adjusted basis in the home at the time of the exchange of $185,000. John and Mary file a joint return for 2010.

Analysis: Because John and Mary had owned and used the University-area home as their principal residence for at least two of the five years preceding the sale of the property, they are entitled to exclude, under Section 121, up to $500,000 of the $715,000 gain realized on the exchange ($900,000 less $185,000 adjusted basis). [Technically, given Section 121(d)(6), the Section 121 exclusion would not apply to the first $15,000 of gain, *i.e.*, the gain in the amount of the depreciation claimed by John and Mary. The exclusion would apply to the remaining $700,000 of gain but not in excess of $500,000.]

John and Mary may defer the remaining $215,000 of gain, including the $15,000 of gain attributable to depreciation, under Section 1031. Although John and Mary received $400,000 in cash (boot) on the exchange, they are not required to recognize gain because the boot is taken into account for purposes of Section 1031(b) only to the extent the boot exceeds the amount of excluded gain. It does not.

Their basis in the River City four-plex will be their basis at the time of the exchange in their University-area property (the relinquished property) of $185,000 increased by the $500,000 (gain excluded under Section 121) and reduced by the $400,000 cash they received. Thus, their basis in the four-plex will be $285,000. Note that this basis will preserve the $215,000 of unrecognized gain.

§ 38.12　SECTION 121(d)(10) — PROPERTY ACQUIRED IN A LIKE KIND EXCHANGE

In 2004, Congress amended Section 121 to provide that, if property is acquired in a like kind exchange, the property must be held for at least five years before gain on its sale or exchange may be excluded under Section 121.[81]

The following example demonstrates the problem Congress sought to address with this new provision.

Example: For many years, Katie and Patrick, a married couple, owned and used as rental property a duplex in Portland, Oregon. On March 1, 2001, they exchanged the Portland apartment building for a large single family home on Lake Washington in Seattle. They intended to hold the Seattle home as rental property with the idea of renting it on a weekly or monthly basis to corporate executives, academics, or medical doctors whose work brought them to Seattle for short periods of time. At the time of the exchange, the Portland duplex had a fair market value of $800,000 and an

---

[81] I.R.C. § 121(d)(10).

adjusted basis of $300,000. The Seattle home they acquired in the exchange also had a fair market value of $800,000. Neither the Portland duplex nor the Seattle home was encumbered by any mortgage. As a result of Section 1031, Katie and Patrick, although realizing a gain on the exchange of $500,000, did not recognize any gain. Instead, under Section 1031, they took a $300,000 basis in the Seattle home, thus preserving the $500,000 of unrecognized gain associated with the duplex. In other words, the effect of Section 1031 was to defer recognition of the $500,000 of gain inherent in the duplex.

Katie and Patrick rented the Seattle home for six months. On September 1, 2001, they decided to move from Portland, where they had lived for a number of years, to Seattle. After looking for homes in Seattle, they finally decided that, instead of continuing to rent the home on Lake Washington, they would move into it themselves and establish it as their principal residence. During the period from October 1, 2001 through October 2003, the Lake Washington home served as their principal residence. On November 1, 2003, they sold that home for $800,000. Under Section 121, they were able to exclude all $500,000 of the realized gain on the sale of the home. (Assume that their adjusted basis in the Lake Washington home had remained $300,000.)

Note that Section 121 combined with the deferral previously accorded them under Section 1031, in effect enabled Katie and Patrick to exclude all of the gain ($500,000) that had been associated with the Portland duplex. Under Section 121 as amended, if the exchange took place after the effective date of the 2004 amendment, Katie and Patrick would not be eligible to exclude any portion of the realized gain from the sale of the Lake Washington home acquired in the exchange until they had owned that home for 5 years. (Note: Katie and Patrick still only need to use the Lake Washington home as their principal residence for periods aggregating 2 years.)

In 2005, Congress extended Section 121(d)(10) so as to apply not only to the taxpayer who acquired property in a Section 1031 exchange, but also to any person whose basis in the property is determined by reference to the taxpayer's basis. A prime target of this extension is presumably those who may receive the property from the taxpayer as a gift. Thus, in the above example, assume Katie and Patrick, after living from October 2001 through October 2003 in the Lake Washington home (acquired March 1, 2001, in a Section 1031 exchange), give the home to their daughter, Donna. Under the 2005 Act, on a subsequent sale of the home, in order for Donna to be entitled to exclusion of gain under Section 121, she would not only have to satisfy the two-year use and ownership requirements of Section 121, but, as the donee of the home, would also have to satisfy the five-year rule of Section 121(d)(10).

Chapter 39

INVOLUNTARY CONVERSIONS

§ 39.01 GENERAL POLICY

The Internal Revenue Code contains a number of relief provisions, some of which have been examined in prior chapters of this text. Section 1033 is an important relief provision affording taxpayers the benefit of nonrecognition of gain in circumstances where recognition could create severe hardship.

Consider a common example: a state condemns farm land for highway use. The farmer's adjusted basis in the land is minimal relative to the value of the land. The farmer, who is compensated by the state for the taking, immediately uses the compensation to purchase replacement land. Technically, as a result of the condemnation, the farmer has realized gain in the amount of the difference between the condemnation award received and the farmer's adjusted basis in the condemned property. Because the farmer received cash when the farm was condemned, Section 1031 nonrecognition[1] will not apply, even though the farmer immediately replaced the condemned land with other land of a like kind. However, a different provision, Section 1033, affords the farmer the opportunity to defer the gain realized on the condemnation.

Originally enacted in 1921, Section 1033 provides taxpayers the opportunity to avoid the forced recognition of gain which, as the above hypothetical demonstrates, might otherwise result when the taxpayer's property is "compulsorily or involuntarily converted" as a result of destruction, theft, seizure, or requisition or condemnation or threat or imminence thereof. Congress recognized the recognition of gain and the resulting imposition of tax liability in a case such as that of the farmer might frustrate the taxpayer's efforts to replace the condemned land.

The farmer has the option of avoiding the recognition of gain by reinvesting the condemnation award in other property "similar or related in service or use" to the property condemned. To the extent that the farmer *elects* Section 1033 treatment and completely invests the condemnation award in property meeting that standard (hereinafter *qualified replacement property*), the farmer will, in effect, be permitted to defer the payment of tax upon the gain from the condemned farmland. Even if the farmer elects Section 1033 treatment, gain will be recognized to the extent the proceeds from the condemnation are not completely reinvested in qualified replacement property.

While initially Section 1033 also applied to losses, Congress in 1942 specifically exempted losses from the nonrecognition rule of Section 1033. This is one of the

---

[1] *See* Chapter 38, *supra.*

significant differences between Sections 1033 and 1031. Another significant difference is that, unlike Section 1031, Section 1033 is applicable not only to property held for use in a trade or business or for investment but also to property held for personal uses, *e.g.*, one's home.

§ 39.02 THE MANDATORY AND ELECTIVE RULES OF SECTION 1033

§ 1033.   Involuntary conversions —

(a)   **General rule — If property (as a result of its destruction in whole or in part, theft, seizure, or requisition or condemnation or threat or imminence thereof) is compulsorily or involuntarily converted —**

(1)   **Conversion into similar property — Into property similar or related in service or use to the property so converted, no gain shall be recognized.**

(2)   **Conversion into money — Into money or into property not similar or related in service or use to the converted property, the gain (if any) shall be recognized except to the extent hereinafter provided in this paragraph:**

(A)   **Nonrecognition of gain — If the taxpayer during the period specified in subparagraph (B), for the purpose of replacing the property so converted, purchases other property similar or related in service or use to the property so converted, or purchases stock in the acquisition of control of a corporation owning such other property, at the election of the taxpayer the gain shall be recognized only to the extent that the amount realized upon such conversion (regardless of whether such amount is received in one or more taxable years) exceeds the cost of such other property or such stock. Such election shall be made at such time and in such manner as the Secretary may by regulations prescribe. For purposes of this paragraph —**

(i)   **no property or stock acquired before the disposition of the converted property shall be considered to have been acquired for the purpose of replacing such converted property unless held by the taxpayer on the date of such disposition; and**

(ii)   **the taxpayer shall be considered to have purchased property or stock only if, but for the provisions of subsection (b) of this section, the unadjusted basis of such property or stock would be its cost within the meaning of section 1012.**

Section 1033(a) actually provides two separate rules: Section 1033(a)(l) applies to those relatively rare situations in which property is directly converted into qualified replacement property; Section 1033(a)(2) applies to the more common situation in which property is first converted into money or nonqualified property and is subsequently replaced with qualified property. In the case of the direct conversion of property into qualified replacement property, nonrecognition of gain is mandatory. In the case of the conversion of property into nonqualified property or a combination of qualified and nonqualified property, nonrecognition is elective. The difference between the two rules is likely a function of the fact that a direct conversion of property into qualified replacement property seems so akin to a Section 1031 exchange that Congress believed it should be treated as such for tax purposes. Thus, just as Section 1031 nonrecognition treatment is mandatory in the case of like kind exchanges, nonrecognition treatment is mandatory in the case of a direct replacement under Section 1033. Because cases and rulings involving direct replacement are rare, the focus of this involuntary conversion discussion will be on the elective nonrecognition rule of Section 1033.

§ 39.03 INVOLUNTARY CONVERSION EVENTS

The involuntary conversion events listed in Section 1033(a) have not created significant controversy. This is not to suggest, however, that in considering Section 1033 problems, one need not be concerned with the kind of event that has resulted in a conversion. A few comments are therefore in order regarding involuntary conversion events. The term "destruction" in Section 1033 has been analogized to the term "casualty" as discussed in Chapter 24. Thus, destruction as a result of fire, storm or shipwreck would be an involuntary conversion within the meaning of Section 1033. The Service has issued numerous rulings finding that specific casualties such as the destruction of livestock by lightning[2] and the destruction of crops by hail[3] constitute involuntary conversion events. For Section 165(c)(3) purposes, a casualty is defined as an event that is sudden, unusual and unexpected. However, the Service has ruled that destruction need not be sudden under Section 1033.[4] Property rendered unsafe for its intended use due to chemical contamination is regarded as destroyed under Section 1033(a).[5] The Service has also ruled that, where a principal residence was destroyed by a tornado — clearly an involuntary conversion event — and the owner subsequently sold the land on which the residence was located, the sale of the land would be treated as part of a single involuntary conversion of the residence.[6] In one case, the Service argued that, by processing damaged trees into end products which it then sold, rather than simply selling the damaged trees themselves, a timber company lost the ability to use Section 1033 to defer the gain inherent in the trees prior to processing. The Tax Court disagreed, holding that, where the taxpayer's property was involuntarily damaged and was no longer available for its intended business purpose, the general elements of Section 1033 were satisfied, regardless of whether the damaged property was sold as is or further processed before being sold.[7]

The term "seizure" in Section 1033(a) is generally accorded the meaning of confiscation of property by a governmental entity without the payment of compensation. For example, the seizure of a boat or car used in an illegal drug operation would be a seizure contemplated by the language of Section 1033. By contrast, the terms "requisition" and "condemnation" suggest a taking of property by a government agency for a public use. Involuntary conversions as a result of requisition or condemnation account for the majority of the reported Section 1033

---

[2] Rev. Rul. 53-195, 1953-2 C.B. 169.

[3] Rev. Rul. 59-8, 1959-1 C.B. 202.

[4] Rev. Rul. 59-102, 1959-1 C.B. 200.

[5] Rev. Rul. 89-2, 1989-1 C.B. 259.

[6] Rev. Rul. 96-32, 1996-1 C.B. 177.

[7] Willamette Industries, Inc. v. Commissioner, 118 T.C. 126 (2002) (relying in part on the Service's own prior ruling, Rev. Rul. 80-175, 1980-2 C.B. 230).

decisions and rulings. As the Court of Claims noted in *American Natural Gas Co. v. United States*,[8] the words "requisition or condemnation" mean "the taking or the threat of taking property by some public or quasi-public corporation — by some instrumentality that has the power to do so against the will of the owner, and for the use of the taker. That is the common, well-recognized meaning of those words and there is nothing to indicate that Congress used them in any other sense."[9]

§ 39.04 SIMILAR OR RELATED IN SERVICE OR USE

Most of the litigation with respect to Section 1033 addresses the issue of whether the property acquired to replace the converted property satisfies the "similar or related in service or use" standard of Section 1033(a)(2). Just as the like kind standard and the holding requirements of Section 1031 are intended to insure that nonrecognition is accorded only when there is continuity of investment, so too the "similar or related in service or use" standard limits the scope of Section 1033 treatment.[10] As the Tax Court noted in explaining the "similar or related in service or use" standard, "it is not necessary to acquire property which duplicates exactly that which was converted, [but] the fortuitous circumstance of involuntary conversion does not permit a taxpayer to change the character of his investment without tax consequences."[11]

Considering the central role the "similar or related in service or use" standard plays in Section 1033, it is surprising that, in enacting the predecessor to Section 1033, Congress did not provide any guidance as to its application. Considerable disagreement exists regarding the meaning of the standard, and its application. But the Service has recognized that, in applying the "similar or related in service or use" standard, the analysis used with respect to owner-occupied property will differ from the analysis employed with respect to rental situations.

> In previous litigation, the Service has taken the position that the statutory phrase, "similar or related in service or use," means that the property acquired must have a close "functional" similarity to the property converted. Under this test, property was not considered similar or related in service or use to the converted property unless the physical characteristics and end uses of the converted and replacement properties were closely similar. Although this "functional use test" has been upheld in lower courts, it has not been sustained in the appellate courts with respect to investors in property, such as lessors.

---

[8] 279 F.2d 220 (Ct. Cl.), *cert. denied*, 364 U.S. 900 (1960).

[9] *Id.* at 225.

[10] As noted previously, Section 1033 does not require that the property be business or investment property. Thus, the involuntary conversion of personal use property, such as one's home, can entitle a taxpayer to the nonrecognition treatment of Section 1033. For example, if the fire insurance proceeds received as a result of the destruction of one's summer cabin were invested in the construction of a new cabin, Section 1033 would apply and defer any gain realized to the extent the requirements of Section 1033 were satisfied.

[11] Maloof v. Comm'r, 65 T.C. 263, 269–270 (1975).

In conformity with the appellate court decisions, in considering whether replacement property acquired by an investor is similar in service or use to the converted property, attention will be directed primarily to the similarity in the relationship of the service or use which the original and replacement properties have to the taxpayer-owner. In applying this test, a determination will be made as to whether the properties are of a similar service to the taxpayer, the nature of the business risks connected with the properties, and what such properties demand of the taxpayer in the way of management, services and relations to his tenants.

For example, where the taxpayer is the lessor, who rented out the converted property for a light manufacturing plant and then rents out the replacement property for a wholesale grocery warehouse, the nature of the taxpayer-owner's service or use of the properties may be similar although that of the end users change. The two properties will be considered as similar or related in service or use where, for example, both are rented and where there is a similarity in the extent and type of the taxpayer's management activities, the amount and kind of services rendered by him to his tenants, and the nature of his business risks connected with the properties.

In modifying its position with respect to the involuntary conversion of property held for investment, the Service will continue to adhere to the functional test in the case of owner-users of property. Thus, if the taxpayer-owner operates a light manufacturing plant on the converted property and then operates a wholesale grocery warehouse on the replacement property, by changing his end use he has so changed the nature of his relationship to the property as to be outside the nonrecognition of gain provisions.[12]

Example 1: John purchased a commercial building several years ago. He leased the building to the American Red Cross. Under the terms of the long term lease, the Red Cross was responsible for all utilities, sewer, garbage collection and maintenance. As a result of an early morning fire in January of this year, the building was completely destroyed. The building was insured for its fair market value. Because the Red Cross was interested in locating in another area of the city, John was under no obligation to rebuild for the benefit of the Red Cross. Instead, John used the insurance proceeds to purchase an apartment building. He kept an apartment for himself in the building and used that apartment as his office. He personally handled all aspects of renting the apartments and addressing specific problems raised by tenants with respect to their units. John realized a substantial amount of gain as a result of the conversion of the commercial building. Will John be eligible for nonrecognition treatment under Section 1033?

Analysis: John will likely not be eligible for nonrecognition treatment under Section 1033. John's relationship to the commercial building destroyed in the fire was not that of an owner/user but rather that of an

---

[12] Rev. Rul. 64-237, 1964-2 C.B. 319.

owner/investor. Therefore, in applying the "similar or related in service or use" standard of Section 1033, the focus will be on the nature of the business risk connected with the properties and on what the properties demand of John as lessor in terms of management, service, and relation to the tenants. With respect to the commercial building, John's obligations appear to have been minimal. The tenant was responsible for the maintenance of the building and for all matters associated with utilities, etc. By contrast, John has assumed considerably more responsibility with respect to the apartment complex. Not only is he responsible for maintaining the complex, he is the one who handles all aspects of renting the apartments. Had John used the insurance proceeds to build another commercial building he leased to a business under terms similar to those of the Red Cross lease, he would have satisfied the "similar or related in service or use standard." That is not the case in this example and, as a result, John does not appear eligible for Section 1033 nonrecognition.

Example 2: Finn owns a commercial building in which he conducts a retail clothing business featuring clothing for both men and women. The building is destroyed by fire and Finn uses the insurance proceeds to build another building. He uses the opportunity to change the focus of his retail clothing business from a more general business to one focusing exclusively on designer clothing for women. Will Finn be entitled to the benefit of nonrecognition treatment under Section 1033 with respect to the gain realized on the conversion of the commercial building?

Analysis: Finn's relation to the commercial building was that of owner/user. As a result, the "similar or related in service or use" standard will be applied by using a functional or end use test. The likelihood is that Finn will satisfy the test. The commercial building was used for retail clothing sales; the new building will likewise be used for a retail clothing business conducted by Finn. Although the specific type of clothing sold in the business has changed, Finn's relationship to the property has not changed and there is enough similarity between the businesses that the new property should be viewed as "similar or related in service or use" to the destroyed property. Nonrecognition treatment under Section 1033 appears to be appropriate in this example.

The regulations provide limited assistance in applying the "similar or related in service or use" standard, and at the same time suggest the narrowness of that standard.[13] The regulation specifically identifies the following three circumstances as examples of when replacement property will not satisfy the "similar or related in service or use" standard.

(1)   The proceeds of unimproved real estate, taken upon condemnation proceedings, are invested in improved real estate. [Note that, under the special rule of Section 1033(g), however, the replacement property could qualify as property "similar or related in service or use." Section 1033(g) was enacted after the regulation and is discussed *infra*.

---

[13] Treas. Reg. § 1.1033(a)-2(c)(9).

(2)   The proceeds of conversion of real property are applied in reduction of indebtedness previously incurred in the purchase of a leasehold. (Nonetheless, a leasehold interest may be similar or related in service or use to a fee interest. For example, a fee interest acquired to replace an involuntarily converted 15-year leasehold was held to be similar or related in service or use to the leasehold where the fee interest and the leasehold were used for the same purposes in the same business.)[14]

(3)   The owner of a requisitioned tug uses the proceeds to buy barges.

Qualifying replacement property can consist of a controlling interest in the stock of a corporation that owns property similar or related in service or use to the converted property.[15]

[A]   Special Rule for Condemnation of Real Property Used for Business or Investment

There is a distinction between the "like kind" standard of Section 1031 and the "similar or related in service or use" standard of Section 1033. That these standards are different is obvious from the fact the Congress used different language. In 1958 Congress recognized the difference between the standards when it amended Section 1033 by adding a new subsection — Section 1033(g).

§ 1033.   Involuntary conversions —

(g)   Condemnation of real property held for productive use in trade or business or for investment —

(1)   Special rule — For purposes of subsection (a), if real property (not including stock in trade or other property held primarily for sale) held for productive use in trade or business or for investment is (as the result of its seizure, requisition, or condemnation, or threat or imminence thereof) compulsorily or involuntarily converted, property of a like kind to be held either for productive use in trade or business or for investment shall be treated as property similar or related in service or use to the property so converted.

Section 1033(g) provides, in part, that, if real property held for productive use in a trade or business or for investment is, as the result of seizure, requisition, or condemnation, or threat or imminence thereof, compulsorily or involuntarily converted after December 31, 1957, property of a like kind to be held either for productive use in a trade or business or for investment shall be treated as property similar or related in service or use to the property so converted.[16] The enactment of this provision afforded Congress the opportunity to compare the "similar or related in service or use" standard of Section 1033(a) with the "like kind" standard of Section 1031. The legislative history of Section 1033(g) provides the following instructive discussion:

---

[14]   Rev. Rul. 83-70, 1983-1 C.B. 189.

[15]   I.R.C. § 1033(a)(2)(A). Special basis rules apply in such cases. I.R.C. § 1033(b)(3).

[16]   Section 1.1033 (g)-1(a) of the Income Tax Regulations provides that the principles set forth in Regulation Section 1.1031 (a)-1(b) shall be used in determining whether replacement property is property of like kind.

The Internal Revenue Service and courts have held that Section 1033 requires a relatively narrow construction of the words "property similar or related in service or use" with the result that the converted property must be substantially similar to that destroyed. It has been held not to include, for example, improved real estate which is converted into unimproved realty, nor a barge substituted for a tug. Similarly, it has been held not to include property used in the operation of a business which was substituted for rented property. Likewise, it has been held not to include city real estate exchanged for a farm or a ranch.

Present law also provides for the nonrecognition of gain where property held for productive use in trade or business or for investment . . . is exchanged for property of a "like kind to be held either for productive use in trade or business or for investment." The phrase "like kind to be held either for productive use in trade or business or for investment" has been given a broader interpretation than the "similar or related" phrase. "Like kind," for example, has been held to include unimproved real estate which is exchanged for improved real estate, so long as both properties are held either for productive use in trade or business or for investment. Thus, the "like kind" phrase has been held to include the exchange of city real estate (used in a trade or business) for a farm or ranch.

Both in the case of property involuntarily converted and in the case of the exchange of property held for productive use in trade or business or for investment, gain is not recognized because of the continuity of the investment. Your committee sees no reason why substantially similar rules should not be followed in determining what constitutes a continuity of investment in these two types of situations where there is a condemnation of real property. Moreover, it appears particularly unfortunate that present law requires a closer identity of the destroyed and converted property where the exchange is beyond the control of the taxpayer than that which is applied in the case of the voluntary exchange of business property.[17]

As a result of Section 1033(g), a significant disparity in the tax treatment of involuntary conversions will result depending on the nature of the conversion event.

Example 1: A fire destroys the building that Mary owns and uses to operate her dance studio. Mary collects the insurance proceeds realizing a large gain, and, within the next 12 months, uses these proceeds to purchase an apartment building; she then commences to rent apartments to residential tenants.

Analysis: As indicated in the foregoing Senate Committee report, and in the above excerpt from Revenue Ruling 64-237, the replacement property is unlikely to be considered "similar or related in service or use" to the converted property under Section 1033(a). Mary's gain will be recognized.

---

[17] S. Rep. No. 1983, 85th Cong. 2d Sess.; 1958-3 C.B. 993–94.

Example 2: Suppose the facts are the same as in the prior example, except the building housing the dance studio is condemned by the State instead of being destroyed by fire.

Analysis: This involuntary conversion appears to fall within Section 1033(g) because there is a condemnation of real property used in trade or business, and the new properties satisfy the "like kind" standard, *i.e.*, the taxpayer has replaced one type of real estate with another type of real estate. As discussed in Chapter 38, the term "like kind" is given a broad definition in the context of real property. Because the replacement property acquired by Mary satisfies the "like kind" standard, the replacement property will be treated as property "similar or related in service or use" to the converted property. Accordingly, the gain on the conversion would not be recognized.

Under certain circumstances, because of the replacement property acquired by taxpayer, the "similar or related in service or use" standard will prove broader than the "like kind" standard of Section 1031. For example, in Revenue Ruling 83-70,[18] a city condemned land that a taxpayer used in its business of hauling, handling, and storing furniture. The taxpayer did not own the land but held a long-term lease on the land. There were 15 years remaining on the taxpayer's leasehold interest in the land at the time of the condemnation. As a result of the compensation the taxpayer received from the city for the taking of taxpayer's leasehold interest, the taxpayer realized a gain. Within the period specified in Section 1033 (a)(2)(B) of the Code, the taxpayer acquired a fee simple interest in real property improved with a warehouse and an office building and used this replacement property in the same business and for the identical purposes the taxpayer had used the condemned leasehold. Revenue Ruling 83-70 first addressed the applicability of Section 1033(g) and concluded that the "like kind" standard afforded by that provision was inapplicable. The ruling noted that, pursuant to Treas. Reg. § 1031(a)-1(b), "the leasehold interest must have a remaining term of at least 30 years in order to be of the same "nature" as a fee interest in real property." Thus, the "like kind" standard of Section 1031 would not be satisfied were a leasehold of less than 30 years exchanged for a fee simple interest. Under the facts of Rev. Rul. 83-70, the condemned leasehold had a remaining term of only 15 years and therefore the taxpayer could not rely on the "like kind" provisions of Section 1033 (g) to defer recognition of the gain realized on the condemnation.

Revenue Ruling 83-70 then addressed the issue whether, under Section 1033(a), a leasehold interest may be "similar or related in service or use" to a fee interest. The ruling noted that, in *Davis Regulator Company v. Commissioner*,[19] the United States Board of Tax Appeals held that a taxpayer did not have to recognize gain on the receipt of proceeds received with respect to the condemnation of a leasehold interest to the extent the proceeds were invested in the construction of a building on land owned by the taxpayer. The new building was used for the identical purpose as the converted leasehold. The court's decision was based on the "similar or related in service or use" standard currently found in Section 1033(a)(2)(A) of the Code."

---

[18] 1983-1 C.B. 189.

[19] 36 B.T.A. 437 (1937), *acq.*, 1937-2 C.B. 7.

Based on that decision, the Service in Revenue Ruling 83-70 concluded the taxpayer qualified for non-recognition of gain under Section 1033(a) because the fee property acquired by the taxpayer with the proceeds from the involuntarily converted 15-year leasehold interest was to be used by the taxpayer in the same business and for the identical purposes as the condemned leasehold.

The replacement property acquired in some circumstances will qualify under neither the "similar or related in service" standard or the "like kind" standard. For example, in Rev. Rul. 76-390,[20] a state condemned some of the land taxpayer owned and used for a mobile home park. The taxpayer used the condemnation proceeds to build a motel on the remaining mobile home park land taxpayer owned. Citing the owner-user standard of Rev. Rul. 64-237, the Service concluded the motel to be constructed on land already owned by the taxpayer could not qualify under the Section 1033(a) "similar or related in service or use" standard because the physical characteristics and end uses of a motel are not closely similar to those of a mobile home park. Similarly, the Service held the "like kind" standard of Section 1033(g) was inapplicable. In regard to the latter standard, the Service relied on Rev. Rul. 67-255,[21] which concluded an office building taxpayer constructed upon land he already owned would not qualify as being of a like kind to land of the taxpayer that was involuntarily converted. "Although the term "real estate" is often used to embrace land and improvements thereon, land and improvements are by nature not alike merely because one term is used to describe both. Land is not of the same nature or character as a building."

[B] Federally Declared Disasters

There are special rules relating to property damaged in federally declared disasters.

§ 1033. Involuntary conversions —

(h) Special rules for property damaged by federally declared disasters —

(1) Principal residences — If the taxpayer's principal residence or any of its contents is located in a disaster area and is compulsorily or involuntarily converted as a result of a federally declared disaster —

(A) Treatment of insurance proceeds —

(i) Exclusion for unscheduled personal property — No gain shall be recognized by reason of the receipt of any insurance proceeds for personal property which was part of such contents and which was not scheduled property for purposes of such insurance.

(ii) Other proceeds treated as common fund — In the case of any insurance proceeds (not described in clause (i)) for such residence or contents —

(I) such proceeds shall be treated as received for the conversion of a single item of property, and

---

[20] 1976-2 C.B. 243.

[21] 1967-2 C.B. 270.

(II) any property which is similar or related in service or use to the residence so converted (or contents thereof) shall be treated for purposes of subsection (a)(2) as property similar or related in service or use to such single item of property.

(B)   Extension of replacement period — Subsection (a)(2)(B) shall be applied with respect to any property so converted by substituting "4 years" for "2 years".

(2)   Trade or business and investment property — If a taxpayer's property held for productive use in a trade or business or for investment is located in a disaster area and is compulsorily or involuntarily converted as a result of a federally declared disaster, tangible property of a type held for productive use in a trade or business shall be treated for purposes of subsection (a) as property similar or related in service or use to the property so converted.

(3)   Federally declared disaster; disaster area — The terms "federally declared disaster" and "disaster area" shall have the respective meaning given such terms by Section 165(h)(3)(C).

(4)   Principal residence — For purposes of this subsection, the term "principal residence" has the same meaning as when used in section 121, except that such term shall include a residence not treated as a principal residence solely because the taxpayer does not own the residence.

Congress has provided special relief for taxpayers whose property is damaged in federally declared disasters. Thus, for example, Section 1033(h)(1)(A)(i) provides that taxpayers will have no gain from insurance proceeds for personal property that was part of the contents of the taxpayer's principal residence[22] if the personal property was not "scheduled property" for purposes of insurance. ("Scheduled property" is an insurance term generally referring to property identified on an itemized list of property attached to an insurance policy. In addition to identifying each item of personal property specially covered by the policy, the "scheduled property" list typically reflects the value of each item of "scheduled property.") As a result of Section 1033(h)(1)(A)(i), taxpayers are not limited in their use of the insurance proceeds attributable to unscheduled personal property. With respect to insurance proceeds for the residence itself and for any scheduled property, Section 1033(h)(1)(A)(ii) treats the insurance proceeds for these properties as a common fund received for the conversion of a single item of property. Any replacement property that is "similar or related in service or use" to the residence or its contents will be treated as "similar or related in service or use" to the deemed single item of property. Thus, if a taxpayer were to receive fire insurance proceeds of $500,000 for the destruction of taxpayer's residence and $150,000 for the destruction of the "scheduled property" contents of that residence, the taxpayer could avoid reporting any gain if the taxpayer spent at least a total of $650,000 on a replacement residence and contents for that residence. If, for example, the taxpayer spent $600,000 on the new residence and only $50,000 on contents for that residence, taxpayer would avoid reporting any gain. In other words, given the "single item" treatment of Section 1033(h)(1)(A)(ii), the taxpayer need not replace the $150,000 of "scheduled prop

---

[22] "Principal residence" is defined for § 1033(h) purposes the same as it is for § 121 purposes except that the term includes a residence that would not be treated a principal residence solely because the taxpayer does not own the residence.

erty" with $150,000 of replacement contents for the replacement residence.

Section 1033(h)(2) provides significant relief if a taxpayer's property held for productive use in a trade or business or for investment is located in a disaster area and is compulsorily or involuntarily converted as a result of a federally declared disaster. Under this provision, any replacement property that is tangible property held for productive use in a trade or business will be treated as property "similar or related in service or use" to the converted property. In explaining the reason for that provision, the legislative history of Section 1033(h)(2) states:[23]

> The property damage in a [federally] declared disaster may be so great that businesses may be forced to suspend operations for a substantial time. During that hiatus, valuable markets and customers may be lost. If this suspension causes the businesses to fail, and the owners of the business wish to reinvest their capital in a new business venture, the involuntary conversion rules will force them to recognize gain when they buy replacement property that is needed for the new business but not similar to that used in the failed business. This provision will offer relief to such businesses by allowing them to reinvest their funds in any tangible business property without being forced to recognize gain.

§ 39.05 TIME FOR REPLACEMENT

§ 1033. Involuntary conversions —

(a) General rule — If property (as a result of its destruction in whole or in part, theft, seizure, or requisition or condemnation or threat or imminence thereof) is compulsorily or involuntarily converted —

(2) Conversion into money — Into money or into property not similar or related in service or use to the converted property, the gain (if any) shall be recognized except to the extent hereinafter provided in this paragraph:

(B) Period within which property must be replaced — The period referred to in subparagraph (A) shall be the period beginning with the date of the disposition of the converted property, or the earliest date of the threat or imminence of requisition or condemnation of the converted property, whichever is the earlier, and ending —

(i) 2 years after the close of the first taxable year in which any part of the gain upon the conversion is realized, or

(ii) subject to such terms and conditions as may be specified by the Secretary, at the close of such later date as the Secretary may designate on application by the taxpayer. Such application shall be made at such time and in such manner as the Secretary may by regulations prescribe.

As noted previously, the relief accorded by Section 1033 is premised on the notion that, where a taxpayer's investment in property continues, it is not appropriate to recognize gain that may have been involuntarily realized by the taxpayer. This continuity of investment rationale underlies the nonrecognition treatment accorded by Section 1031 and accounts for the holding requirements imposed by Section

---

[23] S. Rept. 104-281, at 14.

1031. Unlike Section 1031, however, Section 1033 does not specifically impose any holding requirements. Instead, to assure that continuity of investment exists, Section 1033(a)(2)(B) generally requires that converted property be replaced within a two-year period following the conversion of the property. (A three-year replacement period is provided for Section 1033(g) involuntary conversions.[24] A four-year replacement period is provided under Section 1033(h)(1)(B) for personal residences and their contents damaged in federally declared disasters.)

Section 1033(a)(2)(A) specifically requires that the replacement property be purchased "for the purpose of replacing the property so converted." (Property acquired before the disposition of the converted property will not be deemed to have been acquired as replacement property unless it is held by the taxpayer on the date of the disposition of the converted property.) Furthermore, property will be considered "purchased" only if, but for the special basis rule of Section 1033(b), discussed below, the unadjusted basis of such property would be its cost within the meaning of Section 1012. Thus, for example, property received by gift will not satisfy the "purchased" requirement because the basis of that property will be determined under Section 1015 and not Section 1012.[25]

Finally, if the replacement property is acquired from a related person, nonrecognition treatment may be lost.[26] This rule applies to individual taxpayers if the aggregate realized gain for the year, on all involuntarily converted property on which there is realized gain, exceeds $100,000. The rule, however, does not apply if the related person acquired the replacement property from an unrelated person during the replacement period.

§ 39.06   PARTIAL RECOGNITION OF GAIN UNDER SECTION 1033

Just as there may be partial recognition of gain in the case of a like kind exchange under Section 1031, realized gain will be recognized under Section 1033(a)(2) to the extent that the amount received upon the conversion exceeds the cost of the replacement property.

Example: Assume the farmer in the hypothetical at the outset of this Chapter received a condemnation award in the amount of $50,000, and replaced the converted property with property costing $40,000. Will any gain be recognized?

Analysis: If a Section 1033 election is made, a maximum of $10,000 of the realized gain would be recognized. If the farmer's basis in the converted property had been $10,000, then $10,000 of the $40,000 of realized gain would be recognized. By contrast, if the farmer's basis in the converted property had been $45,000, then only $5,000 of gain would have been realized and thus only $5,000 of gain would be recognized.

---

[24] I.R.C. § 1033(g)(4).

[25] Treas. Reg. § 1.1033(a)-2(c)(4).

[26] I.R.C. § 1033(i).

§ 39.07 BASIS OF REPLACEMENT PROPERTY

§ 1033. Involuntary conversions —

(b) Basis of property acquired through involuntary conversion —

(1) Conversions described in subsection (a)(1)— If the property was acquired as the result of a compulsory or involuntary conversion described in subsection (a)(1), the basis shall be the same as in the case of the property so converted —

(A) decreased in the amount of any money received by the taxpayer which was not expended in accordance with the provisions of law (applicable to the year in which such conversion was made) determining the taxable status of the gain or loss upon such conversion, and

(B) increased in the amount of gain or decreased in the amount of loss to the taxpayer recognized upon such conversion under the law applicable to the year in which such conversion was made.

(2) Conversions described in subsection (a)(2)— In the case of property purchased by the taxpayer in a transaction described in subsection (a)(2) which resulted in the nonrecognition of any part of the gain realized as the result of a compulsory or involuntary conversion, the basis shall be the cost of such property decreased in the amount of the gain not so recognized; and if the property purchased consists of more than 1 piece of property, the basis determined under this sentence shall be allocated to the purchased properties in proportion to their respective costs.

At first glance, the basis rules of Section 1033(b) may seem quite confusing. Just as there are both mandatory and elective nonrecognition rules in Section 1033(a), there are two separate basis rules contained in Section 1033(b)(1) and (2). The rule provided in Section 1033(b)(1) is applicable only to those rare cases in which property is directly converted into qualified replacement property. Note that this basis rule is very similar to the Section 1031 basis rule.

The more common basis rule of Section 1033(b)(2) is applicable in cases where the taxpayer elects Section 1033 nonrecognition, i.e., it is applicable only when property is converted into nonqualified property, such as insurance proceeds or cash, and qualified replacement property is subsequently purchased. Thus, for example, the farmer in the hypothetical at the outset of this chapter would use this basis provision in computing the adjusted basis in the farm land purchased with the condemnation award. The basis rule is simple: the basis of the replacement property shall be the cost of such property decreased by the amount of gain realized on the conversion but not recognized as a result of Section 1033.

Example 1: Assume the farmer's adjusted basis in the condemned land was $10,000 and the amount of the condemnation award was $50,000. Further assume the farmer, in a timely manner, replaced the condemned farm land with farm land purchased for $60,000. What basis will the farmer take in the new farm land?

Analysis: If the farmer elects Section 1033 treatment, none of the $40,000 in gain realized would be recognized. Applying Section 1033(b), the farmer's basis in the replacement property would be $20,000, i.e., the replacement land's cost of $60,000 less the $40,000 of unrecognized gain. The $40,000 gain is thus not permanently excluded, but is merely deferred.

Example 2: Assume the facts of Example 1 except the farmer replaced the condemned farm land with farm land purchased for $40,000. What basis will the farmer take in the new farm land?

Analysis: Assuming a Section 1033 election is made, the farmer will be required to recognize $10,000 of the $40,000 realized gain because the farmer only invested $40,000 of the $50,000 in condemnation proceeds in qualifying property. Under Section 1033(b), the farmer's basis in the replacement property will be $10,000, *i.e.*, the replacement land's cost of $40,000 less the $30,000 of unrecognized gain.

§ 39.08   HOLDING PERIOD OF REPLACEMENT PROPERTY

For purposes of characterizing gains or losses realized and recognized on the subsequent disposition of replacement property, the holding period of that property may be critical. Not surprisingly, Section 1223(1) provides for the tacking of the holding period of the converted property onto the replacement property if the converted property was a capital asset under Section 1221 or a Section 1231 asset.

§ 39.09   INVOLUNTARY CONVERSION OF PRINCIPAL RESIDENCE

As discussed in Chapter 6, Section 121 excludes up to $250,000 ($500,000 in the case of a joint return) of the gain on the sale or exchange of a principal residence if certain requirements are met. Section 121(d)(5)(A) generally provides that an involuntary conversion will be treated as a sale for purposes of Section 121. Thus, the possibility exists that a taxpayer whose principal residence is involuntarily converted could take advantage of Section 121 to exclude some or all of the realized gain; any realized gain not excluded under Section 121 could be deferred under Section 1033 if the requirements of that provisions were satisfied. Section 121(d)(5)(B) provides that for purposes of applying Section 1033, the amount realized will be treated as equaling the difference between the proceeds of the involuntary conversion and the amount of gain excluded under Section 121. In effect, Section 121(d)(5)(B) requires that Section 121 be applied before applying Section 1033.

Example 1: Aaron's principal residence is destroyed by fire. Aaron, who is single, had an adjusted basis of $200,000 in the residence which had a fair market value of $800,000. Within six months of the fire, Aaron receives insurance proceeds of $800,000. Aaron uses the $800,000 plus an additional $100,000 of other money to construct a new principal residence on the same property. He completes and moves into the new residence exactly eighteen months after the fire.

Analysis: Assuming Aaron is eligible for the Section 121 exclusion and does not make the election under Section 121(f), Aaron will exclude $250,000 of the $600,000 gain realized on the involuntary conversion of the residence. For Section 1033 purposes, Aaron's amount realized is $550,000 (*i.e.*, $800,000 insurance proceeds less the $250,000 of gain excluded under Section 121). Therefore, after applying Section 121, Aaron's gain realized for Section 1033 purposes is only $350,000 ($550,000 amount realized less $200,000 basis). [Note that one could also arrive at this $350,000 figure by subtracting the $250,000 gain excluded under Section 121 from the $600,000 gain realized on the conversion of the residence.] Since Aaron invested over $550,000 in the new principal residence (in this case he invested $900,000), he may elect to defer all $350,000 of the gain realized for Section 1033 purposes. Assuming Aaron makes that election, Aaron's basis in the new residence will be $550,000, *i.e.*, the $900,000 cost of the residence less the $350,000 of unrecognized gain. [Note that if Aaron elected under Section 121(f) not to have Section 121 apply, Aaron could still defer all of his gain realized. In that case, Aaron's amount realized for Section 1033 purposes would be the full $800,000 of insurance proceeds he received. Aaron's gain realized for Section 1033 purposes would be $600,000 (*i.e.*, $800,000 less the $200,000 adjusted basis Aaron had in the destroyed residence). None of this gain realized would be recognized since Aaron invested more than $800,000 in the replacement residence. Aaron's basis therefore in the new residence would be $300,000, *i.e.*, the $900,000 cost of the new residence less the $600,000 of unrecognized gain. Note that, if Aaron subsequently sells this new residence, since its basis is determined under Section 1033(b), Aaron's ownership and use of the old residence will be attributed to the new residence for purposes of applying Section 121.[27]]

Example 2: Assume the same facts as Example 1 except Aaron constructs a replacement home that costs him only $450,000. He uses the other $350,000 of insurance proceeds to invest in the stock market.

Analysis: Again, disregarding any application of Section 121(f), $250,000 of the $600,000 gain realized by Aaron will be excluded under Section 121. Just as in Example 1, for Section 1033 purposes, Aaron's amount realized is $550,000 and his gain realized is $350,000. Since Aaron invested only $450,000 in qualifying replacement property, under Section 1033 he must recognize $100,000 of this $350,000 of realized gain. Aaron's basis in the replacement home will be $200,000, *i.e.*, the cost of the new residence ($450,000) less the unrecognized gain ($250,000). [If Aaron elected not to have Section 121 apply, his amount realized for Section 1033 purposes would be the full $800,000 in insurance proceeds and his gain realized would be $600,000. Since he only invested $450,000 in the replacement residence, he would have to recognize $350,000 of gain. There would be $250,000 of unrecognized gain. Under these circumstances, Aaron's basis in the new residence would be $200,000, *i.e.*, $450,000 cost less the $250,000 of unrecognized gain.]

---

[27] *See* I.R.C. § 121(d)(5)(C).

Chapter 40

INSTALLMENT SALES

§ 40.01 STATUTORY FRAMEWORK

§ 453. Installment method.

(a) **General rule** — Except as otherwise provided in this section, income from an installment sale shall be taken into account for purposes of this title under the installment method.

(b) **Installment method defined.** For purposes of this section —

(1) **In general.** The term "installment sale" means a disposition of property where at least 1 payment is to be received after the close of the taxable year in which the disposition occurs.

(2) **Exceptions.** The term "installment sale" does not include —

(A) Dealer dispositions. . . .

(B) **Inventories of personal property.** A disposition of personal property of a kind which is required to be included in the inventory of the taxpayer if on hand at the close of the taxable year.

(c) **Installment method defined.** For purposes of this section, the term "installment method" means a method under which the income recognized for any taxable year from a disposition is that proportion of the payment received in that year which the gross profit (realized or to be realized when payment is completed) bears to the total contract price.

Under the ordinary rules of the Code, a taxpayer who sells property recognizes gain or loss at the time of the sale.[1] Suppose, however, the property is sold at a gain on a deferred payment or installment basis, with all or part of the selling price to be paid following the year of sale. In these circumstances, it may seem harsh to apply the ordinary rules and tax all the gain currently since "possible liquidity problems . . . might arise from the bunching of gain in the year of sale when a portion of the selling price has not been actually received."[2] Accordingly, the installment sales rules of Section 453 provide the gain on the sale — and the tax liability it generates — is spread over the period during which the payments are received. In addition to spreading or deferring income, Section 453 addresses characterization of the income as well. Income recognized under the installment method, whether in the year of sale or thereafter, is income from a disposition of property, rather than income from the collection of an obligation. For example, if

---

[1] I.R.C. § 1001(a), (c).

[2] S. Rep. No. 96-1000, at 7 (1980).

the property disposed of was a capital asset and the disposition was a sale, the gain recognized both in the year of sale and later years will be capital gain.

The basic statutory framework is as follows: income from an "installment sale" is to be reported under the "installment method."[3] The statute does not apply to an installment sale at a loss. An "installment sale" is generally defined as a disposition of property where at least one payment is to be received following the year of disposition.[4] Thus, there is no requirement that any payment be received in the year of disposition. Similarly, there is no prohibition on the use of the installment method even where a substantial percentage of the total payments is received in the year of disposition. The "installment method" prorates the total gain on the sale over the total payments to be received.[5] Note that the installment method applies to both cash method and accrual method taxpayers.

In the language of the statute, income from an installment sale recognized in any year is "that proportion of the payments received in that year which the gross profit (realized or to be realized when payment is completed) bears to the total contract price."[6] "Gross profit" means the selling price less the adjusted basis as defined in section 1011 and the regulations thereunder.[7] "Contract price" means the total contract price equal to selling price reduced by that portion of any qualifying indebtedness assumed or taken subject to by the buyer, which does not exceed the seller's basis in the property.[8] "Selling price" means the gross selling price without reduction to reflect any existing mortgage or other encumbrance on the property.[9]

> **Example 1:** Taxpayer sells qualifying property, which has an adjusted basis of $40, for $100, payable at the rate of $20 per year plus adequate interest on the unpaid balance.[10] When will Taxpayer report the gain?

> **Analysis:** Taxpayer's total gain on the sale is $60, and the total payments to be received are $100. Pursuant to Section 453(c), 60/100ths, or 60% of each $20 payment ($12 of each $20 payment) constitutes income from the sale. The remaining portion of each payment ($8) constitutes a tax-free return of basis. Over the five payments, taxpayer will recover the $40 basis tax-free ($8 × 5), and will report $60 of income ($12 × 5) at the rate of $12 per year.

The ratio of gross profit to total contract price is known as the "gross profit ratio." Once the gross profit ratio is determined — 60% in the above

---

[3] I.R.C. § 453(a).

[4] I.R.C. § 453(b)(1).

[5] I.R.C. § 453(c).

[6] I.R.C. § 453(c).

[7] Treas. Reg. § 15A.453-1(b)(2)(v).

[8] Treas. Reg. § 15A.453-1(b)(2)(iii).

[9] Treas. Reg. § 15A.453-1(b)(2)(ii).

[10] If adequate interest were not charged and paid annually, a portion of the purchase price could be recharacterized as interest. See Sections 1274 and 483. It will be assumed throughout this chapter that adequate interest is stated and paid on all installment sales.

example — then the income portion of any payment is determined simply by multiplying the amount of the payment by the gross profit ratio.

Example 2: Same facts as Example 1, except the $100 selling price is payable in four annual installments of $10, $20, $30, and $40. How much of each payment will constitute gain?

Analysis: Since the total contract price and gross profit are still the same, so is the gross profit ratio: 60%. Applying that ratio to each payment means the income recognized on each payment is $6, $12, $18, and $24, respectively. The balance of each payment represents a return of capital.

§ 40.02 PAYMENTS AND LIABILITIES

The above example involved the sale of property that was not subject to any mortgages or other liabilities. If the property is encumbered by "qualifying indebtedness"[11] and such indebtedness is assumed, or taken subject to, by the buyer, such assumption of debt is not treated as a "payment" to the seller.[12] In effect, all of the mortgage relief is treated as tax-free return of basis, an approach favorable to the taxpayer and consistent with the underlying policy objective of alleviating potential liquidity problems on installment sales.

Example 1: Property worth $100 and has a basis of $40 is subject to a mortgage of $20. Buyer agrees to purchase the property and assume the mortgage. Since the equity in the property is $80, the buyer will make cash payments totaling $80, in addition to assuming the $20 mortgage. The cash payments will consist of four annual payments of $20 each, together with stated interest. How will each payment be taxed?

Analysis: The seller's amount realized, of course, remains $100; the liability relief of $20 is as much a part of the amount realized as are the cash payments. The gross profit is therefore still $60. However, since the liability relief is not treated as a "payment" for purposes of Section 453(c), the "payments" total only $80. The "total contract price" is $80, since it is determined by subtracting the qualifying indebtedness of $20 from the $100 selling price.[13] The gross profit ratio is thus 75% (gross profit of $60,

---

[11] "Qualifying indebtedness" is defined in Regulation § 15A.453-1(b)(2)(iv) as "a mortgage or other indebtedness encumbering the property and indebtedness, not secured by the property but incurred or assumed by the purchaser incident to the purchaser's acquisition, holding, or operation in the ordinary course of business or investment of the property. The term 'qualifying indebtedness' does not include an obligation of the taxpayer incurred incident to the disposition of the property (e.g., legal fees relating to the taxpayer's sale of the property) or an obligation functionally unrelated to the acquisition, holding, or operating of the property (e.g., the taxpayer's medical bill). Any obligation created subsequent to the taxpayer's acquisition of the property and incurred or assumed by the taxpayer or placed as an encumbrance on the property in contemplation of disposition of the property is not qualifying indebtedness if the arrangement results in accelerating recovery of the taxpayer's basis in the installment sale."

[12] Treas. Reg. § 15A.453-1(b)(3)(i).

[13] Treas. Reg. § 15A.453-1(b)(2)(iii), (iv).

divided by total contract price of $80) and as a result, $15 of each $20 cash payment constitutes income. Total recognized gain from the 4 payments will again be $60.

Example 2: Same as Example 1, except the mortgage in question secured a debt of $50 rather than $20. The purchaser, who is assuming the mortgage, will thus agree to make cash payments totaling only $50, the amount of the seller's equity in the property. How will the seller be taxed?

Analysis: Since the amount realized ($100) and basis ($40) are unchanged, the seller's gain is still $60. That gain, however, now exceeds the total cash payments to be received. Thus, even if 100% of each cash payment is taxed as income, the total gain of $60 will not be accounted for. Put another way, if the entire amount of mortgage relief is treated as return of basis, the taxpayer would recover too much basis. In these circumstances, the regulations treat as a payment the "excess" liability — that is, the amount by which the qualifying indebtedness exceeds the basis; in this instance, $10.[14] Total payments will thus be $60 — the cash payments of $60 and the "excess" liability relief of $10. In determining the total contract price, note that qualifying indebtedness offsets the selling price only to the extent of basis.[15] Therefore, the total contract price is $60 — that is, the $100 selling price reduced by only $40 of qualifying debt. The gross profit on the sale is also $60, so the gross profit ratio is 100%. Thus, all $10 of the excess-liability "payment" and all $50 of the actual cash payments constitute income, and the total gain of $60 is properly accounted for.

To this point, "payments" have consisted either of cash or of liability relief in excess of basis. If, at the time of the sale, the buyer issues a promissory note, or notes, to the seller in the amount of the unpaid purchase price, the buyer's own notes do not themselves constitute payment, even if such debt is guaranteed by a third party.[16] The term "payment", however, does include instruments payable on demand and certain readily tradable debt instruments.[17] In other words, in some circumstances a debt instrument is so close to cash that deferral of gain is inappropriate. Third-party notes constitute payment, as does the "securing" of the buyer's own notes by cash or a cash equivalent.[18]

Qualifying indebtedness is typically debt the seller incurred to purchase or to improve the property; the buyer's assumption of qualifying indebtedness, as we have noted, does not constitute payment (except to the extent the debt exceeds basis). However, the buyer's assumption of nonqualifying debt will constitute payment. In effect, favorable treatment for the seller may be appropriate with respect to the buyer's assumption of acquisition debt, but is not appropriate with respect to the buyer's assumption of nonqualifying debt; such an assumption may be

---

[14] Treas. Reg. § 15A.453-1(b)(3)(i).

[15] Treas. Reg. § 15A.453-1(b)(2)(iii).

[16] I.R.C. § 453(f)(3).

[17] I.R.C. § 453(f)(4), (5).

[18] Treas. Reg. § 15A.453-1(bb)(3)(i). See the discussion of constructive receipt and cash equivalency in Chapter 28, *supra*.

regarded as a partial cashing-out of the seller's interest in the property, and should therefore be treated as a payment. For example, post-acquisition debt taken on in contemplation of disposition of the property may not constitute qualifying indebtedness, and debts that are incurred incident to disposition of the property or that are unrelated to the property will not qualify.[19]

Example 1: Taxpayer agrees to sell property to Buyer for $100,000. Taxpayer's adjusted basis in the property is $40,000. The property is not encumbered by any liabilities. Buyer agrees to pay Taxpayer $60,000 in Year 1 and $20,000 in each of the next two years plus adequate interest. How will the payments be taxed?

Analysis: The gross profit ratio will be 6/10, *i.e.*, 60% of each payment (disregarding interest) will constitute gain and the other 40% of each payment will constitute a return of capital. Thus, in Year 1, Taxpayer will receive $60,000 from Buyer and will report $36,000 of income.

Example 2: Assume the facts of Example 1, except that, in contemplation of the sale to Buyer, Taxpayer borrowed $40,000 from a bank, using the property as security. Taxpayer then entered into the sale with Buyer. Buyer agrees to pay Taxpayer $100,000 for the property as follows: Buyer will assume the $40,000 debt encumbering the property, will pay Taxpayer $20,000 in cash at the time of closing, and will pay Taxpayer $20,000 in each of the next two years together with appropriate interest. How will Taxpayer be taxed?

Analysis: When the dust settles, Taxpayer has $60,000 of cash in hand (*i.e.*, $40,000 in loan proceeds and $20,000 downpayment from Buyer). If the debt encumbering the property were treated as qualified indebtedness, Buyer's assumption of the $40,000 debt would not be considered a payment, since the amount does not exceed Taxpayer's adjusted basis in the property. The gross profit ratio in that case would be 100%, *i.e.*, the gross profit would still be $60,000 and the total contract price would also be $60,000 ($100,000 less the liability of $40,000). Thus, 100% of each payment (and there will only be three $20,000 payments) would constitute income. In Year 1 therefore Taxpayer would report $20,000 of income on a $20,000 payment, but the Taxpayer would have been able to "cash-out" to the extent of an additional $40,000, via the loan and the buyer's assumption thereof, without tax liability. This result is far superior to the $36,000 of income Taxpayer has if the property is not encumbered and Buyer makes a $60,000 payment in Year 1. Although Taxpayer ultimately reports the same aggregate gross profit under either approach, borrowing can put the same total dollars in Taxpayer's hands now, but defer the tax liability to later years. To prevent the kind of game playing suggested by this example, the regulations define "qualifying indebtedness" narrowly to preclude the debt in this example from qualifying. Thus, the assumption of the debt by Buyer constitutes a payment. Taxpayer must therefore report in Year 1 not only the $20,000 cash paid by Buyer but also the $40,000 in loan proceeds. The gross profit

---

[19] Treas. Reg. § 15A.453-1(b)(2)(iv).

ratio is the same as it would have been had there been no liability encumbering the property, *i.e.*, 6/10 or 60%. Thus, Taxpayer must report $36,000 of gain in Year 1, as in Example 1.

§ 40.03 RECAPTURE INCOME

§ 453(i). Recognition of recapture income in year of disposition —

(1) In general. In the case of any installment sale of property to which subsection (a) applies —

(A) notwithstanding subsection (a), any recapture income shall be recognized in the year of disposition, and

(B) any gain in excess of the recapture income shall be taken into account under the installment method.

(2) Recapture income. For purposes of paragraph (1), the term "recapture income" means, with respect to any installment sale, the aggregate amount which would be treated as ordinary income under section 1245 or 1250 . . . for the taxable year of the disposition if all payments to be received were received in the taxable year of disposition.

Section 453(i) is an exception to the normal rules of installment method reporting. Since the seller has already benefitted taxwise from the depreciation taken on the property prior to the sale, Section 453(i) requires recognition in the year of sale of any "recapture income," defined as the amount that Sections 1245 or 1250 would classify as ordinary income if all payments to be received were received in the year of sale.[20] Because recapture income is recognized independently of any payments, it is necessary to add the recaptured amount to the seller's basis so as to avoid over-reporting of income. The legislative history to Section 453(i) recognizes the need for, and authorizes, such a basis adjustment.

> **Example:** Property with an adjusted basis of $40 is sold for $100, payable at the rate of $20 per year. Assume $20 of the gain realized would be characterized as ordinary income under Section 1245. When will the seller report the gain?
>
> **Analysis:** Under Section 453(i)(1)(A), the Section 1245 recapture income of $20 is recognized currently, regardless of whether any payments are received in the year of sale. The $20 of recapture income would be added to the pre-sale basis of $40. Given a selling price of $100, the seller's gross profit would now be $40 rather than $60. The gross profit ratio applied to each $20 payment would therefore be 40%, resulting in $8 of installment method income each year. After all five annual payments had been made, the appropriate total gain — $60 — would have been reported: $20 of recapture income and $40 of gain on the five payments of $20 each.

---

[20] See Chapter 33, *supra*, for a complete discussion of depreciation recapture.

§ 40.04 ELECTING OUT OF THE INSTALLMENT METHOD

Installment method reporting is not mandatory. Under Section 453(d), a taxpayer may elect out of the installment method, and report the gain on the sale in accordance with the taxpayer's normal method of accounting. The election must be made in a timely manner and may be revoked only with the consent of the Internal Revenue Service.[21] Prior to the Installment Sales Revision Act of 1980, a taxpayer seeking the benefit of Section 453(a) had to make an affirmative election. Since a taxpayer would ordinarily prefer such reporting, the 1980 Act reversed the pre-1980 rule and provided for the automatic application of Section 453(a), subject to the election out.

The question arises of how to report income if the taxpayer elects out of Section 453. Under the regulations, if an election out of Section 453 is made, an installment obligation is treated as property and is valued at its fair market value, regardless of whether it is a cash equivalent.[22] In addition, a cash method taxpayer is directed to treat the fair market value of the obligation as having been realized in the year of sale, and to treat that value as not less than the fair market value of the property sold (less other consideration received); an accrual method taxpayer is directed to treat the total amount payable on the obligation as realized in the year of sale.[23] The regulations clearly reject the election-out as a deferral of income technique, and instead make it, in effect, an occasion for acceleration of income.

§ 40.05 EXCLUSIONS

The use of installment method reporting is not allowed for certain deferred payment sales. Section 453(k) denies installment reporting for sales of publicly traded property and for sales pursuant to a revolving credit plan. The legislative history of Section 453(k) provides the following reasons for these two limitations:

> First, the committee believes that sales under a revolving credit plan should not be permitted to be accounted for under the installment method. The committee believes that such sales more closely resemble the provision of a flexible line of credit accompanied by cash sales by the seller, and therefore is not appropriately afforded the use of the installment method. Second, the committee believes that the installment method should not be available for sales of certain publicly traded property. In general, publicly traded property is considered to be a sufficiently liquid asset to be treated the same as a payment of cash for purposes of applying the installment method. Moreover, since the taxpayer can easily sell such property for cash

---

[21] *See generally* Treas. Reg. § 15A.453-1(d)(3), (4). The Service has provided some guidance in Rev. Rul. 90-46, 1990-1 C.B. 107, on when it will grant permission to make a late election out of the installment method. A "subsequent change in circumstances or law" — such as a change in tax rates — or a taxpayer "change of mind" will not constitute good cause for a late election. However, where taxpayer's timely attempt to elect out is "thwarted by a mistake," *e.g.*, taxpayer's agent failed to follow written instructions to make the election out, and the taxpayer promptly tries to correct the mistake, the Service may find good cause and permit the late election.

[22] Treas. Reg. § 15A.453-1(d)(2)(i).

[23] Treas. Reg. § 15A.453-1(d)(2)(ii).

in the public market, the committee believes that such property does not present the same liquidity problem that the installment method is intended to alleviate.[24]

All payments to be received on such sales are to be treated as received in the year of disposition. The term "payment to be received" is defined as the aggregate amount of all payments not contingent as to amount, plus the fair market value of contingent-amount payments.[25]

In addition, installment reporting is generally not permitted for so-called "dealer dispositions."[26] Dispositions of personal property includable in inventory also do not qualify as installment sales.[27]

A "dealer disposition" is defined as any disposition of personal property by a person who regularly sells or otherwise disposes of personal property of the same type on the installment plan, or any disposition of real property held by the taxpayer for sale to customers in the ordinary course of business.[28] Exceptions are provided for dispositions of property used or produced in a farming business, and for dispositions of residential lots or timeshares if the taxpayer elects to pay interest on the tax deferred by reason of the use of installment method reporting.[29]

§ 40.06   CONTINGENT PAYMENT SALES

In some instances, a property's selling price is made contingent on future events, such as future profits or rents, and the aggregate selling price thus cannot be determined in the year of the sale. The question then arises as to how to account for the gain on such a contingent payment sale. One approach, given the uncertainty as to the ultimate amount to be realized, would be to hold the transaction "open" until all the payments had been made. Under this approach, no gain would arise and no tax liability would be imposed until the taxpayer had first fully recovered basis in the property. Once the basis had been recovered, remaining payments would constitute taxable gain. The taxpayer in *Burnet v. Logan*[30] successfully argued for open transaction treatment on a 1916 sale of stock for a price that was in part contingent on future mining operations. The Supreme Court concluded that the purchaser's promise of future money payments had no ascertainable fair market value and could not be considered a cash equivalent. The Court rejected the Commissioner's approach under which — despite valuation difficulties — a value would be placed on the purchaser's promise of future payments, and the transaction would thus be treated as "closed." The Court, noting the taxpayer might never recover her capital investment, indicated the taxpayer's proposed method ensured that the liability for tax would ultimately be fairly determined without reliance on

---

[24] S. Rep. No. 99-913, 99th Cong., 2d Sess., p. 124 (1986).

[25] I.R.C. § 453(f)(8).

[26] I.R.C. § 453(b)(2)(A).

[27] I.R.C. § 453(b)(2)(B).

[28] I.R.C. § 453(l)(1).

[29] I.R.C. § 453(l)(2), (3).

[30] 283 U.S. 404 (1931).

mere estimates, assumptions and speculation as proposed by the Commissioner.

Open transaction accounting is of limited applicability today. Section 453(j)(2) directs Treasury to provide regulations for ratable basis recovery in a situation where gross profit or total contract price is not readily ascertainable. Treasury has done so. Thus, unless the taxpayer elects out of Section 453, contingent payment sales are to be reported on the installment method.[31] If the sale is subject to a "stated maximum selling price," the maximum selling price is generally treated as the "selling price" for purposes of computing the gross profit ratio and determining the income portion of each payment.[32]

> **Example 1:** Taxpayer sells property with a $10,000 adjusted basis for payments equal to 10 percent of the property's profits over the next five years (together with adequate interest), but not to exceed the total payment of $100,000. In Year 1, payment under the formula is $15,000. How will Taxpayer report gain on the sale?
>
> **Analysis:** The selling price is considered to be $100,000. Gross profit is therefore $90,000, and the gross profit ratio is $90,000 ($100,000, or 90%). Accordingly, 90%, or $13,500, of the $15,000 payment is recognized as gain in Year 1. The remaining $1,500 is recovery of basis.[33]

If a maximum selling price cannot be determined, but there is a maximum period of time over which payments may be received, the taxpayer's basis is generally allocated over that "fixed period" in equal annual amounts.[34] However, no loss is allowed ordinarily until the final payment year. Thus, if payments in any year were less than the basis allocated to that year, the unrecovered basis would carryover to the following year.

> **Example 2:** Taxpayer sells property with a $10,000 adjusted basis for payments determined as a percentage of income generated by the property, together with adequate stated interest. The payments are to be made over a ten-year period, and are not subject to any maximum selling price. Payment under the formula in Year 1 is $1,500. How will Taxpayer report the payment?
>
> **Analysis:** $1,000 of the property's adjusted basis will be allocated to each of the ten years, and annual payments in excess of $1,000 constitute gain. Thus, Taxpayer will report $500 of income in Year 1.
>
> **Example 3:** Same facts as Example 2, except the Year 1 payment is only $900.
>
> **Analysis:** The Year 1 unrecovered basis is $100; however, no loss is allowed in Year 1, since it is not the final payment year. Instead, the unrecovered

---

[31] Treas. Reg. § 15A.453-1(c)(1).

[32] Treas. Reg. § 15A.453-1(c)(2)(i).

[33] If the maximum selling price is reduced, pursuant to the terms of the sale or otherwise, the gross profit and gross profit ratio must be recalculated, requiring adjustments beyond the scope of this chapter.

[34] Treas. Reg. § 15A.453-1(c)(3)(i).

basis is added to the following year's allocation, and the Year 2 basis allocation becomes $1100. Loss will be reported only at the end of the 10-year period if there is any basis left to be recovered.

In those circumstances in which neither a maximum selling price nor a fixed period limits the payments, the transaction "will be closely scrutinized" to see whether a sale has in fact occurred, and if so, basis will be ordinarily be allocated in equal amounts over a 15-year period.[35] In this case, no loss is allowed unless the payment obligation has become worthless and all basis has not yet been recovered.

The foregoing discussion of contingent payment sales assumed that the taxpayer had not made an election out of Section 453. If such an election is made, gain or loss is computed on the sale under the ordinary rules of Section 1001, and the "contingent payment obligation" is valued at its fair market value.[36] However, the fair market value of a contingent payment obligation shall "in no event" be less than the fair market value of the property sold. Only in those "rare and extraordinary cases" where the fair market value of an obligation cannot be ascertained will the transaction be treated as "open," and even then the transaction will be scrutinized to see if it in fact constitutes a sale.[37]

§ 40.07   DISPOSITIONS OF INSTALLMENT OBLIGATIONS

§ 453B(a).   General rule.

If an installment obligation is satisfied at other than its face value or distributed, transmitted, sold, or otherwise disposed of, gain or loss shall result to the extent of the difference between the basis of the obligation and —

(1) the amount realized, in the case of satisfaction at other than face value or a sale or exchange, or

(2) the fair market value of the obligation at the time of distribution, transmission, or disposition, in the case of the distribution, transmission, or disposition otherwise than by sale or exchange.

Any gain or loss so resulting shall be considered as resulting from the sale or exchange of the property in respect of which the installment obligation was received.

(b)   Basis of obligation. The basis of an installment obligation shall be the excess of the face value of the obligation over an amount equal to the income which would be returnable were the obligation satisfied in full.

In general, when a taxpayer disposes of an installment obligation, the tax deferral authorized by Section 453 with respect to that obligation ends. To determine the gain (or loss) recognized on this disposition, one must subtract the basis of the obligation from either the fair market value of the obligation or the amount realized on its disposition, depending on the type of disposition.

---

[35] Treas. Reg. § 15A.453-1(c)(4).

[36] Treas. Reg. § 15A.453-1(d)(2)(i).

[37] Treas. Reg. § 15A.453-1(d)(2)(iii).

The basis of an obligation is the difference between its face value and the amount that would constitute income were the obligation satisfied in full.[38] Assume, for example, a taxpayer sells property with an adjusted basis of $10, for $50 in cash, plus the buyer's promissory note for $50 payable in a subsequent year. On these facts, the gross profit ratio is 90% (*i.e.*, there is gross profit of $90 built into the transaction, and the total contract price is $100 — the gross profit ratio is therefore 90/100, or 90%). If the $50 note were paid in full, $45 of the payment would be reportable as income. Accordingly, the note's basis is $50 minus $45, or $5.

If the taxpayer sells or exchanges the note, or it is satisfied at other than face value, gain or loss is recognized in an amount equal to the difference between the amount realized and the basis of the note.[39] If the note is otherwise disposed of, such as by gift, the recognized gain or loss equals the difference between its fair market value and its basis.[40] Cancellation of a note is treated as a disposition other than by sale or exchange, and if the parties are related,[41] the fair market value will not be less than the face amount of the note.[42] The character of the recognized gain or loss will turn on the character of the underlying property.[43] In the case of a transfer of an installment obligation between spouses or incident to divorce, the rules of Section 453B(a) do not apply, and no gain or loss is recognized. The transferee instead steps into the shoes of the transferor for purposes of reporting gain on the receipt of payments on the installment obligations.[44]

Revenue Ruling 79-371[45] addresses the question of the transferee's basis in an installment obligation following a disposition by gift under Section 453B(a)(2). The transferee's basis is the transferor's basis, augmented to reflect the income recognized by the transferor.

> **Example:** Tom sold property and is using the installment method to report gain on the sale. The installment notes held by Tom have a face value of $100,000 and a fair market value of $90,000. Tom's basis in the installment notes determined under Section 453B(b) is $40,000. Tom gives the installment notes to his child as a graduation gift. What are the tax consequences to Tom, and what basis will the child take in the note?

> **Analysis:** Under Section 453B(a), Tom will be required to report $50,000 of gain (*i.e.*, $90,000 — the fair market value of the notes — less $40,000 — Tom's basis in the notes). Tom's child's basis in the notes will be $90,000, *i.e.*, the $40,000 basis of Tom plus the gain reportable by Tom as a result of the transfer of the notes to the child.

---

[38] I.R.C. § 453B(b).

[39] I.R.C. § 453B(a)(1).

[40] I.R.C. § 453B(a)(2).

[41] *See* I.R.C. § 453(f)(1).

[42] I.R.C. § 453B(f).

[43] I.R.C. § 453B(a).

[44] I.R.C. § 453B(g).

[45] 1979-2 C.B. 294.

§ 40.08   SECOND DISPOSITIONS BY RELATED PERSONS

§ 453(e).   Second dispositions by related persons.

(1)   In general — If

(A) any person disposes of property to a related person (hereinafter in this subsection referred to as the "first disposition") and,

(B) before the person making the first disposition receives all payments with respect to such disposition, the related person disposes of the property (hereinafter in this subsection referred to as the "second disposition"),

then, for purposes of this section, the amount realized with respect to such second disposition shall be treated as received at the time of the second disposition by the person making the first disposition.

(2) 2-year cutoff for property. . . .

(A)   In general. . . . paragraph (1) shall apply only if the date of the second disposition is not more than 2 years after the date of the first disposition.

. . .

(3)   Limitation on amount treated as received. The amount treated for any taxable year as received by the person making the first disposition by reason of paragraph (1) shall not exceed the excess of —

(A) the lesser of —

(i) the total amount realized with respect to any second disposition of the property occurring before the close of the taxable year, or

(ii) the total contract price for the first disposition, over

(B) the sum of —

(i) the aggregate amount of payments received with respect to the first disposition before the close of such year, plus

(ii) the aggregate amount treated as received with respect to the first disposition for prior taxable years by reason of this subsection.

. . .

(5)   Later payment treated as receipt of tax paid amounts. If paragraph (1) applies for any taxable year, payments received in subsequent taxable years by the person making the first disposition shall not be treated as the receipt of payments with respect to the first disposition to the extent that the aggregate of such payments does not exceed the amount treated as recevied by reason of paragraph (1).

Section 453(e) is applicable when a taxpayer makes an installment sale to a related party, and the related party then sells the property for cash to an unrelated third party. In these circumstances, the taxpayer (the initial seller) must recognize gain as payments are made by the third party. This rule prevents a family unit from deferring the gain by use of an installment sale. The Senate Finance Committee summarized the operation of Section 453(e) as follows:

Under the bill, the amount realized upon certain resales by the related party installment purchaser will trigger recognition of gain by the initial seller, based on his gross profit ratio, only to the extent the amount realized from the second disposition exceeds actual payments made under the installment sale. Thus, acceleration of recognition of the installment gain from the first sale will generally result only to the extent additional cash and other property flows into the related group as a result of a second disposition of the property. In the case of a second disposition which is not a sale or exchange, the fair market value of the property disposed of is treated as the amount realized for this purpose. . . .[46]

Example 1: Assume Father has property with an adjusted basis of $10, which he sells to Daughter for $100, payable ten years later. Daughter, who takes a cost basis in the property of $100, promptly resells the property for $100 cash. What are the tax consequences to Father and Daughter?

Analysis: As a result of Daughter's resale for $100 and her receipt of that amount, Father is treated as receiving a payment of $100 under Section 453(e)(1), (Note that in this case the Section 453(e)(3) limitation is also $100 — Father's total contract price of $100 is the same as the Daughter's amount realized this year, and no payments had been received by Father or Daughter in a prior year.) Since Father's gross profit ratio is 90%, Father will recognize $90 of income. Daughter's basis in the property was $100; she therefore has no gain in the sale.

The Senate Finance Committee report continued:

If . . . a resale results in the recognition of gain to the initial seller, subsequent payments actually received by the seller would be recovered tax-free until they have equaled the amount realized from the resale which resulted in the acceleration of recognition of gain.[47]

Thus, in the above example, when Father actually receives the $100 payment from Daughter, no further gain is recognized since for tax purposes Father was treated as receiving the $100 payment at the time of Daughter's sale to the third party.

An important limitation on the general rule regarding second dispositions of the property by a related party is set forth in Section 453(e)(2), limiting the application of the general rule to second dispositions ocurring not more than two years after the date of the first disposition. The statute contains special rules to prevent manipulation of this two-year rule.[48] The theory behind the two-year rule is essentially that, if the related purchaser is willing to bear the risk of loss vis-a-vis the property for a substantial period of time, the kind of game playing which Section 453(e) is intended to address is unlikely to occur.

---

[46] S. Rep. No. 96-1000, at 14–15 (1980).

[47] *Id.* at 15. I.R.C. § 453(e)(5).

[48] I.R.C. § 453(e)(2)(B).

Example 2: Assume the same facts as in Example 1, except Daughter does not sell the property until three years after the purchase of the property from Father.

Analysis: Under these circumstances, Section 453(e) would not be applicable and Father would report gain as installment payments are received from Daughter. By contrast, if during the second year following her purchase of the property Daughter entered into a contract to sell the property for a fixed price during the third year following her purchase, Section 453)(e) would apply. Thus, even though the sale by Daughter took place more than two years after her purchase of the property from Father, the sale will be treated as a second disposition subject to the general rule of Section 453(e) because Daughter took steps in the two year period following her purchase to reduce her risk of loss associated with the property.

Section 453(e)(6)(C) presents another important limitation on the general rule. This provision essentially makes Section 453(e) inapplicable to transfers after the earlier of the death of the person making the first disposition or the person acquiring the property in the first disposition.

Example 3: As in Example 1, Father sells property to Daughter on an installment contract. Within a year of purchase, Daughter dies in a car accident and her estate sells the property Daughter acquired from Father. What tax results?

Analysis: Although the sale of the property by the estate occurred within two years of Daughter's purchase of the property from Father, the general rule of Section 453(e)(1) will not be applicable. Father will report gain only as payments are made to him by Daughter's estate.

The Senate Finance Committee Report comments on additional limitations included in Section 453(e):

> The bill also contains several exceptions to the application of these rules. . . . [Under one exception] there would be no acceleration of recognition of gain as a result of a second disposition which is an involuntary conversion of the property if the first sale occurred before the threat or imminence of the conversion. . . . [F]inally the resale rules will not apply in any case where it is established to the satisfaction of the Internal Revenue Service that none of the dispositions had as one of its principal purposes the avoidance of Federal income taxes.

> In the exceptional cases to which the nonavoidance exception may apply, it is anticipated that regulations would provide definitive rules so that complicated legislation is not necessary to prescribe substituted property or taxpayer rules which would not be of general application. In appropriate cases, it is anticipated that the regulations and rulings under the nontax avoidance exception will deal with certain tax-free transfers which normally would not be treated as a second disposition of the property, *e.g.*, charitable transfers, like kind exchanges, gift transfers, and transfers to a controlled corporation or a partnership. Generally it is intended that a second

disposition will qualify under the nontax avoidance exception when it is of an involuntary nature, *e.g.*, foreclosure upon the property by a judgment lien creditor of the related purchaser or bankruptcy of the related purchaser. In addition, it is intended that the exception will apply in the case of a second disposition which is also an installment sale if the terms of payment under the installment resale are substantially equivalent to, or longer than, those for the first installment sale. However, the exception would not apply if the resale terms would permit significant deferral of recognition of gain from the initial sale when proceeds from the resale are being collected sooner. . . . It is to be understood that the provisions governing the use of the installment method to report sales between related parties, and the definition of such relationships, are not intended to preclude the Internal Revenue Service from asserting the proper tax treatment of transactions that are shams.[49]

§ 40.09   SALES OF DEPRECIABLE PROPERTY TO RELATED PERSONS

The installment method is not available in the case of installment sales of depreciable property between "related persons."[50] Section 453(g)(2) provides that "related persons" shall have the meaning given that term by Section 1239(b). Thus, the installment method cannot be used with respect to a sale between (1) a taxpayer and a controlled entity within the meaning of Section 1239(c), (2) a taxpayer and a trust in which the taxpayer or her spouse is a beneficiary, or (3) an executor of an estate and a beneficiary of the estate.[51] The purpose of the rule is "to deter transactions which are structured in such a way as to give the related purchaser the benefit of depreciation deductions (measured from a stepped-up basis) prior to the time the seller is required to include in income the corresponding gain on the sale."[52] The rule does not apply where the sale does not have the avoidance of Federal income tax as one of its principal purposes.[53] Where the rule applies, the seller is generally required to treat all payments to be received as received in the year of sale. Furthermore, Section 1239(a), if applicable, will characterize the gain on the sale as ordinary income.

> **Example:** Kate sells a valuable piece of equipment to a corporation in which she owns over 50% of the stock. The corporation agrees to pay Kate the purchase price in installments payable over a number of years. What are the tax consequences to Kate?

> **Analysis:** Under Section 1239(c)(1), a corporation is a controlled corporation with respect to a person if more than 50% of the corporation's outstanding stock is owned by or for such person. Here, Kate owns more

---

[49] S. Rep. No. 96-1000, at 15–17 (1980).

[50] I.R.C. § 453(g)(1).

[51] I.R.C. § 1239(b).

[52] S. Rep. No. 96-1000, at 17 (1980).

[53] I.R.C. § 453(g)(2).

than 50% of the stock of the corporation to which she sold the equipment. Therefore, because of Kate's stock ownership, the corporation is treated as a related party for purposes of Section 453(g). Unless it is determined the sale does not have tax avoidance as a principal purpose, the installment method will be unavailable to Kate and she will be treated as having received the entire purchase price in the year of the sale. Furthermore, assuming the equipment is depreciable in the hands of the corporation, Kate's gain will be treated as ordinary income under Section 1239(a).

§ 40.10 SPECIAL RULES FOR NONDEALERS

Section 453A provides two special rules for certain installment obligations (hereinafter, "Section 453A installment obligations") arising from nondealer dispositions of property. These specially-treated installment obligations are those arising from dispositions of property where the sales price of the property exceeds $150,000.[54]

Under one of the special rules, if a Section 453A installment obligation is itself pledged as security for any debt, the net proceeds of the secured debt are treated as payment on the obligation.[55] In effect, to the extent of the net proceeds, the taxpayer is treated as cashing in the installment obligation. Subsequent payments on the installment obligation are then disregarded up to the aggregate amount of the deemed payment.[56]

> **Example:** George enters into an installment sale of land and receives from the purchaser notes payable over a 10 year period. The notes have a face value of $1,000,000 representing the purchase price of the land. Subsequent to receiving the notes, George pledges them to secure a loan of $250,000. What are the tax consequences, if any, of the pledge?

> **Analysis:** While George's pledge of the notes does not constitute a "disposition" of the installment notes, Section 453A(d) treats the net proceeds from the pledging of the notes as a payment. Thus, George will be deemed to have received a $250,000 payment and will be required to report as a gain a fraction of the deemed payment determined by applying the gross profit ratio determined for purposes of the sale. For example, if George's adjusted basis in the land were $500,000 when the installment sale occurred, the gross profit ratio (assuming no liabilities encumbering the property) would be 5/10 or 50%. Thus, George would have to report $125,000 in gain as a result of pledging the notes to secure the $250,000 loan.

---

[54] I.R.C. § 453A(b)(1). Installment obligations arising from the disposition of personal use property or the disposition of property used or produced in the farming business are excluded from the special rules of Section 453A. I.R.C. § 453A(b)(3). Another exclusion is available under Section 453A(b)(4) with respect to timeshares and residential lots.

[55] I.R.C. § 453A(d)(1).

[56] I.R.C. § 453A(d)(3).

The other rule requires the taxpayer to pay interest[57] on the deferred tax liability attributable to Section 453A installment obligations under certain limited circumstances.[58] The sales price of property must exceed $150,000 before an installment obligation arising from such a sale is even potentially subject to Section 453A. In addition, no interest is charged on the deferred tax liability attributable to such obligations unless the aggregate face amount of all such installment obligations, which arose during the taxable year in question, and are outstanding at its close, exceeds $5,000,000.[59] If this $5,000,000 threshold is not reached, no interest is payable.

The statute defines the "deferred tax liability" as the unrecognized gain on Section 453A installment obligations, multiplied by the maximum tax rate in effect for the year in question.[60] Interest is payable, however, not on the entire deferred tax liability attributable to such an obligation, but only on an "applicable percentage" of it; this percentage is determined in a manner that effectively incorporates the $5,000,000 no-interest threshold.[61] If interest is payable with respect to a Section 453A installment obligation that arises during any year, interest is payable in subsequent years as long as there remains an unpaid balance on the obligation. If interest is not payable with respect to such an installment obligation arising during a year, because the $5,000,000 threshold was not reached, then interest on the obligation is not payable in a subsequent year.[62]

Example: In Year 1, William and Nora enter into an installment sales contract whereby William agrees to sell to Nora a large tract of land for $20,000,000. William's adjusted basis in the land is $4,000,000. Assume the land is free of any encumbrances. Nora pays William $1,000,000 as a downpayment with the balance of $19,000,000 to be paid (with adequate interest on the unpaid balance) over the next 10 years. How much, if any, interest must William pay on the deferred tax liability in Year 1?

Analysis: The gross profit is $16,000,000, and the total contract price is $20,000,000. The gross profit ratio for this transaction will thus be $16,000,000/$20,000,000 or 8/10. The interest to be paid in the year of sale is computed pursuant to Section 453A(c). The deferred tax liability in this example is the unrecognized gain at the close of the year — $15,200,000 (the total gain realized was $16,000,000, but $800,000 of gain was recognized on the $1,000,000 down payment). This unrecognized gain is multiplied by the maximum Section 1 tax rate (assume 15% maximum capital gain rate).[63] The deferred tax liability here thus equals $2,280,000. The "applicable percentage" of this deferred tax liability is about 73.68%, determined under Section 453A(c)(4) by dividing $14,000,000 (the amount by which the

---

[57] The rate of interest is set forth in Section 453A(c)(2)(B).

[58] I.R.C. § 453A(a)(1).

[59] I.R.C. § 453A(b)(2).

[60] I.R.C. § 453A(c)(3).

[61] I.R.C. § 453A(c)(4).

[62] I.R.C. § 453A(b)(2).

[63] I.R.C. § 453A(c)(3).

outstanding balance of $19,000,000 exceeds $5,000,000) by $19,000,000 (the aggregate face amount of the outstanding obligations at the close of the year). The "applicable percentage of the deferred tax liability" is thus 73.68% of $2,280,000, or approximately $1,679,904. If the underpayment rate is 10%, then the interest for the taxable year is 10% of $1,679,904, or $167,990. This is the interest that must be paid for Year 1 on the deferred tax liability. These calculations will have to be repeated in later years based upon the deferred tax liability, applicable percentage and underpayment rates applicable in those years.

§ 40.11 INSTALLMENT OBLIGATIONS AND LIKE KIND EXCHANGES

Suppose a taxpayer engages in an exchange of like kind property and, as part of the transaction, receives as "boot" an installment obligation issued by the other party. Conceptually, the policies of both Sections 1031 and 453 should be carried out; the taxpayer should receive nonrecognition treatment with respect to the like kind exchange and (assuming no exceptions apply) should receive deferral of tax liability with respect to the income inherent in the installment obligation, pending the receipt of payments on it. Accordingly, in a like kind exchange in which an installment obligation is part of the boot received, Section 453(f)(6) provides that (1) the like kind property is not treated as a "payment," and (2) the gross profit ratio is specially determined, with the total contract price reduced by the amount of like kind property received and the gross profit reduced by the amount of gain not recognized under Section 1031. The legislative history to this provision elaborates:

> The basis of the like kind property received (determined under section 1031(d)), will be determined as if the obligation had been satisfied at its face amount. Thus, the taxpayer's basis in the property transferred will first be allocated to the like kind property received (but not in excess of its fair market value) and any remaining basis will be used to determine the gross profit ratio. . . .[64]

The legislative history illustrates this provision with an example under which property with a basis of $400,000 is exchanged for like kind property worth $200,000 and an installment obligation for $800,000. The like kind property takes a basis of $200,000, pursuant to the direction that basis allocations be made first to like kind property, but not in excess of fair market value. For Section 453 purposes, the total contract price is only $800,000, since the value of the like kind property is not included. Because $200,000 of the $400,000 total basis has been allocated to the like kind property, the "remaining basis" for Section 453 purposes is $200,000. With a total contract price of $800,000, and remaining basis of $200,000, the gross profit for Section 453 purposes is $600,000, and the gross profit ratio is therefore 75%.

---

[64] S. Rep. No. 96-1000, at 19–20 (1980).

Accordingly, 75% of each payment will constitute income, and a total of $600,000 of income will have been recognized when the note is fully paid.[65]

---

[65] See also Proposed Regulation § 1.453-1(f)(1), which dictates the same approach as employed in this example from the legislative history. Final regulations have been issued coordinating the deferred like-kind exchange rules of Section 1031 with the Section 453 installment sales rules. Treas. Reg. §§ 1.1031(k)-1(j)(2), 1.1031(b)-2.

Chapter 41

SALE OF A BUSINESS AND SALE-LEASEBACKS

The sale or purchase of an unincorporated business can produce various tax consequences, depending on the structure of the sale or purchase. This chapter addresses the major tax issues related to the sale or purchase of an unincorporated business, as well as sale-leaseback arrangements.

§ 41.01 SALE OF A SOLE PROPRIETORSHIP

[A] The Standard of *Williams v. McGowan*

Is the sale of a sole proprietorship the sale of a single asset or of the separate assets of the business? In the seminal case of *Williams v. McGowan*,[1] the Second Circuit concluded that the sale of an unincorporated hardware business could not be treated as the sale of a unified asset. Despite the functional interrelationship of the business' assets and the fact that the assets would not be as valuable if sold separately, the court held that a separate tax analysis had to be made with respect to each business asset sold. Thus, the character of each business asset must be determined — i.e., is it an ordinary asset, a capital asset, or a Section 1231 asset — and the gain or loss recognized with respect to each asset's disposition must be calculated. To calculate the gain or loss, a portion of the purchase price must be allocated to each asset. Obviously, this approach complicates matters for the buyer, seller and their tax advisors.

The Service's concern in *Williams v. McGowan* was that to view the sale of a business as a sale of single asset would distort the operation of our tax system and enable taxpayers to avoid tax. If capital gains and losses are accorded special treatment, it may make a significant difference whether one's income is ordinary or long-term or short-term capital gain and whether one's losses are ordinary or long-term or short-term capital losses.[2] To permit a taxpayer to treat a business sale as a sale of a single asset would negate in part these significant distinctions.

> **Example:** Steve decides to sell a bowling alley he has owned and operated as a sole proprietor for a number of years. Housed in the same building as and associated with the bowling operation are a pro shop and a bar. Steve intends to sell the entire operation, including the building, equipment, receivables, liquor license, a long term lease on pinsetting equipment, inventory, etc. What is the character of Steve's gain or loss on the sale of his bowling operation?

---

[1] 152 F.2d 570 (2d Cir. 1945).

[2] *Cf.* I.R.C. § 1(h).

Analysis: Considering the Section 1211 limitation on the deduction of capital losses, if the sale of Steve's bowling business would generate a net loss, Steve would benefit from the characterization of the overall loss as an ordinary loss. Such characterization would be possible if the sale of the business were treated as a sale of a single non-capital asset. By contrast, if Steve were required to fragment the sale, Steve might have ordinary income from the sale of inventory, capital gain and loss from the sale of investment property, and Section 1231 gains and losses from the sale of business equipment. This fragmentation approach might result in capital losses exceeding Steve's capital gains, thereby triggering the Section 1211 loss limitation rules. Applying the rule of *Williams v. McGowan*, Steve will be required to fragment the sale; gain or loss will be determined with respect to each asset comprising the business, and the character of the resulting gains and losses will be determined by reference to the character and holding period of each asset.

[B] Goodwill, Going Concern Value and Covenants Not to Compete

Valuable intangible items are often included in the sale of a business. Under the *Williams v. McGowan* analysis, part of the purchase price must be allocated to these items. For example, if Steve has a transferable lease on the pinsetting equipment used in his bowling operation, part of the purchase price of the business must be allocated to the transfer of that lease. In addition to intangibles such as leases, patents, and copyrights, there may also be goodwill, going concern value, and a covenant not to compete reflected in the purchase price of the business.[3] Before considering the tax consequences of allocating the purchase price of a business to intangibles, the nature of goodwill, going concern value and covenants not to compete must first be examined.

[1] Goodwill

A business that has been operating for many years and has a number of loyal patrons will likely sell at a premium attributable to the "goodwill" of the business. Goodwill has been defined to mean "the expectancy that the old customers will resort to the old place. It is the sum total of all the imponderable qualities that attract customers and bring patronage to the business without contractual compulsion."[4] More recently, regulations under Section 197 have defined goodwill as "the value of a trade or business attributable to the expectancy of continued customer patronage."[5]

Not all businesses have goodwill. Typically, goodwill is associated with businesses with an established reputation in an area, a good location, or a well-recognized trademark or tradename. For example, if a business is sold and the purchaser bargains for the right to continue using the tradename of the business, it is likely

---

[3] See Section 197(d) for an expanded list of intangibles commonly included in the sale of a business.

[4] Richard Miller and Sons, Inc. v. Comm'r, 537 F.2d 446, 451 (Ct. Cl. 1976).

[5] Treas. Reg. § 1.197-2(b)(1).

that goodwill has been transferred with the business. Similarly, the long and successful nature of a business indicates substantial goodwill will be transferred with the sale of the business. A purchase price in excess of the fair market value of the tangible and identifiable intangible items of a business indicates a payment for goodwill.

[2] Going Concern Value

In cases where the existence of goodwill was questionable, courts have held a portion of the purchase price should be allocated to "going concern value." According to the regulations under Section 197, going concern value is "the additional value that attaches to property by reason of its existence as an integral part of an ongoing business activity" and "includes the value attributable to the ability of a trade or business to continue functioning or generating income without interruption notwithstanding a change in ownership."[6] For example, assume an owner has a variety of fixtures and furniture used in conjunction his business. When sold with his business, these assets are likely to have more value than if they were sold separately.

[3] Covenant Not to Compete

Before purchasing a business, a buyer may require the seller to agree not to compete with the buyer in the same kind of business for a stated period of time. Such assurance is often necessary to insure that a business' goodwill is effectively transferred to the buyer. For example, if a business prospered because of the owner's expertise and reputation, a buyer of that business would want to be assured that the owner would not open a competing business in the same town.

Given the close relationship that may exist between goodwill and a covenant not to compete, the issue arises as to whether the covenant should be viewed as a separately bargained-for asset to which part of the purchase price of a business must be allocated. Because the tax treatment of amounts allocated to a covenant not to compete differs from that of amounts allocated to goodwill (i.e., a seller may claim capital gain treatment with respect to goodwill whereas the seller must report as ordinary income amounts received for a covenant not to compete), courts have had to consider whether the facts justify a separate allocation of the purchase price to a covenant not to compete. In resolving this issue, some courts have applied a "severability test" focusing on the question of whether a covenant not to compete could be segregated and valued independently from other assets transferred, particularly goodwill.[7] Under a "severability" analysis, if the covenant serves only to assure the transferor will enjoy the benefit of the goodwill he has acquired, no part of the purchase price will be allocated to it.[8] By contrast, if the covenant not to compete is understood by the parties to be a separate and distinct item, courts adopting the "severability analysis" will respect allocations to the covenant. The test more commonly applied is the so-called "economic reality" test. Under this test,

---

[6] Treas. Reg. § 1.197-2(b)(2).

[7] Michaels v. Comm'r, 12 T.C. 17 (1949).

[8] Id. at 19.

courts seek to determine whether the buyer and seller intended part of the purchase price be allocated to the covenant and whether the covenant has some independent basis in fact or some relationship to business reality.[9]

[C] Tax Consequences of Allocation of Purchase Price

The allocation of a part of the purchase price to goodwill, going concern value or a covenant not to compete has significantly different tax consequences to the buyer and the seller. From the seller's standpoint, the allocation will determine the amount realized with respect to each asset and, in turn, the amount and character of the gain or loss to be reported. From the buyer's standpoint, the allocation will determine the buyer's basis in the acquired assets, thus affecting the depreciation deductions the buyer claims and the amount and character of the buyer's gain or loss on any subsequent sale. With the enactment of Section 197 in 1993, Congress radically changed the tax treatment of these and other business intangibles. As a result, the stakes associated with purchase price allocations have also changed. An understanding of the historic tax treatment of business intangibles and the strategies employed by sellers and buyers to enhance their tax positions is necessary to appreciate the significance of the changes wrought by Section 197.

[1] Historic Allocation Strategies

Until 1993, goodwill and going concern value were considered assets without a determinable useful life and therefore not depreciable. Consequently, buyers of businesses sought to minimize the amount of the purchase price allocated to those assets. As part of their allocation strategy, they attempted to carve out of goodwill and going concern value items like customer subscription lists, insurance expirations lists, workforce in place, etc. By treating these items as separate intangible assets with limited useful lives, buyers could amortize the purchase price allocated to those items.[10] From their standpoint, sellers were willing to accommodate the buyers' carve-out efforts because the sellers' gain from the sale of such carved-out items was still characterized as capital gain.

The most significant case testing such taxpayer carve-out efforts was *Newark Morning Ledger Co. v. U.S.*,[11] in which the Supreme Court held a taxpayer could depreciate subscription lists acquired as a result of the purchase of other newspapers. While recognizing the difficulty in separating depreciable intangible assets from goodwill, the Court nevertheless emphasized:

> . . . [I]f a taxpayer can prove with reasonable accuracy that an asset used in the trade or business or held for the production of income has a value that wastes over an ascertainable period of time, that asset is depreciable under § 167, regardless of the fact that its value is related to the expectancy of continued patronage. The significant question for purposes of depreciation is not whether the asset falls "within the core of the

---

[9] Schultz v. Comm'r, 294 F.2d 52, 55 (9th Cir. 1961).

[10] *See* Treas. Reg. § 1.167(a)-3.

[11] 507 U.S. 546 (1993).

concept of goodwill,". . . . but whether the asset is capable of being valued and whether that value diminishes over time.[12]

The majority of the Court concluded Newark Morning Ledger had carried its "substantial burden" of proving that the subscription lists had an ascertainable value and a limited, reasonably predictable useful life.[13] Indicative, however, of the closeness of the question raised by the case, four justices dissented. Justice Souter writing for the dissenters noted:

> Ledger would have us scrap the accepted and substantive definition of "goodwill" as an expectation of continued patronage, in favor of a concept of goodwill as a residual asset of ineffable quality, whose existence and value would be represented by any portion of a business's purchase price not attributable to identifiable assets with determinate lives. Goodwill would shrink to an accounting leftover.[14]

Indeed, Justice Souter's description of Ledger's effort was equally applicable to many other purchasers of businesses who had attempted to use similar carve-outs to limit the amount allocable to goodwill.

Goodwill and going concern value, however, were not the only business intangibles which generated allocation controversies. Buyers and sellers were often at odds regarding the allocation of the purchase price to covenants not to compete. Because covenants not to compete have a limited life (typically a few years), amounts allocated to the covenant are amortizable over that period. Buyers therefore sought to allocate as much of the purchase price as possible to such covenants. Because amounts received by sellers for their agreement not to compete constitute ordinary income, sellers preferred minimal allocation to covenants not to compete.

[2] Section 197 — Amortization of Business Intangibles

§ 197. Amortization of goodwill and certain other intangibles —

(a) **General rule. A taxpayer shall be entitled to an amortization deduction with respect to any amortizable section 197 intangible. The amount of such deduction shall be determined by amortizing the adjusted basis (for purposes of determining gain) of such intangible ratably over the 15-year period beginning with the month in which such intangible was acquired.**

(b) **No other depreciation or amortization deduction allowable. Except as provided in subsection (a), no depreciation or amortization deduction shall be allowable with respect to any amortizable section 197 intangible.**

(c) **Amortizable section 197 intangible. For purposes of this section —**

(1) **In general. Except as otherwise provided in this section, the term**

---

[12] *Id.* at 566.

[13] *Newark Morning Ledger* was followed in *Charles Schwab v. Comm'r*, 122 T.C. 191 (2004), a case involving a pre-Section 197 year, where the Tax Court held that the brokerage customer lists acquired by the purchaser were indistinguishable for tax purposes from the newspaper subscriber lists in *Newark Morning Ledger*, and were this amortizable.

[14] *Id.* at 574.

"amortizable section 197 intangible" means any section 197 intangible —

(A) which is acquired by the taxpayer after the date of the enactment of this section, and

(B) which is held in connection with the conduct of a trade or business or an activity described in section 212.

(2) Exclusion of self-created intangibles, etc. The term "amortizable section 197 intangible" shall not include any section 197 intangible —

(A) which is not described in subparagraph (D), (E), or (F) of subsection (d)(1), and

(B) which is created by the taxpayer.

This paragraph shall not apply if the intangible is created in connection with a transaction (or series of related transactions) involving the acquisition of assets constituting a trade or business or substantial portion thereof.

(d) Section 197 intangible. For purposes of this section —

(1) In general. Except as otherwise provided in this section, the term "section 197 intangible" means —

(A) goodwill,

(B) going concern value,

(C) any of the following intangible items:

(i) workforce in place including its composition and terms and conditions (contractual or otherwise) of its employment,

(ii) business books and records, operating systems, or any other information base (including lists or other information with respect to current or prospective customers),

(iii) any patent, copyright, formula, process, design, pattern, know-how, format or other similar item,

(iv) any customer-based intangible,

(v) any supplier-based intangible, and

(vi) any other similar item,

(D) any license, permit, or other right granted by a governmental unit or an agency or instrumentality thereof,

(E) any covenant not to compete (or other arrangement to the extent such arrangement has substantially the same effect as a covenant not to compete) entered into in connection with an acquisition (directly or indirectly) of an interest in a trade or business or substantial portion thereof, and

(F) any franchise, trademark, or trade name.

(e) Exceptions. For purposes of this section, the term "section 197 intangible" shall not include any of the following:

(1) Financial interests. Any interest —

(A) in a corporation, partnership, trust, or estate, or

(B) under an existing futures contract, foreign currency contract, notional principal contract, or other similar financial contract.

(2) Land. Any interest in land.

(3) Computer software.

In response to cases like *Newark Morning Ledger* and recurring issues regarding appropriateness of allocations to covenants not to compete and other business intangibles, Congress enacted Section 197, authorizing the amortization of goodwill, going concern value, covenants not to compete and a broad range of other business intangibles over a 15-year period. Although negating the incentive for the kind of carve-outs made by taxpayers in cases like *Newark Morning Ledger*, Section 197 creates new planning considerations for buyers and sellers.

Section 197 eliminates much of the historic tension between buyers and sellers regarding allocations to goodwill and going concern. To the extent amounts are allocated to those items, buyers benefit from the opportunity Section 197 affords for amortization. As amortizable items, goodwill and going concern value are Section 1231 items in the hands of buyers. Assuming goodwill and going concern value are self-created items of sellers, those items are not amortizable by sellers and constitute capital assets in the hands of sellers. Sellers thus may claim capital gain treatment for amounts allocated to those items.

Nonetheless, buyers may view the 15-year amortization period as relatively long and prefer to allocate the purchase price to depreciable assets with shorter lives, thereby accelerating the write-off of the purchase price of the business. For similar reasons, the buyer may find allocations to covenants not to compete to be less attractive than they were before the 1993 legislation. For example, while historically a five-year covenant not to compete was amortized on a pro rata basis over a five-year period, Section 197 now requires that amortization to occur over a 15-year period.

Sellers, of course, welcome the diminished tax advantages to buyers of allocations to covenants not to compete. To the extent less of the purchase price is allocated to covenants not to compete, sellers will report less ordinary income on sales. At the same time, sellers in some circumstances may be concerned about buyers' efforts to maximize allocations to depreciable assets with a short useful life, *e.g.*, 3-, 5- or 7-year property. Because of Section 1245 recapture potential, increased allocation to such property might mean increased ordinary income.[15]

> **Example:** Kevin purchased for $100,000 a piece of equipment for use in his business. The equipment was 5-year property under Section 168(c) for depreciation purposes. Seven years later, after Kevin had completely depreciated the equipment, Kevin sells his business to Ron. In valuing the assets of the business, Kevin and Ron disagree over the value to be accorded the piece of equipment. Ron believes that $50,000 of the purchase price should be allocated to the equipment while Kevin argues the equipment is not worth more than $20,000. What significance does the valuation of the equipment have to the parties?

---

[15] See the Section 1245 recapture rules discussed in Chapter 33, *supra*.

Analysis: Assuming all of the gain realized on the equipment would be Section 1245 gain, Kevin will want the lowest value possible allocated to the equipment. Since the adjusted basis of the equipment is zero, if Kevin prevails in having $20,000 of the purchase price allocated to the equipment, Kevin will report $20,000 of ordinary income; if Ron prevails, Kevin will have $50,000 of ordinary income. Assuming the equipment will be depreciable property in Ron's hands, Ron will prefer to have more of the purchase price allocated to an asset like the equipment which will be depreciated over a five year period than to goodwill which would be amortized over a fifteen year period.

Section 197 specifically excludes a number of intangibles from the 15-year amortization rule: intangibles such as patents and copyrights which are not acquired as part of the acquisition of assets constituting a trade or business or substantial portion thereof,[16] and certain computer software.[17] This exclusion of computer software must be read in conjunction with the favorable depreciation treatment accorded software,[18] *i.e.*, computer software excluded from Section 197 is depreciable over a 36-month period using the straight line method of depreciation.

Certain self-created Section 197 intangibles are also excluded from "amortizable Section 197 intangible" status.[19] Thus, for example, advertising expenditures will not be subject to the rules of Section 197 but will generally continue to be deducted in the year incurred or paid even though they may provide a benefit beyond that year.

If a buyer, having appropriately allocated a portion of the purchase price to each Section 197 intangible acquired in the purchase of a business, subsequently sells one of the intangibles at a loss, the buyer may not recognize a loss on the sale if she still retains the other amortizable Section 197 intangibles.[20] Instead, the loss will be allocated among the remaining intangibles, thereby increasing their basis.

Amortizable Section 197 intangibles will be treated as properties "of a character subject to the allowance for depreciation under Section 167."[21] Thus, for example, if the sale of a Section 197 intangible results in a gain to the taxpayer, the gain may be subject to the recapture rules of Section 1245 and/or characterization under Section 1231.

---

[16] I.R.C. § 197(e)(4).

[17] I.R.C. § 197(e)(3).

[18] I.R.C. § 167(f).

[19] I.R.C. § 197(c)(2).

[20] I.R.C. § 197(f)(1).

[21] I.R.C. § 197(f)(7).

§ 41.02   VALUING GOODWILL, GOING CONCERN VALUE, AND COVENANTS NOT TO COMPETE

§ 1060.   Special Allocation Rules for Certain Asset Acquisitions.

(a)   **General Rule.** — In the case of any applicable asset acquisition, for purposes of determining both —

(1) the transferee's basis in such assets, and

(2) the gain or loss of the transferor with respect to such acquisition,

the consideration received for such assets shall be allocated among such assets acquired in such acquisition in the same manner as amounts are allocated to assets under section 338(b)(5). If in connection with an applicable asset acquisition, the transferee and transferor agree in writing as to the allocation of any consideration, or as to the fair market value of any of the assets, such agreement shall be binding on both the transferee and transferor unless the Secretary determines that such allocation (or fair market value) is not appropriate.

(c)   **Applicable asset acquisition.** — For purposes of this section, the term "applicable asset acquisition" means any transfer (whether directly or indirectly)—

(1) of assets which constitute a trade or business, and

(2) with respect to which the transferee's basis in such assets is determined wholly by reference to the consideration paid for such assets.

A transfer shall not be treated as failing to be an applicable asset acquisition merely because section 1031 applies to a portion of the assets transferred.

Generally, the Service will respect the values established by contracting parties in their sales agreement, particularly where the interests of the parties are adverse. As a result, the allocation of the purchase price to the various tangible and intangible items transferred in a sale of a business should generally be negotiated by the parties and should be specifically reflected in their agreement. The Service, of course, cannot be precluded from attacking allocations in an agreement that have no basis in economic reality.[22]

In 1986, Congress added Section 1060 to the Code. This provision requires that the "residual method" of valuation be used in valuing goodwill and going concern value in "applicable asset acquisitions."[23] As its name suggests, the residual method provides that the value of goodwill and going concern value is the excess of the purchase price over the aggregate fair market value of the tangible and identifiable intangible assets (other than goodwill or going concern value). In the Senate Finance Committee report, the reason for requiring the residual method was explained as follows:

---

[22]   Concord Control Inc. v. Comm'r, 78 T.C. 742, 745 (1982).

[23]   An applicable asset acquisition is, essentially, the purchase of the assets of a trade or business. *See* I.R.C. § 1060(c).

The committee is aware that the allocation of purchase price among the assets of a going business has been a troublesome area of the tax law. Purchase price allocations have been an endless source of controversy between the Internal Revenue Service and taxpayers, principally because of the difficulty of establishing the value of goodwill and going concern value. The Service lacks the resources to challenge allocations to goodwill or going concern value in all or even a substantial portion of the cases in which it would otherwise assert that the value of those assets is misstated.

. . .

The committee is also concerned about the potential for abuse inherent in the sale of a going business where there is no agreement between the parties as to the value of specific assets. In many instances, the parties' allocations for tax reporting purposes are inconsistent, resulting in a whipsaw of the government. The committee expects that requiring both parties to use the residual method for allocating amounts to nonamortizable goodwill and going concern value may diminish some of this "whipsaw" potential.[24]

Regulations issued under Section 1060 provide that the purchase price must be allocated among seven classes of assets in the following order:[25]

Class I: Cash and cash equivalents;

Class II: Actively traded personal property as defined in Section 1092(d), certificates of deposit, and foreign currency;

Class III: Accounts receivable, mortgages and credit card receivables which arise in the ordinary course of business;

Class IV: Stock in trade of the taxpayer or other property of a kind which would properly be included in the inventory of taxpayer if on hand at the close of the taxable year, property primarily held for sale to customers in the ordinary course of a trade or business;

Class V: All assets not included in I, II, III, IV, VI, or VII;

Class VI: All section 197 intangibles except goodwill or going concern value; and

Class VII: Goodwill and going concern value.[26]

As the legislative history of Section 1060 reflects, Congress was concerned that the government might be whipsawed as a result of inconsistent reporting by taxpayers. This was often the case where parties did not allocate the purchase price to the various assets of the business. In such cases, it was not uncommon for a buyer to allocate less to goodwill than a seller. Even where the parties had made an allocation of the purchase price in the agreement, it was not uncommon for parties

---

[24] S. Rep. No. 99-313, 99th Cong. 2d Sess, p. 253–54 (1986).

[25] The regulations incorporate the residual method set out in Regulation §§ 1.338-6 and 1.1060-1(c)(2).

[26] Treas. Reg. § 1.1060-1(a).

to report the transaction in a manner inconsistent with that allocation.

For example, in *Brams v. Commissioner*,[27] the taxpayer sold his commercial salad making business pursuant to an agreement allocating $80,000 of the purchase price to the name "Salad House, Inc." and its accompanying goodwill, $150,000 to a ten-year covenant not to compete, and the remaining $130,000 of the purchase price to the other assets of the business. The taxpayer on his tax return, however, reported the $150,000 as allocable to business assets, primarily goodwill, instead of to the covenant not to compete as provided in the agreement. As a result, the taxpayer claimed capital gain treatment. The Service argued that the taxpayer should have reported $150,000 of ordinary income attributable to the covenant not to compete. The issue before the court was whether the taxpayer was bound by the allocations in the agreement, specifically the allocation of $150,000 of the purchase price to the covenant not to compete. The court noted two different standards have evolved to resolve this issue. Under the rule of *Danielson v. Commissioner*,[28] a taxpayer can avoid the tax consequences of his agreement if he can establish its terms are unenforceable because of mistake, undue influence, fraud, duress, etc. The Tax Court refused to follow this rule, and instead applied the "strong proof" rule, requiring the taxpayer to establish that the allocation was not intended by the parties or did not reflect economic reality. The court concluded there was evidence establishing both intent and economic reality with respect to the allocation in the agreement of $150,000 of the purchase price to the covenant not to compete. The court therefore agreed with the Service that the taxpayer should report $150,000 of ordinary income attributable to the covenant not to compete.

Section 1060(a) provides the parties will be bound by a written allocation of any consideration or by a written agreement regarding fair market value of any asset, unless the Treasury determines such allocation or value is inappropriate. The legislative history of this provision indicates that, while the Service is free to challenge any allocation or the valuation of any asset, particularly where the parties' interests are not adverse, the parties themselves are bound by their written agreement, unless they are "able to refute the allocation or valuation under the standards set forth in the *Danielson* case."[29] Apparently, the "strong proof" test is no longer to be applied to written agreements in Section 1060(a) acquisitions. Thus, while the allocation of the purchase price in a sales agreement is recommended, it behooves the parties to consider carefully the tax consequences of those allocations.

As noted, the legislative history of Section 1060 makes it clear the Service may challenge the taxpayer's determination of the value of any asset. For example, a taxpayer may place an unduly high value on goodwill or another depreciable or amortizable asset, thereby hoping to secure some tax advantage. The Service, however, may challenge that value using any appropriate means.

Example: Mark will sell Ellen a medical supply business Mark has operated as a sole proprietor for the last ten years. The following table lists

---

[27] T.C. Memo 1980-584.

[28] 378 F.2d 771, 775 (3d Cir. 1967).

[29] House Ways and Means Comm. Rep., H.R. 5835, p. 103.

the assets to be sold, Mark's adjusted basis (A/B) in each asset and the fair market value (FMV) of the assets:

Asset	A/B	FMV
Accounts Receivable	$0	$60,000
Building	0	240,000
Land	30,000	100,000
Inventory	250,000	230,000
Light truck	0	20,000

Ellen agrees to pay Mark $800,000 for the business. Under the terms of the agreement, Ellen will be entitled to continue to use the name "Mark's Medical Supplies" and Mark agrees not to engage in the medical supply business for the next five years within a 30-mile radius of the current business location. The agreement specifically allocates the $800,000 purchase price to the above items in the amount of the fair market value indicated. In addition, their agreement allocates $50,000 to the covenant not to compete and $100,000 to goodwill. What are the tax consequences to Mark of the sale of the business? Assume the gain inherent in the truck would be characterized entirely as Section 1245 gain. Assume also that Mark had an adjusted basis of $0 in the goodwill of his business.

Analysis: Mark's aggregate basis in the assets sold is $280,000. The total amount realized is $800,000. Mark has $520,000 of gain that, according to *Williams v. McGowan*, must be allocated to the individual assets of the business.[30] The example provides the fair market values of the listed assets, which are assumed to be accurate. The Service has the right to challenge allocations and valuations, whereas the parties themselves will ordinarily be bound by their written allocations and agreements.

Accounts receivable: The amount realized from the accounts receivable presumably is $60,000. The adjusted basis of the accounts is $0. The gain realized and recognized is therefore is $60,000. Accounts receivable are not capital assets and the gain is therefore ordinary.[31]

Building: The amount realized on the building is $240,000 and the adjusted basis of the building is $0. The gain realized and recognized is $240,000. The building is a depreciable asset used in the trade or business and as such is Section 1231(b) property. The gain will likely be long-term capital gain but its characterization will depend on the other Section 1231 gains and losses Mark has during the taxable year. (The possibility of Section 1231(c) recapture might be raised; also the possibility of Section 1250 recapture might be raised if accelerated depreciation had been claimed with respect to the building.)

Land: The amount realized on the land is $100,000 and the adjusted basis in the land is $30,000. The gain realized and recognized will be

---

[30] See Section 1060 and the purchase price allocation rules of Regulation § 1.1060-1(d).

[31] I.R.C. § 1221(4).

$70,000. Like the building, the land is not a capital asset.[32] Rather, it is a Section 1231(b) asset. The characterization of the gain on the land will therefore depend on the other Section 1231 gains and losses Mark has during the taxable year.

Inventory: A loss of $20,000 is realized on the inventory. Inventory is not a capital asset (Section 1221(a)(1)) nor is it a Section 1231(b) asset. Therefore, the loss will be treated as an ordinary loss deductible under Section 165.

Light truck: Mark will realize and recognize a gain of $20,000 on the truck, which is Section 1245 property. All of the gain will therefore be recaptured as ordinary income.

Goodwill and Covenant Not to Compete: Since goodwill is treated as a capital asset, the $100,000 allocation to the zero-basis goodwill produces $100,000 of capital gain for Mark. The $50,000 allocation to the covenant not to compete results in $50,000 of ordinary income. This assumes the allocation to these items is respected by the Service.

Note that for Ellen, both the goodwill and the covenant not to compete are Section 197 intangibles amortizable ratably over 15-year periods.[33] Ellen is therefore indifferent as to how the $150,000 total is allocated between goodwill and the covenant; Mark, of course, is not. For him, allocations to goodwill are preferable to allocations to the covenant not to compete.

Even though the purchase price paid by Ellen exceeds the fair market value of the tangible assets analyzed above by $150,000, the parties cannot disregard the actual fair market value of the assets in allocating the purchase price and simply allocate the $150,000 excess to certain tangible depreciable assets being purchased by Ellen. As noted above, a premium may be paid for intangibles such as goodwill, covenant not to compete or gong concern value. The Service will not permit the seller and buyer to disguise what is in essence a goodwill payment by calling it part of the purchase price for fixtures or equipment.

Assuming the purchase price is allocated according to the fair market values indicated in the example, Ellen's basis in the accounts receivable, building, land, inventory and fixtures will be the fair market value of each of those assets.[34] Ellen will also have a $50,000 fair market value basis in the covenant not to compete, and a $100,000 fair market value basis in the goodwill.

As noted, Ellen is indifferent to allocations between goodwill and covenants not to compete. But Ellen is not indifferent to allocations generally. Allocations to short-life assets entitled to accelerated depreciation are much more attractive to Ellen than allocations to Section 197

---

[32] I.R.C. § 1221(2).

[33] I.R.C. § 197(a), (d)(1)(A), (E).

[34] I.R.C. § 1012.

intangibles: hence, the incentive to boost the allocations to the truck but not to buildings or land, which are long-life or nondepreciable assets. Allocations to inventory items may also be attractive, however, in generating relatively prompt ordinary losses or reducing amounts of ordinary income. Clearly the Service is not bound by the parties' self-serving allocations.

§ 41.03 SALE-LEASEBACK

The issue may sometimes arise as to whether a given transaction should be characterized as a sale or a lease.[35] Casting a purchase as a lease could prove beneficial to a taxpayer, if as a "lessee" he would be entitled to claim rental deductions in excess of the depreciation and interest deductions available to a purchaser of the same property. Sale-leaseback arrangements raise comparable characterization questions. If respected, the sale of property to the purchaser, followed by the leaseback of the property to the seller, may provide a valuable mechanism for shifting tax benefits from one taxpayer to another. The seller-lessee in such a situation may claim a deduction for rent that may be greater than the tax deductions available to it as an owner of the property.

Assume, for example, a tract of land, a nondepreciable asset, is the subject of a sale-leaseback. Assume also the seller-lessee has substantial net operating losses and cannot use other available deductions, e.g., the deduction for real property taxes. The sale-leaseback in such circumstances may enable the seller-lessee to raise a substantial amount of cash, continue to possess and use the property, and pay "rent" lower than the interest expense that might be incurred if standard financing had been sought. Obviously, the Service is anxious to prevent the shifting of tax benefits and the resulting decrease in tax revenues which can result from such arrangements. There are various ways which sale-leaseback transactions may be recharacterized.

[A] Sale-Leaseback Characterized as Financing Arrangement

A taxpayer owning business property may need substantial cash to finance business operations. One alternative, of course, would be to borrow the funds, using the business property as security. However, this method of acquiring necessary financing may not be desirable for a variety of reasons, including local usury laws, adverse impact of debt on the borrower's financial statements, etc. Another alternative might be a sale of the property to the would-be lender and a simultaneous leasing of the property by the borrower combined with an option to purchase. This method enables the taxpayer to raise the cash necessary to continue its business while retaining possession of the property.

Assuming a sale-leaseback of depreciable property, the question arises as to who is entitled to claim the depreciation deductions. This issue was considered by the Supreme Court in *Helvering v. Lazarus & Co.*[36] There the taxpayer deeded

---

[35] *See, e.g.,* Starr's Estate v. Comm'r, 274 F.2d 294 (9th Cir. 1959).

[36] 308 U.S. 252 (1939), *aff'g* 101 F.2d 728 (6th Cir. 1939).

developed real property to a bank and leased the property back from the bank under a 99-year renewable lease with an option to buy. The taxpayer sought to deduct the depreciation allowable on the leased property; the Service argued that the bank as titleholder was entitled to the depreciation deductions. The Supreme Court affirmed the decision of the Sixth Circuit disregarding the sale-leaseback form of the transaction and recharacterizing it as merely a financing arrangement akin to a mortgage. The evidence established that the "sale" proceeds amounted to about half the actual worth of the property and that the parties understood the arrangement to be a financing arrangement. The rental payments were viewed as simply constituting interest payments on a loan. Under these circumstances, the Court concluded the taxpayer, and not the titleholder, was entitled to the depreciation deductions.

In *Frank Lyon Co. v. U.S.*,[37] the taxpayer took title to a building being constructed by Worthen Bank and Trust, and leased the building back to Worthen. Financing of the purchase price was provided by a third party. The Supreme Court concluded the sale-leaseback would be respected as such. As a result, the taxpayer could claim both depreciation and interest deductions.

> The *Lazarus* case, we feel, is to be distinguished from the present one and is not controlling here. Its transaction was one involving only two (and not multiple) parties, the taxpayer-department store and the trustee-bank. . . . The present case, in contrast, involves three parties, Worthen, Lyon, and the finance agency. . . . Despite Frank Lyon's presence on Worthen's board of directors, the transaction, as it ultimately developed, was not a familial one arranged by Worthen, but one compelled by the realities of the restrictions imposed upon the bank. Had Lyon not appeared, another interested investor would have been selected. The ultimate solution would have been essentially the same. Thus, the presence of the third party, in our view, significantly distinguishes this case from *Lazarus* and removes the latter as controlling authority. . . . Most significantly, it was Lyon alone, and not Worthen, who was liable on the notes. . . . No matter how the transaction could have been devised otherwise, it remains a fact as the agreements were placed in final form, the obligation on the notes fell squarely on Lyon. Lyon, an ongoing enterprise, exposed its very business well-being to this real and substantial risk. . . .

> In short, we hold that where, as here, there is a genuine multiple-party transaction with economic substance which is compelled or encouraged by business or regulatory realities, is imbued with tax-independent consider-ations, and is not shaped solely by tax-avoidance features that have meaningless labels attached, the Government should honor the allocation of rights and duties effectuated by the parties. Expressed another way, so long as the lessor retains significant and genuine attributes of the traditional lessor status, the form of the transaction adopted by the parties governs for tax purposes. What those attributes are in any particular case will necessarily depend upon its facts. It suffices to say that, as here, a

---

[37] 435 U.S. 561 (1978).

sale-and-leaseback, in and of itself, does not necessarily operate to deny a taxpayer's claim for deductions.[38]

[B] Sale-Leaseback Characterized as a Tax-Free Exchange

Assume a taxpayer owns and uses real estate in its day-to-day operations. The real estate has a current fair market value less than its adjusted basis. Seeking additional operating capital, the taxpayer sells the property for its fair market value and then immediately leases the property back for a period in excess of thirty years. If this arrangement is respected, the taxpayer will have raised the desired amount of cash and will also be entitled to claim a loss deduction on the transfer of the property. As a result of the leaseback, taxpayer's possession and use of the property will continue uninterrupted. The Service, as discussed previously, could attack this arrangement claiming it constitutes a mere financing arrangement. Another route of attack may also be available: treatment of the arrangement as a tax free exchange under Section 1031.

The Service first raised the Section 1031 argument in a sale-leaseback situation in *Century Electric Co. v. Commissioner*.[39] There, Century Electric Company transferred its foundry building to William Jewell College. Under the sales agreement, William Jewell paid $150,000 cash and gave Century Electric a lease which enabled Century Electric to continue using the property for a 95-year period. The foundry building had an adjusted basis of approximately $532,000 and a fair market value considerably less than that. The taxpayer claimed a deductible loss of almost $382,000 on the transaction.

The Service, relying on Regulation Section 1.1031(a)-1(c), argued the transaction constituted a like kind exchange. That regulation provides that a lease with 30 or more years to run and a fee interest in real estate are like kind properties. The court agreed with the Service, noting the purpose of Section 1031 was to negate gain or loss in transactions where the taxpayer is in essentially the same economic position after the transaction as before. With respect to Century Electric's economic position, the court reasoned:

> It is undisputed that the foundry property before the transaction was held by petitioner for productive use in petitioner's business. After the transaction, the same property was held by the petitioner for the same use in the same business. Both before and after the transaction the property was necessary to the continued operation of petitioner's business. The only change brought by the transaction was in the estate or interest of petitioner in the foundry property.[40]

A more recent sale-leaseback case in which the Service argued Section 1031 is *Leslie Co. v. Commissioner*.[41] Unlike the taxpayer in *Century Electric*, the taxpayer in *Leslie* successfully overcame the Service's challenge. The *Leslie* court

---

[38] *Id.* at 575–576, 583–584.

[39] 192 F.2d 155 (8th Cir. 1951), *cert. denied*, 342 U.S. 954 (1952).

[40] *Id.* at 159–160.

[41] 539 F.2d 943 (3d Cir. 1976).

relied on *Jordon Marsh Co. v. Commissioner*,[42] a case holding a similar sale and leaseback constituted a sale on which a loss was recognized.

Thus we may interpret the essential difference between *Jordan Marsh* and *Century Electric* as centering on their respective views of the need to value property involved in a sale and leaseback.[43] *Jordan Marsh*, viewing the Congressional purpose behind the nonrecognition provision as one of avoiding taxation of paper gains and losses, would value the properties involved in order to determine whether the requirements of an "exchange" have been met. *Century Electric*, on the other hand, viewing the legislative enactment as one to relieve the administrative burden of valuation, would regard the value of the properties involved as irrelevant. . . . We are persuaded that the *Jordan Marsh* approach is a more satisfactory one.

It seems to us, therefore, that, in order to determine whether money was the sole consideration of a transfer, the fair market value of the properties involved must be ascertained. Here, the Tax Court found that Leslie had sold its property unconditionally for cash equal to its fair market value, and had acquired a leasehold for which it was obligated to pay fair rental value. . . . Nor do we think the Tax Court erred in concluding that the leasehold acquired by Leslie had no capital value. Among other considerations, the rental charged at fair market rates, the lack of compensation for the leasehold interest in the event of condemnation, and the absence of any substantial right to control over the property all support this conclusion. On this record, we agree with the Tax Court that the conveyance was not an exchange, "a reciprocal transfer of property," but was rather "a transfer of property for a money consideration only," and therefore a sale.[44]

---

[42] 269 F.2d 453 (2d Cir. 1959).

[43] The Court in *Jordan Marsh* also distinguished *Century Electric* on its facts, since in that case there had been no finding that the cash received by the taxpayer was the full equivalent of the value of the fee which had been conveyed. Nor had there been a finding that the leaseback was at a rental which was a fair rental for the premises.

Indeed, as noted in *Jordan Marsh*, the record in *Century Electric* indicated the sales price was substantially less than the fair market value. There was also evidence from which the court could have found the leasehold had a separate capital value, since the conveyance to a nonprofit college avoided considerable tax liabilities on the property.

[44] 539 F.2d at 949.

Chapter 42

AN INTRODUCTION TO ORIGINAL ISSUE DISCOUNT

Various provisions of the Code address the issue of the time value of money. This chapter deals with this topic principally by introducing the concept of "original issue discount" and outlining the computation and treatment of original issue discount on debt instruments issued for cash.[1]

§ 42.01 ORIGINAL ISSUE DISCOUNT: INTRODUCTION

The original issue discount Code provisions, in general, impute an interest equivalent — called "original issue discount" — to debt instruments that do not bear an adequate rate of interest, and require that this interest equivalent be included in income on a current basis. The original issue discount provisions are among the most complex provisions to be found in the Code, and their complexity is exacerbated by unique terminology.

A bond that will pay a specific sum at a future date, but no interest in the interim (otherwise known as a "zero coupon bond") will obviously sell at issuance date for less than its face value. The value of the bond will move closer and closer to the face amount as the maturity date draws nearer, but its value will be considerably less than face amount initially. If an investor purchases the bond on issuance for less than its face amount, and then holds the bond until it is redeemed at maturity for its face amount, the difference between the amount paid on issuance and the amount paid on redemption — that is, the "original issue discount" on the bond — serves the same purpose as interest, even though the bond nominally pays no interest.

The investor's gain is taxed as ordinary income whether the investor simply collects the proceeds on maturity or sells the bond for something less than its face amount prior to maturity. A sale, in other words, does not convert the "earned" original issue discount to capital gain, even if the bond is a capital asset. The Supreme Court rejected a claim to the contrary in *United States v. Midland-Ross Corporation*[2] with respect to notes sold there at a gain that was attributable to original issue discount. The *Midland-Ross* decision, based on the "application of

---

[1] I.R.C. §§ 1271–1273. This chapter considers only briefly (1) original issue discount on debt instruments issued for property (I.R.C. §§ 1271–1275); (2) the computation and treatment of "unstated interest" on certain deferred-payment sales of property (I.R.C. § 483); and (3) the tax treatment of certain deferred-payment rental agreements (I.R.C. § 467). These provisions are of particular complexity and are beyond the scope of this book.

[2] 381 U.S. 54 (1965).

general principles" of tax law, is confirmed in the statutory provisions discussed below.

The investor's gain is thus to be taxed as ordinary income, but the question remains as to when it will be so taxed. When Congress first legislated in this area in 1954, the earned original issue discount (henceforth, OID) was taxed on receipt — that is, when the bond was redeemed, sold or otherwise disposed of. (This rule applied to cash mathod taxpayers; an accrual method taxpayer would report interest income as it accrued.) Congress eventually decided this approach presented too much opportunity for mismatching of income and deductions. The bond-issuing corporation, presumably on the accrual method, could deduct as interest the accrued, unpaid OID, while the cash method investor reported no income until payment was made. This deduction-now, income-later arrangement was satisfactory to the two taxpayers, of course, but not to the Treasury.

In 1969 Congress acted again, changing the rule to require the OID be treated as earned *ratably* over the term of the bond. This approach corrects the mismatching of income and deductions permitted by the earlier legislation, requiring current reporting of the OID by both lender and borrower. The 1969 legislation required original issue discount income to be reported as earned, but treated the income as earned in equal amounts throughout the period. This approach, in effect, put both parties on the accrual method. The investor was required to report ordinary income each year; the corporation would have a comparable interest expense each year.

There is a major problem with the ratable accrual method, and the 1969 provisions that embodied it have been repealed. Economically speaking, it is unrealistic to treat the interest as accruing in equal amounts each year. By purchasing the bond at a discount, the investor in effect loaned money to the issuing corporation for a period of years. From an economic standpoint, unpaid interest itself earns interest — that is, interest is "compounded" on some periodic basis. Therefore, whatever amount of interest is treated as earned in the first year of the loan, a greater amount should be treated as earned in the second year, and increasingly greater amounts should be treated as earned in subsequent years. If the compounding period is an annual one, at the end of Year 1, the unpaid Year 1 interest is added to the principal amount. The interest earned in Year 2 is not only interest on the principal but also interest on the unpaid Year 1 interest. Similarly, interest earned in Year 3 will be greater than interest earned in Year 2 because the Year 3 interest includes interest on the unpaid Year 2 interest. Because interest is not paid until the end of Year 10, the corporate obligor's real debt, consisting of principal and unpaid interest, increases each year; hence the interest on the debt also increases.

> **Example:** Corporation issues a 10-year, $1,000,000 noninterest bearing bond. Investor purchases the bond on issuance for $385,000 and holds the bond until it is redeemed at maturity, 10 years later, for $1,000,000.

> **Analysis:** An interest rate of about 10%, compounded annually, will result in a $1,000,000 payment on a 10-year loan of $385,000. The table below compares the annual interest amounts under the ratable accrual approach (column 1) and the annual compounding approach (column 2). The third column shows the total debt on which the column 2 interest is charged. For

example, the Year 6 interest charge under annual compounding is $62,005. This is 10% of $620,047, which is the total of the combined unpaid principal ($385,000) and the unpaid interest earned in the five *prior* years ($235,047). (The slight difference between columns 1 and 2 in total interest accrued reflects the fact that the interest rate under annual compounding is actually a bit greater than 10%. The 10% figure is used here only for ease of computation. If the exact figure were used, column 2 would also total $615,000.) Thus, after 10 years, the same total amount is paid to the bond holder, but the interest portion accrues on quite different schedules.

		(1)	(2)			(3)
		Interest ratably accrued	Interest at 10% annually compounded	Unpaid Principal +	Unpaid Interest =	Total Debt
Year	1	$ 61,500	$ 38,500	$385,000 +	$0 =	$385,000
	2	61,500	42,350	385,000 +	38,500 =	423,500
	3	61,500	46,585	385,000 +	80,850 =	465,850
	4	61,500	51,244	385,000 +	127,435 =	512,435
	5	61,500	56,368	385,000 +	178,679 =	563,679
	6	61,500	62,005	385,000 +	235,047 =	620,047
	7	61,500	68,205	385,000 +	297,052 =	682,052
	8	61,500	75,026	385,000 +	365,257 =	750,257
	9	61,500	82,528	385,000 +	440,283 =	825,283
	10	61,500	90,781	385,000 +	522,811 =	907,811
TOTAL		$615,000	$613,592			

The ratable accrual approach of the 1969 legislation thus did not reflect an "economic accrual" of interest. To treat $61,500 of interest as accruing each year overstated the accrual in the early years and understated it in the later years. Such a distortion was quite satisfactory from the standpoint of the obligor — accelerating deductions into the early years increases their value by generating tax savings now rather than later. By contrast, for the ordinary investor, the arrangement was unattractive; it accelerated income recognition, but without any cash payments. However, for tax-exempt investors, for other investors in low tax brackets, or for investors with sufficient deductions to offset the OID income, the income acceleration was acceptable. As a result, the practical effect of the ratable accrual method for OID was to accelerate corporate interest deductions, while the accelerated OID income (given the investors who purchased the OID bonds) would be taxed lightly or not at all.

This third approach to OID, the annual compounding approach demonstrated in the above example, adopted by Congress in 1982 and expanded upon in 1984, reflects the status of the law today. This approach to the timing of the investor's income of $615,000 — and not so incidentally, to the timing of the corporate obligor's interest expense of $615,000 — retains the matching concept of the 1969 legislation. It continues to place both parties on the accrual method for OID purposes, but it rejects ratable accrual in favor of "economic accrual" of OID.

As noted above, compound interest is interest upon unpaid interest. The more often interest is compounded (*i.e.*, calculated and added to the principal), the greater the aggregate amount of interest earned will be. If interest is compounded daily, the interest earned today itself starts earning interest tomorrow. If interest is compounded annually, however, the interest earned on Day 1 earns nothing for the next 364 days, the interest earned on Day 2 waits 363 days before itself earning interest, etc. As the frequency of compounding decreases, the interest rate must increase in order to earn the same total interest over the same time period.

§ 42.02 OID: DEBT INSTRUMENTS ISSUED FOR CASH

§ 1271. **Treatment of amounts received on retirement or sale or exchange of debt instruments —**

(a) **General rule — For purposes of this title —**

(1) **Retirement — Amounts received by the holder on retirement of any debt instrument shall be considered as amounts received in exchange therefor.**

---

§ 1272. **Current inclusion in income of original issue document —**

(a) **Original issue discount on debt instruments issued after July 1, 1982, included in income on basis of constant interest rate —**

(1) **General rule — For purposes of this title, there shall be included in the gross income of the holder of any debt instrument having original issue discount issued after July 1, 1982, an amount equal to the sum of the daily portions of the original issue discount for each day during the taxable year on which such holder held such debt instrument.**

(2) **Exceptions — Paragraph (1) shall not apply to —**

(A) **Tax-exempt obligations — Any tax-exempt obligation.**

(B) **United States savings bonds — Any United States savings bond.**

(C) **Short-term obligations — Any debt instrument which has a fixed maturity date not more than 1 year from the date of issue.**

(D) **Obligations issued by natural persons before March 2, 1984 — Any obligation issued by a natural person before March 2, 1984.**

(E) **Loans between natural persons —**

(i) **In general — Any loan made by a natural person to another person if —**

(I) **such loan is not made in the course of a trade or business of the lender, and**

(II) **the amount of such loan (when increased by the outstanding amount of prior loans by such natural person to such other natural person) does not exceed $10,000.**

(ii) Clause (i) not to apply where tax avoidance a principal purpose — Clause (i) shall not apply if the loan has as 1 of its principal purposes the avoidance of any Federal tax.

(iii) Treatment of husband and wife — For purposes of this sub-paragraph, a husband and wife shall be treated as 1 person. The preceding sentence shall not apply where the spouses lived apart at all times during the taxable year in which the loan is made.

(3) Determination of daily portions — For purposes of paragraph (1), the daily portion of the original issue discount on any debt instrument shall be determined by allocating to each day in any accrual period its ratable portion of the increase during such accrual period in the adjusted issue price of the debt instrument. For purposes of the preceding sentence, the increase in the adjusted issue price for any accrual period shall be an amount equal to the excess (if any) of —

(A) The product of — (i) the adjusted issue price of the debt instrument at the beginning of such accrual period, and (ii) the yield to maturity (determined on the basis of compounding at the close of each accrual period and properly adjusted for the length of the accrual period), over

(B) the sum of the amounts payable as interest on such debt instrument during such accrual period.

(4) Adjusted issue price — For purposes of this subsection, the adjusted issue price of any debt instrument at the beginning of any accrual period is the sum of —

(A) the issue price of such debt instrument, plus

(B) the adjustments under this subsection to such issue price for all periods before the first day of such accrual period.

(5) Accrual period — Except as otherwise provided in regulations prescribed by the Secretary, the term "accrual period" means a 6-month period (or shorter period from the date of original issue of the debt instrument) which ends on a day in the calendar year corresponding to the maturity date of the debt instrument or the date 6 months before such maturity date.

---

§ 1273. Determination of amount of original issue discount —

(a) General rule — For purposes of this subpart —

(1) In general — The term "original issue discount" means the excess (if any) of —

(A) the stated redemption price at maturity, over

(B) the issue price.

(2) Stated redemption price at maturity — The term "stated redemption price at maturity" means the amount fixed by the last modification of the purchase agreement and includes interest and other amounts payable at that time (other than any interest based on a fixed rate, and payable unconditionally at fixed periodic intervals of 1 year or less during the entire term of any

debt instrument.)

(3)   ¼ of 1 percent de minimis rule — If the original issue discount determined under paragraph (1) is less than —

(A) ¼ of 1 percent of the stated redemption price at maturity, multiplied by

(B) the number of complete years to maturity, then the original issue discount shall be treated as zero.

(b)   Issue price — For purposes of this subpart —

(1)   Publicly offered debt instruments not issued for property — In the case of any issue of debt instruments —

(A) publicly offered, and

(B) not issued for property, the issue price is the initial offering price to the public (excluding bond houses and brokers) at which price a substantial amount of such debt instruments was sold.

(2)   Other debt instruments not issued for property — In the case of any issue of debt instruments not issued for property and not publicly offered, the issue price of each such instrument is the price paid by the first buyer of such debt instrument.

(3)   Debt instruments issued for property where there is public trading — In the case of a debt instrument which is issued for property and which —

(A) is part of an issue a portion of which is traded on an established securities market, or

(B) (i) is issued for stock or securities which are traded on an established securities market, or

(ii) to the extent provided in regulations, is issued for property (other than stock or securities) of a kind regularly traded on an established market, the issue price of such debt instrument shall be the fair market value of such property.

(4)   Other cases — Except in any case —

(A) to which paragraph (1), (2), or (3) of this subsection applies, or

(B) to which section 1274 applies, the issue price of a debt instrument which is issued for property shall be the stated redemption price at maturity.

(5)   Property — In applying this subsection, the term "property" includes services and the right to use property, but such term does not include money.

[A]   Determining the Amount of OID

Original issue discount on a debt instrument is defined as "the stated redemption price at maturity" over "the issue price."[3] The stated redemption price at maturity is generally the total of all payments under the debt instrument,

---

[3] I.R.C. § 1273(a)(1).

including interest payments, except for interest based on a fixed rate and unconditionally payable at fixed periods of one year or less.[4] (Under the regulations to Section 1273, the interest that is not included in the stated redemption price at maturity is called "qualified stated interest."[5]) The issue price of a debt instrument issued for cash is generally the amount paid on issuance.[6] If the issue of debt instruments is publicly offered, the issue price is the initial public offering price at which a substantial amount of the debt instruments was sold.[7]

Example 1: Assume on January 1, Year 1, Corporation issues a 10-year bond to Investor for $100,000. The bond bears no interest and will pay $265,330 at maturity. How much OID?

Analysis: On these facts, the stated redemption price at maturity is $265,330, and the issue price is $100,000. Thus, the OID is $165,330, the excess of the stated redemption price at maturity over the issue price.

Example 2: Assume (unrealistically) that the bond in Example 1 will pay $102,000 at maturity. How much OID?

Analysis: Under a special *de minimus* rule, OID is treated as zero if OID is less than ¼% of the stated redemption price at maturity, multiplied by the number of years to maturity.[8] Since ¼% of $102,000 × 10 years equals $2,550, and since this amount exceeds the OID determined under the general rule of Section 1273(a)(1), OID is treated as zero.[9]

Example 3: A bond issued for cash can bear both stated and unstated interest. Assume Corporation issues a 5-year bond for $80,000 that will pay $100,000 at maturity and that bears interest of 5% per year, compounded and paid semiannually. How much OID?

Analysis: Since the stated interest is a fixed rate, unconditionally payable at least annually through the term of the debt, it is not included in determining the stated redemption price at maturity; in the language of the regulations it is qualified stated interest. Thus, the stated redemption price at maturity is $100,000, the issue price is $80,000, and the difference, the OID, is $20,000.[10]

---

[4] I.R.C. § 1273(a)(2).

[5] Treas. Reg. § 1.1273-1(b), (c)(i).

[6] *See* I.R.C. § 1273(b)(2).

[7] I.R.C. § 1273(b)(1). The regulations under Section 1273 provide a common general rule for determining the issue price of debt instruments issued for money, whether publicly traded or not. The regulations provide that, where a "substantial amount of the debt instruments in an issue is issued for money," the issue price will be "the first price at which a substantial amount of the debt instruments is sold for money." Treas. Reg. § 1.1273-2(a)(1).

[8] I.R.C. § 1273(a)(3).

[9] *De minimis* OID is generally included in income as principal payments are made. Treas. Reg. § 1.1273-1(d)(5)(i). The character of such income may be capital gain. Treas. Reg. § 1.1273-1(d)(5)(ii). *De minimis* OID, however, can also be characterized as qualified stated interest. *See* Treas. Reg. § 1.1273-1(d)(1).

[10] I.R.C. § 1273(a)(1), (2). The regulations, however, permit both cash method and accrual method holders of debt instruments to elect to treat all interest as OID, including stated interest, *de minimis*

Example 4: Assume the facts of Example 3, except the stated interest is not payable until maturity. How much OID?

Analysis: Since the stated interest payment of 5% per year, compounded semiannually, is not payable annually, but is payable only at maturity, the amount of the stated interest payment — which turns out to be slightly more than $28,000 — is not qualified stated interest. It will therefore be part of the stated redemption price at maturity, which now totals about $128,000. Given the issue price of $80,000, OID will thus be $48,000.

[B]   Current Inclusion of OID

In general, the holder of any debt instrument having OID must *currently* include the earned portion in income.[11] Specifically, the holder must currently include "the sum of the daily portions of the original issue discount for each day during the taxable year on which such holder held such debt instrument."[12] The term "debt instrument" is defined very broadly to encompass any "bond, debenture, note, or certificate or other evidence of indebtedness."[13] Certain annuity contracts are excluded.[14]

To calculate the "daily portions of OID" that must be currently included in income[15] it is necessary to determine (with the help of a calculator!) the debt instrument's "yield to maturity" — that is, the *constant interest rate*, applied to the issue price and compounded at least annually, that will produce the necessary OID over the period to maturity.[16] For consistency, the examples used throughout this chapter will assume semiannual compounding.[17] On the facts of Example 1, where a 10-year zero interest bond, purchased for $100,000, paid $265,330 at

---

OID, etc. Treas. Reg. § 1.1272-3(a). In that event, none of the interest will be treated as qualified stated interest.

[11] The current-inclusion-in-income rule of Section 1272(a)(1) does not apply to certain debt instruments, including (1) tax-exempt obligations; (2) U.S. savings bonds; (3) debt instruments with fixed terms of one year or less; (4) obligations issued by natural persons prior to March 2, 1984; and (5) in general, outstanding loans between natural persons not in excess of $10,000 in the aggregate, not issued in the course of the lender's trade or business, or for a tax avoidance purpose. In addition, Section 1272 does not apply to one who purchases a debt instrument at a premium — that is, for an amount in excess of the principal amount. Generally, however, the current-inclusion rule of Section 1272(a)(1) applies to the holder of "any debt instrument" having OID.

[12] I.R.C. § 1272(a)(1).

[13] I.R.C. § 1275(a)(1)(A). The regulations define a debt instrument as, in general, any instrument or contractual arrangement that constitutes indebtedness under general tax principles. Treas. Reg. § 1.1275-1(d).

[14] I.R.C. § 1275(a)(1)(B).

[15] *See* I.R.C. § 1272(a)(3).

[16] The regulations define "yield to maturity" in terms of a "constant yield method." This yield is the discount rate, constant over the term of the instrument, that when used to compute the present value of all principal and interest payments under the debt instrument, produces a total equal to the issue price of the instrument. Treas. Reg. § 1.1272-1(b)(1)(i). For ease of computation, we shall use the equivalent definition expressed in terms of a constant interest rate applied to the issue price.

[17] The statute contemplates semiannual compounding — that is, 6-month accrual periods — but permits the regulations to provide other accrual periods. I.R.C. § 1272(a)(5). The regulations in turn authorize accrual periods that vary and may be of any length up to one year. Treas. Reg. § 1.1272-

maturity, the yield to maturity, based on semiannual compounding, turns out to be 10% — in other words, $100,000, invested at 10%, compounded semiannually, will grow to $265,330 at the end of 10 years.

The daily portions of OID are determined by allocating to each day in the accrual period its ratable portion of the "increase in the adjusted issue price" during such period.[18] The "adjusted issue price" is the issue price plus the adjustments in prior accrual periods.[19] In Example 1, at the outset, the "adjusted issue price" is $100,000 — that is, the issue price ($100,000) plus adjustments thereto ($0). The OID attributable to the first six-month accrual period is therefore $5,000 (½ × 10% × $100,000). Each day in that six-month period is allocated a ratable portion of that $5,000 — or somewhat less than $27.50 per day. If Investor holds the bond for the entire six-month period, Investor is charged with $5,000 of income.

At the beginning of the second six-month accrual period, the adjusted issue price is $105,000 — the issue price of $100,000 plus $5,000 of adjustments for the prior accrual period. The "increase" in the adjusted issue price for the first six-month accrual period is thus $5,000. The increase in the adjusted issue price in the second six-month accrual period is determined by multiplying the yield to maturity (here, 10%, compounded semiannually) by the adjusted issue price at the beginning of the period ($105,000 at the beginning of the second six-month period); thus, the increase in the second accrual period is $5,250 (½ year × 10% × $105,000), and it is ratably allocated to each day in the period. The daily portions of OID will accordingly be somewhat greater than they were in the first six months. If Investor holds the bond for one year, the total OID inclusion is thus $10,250.

The adjusted issue price at the beginning of the third six-month accrual period is therefore $110,250, and the increase in the adjusted issue price during that third period is $5,512.50 (½ × 10% × $110,250), allocated ratably to each day in that period and included in the holder's gross income. Similar computations are done for each succeeding accrual period. If investor holds the bond until maturity, all $165,330 of OID will have been included in income.[20]

[C] Deduction of OID

The OID rules are designed to match interest income and expense by putting both parties on the accrual basis with respect to the interest. The issuer of a debt instrument having OID is thus treated as having an interest expense equal to the

---

1(b)(1)(ii). Accrual periods chosen must be such that scheduled payments of principal or interest occur either on the first or the last day of an accrual period. For the sake of simplicity, we shall assume accrual periods that are always 6 months long. It might be noted, however, that if accrual periods vary in length, it will be necessary to convert a yield based on one length into the equivalent yield based on different lengths. *See, e.g.,* Treas. Reg. § 1.272-1(b)(1)(iii), -1(j) Ex. 1.

[18] I.R.C. § 1272(a)(3).

[19] I.R.C. § 1272(a)(4).

[20] The regulations describe the general rule for accrual of OID as a four-step process: (1) determine the yield to maturity; (2) determine the accrual periods; (3) determine the OID allocable to each accrual period; (4) determine the daily portions of OID. Treas. Reg. § 1.1273-1(b)(1).

aggregate daily portions of OID for days during the issuer's tax year.[21] Its deductibility is subject to any other rules that may deny, limit or defer the deduction.[22]

[D]   Gain or Loss on Sale, Exchange or Retirement

Assume the bond in Example 1 is a capital asset and that OID is properly accounted for. As is the case with other capital assets, the sale or exchange of the bond will generate capital gain or loss to the extent of the difference between the adjusted basis and the amount realized. Suppose the bond is held to maturity, however. Absent legislation to the contrary, the retirement of the bond would not constitute a sale or exchange and thus would not produce capital gain or loss.[23] This result has, however, been legislatively reversed. In general, amounts received on retirement of a debt instrument are to be treated as amounts received on an exchange.[24] Capital gain treatment on a retirement is thus made possible, and there is no need for a bond holder to sell a bond prior to maturity simply to avoid ordinary income treatment. (Special rules apply where there is an intention to call a debt instrument before maturity.)[25]

> **Example 5:** On January 1, Year 1, Corporation issues a 10-year bond to Investor for $100,000. The bond bears no interest and will pay $265,330 at maturity. As noted in Example 1, on these facts, the stated redemption price at maturity is $265,330, the issue price is $100,000, and the OID is

---

[21] I.R.C. § 163(e)(1). See the general rule of deductibility, expressed by reference to the "constant yield method" for accrual of OID, at Regulation § 1.163-7(a). *De minimis* OID may be deducted using a straight line method over the terms of the debt instrument, or in proportion to stated interest payments, or at maturity. Treas. Reg. § 1.163-7(b)(2).

[22] An exception to this general rule of deductibility should be noted. In 1989 Congress placed an added limitation on the deduction of OID on certain "high yield" obligations. The general rule of Section 163(e)(1) provides that the issuer of a debt instrument having OID is (potentially, at least) entitled to an interest deduction equal to the OID accruing during that year's accrual periods. The enactment in 1989 of Sections 163(e)(5) and 163(i), which limit the general rule, reflected the concern that developed about high yield, "junk bonds" that were issued with significant OID, and that thus provided significant interest deductions in advance of payment. The 1989 legislation thus provided that with respect to an "applicable high yield discount obligation" issued by a corporation (other than an S corporation), no deduction at all is allowed for the "disqualified portion" of OID, and a deduction for the remaining portion of OID is not allowed until the OID is paid. I.R.C. § 163(e)(5)(A). An applicable high yield discount obligation is a debt instrument with statutorily-defined "significant" OID, plus a maturity date more than five years from issuance and a yield to maturity at least five points greater than the applicable Federal rate at issuance. I.R.C. § 163(i)(1). (Thus, the 10-year bond in Example 1 above could be an applicable high yield discount obligation.) The theory underlying the harsh treatment given such instruments — which will obviously discourage their issuance — is expressed in the legislative history as follows:

> This . . . approach is adopted because . . . a portion of the return on certain high-yield OID obligations is similar to a distribution of corporate earnings with respect to equity. Thus, [the statute] bifurcates the yield on applicable instruments, creating an interest element that is deductible when paid and a return on equity element for which no deduction is granted. . . . Conference Committee Report to the Revenue Reconciliation Act of 1989, p. 46.

The OID *inclusion* rules are not affected by these restrictions on the deduction of OID.

[23] *See* Fairbanks v. U.S., 306 U.S. 436 (1939).

[24] I.R.C. § 1271(a)(1).

[25] I.R.C. § 1271(a)(2).

thus $165,330. Assume Investor holds the bond until maturity, and collects $265,330. Is there any gain or loss at that point?

Analysis: To answer this question, it is necessary to determine the investor's basis in the bond. Pursuant to Section 1272(d)(2), the original basis is appropriately increased by the OID included in income. Over 10 years, the daily portions of OID will total $165,330. Accordingly, the basis in the bond after 10 years will be the $265,330 the corporation pays on maturity; the deemed exchange on retirement thus produces no gain or loss.

Example 6: Assume, the facts of Example 5, except that Investor sells the bond after two years for $125,000. Any gain or loss?

Analysis: After two years, the daily portion of OID included in income would total $21,551 (based on $100,000 at 10% per annum, compounded semiannually). The bond's adjusted basis would thus be $121,551. Investor would thus recognize long term capital gain of $3,449, the difference between $125,000 and $121,551.

This last example points up the obvious fact that debt instruments having OID can change hands. A subsequent holder of a debt instrument having OID must include OID in income pursuant to Section 1272(a)(1). Note, however, the potential problem that would arise in this example if the subsequent holder purchased the bond two years after issuance for $125,000. If the original holder had retained the bond until maturity, the OID inclusion for Years 3 through 10 would have been $143,779 ($265,330 stated redemption price, less $121,551 basis at the end of Year 2). However, if the subsequent holder includes $143,779 of OID, the adjusted basis in the bond on retirement will be $268,779 ($125,000 of original basis plus $143,779 OID). If no adjustment is made, the subsequent holder's basis in the bond on retirement will exceed the redemption price by $3,449; a capital loss would be built into the bond. Accordingly, under Section 1272(a)(7), the daily portions of OID are reduced to take this "premium" into account and eliminate the built-in loss and "excess" OID. As a result, if a subsequent holder holds the bond until retirement, the OID inclusion will total only $140,330, the difference between the basis of $125,000 and the stated redemption price of $265,330.[26]

[E]   Market Discount

Assume a 10-year bond has a face amount of $100,000, pays 10% interest semiannually, and has an issue price of $100,000. Because the interest is at a fixed rate, unconditionally payable at least annually, the stated redemption price at maturity does not include the interest payments and is therefore $100,000. Since the issue price equals or exceeds the stated redemption price at maturity, the bond has no OID. Assume now that, subsequent to issuance, interest rates rise and the already-issued bond is now sold by the original holder for $90,000. The $10,000 decline in value constitutes "market discount."[27] Alternatively, suppose this

---

[26] *See generally* Treas. Reg. § 1.1272-2.

[27] *See* I.R.C. § 1278(a)(2)(A).

$100,000 face amount bond had an issue price of $95,000. It would thus have $5,000 of OID. Again, assume a subsequent rise in interest rates (or decline in the creditworthiness of the corporation issuing the bond) such that the sales price of the bond, on a sale to a subsequent holder, is only $90,000. The $5,000 decline in value again constitutes market discount.[28] In this latter scenario, then, the bond has both OID and market discount. Assuming no exceptions apply, the subsequent holder must currently include the $5,000 of OID in income in accordance with Section 1272(a). From the standpoint of the subsequent holder, market discount, like OID, is the functional equivalent of interest. Thus, in general, to the extent any gain on disposition reflects market discount, it must be treated, like OID, as ordinary income.[29] However, unlike OID, market discount accrues ratably, although an election may be made to accrue market discount in the same manner as OID accrues.[30] Moreover, again unlike OID, market discount is not currently included in income as accrued by the subsequent holder.[31] In addition, interest incurred by the holder of the market discount bond, in order to purchase or carry the bond, may be subject to a special provision deferring the allowance of a deduction for such interest.[32]

§ 42.03   SALES AND EXCHANGES OF PROPERTY AND SECTION 467 RENTAL AGREEMENTS

The preceding section dealt with OID with respect to debt instruments issued for cash. OID may also arise in connection with a debt instrument issued on a sale or exchange of property. For example, assume Seller and Purchaser agree that certain property is worth $5,000,000; also assume the current interest rate is 10%, compounded annually. Among various possibilities, Seller and Purchaser could provide that the sales price is $5,500,000, payable one year later without interest; alternatively, they could provide that the sales price is $5,000,000, payable one year from now, plus $500,000 interest. From an economic standpoint, the choice hardly matters: either way, $5,500,000 will be paid one year from now. From a tax standpoint, however, the choices could have very different consequences. For example, for the seller, a $5,500,000 sales price might produce an extra $500,000 in capital gain in lieu of $500,000 of ordinary interest income. For the purchaser, if the property were depreciable, a $5,500,000 sales price would mean an additional $500,000 basis for depreciation, rather than $500,000 in interest expense. The parties will generally not be permitted to put whatever tax labels they wish on the dollar amounts paid. Instead, when property is sold on a deferred payment basis, the parties will generally be required to provide for adequate interest, payable currently, on the unpaid balance; if adequate stated interest is not provided, or is not payable currently, it may give rise to OID or to unstated interest and may

---

[28] I.R.C. § 1278(a)(2)(B), (4).

[29] I.R.C. § 1276(a)(1).

[30] I.R.C. § 1276(b).

[31] But see Regulation § 1.1272-3(a), generally permitting an election to treat all interest on a debt instrument, including market discount, as OID.

[32] I.R.C. § 1277.

require, in effect, an adjustment of the nominal selling price.[33] These tasks are the province of the complex rules of Sections 1274 and 483, among others, the examination of which is beyond the scope of this chapter.

In 1984, Congress extended the imputed interest concept to rentals with the enactment of Section 467. As an illustration of some of the practices Congress was concerned with, assume a cash method landlord rents a commercial building to an accrual method tenant for five years for $500,000, with all the rent to be paid in a single lump sum payment at the end of the five-year period. The accrual method tenant will claim annual rental deductions, each presumably equal to one-fifth of the lump sum payment, while the cash method landlord will report no income until payment is actually made at the end of the five-year period. This arrangement is yet another illustration of the deduction-now, income-later mismatching game, played at the expense of the Treasury. Beyond the mismatching, it can also reasonably be concluded that the lump sum payment at the end of Year five is not entirely rent. Part of the rent payment could be characterized as compensation for the delayed payment of the rent attributable to the four prior years; part of the "rent," in other words, could be seen as interest on the unpaid rent of prior years. Accordingly, Section 467 takes the following approach to the rental arrangements it covers: (1) it places both landlord and tenant on the accrual method with respect to their rental agreement; (2) it provides for the accrual and current reporting of rent each year; and (3) it provides for the accrual and reporting of interest on unpaid rent — as was done with deferred interest under the OID rules. Section 467 does not apply to rental agreements involving payments of $250,000 or less. The rules that apply to Section 467 rental agreements can be quite complex, and as with Sections 1274 and 483, go beyond the scope of this chapter.

---

[33] See Regulation §§ 1.1001-1(g) and 1.1012-1(g) for the determination of the seller's amount realized and the buyer's basis when a debt instrument is issued in exchange for property.

Chapter 43

LIMITATIONS ON TAX SHELTERS

§ 43.01   THE AT RISK RULES — SECTION 465

[A]   General Background

A taxpayer's basis in property generally limits the amount of deductions allowable with respect to that property. For example, a loss deduction under Section 165 cannot exceed a taxpayer's adjusted basis in the property.[1] Likewise, depreciation deductions are determined with reference to (and cannot exceed) a taxpayer's adjusted basis in the depreciable property. Thus, a direct correlation exists between the amount of one's basis in property and the amount potentially deductible with respect to that property.

In computing basis, one generally begins with the cost of the property. As discussed in Chapter 37, *Crane v. Commissioner*[2] and its progeny established that the cost basis of acquired property includes that part of the purchase price financed by nonrecourse borrowing. In other words, a taxpayer's basis may reflect borrowed funds with respect to which the taxpayer has no personal liability. This treatment of nonrecourse liabilities sets the stage for the modern tax shelter by enabling taxpayers to claim deductions far in excess of the dollars they actually had at risk. For example, assume that a taxpayer purchases a piece of equipment for business use. The purchase price is $100,000, and the taxpayer finances the equipment entirely through a nonrecourse loan. Applying *Crane*, the taxpayer will have a $100,000 basis in the equipment. In turn, that basis will enable the taxpayer to claim substantial depreciation deductions under Sections 167 and 168 despite the fact that the taxpayer has not personally invested a single dollar in the equipment and cannot be forced to do so. The depreciation deductions generated by the equipment can be used by the taxpayer to offset income from other sources.

There is, of course, a downside to this arrangement. If the taxpayer never pays the nonrecourse loan, the taxpayer will ultimately be taxed on the loan proceeds when the taxpayer disposes of or abandons the property.[3] For example, if the taxpayer never paid a single penny on the loan, completely depreciated the equipment, and then sold the equipment for $100,000, the taxpayer's gain on the

---

[1] I.R.C. § 165(b).

[2] 331 U.S. 1 (1947).

[3] As discussed in Chapter 38, *supra*, upon a sale of an asset, the seller must include in her amount realized any liabilities, recourse or nonrecourse, that a purchaser assumes or takes subject to.

sale would be $100,000.[4] Thus, the taxpayer would have claimed $100,000 in depreciation (all of which is attributable to the basis provided by the nonrecourse financing) and upon the sale would report $100,000 of income. Note, however, that the taxpayer, as a result of the $100,000 in depreciation deductions, would have been allowed to defer tax on $100,000 of income (i.e., the income offset by the depreciation deductions) until taxpayer finally disposed of the equipment.

The opportunity for tax deferral afforded by nonrecourse financing of investments encouraged taxpayers to invest in activities which were economically unsound. For example, in *Estate of Franklin*,[5] a group of doctors entered into a transaction to purchase a motel for a price far in excess of the fair market value of the property. The doctors, who were not personally liable for the purchase price, clearly had no interest in operating a motel. Rather, they sought to generate substantial depreciation deductions computed with reference to the inflated purchase price. Simply stated, the doctors engaged in the transaction only because of the tax benefits available.

In 1976, Congress enacted the Section 465 "at risk" limitations to prevent taxpayers from claiming such artificial deductions. Congress enacted the legislation because "it was not equitable to allow individual investors to defer tax on income from other sources through losses generated by tax sheltering activities. One of the most significant problems in tax shelters was the use of nonrecourse financing and other risk-limiting devices [such as guarantees, stop-loss agreements, guaranteed repurchase agreements, etc.] which enabled investors in these activities to deduct losses from the activities in amounts which exceeded the total investment the investor actually placed at risk in the activity. The Act consequently provides an 'at risk' rule to deal directly with this abuse in tax shelters."[6]

[B] Operation of the at Risk Rules

§ 465. Deductions limited to amount at risk.

(a) Limitation to amount at risk.

(1) In general. In the case of

(A) an individual . . .

. . . engaged in an activity to which this section applies, any loss from such activity for the taxable year shall be allowed only to the extent of the aggregate amount with respect to which the taxpayer is at risk (within the meaning of subsection (b)) for such activity at the close of the taxable year.

---

[4] Applying *Crane*, the taxpayer's amount realized would be $100,000, *i.e.*, the amount of the nonrecourse liability taken subject to by the purchaser; the taxpayer's adjusted basis would be $0; and the taxpayer's Section 1001(a) gain would be $100,000. All of the gain would be characterized as ordinary income under the Section 1245 recapture rules.

[5] 544 F.2d 1045 (9th Cir. 1976) (discussed in Chapter 38, *supra*).

[6] Staff of the Joint Committee on Taxation, General Explanation of the Tax Reform Act of 1976, 94th Cong. 2d Sess.; 1976-3 C.B. 47.

(2) Deduction in succeeding year. Any loss from an activity to which this section applies not allowed under this section for the taxable year shall be treated as a deduction allocable to such activity in the first succeeding taxable year.

(b) Amounts considered at risk.

(1) In general. For purposes of this section, a taxpayer shall be considered at risk for an activity with respect to amounts including —

(A) the amount of money and the adjusted basis of other property contributed by the taxpayer to the activity, and

(B) amounts borrowed with respect to such activity (as determined under paragraph (2)).

(2) Borrowed amounts. For purposes of this section, a taxpayer shall be considered at risk with respect to amounts borrowed for use in an activity to the extent that he —

(A) is personally liable for the repayment of such amounts, or

(B) has pledged property, other than property used in such activity, as security for such borrowed amount (to the extent of the net fair market value of the taxpayer's interest in such property). No property shall be taken into account as security if such property is directly or indirectly financed by indebtedness which is secured by property described in paragraph (1).

. . .

(4) Exception. Notwithstanding any other provision of this section, a taxpayer shall not be considered at risk with respect to amounts protected against loss through nonrecourse financing, guarantees, stop loss agreements, or other similar arrangements.

(5) Amounts at risk in subsequent years. If in any taxable year the taxpayer has a loss from an activity to which subsection (a) applies, the amount with respect to which a taxpayer is considered to be at risk within the meaning of subsection (b)) in subsequent years with respect to that activity shall be reduced by that portion of the loss which (after the application of subsection (a)) is allowable as a deduction.

. . .

(d) Definition of loss. For purposes of this section, the term "loss" means the excess of the deductions allowable under this chapter for the taxable year determined (without regard to the first sentence of subsection (a)) and allocable to an activity to which this section applies over the income received or accrued by the taxpayer during the taxable year from such activity (determined without regard to subsection (e)(1)(A)).

(e) Recapture of losses where amount at risk is less than zero.

(1) In general. If zero exceeds the amount for which the taxpayer is at risk in any activity at the close of any taxable year —

(A) the taxpayer shall include in his gross income for such taxable year (as income from such activity) an amount equal to such excess, and

(B) an amount equal to the amount so included in gross income shall be treated as a deduction allocable to such activity for the first succeeding taxable year.

(2) Limitation. The excess referred to in paragraph (1) shall not exceed

(A) the aggregate amount of the reductions required by subsection (b)(5) with respect to the activity by reason of losses for all prior years beginning after December 31, 1978, reduced by

(B) the amounts previously included in gross income with respect to such activity under this subsection.

While quite complex, the at risk rules essentially provide that a taxpayer may not deduct losses generated by certain business or income producing activities in excess of the aggregate amount with respect to which the taxpayer is at risk (*i.e.*, the amount the taxpayer could actually lose) in each activity. For Section 465 purposes, a loss is the excess of the deductions attributable to the activity over the income from the activity.[7] The rules are applicable to individuals, estates, trusts, and to most closely held corporations.[8]

[1] Activities Subject to the at Risk Rules

Initially, the at risk rules were applicable only to a narrow range of activities.[9] Today, any business or income producing activity, including real estate activity, engaged in by a taxpayer is covered.[10] However, as explained herein, Section 465 provides an important exception for real estate activity.

[2] Determination of the Initial Amount at Risk

Section 465(b) defines the taxpayer's initial amount at risk as the sum of (1) the taxpayer's cash contributions to the activity; (2) the adjusted basis of other property contributed by the taxpayer to the activity; and (3) amounts borrowed for use in the activity for which the taxpayer is personally liable or has pledged property (other than property used in the activity) as security. Amounts borrowed from any person who has an interest in the activity or from a person related to such person will not be considered amounts at risk.[11] Likewise, a taxpayer is not at risk with respect to amounts protected against loss through nonrecourse financing, guarantees or other similar arrangements.[12]

---

[7] I.R.C. § 465(d).

[8] I.R.C. § 465(a)(1).

[9] *See* I.R.C. § 465(c)(1).

[10] I.R.C. § 465(c)(3)(A).

[11] I.R.C. § 465(b)(3)(A). *See also* I.R.C. § 465(c)(3)(O); Treas. Reg. § 1.465-8(a).

[12] I.R.C. § 465(b)(4).

[3] Qualified Nonrecourse Financing

In extending the at risk rules to the activity of holding real property, Congress created a special exception, applicable only to that activity, which allows certain nonrecourse financing to be considered in computing a taxpayer's amount at risk. "Qualified nonrecourse financing" is financing with respect to the activity of holding real property and with respect to which no person is personally liable. It includes (1) amounts borrowed by the taxpayer from any Federal, State, or local government or instrumentality thereof; (2) borrowed amounts guaranteed by a Federal, State or local government; and (3) amounts borrowed from a "qualified person."[13] As described by the Staff of the Joint Committee on Taxation, the term "qualified person" includes "any person actively and regularly engaged in the business of lending money. Such persons generally include, for example, a bank, savings and loan association, credit union, or insurance company regulated under Federal, State, or local law, or a pension trust. However, qualified persons do not include (1) any person from whom the taxpayer acquired the property (or a pers on related to such person)[14] or (2) any person who receives a fee (*e.g.*, a promoter) with respect to the taxpayer's investment in the property (or a person related to such person). For example, no portion of seller financing and promoter financing is qualified nonrecourse financing."[15]

Nonrecourse financing obtained from a related person will constitute "qualified nonrecourse financing" if it is commercially reasonable and is provided on substantially the same terms as loans involving unrelated persons.[16] According to the Staff of the Joint Committee on Taxation, "Congress intends that terms of nonrecourse financing are commercially reasonable if the financing is a written unconditional promise to pay on demand or on a specified date or dates a sum or sums certain in money, and the interest rate is a reasonable market rate of interest (taking into account the maturity of the obligation). . . . The terms of the financing will also not be considered commercially reasonable if, for example, the term of the loan exceeds the useful life of the property, or if the right to foreclosure or collection with respect to the debt is limited (except to the extent provided under applicable local law)."[17]

[4] Adjustments to the Amount at Risk

The amount a taxpayer has at risk in an activity is adjusted each year for income and losses generated by the activity and for withdrawals from the activity. The various adjustments which must be made to a taxpayer's amount at risk can be best explained by the use of the following examples:

> **Example 1:** In Year 1, Eric purchases property and uses it in a business activity (other than the activity of holding real property). The purchase price of the property is $100,000 and Eric makes a downpayment of $10,000

---

[13] I.R.C. § 465(b)(6).

[14] Related persons generally include family members, fiduciaries, and corporations or partnerships in which a person has at least a 10% interest. I.R.C. § 465(b)(3)(C).

[15] General Explanation of the Tax Reform Act of 1986, p. 258. *See* I.R.C. § 49(a)(1)(D)(iv).

[16] I.R.C. § 465(b)(6)(D)(ii).

[17] General Explanation of the Tax Reform Act of 1986, pp. 258–259.

and borrows $90,000 of the purchase price on a nonrecourse basis. Assume in Year 1 the activity suffers a loss of $5,000[18] What are the tax consequences to Eric in view of Section 465?

Analysis: Applying Section 465, Eric's initial amount at risk is $10,000. The at risk rules will not prevent the $5,000 loss from being fully deductible in Year 1. Assuming the activity is not a passive activity (see discussion of the passive activity rules below), the loss will be deductible against Eric's income from other sources. Under Section 465(b)(5), Eric's amount at risk is reduced from $10,000 to $5,000 as a result of the loss.

Example 2: Assume the facts of Example 1. Assume in Year 2 another $8,000 loss is generated. Assume also $5,000 of the cash generated by the activity in Year 2 is used to make a payment on the nonrecourse indebtedness and Eric withdraws $2,000 of cash from the activity.

Analysis: As noted, Eric began Year 2 with an at risk amount of $5,000. Eric must reduce his amount at risk from $5,000 to $3,000 by the $2,000 of cash which he has withdrawn.[19] The $5,000 payment made on the nonrecourse loan will not increase Eric's amount at risk, because the repayment of a nonrecourse loan from cash generated by the activity has no effect on the amount at risk.[20] That result makes sense because the repayment does not represent any increase in Eric's investment in the business activity. Thus, in Year 2 there is only $3,000 at risk. Accordingly, Section 465(a)(1) limits Eric's loss deduction in Year 2 to $3,000. The remaining $5,000 of the $8,000 loss is disallowed by the at risk rules and is treated as a deduction allocable to the activity in Year 3.[21] Eric's amount at risk is reduced to $0 as a result of the $3,000 deduction allowed in Year 2.

Example 3: Assume the facts in the prior examples. Assume in Year 3 the income from the activity exactly equals the deductions available (other than the $5,000 deduction carried over from Year 2). Assume Eric also withdraws an additional $2,000 from the business.

Analysis: Eric began Year 3 with an at risk amount of $0. Obviously, the $5,000 deduction carried over from Year 2 cannot be used and must be carried over to the following year. Furthermore, Eric's withdrawal of an additional $2,000 in cash from the activity creates a negative $2,000 balance in the at risk account. This withdrawal will trigger application of the Section 465(e) recapture rule requiring Eric to include $2,000 in gross income. Section 465(e)(1) requires a taxpayer to include in income an amount equal to the deductions taken in excess of the taxpayer's amount at risk. Here, Eric in Years 1 and 2 had taken loss deductions totaling $8,000. Eric originally contributed and had at risk $10,000. In Years 2 and 3, he

---

[18] For purposes of this example, assume all losses are a function of depreciation and interest deductions. Under Section 465(d), losses are the excess of deductions over income.

[19] Prop. Treas. Reg. § 1.465-22(b). The downward adjustment of the amount at risk is obviously appropriate since Eric now only has $8,000 in the activity. *See* Prop. Treas. Reg. § 1.465-22(b), (c).

[20] Prop. Treas. Reg. § 1.465-25(b)(2)(i).

[21] I.R.C. § 465(a)(2).

withdrew a total of $4,000. Thus, he had only $6,000 of his own money in the activity and yet had claimed a total of $8,000 in deductions. Section 465(e) requires a restoration of $2,000 of those deductions by means of a $2,000 inclusion in gross income. Under Section 465(e)(1)(B), Eric may treat this $2,000 amount included in gross income as a deduction allocable to such activity in Year 4. Thus, there will be a total of $7,000 of deduction carried over to Year 4. With the inclusion of $2,000 in income, Eric's at risk amount will be returned to $0.[22]

Example 4: Assume the facts of the prior examples. Assume also that in Year 4 the activity generates net income of $5,000 (not taking into account the $7,000 of loss deductions carried over from prior years under Section 465(a)(2)).

Analysis: Eric may use $5,000 of the $7,000 loss deduction carryover to offset this $5,000 of net income in Year 4.[23] Because Eric's amount at risk remains at $0, the other $2,000 of loss deduction carryover cannot be used and must be carried over to the following year.

Example 5: Assume the facts of the prior examples. Assume also that in Year 5 the activity generates income of $5,000 and there are no deductions other than the $2,000 of deductions carried over from Year 4.

Analysis: Eric will be entitled to offset the $5,000 of income by the $2,000 of carryover deductions and will have income from the activity of $3,000 to report. In turn, the inclusion of $3,000 in income will increase Eric's amount at risk by $3,000.[24] Thus, if Eric chose to withdraw $3,000 of the cash in the activity, he could do so without triggering the recapture rule of Section 465(e), discussed previously.

Eric's amount at risk will be increased not only by income from the activity which he reports but also by (1) Eric's direct payment of the nonrecourse indebtedness; (2) additional cash contributions from Eric; and (3) additional property contributions by Eric.[25] If a taxpayer transfers or otherwise disposes of part or all of an activity or an interest in an activity during the taxable year, the gain, if any, recognized on the transfer or disposition will be considered as income from the activity.[26] This rule, in effect, will generally enable taxpayers to deduct losses suspended as a result of Section 465 when the taxpayer disposes of the activity.

As these examples demonstrate, the at risk rules successfully limit a taxpayer's ability to use losses in excess of the amounts the taxpayer actually could lose in an activity. The at risk rules thus reduce the use of the deferral benefits historically afforded by tax shelters. However, losses not disallowed by Section 465 could, as noted, be used to offset income from other sources. As discussed in the next section

---

[22] Prop. Treas. Reg. § 1.465-3(b).

[23] I.R.C. § 465(a)(2), (e)(1)(B).

[24] Prop. Treas. Reg. § 1.465-22(c)(1).

[25] Prop. Treas. Reg. §§ 1.465-22(a), -23(a), -25(a)(2).

[26] Prop. Treas. Reg. § 1.465–66.

of this Chapter, Congress in enacting Section 469 sought to eliminate this additional benefit long associated with tax shelter activity.

§ 43.02   SECTION 469 — LIMITATION ON PASSIVE ACTIVITY LOSSES AND CREDITS

[A]   Background

Prior to the 1986 Tax Reform Act, taxpayers were essentially free to offset income from one source with deductions (or credits) from tax shelter activities. For example, a taxpayer owning an interest in a real estate limited partnership could use the deductions generated by that tax shelter to offset the taxpayer's income from other sources, *e.g.*, salary, dividends, interest. Not only did such arrangements reduce federal tax revenues, they also contributed to a perception that the tax system was inequitable and benefitted the wealthy who could afford to invest in tax shelters. In turn, compliance suffered and tax shelters flourished. The various anti-tax shelter weapons available to the Service, *e.g.*, Sections 465 and 183, were not adequate to solve these problems. While measuring the maximum amount that a taxpayer might lose in an activity, the at risk rules of Section 465 (discussed above) did not address whether and when deductions from one activity could be used to offset income from another activity. Section 183, limiting deductions attributable to activities not engaged in for profit,[27] was likewise too narrow in focus and was also cumbersome administratively.[28]

In 1986, Congress enacted a new set of rules intended to address the problems associated with the burgeoning tax shelter industry. As noted by the Staff of the Joint Committee on Taxation:[29]

> Congress determined that decisive action was needed to curb the expansion of tax sheltering and to restore to the tax system the degree of equity that was a necessary precondition to a beneficial and widely desired reduction in rates. So long as tax shelters were permitted to erode the Federal tax base, a low-rate system could provide neither sufficient revenues, nor sufficient progressivity, to satisfy the general public that tax liability bore a fair relationship to the ability to pay. In particular, a provision significantly limiting the use of tax shelter losses was viewed as unavoidable if substantial rate reductions were to be provided to high-income taxpayers without disproportionately reducing the share of total

---

[27] *See* Chapter 20, *supra.*

[28] The Commissioner used Section 183 effectively in a number of tax shelter cases where taxpayers sought to use deductions from one activity to offset income from other activities. For example, in *Estate of Baron v. Commissioner*, 83 T.C. 542 (1984), the Commissioner successfully argued that the acquisition of rights in a master recording did not constitute an activity engaged in for profit. As a result, the taxpayer was not allowed to claim depreciation deductions which were far in excess of the income anticipated from the activity. *See also* Soriano v. Commissioner, 90 T.C. 44 (1988). As the decisions in these cases suggest, however, the application of Section 183 requires complicated economic analysis to determine whether profit motivation exists.

[29] General Explanation of the Tax Reform Act of 1986, pp. 210–213.

liability under the individual income tax borne by high-income taxpayers as a group.

Congress viewed the question of how to prevent harmful and excessive tax sheltering as not a simple one. One way to address the problem would have been to eliminate substantially all tax preferences in the Internal Revenue Code. For two reasons, however, this course was determined by Congress to be inappropriate.

First, while the Act reduces or eliminates some tax preference items that Congress decided did not provide social or economic benefits commensurate with their cost, there were many preferences that Congress concluded were socially or economically beneficial. It was determined that certain preferences were particularly beneficial when used primarily to advance the purposes upon which Congress relied in enacting them, rather than to avoid taxation of income from sources unrelated to the preferred activity.

Second, Congress viewed as prohibitively difficult, and perhaps impossible, the task of designing a tax system that measured income perfectly. For example, the statutory allowance for depreciation . . . reflects broad industry averages, as opposed to providing precise item-by-item measurements. Accordingly, taxpayers with assets that depreciate less rapidly than the average, or that appreciate over time (as may be the case with certain real estate), could engage in tax sheltering even under the minimum tax, in the absence of direct action regarding the tax shelter problem.

. . .

The question of what constituted a tax shelter that should be subject to limitations was viewed as closely related to the question of who Congress intends to benefit when it enacts a tax preference. For example in providing preferential depreciation for real estate or favorable accounting rules for farming, it was not Congress's primary intent to permit outside investors to avoid tax liability with respect to their salaries by investing in limited partnership syndications. Rather, Congress intended to benefit and provide incentives to taxpayers active in the businesses to which the preferences were directed.

. . .

Moreover, Congress concluded that restricting the use of losses from business activities in which the taxpayer did not materially participate against other sources of positive income (such as salary and portfolio income) would address a fundamental aspect of the tax shelter problem. Instances in which the tax system applies simple rules at the expense of economic accuracy encouraged the structuring of transactions to take advantage of the situations in which such rules gave rise to undermeasurement or deferral of income. Such transactions commonly were marketed to investors who did not intend to participate in the transactions, as devices for sheltering unrelated sources of positive income (e.g., salary and portfolio income). Accordingly, by creating a bar against the use of losses from business activities in which the taxpayer does not materially participate to offset positive income sources such as salary and portfolio income, Congress believed that it was possible to significantly reduce the tax shelter problem.

[B]   Section 469 — In General

§ 469.   Passive activity losses and credits limited.

(a)   Disallowance.

(1)   In general. If for any taxable year the taxpayer is described in paragraph (2), neither

(A) the passive activity loss, nor

(B) the passive activity credit, for the taxable year shall be allowed.

(2)   Persons described. The following are described in this paragraph:

(A) any individual, estate, or trust,

. . .

(b)   Disallowed loss or credit carried to next year. Except as otherwise provided in this section, any loss or credit from an activity which is disallowed under subsection (a) shall be treated as a deduction or credit allocable to such activity in the next taxable year.

(c)   Passive activity defined. For purposes of this section

(1)   In general. The term "passive activity" means any activity —

(A) which involves the conduct of any trade or business, and

(B) in which the taxpayer does not materially participate.

(2)   Passive activity includes any rental activity. The term "passive activity" includes any rental activity.

(d)   Passive activity loss and credit defined. For purposes of this section —

(1)   Passive activity loss. The term "passive activity loss" means the amount (if any) by which

(A) the aggregate losses from all passive activities for the taxable year, exceed

(B) the aggregate income from all passive activities for such year.

. . .

(h)   Material participation defined. For purposes of this section —

(1)   In general. A taxpayer shall be treated as materially participating in an activity only if the taxpayer is involved in the operations of the activity on a basis which is

(A) regular,

(B) continuous, and

(C) substantial.

Section 469 represents the most significant anti-tax shelter legislation enacted by Congress. Section 469 is applicable to individuals, estates and trusts, and certain corporations. Essentially, it requires taxpayers to classify their income, losses and credits as being generated either by so-called "passive activities" or "nonpassive activities." Passive activity deductions may only be used to offset income from passive activities; and tax credits related to passive activities may only offset tax liability of passive activities.[30] Those passive activity losses which cannot be used currently because of the limitations imposed by Section 469 will be carried forward to the next year and will be treated as passive activity losses in that year.[31] There are no limits to the carryover of passive activity losses. As a general rule, suspended losses are allowed in full when the taxpayer disposes of the interest in the passive activity.[32] Special rules govern the treatment of passive activity losses and credits when the taxpayer makes a gift of the passive activity or when the taxpayer dies. As this brief summary suggests, the passive activity rules result in the deferral and not the permanent disallowance of excess deductions and credits generated by passive activities.

[C]   Passive Activities

A passive activity involves the conduct of any trade or business in which the taxpayer does not materially participate.[33] The reference to "trade or business" includes those activities involving the conduct of a trade or business within the meaning of Section 162.[34]

[1]   Material Participation

The rationale for limiting passive activities to those in which the taxpayer does not "materially participate" is explained by the Staff of the Joint Committee as follows:[35]

> Congress determined that, in order for tax preferences to function as intended, their benefits should be directed primarily to taxpayers with a substantial and *bona fide* involvement in the activities to which the preference related. Congress also determined that it was appropriate to encourage nonparticipating investors to invest in particular activities, by permitting the use of preferences to reduce the rate of tax on income from those activities; however, such investors were viewed as not appropriately permitted to use tax benefits to shelter unrelated income.

> Congress believed that there were several reasons why it was appropriate to examine the materiality of a taxpayer's participation in an activity in determining the extent to which such taxpayer should be permitted to use

---

[30] I.R.C. § 469(a)(1), (d)(1),(2).

[31] I.R.C. § 469(b).

[32] I.R.C. § 469 (g)(1)(A).

[33] I.R.C. § 469(c)(1).

[34] Temp. Treas. Reg. § 1.469-1T(e)(1)(i).

[35] General Explanation of the Tax Reform Act of 1986, p. 212.

tax benefits from the activity. A taxpayer who materially participated in an activity was viewed as more likely than a passive investor to approach the activity with a significant nontax economic profit motive, and to form a sound judgment as to whether the activity had genuine economic significance and value.

A material participation standard identified an important distinction between different types of taxpayer activities. It was thought that, in general, the more passive investor seeks a return on capital invested, including returns in the form of reductions in the tax owed on unrelated income, rather than an ongoing source of livelihood. A material participation standard reduced the importance, for such investors, of the tax-reduction features of an investment, and thus increased the importance of the economic features in an investor's decision about where to invest his funds.

For a taxpayer's participation to be considered material, it must be regular, continuous and substantial.[36] The temporary regulations provide seven alternative tests to satisfy this statutory requirement. For example, an individual materially participates in an activity for a given tax year if the individual's participation in the activity exceeds 500 hours during the year.[37] Alternatively, material participation exists when the individual's participation for the year constitutes "substantially all of the participation" in that activity, or when the individual's participation for the year exceeds 100 hours and is also not less than the participation of any other individual.[38] Under yet another test, material participation in any activity for any five of the immediate past ten years constitutes material participation for the current year.[39] Separate tests are also provided for "significant participation activities" and "personal service activities."[40] Finally, the temporary regulations also provide that material participation may be found based on "all the facts and circumstances."[41] Each of the tests must be examined before concluding that an individual did not materially participate in an activity in a given tax year.[42]

---

[36] I.R.C. § 469(h)(1).

[37] Temp. Treas. Reg. § 1.469-5T(a)(1).

[38] Temp. Treas. Reg. § 1.469-5T(a)(2), (3).

[39] Temp. Treas. Reg. § 1.469-5T(a)(5).

[40] Material participation exists if the activity is a significant participation activity — essentially a trade or business activity in which the individual participates for more than 100 hours during the year but not enough to achieve material participation under the other tests — and the individual's aggregate participation in all significant participation activities exceeds 500 hours. Temp. Treas. Reg. § 1.469-5T(a)(4), (c). Personal service activities are trades or businesses, such as law, in which capital is not a material income-producing factor. An individual materially participates in a personal service activity if the individual materially participated in the activity for any three prior years. Temp. Treas. Reg. § 1.469-5T(a)(6), (d).

[41] Temp. Treas. Reg. § 1.469-5T(a)(7), (b).

[42] Note that as a threshold matter in satisfying the material participation requirement, the taxpayer's involvement with the activity must constitute "participation." Ordinarily, any work done in connection with the activity will suffice, but the temporary regulations define the term to exclude certain work not customarily done by owners and participation as an investor. Temp. Treas. Reg. § 1.469-5T(f)(2).

Special rules exist for limited partners. Except as provided by regulation, a limited partner does not materially participate with respect to his interest in the limited partnership.[43] Thus, as a general matter, a limited partnership interest generates passive income or passive loss. The temporary regulations, however, create significant exceptions to this general rule by providing that a limited partner can materially participate by satisfying one of three material participation tests: the 500-hour test, the five-years-out-of-ten test, or the personal-service-activity test.[44] Despite the Service's arguments to the contrary, courts have ruled that, for purposes of Section 469(h)(2), an interest in a limited liability company will not be treated as an "interest in a limited partnership as a limited partner."[45]

[2] Rental Activities

Regardless of whether the taxpayer is a material participant, a rental activity is generally a passive activity subject to Section 469.[46] A rental activity is any activity "where payments are principally for the use of tangible property."[47] However, if significant services are rendered in connection with the rental of property, the activity will not be treated as a rental activity. "For example, an activity consisting of the short-term leasing of motor vehicles, where the lessor furnishes services including maintenance of gas and oil, tire repair and changing, cleaning and polishing, oil changing and lubrication and engine and body repair, is not treated as a rental activity. Based on similar considerations, renting hotel rooms or similar space used primarily for lodging of transients where significant services are provided generally is not a rental activity. By contrast, renting apartments to tenants pursuant to leases (with, e.g., month-to-month or yearly lease terms) is treated as a rental activity. Similarly, being the lessor of property subject to a net lease is a rental activity."[48]

In 1993, Congress amended Section 469 to provide that rental real estate activities of a taxpayer would not be considered per se passive activities under Section 469(c)(2) if the taxpayer met the following requirements:

(1) more than half of the personal services the taxpayer performs in trades or businesses during the taxable year are performed in real property trades or businesses in which the taxpayer materially participates; and

(2) the taxpayer performs more than 750 hours of service during the taxable

---

[43] I.R.C. § 469(h)(2).

[44] Temp. Treas. Reg. § 1.469-5T(e)(2).

[45] Newell v. Commissioner, T.C. Memo 2010-23; Garnett v. Commissioner, 132 T.C. 368 (2009). In November 2011, Treasury issued proposed regulations to address this status issue. The proposed regulations eliminate the current regulation's reliance on limited liability for purposes of determining whether an interest is that of a limited partner and focus instead on the right to participate in the management of the entity. See Prop. Treas. Reg. § 1.469-5(a)(3).

[46] I.R.C. § 469(c)(2).

[47] I.R.C. § 469(j)(8).

[48] General Explanation of the Tax Reform Act of 1986, p. 249. Temporary Regulation § 1.469-1T(e)(3) discusses in detail what constitutes a rental activity and what services rendered in connection with the rental of property will be considered "significant."

year in real property trades or businesses in which the taxpayer materially participates.[49]

"Real property trade or business" is defined in Section 469(c)(7)(C) to include "real property development, redevelopment, construction, reconstruction, acquisition, conversion, rental operation, management, leasing, or brokerage trade or business." Thus, a taxpayer meeting the above requirements who is engaged in rental real estate activities in which she materially participates may offset losses from those activities against nonpassive income including salary, portfolio income, etc.

[D]   Scope of Passive Activities

Defining the scope of a passive activity is critical to the operation of Section 469. The scope of an activity must be determined in order to assess whether a taxpayer is a material participant in the activity. Furthermore, the precise scope of the passive activity must be known before one can apply Section 469(g), discussed herein, allowing the deduction of suspended losses of a passive activity when a taxpayer disposes of the entire interest in that activity.

As noted by the Staff of the Joint Committee, "[d]efining separate activities either too narrowly or too broadly could lead to evasion of the passive loss rule. For example, an overly narrow definition would permit taxpayers to claim losses against salary, portfolio, or active business income by selectively disposing of portions of their interests in activities with respect to which there has been depreciation or loss of value, while retaining any portion with respect to which there has been appreciation. An overly broad definition would permit taxpayers to amalgamate undertakings that in fact are separate, and thus to use material participation in one undertaking as a basis for claiming without limitation losses and credits from another undertaking."[50]

The Senate Finance Committee noted that "[t]he determination of what constitutes a separate activity is intended to be made in a realistic economic sense. The question to be answered is what undertakings consist of an integrated and interrelated economic unit, conducted in coordination with or reliance upon each other, and constituting an appropriate unit for the measurement of gain or loss."[51] In determining the scope of an activity, one must consider the specific nature of the activity and identify an appropriate unit for determining gain and loss. For example, where different products or services are provided to customers, it is likely that there is more than one activity. Of course, if it is customary that such products or services are provided together, there will only be one activity. Normal commercial practices will be relevant in determining the scope of an activity.[52]

The Treasury has set forth a facts and circumstances test for determining what constitutes an activity and the scope of a given activity.[53] The factors given the

---

[49] I.R.C. § 469(c)(7)(B).

[50] General Explanation of the Tax Reform Act of 1986, p. 245.

[51] Sen. Rep. No. 99-313, 99th Cong., 2d Sess., p. 739.

[52] General Explanation of the Tax Reform Act of 1986, p. 246.

[53] Treas. Reg. § 1.469-4.

greatest weight "in determining whether activities constitute an appropriate economic unit for purposes of section 469" include: (1) similarities and differences in types of business; (2) the extent of common control; (3) geographical location; and (4) interdependence between the activities.[54]

[E]   Treatment of Losses and Credits

Section 469 requires a taxpayer to compute the gains and losses from each passive activity. The losses from an activity are first offset against the gains from that activity and any excess loss is then offset against excess gains from other passive activities. In other words, a taxpayer may deduct all the losses from passive activities from all the gains from passive activities. The excess of the aggregate losses from one's passive activities over the aggregate gains from such activities, referred to as a "passive activity loss," cannot be used in the current taxable year. Rather, it may be carried forward and used in subsequent years. The disallowed passive activity loss must be apportioned among the various passive activities in which taxpayers realized a loss during the taxable year.

The regulations provide the following simple but instructive example:[55]

An individual holds interests in three passive activities, A, B, and C. The gross income and deductions from these activities for the taxable year are as follows:

	A	B	C	Total
Gross Income	$7,000	$4,000	$12,000	$23,000
Deductions	($16,000)	($20,000)	($8,000)	($44,000)
Net Income (Loss)	($9,000)	($16,000)	$4,000	($21,000)

The taxpayer's $21,000 passive activity loss for the taxable year is disallowed. Therefore, a ratable portion of the losses from activities A and B is disallowed. The disallowed portion of each loss is determined as follows:

A: $21,000   × $9,000/$25,000   = $7,560
B: $21,000   × $16,000/$25,000   = $13,440

Total $21,000

The regulation provides specific rules for determining which part of each passive activity deduction for each loss activity is disallowed.[56] Thus, in the example the $7,560 of disallowed loss in activity A would in turn be allocated to the passive activity deductions claimed by A. The detail of these allocations is complex and is beyond the scope of this chapter.

---

[54] Treas. Reg. § 1.469-4(c)(2).

[55] Temp. Treas. Reg. § 1.469-1T(f)(2)(i)(D).

[56] Temp. Treas. Reg. § 1.469-1T(f)(2)(ii).

[F] Portfolio Income and Expenses

§ 469(e). Special rules for determining income or loss from a passive activity.

For purposes of this section —

(1) Certain income not treated as income from passive activity. In determining the income or loss from any activity —

(A) In general. There shall not be taken into account —

(i) any

(I) gross income from interest, dividends, annuities, or royalties not derived in the ordinary course of a trade or business,

(II) expenses (other than interest) which are clearly and directly allocable to such gross income, and

(III) interest expense properly allocable to such gross income and

(ii) gain or loss not derived in the ordinary course of a trade or business which is attributable to the disposition of property

(I) producing income of a type described in clause (i), or

(II) held for investment.

For purposes of clause (ii), any interest in a passive activity shall not be treated as property held for investment.

(3) Compensation for personal services. Earned income . . . shall not be taken into account in computing the income or loss from a passive activity for any taxable year.

A special rule found in Section 469(e)(1) excludes portfolio income and expenses from the determination of passive activity gains and losses. As noted in the legislative history, "[p]ortfolio income generally includes interest, dividends, and royalties. Also included in portfolio income are gain or loss attribute to disposition of (1) property that is held for investment (and that is not a passive activity) and (2) property that normally produces interest, dividend, or royalty income."[57] The regulations define "portfolio income" in some detail.[58] The Senate Report on the Tax Reform Act explains the reason for excluding portfolio income as follows: "Portfolio investments ordinarily give rise to positive income, and are not likely to generate losses which could be applied to shelter other income. Therefore, for purposes of the passive loss rule, portfolio income generally is not treated as derived from a passive loss activity, but rather is treated like other positive income sources such as salary. To permit portfolio income to be offset by passive losses or credits would create the inequitable result of restricting sheltering by individuals dependent for support on wages or active business income, while permitting sheltering by those whose income is derived from an investment portfolio."[59]

---

[57] Sen. Rep No. 99-313, 99th Cong., 2d Sess., p. 728.

[58] Temp. Treas. Reg. § 1.469-2T(c)(3).

[59] Sen. Rep No. 99-313, 99th Cong., 2d Sess., p. 728. Income from a covenant not to compete is also

[G] Exception for Active Participation in Rental Real Estate

As noted previously, under Section 469(c)(2), all rental activity, except rental real estate activity that satisfies the special rule of Section 469(c)(7), will be passive activity regardless of the taxpayer's material participation. Congress nonetheless has provided a limited exception from the Section 469 limitations for certain rental real estate activity, despite its status as passive activity. If a taxpayer, who is a natural person, *actively participates* in rental real estate activity, the taxpayer may apply the losses and credits from that activity against up to $25,000 of the taxpayer's nonpassive income.[60] The relief is phased-out for taxpayers whose adjusted gross income exceeds $100,000.[61]

As noted by the Staff of the Joint Committee on Taxation, this exception was created "because rental real estate is held, in many instances, to provide financial security to individuals with moderate incomes. In some cases, for example, an individual may hold for rental a residence that he uses part time, or that previously was and at some future time may be his primary residence. Even absent any such residential use of the property by the taxpayer, Congress believed that a rental real estate investment in which the taxpayer has significant responsibilities with respect to providing necessary services, and which serves significant nontax purposes of the taxpayer, is different in some respects from the activities that are meant to be fully subject to limitation under the passive loss provision."[62]

To be an *active participant* in a rental real estate activity, a taxpayer must own at least a 10 percent interest in it.[63] The "active participation" standard is more lenient than the "material participation" standard considered before. A taxpayer may be an active participant without regular, continuous, and substantial involvement in the operations. A taxpayer is an active participant if the taxpayer participates in a significant and bona fide sense in making management decisions or arranges for the provision of services such as repairs. Examples of management decisions that would establish a taxpayer as an active participant include selecting or approving new tenants, establishing rental terms, hiring a rental agent, hiring a person to provide repair services, and approving capital or repair expenditures.[64]

[H] Disposition of Taxpayer's Entire Interest in Passive Activity

If a taxpayer disposes of the entire interest in a passive activity, any suspended losses allocable to that activity (as well as any loss realized on the disposition of a passive activity) no longer are treated as passive activity losses. Instead, they are

---

passive income, per Temporary Regulation § 1.469-2 T(c)(7)(iv). The validity of that regulation was upheld in *Schaefer v. Commissioner*, 105 T.C. 227 (1995).

[60] I.R.C. § 469(i)(1), (2).

[61] I.R.C. § 469(i)(3)(A).

[62] General Explanation of the Tax Reform Act of 1986, p. 243.

[63] I.R.C. § 469(i)(6).

[64] Sen. Rep. No. 99-313, 99th Cong., 2d Sess., p. 738.

deductible against income (whether passive or nonpassive) as set forth in Section 469(g)(1)(A). Under this provision, any net passive loss from the activity is first applied against passive income, with any remaining loss classified as nonpassive and available to offset nonpassive income. This release of suspended passive activity losses, however, is applicable only in the case of a fully taxable disposition of the taxpayer's interest in the activity to an unrelated party.[65] An arm's length sale of the property for fair market value is the kind of fully taxable disposition envisioned by Section 469(g)(1).[66]

The following excerpt from the legislative history explains the reason for releasing suspended losses upon the disposition of taxpayer's entire interest:[67]

> When a taxpayer disposes of his entire interest in a passive activity, the actual economic gain or loss on his investment can be finally determined. . . . [P]rior to a disposition of the taxpayer's interest, it is difficult to determine whether there has actually been gain or loss with respect to the activity. For example, allowable deductions may exceed actual economic costs, or may be exceeded by untaxed appreciation. Upon a taxable disposition, net appreciation or depreciation with respect to the activity can be finally ascertained.

As noted previously, the determination of the scope of a passive activity is critical to the operation of this special rule regarding dispositions, since the taxpayer must establish that she has disposed of her "entire" interest. To dispose of her "entire" interest, a sole proprietor must dispose of all assets created or used in the activity.[68]

If a passive activity is transferred as a result of taxpayer's death, the suspended losses are allowed only to the extent that they exceed the amount, if any, by which the basis of the property in the activity is increased at death by Section 1014.[69] To the extent that the basis of property in the activity is increased by Section 1014, suspended losses of the activity are forever disallowed.[70]

Because a gift is not a fully taxable disposition of property, a gift of part or all of a taxpayer's interest in an activity will not cause the release of the suspended losses allocable to the activity.[71] However, the donor's basis in any gifted property will be increased by the suspended losses allocable to that property. Under Section 1015, the donee's basis in the gifted property will reflect this increase, subject, of course,

---

[65] I.R.C. § 469(g)(1)(A),(B). If a taxpayer disposes of the entire interest in the property in a related party transaction (as defined in Section 469(g)(1)(B), the suspended losses allocable to such interest will not be released under the general rule of Section 469(g)(1)(A) until the transferred interest is acquired in another fully taxable transaction by a person not related to the taxpayer. In the meantime, the taxpayer can continue to use these suspended passive losses against income from other passive activities.

[66] Sen. Rep. No. 99-3123, 99th Cong., 2d Sess., p. 725. By contrast, if a taxpayer were to transfer the interest in a passive activity to a corporation or a partnership in a nonrecognition transfer under Section 351 or 721, the suspended losses would not be released.

[67] Sen. Rep. No. 99-313, 99th Cong., 2d Sess., p. 725.

[68] Id.

[69] I.R.C. § 469(g)(2).

[70] Id.

[71] I.R.C. § 469(j)(6).

to the special rule in Section 1015(a) limiting a donee's basis for purposes of the computation of loss. To the extent suspended losses are so used to increase the donor's basis in gifted property, they are eliminated.[72]

---

[72] I.R.C. § 469(j)(6)(B).

Chapter 44

THE ALTERNATIVE MINIMUM TAX

The alternative minimum tax reflects a congressional determination that certain provisions of the Code constitute tax preferences, apt to be utilized disproportionately by high income persons, and that a taxpayer's ability to reduce tax liability through the use of certain tax preferences should be restricted. When Congress substantially revised the alternative minimum tax in 1986, committee reports described the tax's purpose as follows:

> The committee believes that the minimum tax should serve one overriding objective: to ensure that no taxpayer with substantial economic income can avoid significant tax liability by using exclusions, deductions, and credits. Although these provisions may provide incentives for worthy goals, they become counterproductive when taxpayers are allowed to use them to avoid virtually all tax liability. The ability of high-income taxpayers to pay little or no tax undermines respect for the entire tax system and, thus, for the incentive provisions themselves. In addition, even aside from public perceptions, the committee believes that it is inherently unfair for high-income taxpayers to pay little or no tax due to their ability to utilize tax preferences.[1]

A problem that has arisen in recent years involves the potential reach of the minimum tax to apply to middle-income taxpayers, a point discussed below. In any event, tax computations are not completed when a taxpayer's regular tax liability has been calculated; it still remains necessary to determine whether the type and amount of tax preferences render the taxpayer subject to the alternative minimum tax.

§ 44.01 MECHANICS

§ 55. **Alternative minimum tax imposed —**

(a) **General rule.**

There is hereby imposed (in addition to any other tax imposed by this subtitle) a tax equal to the excess (if any) of —
the tentative minimum tax for the taxable year, over the regular tax for the taxable year.

(b) **Tentative minimum tax.**

For purposes of this part —

---

[1] H. Rep. No. 99-426, at 305–306 (1986). *See also* S. Rep. No. 99-313, at 518–519 (1986).

(1)   Amount of tentative tax —

(A)   Noncorporate taxpayers —

(i)   In general — In the case of a taxpayer other than a corporation, the tentative minimum tax for the taxable year is the sum of —

(I) 26 percent of so much of the taxable excess as does not exceed $175,000 [indexed for inflation after 2012], plus

(II) 28 percent of so much of the taxable excess as exceeds $175,000 [indexed for inflation after 2012]. The amount determined under the preceding sentence shall be reduced by the alternative minimum tax foreign tax credit for the taxable year.

(ii)   Taxable excess — For purposes of this subsection, the term "taxable excess" means so much of the alternative minimum taxable income for the taxable year as exceeds the exemption amount.

(iii)   Married individual filing separate return — In the case of a married individual filing a separate return, clause (i) shall be applied by substituting 50 percent of the dollar amount otherwise applicable under subclause (I) and subclause (II) thereof. For purposes of the preceding sentence, marital status shall be determined under section 7703.

(B)   Corporations —

In the case of a corporation, the tentative minimum tax for the taxable year is —

(i) 20 percent of so much of the alternative minimum taxable income for the taxable year as exceeds the exemption amount, reduced by

(ii) the alternative minimum tax foreign tax credit for the taxable year.

(2)   Alternative minimum taxable income —

The term "alternative minimum taxable income" means the taxable income of the taxpayer for the taxable year — (A) determined with the adjustments provided in section 56 and section 58, and (B) increased by the amount of the items of tax preference described in section 57.

If a taxpayer is subject to the regular tax, such taxpayer shall be subject to the tax imposed by this section (and, if the regular tax is determined by reference to an amount other than taxable income, such amount shall be treated as the taxable income of such taxpayer for purposes of the preceding sentence).

(c)   Regular tax.

(1)   In general — For purposes of this section, the term "regular tax" means the regular tax liability for the taxable year (as defined in section 26(b)) reduced by [specified credits and not including specified additions to tax] . . . .

. . .

(d)   Exemption amount. For purposes of this section —

(1)   Exemption amount for taxpayer other than corporations —

In the case of a taxpayer other than a corporation, the term "exemption amount" means —

  (A) $78,750 [indexed for inflation after 2012] in the case of —

   (i) a joint return, or

   (ii) a surviving spouse,

  (B) $50,650 [indexed for inflation after 2012] in the case of an individual who —

   (i) is not a married individual, and

   (ii) is not a surviving spouse,

  (C) 50% of the dollar amount applicable under subparagraph (A) in the case of a married individual who files a separate return. . . .

For purposes of this paragraph, the term "surviving spouse" has the meaning given to such term by section 2(a), and marital status shall be determined under section 7703.

  (2) Corporations — In the case of a corporation, the term "exemption amount" means $40,000.

  (3) Phase-out of exemption amount —

The exemption amount of any taxpayer shall be reduced (but not below zero) by an amount equal to 25 percent of the amount by which the alternative minimum taxable income of the taxpayer exceeds —

  (A) $150,000 [indexed for inflation after 2012] in the case of a taxpayer described in paragraph (1)(A),

  (B) $112,500 [indexed for inflation after 2012] in the case of a taxpayer described in paragraph (1)(B),

  (C) 50 percent of the dollar amount applicable under subparagraph (A) in the case of a taxpayer described in subparagraph (C) . . .

In the case of a taxpayer described in paragraph (1)(C), alternative minimum taxable income shall be increased by the lesser of (i) 25 percent of the excess of alternative minimum taxable income (determined without regard to this sentence) over the minimum amount of such income (as so determined) for which the exemption amount under paragraph 1(C) is zero or (ii) such exemption amount determined without regard to this paragraph.

 The alternative minimum tax is defined as the excess of the "tentative minimum tax" over the regular tax for the year.[2] In effect, this simply means the taxpayer pays the regular tax or the tentative minimum tax, whichever is greater. For example, if the regular tax is $40,000 and the tentative minimum tax is $30,000, the alternative minimum tax is zero; the taxpayer would simply pay the regular tax of $40,000. However, if the tentative minimum tax is $50,000, the tax imposed consists of a regular tax of $40,000 and an alternative minimum tax of $10,000.

---

[2] I.R.C. § 55(a).

The tentative minimum tax for individuals is generally equal to 26% of the first $175,000 (inflation-adjusted beginning in 2013) in "taxable excess" plus 28% thereafter.[3] (For married individuals filing separate returns, the 26% rate applies to the first $87,500, inflation-adjusted, beginning in 2013.) There are separate lower maximum rates, drawn from Section 1(h), on that portion of the taxable excess that consists of net capital gain.[4] "Taxable excess," in turn, is the excess of "alternative minimum taxable income" over the "exemption amount."[5] For 2013, the exemption amount is $78,750 on joint returns (or for surviving spouses), $50,600 for an individual not married and not a surviving spouse, and $39,375 for married individuals filing separately.[6] (These amounts are inflation-adjusted beginning in 2013.) For example, if a single taxpayer in 2013 had alternative minimum taxable income of $91,600, none of which consisted of net capital gain, the tentative minimum tax would be 26% of a taxable excess of $41,000 ($91,600 less the $50,600 exemption amount), or $10,660.[7] If the taxpayer's regular tax liability were less than $10,660, the alternative minimum tax would be applicable.

The exemption amount phases out when alternative minimum taxable income reaches sufficiently high levels.[8] For example, with respect to single taxpayers, the phase-out begins when alternative minimum taxable income exceeds $112,500 (indexed for inflation beginning in 2013). Every $4 in excess of this amount reduces the exemption amount by $1 (but not below zero).

> **Example:** Assume a single taxpayer has alternative minimum taxable income of $152,500 and an exemption amount of $112,500. What is the taxpayer's tentative minimum tax?
>
> **Analysis:** Because the taxpayer's alternative minimum taxable income exceeds the exemption amount, the exemption amount would be reduced by $10,000 (25% of $40,000, the excess of $152,500 over $112,500). The exemption amount would thus be reduced from $48,450 to $38,450, and the tentative minimum tax rate of 26%, assuming no net capital gain, would be applied to a base of $114,050 ($152,500 less the $38,450 exemption amount), resulting in a tentative minimum tax of $29,653.

§ 44.02   DETERMINING ALTERNATIVE MINIMUM TAXABLE INCOME

§ 56.   Adjustments in computing alternative minimum taxable income —

(a)   Adjustments applicable to all taxpayers —

In determining the amount of the alternative minimum taxable income for any

---

[3] I.R.C. § 55(b)(1)(A).

[4] I.R.C. § 55(b)(3).

[5] I.R.C. § 55(b)(1)(A).

[6] I.R.C. § 55(d)(1). There is a special rule for computing the exemption amount of a child subject to the "kiddie tax" of Section 1(g). *See* I.R.C. § 59(j).

[7] Technically, the tentative minimum tax is $10,660, less certain specified credits and with the addition of specified taxes — none of which are applicable to the average taxpayer. I.R.C. § 55(b)(1)(A).

[8] I.R.C. § 55(d)(3).

taxable year the following treatment shall apply (in lieu of the treatment applicable for purposes of computing the regular tax):

(1) Depreciation — (A) In general —

(ii) 150-percent declining balance method for certain property — The method of depreciation used shall be —

(I) the 150 percent declining balance method,

(II) switching to the straight line method for the 1st taxable year for which using the straight line method with respect to the adjusted basis as of the beginning of the year will yield a higher allowance. The preceding sentence shall not apply to any section 1250 property (as defined in section 1250(c)) or to any other property if the depreciation deduction determined under section 168 with respect to such other property for purposes of the regular tax is determined by using the straight line method.

. . .

(b) Adjustments applicable to individuals — In determining the amount of the alternative minimum taxable income of any taxpayer (other than a corporation), the following treatment shall apply (in lieu of the treatment applicable for purposes of computing the regular tax):

(1) Limitation on itemized deductions —

(A) In general no deductions shall be allowed —

(i) for any miscellaneous itemized deduction (as defined in section 67(b)), or

(ii) for any taxes described in paragraph (1), (2), or (3) of section 164(a) or clause (ii) of section 164(b)(5)(A). Clause (ii) shall not apply to any amount allowable in computing adjusted gross income.

(B) Medical expenses —

In determining the amount allowable as a deduction under section 213, subsection (a) of section 213 shall be applied [by substituting 10 percent without regard to the special rule applicable to individuals 65 or older.]

. . .

(E) Standard deduction and deduction for personal exemptions not allowed — The standard deduction under section 63(c), the deduction for personal exemptions under section 151, and the deduction under section 642(b) shall not be allowed.

§ 57. Items of tax preference —

(a) General rule — For purposes of this part, the items of tax preference determined under this section are —

(1) Depletion —

With respect to each property (as defined in section 614), the excess of the deduction for depletion allowable under section 611 for the taxable year over the adjusted basis of the property at the end of the taxable year (determined without regard to the depletion deduction for the taxable year). Effective with respect to taxable years beginning after December 31, 1992, this paragraph shall not apply to any deduction for depletion computed in accordance with section 613A(c).

. . .

(5) Tax-exempt interest —

(A) In general — Interest on specified private activity bonds reduced by any deduction (not allowable in computing the regular tax) which would have been allowable if such interest were includible in gross income.

. . .

(7) Exclusion for gains on sale of certain small business stock — An amount equal to 7 percent of the amount excluded from gross income for the taxable year under section 1202.

The determination of "alternative minimum taxable income" (hereinafter, AMTI) is central to the tentative minimum tax, and hence, to the alternative minimum tax. AMTI is defined as taxable income, adjusted as set forth in Sections 56 and 58, and increased by the items of tax preference in Section 57.[9] Since the starting point in determining AMTI is taxable income, it is first necessary to determine gross income and allowable deductions; to determine whether deductions are allowable above the line or below the line; to subject the "miscellaneous itemized deductions" to the 2% floor of Section 67; to apply the overall limitation on itemized deductions of Section 68; to determine the standard deduction for nonitemizers; and to determine personal exemptions.[10]

[A] Section 56 and 58 Adjustments

Once the taxpayer's taxable income has been determined, the Sections 56 and 58 adjustments are made. Some of the required adjustments deal with corporate tax, including a special exemption for small corporations, and other matters beyond the scope of this chapter, and they are not discussed here at all. Among the other adjustments are the following:

---

[9] I.R.C. § 55(b)(2).

[10] See Chapter 1, supra.

[1]   Depreciation

For purposes of determining AMTI, a depreciation adjustment will sometimes be required. Starting in 1999, the same recovery period is used for both regular tax and minimum tax purposes. However, except for Section 1250 property (generally real property) and property otherwise depreciated under the straight line method, depreciation for minimum tax purposes must be calculated using the 150% declining balance method. The practical effect is that depreciation deductions will be the same under both the regular tax and alternative minimum tax for Section 1250 real property, other straight line property, and property depreciated under the 150% declining balance method. However, tangible personal property depreciated under the 200% declining balance method for regular tax purposes, i.e., 3-year, 5-year, 7-year and 10-year property, must use the less accelerated 150% declining balance method for alternative minimum tax purposes.[11] Total depreciation deductions over the life of the property are of course the same under both the regular tax and the alternative minimum tax. This means that for some property the taxpayer must maintain two depreciation schedules — one for regular tax purposes, and one for alternative minimum tax purposes. (Since in these cases the property's AMTI basis will exceed its regular tax basis — assuming the basis has not been reduced to zero under both schedules — the gain on a sale of the property will be less (or the loss greater) when determining AMTI than when computing regular tax liability.)[12]

[2]   Limitation on Itemized Deductions, Standard Deductions and Personal Exemptions

Miscellaneous itemized deductions, as defined in Section 67(b), are not allowed in computing AMTI, nor are those state and local taxes that were deductible below the line for regular tax purposes.[13] In some cases, disallowance of miscellaneous itemized deductions can have a substantial impact. Consider, for example, the situation where substantial attorney's fees are incurred to pursue a claim for taxable damages. The taxable damages are part of the tax base for regular tax and alternative minimum tax purposes, but if the attorney's fees are deductible under Section 212, not Section 162, and if the fees do not qualify for above-the-line treatment under provisions like Section 62(a)(4) (expenses attributable to rents and royalties) or Section 62(a)(20) (fees and costs attributable to claims of unlawful discrimination and certain other claims), the fees will be disallowed as miscellaneous itemized deductions in computing AMTI.

Alexander v. IRS[14] is a good illustration of the sometimes heavy impact of the disallowance of miscellaneous itemized deductions for alternative minimum tax purposes. In *Alexander*, the taxpayer, after initiating a lawsuit against his former employer, received a settlement, most of which was taxable, and paid his own attorney's fees from the proceeds of the settlement. Although the attorney's fees

---

[11]   Section 168(k), however, provides a special rule for qualified property generally acquired after 2007 and before 2013. I.R.C. § 168(k)(2)(G).

[12]   I.R.C. § 56(a)(7).

[13]   I.R.C. § 56(b)(1)(A).

[14]   72 F.3d 938 (1st Cir. 1995), *aff'g* T.C. Memo. 1995-51.

allocable to the taxable portion of the settlement were deductible, the First Circuit held them to be allowable only as a below the line deduction and held that they constituted a miscellaneous itemized deduction under Section 67(b). (With the enactment in 2004 of Sections 62(a)(20) and 62(e), attorney fees in a broad array of non-physical personal injury cases will be treated as above-the-line deductions and thus will not be miscellaneous itemized deductions subject to Section 67 and to disallowance for AMTI purposes.) As such, they were subject to the 2% floor rule of Section 67(a), but much more importantly, as a miscellaneous itemized deduction, the allowable amount constituted an adjustment for alternative minimum tax purposes under Section 56(b)(1)((A)(i). The numbers show why the taxpayer resisted the classification: the taxable portion of the settlement was about $250,000; the legal fees allocable to this taxable portion were about $245,000 — that is, only about $5,000 less than the settlement. After application of the 2% floor rule, the allowable amount was about $240,000, a relatively minor cutback for regular tax purposes. But application of the Section 56 adjustment rules, which inexorably followed, effectively disallowing the deduction in its entirety for alternative minimum tax purposes, resulted in an additional tax liability of some $57,000.[15] (The *Alexander* case pre-dated the enactment of Section 62(a)(20), which would now provide above-the-line treatment for the fees and avoid the AMT.)

Medical expenses are allowed in computing AMTI only to the extent they exceed 10% of adjusted gross income (rather than 7.5% for regular tax purposes of adjusted gross income for years before 2013 and for taxpayers 65 or older in years before 2017.).[16] The interest deduction limitations of Section 163(d) and (h) are modified.[17]

The standard deduction and personal exemptions are also not allowed in computing AMTI.[18] Occasionally, these disallowances can have a substantial impact. For example, the middle income taxpayers in *Klaassen v. Commissioner*,[19] with adjusted gross income of about $83,000 and almost $30,000 in personal exemptions for themselves and their 10 children, were not able to claim the personal exemptions and certain itemized deductions for minimum tax purposes. As a result, they faced minimum tax liability, although they were clearly not the type of "high-income taxpayer" for whom the minimum tax was intended.

The overall limitation on itemized deductions under Section 68 does not apply in computing AMTI.[20]

[B] Section 57 Preferences

Taxable income, as adjusted by these and other provisions of Sections 56 and 58, is then increased by the items of tax preference listed in Section 57.

---

[15] *See also* Benci-Woodard v. Comm'r, T.C. Memo. 1998-39.

[16] I.R.C. § 56(b)(1)(B).

[17] I.R.C. § 56(b)(1)(C).

[18] I.R.C. § 56(b)(1)(E).

[19] 183 F.3d 932 (10th Cir. 1999).

[20] I.R.C. § 56(b)(1)(F).

Certain otherwise tax-exempt interest must be included in income for AMTI purposes. Pursuant to Section 57(a)(5), the interest on "specified private activity bonds" (reduced by deductions that were nondeductible in computing regular tax liability) is an item of tax preference taken into account in computing AMTI.

Seven percent (7%) of the amount excluded under the qualified small business stock rules of Section 1202 is an item of tax preference.[21]

Tax preference items may also include certain depletion deductions, intangible drilling costs, and a portion of the depreciation taken on certain property placed in service prior to 1987.[22]

It is worth noting, however, that a charitable contribution of appreciated "capital gain property" does not generate an item of tax preference for AMTI purposes. As discussed in Chapter 26, a charitable contribution of such property may be deductible in an amount equal to its fair market value.[23] In such cases, the taxpayer gets a deduction that takes into account the property's appreciation in value, but the taxpayer is not similarly required to take the appreciation into account for purposes of determining gross income. This asymmetrical treatment of appreciation in capital gain property was at one time altered, for AMTI purposes, by requiring that the Section 170 deduction be reduced to the amount that would have been allowed had the capital gain property been taken into account at its adjusted basis. However, this provision was repealed in 1993, making such charitable contributions very attractive not only for regular tax purposes, but for minimum tax purposes as well.

§ 44.03 DETERMINING TAX LIABILITY

Once the taxpayer's AMTI has been determined, the appropriate exemption amount is subtracted and the balance is the "taxable excess."[24] Assuming no net capital gain, the tentative minimum tax is simply 26% of the first (inflation-adjusted) $175,000 of this taxable excess, plus 28% of the amount above $175,000 (less any alternative minimum tax foreign tax credit).[25] To the extent of net capital gain, the special lower maximum rates of Section 55(b)(3) must be applied in determining the tentative minimum tax. An alternative minimum tax is imposed only to the extent this tentative minimum tax exceeds the "regular tax."

Under Section 55(c)(1), the regular tax is the taxpayer's specially-defined "regular tax liability," which in turn means "the tax imposed by this chapter," *i.e.*, that is, by Chapter 1, Code Sections 1-1399, less certain specified taxes, including the alternative minimum tax.[26] For our purposes, we shall assume that a taxpayer's regular tax liability, and the regular tax, consist simply of the tax imposed by

---

[21] I.R.C. § 57(a)(7).

[22] *See* I.R.C. § 57(a).

[23] *See* I.R.C. § 170(a), (e).

[24] I.R.C. § 55(b)(1)(A)(ii).

[25] I.R.C. § 55(b)(1)(A)(i).

[26] I.R.C. § 26(b).

Section 1 of the Code. Therefore, upon determining the taxpayer's taxable income and filing status, and upon applying, if necessary, the maximum capital gains rate of Section 1(h), the regular tax may be computed.

> **Example:** John is a single taxpayer. His income consists of $150,000 compensation and $50,000 in tax-exempt "private activity" bonds. His only expense is $40,000 in attorney's fees that John paid to a lawyer representing John in some personal income and estate tax planning. Assume John's personal exemption is $5,000 and his standard deduction is $5,000. Assume his exemption amount for AMT purposes is $50,650.

> **Analysis:** For regular tax purposes, John's taxable income is $100,000. (His gross income is $150,000; the $40,000 in legal fees and the $10,000 for personal exemption and standard deduction reduce his taxable income to $100,000. For simplicity, we are ignoring the 2% cutback rule of Section 67.) Assume John's regular tax liability is approximately $21,000.

> John's alternative minimum taxable income (AMTI) is $200,000. (Under Section 56, John cannot claim the $5,000 personal exemption and the $5,000 standard deduction; he cannot claim the $40,000 in legal fees because it is a Section 212 deduction that constitutes a miscellaneous itemized deduction under Section 67(b). Under Section 57, John must include the $50,000 in interest from private activity bonds in AMTI. These upward adjustments total $100,000 and result in AMTI of $200,000.) In addition, John's AMTI is sufficiently high that his potential exemption amount of $50,650 is reduced to $28,775.[27] Hence his "taxable excess" is $171,225. Applying the Section 55 rates to this amount (26% of the first $175,000, and 28% of the balance — here, none — for a total of $44,518.50) produces a tentative minimum tax of $23,518.50. Thus, the minimum tax results in an increased tax of $23,518.50 over the regular tax, i.e., $44,518.50 less $21,000 (regular tax).

§ 44.04   CREDITS ALLOWED

Once the amount of the tax imposed has been calculated, it is then necessary to determine whether the taxpayer is entitled to claim any credits against it.

Some of the so-called "nonrefundable personal credits" of Sections 21–25B were generally allowed only to the extent, in the aggregate, they did not exceed the excess (if any) of the taxpayer's regular tax liability over the tentative minimum tax. Thus, in effect, they formerly offset only the regular tax. The nonrefundable personal credits are now allowed to offset both regular tax and the alternative minimum tax.[28]

There are a number of other credits allowed by the Code.[29] The most familiar ones include the credit for tax withheld on wages (Section 31) and the earned

---

[27] I.R.C. § 55(d). This calculation assumes a phaseout of the exemption amount beginning at AMTI of $112,500.

[28] I.R.C. § 26(a)(1).

[29] *See generally* I.R.C. §§ 27–53.

income credit for low-income individuals (Section 32). Some other credits are subject to disallowance, as were the nonrefundable personal credits.[30]

Finally, note the minimum tax credit of Section 53. Under this provision, a portion of the alternative minimum tax imposed in a prior year may be allowed as a credit against the current year's regular tax liability. The minimum tax credit addresses a potential whipsawing of the taxpayer between the regular tax and the alternative minimum tax. The whipsawing can occur because some minimum tax provisions essentially make only timing adjustments to regular tax "benefits" rather than disallow them permanently. For example, minimum tax depreciation cuts back on the front-loading of regular tax depreciation, but the total depreciation allowed under both schedules is the same. Thus, as a result of the front-loading differentials, it is possible for the taxpayer to get the worst of both worlds — the minimum tax in the early years (when minimum tax depreciation is less than regular tax depreciation), and the regular tax in the later years (when minimum tax depreciation exceeds regular tax depreciation), In such circumstances, the minimum tax credit of Section 53 may apply to eliminate the "overtaxation" of the taxpayer due to these (and other) timing differentials. The mechanics of the process are in the "adjusted net minimum tax" definition.[31] In any event, the minimum tax credit is allowed only to the extent the taxpayer's regular tax liability, after having been reduced by most other allowable credits, still exceeds the taxpayer's tentative minimum tax for the year.[32] The practical effect, in general, is that the minimum tax credit is not allowed in a year in which the alternative minimum tax is itself imposed.

[30] For an example of a specific disallowance provision, see Section 38(c), relating to the general business credit.

[31] See I.R.C. § 53(d)(1)(B)(i), (ii).

[32] I.R.C. § 53(c).

Appendix A

NOTE ON MISCELLANEOUS EXCLUSIONS

[A] TAX-EXEMPT INTEREST

Interest on state and local bonds is excluded from gross income under Section 103(a). The exclusion has been part of the income tax law since its inception in 1913. Although the primary initial justification for the provision was a concern about the constitutionality of federal taxation of state and local obligations, most scholars today believe there is little doubt that it would be constitutional to impose a federal tax on such interest income.

Determining whether one should invest in a tax-exempt bond calls for a review of the tax bracket of the taxpayer in question and the rate of return on comparable taxable investments. Thus, for example, assume an investor has a choice of two bonds: a taxable corporate bond paying 10% interest and a tax-free municipal bond paying 8% interest. If the investor is in the 15% marginal tax bracket, the after-tax return on the corporate bond exceeds 8%, and it is therefore preferable. For the investor in a marginal tax bracket that exceeds 20%, the after-tax return on the corporate bond is less than 8%, and the municipal bond is the better choice. (Note, however, that interest on certain types of state and local bonds may be subject to the alternative minimum tax of Section 55, which must be considered in making the comparison of after-tax returns.) As the example demonstrates, the exclusion is worth more to taxpayers in higher tax brackets and it has often been criticized on that account.

Section 103(a) makes it possible for state and local governments to sell their bonds at lower interest rates than would be the case if the bonds were taxable. The exclusion is therefore justified by some as a form of federal assistance to local government, a type of revenue sharing in which the federal government forgoes tax revenues in order to reduce local government expenses. It has often been pointed out, however, that if a subsidy is intended, the subsidy is an inefficient one when an investor's marginal tax bracket exceeds the spread between otherwise comparable taxable and non-taxable bonds. The federal tax revenue forgone in these cases does not fully translate into state and local savings realized. For example, if an investor in a 28% bracket purchases a $10,000, 8% municipal bond rather than a comparable 10% corporate bond, the investor saves $280 in federal taxes, but the municipality saves — and the investor forgoes — only $200 worth of interest. Historically, the interest rates on tax-free bonds, as a percentage of the interest rate on taxable bonds, has been such that taxpayers in higher brackets can generally effect such net gains by investing in municipal bonds.

The Section 103(a) exclusion, as might be expected, has been exploited by local governments to such a degree that Congress, concerned with abuse, has imposed various restrictions on the basic exclusion.[1] By way of a brief summary, and without making any attempt to explore the details, one may divide state and local bonds into three categories. In the first category are "governmental bonds," which are bonds issued to finance general governmental operations and facilities such as schools, roads, government buildings, water and sewer facilities and the like. Governmental bonds are tax-exempt, and free of most of the restrictions imposed on non-governmental bonds. The second category consists of "private activi ty bonds" — bonds issued to finance the activities of non-governmental persons. Local governments have often used the Section 103(a) exclusion to issue bonds that financed the development of private businesses and industries, and other activities that were private or only semi-public in nature. The general rule adopted by Congress is that interest on private activity bonds is taxable in the absence of a specific exception to the contrary. A number of exceptions have been provided, and, subject to various restrictions, including an annual volume limitation for most private activity bonds, interest on such "qualified" private activity bonds is tax-exempt. The third category consists of arbitrage bonds. State and local governments are treated by the Treasury as tax-exempt entities under the Internal Revenue Code. It could thus be quite profitable for them to take advantage of their tax-exempt status, and the relatively low interest expense Section 103(a) makes possible, by investing the proceeds of a bond issue — pending disbursement for its given purposes — at a rate of return in excess of the interest rate payable on the bonds. The congressional response, in general terms, is that such "arbitrage profits" belong to the federal government. Thus, all tax-exempt bonds — governmental or private activity — are subject to various arbitrage restrictions, and to a requirement that certain arbitrage profits be rebated to the federal treasury.

[B] SECTIONS 109 AND 1019

Congress enacted Sections 109 and 1019 in 1942 to overturn the Supreme Court's decision in *Helvering v. Bruun*,[2] holding that a lessor was taxable, on forfeiture of the leasehold, on the value of a building erected by the tenant on the lessor's premises. Section 109 excludes from the income of a lessor on termination of a lease the value of improvements made to the property by the lessee (other than as rent). However, since the special basis rule of Section 1019 denies any basis adjustment on account of such exempt income, the gain the lessor realizes is really tax-deferred rather than permanently excluded. Since basis is not adjusted, no increase in depreciaton deductions occurs by reason of the improvement. The tax-deferred gain will be accounted for upon the lessor's sale or other disposition of the property.

The parenthetical clause of Section 109 provides that the exclusion does not apply to rent. The regulations at Section 1.61-8(c) provide that improvements by a lessee which are a "substitue for rent" constitute gross income to the lessor, and further state that whether or not an improvement is a rental substitute depends on the intention of the parties, as indicated by the terms of the lease or surrounding circumstances. The distinction Section 109 requires — between improvements that

---

[1] *See* I.R.C. § 103(b).

[2] 309 U.S. 461 (1940).

are rental substitutes and those that are not — may obviously be a difficult one to make in a given set of circumstances.

[C] CREDIT FOR ADOPTION EXPENSES AND EXCLUSION FOR ADOPTION PAYMENTS MADE BY EMPLOYER

Section 23 provides a tax credit for qualified adoption expenses. The credit increases to a maximum of $10,000 (adjusted for inflation). Section 23(d) defines "qualified adoption expenses" to include reasonable and necessary adoption fees, courts costs, attorney fees and other expenses directly related to the adoption of an "eligible child" (other than the child of the taxpayer's spouse). An "eligible child" means an individual who has not attained the age of 18 or is physically or mentally incapable of caring for himself. There are special provisions for children with "special needs." With respect to the adoption of a child who is not a citizen or resident of the United States, Section 23(e) provides that the credit will not be available until the adoption is finalized. The credit is phased out ratably for taxpayers whose adjusted gross income (as specially modified) exceeds a specified amount ($150,000 adjusted for inflation).

Section 137 authorizes an employee to exclude from gross income amounts paid or expenses incurred by an employer for qualified adoption expenses in connection with the employee's adoption of a child. The maximum amount of the exclusion is $10,000 (adjusted for inflation). Like the credit, the exclusion is phased out once employee's specially modified adjusted gross income exceeds an inflation-adjusted $150,000. "Qualified adoption expenses" has the same meaning as that term is used in Section 23.

[D] GOVERNMENT WELFARE PAYMENTS

Without relying on any explicit statutory authority, the Service has held a variety of government benefits to be excluded from gross income. It was noted in Chapter 2, that unemployment benefits, once treated as non-taxable by the Service, are now fully included in income, and that Social Security benefits, also formerly tax-free in full, are now partially taxable. Taxing these benefits may stem from viewing unemployment compensation as a wage replacement program, and from viewing Social Security as, at least in part, a program of deferred compensation. Welfare-type benefits, on the other hand, tend to lack the nexus to compensation, are seemingly more in the nature of charitable gifts, and thus excludable from gross income on that basis. Moreover, to the extent benefits are based on need, treating them as income would, in any event, likely generate little or no taxable income in the great majority of cases. Thus, government disbursements in the nature of welfare payments are held to be tax-free.[3] However, government transfer payments made without regard to need are likely to be taxed.[4]

---

[3] See, for example, Revenue Ruling 76-144, 1976-1 C.B. 17, excluding disaster relief grants from income.

[4] See, for example, Revenue Ruling 85-39, 1985-1 C.B. 21, *amplified by* Revenue Ruling 90-56, 1990-2 C.B. 102, holding that "dividend payments" made by Alaska to its adult residents were taxable because they were not general welfare program payments, not restricted to those in need, and not characterized as gifts.

[E] EDUCATIONAL SAVINGS BONDS

Section 135, enacted in 1988 to encourage savings for higher education, excludes from income interest on "qualified U.S. savings bonds" used to pay higher education expenses of the taxpayer, spouse or dependent.[5] The exemption is subject to an inflation-adjusted phase-out based on the taxpayer's modified adjusted gross income.[6] The exemption is also limited where the redemption proceeds for the year from qualifying bonds exceed the higher education expenses paid during the year.[7] Qualifying higher education expenses include tuition and required fees at eligible institutions, reduced by certain scholarships and benefits received with respect to the student.[8]

[F] FOREIGN EARNED INCOME

Section 911 excludes from the gross income of United States citizens or residents living abroad, provided certain requirements are met, up to $80,000 per year[9] of foreign-earned income, plus an additional "housing cost amount." Congress has justified this substantial exclusion as encouraging Americans to work abroad in order to help promote the export of American goods and services, and make American business more competitive in foreign markets.

[G] FOSTER CARE PAYMENTS

To provide a tax encouragement to foster care, certain foster care payments are excluded from income by Section 131. Provided various requirements are met, the exclusion applies to amounts paid as reimbursement for expenses and also to "difficulty of care" payments as well — that is, payments in the nature of compensation for caring for a physically, mentally, or emotionally handicapped individual.

[H] SECTION 126 PAYMENTS

Section 126 excludes from income certain federal or state payments under a variety of conservation, environmental, forestry and wildlife programs. No basis adjustment is permitted on account of the exclusion with respect to property acquired or improved with the payment — a provision reminiscent of Section 1019 in connection with the Section 109 exclusion. Disposition of "Section 126 property" is subject to the recapture rules of Section 1255.

[I] CERTAIN LIVING EXPENSES

Section 123 excludes from gross income insurance payments received as reimbursement or compensation for the increase in living expenses incurred on account of casualty to a principal residence. For guidance in determining the scope

---

[5] I.R.C. § 135(a), (c).

[6] I.R.C. § 135(b)(2).

[7] I.R.C. § 135(b)(1).

[8] I.R.C. § 135(c)(2), (d)(1).

[9] This dollar amount is adjusted for inflation. I.R.C. § 911(b)(2)(D).

of the Section 123 exclusion, see the regulations thereunder. For examples applying the exclusion where insurance payments and increased living expenses are spread over a multi-year period, see Revenue Ruling 93-43.[10]

---

[10] 1993-2 C.B. 69.

Appendix B

ADDITIONAL ACCOUNTING CONSIDERATIONS

[A] INVENTORY ACCOUNTING

The gross proceeds from the sale of property do not constitute gross income to the seller, since the seller is entitled to subtract the adjusted basis of the property from the amount realized in computing gain. Similarly, when a manufacturer or retailer sells goods from inventory, the sales proceeds are not gross income. Rather, to determine gross income, it is necessary to subtract from the sale price the "cost of goods sold." In the typical merchandising or manufacturing business, however, it is simply not possible or feasible to identify the specific cost attributable to each individual item sold from inventory. The rules of inventory accounting are designed to address the problem.

The regulations provide that, where it is necessary to use an inventory, accrual method accounting must be used with respect to purchases and sales.[1] Elsewhere, the regulations provide that inventories must be used at the beginning and end of each tax year "in every case in which the production, purchase, or sale of merchandise is an income-producing factor."[2] It should thus be apparent that inventory accounting and the accrual method on purchases and sales will be required of a great many businesses.

The gross income on sales from inventory is equal to total sales, minus the cost of goods sold.[3] Determining total sales, or gross receipts, is straightforward enough. Determining the cost of goods sold is somewhat more complex. The goods sold during the tax year, however, may be expressed as the sum of those on hand at the outset of the year ("opening inventory") plus those purchased during the year ("purchases"), minus the inventory on hand at the end of the year ("closing inventory"). In short, the total inventory on hand during the year consists of opening inventory and purchases. Once we subtract the closing inventory from that total, the balance is the inventory sold, the "goods sold," during the year. Assuming that we know the cost of purchases during the year, we can determine the "cost of goods sold" by converting the opening inventory and closing inventory to dollar amounts. The cost of goods sold (CGS) may thus be expressed as opening inventory (OI) plus purchases (P) less closing inventory (CI).

To summarize:

---

[1] Reg. § 1.446-1(c)(2).

[2] Reg. § 1.471-1. *See* I.R.C. § 471(a).

[3] *See* Reg. § 1.61-3(a).

Gross income = Sales − Cost of Goods Sold

Cost of Goods Sold = Opening Inventory + Purchases − Closing Inventory

Thus:

Gross Income = Sales − (Opening Inventory + Purchases − Closing Inventory)

Or

Gross Income = Sales − Opening Inventory − Purchases + Closing Inventory

It should thus be apparent, for example, that gross income will decrease as opening inventory and purchases increase; but gross income will increase as closing inventory increases. Note, however, that since one year's closing inventory becomes the following year's opening inventory, the impact of closing inventory on the gross income of Year 1 is felt in the opposite direction in Year 2.

Inventory accounting requires a counting or measuring of inventory at the beginning and end of the tax year. As noted, it also requires that we be able to express the inventory count in dollar terms — that is, inventory must not only be identified, it must be valued. The valuation is commonly done in one of two ways. The inventory may be valued at cost.[4] Alternatively, the inventory may be valued at cost or at market value, whichever is lower.[5] This latter approach, which reflects a decline in the market value of inventory in the current year's income, was originally developed for financial accounting purposes, but it may also generally be used for tax accounting purposes (except that it may not be used in conjunction with the so-called LIFO convention, discussed below). A change in the way inventory is valued cannot be made without the consent of the Commissioner.[6]

Assume the taxpayer wishes to value inventory at cost, but inventory is extensive and the cost of acquiring inventory items changes frequently. The taxpayer can determine the closing inventory, but realistically there may be no way to know when each item in it was acquired and thus no way to know the cost to assign to each individual item. This problem is solved by the use of an accounting convention. The most common convention assumes that the inventory first acquired is also the inventory first sold — that is, "first in, first out" or "FIFO." Thus, the closing inventory under FIFO consists of the most recently acquired inventory. If the cost of inventory has been rising, the FIFO convention raises the dollar value assigned to closing inventory and thus also raises gross income. Under the "LIFO" convention, on the other hand, the most recently acquired inventory is treated as the first sold — "last in, first out." The LIFO convention, in a time of rising prices, has the effect of reducing gross income, since it assumes the closing inventory is comprised of the earliest (least expensive) items and thus puts a lower value on closing inventory than would the FIFO convention. Conversely, in a time of falling prices, FIFO would produce a lower-valued closing inventory, thus a lower gross

---

[4] Reg. § 1.471-3.

[5] Reg. §§ 1.471-2(c), -4.

[6] Reg. § 1.471-2(d).

income, than would LIFO. Over the life of the business, of course, the gross income totals are the same under both methods.

The authorization to elect the LIFO method is provided by Section 472, and, once made, the election may not be revoked without the consent of the Commissioner.[7] Valuation of inventory under LIFO must be made at cost.[8] Under the FIFO convention, valuation may be made either at cost or under the lower-of-cost-or-market method.

The LIFO impact in a year of rising prices can be seen in the following examples.

Example 1: Assume the taxpayer has an opening inventory of 50 widgets valued at a cost of $5 each, or $250. During the year, the taxpayer sells 110 widgets for $12 each, or $1,320. The taxpayer purchases 3 shipments of widgets during the year: an April shipment of 40 widgets at $6 each, or $240; an August shipment of 40 widgets at $7 each, or $280; and an October shipment of 40 widgets at $8 each, or $320. The taxpayer's closing inventory is thus 60 widgets. Applying FIFO, what is the taxpayer's gross income?

Analysis: What is the taxpayer's gross income? Under FIFO, those 60 widgets are deemed to consist of the October shipment of 40 ($320) and one-half the August shipment ($140) and are valued at $460. Thus, gross income equals sales ($1,320) less opening inventory ($250), less the three purchases ($240 + $280 + $320, or $840), plus the closing inventory ($460). The resulting gross income is $690.

Example 2: Assume the same facts as Example 1 except that the LIFO method is used.

Analysis: Under LIFO, the 60 widgets in closing inventory are the 50 in opening inventory ($250 value) plus 10 from the April shipment of 40 (at $6 each, a total of $60). Closing inventory under LIFO is thus $310, which is $150 less than the valuation of closing inventory under FIFO. The resulting gross income determined using LIFO will be $540, which is similarly $150 less than the $690 determined with FIFO. Recall, of course, that next year's opening inventory is this year's closing inventory, and the benefit of a relatively low value on closing inventory thus translates into next year's opening inventory burden. There is, nonetheless, a real deferral of income advantage to be gained from LIFO in a time of rising prices.

Inventory accounting, and the Treasury regulations that govern it, are considerably more complex and detailed than the foregoing overview suggests;[9] this discussion merely touches on some salient, general aspects of inventory accounting. Nonetheless, it should be apparent that there is a direct relationship between accounting for inventory costs and the determination of gross income and a real potential for manipulation.

---

[7] Reg. § 1.472-5.

[8] Reg. § 1.472-2(b).

[9] See, for example, the regulations under Section 472 dealing with LIFO accounting; see also those at Regulation § 1.471-11 concerning manufacturing businesses (in contrast to retailers), which must allocate a variety of direct and indirect production costs among their inventory items.

[B]   FINANCIAL VS. TAX ACCOUNTING

Tax accounting and financial accounting principles often produce different results. As noted by the U.S. Supreme Court in *Thor Power Tool Co. v. Commissioner*, the disparities are a function of the "vastly different objectives that financial and tax accounting have."[10] The Supreme Court highlighted those different objectives as follows:

> The primary goal of financial accounting is to provide useful information to management, shareholders, creditors, and others properly interested; the major responsibility of the accountant is to protect these parties from being misled. The primary goal of the income tax system, in contrast, is the equitable collection of revenue; the major responsibility of the Internal Revenue Service is to protect the public fisc. Consistent with its goals and responsibilities, financial accounting has as its foundation the principle of conservatism, with its corollary that "possible error in measurement [should] be in the direction of understatement rather than overstatement of net income and net assets." In view of the Treasury's markedly different goals and responsibilities understatement of income is not destined to be its guiding light. Given this diversity, even contrariety, of objectives, any presumptive equivalency between tax and financial accounting would be unacceptable.

> The difference in objectives is mirrored in numerous differences of treatment. Where the tax law requires that a deduction be deferred until "all the events" have occurred that will make it fixed and certain, *United States v. Anderson*, 269 U.S. 422, 441 (1926), accounting principles typically require that a liability be accrued as soon as it can reasonably be estimated. Conversely, where the tax law requires that income be recognized currently under "claim of right," "ability to pay," and "control" rationales, accounting principles may defer accrual until a later year so that revenues and expenses may be better matched. Financial accounting, in short, is hospitable to estimates, probabilities, and reasonable certainties; the tax law, with its mandate to preserve the revenue, can give no quarter to uncertainty. This is as it should be. Reasonable estimates may be useful, even essential, in giving shareholders and creditors an accurate picture of a firm's overall financial health; but the accountant's conservatism cannot bind the Commissioner in his efforts to collect taxes. . . .

> Finally, a presumptive equivalency between tax and financial accounting would create insurmountable difficulties of tax administration. Accountants have long recognized that "generally accepted accounting principles" are far from being a canonical set of rules that will ensure identical accounting treatment of identical transactions. "Generally accepted accounting principles," rather, tolerate a range of "reasonable" treatments, leaving the choice among alternatives to management. Variances may be tolerable in financial reporting, but they are questionable in a tax system designed to ensure as far as possible that similarly situated taxpayers pay the same tax.

---

[10]   439 U.S. 522, 542 (1979).

If management's election among "acceptable" options were dispositive for tax purposes, a firm, indeed, could decide unilaterally — within limits dictated only by its accountants — the tax it wished to pay. Such unilateral decisions would not just make the Code inequitable; they would make it unenforceable.[11]

---

[11] *Id.* at 542–43.

TABLE OF CASES

[References are to pages]

[References are to pages]

[References are to pages]

[References are to pages]

[References are to pages]

TABLE OF STATUTES

[References are to pages]

[References are to pages]

[References are to pages]

[References are to pages]

[References are to pages]

[References are to pages]

TAX SOURCES

Proposed Treasury Regulations

TABLE OF AGENCY DECISIONS

[References are to pages]

INDEX

[References are to sections.]

A

ACCIDENT
Payment under accident and health insurance policies . . . 10.03

ACCOUNTS RECEIVABLE
Capital asset; accounts receivable for services rendered or inventory-type assets sold . . . . 31.04[D]

ACCRUAL METHOD ACCOUNTING
All events test . . . 29.01
Choice of accounting methods . . . 29.04
Deductions under
    Generally . . . 29.03[A]
    Capitalization . . . 29.03[E]
    Contested liabilities . . . 29.03[F]
    Economic performance test
        Generally . . . 29.03[C]
        Recurring item exception to
        . . . 29.03[D]
    Premature accruals . . . 29.03[B]
    Section 461(h) . . . 29.03[C]
Income, accrual of
    Generally . . . 29.02[A]
    Issues, accrual . . . 29.02[B]
    Prepayments . . . 29.02[C]
    Prior to receipt, income . . . 29.02[B]
    Receipt prior to earning . . . 29.02[C]
Issues . . . 29.02[B]
Prepayments . . . 29.02[C]
Prior to receipt, income . . . 29.02[B]
Receipt prior to earning . . . 29.02[C]

ADJUSTED GROSS INCOME
Calculation of . . . 1.03[B][4]
Concept of . . . 1.03[B][2]

ADOPTION EXPENSES
Exclusions . . . App.A[C]

ADVERTISING EXPENSES
Capital expenditures . . . 13.03[F]

AIRLINE INDUSTRY
No-additional-cost service fringe benefits
    . . . 11.02[A]

ALIMONY
Divorce, tax consequences of . . . 36.01
Tax consequences of divorce . . . 36.01
Trusts . . . 36.04

ALTERNATIVE MINIMUM TAXABLE INCOME (AMTI)
Generally . . . 44.02
Adjustments, Section 56 and 58
    Generally . . . 44.02[A]
    Depreciation . . . 44.02[A][1]
    Itemized deductions, limitations on
        . . . 44.02[A][2]

ALTERNATIVE MINIMUM TAXABLE INCOME (AMTI)—Cont.
Adjustments, Section 56 and 58—Cont.
    Personal exemptions . . . 44.02[A][2]
    Standard deductions . . . 44.02[A][2]
Deductions
    Itemized deductions, limitations on
        . . . 44.02[A][2]
    Standard deductions . . . 44.02[A][2]
Depreciation . . . 44.02[A][1]
Itemized deductions, limitations on . . . 44.02[A][2]
Personal exemptions . . . 44.02[A][2]
Section 57 preferences . . . 44.02[B]
Standard deductions . . . 44.02[A][2]

ALTERNATIVE MINIMUM TAX (AMT)
Generally . . . 44.01
Alternative minimum taxable income (AMTI) (See ALTERNATIVE MINIMUM TAXABLE INCOME (AMTI))
Credits allowed . . . 44.04
Liability, determination . . . 44.03

AMERICAN TAXPAYER RELIEF ACT OF 2012
18.05, 22.02[C], 22.03, 32.03, 36.01

AMORTIZATION
Business start-up business expenses
    . . . 12.01[B][3]

AMT (See ALTERNATIVE MINIMUM TAX (AMT))

AMTI (See ALTERNATIVE MINIMUM TAXABLE INCOME (AMTI))

ANNUAL ACCOUNTING
Claim of right, restoration of amount received under
    Generally . . . 30.01
        Appearance of right . . . 30.01[A]
        Unrestricted right, no . . . 30.01[B]
Net operating losses . . . 30.03
Tax benefit rule
    Generally . . . 30.02
    Erroneous original deduction . . . 30.02[B]
    Fundamental inconsistency test . . . 30.02[A]

ANNUITIES
Generally . . . 8.02

APPRECIATION OF PROPERTY
Charitable contribution of appreciated property
    . . . 26.04
Nonrecourse borrowing and . . . 37.04

ASSETS
Quasi-capital assets (See QUASI-CAPITAL ASSETS)

ASSIGNMENT OF INCOME
Application of assignment rules . . . 34.04
Community property . . . 34.03

I-1

[References are to sections.]

[References are to sections.]

[References are to sections.]

[References are to sections.]

[References are to sections.]

[References are to sections.]

[References are to sections.]

[References are to sections.]

[References are to sections.]

[References are to sections.]

[References are to sections.]

[References are to sections.]

NONRECOURSE BORROWING—Cont.
Insolvency exclusion, and . . . 37.03

O

OID (See ORIGINAL ISSUE DISCOUNT (OID))

ORDINARY INCOME
Depreciation recapture . . . 33.04

ORIGINAL ISSUE DISCOUNT (OID)
Generally . . . 42.01
Amount of, determination of . . . 42.02[A]
Cash, debt instruments issued for (See subhead: Debt instruments issued for cash)
Current inclusion of . . . 42.02[B]
Debt instruments issued for cash
    Generally . . . 42.02
    Amount of original issue discount, determination of . . . 42.02[A]
    Current inclusion of original issue discount . . . 42.02[B]
    Deduction of original issue discount . . . 42.02[C]
    Market discount . . . 42.02[E]
    Sale or exchange of property
        Gain or loss on . . . 42.02[D]
        Rental agreements under IRC Section 467 . . . 42.03
Deduction . . . 42.02[C]
Market discount . . . 42.02[E]
Rental agreements under IRC Section 467 and sale or exchange of property . . . 42.03
Sale or exchange of property
    Gain or loss on . . . 42.02[D]
    Rental agreements under IRC Section 467 . . . 42.03

P

PASSENGER AUTOMOBILES
Deductions . . . 21.03[B]

PASSIVE ACTIVITY LOSSES AND CREDITS
Generally . . . 43.02[A], [B]
Disposition of taxpayer's entire interest in passive activity . . . 43.02[H]
Entire interest of taxpayer in passive activity, disposition of . . . 43.02[H]
Material participation . . . 43.02[C][1]
Passive activities
    Generally . . . 43.02[C]
    Material participation . . . 43.02[C][1]
    Rental activities . . . 43.02[C][2]
    Scope of . . . 43.02[D]
Portfolio income and expenses . . . 43.02[F]
Rental activities . . . 43.02[C][2]
Rental real estate, exception for active participation in . . . 43.02[G]
Scope of activity . . . 43.02[D]
Taxpayer's entire interest in passive activity, disposition of . . . 43.02[H]
Treatment of . . . 43.02[E]

PENSIONS
Annuities . . . 8.02
Disability pensions . . . 10.06

PERSONAL EXEMPTIONS
Alternative minimum taxable income (AMTI) . . . 44.02[A][2]

PERSONAL EXPENSES DEDUCTION
Child care expenses . . . 19.02
Legal expenses . . . 19.03
Moving expenses . . . 19.01

PERSONAL INJURY AND SICKNESS DAM-AGES
Generally . . . 10.01; 10.02[B]
Accident and health insurance policies, payment under . . . 10.03
Awards, allocation of . . . 10.02[F]
Business damages . . . 10.02[A]
Disability pensions . . . 10.06
Exclusion for
    Generally . . . 10.02[D][2]
    Emotional distress . . . 10.02[D][3]
    Individuals other than individuals suffering physical injury or sickness, recoveries by . . . 10.02[D][4]
    Physical versus non-physical injuries . . . 10.02[D][1]
Health insurance policies, payment under accident and . . . 10.03
Medical expenses, previously deducted . . . 10.04
Payment under accident and health insurance policies . . . 10.03
Pensions, disability . . . 10.06
Periodic payments . . . 10.02[G]
Property damages . . . 10.02[A]
Punitive damages . . . 10.02[E]
Supreme court limitations on pre-1996 version of Section 104(a)(2)
    Generally . . . 10.02[C]
    Damages received on account of personal injury . . . 10.02[C][2]
    Personal injury defined . . . 10.02[C][1]
Workers' compensation . . . 10.05

PORTFOLIO INCOME
Passive activity losses and credits . . . 43.02[F]

POST-CONVERSION LOSSES
Generally . . . 15.01[C][2]

PREFERENCES
Alternative minimum taxable income . . . 44.02[B]
Justification for preferential capital gain treatment . . . 31.01[C]
Long term capital gain, preferential treatment for . . . 31.01[A]

PREPAID INTEREST
Allocation for deduction purposes . . . 22.04[A]

[References are to sections.]

[References are to sections.]